# Linux® Bible

## 2010 Edition

## Boot Up to Ubuntu®, Fedora®, KNOPPIX, Debian®, openSUSE®, and 13 Other Distributions

## Christopher Negus

**WILEY**

Wiley Publishing, Inc.

**Linux® Bible 2010 Edition**

Published by
Wiley Publishing, Inc.
10475 Crosspoint Boulevard
Indianapolis, IN 46256
www.wiley.com

Copyright © 2010 by Wiley Publishing, Inc., Indianapolis, Indiana

Published simultaneously in Canada

ISBN: 978-0-470-48505-7

Manufactured in the United States of America

10 9 8 7 6 5 4 3 2 1

For general information on our other products and services please contact our Customer Care Department within the United States at (877) 762-2974, outside the United States at (317) 572-3993 or fax (317) 572-4002.

Wiley also publishes its books in a variety of electronic formats. Some content that appears in print may not be available in electronic books.

**Library of Congress Control Number: 2009937839**

*As always, I dedicate this book to my wife, Sheree.*

# About the Author

**Chris Negus** has written or co-written dozens of books on Linux and UNIX, including Red Hat Linux Bible (all editions), CentOS Bible, Fedora and Red Hat Enterprise Linux Bible, Linux Troubleshooting Bible, Linux Toys and Linux Toys II. Recently, Chris co-authored several books for the new Toolbox series for power users: Fedora Linux Toolbox, SUSE Linux Toolbox, Ubuntu Linux Toolbox, Mac OS X, and BSD UNIX Toolbox.

For eight years Chris worked with the organization at AT&T that developed UNIX before moving to Utah to help contribute to Novell's UnixWare project in the early 1990s. When not writing about Linux, Chris enjoys playing soccer and just hanging out with his family.

Currently, Chris is employed by Red Hat, Inc. as a Linux instructor. He teaches classes and gives exams to those seeking Red Hat Certified Engineer (RHCE) and Red Hat Certified Technician (RHCT) certifications.

# Credits

**Executive Editor**
Carol Long

**Project Editor**
Sara Shlaer

**Technical Editor**
Warren Wyrostek

**Production Editor**
Kathleen Wisor

**Copy Editor**
Paula Lowell

**Editorial Director**
Robyn B. Siesky

**Editorial Manager**
Mary Beth Wakefield

**Marketing Manager**
David Mayhew

**Production Manager**
Tim Tate

**Vice President and Executive Group Publisher**
Richard Swadley

**Vice President and Executive Publisher**
Barry Pruett

**Associate Publisher**
Jim Minatel

**Project Coordinator, Cover**
Lynsey Stanford

**Compositor**
Maureen Forys, Happenstance Type-O-Rama

**Proofreaders**
Josh Chase, Word One
Kristy Eldridge, Word One

**Indexer**
Robert Swanson

**Cover Image**
Joyce Haughey

**Cover Designer**
Michael E. Trent

# Acknowledgments

I consider anyone who has contributed to the free and open source software community to be a contributor to the book you are holding. The backbone of any Linux distribution is formed by the organizations that produce the distributions, the major projects included in Linux, and the thousands of people who give their time and code to support Linux. So, thanks to you all!

I'd like to acknowledge several contributors for their participation in previous editions. Wayne Tucker originally wrote the chapters on Debian, LAMP servers, and mail servers. Bill von Hagen has contributed updates to the SUSE, Yellow Dog, and Ubuntu chapters. Warren Wyrostek served as technical editor to this edition. Thanks to the folks at Wiley for helping me press through the project. Sara Shlaer did an excellent job helping me stay on track as I balanced my work on this book with my new full-time job with Red Hat. Katie Wisor shepherded the book through the production process. Thanks to Margot Maley Hutchison and Maureen Maloney from Waterside Productions for contracting the book for me with Wiley.

And finally, special thanks to my wife, Sheree. There's no way I could do the work I do without the solid support I get on the home front. I love you, and thanks for taking such good care of Seth, Caleb, and me.

# Contents at a Glance

# Contents at a Glance

# Contents

# Contents

# Contents

# Contents

# Contents

# Contents

# Contents

# Contents

# Contents

# Contents

# Contents

# Introduction

Insert the DVD or CD that comes with this book into a PC. Within five minutes, you'll be able to try out Linux with a full range of desktop applications. Within an hour, you can have a full-blown Linux desktop or server system installed on your computer. If you are like most of us who have been bitten by the Linux bug, you won't ever look back.

*Linux Bible 2010 Edition* is here to open your eyes to what Linux is, where it came from, and where it's going. But, most of all, the book is here to hand you Linux and help you get started. Because Linux is the operating system of free speech and free choice, *Linux Bible* gives you choices in selecting the Linux that is right for you.

On the DVD and CD that come with this book are 18 different Linux distributions that you are free to install, try out, and keep. You learn how those distributions are alike or different, and the book leads you through the basics of installing and setting up your Linux system as:

- **A desktop computer user**—You have a full range of office, music, gaming, graphics, and other applications to use.

- **A Linux system administrator**—Learn how to install software, use shell commands, configure system services, and secure your computers and networks.

- **A Linux server administrator**—Using some of the world's best server software, you can set up your computer to be a Web server, file server, mail server, or print server.

- **A software developer**—You can draw on thousands of open source programming tools to develop your own software applications.

The Linux systems you have in your hand don't contain trialware or otherwise-hobbled software. On the contrary, they feature software created by world-class development projects, the same teams that build the software that powers many professional businesses, schools, home desktops, and Internet service providers. In other words, this truly first-rate software is from developers who have made a commitment to producing software that can be used in the ways that you choose to use it.

Most of the Linux distributions offered on the DVD and CD that come with this book are live CDs that let you try a Linux distribution without installing. Almost all of those live CDs include features that let you install the contents of those live CDs to your hard disk. For example, you can try out Fedora, Gentoo, Ubuntu, openSUSE, PCLinuxOS, and Mandriva as live CDs, and then install those distributions permanently to your hard drive from icons on the desktops of those live CDs.

Unlike some other books on Linux, this book doesn't tie you to one Linux distribution. The book teaches you the essentials of Linux graphical desktop interfaces, shell commands, and basic system administration. Separate chapters break down many of the major Linux distributions available today. Then descriptions of the major software projects in most Linux distributions (KDE and GNOME desktops, Apache Web servers, Samba file and printer sharing, and so on) guide you in setting up and using those features, regardless of which Linux you choose.

# Understanding the Linux Mystique

This book is designed to spark your imagination about what is possible with Linux, then give you the software and instruction to jump right into Linux. From there, the approach is to help you learn by using it.

In the first two chapters, you'll learn a lot of exciting ways Linux is being used today and see who many of the major players are in the free and open source software (FOSS) world. You will see how people are adapting Linux to run on handhelds, mini laptops, 32- and 64-bit PCs, Macs, mainframes, and super computers. Linux is truly everywhere!

However, if you are concerned that somehow "free" software is too good to be true, skip ahead for the moment to the brief history of Linux in Appendix B. That appendix guides you through the strange and circuitous path of free and open source software development that led to the Linux phenomenon.

If you are intrigued by what you learn here, I'll tell you how you can become part of the open source and free software communities, whose stars are known by a single name (such as Linus) or a few initials (such as rms). You'll find a staggering number of open source projects, forums, and mailing lists that are thriving today (and always looking for more people to get involved).

# How This Book Is Organized

Learn the basics of what goes into Linux and you will be able to use all sorts of devices and computers in the future. The book is organized in a way that enables you to start off at the very beginning with Linux, but still grow to the point where you can get going with some powerful server and programming features, if you care to.

**Part I** includes two short chapters designed to open your eyes to what you can do with Linux, then get your hands on it quickly. Those two chapters describe

- How others use Linux, how to transition to Linux from Windows, and how to start with Linux using the CD and DVD inside this book (Chapter 1)
- What you can do, what you can make, and what you can become with Linux (Chapter 2)

In **Part II**, you start in with details on how to use Linux desktops and associated applications. Chapters 3–7 describe

- The KDE, GNOME, and other desktop interfaces (Chapter 3)
- Tools for playing music and video (Chapter 4)
- Desktop publishing and Web publishing using word processing, layout, drawing, and image manipulation tools, plus tools such as wikis, blogs, and content management systems for managing content online (Chapter 5)
- Applications for e-mail and Web browsing (Chapter 6)
- Desktop gaming applications (Chapter 7)

In **Part III**, you learn how to administer Linux systems, including

- Installing Linux systems (Chapter 8)
- Using the shell (Chapter 9)
- Doing basic administration (Chapter 10)
- Connecting to the Internet (Chapter 11)
- Securing your Linux system (Chapter 12)

Linux creates powerful servers, and in **Part IV** you learn to

- Set up a Web server using Apache, MySQL, and PHP in Linux (Chapter 13)
- Run a mail server (Chapter 14)
- Share printers with a CUPS print server (Chapter 15)
- Share files with a Samba or NFS file server (Chapter 16)

If you don't have Linux installed yet, this book helps you understand differences in Linux distribution, then install the systems you want from the DVD and CD included in this book. **Part V** (Chapters 17 through 28) describes each of those distributions and how to run them live or install them.

If you are coming to Linux for its programming environment, **Part VI** provides chapters that describe

- Programming environments and interfaces (Chapter 29)
- Programming tools and utilities (Chapter 30)

In addition, Appendix A tells you what's on the DVD and CD, how to install from the DVD or CD, and how to burn additional installation CDs from the software that comes with this book. Appendix B provides history and background information about Linux.

# What You Will Get from This Book

By the time you finish this book, you'll have a good basic understanding of many of the major features in Linux and how you can use them. If you decide then that you want to go a bit deeper, try the *Fedora 12 Bible* or the *Red Hat Enterprise Linux Bible* (both from Wiley, 2010), with content that includes how to set up many different types of Linux servers. You can find similar books for other distributions.

If you are more technically oriented, *Linux Troubleshooting Bible* (Wiley, 2004) can be a good way to learn more advanced skills for securing and troubleshooting Linux systems. Or a *Linux Toolbox* book for Fedora, Ubuntu, BSD, or SUSE (Wiley, 2007 and 2008) can provide you with more than 1,000 Linux command lines to help you become a Linux power user.

If you are looking for some fun, try out some projects with an old PC and free software from *Linux Toys II* (Wiley, 2006).

# Conventions Used in This Book

Throughout the book, special typography indicates code and commands. Commands and code are shown in a monospaced font:

```
This is how code looks.
```

In the event that an example includes both input and output, the monospaced font is still used, but input is presented in bold type to distinguish the two. Here's an example:

```
$ ftp ftp.handsonhistory.com
Name (home:jake): jake
Password: ******
```

As for styles in the text:

- New terms and important words appear in italics when introduced.
- Keyboard strokes appear like this: Ctrl+A.
- Filenames, URLs, and code within the text appear like so: `persistence.properties`.

The following items call your attention to points that are particularly important.

## Note
A Note box provides extra information to which you need to pay special attention. ■

## Tip
A Tip box shows a special way of performing a particular task. ■

## Caution

A Caution box alerts you to take special care when executing a procedure, or damage to your computer hardware or software could result. ■

## Cross-Reference

A Cross-Reference box refers you to further information on a subject that you can find outside the current chapter. ■

## Coming from Windows

A Coming from Windows box provides tips to help you transfer your knowledge of Windows systems to the Linux world. ■

The On the CD and On the DVD icons point out features related to the media that accompany the book.

# Part I

# Getting off the Ground with Linux

# Starting with Linux

With Linux, you are free to erase your computer's entire hard disk and run nothing but free (as in freedom) software on it. As an alternative, you could run Linux from a live CD (ignoring your computer's contents without changing them) or install Linux to dual boot with your Windows or Mac OS X system as you choose. The bottom line is that with Linux you are free to do as YOU choose with your computer.

In only a few years, Linux has advanced from being considered a specialty operating system into the mainstream. Precompiled and configured Linux systems can be installed with no technical expertise. Versions of Linux run on all kinds of devices, from PCs to handhelds (see `www.linuxdevices.com`) to game consoles (such as PlayStation 3) to supercomputers to Mars rovers. In short, Linux has become a system that almost anyone can run almost anywhere.

On both desktop and server computers Linux has become a formidable operating system across a variety of business applications. Today, large enterprises can deploy thousands of systems using Linux distributions from companies such as Red Hat, Inc. and Novell, Inc. Small businesses can put together the mixture of office and Internet services they need to keep their costs down.

The free and open source software (FOSS) development model that espoused sharing, freedom, and openness is now on a trajectory to surpass the quality of other operating systems outside of the traditional Linux servers and technical workstations. What were once weak components of Linux, such as easy-to-use desktops, multimedia codecs and limited driver availability, have improved at a rapid pace. In areas of security, usability, connectivity, and network services, Linux has continued to improve and outshine the competition.

## IN THIS CHAPTER

**Getting started with Linux**

**Understanding Linux**

**Linux features and advantages**

Computer industry heavy-hitters such as Microsoft and Oracle have taken notice of Linux. Microsoft has struck agreements with Linux companies including Novell and Xandros to form partnerships that primarily protect those companies against threatened Microsoft lawsuits. Oracle began producing its own enterprise-targeted Linux system to try to stem the flow of customers to Red Hat Enterprise Linux.

What does this all add up to? A growing swirl of excitement around the operating system that the big guys can't seem to get rid of. For people like yourself, who want the freedom to use your computer software as you like, it means great prospects for the future.

Let this book help you grab your first look at the distributions, applications, services, and community that make up the phenomenon that has become Linux.

# Taking Your First Step

In your hands, you have 18 different Linux distributions (on CD and DVD), thousands of applications, and descriptions for getting it all running on your own computer. For you right now, the worldwide Linux phenomenon is just a reboot away.

*Linux Bible 2010 Edition* brings you into the world of free and open source software that, through some strange twists and turns, has fallen most publicly under the "Linux" banner. Through descriptions and procedures, this book helps you

- Understand what people do with Linux and how you can use Linux for all your computing tasks.
- Sort through the various distributions of Linux to choose one (or more) that is right for you. You get several Linux systems on this book's CD and DVD. (Linux is all about choice, too!)
- Try out Linux as a desktop computer, server computer, or programmer's workstation.
- Become connected to the open source software movement, as well as many separate high-quality software projects that are included with Linux.

## What comes in Linux systems?

Whether you are using Linux for the first time or just want to try out a new Linux distribution, *Linux Bible 2010 Edition* is your guide to using Linux and the latest open source technology. Although different Linux distributions vary in the exact software they include, this book describes the most popular software available for Linux to

- Manage your desktop (menus, icons, windows, and so on)
- Listen to music, watch video, and store and arrange digital photos
- Create, lay out, manipulate, and publish documents and images on paper or on the Web

- Browse the Web and send e-mail
- Play games
- Find thousands of other open source software packages you can get for free

Because most Linux distributions also include features that let them act as servers (in fact, that's one of the things Linux has always been best at), you'll also learn about software available for Linux that lets you do the following:

- Connect to the Internet or other network
- Use Linux as a firewall and router to protect and manage your private network
- Run a Web server (using Apache, MySQL, and PHP)
- Run a mail server (using Exim, Sendmail or other mail transfer agent)
- Run a print server (using Samba or CUPS)
- Run a file server (using vsFTPd or Samba)
- Use the exact same enterprise-quality software used by major corporations (such as Google and Amazon.com), universities, and businesses of all sizes

This book guides you through the basics of getting started with these Linux features, plus many more. After you've been through the book, you should be proficient enough in the basics to track down answers to your more advanced questions through the volumes of man pages, FAQs, HOWTOs, and forums that cover different aspects of the Linux operating system.

To get started with Linux right now, all you need is a standard PC with a bootable CD or DVD drive.

# What do you need to get started?

Although Linux runs great on many low-end computers (even some old 486s and early Pentiums), if you are completely new to Linux, I recommend that you start with a PC that has a little more muscle. Here's why:

- Full-blown Linux operating systems with complete GNOME or KDE desktop environments (see Chapter 3) perform poorly on slow CPUs and less than the recommended amount of RAM. The bells and whistles come at the price of processing power. Lighter-weight options (such as the Xfce or LXDE desktop environments) often run well on computers that have limited resources, but they may offer fewer features.
- You can use streamlined graphical Linux installations that fit on small hard disks (as small as 100MB) and run fairly well on slow processors. Also, small live CD Linux distributions, such as Damn Small Linux (DSL), can be copied to hard disk and run from there (read about some of these small "bootables" in Chapter 28). The 50MB DSL desktop system can run fine on old Pentium machines with little RAM. But if you want to add some of the more demanding applications to these small systems, such as OpenOffice.org office applications, you will find you need more than minimal computer hardware.

If you are starting with a Pentium II, 400 MHz, your desktop will run slowly in default KDE or GNOME configurations with less than 128MB of RAM. A simpler desktop system, with just X and a window manager, will work, but won't give you the full flavor of a Linux desktop. (See Chapter 3 for information about different desktop choices and features.)

The good news is that cheap desktop PCs or netbooks that you can buy from big box retailers start at less than $200. Those systems will perform better than most PCs you have laying around that are more than a few years old, and some even come with Linux pre-installed. The bottom line is that the less you know about Linux, the more you should try to have computer hardware that is up to spec to have a pleasant experience.

## Starting right now

If you are anxious to get started, insert either the DVD or CD accompanying this book into the appropriate drive on your PC and reboot. When you see the boot screen, press Enter. When the DVD or CD boots, the following happens, respectively:

- **KNOPPIX starts up.** A fully functional KNOPPIX desktop Linux system will boot directly from the DVD. From that Linux system, you can do everything you would expect to do from a modern desktop computing system: write documents, play music, communicate over the Internet, work with images, and so on. If you have a wired Ethernet connection that connects to the Internet when you started up Windows, most likely it will also connect automatically when KNOPPIX starts.

- **Damn Small Linux starts up.** This small, amazing desktop-oriented Linux system starts up directly from the CD that comes with this book. Besides being expandable and adaptable, DSL runs on everything from low-end PCs to powerful workstation hardware while being small enough to fit on a mini CD (it's only about 50MB in size).

What you have in front of you is a functioning desktop system that you can install to your hard disk to use permanently, if you like. You can choose to add software from among thousands of software packages available for Linux. Depending on your Linux system, installing extra software might just take a few clicks.

The next sections step you through a few things you can do with KNOPPIX and Damn Small Linux.

### Trying KNOPPIX

When KNOPPIX starts up, you bypass a login screen and go directly to a Lightweight X11 Desktop Environment (LXDE) that is loaded with free software for you to try. Figure 1-1 shows an example of the KNOPPIX LXDE desktop with desktop effects enabled. The image shows a window exploding as it is closed.

## Note

If you have any trouble starting KNOPPIX, see Chapter 21 for descriptions of boot options to help you overcome certain problems (such as a garbled screen or hanging when certain hardware is encountered). That chapter also describes other KNOPPIX features. ■

**FIGURE 1-1**

The KNOPPIX live Linux CD contains the KDE desktop and hundreds of applications.

Here is a quick tour of the KNOPPIX desktop:

- **Browsing**—Select the Web Browser icon from the bottom panel to open the IceWeasel browser. The IceWeasel browser is a version of the Firefox Web browser that was rebranded by the Debian project (http://geticeweasel.org).

- **Managing files**—Select the My Documents icon from the desktop. A PCMan File Manager window opens to show your home folder (/home/knoppix). You will typically save files and folders to your home folder. Because you are running KNOPPIX as a live CD, any files you create will be lost when you reboot if you don't explicitly save them. Chapter 21 describes how to make a persistent desktop, so you can save the files you create in KNOPPIX permanently.

- **Accessing disks**—A live CD, such as KNOPPIX, is designed to run without touching the contents of your hard disk. However, if you have something on your hard disk you want to use with KNOPPIX (such as a music file or document), KNOPPIX makes doing it easy.

  Entries appear in the left column of the file manager, representing every partition on your hard disk, as well as detected removable media (such as a USB flash drive). In Figure 1-1, Volume entries represent several partitions on your hard disk. Select an icon to display the contents of the partition in that file manager window. To add content to that disk partition, simply drag and drop files from the desktop, or copy, move, or otherwise create files from the shell.

- **Special Knoppix features**—Because of the temporary nature of a live CD, you have to configure settings each time you boot, unless you take steps to save those settings. From the LXDE icon on the left side of the bottom panel, you can see a menu of selections to do special things to make KNOPPIX run from your hard disk. Select System Tools ➪ KNOPPIX HD Install to install KNOPPIX so you can run it from your hard disk.

  Other KNOPPIX features are also available from that menu. You can select Install Components to add non-free software, such as Flash plug-ins or Windows fonts. Chapter 21 describes other KNOPPIX features.

- **Running Applications**—Select the LXDE icon from the lower-left corner of the panel to see a menu of available applications. Choose Office to select from several OpenOffice.org office applications for writing documents, using spreadsheets, drawing pictures, and building presentations. Try out some communications applications, such as Icedove mail reader and Pidgin Internet Messenger, from the Network menu.

When you are done trying KNOPPIX, select Log Out from the LXDE menu and choose Shut Down. After KNOPPIX shuts down, it ejects the disc. After you remove the disc, you can use your computer again with whatever operating system you have installed there.

### Trying Damn Small Linux

Because Damn Small Linux (DSL) is based on KNOPPIX, you may notice some similarities. DSL is smaller and faster, however, so you should get to the DSL desktop screen quicker. Instead of LXDE, the DSL desktop features a simple window manager. Figure 1-2 shows an example of a Damn Small Linux desktop with several applications open.

## Note

**Many of the same boot options that come with KNOPPIX will work with DSL, so check Chapter 21 if you have trouble booting DSL. For other descriptions of DSL, see Chapter 28. ■**

**FIGURE 1-2**

Damn Small Linux provides an efficient desktop Linux.

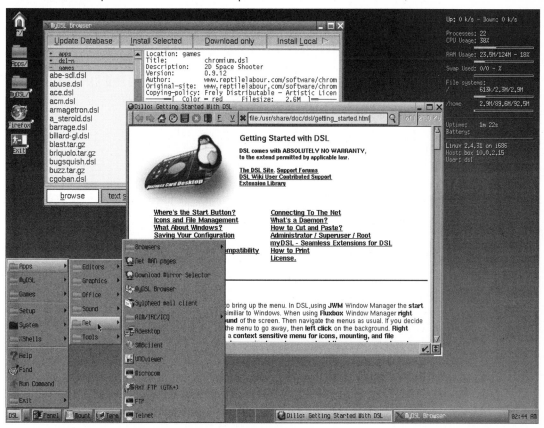

Here are some things to try on your DSL desktop:

- **Web browsing**—With an active wired Internet connection, you should be able to connect to the Internet automatically when DSL boots up. The Dillo Web browser opens to a page of basic DSL information. Continue to browse the Web from Dillo, or open the Firefox icon from the desktop to browse with Firefox instead.

- **Install applications**—Open the MyDSL icon from the desktop and then, when prompted, download the applications database. After that, select categories from the left column to look through listings of hundreds of applications you can add to DSL. When you find one you like, choose Install Selected to download and install it.

- **Check out the desktop**—On the desktop itself, view information about your computer (CPU Usage, RAM, Swap, file systems, and so on) in the upper-right corner. Select DSL in the lower-left corner of the bottom panel to see a menu of available applications. Then try a few applications. You can view the same menu by right-clicking on the desktop.

- **Change settings**—Select Setup from the main menu to adjust the date and time, change your desktop theme, configure your X display server, or set up a wireless or dial-up Internet connection.

- **Control the system**—Select System from the menu and choose Control Panel. From the Control Panel that appears, you can configure your printer, back up your files (remember that files disappear at reboot with live CDs if you don't save them to disk or removable media), or start login (SSH) or FTP services. Return to the main menu and select Apps ⇨ Tools to do some cool, specialized DSL features, such as install to hard disk or portable USB flash drive (pendrive). You can also remaster a MyDSL CD or make a boot floppy.

- **Trying applications**—Figure 1-2 shows a couple of applications open on the DSL desktop. Open the MyDSL folder to see application packages you can install (shown upper left). Select Apps ⇨ Net to see applications you could use to access the Internet (such as email clients, web browsers and instant messaging clients).

Select the Exit icon from the desktop and choose Shutdown or Reboot to exit from DSL. Notice that the Backup box is selected. With that box selected, DSL gives you the option to save your files and settings (provided you set up a location to back up your files earlier from the Control Panel). With that information saved, the next time you boot DSL from that computer, you have those files and settings available.

### Trying other Linux distributions

Of course you can try many other Linux distributions from the CD and DVD that come with this book besides KNOPPIX and Damn Small Linux. Ubuntu has a large, active following and can be run live from the DVD. Try Fedora or openSUSE if you want to try a Linux system that is being prepared for enterprise distros (Red Hat Enterprise Linux and SUSE Linux Enterprise, respectively).

Gentoo and Slackware often appeal to technically oriented users. On small machines, distros such as Puppy Linux or BackTrack may interest you. See Appendix A for information on these and other Linux systems included with this book.

# Understanding Linux

People who don't know what Linux is sometimes ask me whether it's a program that runs on Microsoft Windows. When I tell them that Linux is, itself, an operating system like Windows and that they can remove (or never purchase) Windows, I sometimes get a surprised reaction, "A PC can run with nothing from Microsoft on it?" The answer is yes!

The next question about Linux is often, "How can Linux be free?" Although the full answer to that is a bit longer (and covered later), the short answer is, "Because the people who write the code license it to be freely distributed." Keep in mind, however, that the critical issue relating to the word "free" is "freedom," meaning that you are free to rebuild, reuse, reconfigure, and otherwise do what you like with the code. The only major responsibility is that if you change the software, you pass it forward so that others may benefit from your work as well.

Linux is a full-blown operating system that is a free clone of the powerful and stable UNIX operating system. Start your computer with Linux, and Linux takes care of the operation of your PC and manages the following aspects of your computer:

- **Processor**—Because Linux can run many processes from many different users at the same time (even with multiple CPUs on the same machine), Linux needs to be able to manage those processes. The Linux scheduler sets the priorities for running tasks and manages which processes run on which CPUs (if multiple processors are present). You can tune the scheduler differently for different types of Linux systems. If the scheduler is tuned properly, the most important processes get the quickest responses from the processor. For example, a Linux scheduler on a desktop system gives higher priority to things such as moving a window on the desktop than it does to a background file transfer.

- **Memory**—Linux tries to keep processes with the most immediate need in RAM, while managing how processes that exceed the available memory are moved to swap space. *Swap space* is a defined area on your hard disk that's used to handle the overflow of running processes and data. When RAM is full, processes are placed in swap space. When swap space is full (something that you don't want to happen), new processes can't start up.

- **Devices**—Linux supports thousands of hardware devices, yet keeps the kernel a manageable size by including only a small set of drivers in the active kernel. Using loadable modules, the kernel can add support for other hardware as needed. Modules can be loaded and unloaded on demand, as you add and remove hardware. (The kernel, described in detail a bit later on, is the heart of a Linux operating system.)

- **File systems**—File systems provide the structure in which files are stored on hard disk, CD, DVD, floppy disks, or other media. Linux knows about different file system types (such as Linux ext3 and reiserfs file systems, or VFAT and NTFS from Windows systems) and how to manage them.

- **Security**—Like UNIX, Linux was built from the ground up to enable multiple users to access the system simultaneously. To protect each user's resources, every file, directory, and application is assigned sets of read, write, and execute permissions that define who can access them. In a standard Linux system, the root user has access to the entire system, some special logins have access to control particular services (such as Apache for Web services), and users can be assigned permission individually or in groups. Recent features such as Security Enhanced Linux and AppArmor enable more refined tuning and protection in highly secure computing environments.

What I have just described are components that are primarily managed by what is referred to as the Linux *kernel*. In fact, the Linux kernel (which is still maintained by Linus Torvalds, who created the Linux kernel as a graduate student in Finland) is what gives Linux its name. The kernel is the software that starts up when you boot your computer and interfaces with the programs you use so they can communicate effectively and simply with your computer hardware.

## Note

**See Appendix B for historic details on how the kernel and other free software came together to create the Linux phenomenon.** ■

Components such as administrative commands and applications from other free and open source software projects work with the kernel to make Linux a complete operating system. The GNU project (www.gnu.org), in particular, contributed many implementations of standard UNIX components that are now in Linux. Apache, KDE, GNOME, and other major open source projects in Linux have also contributed to the success of Linux. (See Chapter 2 for an explanation of how open source projects work and how you can get involved in them.) Those other projects added such things as

- **Graphical user interfaces (GUIs)**—Consisting of a graphical framework (typically the X Window System), window managers, panels, icons, and menus. GUIs enable you to use Linux with a keyboard and mouse combination, instead of just typing commands (as was done in the old days).

- **Administrative utilities**—Including hundreds (perhaps thousands) of commands and graphical windows to do such things as add users, manage disks, monitor the network, install software, and generally secure and manage your computer.

- **Applications**—Although no Linux distribution includes all of them, literally thousands of games, office productivity tools, Web browsers, chat windows, multimedia players, and other applications are available for Linux.

- **Programming tools**—Including programming utilities for creating applications and libraries for implementing specialty interfaces.

- **Server features**—Enabling you to offer services from your Linux computer to another computer on the network. In other words, while Linux includes Web browsers to view Web pages, it can also be the computer that serves up Web pages to others. Popular server features include Web, mail, database, printer, file, DNS, and DHCP servers.

After Linus Torvalds and friends had a working Linux kernel, pulling together a complete open source operating system was possible because so much of the available "free" software was

- **Covered by the GNU Public License (GPL) or similar license**—That allowed the entire operating system to be freely distributed, provided guidelines were followed relating to how the source code for that software was made available going forward (see http://www.gnu.org/licenses/gpl.html).

- **Based on UNIX-like systems**—Clones of virtually all the other user-level components of a UNIX system had been created. Those and other utilities and applications were built to run on UNIX or other UNIX-like systems.

Linux has become one of the most popular culminations of the open source software movement. But the traditions of sharing code and building communities that made Linux possible started years before Linux was born. You could argue that it began in a comfortable think tank known as Bell Laboratories. Read Appendix B to learn more about the history of Linux.

Leveraging work done on UNIX and GNU projects helped to get Linux up and running quickly. The culture of sharing in the open source community and adoption of a wide array of tools for communicating on the Internet have helped Linux to move quickly through infancy and adolescence to become a mature operating system.

The simple commitment to share code is probably the single most powerful contributor to the growth of the open source software movement in general, and Linux in particular. That commitment has also encouraged involvement from the kind of people who are willing to contribute back to that community in all kinds of ways. The willingness of Linus Torvalds to incorporate code from others in the Linux kernel has also been critical to the success of Linux.

# What's So Great About Linux?

If you have not used Linux before, you should expect a few things to be different from using other operating systems. Here is a brief list of some Linux features that you might find cool:

- **No constant rebooting**—Uptime is valued as a matter of pride (remember, Linux and other UNIX systems are most often used as servers, which are expected to, and do, stay up 24/7/365). After the original installation, you can install or remove most software without having to reboot your computer for almost any software besides the kernel itself.

- **Start/stop services without interrupting others**—You can start and stop individual services (such as Web, file, and e-mail services) without rebooting or even interrupting the work of any other users or features of the computer. In other words, you should not have to reboot your computer every time someone sneezes. (Installing a new kernel is just about the only reason you need to reboot.)

- **Portable software**—You can usually change to another Linux, UNIX, or BSD system and still use the exact same software! Most open source software projects were created to run on any UNIX-like system and many also run on Windows systems, if you need them to. If it won't run where you want it to, chances are that you, or someone you hire, can port it to the computer you want. (*Porting* refers to modifying an application or driver so it works in a different computer architecture or operating system.)

- **Downloadable applications**—If the applications you want are not delivered with your version of Linux, you can often download and install them with a single command, using tools such as apt, urpmi, and yum.

- **No settings hidden in code or registries**—After you learn your way around Linux, you'll find that (given the right permissions on your computer) most configuration is done in plain text files that are easy to find and change. In recent years, simplified graphical interfaces have been added to make working with configuration files even easier. Because Linux is based on openness, nothing is hidden from you. Even the source code, for GPL-covered software, is available for your review.

- **Mature desktop**—The X Window System (providing the framework for your Linux desktop)' has been around longer than Microsoft Windows. The KDE and GNOME desktop environments provide graphical interfaces (windows, menus, icons, and so forth) that rival those on Microsoft systems. You have the freedom to choose lightweight window managers instead as well. Ease-of-use problems with Linux systems are rapidly evaporating.

- **Freedom**—Linux, in its most basic form, has no corporate agenda or bottom line to meet. You are free to choose the Linux distribution that suits you, look at the code that runs the system, add and remove any software you like, and make your computer do what you want it to do. Linux runs on everything from supercomputers, to cell phones, and everything in between. Many countries are rediscovering their freedom of choice and making the switch at government and educational levels. France, Germany, Korea, and India are just a few that have taken notice of Linux. The list continues to grow.

Some aspects of Linux make it hard for some new users to get started. One is that Linux is typically set up to be secure by default, so you must adjust to using an administrative login (root) to make most changes that affect the whole computer system. Although this can be a bit inconvenient, trust me, it makes your computer safer than just letting anyone do anything. This model was built around a true multi-user system. You can set up logins for everyone who uses your Linux computer, and you (and others) can customize your environment however you see fit without affecting anyone else's settings.

For the same reason, many services are off by default, so you need to turn them on and do at least minimal configuration to get them going. For someone who is used to Windows, Linux can be difficult just because it is different from Windows. But because you're reading this book, I assume you want to learn about those differences.

# Summary

Getting started with Linux can be as easy as inserting the CD or DVD accompanying this book into your PC and rebooting. Using that media, you can try out 18 different Linux systems, either live or by installing them to hard disk.

You can use Linux as a desktop system (like Microsoft Windows); as a Web, file, or print server; or as a programmer's workstation. You have a lot of flexibility when it comes to how Linux is configured and what software you install and run on it.

Because you are free to use open source software as you please, many Linux enthusiasts have come up with interesting and innovative ways to use Linux and benefit from it. Chapter 2 describes what you can do with Linux, what you can make with Linux, and what you can become with Linux.

# Linux Projects, Activities, and Careers

The primary objective of this book is to lead you through the most popular ways of using Linux as a desktop, server, or programmer's workstation. After you become comfortable using Linux, however, you'll begin to see that these uses are just the tip of the iceberg.

Remember that you can modify, rebuild, and reuse free and open source software as you please. This means that you can piece together the projects you like to build the Linux system you want. You could even modify it to run on different types of hardware. To those ends, you can join together with others of like mind to produce software that might be too ambitious to build by yourself.

So, before we head full-speed into the how-to portions of the book, this chapter sets out to spark your imagination and open your eyes to

- **What you can make with Linux**—With free software and a spare PC you can make stand-alone gadgets, such as a music jukebox, game console, telephone answering machine, or home network server. NASA straps Linux on its moon rovers to guide their movements. Some schools use the Linux Terminal Server Project to drive hundreds of old or cheap PCs from a single server. What sort of projects can you come up with?

- **How you can get involved with Linux**—For many Linux enthusiasts, Linux is more than just their computer system. It is what they believe in. It is what they fight for. It is what consumes them. If Linux stirs you up, you have many ways to contribute to open source software projects and advocate the use of free software.

- **What you can become with Linux**—Just because Linux is "free" doesn't mean that you can't make any money from it. Some small

**IN THIS CHAPTER**

**What you can do with Linux**

**What you can make with Linux**

**How you can become involved with Linux**

businesses use Linux for all their office and Web software needs. Linux enterprise software is used to drive thousands of workstations and servers in many major corporations. If you are interested in using Linux as a profession, you can get training and certification to become a skilled participant in the open source revolution.

# Making Things with Linux

To start thinking about the kinds of things you can make or do with Linux, all you have to do is look around you. Linux may already be in your handheld device, in your personal video recorder, and (almost certainly) running your search engine or favorite Web site.

Many people, schools, and companies have adapted Linux in all kinds of fun, educational, and profitable ways. Some have stripped Linux down to its bare essentials (an embedded Linux kernel, a shell, and a few drivers) and added their own software to use Linux in communications devices and robots. Others have put together their own set of software to accomplish a specific goal, such as a kid-safe computer or a portable Web server.

This section describes some fun and interesting ways that people have adapted Linux to suit their needs.

## Linux in outer space

When NASA's Mars Exploration Rovers named Spirit and Opportunity are tooling around Mars and sending back images and data, Linux is driving the rovers in everything from high-level planning to low-level simulation and visualization. NASA chose Linux because of graphics and processor speed, as well its stability and the myriad of software tools available for it.

NASA developed the Roving Sequencing and Visualization Program (RSVP) application suite in Linux to command the Mars rovers, and then tested and deployed that system on Linux as well. In that suite, the Rover Sequence Editor (RoSE) lets NASA send spacecraft commands to the rovers while HyperDrive offers three-dimensional graphics for controlling the rover (such as moving the arms, driving the vehicles and controlling imaging).

Figure 2-1 shows a computer-generated image produced by NASA of how the Mars Exploration Rover appears on Mars.

The Linux system running on each rover is an embedded Linux real-time operating system from TimeSys (www.timesys.com). The RoSE application (for passing messages) was written in Java, whereas HyperDrive elements (image viewer and sequence flow browser) are written in C++ and C languages. An article in *Linux Journal* by NASA scientists Frank Hartman and Scott Maxwell describes in depth how Linux was used on the Mars Rover project (www.linuxjournal.com/article/7570).

**FIGURE 2-1**

Mars Exploration Rovers (MER) gather data, send images, and move around Mars from onboard Linux systems.

*(Photo by NASA)*

Spirit landed on Mars on January 4, 2004 and Opportunity landed on January 25. Both were still in operation after more than five years, at the time of this writing. If you are interested in following the progress of the Mars Exploration Rover Mission, refer to the project's Web site at the NASA Jet Propulsion Laboratory (`http://marsrovers.jpl.nasa.gov`).

## Linux in gadgets

Lots of commercial communications, entertainment, and other kinds of gadgets have Linux running on the inside. Linux makes an excellent operating system for these specialty devices, not only because of its cost, but also because of its stability and adaptability.

Linux enthusiasts love these devices, referred to as *embedded* Linux systems, because they can often adapt, add, or run different Linux software on these devices (whether the manufacturer intended that or not). More and more, however, manufacturers are embracing the Linux enthusiast and hardware hacker and selling open devices for them to use. Here are some examples:

- **Mobile Phones**—OpenMoko (`www.openmoko.com`) produces mass-market mobile phones, such as the Neo FreeRunner, that are based on Linux. Like the software, the FreeRunner's hardware also follows an open design. Although the phone is intended for general consumer use, the phone's software is currently most appropriate for people who want to develop their own software for the phones. Figure 2-2 shows an example of the Neo FreeRunner.

---

**FIGURE 2-2**

Modify software to use the Linux Neo FreeRunner as a phone, GPS device, clock, game player, and media player.

Motorola, OpenMoko, and Tranzda Technologies each offer multiple Linux-based mobile phones. Phone models running Linux on the inside include the Motorola Rokr EM30 (emphasizing music playing), Tranzda Technologies NewPlus phones (with WiFi, GPS, and a camera), Purple Labs Purple Magic phones (sub-$100 phone), and Grunig B700 (with keyboard and e-mail support).

- **Sony PlayStation**—Not only can you install and run Linux on PlayStation, but Sony encourages you to do it. In 2002, Sony released Linux Kit for PlayStation 2. Included in that kit is a derivative of the Japanese Kondara MNU/Linux (which is based on Red Hat Linux). For PlayStation 3, several Linux distributions have been modified (ported) to run on that hardware, including Fedora, OpenSUSE, Ubuntu, Gentoo, Debian, and a commercial Yellow Dog Linux product for PlayStation 3. (See Chapter 22 for a description of Yellow Dog Linux.)

- **Personal Video Recorders (PVR)**—If you have a TiVo PVR or a set-top for streaming video from Netflix, you are already running Linux in your home. The Netflix PVR is from Roku, Inc. (`www.roku.com`), which produces a range of Linux-based media players. TiVo has produced Linux-based PVRs for years. The availability of the TiVo Linux source code (`www.tivo.com/linux`) has made TiVo one of the most popular devices for Linux enthusiasts to hack.

- **Netbooks**—Shrinking laptops with shrinking prices have led to Netbooks. These mini laptop computers have proven to be excellent devices for running Linux. With low-powered processors and small screens, Netbooks provide a good partnership with Linux systems that are tuned for these compact, efficient devices.

The Asus Eee PC is one of the most popular Netbooks available today. Many Asus Eee PCs have been sold with Xandros Linux preinstalled. However, industrious Linux enthusiasts have created ports of Fedora, Ubuntu, and other Linux distributions to run on the Eee PC. The Acer Aspire One is another popular netbook. Figure 2-3 shows an Eee PC with Fedora Linux running on it.

**FIGURE 2-3**

An Asus Eee PC can run specially tuned Fedora or other Linux systems.

- **Personal handheld devices**—A whole range of personal digital assistants (PDAs), portable navigation devices (PNAs), and portable media players (PMPs) are available today with Linux inside. The Garmin Nuvi (models 860, 880, and 5000) GPS navigation devices feature GNOME Mobile Linux and GeoClue location technology. The Samsung i70 combines a digital camera with a personal media player built on MontaVista Linux. Inside the Sony mylo Internet Device is the Qtopia Linux system, which lets you connect to WiFi networks, play Adobe Flash video and games, and even record video.

A good place to learn about these and other devices that run Linux is the LinuxDevices site (www.linuxdevices.com).

## Linux in projects

Whole open source projects have been devoted to special-use Linux systems. These projects may be focused on doing one type of activity very well (like building a multimedia center) or solving a problem (like dwindling school computer budgets). Here are some examples of ways people have brought together open source software that you might find interesting:

- **MythTV** (www.mythtv.org)—When it comes to open source personal video recorder (PVR) projects, MythTV leads the way. Like most PVRs, MythTV lets you gather TV channel listings for your area, select shows you want to view or record, and play back recorded shows when you are ready. Beyond that, MythTV lets you pause, fast forward, and rewind live TV, skip commercials, and choose from different types of video compression.

  By integrating other open source software into the MythTV interface, you can do a lot of things you wouldn't expect to do with a PVR. You can rip and play MP3, FLAC, Ogg, and CD audio files and group them into playlists. You can use MAME and other gaming console applications to play games. MythTV also includes an image viewer, weather module, and RSS newsfeeder.

  Mythbuntu (www.mythbuntu.org) and MythDora (www.mythdora.com) projects are available to configure MythTV on a particular Linux distribution. KnoppMyth (www.knoppmyth.net) provides an easy-to-install Knoppix-based MythTV version. Figure 2-4 shows an example of the main MythTV screen.

**FIGURE 2-4**

Manage your TV viewing, recording, and playback with MythTV.

- **Linux Terminal Server Project** (www.ltsp.org)—Using a central server and possibly hundreds of low-end PCs or thin clients, you can create a cost-effective way to fill a school or small business with Linux workstations. Client computers don't need much power because they essentially just run the display, keyboard, and mouse. The server actually stores data, runs applications, and provides access to network devices and other hardware. (The K12 LTSP project is described later in this chapter.)

- **Asterisk Telephony Project** (www.asterisk.org)—Asterisk is an open source telephony project that includes a PBX telephony engine and related applications and tools. With Asterisk, you can create an IP or hybrid PBX that can communicate to callers over the Internet (or other IP networks), analog telephone service, or digital T1 lines. A huge range of features lets you set up call centers, create conference bridges, and manage voicemail.

- **Linux Toys and Make** (www.linuxtoys.net and http://makezine.com)—If you like to tinker, there are places you can go to find instructions for putting together your own free software and random hardware projects. The books *Linux Toys* and *Linux Toys II* (Wiley Publishing) contain instructions to build your own gaming console, weather monitor, home network server, and so on from free software and an old PC. *Make Magazine* and its Web site describe many projects that include open source software, such as building a supercomputer from dozens of old PCs and ParallelKnoppix or turning an old PC into an Internet-enabled DVD burner, CD player, and MP3 Jukebox that's based on KNOPPIX.

As you can see, a lot of people have already gone to the trouble of putting together fun and interesting projects that you can replicate on your own. And, of course, you can always be creative and come up with your own projects, while drawing on the massive amounts of open source software available.

# Getting Involved with Linux

Using and playing with Linux is great fun. Connecting up with others who share your joy in Linux can make the whole Linux experience that much better. So if you want to go beyond just using Linux and become someone who improves it and spreads the word, here are some things you can do:

- Join a Linux User Group (LUG) or Linux community
- Contribute to an open source project
- Ask or answer questions at online Linux forums
- Connect to a Linux IRC chat room

Activity in the Linux and the open source communities has grown so dramatically in recent years that many diverse outlets exist for learning and getting to know other Linux enthusiasts.

Likewise, if you find that Linux is something you enjoy and want to help to flourish in the future, you can become a Linux advocate in a variety of ways.

## Joining a Linux User Group

Linux User Groups (LUGs) have sprung up all over the world. Many LUGs sponsor Linux install-fests (where members help you install the Linux of your choice on your computer) or help non-profit groups and schools use Linux on older computers that will no longer support the latest Microsoft Windows software. Here are some places to help you track down a local LUG:

- **Google** (www.google.com/linux)—I found both of the LUGs I've been associated with by using Google to search for the word "Linux" and the city closest to where I was living.

- **Linux Meetup Groups** (linux.meetup.com)—Enter your ZIP code to search for the nearest LUG in your area.

- **Linux Online** (www.linux.org/groups)—Offers a large, international list of Linux User Groups. Select your country to see a list of available groups.

If no Linux User Group is in your area, you might consider starting one. To get information on what LUGs are all about and some suggestions about starting one, refer to the Linux User Group HOWTO (www.tldp.org/HOWTO/User-Group-HOWTO.html).

## Joining Linux communities

Communities of professionals and enthusiasts have grown around Linux and its related open source projects. Many have shown themselves willing to devote their time, knowledge, and skills on public mailing lists, forums, Wikis, and other Internet venues (provided you ask politely and aren't too annoying).

Free online forums have sprung up to get information on specific Linux topics. Popular general Linux forums are available from www.LinuxQuestions.org, www.LinuxForums.org, and www.LinuxHelp.net. Most major Linux distributions have associated mailing lists and forums. You can go directly to the Web sites for the Red Hat–sponsored Fedora Linux (http://fedoraproject.org/), Debian (www.debian.com), Ubuntu (http://ubuntuforums.org), Gentoo (www.gentoo.org), and others to learn how to participate in forums and contribute to those projects.

## Companies and groups supporting Linux

Some companies and organizations make important contributions to Linux and open source software. Here are some of the most prominent ones:

- **SourceForge** (web.sourceforge.com)—This organization maintains the open source development site Freshmeat (freshmeat.net) as well as SourceForge (`www.sourceforge.net`). It also maintains information technology sites, such as Slashdot (`slashdot.org`), NewsForge (`www.newsforge.com`), and Linux.com (`www.linux.com`).

- **IBM** (`www.ibm.com/linux`)—Because IBM has been the recipient of the lion's share of lawsuits against Linux and done a lot to further Linux, especially in the enterprise area, it deserves a mention here. Many good resources for Linux exist at IBM's Web site, including some excellent white papers covering Linux in business.

- **Ibiblio** (`www.ibiblio.org`)—Contains a massive archive of Linux software and documentation (`www.ibiblio.org/pub/linux`).

- **Software Freedom Law Center** (`www.softwarefreedom.org`)—This organization provides legal representation for most of the major free and open source software (FOSS) projects in existence today. It is the organization that defends the proper use of software covered under the GNU public license.

- **One Laptop Per Child Project** (`www.laptop.org`)—The OLPC project is an organization that is dedicated to helping educate disadvantaged children all over the world by putting laptop computers in their hands. As of this writing, more than 300,000 OLPC XO laptop computers have been shipped worldwide, making it the single largest distributor of Fedora Linux systems.

# Keeping Up with Linux

Although Slashdot.org is probably the news site that most Linux enthusiasts keep track of and participate in, there are many other places to look for Linux and open source news as well:

- **Slashdot** (`slashdot.org`)—Probably the top news site for open source devotees. People submit links to news articles, book reviews, and interviews related to technology, science, politics, or other "news for nerds." Then everyone piles on with their own commentaries. Having your book or project "slashdotted" means you have made the big time—although you are as likely to get crushed as you are to get praised.

- **Digg** (`http://digg.com/linux_unix`)—Some say that Digg.com has become more popular than Slashdot for providing articles relating to Linux. You can vote on which articles are most interesting to you to gain more exposure for an article.

- **Groklaw** (`www.groklaw.net`)—The place to look for information regarding legal issues surrounding open source software.

- **Linux Today** (`www.linuxtoday.com`)—This site gathers news that is of particular interest to software developers and IT managers.

- **LWN.net** (`www.lwn.net`)—Produces a weekly newsletter covering a range of Linux topics.

- **Newsforge** (www.newsforge.com)—Bills itself as the "Online Newspaper for Linux and Open Source." Contains many original articles, as well as links to up-to-the-minute open source stories from other locations on the Web.

- **LinuxInsider** (www.linuxinsider.com)—Covers news articles related to Linux issues around the world.

- **Linux at Wikipedia** (http://en.wikipedia.org/wiki/Linux)—Contains an excellent write-up of what Linux is, and includes other Wikipedia links to related topics, companies, and issues. Also, provides a good understanding of Linux history and relationships.

- **Linux.com** (www.linux.com)—Provides Linux information, news, tips, articles, and reference material.

- **CertCities.com** (http://certcities.com/certs/linux_unix/columns/)—Regularly publishes articles on Linux and UNIX.

If you need help or have questions about Linux, here are a few sites to try:

- **Linux Questions** (www.linuxquestions.org)—In addition to offering forums on different Linux distributions, this is a great place to ask questions related to hardware compatibility, security, and networking. The site also has some good tutorials, as well as reviews of books and Linux distributions.

- **Google Linux** (www.google.com/linux)—Search for Linux-specific information from this part of the Google search site.

- **Linux Forums** (www.linuxforums.org)—Contains active forums on your favorite distributions and has active IRC channels as well.

- **The Linux Documentation Project** (www.tldp.org)—Offers a wide range of HOWTOs, guides, FAQs, man pages, and other documentation related to Linux.

- **Linux Help** (www.linuxhelp.net)—Offers forums, news, and current information about the Linux kernel. Also contains information about finding Linux mailing lists, newsgroups, and user groups.

- **Linux Online** (www.linux.org)—Provides a central source of information related to Linux distributions, documentation, books, and people.

- **Linux Kernel Archives** (www.kernel.org)—The primary site for Linux kernel development. You can get the latest stable or testing versions of the Linux kernel. Not the first place to start with Linux, but I thought you would want to know it's there.

## Major Linux projects

As you may know, the name Linux comes from the Linux kernel created by Linus Torvalds. The desktop, application, server, and other software needed to create a full Linux system are added from other open source projects. The following is a list of some of the major open source software organizations that usually have software included with Linux:

- **Free Software Foundation** (www.fsf.org)—Supports the GNU project, which produces much of the software outside the kernel that is associated with Linux. In particular, open source versions of nearly every early UNIX command have been implemented by the GNU project.

- **Apache Software Foundation** (www.apache.org)—Produces the Apache (HTTP) Web server. It also manages related projects, such as SpamAssassin (spam filtering software) and a variety of modules for serving special Web content (Perl, SSL, PHP, and so on).

- **K Desktop Environment** (www.kde.org)—Develops KDE, one of the two leading desktop environments used with Linux.

- **GNOME** (www.gnome.org)—Develops the other leading Linux desktop environment (used as the default desktop for Red Hat Linux systems).

- **X.Org** (www.x.org) **and XFree86** (www.xfree86.org)—These two organizations provide different implementations of the X Window System graphical desktop framework software.

- **Internet Systems Consortium** (www.isc.org)—Develops several major open source software projects related to the Internet. These include Bind (domain name system server), INN (InterNetNews news server), and DHCP (dynamic host configuration protocol).

- **The Mozilla Project** (www.mozilla.org)—The first major Web browser product was Mozilla Navigator, which was originally based on code released to the open source community from Netscape Communicator. Other open source browsers incorporate Mozilla's engine. The Mozilla project also offered a suite of related Internet clients that included e-mail, composer, IRC Chat, and address book software. New software development from the Mozilla project focuses on the Thunderbird e-mail and news client and Firefox Web browser, which have seen enormous success on Linux, Windows, and Mac OS X platforms in the past few years. The old Mozilla suite is offered today under the name SeaMonkey (www.mozilla.org/projects/seamonkey).

- **The Samba Project** (www.samba.org)—This provides software for sharing files and printers using CIFS and SMB clients. These protocols are the most common means of sharing files and printers with Microsoft Windows operating systems.

- **The Sendmail Consortium** (www.sendmail.org)—This maintains the sendmail mail transport agent, which is the world's most popular software for transporting mail across the Internet.

There are, of course, many more open source projects and organizations that provide software included in various Linux distributions, but the ones discussed here will give you a good feel for the kind of organizations that produce open source software.

## Exploring Linux distributions

Despite the fact that hundreds of Linux distributions exist, you can safely focus on a handful of Linux systems to get a good flavor of what is available. That's because most Linux distributions are derived from a few major ones. For example, Ubuntu, KNOPPIX, Damn Small, and other Linux systems are based on Debian GNU/Linux. CentOS, Red Hat Enterprise Linux, and others are based on Fedora.

Refer to Chapters 17 through 28 for descriptions on most of the major Linux distributions available today, along with procedures for getting and installing them. If you haven't chosen a distribution yet, here are some sites that can help you evaluate, find, and get a Linux distribution that interests you:

- **Distrowatch** (`distrowatch.com`)—Contains information about a few hundred different Linux distributions. The site provides an easy way to find out about different distributions, and then simply connect to the distribution's home page, download site, or related forums.
- **LWN.net Linux Distributions** (`lwn.net/Distributions`)—For succinct descriptions of more than 400 Linux distributions on one page, this is the place to go.

Here are key sites associated with Linux distributions covered in this book:

- **Fedora** (`http://fedoraproject.org`)—Community-driven Linux, supported by Red Hat. Look to Livna.org (`rpm.livna.org`) for downloads of add-on software for Fedora. FedoraForum.org is a popular Forum site for Fedora.
- **Red Hat Enterprise Linux** (`www.redhat.com`)—Check the main Red Hat Web site for information on commercial Linux products.
- **Debian GNU/Linux** (`www.debian.org`)—Get news, documentation, support, and download information about Debian. Try the Debian news site (`www.us.debian.org/News/`) for the latest news articles on Debian.
- **Ubuntu Linux** (`www.ubuntu.com`)—Learn about the Ubuntu Linux distribution, community, and related products from this official Ubuntu site. From the Ubuntu Wiki (`https://wiki.ubuntu.com`) find links to documentation, HOWTOs, community sites, events, and releases.
- **SUSE** (`www.novell.com/linux/`)—Get product and support information from this project's site. The Novell site also provides information about Novell's own Linux offerings and details of its recent alliance with Microsoft.
- **openSUSE** (`www.opensuse.org`)—Get information and downloads, connect to mailing lists and forums, and participate in the community-supported version of SUSE.
- **KNOPPIX** (`www.knopper.net/knoppix/index-en.html`)—The official KNOPPIX page on its creator's (Klaus Knopper's) Web site. An active KNOPPIX forum is available from `www.knoppix.net/forum/`.

- **Yellow Dog** (www.terrasoftsolutions.com/products/ydl)—From this site, sponsored by Terra Soft Solutions, you can purchase Yellow Dog Linux on CDs or get it pre-installed on Mac hardware. The YDL.net site offers some extra services for Yellow Dog Linux users, such as personal e-mail accounts and Web space.

- **Gentoo** (www.gentoo.org)—The center for the very active Gentoo community. The site contains a wealth of information about Gentoo and plenty of forums and IRC channels in which to participate. You'll find a solid and growing documentation set to back up the distribution and tons of software packages to try (in the thousands).

- **Slackware** (www.slackware.org)—Check the changelogs at this site to get a feel for the latest Slackware developments. Try LinuxPackages (www.linuxpackages.net) for a broader range of information about Slackware.

- **Freespire** (www.freespire.org)—Contains information about what was once the community-supported arm of the Linspire Linux system. With the Xandros purchase of Linspire, Freespire now is under the control of Xandros.

- **Mandriva** (www.mandrivalinux.com)—Formed from the merger of Mandrake Linux and Connectiva Linux, the Mandriva Linux Web site gives visitors a variety of Linux products, services, and support.

# Linux in the Real World

To see how Linux and related free and open source software is being used today in the real world, I've provided some short examples that relate to Linux use in schools, small business, and enterprise venues.

## Linux in schools

Cost savings, flexibility, and a huge pool of applications have made Linux a wonderful alternative to proprietary systems for many schools. One project has been particularly successful in schools: the K12 Linux Terminal Server Project (www.k12ltsp.org).

K12LTSP is based on the Linux Terminal Service Project (www.ltsp.org) and Fedora (www.fedoraproject.org), but is tuned to work particularly in schools. With K12LTSP, you centralize all your school's applications on one or more server machines. Then you can use low-end PCs (old Pentiums or thin clients) as workstations. With thin clients starting under $200 or old PCs already hanging around your school, you can service a whole class or even a whole school for little more than the cost of the servers and some networking hardware. Figure 2-5 illustrates the general steps you would go through to configure a Linux LTSP sever to manage multiple workstations.

By centralizing all the school's software on a limited number of servers, K12LTSP can offer both security (only a few servers to watch over) and convenience (no need to reinstall hundreds of Windows machines to upgrade or enhance the software). Each client machine controls the display, mouse, and keyboard, whereas all the user's applications and files are stored on and run from the server.

**FIGURE 2-5**

Configure LTSP on the server, and then boot up workstations to work from that server.

The K12LTSP distribution contains many battle-tested open source applications, including full GNOME and KDE desktops, Evolution e-mail, Firefox browser, OpenOffice.org office suite, and GIMP image application. They also add DansGuardian (open source Web content filtering) and educational software (such as Gcompris). If the Windows application you are looking for is not available in Linux, you can almost surely find a similar Linux application.

Many schools in Oregon have adopted K12LTSP, including those attended by Linus Torvalds' children in Portland, Oregon. Adoption of K12LTSP has also begun in Atlanta, Georgia and many other cities across the United States.

## Linux in small business

Often a small business can consolidate the Web services it needs into one or two Linux servers. It can meet its basic office computing needs with mature open source applications such as OpenOffice.org, The GIMP, and a Firefox browser. But can a small business run entirely on open source software alone?

When Jim Nanney started his Coast Grocery business, where residents of the Mississippi Gulf Coast can order groceries online for delivery, he set out to do just that. In part, he just wanted to see whether he could rely solely on open source software. But he also figured that a cost savings of at least $10,000 by not buying commercial software could help make his small business profitable a lot faster.

To enable customers to order groceries online, Jim selected the open source e-commerce software called osCommerce (www.oscommerce.com). The osCommerce software is built with the PHP Web scripting language and uses a MySQL database. Jim runs the software from a Linux system with an Apache Web server.

On the office side of the business, Jim relies entirely on Fedora Linux systems. He uses OpenOffice.org Writer for documents, GIMP and Inkscape for logos and other artwork, and GnuCash for accounting. For Web browsing, Firefox is used. So far, Jim hasn't had a need to purchase any commercial software.

Here are some of the advantages that Jim has found from his all–open source business:

- **Community support**—The communities surrounding osCommerce and Fedora have been very helpful. With active forums and 24-hour IRC channels, getting help with those projects has been easier than with any proprietary software. Also unlike proprietary software, participants are generally quite knowledgeable and often include the developers of the software themselves.

- **Long-term security**—Jim disputes conventional wisdom that betting your business on proprietary software is safer than relying on open source. If a software company goes out of business, the small business could go down, too. But with open source you have the code, so you could always pay someone to update the code when necessary or fix it yourself.

- **Easier improvements**—By doing some of his own PHP programming, Jim had a lot of flexibility related to adding features. In some cases, he could take existing code and modify it to suit his needs. In the case of creating a special shopping list feature, he found it easiest to write code from scratch. In the process of using the software, when he found exploitable bugs, he submitted the code fixes back to the project.

- **No compatibility problems**—On those occasions where he needed to provide information to others, compatibility has not been a problem. When he makes business cards, door hangers or other printed material, he saves his artwork to PDF or SVG formats to send to a commercial printer. Regular documents can be exported to Word, Excel, or other common formats.

For businesses starting on a shoestring, in many cases open source software can offer both the cost savings and flexibility needed to help the business survive during the difficult start-up period. Later, it can help those same businesses thrive, as open source solutions can often be easily scaled up as the business grows.

## Linux in the enterprise

Building a company's computer infrastructure on open source software represents a huge amount of confidence that it will provide the level of reliability, security, and features that a company needs. That's why most large companies converting to open source infrastructures have gone with products from enterprise Linux providers, such as Red Hat, Inc. (Red Hat Enterprise Linux) and Novell, Inc. (SUSE Linux Enterprise).

Built into Red Hat's open source enterprise products are features such as Red Hat Directory Server, Global File System (GFS), and Cluster Suite. Directory Server can scale up to handle millions of identities, representing settings for applications' user profiles, access control, and policies across thousands of machines and users. Using GFS and Cluster Suite, an enterprise can treat its entire storage infrastructure as a common pool, to minimize data duplication and simplify backups, system recovery, and adding storage and servers.

Companies moving their infrastructures to Linux include Apoteket (Sweden's government-run pharmacy), which is moving more than 900 pharmacies to Red Hat Enterprise Linux (RHEL) on Intel servers. Governments that are migrating to RHEL include cities such as Chicago and Bloomington, Illinois. You can read about other organizations migrating to RHEL on Red Hat's Success Stories page (www.redhat.com/solutions/info/casestudies).

# Becoming a Linux Professional

Pursuing a career based on something that people give away for free may not seem like a brilliant idea. But the truth is that thousands of jobs exist for Linux professionals if you have the skills to get the job done.

Contributing to open source projects has long been one of the best ways to gain the skills you need to gain entry to a Linux career. When the Ubuntu project started up, it hired many of the best contributors to the Debian GNU/Linux project. When Red Hat, Inc. looks to hire a Linux professional, it often looks to the ranks of Fedora contributors.

Formal Linux training and certification opportunities have grown considerably in the past few years. If you want to work for companies that use Red Hat Enterprise Linux, you can get training and certification directly from Red Hat (www.redhat.com/training). Red Hat offers classes in everything from Red Hat Linux Essentials to Red Hat Enterprise Deployment, Virtualization, and Systems Management. You can train for certifications such as

- **Red Hat Certified Technician (RHCT)**—Those who have never used Linux or other UNIX-like systems can transition their skills to Linux with an RHCT certification.
- **Red Hat Certified Engineer (RHCE)**—More advanced Linux professionals in the area of systems administration usually take the RHCE certification.
- **Red Hat Certified Datacenter Specialist (RHCDS)**—The RHCDS certification demonstrates skills to build mission-critical data center environments. Emphasis is put on

using Red Hat technologies to create data centers that are scalable, reliable, available, and manageable.

- **Red Hat Certified Security Specialist (RHCSS)**—Skills emphasized in the RHCSS program focus on SELinux, Red Hat Enterprise Linux, and Red Hat Directory Server.
- **Red Hat Certified Architect (RHCA)**—This credential is for technical professionals that have skills deploying large-scale enterprise environments.

Although Red Hat offers one of the most popular programs for Linux certifications, it is by no means the only place to get Linux certification. Sun Microsystems offers training for Linux system administrators (www.sun.com/training/). CompTIA offers Linux+ certification that is not tied to a particular Linux distribution. Likewise, Novell and Linux Professional Institute both offer Linux certifications. Ubuntu offers Ubuntu Certified Professional training and certification (www.ubuntu.com/training/certificationcourses).

# Summary

Although most people use Linux as a desktop, server, or programmer's workstation, many have also found that the freedom open source software provides can be used in many creative ways. This chapter describes ways that projects ranging from NASA's Mars Rover to the MythTV personal video recorder have adapted Linux systems and software to meet their needs.

If you get excited about the prospects of open source software as you read this book, you may find you want to pursue ways of getting more involved. Some ways of getting involved include joining a Linux User Group, contributing to open source projects, or participating in mailing lists or forums.

As you increase your skills with open source software, you may find the idea of a career in Linux interesting. Many companies offer training and certification in Linux. This includes enterprise-oriented companies such as Red Hat and Novell, as well as specialized Linux training companies such as CompTIA and Linux Professional Institute.

# Part II

# Running a Linux Desktop

# Getting into the Desktop

In the past few years, graphical user interfaces (GUIs) available for Linux have become as easy to use as those on the Apple Mac or Microsoft Windows systems. With these improvements, even a novice computer user can start using Linux without needing to have an expert standing by.

You don't need to understand the underlying framework of the X Window System, window managers, widgets, and whatnots to get going with a Linux desktop system. That's why I start by explaining how to use the two most popular desktop environments: KDE (K desktop environment) and GNOME. After that, if you want to dig deeper, I tell you how you can put together your own desktop by discussing how to choose your own X-based window manager to run in Linux.

## Understanding Your Desktop

When you install Linux distributions such as Fedora, SUSE, Mandriva, or Ubuntu, you have the option to choose a desktop environment. Distributions such as Gentoo and Debian GNU/Linux give you the option to go out and get whatever desktop environment you want (without an installer particularly prompting you for it). When you are given the opportunity to select a desktop during installation, your choices usually include one or more of the following:

- **K desktop environment** (www.kde.org)—In addition to all the features you would expect to find in a complete desktop environment (window managers, toolbars, panels, menus, keybindings, icons, and so on), KDE has many bells and whistles available.

Applications for graphics, multimedia, office productivity, games, system administration, and many other uses have been integrated to work smoothly with KDE, which is the default desktop environment for SUSE and various other Linux distributions.

- **GNOME desktop environment** (www.gnome.org)—GNOME is a more streamlined desktop environment. It includes a smaller feature set than KDE and runs faster in many lower-memory systems. Some think of GNOME as a more business-oriented desktop. It's the default desktop for Red Hat–sponsored systems such as Fedora and RHEL, as well as Ubuntu, and others.

## Note

The KDE 4 Desktop is based on the Qt 4.5 graphical toolkit. GNOME is based on GTK+ 2.12. Although graphical applications are usually written to either QT or GTK+, by installing both desktops you will have the libraries needed to run applications written for both toolkits from either environment. ■

- **Lightweight desktop environments**—Xfce (www.xfce.org) and LXDE (www.lxde.org) are examples of desktop environments that are built to run well with low-powered processors and less RAM. LXDE is currently the desktop environment used with KNOPPIX.
- **X and a window manager** (X.org or XFree86.org + WM)—You don't need a full-blown desktop environment to operate Linux from a GUI. The most basic, reasonable way of using Linux is to simply start the X Window System server and a window manager of your choice (you have dozens to choose from). Many advanced users go this route because it can offer more flexibility in how they set up their desktops. Window managers such as Xfce and fluxbox are particularly good on low-end, low-resource machines.

The truth is that most X applications run in any of the desktop environments just described (provided that proper libraries are included with your Linux distribution, as noted earlier). So you can choose a Linux desktop based on the performance, customization tools, and controls that best suit you. Each of these three types of desktop environments is described in this chapter.

# Starting the Desktop

Because the way that you start a desktop in Linux is completely configurable, different distributions offer different ways of starting up the desktop. After your Linux distribution is installed, it may just boot to the desktop, offer a graphical login, or offer a text-based login. Bootable Linux systems (which don't have to be installed at all) typically just boot to the desktop.

## Boot to the desktop

Some bootable Linux systems boot right to a desktop without requiring you to log in so you can immediately start working with Linux. KNOPPIX is an example of a distribution that boots straight to a Linux desktop from a CD. That desktop system usually runs as a particular user-name (such as knoppix, in the case of the KNOPPIX distribution). To perform system admin-istration, you have to switch to the administrator's account temporarily (using the su or sudo command).

## Caution

**Using any computer operating system without password protection violates all basic security rules. Use a sys-tem without password protection only on a temporary basis on computers that have no access to critical data. To be more secure, you can assign a password to a live CD's primary user account, and certainly assign one if you install that live CD to hard disk. ■**

## Boot to graphical login

Most desktop Linux systems that are installed on your hard disk boot up to a graphical login screen. Although the X display manager (xdm) is the basic display manager that comes with the X Window System, KDE and GNOME each have their own graphical display managers that are used as login screens (kdm and gdm, respectively).

So chances are that you will see the login screen associated with KDE or GNOME (depending on which is the default on your Linux system). Display managers such as gdm offer you the oppor-tunity to log in to different types of desktops, depending on what is installed on your system (GNOME, KDE, Xfce, or others).

## Note

**When Linux starts up, it enters into what is referred to as a run level or system state. Typically, a system set to start at run level 5 boots to a graphical login prompt. A system set to run level 3 boots to a text prompt. The run level is set by the** initdefault **line in the** /etc/inittab **file. Change the number on the** initde-fault **line as you please between 3 and 5. Don't use any other number unless you know what you are doing. Never use 0 or 6. Those numbers are used to shut down and reboot the system, respectively. ■**

Because graphical login screens are designed to be configurable, you often find that the distribu-tion has its own logo or other graphical elements on the login screen. With Fedora Linux, the default login screen is based on the GNOME display manager (gdm). To begin a session, you can just enter your login (username) and password to start up your personal desktop environment.

Your selected desktop environment—KDE, GNOME, Xfce, or other—comes up ready for you to use. Although the system defines a desktop environment by default, you can typically change desktop environments on those Linux systems, such as Fedora, that offer multiple desktop environments.

Figure 3-1 shows a basic graphical login panel displayed by the gdm graphical display manager in Fedora.

To end a session, you can choose to log out. Figure 3-2 shows the graphical menu from a Fedora GNOME desktop for ending a session or changing the computer state (System ⇨ Shut Down).

FIGURE 3-1

A simple GNOME display manager (gdm) login screen

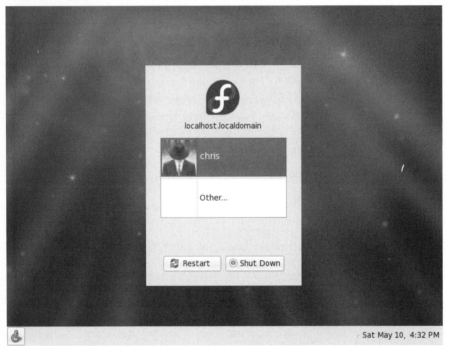

FIGURE 3-2

The Session menu in Fedora

X display managers can enable you to do a lot more than just get to your desktop. Although different graphical login screens offer different options, here are some you may encounter:

- **Session/Options**—Look for a Session or Options button on the login screen. From there, you can choose to start your login session with a GNOME, KDE, or other desktop environment.

- **Language**—Linux systems that are configured to start in multiple languages may give you the opportunity to choose a language (other than the default language) to boot into. For this to work, however, you must have installed support for the language you choose.

- **Accessibility**—Some display managers let you choose accessibility preferences. These selections let you hear text read aloud, magnify parts of the screen, use an onscreen keyboard, or do other things to overcome difficulty hearing, seeing, or using a keyboard.

If you don't like the way the graphical login screen looks, or just want to assert greater control over how it works, you can configure and secure X graphical login screens in many ways. Later, after you are logged in, you can use the following tools (as root user) to configure the login screen:

- **KDE login manager**—From the KDE Control Center, you can modify your KDE display manager using the Login Manager screen (from KDE Control Center, select System Administration ➪ Login Manager). You can change logos, backgrounds, color schemes, and other features related to the look-and-feel of the login screen.

- **GNOME login manager**—The GNOME display manager (gdm) comes with a Login Window Preferences utility (from the desktop, run the gdmsetup command as root user). From the Login Window Preferences window, you can select the Local tab and choose a whole different theme for the login manager. On the Security tab, you may notice that all TCP connections to the X server are disallowed. Don't change this selection because no processes other than those handled directly by your display manager should be allowed to connect to the login screen. (The gdmsetup utility is not available in the current release of Fedora.)

After your login and password have been accepted, the desktop environment configured for your user account starts up. Users can modify their desktop environments to suit their tastes (even to the point of changing the entire desktop environment used).

## Boot to a text prompt

Instead of a nice graphical screen with pictures and colors, you might see a login prompt that looks like this:

```
Welcome to XYZ Linux
yourcomputer login:
```

This is the way all UNIX and older Linux systems used to appear on the screen when they booted up. Now this is the login prompt that is typical for a system that is installed as a server or, for some reason, was configured not to start an X display manager for you to log in. Run level 3 boots to a plain-text login prompt in multiuser mode.

Just because you have a text prompt doesn't necessarily mean you can start a desktop environment. Many Linux experts boot to a text prompt because they want to bypass the graphical login screen or use the GUI only occasionally. Some Linux servers may not even have a desktop environment installed. However, if X and the necessary other desktop components are installed on your computer, you can typically start the desktop after you log in by typing the following command:

```
$ startx
```

The default desktop environment starts up, and you should be ready to go. What you do next depends on whether you have a KDE, GNOME, or some sort of homespun desktop environment.

## Note

**In most cases, the GUI configuration you set up during installation for your video card and monitor gets you to a working desktop environment. If, for some reason, the screen is unusable when you start the desktop, you need to do some additional configuration. The "Configuring Your Own Desktop" section later in this chapter describes some tools you can use to get your desktop working. ■**

# K Desktop Environment

KDE was created to bring a high-quality desktop environment to UNIX (and now Linux) workstations. Integrated within KDE are tools for managing files, windows, multiple desktops, and applications. If you can work a mouse, you can learn to navigate the KDE desktop.

The lack of an integrated, standardized desktop environment once held back Linux and other UNIX systems from acceptance on the desktop. While individual applications ran well, you mostly could not drag-and-drop files or other items between applications. Likewise, you couldn't open a file and expect the machine to launch the correct application to deal with it or save your windows from one login session to the next. With KDE, you can do all those things and much more. For example, you can

- Drag-and-drop a document from one folder window to another (to move it) or on an OpenOffice.org Writer icon (to open it for editing).
- Right-click an image file (JPEG, PNG, and so on), and the OpenWith menu lets you choose to open the file using an image viewer (KView), editor (The GIMP), slideshow viewer (KuickShow), or other application.

To make more applications available to you in the future, KDE provides a platform for developers to create programs that easily share information and detect how to deal with different data types. The things you can do with KDE increase in number every day.

KDE is the default desktop environment for Mandriva and several other Linux systems. SUSE, openSUSE, and related distributions moved from KDE to GNOME as the default desktop, but still make KDE available. Red Hat Enterprise Linux and Fedora, which used to place less emphasis on KDE, now have much improved support for KDE desktops, even offering a custom KDE desktop live CD/installer disk.

The past year has seen several point releases to improve the KDE 4 desktop. Despite many bold new features for managing the desktop, KDE 4 suffered from some instability. The latest version of KDE is much improved. The following section describes how to get started with KDE.

## Using the KDE desktop

The KDE 4 desktop, now available with Fedora, Ubuntu, and other major Linux distributions, offers the Plasma desktop and a relatively new framework for developing KDE applications. Some Linux distributions still use the more stable KDE 3.5, so you may have a choice of which KDE you use.

KDE 4 marked some major innovations for the KDE desktop. New libraries were added to support multimedia applications and improve handling of removable devices. There are new applications for viewing documents (such as Okular) and managing files (such as Dolphin). The most important new feature, however, was the Plasma desktop shell.

The Plasma desktop shell gives the KDE 4 desktop a whole new look-and-feel from the KDE 3.5 desktop. It featured improved ways of finding and presenting information, such as KRunner and KickOff. The Plasma Panel incorporates lots of applets, as well as clocks, pagers, and other useful applications.

Elements in the Plasma desktop shell are referred to as *plasmoids*. What makes plasmoids different from components on many of today's desktop systems is that they can be combined in various ways to interact with each other and can be placed in different locations. For example, if a particular widget (such as a clock or a news ticker) is important to you, instead of having it represented by a tiny icon on the panel, you can put a big version of the applet on your desktop.

Figure 3-3 shows an example of a KDE desktop in Fedora.

Some of the key elements of the KDE desktop include

- **Plasmoids**—Applets that you can add to the desktop as well as the panel are referred to as *plasmoids* in KDE 4. In Figure 3-3 you can see the clock, picture frame, and news ticker all added to the desktop. You can drag plasmoids around, group them together, and arrange them as you like on your desktop.

- **Konqueror**—The default Web browser for KDE, which can also be used as a file manager.

- **Dolphin**—A new file manager for KDE.

- **Panel**—The panel provides some quick tools for launching applications and managing the desktop. You can adapt the panel to your needs by resizing it, adding tools, and changing its location. By default, you start with an application launcher, taskbar, desktop pager, some mini applets, new device modifier, and a clock.

## FIGURE 3-3

The KDE desktop includes a panel, desktop icons, and much more.

- **Application Launcher/Menu**—This panel button is the new KickOff Application menu, which helps you search for applications installed on your system and launch them. Choose between Favorites (applications you use often), Applications (application menus), Computer (places and storage devices), or Recently Used applications. Right-click the button and select Switch to Classic Menu Style to return to a classic view of application categories and menus.

- **Taskbar**—This button shows the tasks that are currently running on the desktop. The button for the window that is currently active appears pressed in. Click a task to toggle between opening and minimizing the window.

- **Desktop Pager**—This box on the panel consists of your virtual desktops, which contain small views of each desktop. Four virtual desktops are available to you by default. These are labeled 1, 2, 3, and 4. You begin your KDE session on virtual desktop 1. If windows are on the desktop, small icons representing them may cover the desktop number. You can change to any of the four desktops by clicking it.

- **Mini applets**—Some applications, such as media players, clipboards, and battery power managers, will keep running after you have closed the related window. Some of those applications maintain a tiny applet in the panel. Clicking on these applets often restores the windows they represent. This feature is convenient for music players if you don't want to take up desktop space while you play music, but you want to be able to open the player quickly to change songs.

- **Clock**—The current time appears on the far-right side of the panel. Click it to see a calendar for the current month. Click the arrow keys on the calendar to move forward and back to other months.

To navigate the KDE desktop, you can use the mouse or key combinations. The responses from the desktop to your mouse depend on which button you click and where the mouse pointer is located.

Table 3-1 shows the results of clicking each mouse button with the mouse pointer placed in different locations. (You can change these and other behaviors from the KDE menu by selecting System Settings, and then choosing Keyboard & Mouse.)

**TABLE 3-1**

## Single-Click Mouse Actions

| Pointer Position | Mouse Button | Result |
| --- | --- | --- |
| Window title bar or frame (current window active) | Left | Raises current window |
| Window title bar or frame (current window active) | Middle | Lowers current window |
| Window title bar or frame (current window active) | Right | Opens operations menu |
| Window title bar or frame (current window not active) | Left | Activates current window and raises it to the top |
| Window title bar or frame (current window not active) | Middle | Activates current window and lowers it |
| Window title bar or frame (current window not active) | Right | Opens operations menu without changing position |
| Inner window (current window not active) | Left | Activates current window, raises it to the top, and passes the click to the window |

*continued*

**TABLE 3-1**     (continued)

| Pointer Position | Mouse Button | Result |
|---|---|---|
| Inner window (current window not active) | Middle or Right | Activates current window and passes the click to the window |
| Any part of a window | Middle (plus hold Alt key) | Toggles between raising and lowering the window |
| Any part of a window | Right (plus hold Alt key) | Resizes the window |
| On the desktop area | Left (hold and drag) | Selects a group of icons |
| On the desktop area | Right | Opens system pop-up menu |

Click a desktop icon to open it. Double-clicking a window title bar results in a window-shade action, where the window scrolls up and down into the title bar.

If you don't happen to have a mouse or you just like to keep your hands on the keyboard, you can use several keystroke sequences to navigate the desktop. Table 3-2 shows some examples.

**TABLE 3-2**

## Keystrokes

| Key Combination | Result | Directions |
|---|---|---|
| Alt+Tab | Step through windows | To step through each of the windows that are running on the current desktop, hold down the Alt key and press the Tab key until you see the one you want. Then release the Alt key to select it. |
| Alt+F2 | Open Run Command box | To open a box on the desktop that lets you type in a command and run it, hold the Alt key and press F2. Next, type the command in the box and press Enter to run it. You can also type a URL into this box to view a Web page. |
| Alt+F4 | Close current window | To close the current window, press Alt+F4. |
| Ctrl+Alt+Esc | Close another window | To close an open window on the desktop, press Ctrl+Alt+Esc. When a skull and crossbones appear as the pointer, move the pointer over the window you want to close and click the left mouse button. (This technique is good for killing a window that has no borders or menu.) |

| Key Combination | Result | Directions |
|---|---|---|
| Ctrl+F1, F2, F3, or F4 key | Switch virtual desktops | Go directly to a particular virtual desktop by pressing and holding the Ctrl key and pressing one of the following: F1, F2, F3, or F4. These actions take you directly to desktops one, two, three, and four, respectively. You could do this for up to eight desktops, if you have that many configured. |
| Alt+F3 | Open window operation menu | To open the operations menu for the active window, press Alt+F3. When the menu appears, move the arrow keys to select an action (Move, Size, Minimize, Maximize, and so on), and then press Enter to select it. Press Esc to close the menu. |

## Managing files with Dolphin and Konqueror

With KDE 4, the KDE desktop offers two file managers: the newer Dolphin File Manager and the existing Konqueror File Manager/Browser. Dolphin is a streamlined file manager that is now used by default when you open a folder in KDE. Konqueror can handle a wide range of content from local files and folders to remote Web content. The two applications are described in the sections that follow.

### Note

**For further information on Dolphin, refer to the Dolphin File Manager home page** (http://enzosworld .gmxhome.de). ■

## Using the Dolphin file manager

By adding Dolphin to KDE, the KDE project now offers an efficient way to manage your files and folders, without the overhead of a full-blown Web browser (such as Konqueror). With Dolphin, you have a lot of flexibility and features for getting around your file system and working with the files and folders you encounter. Features in Dolphin include

- **Navigation**—The navigation bar lets you see the current folder in relation to your home directory or to the root of the file system. Select View ➪ Navigation Bar ➪ Show Full Location to see (and change) the full path to your current folder. Select folders from the left column to go straight to that folder.

- **Listing Files and Folders**—Select icons in the toolbar to display files and folders as icons, with filename, size, and date, or with small icons in columns.

- **Properties**—Right-click on a file or folder and select Properties. Properties displayed include file type (such as folder or Ogg Vorbis audio), location (such as /home/joe), file/folder size, date/time modified, date/time accessed, and permissions. For folders, there are also some nice features that let you refresh the amount of disk space used by the folder or configure file sharing to share the folder with other computers on the network. Both Samba and NFS file sharing are supported.

- **Filter and Search**—Select Tools ➪ Show Filter Bar from the Dolphin toolbar. In the Filter box that appears, type a string of text to display any file or folder name containing that text string (for example, usi would match Music). Select Tools ➪ Find Files to open the kfind window to search for files (described later).

- **Preview**—Typically, files are represented by generic icons (text file, image file, and so on) in the Dolphin window. Click the Preview button on the toolbar and you can see small representations of the text or image contained in the file, instead of a generic icon.

To open the Dolphin file manager, select File Manager from the main KDE menu. Figure 3-4 shows an example of the Dolphin file manager.

### Working with files

Because most of the ways of working with files in Dolphin are quite intuitive (by intention), Table 3-3 provides a quick rundown of how to do basic file manipulation.

**FIGURE 3-4**

Dolphin is an efficient file manager for KDE.

TABLE 3-3

## Working with Files in Dolphin

| Task | Action |
|---|---|
| Open a file | Left-click the file. The contents of that file will open in the application window defined for that content. For example, images open in Gwenview and text files open in KWrite. You also can open directories, applications, and links by left-clicking them. |
| Open a file with a specific application | Right-click a data file, choose Open With from the pop-up menu, and then select one of the available applications to open the file. The applications listed are those that are set up to open the file. Select Other to choose a different application. |
| Delete a file | Right-click the file and select Move to Trash. You are asked whether you really want to move the file to trash. Click Yes to move the file to the trash. |
| Copy a file | Right-click the file and select Copy. This copies the file to your clipboard. After that, you can paste it to another folder. Click the Klipper (clipboard) icon in the panel to see a list of copied files. Klipper holds the seven most recently copied files, by default. Click the Klipper icon and select Configure Klipper to change the number of copied files Klipper will remember. |
| Paste a file | Right-click (an open area of a folder) and select Paste. A copy of the file you copied previously is pasted in the current folder. |
| Link a file | Drag-and-drop a file from one folder to another. When the menu appears, click Link Here. (A linked file lets you access a file from a new location without having to make a copy of the original file. When you open the link, a pointer to the original file causes it to open.) |
| Move a file Copy a file Create a link to a file | With the original folder and target folder both open on the desktop, click and hold the left mouse button on the file you want to move, drag the file to an open area of the new folder, and release the mouse button. From the menu that appears, click Move. (You also can use this menu to copy or create a link to the file.) |

There are also several features for viewing information about the files and folders in your Dolphin windows:

- **View quick file information**—Positioning the mouse pointer over the file displays information such as its filename, size, and type in the window footer.

- **View hidden files**—Selecting View ⇨ Show Hidden Files enables you to see files that begin with a dot (.). Dot files tend to be used for configuration and don't generally need to be viewed in your daily work.

- **View file details**—Selecting View ⇨ View Mode ⇨ Details provides a list of details regarding the contents of the current folder. You can click a folder in the details view to jump directly to that folder. Select View ⇨ Additional Information to add more information about each file to the view, such as permissions, owner, group, and type. Columns and Icon views are also available.

To act on a group of files at the same time, you can take a couple of actions. Choose Edit ⇨ Select All to highlight all files and folders in the current folder so they are ready for you to act on. Or, you can select a group of files by clicking in an open area of the folder and dragging the pointer across the files you want to select. All files within the box will be highlighted. When files are highlighted, you can move, copy, or delete the files as described earlier.

### Searching for files

If you are looking for a particular file or folder, use the Dolphin Find feature. To open a Find window to search for a file, open a local folder (such as /home/chris) and choose Tools ⇨ Find File. The Find Files/Folders (kfind) window appears. You can also open this window by typing **kfind** from a Terminal window.

Figure 3-5 shows the Find Files/Folders window.

**FIGURE 3-5**

Search for files and folders from the kfind window.

Simply type the name of the file you want to search for (in the Named text box) and the folder, including all subfolders, you want to search in (in the Look in text box). Then click the Find button. Use metacharacters, if you like, with your search. For example, search for *.rpm to find all files that end in .rpm or z*.doc to find all files that begin with z and end with .doc. You can also select to have the search be case-sensitive or click the Help button to get more information on searching. The example in Figure 3-5 shows a search for Ogg music files (ending in .ogg).

To further limit your search, you can click the Properties tab and then enter a date range (between), a number of months before today (during the previous *x* months), or the number of days before today (during the previous *x* days). You can also search for files that are of a certain size (File size is) in kilobytes, megabytes, or gigabytes. Select the Contents tab to choose to limit the search to files of a particular type (File Type) or files that include text that you enter (Containing Text).

## Creating new files and folders

You can create a variety of file types when using the Dolphin window. Choose File ➪ Create New, and select Folder (to create a new folder) or one of several different types under the File or Device submenu. Depending on which version of Dolphin you are using, you might be able to create some or all of the file types that follow:

- **Text File**—Opens a dialog box that lets you create a document in text format and place it in the Dolphin window. Type the name of the text document to create and click OK.

- **HTML File**—Opens a dialog box that lets you type the name of an HTML file to create.

- **Link to Location (URL)**—Selecting this menu item opens a dialog box that lets you create a link to a Web address. Type a name to represent the address and type the name of the URL (Web address) for the site. (Be sure to add the http://, ftp://, or other prefix.)

- **Link to Application**—Opens a window that lets you type the name of an application. Click the Permissions tab to set file permissions (Exec must be on if you want to run the file as an application). Click the Execute tab and type the name of the program to run (in the field Execute on click) and a title to appear in the title bar of the application (in the field Window Title). If it is a text-based command, select the Run in terminal check box. Select the check box to Run as a different user and add the username. Click the Application tab to assign the application to handle files of particular MIME types. Click OK.

Under the Link to Device submenu, you can make the following selections:

- **CD-ROM Device**—Opens a dialog box that lets you type a new CD-ROM device name. Click the Device tab and type the device name (/dev/cdrom), the mount point (such as /mnt/cdrom), and the file system type (you can use iso9660 for the standard CD-ROM file system, ext2 for Linux, or msdos for DOS). When the icon appears, you can open it to mount the CD-ROM and display its contents.

- **CDWRITER Device**—From the window that opens, enter the device name of your CD writer.

- **Camera Device**—In the dialog box that opens, identify the device name for the camera devices that provide access to your digital camera.

- **DVD-ROM Device**—Opens a dialog box that lets you type a new CD-ROM or DVD-ROM device name. Click the Device tab and type the device name (such as /dev/cdrom), the mount point (such as /mnt/cdrom), and the file system type (you can use iso9660 for the standard CD-ROM file system, ext2 for Linux, or msdos for DOS). When the icon appears, you can open it to mount the CD-ROM or DVD-ROM and display its contents.

- **Floppy Device**—Opens a dialog box in which you type a new floppy name. Click the Device tab and type the device name (/dev/fd0), the mount point (such as /mnt/floppy), and the file system type (you can use auto to autodetect the contents, ext2 for Linux, or msdos for DOS). When the icon appears, open it to mount the floppy and display its contents.

- **Hard Disc Device**—Opens a dialog box that lets you type the name of a new hard disk or hard-disk partition. Click the Device tab and type the device name (/dev/hda1), the mount point (such as /mnt/win), and the file system type (you can use auto to autodetect the contents, ext2 or ext3 for Linux, or vfat for a Windows file system). When the icon appears, you can open it to mount the file system and display its contents.

Creating MIME types and applications is described later in this chapter.

## Using the Konqueror Web browser/file manager

Although Dolphin is now intended for pure file manager features, Konqueror is an excellent tool if you want to move between local and Web content. Konqueror's greatest strengths over earlier file managers include the following:

- **Network desktop**—If your computer is connected to the Internet or a LAN, features built into Konqueror enable you to create links to files (using FTP) and Web pages (using HTTP) on the network and open them in the Konqueror window. Those links can appear as file icons in a Konqueror window or on the desktop. Konqueror also supports WebDAV, which you can configure to allow local read and write access to remote folders (which is a great tool if you are maintaining a Web server).

- **Web browser interface**—The Konqueror interface works like Firefox, Internet Explorer, or other Web browsers in the way you select files, directories, and Web content. Because Konqueror is based on a browser model, a single click opens a file, a link to a network resource, or an application program. You can also open content by typing Web-style addresses in the Location box. The rendering engine used by Konqueror, called KHTML, is also used by Safari (the popular Web browser for Apple Mac OS X systems) and supports advanced features, such as Cascading Style Sheets (CSS) 3.

## Tip

Web pages that contain Java and JavaScript content run by default in Konqueror. To check that Java and JavaScript support is turned on, choose Settings ⇨ Configure Konqueror. From the Settings window, click Java & JavaScript and select the Java tab. To enable Java, click the Enable Java Globally box and click Apply. Repeat for the JavaScript tab. ∎

- **File types and MIME types**—If you want a particular type of file to always be launched by a particular application, you can configure that file yourself. KDE already has dozens of MIME types defined so that particular file and data types can be automatically detected and opened in the correct application. There are MIME types defined for audio, image, text, video, and a variety of other content.

Of course, you can also perform many standard file manager functions with Konqueror. For example, you can manipulate files by using features such as select, move, cut, paste, and delete; search directories for files; create new items (files, folders, and links, to name a few); view histories of the files and Web sites you have opened; and create bookmarks. Most of these features work the same way as they do in Dolphin (as described earlier).

## Using bookmarking features in Konqueror

Because Konqueror performs like a Web browser as well as a file manager, it includes several browser features. For example, the bookmarks feature enables you to keep a bookmark list of Web sites you have visited. Click Bookmarks, and a drop-down menu of the sites you have bookmarked appears. Select from that list to return to a site. There are several ways to add and change your bookmarks list:

- **Add Bookmark**—To add the address of the page currently being displayed to your bookmark list, choose Bookmarks ➪ Add Bookmark. The next time you click Bookmarks, you will see the bookmark you just added on the Bookmarks menu. In addition to Web addresses, you can also bookmark any file or folder.

- **Edit Bookmarks**—Select Bookmarks ➪ Edit Bookmarks to open a tree view of your bookmarks. From the Bookmark Editor window that appears, you can change the URLs, the icon, or other features of the bookmark. Another nice feature lets you check the status of the bookmark (that is, the address available).

- **New Bookmark Folder**—You can add a new folder of bookmarks to your Konqueror bookmarks list. To create a bookmarks folder, choose Bookmarks ➪ New Folder. Then type a name for the new Bookmarks folder, and click OK. The new bookmark folder appears on your bookmarks menu. You can add the current location to that folder by clicking on the folder name and selecting Add Bookmark.

## Configuring Konqueror options

You can change many of the visual attributes of the Konqueror window, including which menu bars and toolbars appear. You can have any of the following bars appear on the Konqueror window: Menubar, Toolbar, Extra Toolbar, Location Toolbar, and Bookmark Toolbar. Select Settings, and then click the bar you want to have appear (or not appear). The bar appears when a check mark is shown next to it.

You can modify a variety of options for Konqueror by choosing Settings ➪ Configure Konqueror. The Konqueror Settings window appears, offering the following options:

- **Performance**—Display configuration settings that can be used to improve Konqueror performance. You can preload an instance after KDE startup or minimize memory usage.

- **File Management**—Configure features such as file tips, previews, and how trash is handled.

- **Previews & Meta-Data**—An icon in a Konqueror folder can be made to resemble the contents of the file it represents. For example, if the file is a JPEG image, the icon representing the file could be a small version of that image. Using the Previews features, you can limit the size of the file used (1MB is the default) because many massive files could take too long to refresh on the screen. You can also choose to have any thumbnail embedded in a file to be used as the icon or have the size of the icon reflect the shape of the image used.

- **File Associations**—Describes which programs to launch for each file type. If you prefer a certain image viewer, text editor, or other application for handling your data, you should configure those applications to launch for those data types.

- **Web Browsing**—Click the Browsing selection to open a window to configure the Web browser features of Konqueror. By enabling Form Completion, Konqueror can save form data you type and, at a later time, fill that information into other forms. If your computer has limited resources, you can speed up page display by clearing the Automatically Load Images check box or by disabling animations.

- **AdBlock Filters**—Click here to create a list of URLs that are filtered as you browse the Web. Filtering is based on frame and image names. Filtered URLs can be either thrown away or replaced with an image. You can also import and export lists of filters here.

- **Web Shortcuts**—Display a list of keyword shortcuts you can use to go to different Internet sites. For example, follow the word "ask" with a search string to search the Ask (www.ask.com) Web site.

- **Cache**—Indicate how much space on your hard disk can be used to store the sites you have visited (based on the value in the Disk Cache Size field).

- **Proxy**—Click Proxy to configure Konqueror to access the Internet through a proxy server (by default, Konqueror tries to connect there directly). You need to enter the address and port number of the computer providing HTTP and/or FTP proxy services. Alternatively, you can have Konqueror try to automatically detect the proxy configuration.

- **Fonts**—Choose which fonts to use, by default, for various fonts needed on Web pages (standard font, fixed font, serif font, sans serif font, cursive font, and fantasy font). The serif fonts are typically used in body text, whereas sans serif fonts are often used in headlines. You can also set the Minimum and Medium font sizes.

- **Stylesheets**—Choose whether to use the default stylesheet, a user-defined stylesheet, or a custom stylesheet. The stylesheet sets the font family, font sizes, and colors that are applied to Web pages. (This won't change particular font requests made by the Web page.) If you select a custom stylesheet, click the Customize tab to customize your own fonts and colors.

- **History Sidebar**—Modify the behavior of the list of sites you have visited (the history). By default, the most recent 500 URLs are stored, and after 500 days (KNOPPIX) or 90 days (Fedora), a URL is dropped from the list. There's also a button to clear your history. (To view your history list in Konqueror, open the left panel, and then click the tiny scroll icon.)

- **Cookies**—Choose whether cookies are enabled in Konqueror. By default, you are asked to confirm that it is okay each time a Web site tries to create or modify a cookie. You can change that to either accept or reject all cookies. You can also set policies for acceptance or rejection of cookies based on host and domain names.

- **Crypto**—Display a list of secure certificates that the Konqueror browser can accept. By default, Secure Socket Layer (SSL) versions 2 and 3 certificates are accepted, as is TLS support (if supported by the server). You can also choose to be notified when you are entering or leaving a secure Web site.

- **Browser Identification**—Set how Konqueror identifies itself when it accesses a Web site. By default, Konqueror tells the Web site that it is the Mozilla Web browser. You can select Konqueror to appear as different Web browsers to specific sites. You must sometimes do this when a site denies you access because you do not have a specific type of browser (even though Konqueror may be fully capable of displaying the content).

- **Java and JavaScript**—Enable or disable Java and JavaScript content contained in Web pages in your Konqueror window.

- **Plugins**—Display a list of directories that Konqueror will search to find plug-ins. Konqueror can also scan your computer to find plug-ins that are installed for other browsers in other locations.

# Managing the KDE desktop

If you have a lot stuff open at the same time, organizing those items can make managing your desktop much easier. The KDE 4 Plasma desktop offers many of the traditional ways of managing desktop elements (windows, workspaces, panels, icons, menus, and so on). However, it also offers new ways of grouping and managing your desktop elements.

## Managing windows in the taskbar

When you open a window, a button representing the window appears in the panel at the bottom of the screen. Here is how you can manage windows from the taskbar appearing on that panel:

- **Toggle windows**—Left-click any running task in the taskbar to toggle between opening the window and minimizing it.

- **Position windows**—You can choose to have the selected window be above or below other windows or displayed in full screen. Right-click the running task in the taskbar and select Advanced. Then choose Keep Above Others, Keep Below Others, or Fullscreen.

- **Move windows**—Move a window from the current desktop to any other virtual desktop. Right-click any task in the taskbar, select To Desktop, and then select any desktop number. The window moves to that desktop.

All the windows that are running, regardless of which virtual desktop you are on, appear in the taskbar.

### Uncluttering the desktop

If you find yourself with icons all over the desktop, you also can organize them from the desktop menu. Right-click the desktop, and then select Align Horizontally or Align Vertically. You can also choose to simply line up all icons vertically or horizontally.

### Moving windows

The easiest way to move a window from one location to another is to place the cursor on the window's title bar, hold down the mouse button and drag the window to a new location, and release the mouse button to drop the window. Another way to do it is to click the window menu button (top-left corner of the title bar), select Move, move the mouse to relocate the window, and then click again to place it.

## Tip

**If somehow the window gets stuck in a location where the title bar is off the screen, you can move it back to where you want it by holding down the Alt key and clicking the left mouse button in the inner window. Then move the window where you want it and release. ■**

### Resizing windows

To resize a window, grab anywhere on the outer edge of the window border, and then move the mouse until the window is the size you want. Grab a corner to resize vertically and horizontally at the same time. Grab a side to resize in only one direction.

You can also resize a window by clicking the window menu button (top-left corner of the title bar) and selecting Resize. Move the mouse until the window is resized and click to leave it there.

### Pinning windows on top or bottom

You can set a window to always stay on top of all other windows or always stay under them. Keeping a window on top can be useful for a small window that you want to always refer to (such as a clock or a small TV viewing window). To pin a window on top of the desktop, click in the window title bar. From the menu that appears, select Advanced ➪ Keep Above Others. Likewise, to keep the window on the bottom, select Advanced ➪ Keep Below Others.

### Using virtual desktops

To give you more space to run applications than will fit on your physical screen, KDE gives you access to several virtual desktops at the same time. Using the 1, 2, 3, and 4 buttons on the panel, you can easily move between the different desktops. Just click the one you want.

If you want to move an application from one desktop to another, you can do so from the window menu. Click the window menu button for the window you want to move, click To Desktop, and then select Desktop 1, 2, 3, or 4. The window will disappear from the current desktop and move to the one you selected.

### Adding widgets

You want to be able to quickly access the applications that you use most often. One of the best ways to make that possible is to add widgets to the panel or the desktop that can either run continuously (such as a clock or news ticker) or launch the applications you need with a single click.

To add a KDE widget to the panel:

**1.** Right-click anywhere on the panel.

**2.** Click Add Widgets.

**3.** Select the widget you want to add and click Add Widget.

An icon representing the widget should immediately appear on the panel. (If the panel seems a bit crowded, you might want to remove some widgets you don't use or add a widget directly to the desktop.) At this point, you can change any properties associated with the widget by right-clicking the widget in the panel and then selecting to change its settings.

If you decide later that you no longer want this widget to be available on the panel, right-click it and click Remove.

To add a widget to the desktop:

**1.** Right-click an open area of the desktop.

**2.** Select Add Widgets from the menu.

**3.** Select the widget you want from the list that appears and click Add Widget.

If you decide later that you no longer want this widget to be available on the desktop, hover the mouse over it and click the red X to delete it.

## Configuring the desktop

If you want to change the look, feel, or behavior of your KDE desktop, the best place to start is the System Settings window. The System Settings window lets you configure dozens of attributes associated with colors, fonts, and screensavers used by KDE. Selections from that window also let you do basic computer administration, such as changing date/time settings and modifying your display.

To open the System Settings window, select the KickOff menu button (represented by a Fedora logo icon in Fedora) at the lower-left corner of the panel and choose System Settings. The System Settings window appears, as shown in Figure 3-6.

**FIGURE 3-6**

Configure your system in KDE from the System Settings window.

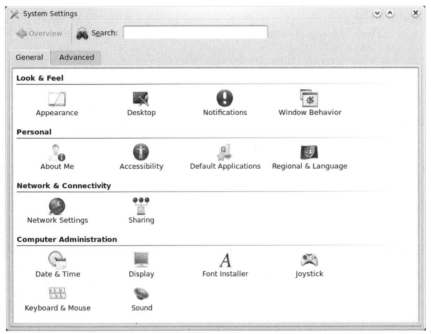

Click any item you want to configure, or type into the Search box to find a selection that matches what you type.

There are several ways you can change the look-and-feel of your desktop display from the System Settings window. Under the Look & Feel topic, you can select to change the appearance, desktop, notifications, or window behavior.

Here are a few of the individual desktop features you may want to change:

- **Change the screensaver**—Under the Look & Feel heading, select Desktop ➪ Screen Saver. From the window that appears, only a few screensavers are available by default. However, by installing the kdeartwork-extras package, you can get a lot more screensavers to choose from. Under the Start Automatically box, select how many minutes of inactivity before the screensaver turns on. You can also click Require Password to require that a password be entered before you can access your display after the screensaver has come on.

## Tip

**If you are working in a place where you want your desktop to be secure, be sure to turn on the Require Password feature. This prevents others from gaining access to your computer when you forget to lock it or shut it off. If you have any virtual terminals open, switch to them and type vlock to lock each of them as well. (You need to install the vlock package if the `vlock` command isn't available.)** ∎

- **Change fonts**—You can assign different fonts to different places in which fonts appear on the desktop. Under the Look & Feel heading, select Appearance ➪ Fonts. Select one of the categories of fonts (General, Fixed width, Small, Toolbar, Menu, Window title, Taskbar, and Desktop fonts). Then click the Choose box to select a font from the Select Font list box that you want to assign to that category. If the font is available, you will see an example of the text in the Sample text box.

- **Change the colors**—Under the Look & Feel heading in the System Settings window, select Appearance ➪ Colors. The window that appears lets you change the color of selected items on the desktop. Select a whole color scheme from the Color Scheme list box. Or select an item from the Colors tab to change a particular item. Items you can change include text, backgrounds, links, buttons, and title bars.

- **Fonts**—You can assign different fonts to different places in which fonts appear on the desktop. Under the Appearance & Themes heading, select Fonts. Select one of the categories of fonts (General, Fixed width, Toolbar, Menu, Window title, Taskbar, and Desktop fonts). Then click the Choose check box to select a font from the Select Font list box that you want to assign to that category. If the font is available, an example of the text appears in the Sample text box.

## Tip

**To use 100 dpi fonts, you must add an entry for 100 dpi fonts to `/etc/X11/xorg.conf` file. After you make that change, you must restart the X server for it to take effect.** ∎

### Changing panel attributes

For most people, the panel is the place where they select which desktop is active and which applications are run. You can change panel behavior from the Configure Panel window. Right-click any empty space on your panel, and then select Panel Settings. You can change these features from the Settings window that appears:

- **Size**—The Size selection lets you change the size of the Panel from Normal to Tiny, Small, Large, or Custom. With Custom, select the exact point size (48 is the default).

- **Location**—Change the location of the panel from Bottom to Top, Right, or Left.

# The GNOME Desktop

GNOME (pronounced *guh-nome*) provides the desktop environment that you get by default when you install Fedora, Ubuntu, and other Linux systems. This desktop environment provides the software that is between your X Window System framework and the look-and-feel provided by the window manager. GNOME is a stable and reliable desktop environment, with a few cool features.

As of this writing, GNOME 2.26 is the most recent version available, although the distribution you are using may or may not include this latest version. Recent GNOME releases include advancements in 3D effects (see "3D effects with AIGLX" later in this chapter), improved usability features, and an application for using your Webcam.

To use your GNOME desktop, you should become familiar with the following components:

- **Metacity (window manager)**—The default window manager for GNOME in Ubuntu, Fedora, RHEL, and others is Metacity. Metacity configuration options let you control such things as themes, window borders, and controls used on your desktop.

- **Compiz (window manager)**—You can enable this window manager in GNOME to provide 3D desktop effects.

- **Nautilus (file manager/graphical shell)**—When you open a folder (by double-clicking the Home icon on your desktop, for example), the Nautilus window opens and displays the contents of the selected folder. Nautilus can also display other types of content, such as shared folders from Windows computers on the network (using SMB).

- **GNOME panels (application/task launcher)**—These panels, which line the top and bottom of your screen, are designed to make it convenient for you to launch the applications you use, manage running applications, and work with multiple virtual desktops. By default, the top panel contains menu buttons (Applications, Places, and System), desktop application launchers (Evolution e-mail and Firefox Web browser), a workspace switcher (for managing four virtual desktops), and a clock. Icons appear in the panel when you need software updates or SELinux detects a problem. The bottom panel has a Show Desktop button, window lists, a trashcan and workspace switcher.

- **Desktop area**—The windows and icons you use are arranged on the desktop area, which supports drag-and-drop between applications, a desktop menu (right-click to see it), and icons for launching applications. A Computer icon consolidates CD drives, floppy drives, the file system, and shared network resources in one place.

Here are some feature additions you will find useful in the most recent versions of GNOME:

- **XSPF playlists in Totem**—The Totem video/audio player now includes support for open standard XSPF playlists (www.xspf.org). Other improvements to Totem allow it to interact with content from Web sites.

- **Screensaver previews**—Previewing screen savers in full-screen mode is now supported.

- **Direct DVD burning**—Use the Nautilus CD burner feature to burn DVDs directly, without needing first to create an ISO image.

- **Drag from taskbar**—Drag an application from the taskbar to workspaces represented in the panel Workspace Switcher to move the application to a new workspace.

- **Nautilus text or button browsing**—When saving or opening files or folders in Nautilus, a new toggle button enables you to choose between browsing by clicking on buttons or by typing full pathnames.

GNOME also includes a set of Preferences windows that enable you to configure different aspects of your desktop. You can change backgrounds, colors, fonts, keyboard shortcuts, and other features related to the look and behavior of the desktop. Figure 3-7 shows how the GNOME desktop environment appears the first time you log in, with a few windows added to the screen.

**FIGURE 3-7**

The GNOME desktop environment

The desktop shown in Figure 3-7 is for Ubuntu. The following sections provide details on using the GNOME desktop.

## Using the Metacity window manager

The Metacity window manager seems to have been chosen as the default window manager for GNOME because of its simplicity. The creator of Metacity refers to it as a "boring window manager for the adult in you"—and then goes on to compare other window managers to colorful, sugary cereal, whereas Metacity is characterized as Cheerios.

## Note

To use 3D effects, your best solution is to use the Compiz window manager, described later in this chapter. ■

There really isn't much you can do with Metacity (except get your work done efficiently). You assign new themes to Metacity and change colors and window decorations through the GNOME preferences (described later). A few Metacity themes exist, but expect the number to grow.

Basic Metacity functions that might interest you are keyboard shortcuts and the workspace switcher. Table 3-4 shows keyboard shortcuts to get around the Metacity window manager.

**TABLE 3-4**

### Metacity Keyboard Shortcuts

| Actions | Keystrokes | |
|---|---|---|
| Window focus | Cycle forward, with pop-up icons | Alt+Tab |
| | Cycle backward, with pop-up icons | Alt+Shift+Tab |
| | Cycle forward, without pop-up icons | Alt+Esc |
| | Cycle backward, without pop-up icons | Alt+Shift+Esc |
| Panel focus | Cycle forward among panels | Alt+Ctrl+Tab |
| | Cycle backward among panels | Alt+Ctrl+Shift+Tab |
| Workspace focus | Move to workspace to the right | Ctrl+Alt+right arrow |
| | Move to workspace to the left | Ctrl+Alt+left arrow |
| | Move to upper workspace | Ctrl+Alt+up arrow |
| | Move to lower workspace | Ctrl+Alt+down arrow |
| | Minimize/maximize all windows | Ctrl+Alt+D |
| | Show window menu | Alt+Spacebar |
| | Close menu | Esc |

Another Metacity feature of interest is the workspace switcher. Four virtual workspaces appear in the workspace switcher on the GNOME panel. You can do the following with the Workspace Switcher:

- **Choose current workspace**—Four virtual workspaces appear in the Workspace Switcher. Click any of the four virtual workspaces to make it your current workspace.

- **Move windows to other workspaces**—Click any window, each represented by a tiny rectangle in a workspace, to drag-and-drop it to another workspace. Likewise, you can drag an application from the Window List to move that application to another workspace.

- **Add more workspaces**—Right-click the Workspace Switcher, and select Preferences. You can add workspaces (up to 32).

- **Name workspaces**—Right-click the Workspace Switcher and select Preferences. Click in the Workspaces pane to change names of workspaces to any names you choose.

You can view and change information about Metacity controls and settings using the gconf-editor window (type **gconf-editor** from a Terminal window). As the window says, it is not the recommended way of changing preferences, so when possible, you should change the desktop through GNOME preferences. However, gconf-editor is a good way to see descriptions of each Metacity feature.

From the gconf-editor window, select apps ⇨ metacity, and then choose from general, global_keybindings, keybindings_commands, window_keybindings, and workspace_names. Click each key to see its value, along with short and long descriptions of the key.

## Using the GNOME panels

The GNOME panels are placed on the top and bottom of the GNOME desktop. From those panels you can start applications (from buttons or menus), see what programs are active, and monitor how your system is running. There are also many ways to change the top and bottom panels—by adding applications or monitors or by changing the placement or behavior of the panel, for example.

Right-click any open space on either panel to see the Panel menu. Figure 3-8 shows the Panel menu on the top.

**FIGURE 3-8**

The GNOME Panel menu

From GNOME's Panel menu, you can choose from a variety of functions, including:

- **Use the menus**—The Applications menu displays most of the applications and system tools you will use from the desktop. The Places menu lets you select places to go, such as the Desktop folder, home folder, removable media, or network locations. The System menu lets you change preferences and system settings, as well as get other information about GNOME.

- **Add to Panel**—Add an applet, menu, launcher, drawer, or button.

- **Properties**—Change the panel's position, size, and background properties.

- **Delete This Panel**—Delete the current panel.

- **New Panel**—Add panels to your desktop in different styles and locations.

You can also work with items on a panel. For example, you can

- **Move items**—To move an item on a panel, right-click it, select Move, and then drag-and-drop it to a new position.

- **Resize items**—You can resize some elements, such as the Window List, by clicking an edge and dragging it to the new size.

- **Use the Window List**—Tasks running on the desktop appear in the Window List area. Click a task to minimize or maximize it.

The following sections describe some things you can do with the GNOME panel.

## Using the Applications and System menus

Click Applications on the panel, and you see categories of applications and system tools that you can select. Click the application you want to launch. To add an item from a menu so that it can launch from the panel, drag-and-drop the item you want to the panel.

You can add items to your GNOME menus. To do that, right-click on any of the menu names, and then select Edit Menus. The window that appears lets you add or delete menus associated with the Applications and System menus. You can also add items to launch from those menus by selecting New Item and typing the Name, Command, and comment for the item.

## Adding an applet

You can run several small applications, called *applets,* directly on the GNOME panel. These applications can show information you may want to see on an ongoing basis or may just provide some amusement. To see what applets are available and to add applets that you want to your panel, perform the following steps:

1. Right-click an open space in the panel so that the Panel menu appears.

2. Select Add to Panel. An Add to Panel window appears.

3. Select from among several dozen applets, including a clock, dictionary lookup, stock ticker, and weather report. The applet you select appears on the panel, ready for you to use.

Figure 3-9 shows (from left to right) eyes, system monitor, weather report, network monitor, and wanda the fish.

**FIGURE 3-9**

Placing applets on the panel makes accessing them easy.

After an applet is installed, right-click it on the panel to see what options are available. For example, select Preferences for the stock ticker, and you can add or delete stocks whose prices you want to monitor. If you don't like the applet's location, right-click it, click Move, slide the mouse until the applet is where you want it (even to another panel), and click to set its location.

If you no longer want an applet to appear on the panel, right-click it, and then click Remove From Panel. The icon representing the applet disappears. If you find that you have run out of room on your panel, you can add a new panel to another part of the screen, as described in the next section.

## Adding another panel

You can have several panels on your GNOME desktop. You can add panels that run along the entire bottom, top, or side of the screen. To add a panel, do the following:

1. Right-click an open space in the panel so that the Panel menu appears.
2. Select New Panel. A new panel appears on the side of the screen.
3. Right-click an open space in the new panel and select Properties.
4. From the Panel Properties, select where you want the panel from the Orientation box (Top, Bottom, Left, or Right).

After you've added a panel, you can add applets or application launchers to it as you did to the default panel. To remove a panel, right-click it and select Delete This Panel.

## Adding an application launcher

Icons on your panel represent a Web browser and several office productivity applications. You can add your own icons to launch applications from the panel as well. To add a new application launcher to the panel, do the following:

1. Right-click in an open space on the panel.

2. Select Add to Panel ⇨ Application Launcher from the menu. All application categories from your Applications and System menus appear.

3. Select the arrow next to the category of application you want, and then select Add. An icon representing the application appears on the panel.

To launch the application you just added, simply click the icon on the panel.

If the application you want to launch is not on one of your menus, you can build a launcher yourself as follows:

1. Right-click in an open space on the panel.

2. Select Add to Panel ⇨ Custom Application Launcher ⇨ Add. The Create Launcher window appears.

3. Provide the following information for the application that you want to add:

   - **Type**—Select Application (to launch a regular GUI application) or Application in Terminal. Use Application in Terminal if the application is a character-based or ncurses application. (Applications written using the ncurses library run in a Terminal window but offer screen-oriented mouse and keyboard controls.)

   - **Name**—A name to identify the application (this appears in the tooltip when your mouse is over the icon).

   - **Command**—The command line that is run when the application is launched. Use the full path name, plus any required options.

   - **Comment**—A comment describing the application. It also appears when you later move your mouse over the launcher.

4. Click the Icon box (it might say No Icon). Select one of the icons shown and click OK. Alternatively, you can browse your file system to choose an icon.

5. Click OK.

The application icon should now appear in the panel. Click it to start the application.

# Note

Icons available to represent your application are contained in the /usr/share/pixmaps directory. These icons are either in .png or .xpm formats. If there isn't an icon in the directory you want to use, create your own (in one of those two formats) and assign it to the application. ∎

## Adding a drawer

A drawer is an icon that you can click to display other icons representing menus, applets, and launchers; it behaves just like a panel. Essentially, any item you can add to a panel you can add to a drawer. By adding a drawer to your GNOME panel, you can include several applets and launchers that together take up the space of only one icon. Click on the drawer to show the applets and launchers as if they were being pulled out of a drawer icon on the panel.

To add a drawer to your panel, right-click the panel and select Add to Panel ➪ Drawer. A drawer appears on the panel. Right-click it, and add applets or launchers to it as you would to a panel. Click the icon again to retract the drawer.

Figure 3-10 shows a portion of the panel with an open drawer that includes an icon for launching a volume monitor, a weather report, and Tomboy sticky notes.

**FIGURE 3-10**

Add launchers or applets to a drawer on your GNOME panel.

## Changing panel properties

Those panel properties you can change are limited to the orientation, size, hiding policy, and background. To open the Panel Properties window that applies to a specific panel, right-click on an open space on the panel and choose Properties. The Panel Properties window that appears includes the following values:

- **Orientation**—Move the panel to different locations on the screen by clicking on a new position.

- **Size**—Select the size of your panel by choosing its height in pixels (48 pixels by default).

- **Expand**—Select this check box to have the panel expand to fill the entire side, or clear the check box to make the panel only as wide as the applets it contains.

- **AutoHide**—Select whether a panel is automatically hidden (appearing only when the mouse pointer is in the area).

- **Show Hide buttons**—Choose whether the Hide/Unhide buttons (with pixmap arrows on them) appear on the edges of the panel.

- **Arrows on hide buttons**—If you select Show Hide Buttons, you can choose to have arrows on those buttons.

- **Background**—From the Background tab, you can assign a color to the background of the panel, assign a pixmap image, or just leave the default (which is based on the current system theme). Click the Background Image check box if you want to select an image for the background, and then select an image, such as a tile from /usr/share/backgrounds/tiles or other directory.

## Tip

**I usually turn on the AutoHide feature and turn off the Hide buttons. Using AutoHide gives you more desktop space to work with. When you move your mouse to the edge where the panel is, the panel pops up—so you don't need Hide buttons. ■**

# Using the Nautilus file manager

At one time, file managers did little more than let you run applications, create data files, and open folders. These days, as the information a user needs expands beyond the local system, file managers are expected to also display Web pages, access FTP sites, and play multimedia content. The Nautilus file manager, which is the default GNOME file manager, is an example of just such a file manager.

When you open the Nautilus file manager window (for example, by opening the Home icon or other folder on your desktop), you see the name of the location you are viewing (such as the folder name) and what that location contains (files, folders, and applications). Double-click a folder to open that folder in a new window.

Select your folder name in the lower-left corner of the window to see the file system hierarchy above the current folder. GNOME remembers whatever size, location, and other setting you had for the folder the last time you closed it and returns it to that state the next time you open it.

To see more controls, right-click a folder and select Browse Folder to open it. Icons on the toolbar of the Nautilus window let you move forward and back among the directories and Web sites you visit. To move up the directory structure, click the up arrow. If you prefer to type the path to the folder you want, instead of clicking icons, you can toggle between button and text-based location bars (click the paper and pencil icon next to the location buttons to change the view). Figure 3-11 is an example of the file manager window displaying the home directory of a user named chris in browse mode.

## FIGURE 3-11

The Nautilus file manager enables you to move around the file system, open directories, launch applications, and open Samba folders.

To refresh the view of the folder, click the Reload button. The Home button takes you to your home page, and the Computer button lets you see the same type of information you would see from a My Computer icon on a Windows system (CD drive, floppy drive, hard disk file systems, and network folders).

Icons in Nautilus often indicate the type of data that a particular file contains. The contents or file extension of each file can determine which application is used to work with the file, or you can right-click an icon to open the file it represents with a particular application or viewer.

Here are some of the more interesting features of Nautilus:

- **Sidebar**—From the Browse Folder view described previously, select View ➪ Side Pane to have a sidebar appear in the left column of the screen. From the sidebar, you can click a pull-down menu that represents different types of information you can select one at a time.

  The Tree tab, for example, shows a tree view of the directory structure, so you can easily traverse your directories. The Notes tab lets you add notes that become associated with the current Directory or Web page, and the History tab displays a history of directories you have visited, enabling you to click those items to return to the sites they represent. There is also an Emblems tab that lets you drag-and-drop emblems on files or folders to indicate something about the file or folder (emblems include icons representing drafts, urgent, bug, and multimedia).

- **Windows file and printer sharing**—If your computer is connected to a LAN on which Windows computers are sharing files and printers, you can view those resources from Nautilus. Type **smb:** in the Open Location box (select File ➪ Open Location to get there) to see available workgroups. Click a workgroup to see computers from that workgroup that are sharing files and printers. Figure 3-12 shows an example of a local Nautilus window displaying icons representing folders shared from a Window computer named bluestreak that is accessible on the local LAN. The shared folder from that computer is named My Doc Blue.

**FIGURE 3-12**

Display shared Windows file and printer servers (SMB) in Nautilus.

- **MIME types and file types**—To handle different types of content that may be encountered in the Nautilus window, you can set applications to respond based on MIME type and file type. With a folder displayed, right-click a file for which you want to assign an application. Click either Open With an Application or Open With a Viewer. If no application or viewer has been assigned for the file type, click Associate Application to be able to select an application. From the Add File Types window, you can add an application based on the file extension and MIME type representing the file.

- **Drag-and-drop**—You can use drag-and-drop within the Nautilus window, between the Nautilus and the desktop, or among multiple Nautilus windows. As other GNOME-compliant applications become available, they are expected to also support the drag-and-drop feature.

If you would like more information on the Nautilus file manager, visit the GNOME Web site (www.gnome.org/nautilus).

## 3D effects with AIGLX

Several different initiatives have made strides in recent years to bring 3D desktop effects to Linux. Ubuntu and Fedora used AIGLX (http://fedoraproject.org/wiki/RenderingProject/aiglx). The openSUSE project originally backed the Xgl approach (http://en.opensuse.org/Xgl), but has recently also moved to supporting AIGLX.

The goal of the Accelerated Indirect GLX project (AIGLX) is to add 3D effects to everyday desktop systems. It does this by implementing OpenGL (http://opengl.org) accelerated effects using the Mesa (www.mesa3d.org) open source OpenGL implementation.

Currently, AIGLX supports a limited set of video cards and implements only a few 3D effects, but it does offer some insight into the eye candy that is in the works.

Direct rendering infrastructure (DRI) is required for most video cards supporting AIGLX. However, some NVidia cards that don't support DRI can be used, but they require that you get the closed source binary drivers made available from NVidia. Cards that are known to *not* work with AIGLX include ATI Rage 128 and Mach 64, Matrox G200 through G550, and 3DFX Voodoo 1 and 2.

If your video card was properly detected and configured, you may be able to simply turn on the Desktop Effects feature to see the effects that have been implemented so far. To turn on Desktop Effects, select System ➪ Preferences ➪ Look and Feel ➪ Desktop Effects. When the Desktop Effects window appears, select Enable Desktop Effects. Enabling this does the following:

- Stops the current window manager and starts the Compiz window manager.
- Enables the Windows Wobble When Moved effect. With this effect on, when you grab the title bar of the window to move it, the window will wobble as it moves. Menus and other items that open on the desktop also wobble.

- Enables the Workspaces on a Cube effect. Drag a window from the desktop to the right or the left and the desktop will rotate like a cube, with each of your desktop workspaces appearing as a side of that cube. Drop the window on the workspace where you want it to go. You can also click on the Workspace Switcher applet in the bottom panel to rotate the cube to display different workspaces.

Other nice desktop effects result from using the Alt+Tab keys to tab among different running windows. As you press Alt+Tab, a thumbnail of each window scrolls across the screen as the window it represents is highlighted.

Figure 3-13 shows an example of a Compiz desktop with AIGLX enabled. The figure illustrates a Web browser window being moved from one workspace to another as those workspaces rotate on a cube.

**FIGURE 3-13**

Rotate workspaces on a cube with AIGLX desktop effects enabled.

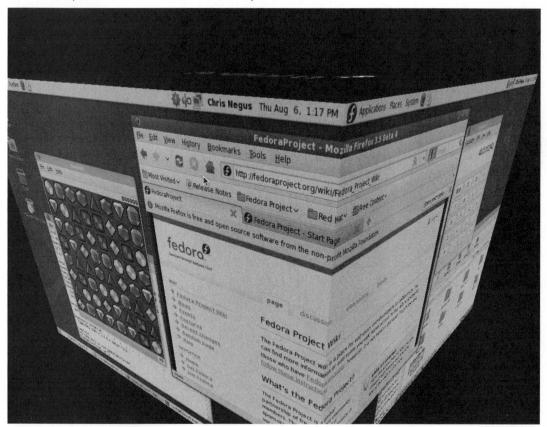

The following are some interesting effects you can get with your 3D AIGLX desktop:

- **Spin cube**—Hold Ctrl+Alt keys and press the right and left arrow keys. The desktop cube spins to each successive workspace (forward or back).

- **Slowly rotate cube**—Hold the Ctrl+Alt keys, press and hold the left mouse button, and move the mouse around on the screen. The cube will move slowly with the mouse among the workspaces.

- **Tab through windows**—Hold the Alt key and press the Tab key. You will see reduced versions of all your windows in a strip in the middle of your screen, with the current window highlighted in the middle. Still holding the Alt key, press Tab or Shift+Tab to move forward or backwards through the windows. Release the keys when the one you want is highlighted.

- **Scale and separate windows**—If your desktop is cluttered, hold Ctrl+Alt and press the up arrow key. Windows will shrink down and separate on the desktop. Still holding Ctrl+Alt, use your arrow keys to highlight the window you want and release the keys to have that window come to the surface.

- **Scale and separate workspaces**—Hold Ctrl+Alt and press the down arrow key to see reduced images of the workspace shown on a strip. Still holding Ctrl+Alt, use right and left arrow keys to move among the different workspaces. Release the keys when the workspace you want is highlighted.

- **Send current window to next workspace**—Hold Ctrl+Alt+Shift keys together and press the left and right arrow keys. The current window will move to the next workspace to the left or right, respectively.

- **Slide windows around**—Press and hold the left mouse button, and then press the left, right, up, or down arrow keys to slide the current window around on the screen.

If you get tired of wobbling windows and spinning cubes, you can easily turn off the AIGLX 3D effects and return Metacity as the window manager. Select System ➪ Preferences ➪ Desktop Effects again and toggle off the Enable Desktop Effects button to turn off the feature.

If you have a supported video card, but find that you are not able to turn on the Desktop Effects, check that your X server started properly. In particular, make sure that your /etc/X11/xorg.conf file is properly configured. Make sure that dri and glx are loaded in the Module section. Also, add an extensions section anywhere in the file (typically at the end of the file) that appears as follows:

```
Section ""extensions""
 Option ""Composite""
EndSection
```

Another option is to add the following line to the /etc/X11/xorg.conf file in the Device section:

```
Option ""XAANoOffscreenPixmaps""
```

The XAANoOffscreenPixmaps option will improve performance. Check your /var/log/ Xorg.log file to make sure that DRI and AIGLX features were started correctly. The messages in that file can help you debug other problems as well.

# Changing GNOME preferences

There are many ways to change the behavior, look, and feel of your GNOME desktop. You can modify most GNOME preferences from submenus on the Preferences menu (select System ➪ Preferences).

Unlike earlier versions of GNOME, boundaries between preferences related to the window manager (Metacity), file manager (Nautilus), and the GNOME desktop itself have been blurred. Preferences for all of these features are available from the Preferences menu.

The following items highlight some of the preferences you might want to change:

- **Accessibility**—If you have difficulty operating a mouse or keyboard or seeing the screen, the Assistive Technologies window lets you adapt mouse and keyboard settings to make operating your computer easier for you. It also lets you magnify selected applications. (Select System ➪ Preferences ➪ Personal ➪ Assistive Technologies.)

- **Desktop Background**—You can choose a solid color or an image to use as wallpaper. Select System ➪ Preferences ➪ Look and Feel ➪ Appearance and then the Background tab. If you choose to use a solid color (by selecting No Wallpaper), click the Color box, select a color from the palette, and click OK.

  To use wallpaper for your background, open the folder containing the image you want to use, and then drag the image into the Desktop Wallpaper pane on the Desktop Preferences window. You can choose from a variety of images in the /usr/share/nautilus/patterns and /usr/share/backgrounds/tiles directories. Then choose to have the wallpaper image tiled (repeated pattern), centered, scaled (in proportion), or stretched (using any proportion to fill the screen).

- **Screensaver**—Choose from dozens of screen savers from the Screensaver window. Select System ➪ Preferences ➪ Look and Feel ➪ Screensaver. Choose Random to have your screen saver chosen randomly from available screen savers, or select one that you like from the list to use all the time. Next, choose how long your screen must be idle before the screen saver starts (default is 10 minutes). You can also choose to lock the screen when the screen saver is active, so a password is required to return to the desktop. If you only see a few screen savers, you might want to install the xscreensaver-extras and xscreensaver-gl-extras packages to get a bunch more.

- **Theme**—Choose an entire theme of elements to be used on your desktop, if you like. From the Appearance window, select the Theme tab. A desktop theme affects not only the background but also the way that many buttons and menu selections appear. Only a few themes are available for the window manager (Metacity) in the Fedora distribution, but you can get a bunch of other themes from themes.freshmeat.net (click Metacity).

To modify a theme, select the Customize button and then click the Controls tab to choose the type of controls to use on your desktop. Click the Window Border tab to select from different themes that change the title bar and other borders of your windows. Click the Icons tab to choose different icons to represent items on your desktop. Themes change immediately as you click or when you drag a theme name on the desktop.

## Exiting GNOME

When you are done with your work, you can either log out from your current session or shut down your computer completely. To exit from GNOME, do the following:

1. Click the System button from the panel (in Fedora) or the red button icon in the upper-right corner (in Ubuntu).

2. Select Log Out from the menu. A pop-up window appears, asking whether you want to Log Out. Some versions will also ask whether you want to Shut Down or Restart the computer.

3. Select Log Out from the pop-up menu. This logs you out and returns you to either the graphical login screen or to your shell login prompt. (If you select Shut Down, the system shuts down, and if you select Reboot, the system restarts.)

4. Select OK to finish exiting from GNOME.

If you are unable to get to the Log Out button (if, for example, your panel crashed), two other exit methods are available. Try one of these ways, depending on how you started the desktop:

- If you started the desktop from the graphical display manager or by typing **startx** from your login shell, press Ctrl+Backspace to end your GNOME session.

- If your screen is completely unresponsive (mouse and keyboard aren't working), you might just have to reboot your computer. If possible, log in to the computer over the network and type **init 6** (as root user) to reboot.

Although these ways are not the most graceful for exiting the desktop, they work. You should be able to log in again and restart the desktop.

## Configuring Your Own Desktop

Today's modern desktop computer systems are made to spoon-feed you your operating system. In the name of ease of use, some desktop environments spend a lot of resources on fancy panels, complex control centers, and busy applets. In short, they can become bloated.

Many technically inclined people want a more streamlined desktop—or at least want to choose their own bells and whistles. They don't want to have to wait for windows to redraw or menus to come up. Linux enables those people to forget the complete desktop environments and configure the main elements:

- **X**—The X Window System provides the framework of choice for Linux and most UNIX systems. When you configure X yourself, you can choose the video driver, monitor settings, mouse configuration, and other basic features needed to get your display working properly.

- **Window manager**—Dozens of window managers are available to use with X on a Linux system. Window managers add borders and buttons to otherwise bare X windows. They add colors and graphics to backgrounds, menus, and windows. Window managers also define how you can use keyboard and mouse combinations to operate your desktop.

You need to configure X directly only if your desktop isn't working (the desktop may appear scrambled or may just plain crash). You may choose to configure X if you want to tune it to give you higher resolutions or more colors than you get by default.

Still to come in this chapter: examining tools for tuning X and, in particular, working with the `xorg.conf` file. You'll also explore a few popular window managers that you might want to try out. Slackware Linux is used to illustrate how to choose and configure a window manager because Slackware users tend to like simple, direct ways of working with the desktop (when they need a desktop at all).

## Configuring X

Before 2004, most Linux distributions used the X server from the XFree86 project (`www.xfree86.org`). Because of licensing issues, many of the major Linux vendors (including Red Hat, SUSE, and Slackware) changed to the X server from X.Org (`www.X.org`). The descriptions of how to get X going on your machine assume you are using the X.Org X server.

## Note

To determine which X server is installed on your system, from a Terminal window type **man Xorg** and **man XFree86**. If you have only one X server installed on your computer (which you probably do) only the one installed will show a man page. While you are there, press the spacebar to page through the features of your X server. ■

If you are able to start a desktop successfully, and your mouse, keyboard, and screen all seem to be behaving, you may not have to do anything more to configure X. However, if you can't start the desktop or you want to adjust some basic features (such as screen resolution or number of colors supported), the following sections offer some ideas on how to go about doing those things.

### Creating a working X configuration file

If your desktop crashes immediately or shows only garbled text, try to create a new X configuration file. With the X.Org X server, that file is `/etc/X11/xorg.conf`.

## Note

**In XFree86, the configuration file, which has basically the same format, is** `/etc/X11/XF86Config`. ∎

Before you try to reconfigure X, be sure that you are not in run level 5. That run level will continuously try to restart X. I recommend you change to run level 3 before reconfiguring X. Press Ctrl+Alt+F1 and log in as root. Then type the following:

```
# init 3
```

To have X try to create a working `xorg.conf` file for you to use, do the following from a Terminal window as root user:

1. If Linux booted to a command prompt, go to the next step. However, if it tried to start X automatically, you might have an illegible screen. In that case, press these keys together: Ctrl+Alt+Backspace. It should kill your X server and get you back to a command prompt. If X tries to restart (and is still messed up), press Ctrl+Alt+F2. When you see the command prompt, log in as root and type **init 3**. This temporarily brings you down to a nongraphical state.

2. To have X probe your video hardware and create a new configuration file, type

```
# Xorg -configure
```

3. The file `x.org.conf.new` should appear in your home directory. To test whether this new configuration file works, type the following to start the X server:

```
# X -xf86config /root/xorg.conf.new
```

A gray background with an X in the middle should appear. Move the mouse to move the X pointer. If that succeeds, you have a working `xorg.conf` file to use.

4. Press Ctrl+Alt+Backspace to exit the X server.

5. Copy the new configuration file to where it is picked up the next time X starts.

```
# cp /root/xorg.conf.new /etc/X11/xorg.conf
```

Chances are that you have a very basic X configuration that you may want to tune further. After X is working you can return to run level 5 by typing the following as root user:

```
# init 5
```

## Getting new X drivers

Working video drivers in Linux are available with most video cards you can purchase today. However, to get some advanced features from your video cards (such as 3D acceleration) you may need to get proprietary drivers directly from the video manufacturers. In particular, you may want to get drivers from NVidia and ATI.

For Ubuntu, Fedora, and many other major Linux distributions, NVidia and ATI drivers have been packaged for the particular kernel you are running. Because these drivers are not open source, however, you typically have to enable third-party or non-free software repositories to get them to work.

If your Linux system doesn't have such repositories available, to get new drivers for video cards or chipsets from NVidia, go to the NVidia site (www.nvidia.com) and select the Download Drivers button. Follow the link to Linux and FreeBSD drivers. Links from the page that appears will take you to a Web page from which you can download the new driver and get instructions for installing it.

For ATI video cards and chipsets, go to www.ati.com and select Drivers & Software. Follow the links to Linux drivers and related installation instructions.

## Tuning up your X configuration file

The xorg.conf file might look a bit complicated when you first start working with it. However, chances are that you will need to change only a few key elements in it. As root user, open the /etc/X11/xorg.conf file in any text editor. Here are some things you can look for:

- **Mouse**—Look for an InputDevice section with a Mouse0 or Mouse1 identifier. That section for a simple two-button, PS2 mouse might look as follows:

```
Section ""InputDevice""
    Identifier    ""Mouse0""
    Driver        ""mouse""
    Option        ""Protocol"" ""PS/2""
    Option        ""Device"" ""/dev/psaux""
EndSection
```

  If you are unable to use some feature of the mouse, such as a middle wheel, you might be able to get it working with an entry that looks more like the following:

```
Section ""InputDevice""
    Identifier    ""Mouse0""
    Driver        ""mouse""
    Option        ""Protocol"" ""IMPS/2""
    Option        ""Device"" ""/dev/psaux""
    Option        ""ZAxisMapping"" ""4 5""
EndSection
```

Don't change the mouse identifier, but you can change the protocol and add the ZAxisMapping line to enable your wheel mouse. Try restarting X and trying your mouse wheel on something like a Web page to see whether you can scroll up and down with it.

Your mouse might be connected in a different way (such as a bus or serial mouse) or may have different buttons to enable. Tools for configuring your mouse are distribution-specific. Try mouseconfig, mouseadmin, or system-config-mouse to reconfigure your mouse from the command line.

- **Monitor**—The monitor section defines attributes of your monitor. You can use some generic settings if you don't know the exact model of your monitor. Changing the Horizontal Sync and Vertical Refresh rates without checking your monitor's technical specifications is not recommended; you could damage the monitor. Here's an example of an entry that will work on many LCD panels:

```
Section ""Monitor""
    Identifier    ""Monitor0""
    VendorName    ""Monitor Vendor""
    ModelName     ""LCD Panel 1024x768""
    HorizSync     31.5--48.5
    VertRefresh   40.0--70.0
EndSection
```

Here's an entry for a generic CRT monitor that will work on many CRTs:

```
Section ""Monitor""
    Identifier    ""Monitor0""
    VendorName    ""Monitor Vendor""
    ModelName     ""Generic Monitor, 1280x1024 @ 74 Hz""
    HorizSync     31.5--79.0
    VertRefresh   50.0--90.0
EndSection
```

If a tool is available to select your monitor model directly, that would be the best way to go. For example, in Red Hat systems, you would run system-config-xfree86 to change monitor settings.

- **Video device**—The Device section is where you identify the driver to use with your video driver and any options to use with it. It is important to get this section right. The Xorg command described earlier usually does a good job detecting the driver. If you want to change to a different one, this is where to do so. Here's an example of the Device section after I added a video driver from NVIDIA to my system (the driver name is nv):

```
Section ""Device""
```

```
        Identifier      ""Card0""
        Driver          ""nv""
        VendorName      ""nVidia Corporation""
        BoardName       ""Unknown Board""
        BusID           ""PCI:1:0:0""
EndSection
```

- **Screen resolution**—The last major piece of information you may want to add is the screen resolution and color depth. There will be a screen resolution associated with each video card installed on your computer. The Screen section defines default color depths (such as 8, 16, or 24) and modes (such as 1024 × 768, 800 × 600, or 640 × 480). Set the DefaultDepth to the number of bits representing color depth for your system, and then add a Modes line to set the screen resolution.

To read more about how to set options in your xorg.conf file, type **man xorg.conf**. If your X server is XFree86, type **man XF86Config**.

# Choosing a window manager

Fully integrated desktop environments have become somewhat unfriendly to changing out window managers. However, you can completely bypass KDE or GNOME, if you like, and start your desktop simply with X and a window manager of your choice.

Although I'm using Slackware as the reference distribution for describing how to change window managers, the concept is the same on other Linux systems. In general, if no desktop environment is running in Linux, you can start it by typing the following:

```
$ startx
```

This command starts up your desktop environment or window manager, depending on how your system is configured. Although a variety of configuration files are read and commands are run, essentially which desktop you get depends on the contents of two files:

- /etc/X11/xinit/xinitrc—If a user doesn't specifically request a particular desktop environment or window manager, the default desktop settings will come from the contents of this file. The xinitrc file is the system-wide X configuration file. Different Linux systems use different xinitrc files.

- $HOME/.xinitrc—The .xinitrc file is used to let individual users set up their own desktop startup information. Any user can add a .xinitrc file to his or her own home directory. The result is that the contents of that file will override any systemwide settings. If you do create your own .xinitrc file, it should have as its last line exec *windowmanager*, where *windowmanager* is the name of your window manager; for example:

```
exec /usr/bin/blackbox
```

Slackware has at least seven different window managers from which you can choose, making it a good place to try out a few. It also includes a tool called xwmconfig, which lets you change the window manager systemwide (in the /etc/X11/xinit/xinitrc file). To use that tool, as the root user simply type **xwmconfig** from any shell on a Slackware system.

Select the window manager you want to try from that screen and select OK. That window manager will start the next time you run startx (provided you don't override it by creating your own .xinitrc file). Here are your choices:

- **LXDE** (www.lxde.org)—The Lightweight X11 Desktop Environment was created to perform quickly and elegantly, even in less powerful machines. These qualities make it particularly suitable for mobile devices, netbooks, and other hardware directed toward cloud computing. KNOPPIX now uses LXDE as its desktop environment (see Chapter 12 for some neat ways of using LXDE with Compiz for 3D desktop effects). Figure 3-14 shows an example of an LXDE desktop running in KNOPPIX:

**FIGURE 3-14**

Get special effects on low-powered machines with the Lightweight X11 Desktop Environment.

● **Xfce** (`www.xfce.org`)—The Xfce window manager is designed to be lightweight and fast. Xfce is very popular for running Linux on inexpensive PCs, such as the ASUS EeePC. Figure 3-15 shows an example of an Xfce desktop in Fedora.

Xfce offers many powerful features in an efficient desktop.

● **Blackbox** (`http://blackboxwm.sourceforge.net`)—Another lightweight window manager that strives to require few library dependencies so it can run in many environments. Offers many features for setting colors and styles.

● **FluxBox** (`http://fluxbox.sourceforge.net`)—Based on Blackbox (0.61.1), FluxBox adds nice features such as window tabs (where you can join together multiple windows so they appear as multiple tabs on a single window). It also includes an icon bar and adds some useful mouse features (such as using your mouse wheel to change workspaces).

- **Window Maker** (www.windowmaker.info)—Window Maker is a clone of the NEXTSTEP graphical interface, a popular UNIX workstation of the 1980s and 1990s. It is a particularly attractive window manager, with support for themes, various window decorations, and features for changing backgrounds and animations, and adding applets (called docapps).

- **FVWM** (www.fvwm.org)—This window manager supports full internationalization, window manager hints, and improved font features. Interesting features include window shading in all directions (even diagonal) and side titles (including text displayed vertically).

- **FVWM-95** (http://fvwm95.sourceforge.net)—A version of FVWM that was created to look and feel like Windows 95.

- **Twm (Tabbed Window Manager)**—Although no longer actively maintained, some people still use twm when they want a truly bare-bones desktop. Until you click the left mouse button in twm, there's nothing on the screen. Use the menu that pops up to open and close windows.

Many other window managers are available for Linux as well. To check out some more, visit the Xwinman Web site (http://xwinman.org).

After the system default is set for your window manager, users can set their own window manager to override that decision. The following section describes how to do that.

## Choosing your personal window manager

Simply adding an exec line with the name of the window manager you want to use to your own .xinitrc file in your home directory causes startx to start that window manager for you. Here is an example of the contents of a .xinitrc to start the Window Maker window manager:

```
exec /usr/bin/wmaker
```

Make sure that the file is executable (chmod 755 $HOME/.xinitrc). The Window Maker window manager should start the next time you start your desktop. Other window managers you can choose include Blackbox (/usr/X11R6/bin/blackbox), FluxBox (/usr/X11R6/bin/fluxbox), FVWM (/usr/X11R6/bin/fluxbox), FVWM-95 (/usr/X11R6/bin/fvwm95), and twm (/usr/X11R6/bin/twm).

# Getting More Information

If you tried configuring X and you still have a server that crashes or has a garbled display, your video card may either be unsupported or may require special configuration. Here are a couple of locations you can check for further information:

- **X.Org** (www.x.org)—The latest information about the X servers that come with Fedora is available from the X.Org Web site. X.Org is the freeware version of X recently used by many major Linux distributions to replace the XFree86 X server.

- **X documentation**—README files specific to different types of video cards are delivered with the X.Org X server. Visit the X `doc` directory (`/usr/X11R6/lib/X11/doc`) for a README file specific to the type of video card (or more specifically, the video chipset) you are using. You can also find a lot of good information on the `xorg.conf` man page (type **man xorg.conf**).

# Summary

Complete desktop environments that run in Linux can rival desktop systems from any operating system. KDE and GNOME are the most popular desktop environments available today for Linux. For people who want a sleeker, more lightweight desktop environment, Xfce and LXDE desktops and a variety of simple window managers (Blackbox, Xfce, FVWM, twm, FluxBox, and many others) are available to use in Linux as well.

The KDE desktop is well known for its large set of integrated applications (office productivity tools, games, multimedia, and other applications). The latest KDE offers a more efficient file manager called Dolphin and desktop applets called plasmoids.

GNOME has the reputation of being a more basic, business-oriented desktop. Most Linux distributions such as Slackware and Gentoo offer GNOME and KDE desktops that aren't changed much from how they are delivered from those desktop projects. Other Linux systems (such as Fedora) put their own look-and-feel over GNOME and KDE desktops.

Although the latest Windows systems won't run on many older 486 and Pentium machines, you can use an efficient Linux system such as Slackware, add a lightweight window manager, and get reasonably good performance with your desktop system on those machines.

# Playing Music and Video

One of the most popular and enjoyable activities on a computer is playing audio and video. With improved multimedia players and tools for storing and managing content, Linux has become a great platform for storing, playing, and managing your music and video files.

In this chapter, you learn to use the sound, video, digital imaging, and other multimedia tools available for Linux. You explore the process of configuring audio and select video devices and examine the kinds of media formats available for the Linux platform, how they work, and how to make the most of them by using the right applications.

Linux is an excellent platform for taking advantage of widely used formats such as MPEG, AVI, Ogg Vorbis, and QuickTime. A wide variety of players are available for the various formats, and this chapter discusses several of them to help you determine which might be the right one (or combination) for your interests and/or needs.

## Note

Because many devices holding multimedia content are removable (CDs, DVDs, digital cameras, Webcams, and so on), recent features in Linux to automatically handle removable hardware and media have greatly improved the Linux desktop experience. See the section on managing hardware in Chapter 3 for descriptions of how features such as Udev and HAL are used to manage removable media. ∎

Some Linux distributions are more multimedia-friendly right after the install than others. An example of this is Ubuntu, which gives you the opportunity to enable "non-free" repositories from which you can get software that cannot be freely distributed or, in some cases, allow you to purchase "non-free" software from the Ubuntu store (http://shop.canonical.com). This can save you a great deal of time trying to track down licensing issues and resolve problems.

# Playing Digital Media and Obeying the Law

Debate about just what an end user can legally do with digital media continues to be a hot topic. What exactly can you do as far as making copies of your CDs, DVDs, and other media? What proprietary media (MP3s, commercial DVD movies, and so on) is even legal to play back in Linux? Unfortunately, there is no really good answer. This issue affects just about every computer user, either directly or indirectly.

How you are allowed to use the audio, video, and other media you keep on your computer is increasingly dictated by national and international law. There was a time when you could essentially disregard this issue for personal use, but in the era where individual computer users have been successfully sued by corporations and industry groups, a little more caution is required.

## Copyright protection issues

The biggest factor in the world of digital media policy is the 1998 Digital Millennium Copyright Act (DMCA). This law ostensibly establishes a framework for implementing several international treaties concerning copyright protection.

The DMCA has been widely criticized because it seems to intrude on the free-speech provisions of the U.S. Constitution. Many people view computer code as a protected form of speech. A conflict arises because the DMCA forbids the development of applications that are designed to intentionally circumvent content security. For example, Dmitry Sklyarov, a Russian cryptographer employed by a Russian software company, ElcomSoft, was arrested by the FBI while attending a conference in Las Vegas because he demonstrated an application that could decrypt Adobe eBooks. A jury found Sklyarov and ElcomSoft not guilty in December 2002, but the point is that companies *will* use the DMCA to litigate against those who publicize methods to decrypt encrypted content.

If nothing else, this event demonstrated that the DMCA had teeth. Unfortunately, these teeth have been used not only to protect legitimate commerce, but to pursue computer scientists at academic institutions researching content protection schemes, encryption, and a range of other technologies. Because the DMCA makes it a crime to manufacture and transport technology used to circumvent copyright protection schemes, many researchers have abandoned valuable research that could yield better (stronger and more useful) protection schemes or reveal critical flaws in existing ones.

Although DCMA has provided some clout for content providers to legitimately protect their material, such as persuading search engines to drop information about links to illegally posted and copyrighted information, there are times when that clout has been abused. Some copyright holders, it seems, are more than willing to use the DMCA to curtail three "rights" allowed under pre-DMCA copyright law. Copyright law stipulates the following:

- Users can make a copy of any copyrighted work for academic purposes, reporting, or critique. This includes a wide range of uses, from students or instructors copying materials for research to someone creating a parody of published materials. But what about a student making a copy of some DVD materials for a multimedia presentation? The student has fair-use access to the material on the DVD, but the DMCA makes it illegal for the student to break the DVD encryption that would allow the student to copy the material.

## Note

**The fair-use rule is a privilege that permits someone other than the owner of the copyright to use the copyrighted material in a reasonable and limited manner without his consent. ■**

- Users can sell copyrighted works that they own. You can sell your books, DVDs, audio CDs, and other materials as long as you are not retaining a copy for yourself, or (of course) selling copies of the work without permission from the copyright holder. Some people arguing in favor of file trading with copyrighted materials claim that the DMCA infringes on their ability to "share" content they "own." In fact, under existing copyright law they do not "own" the copyrighted material and certainly do not possess the rights to redistribute the content unless they are reselling it in an allowed manner.

- All copyrights expire at some time in the future and fall into the public domain. Basically, this point raises the same issue as with the first item: Your DVD movie falls into the public domain (eventually), but to freely copy the content you must again circumvent the protection inherent on the DVD and by doing so, you run afoul of the DMCA.

It is important to realize the DMCA is very vague about how it defines many of the acts that are illegal. What is a "protection scheme?" Some argue that it could be nearly anything. Many pundits fear that the DMCA can be used to curtail the use of nondigital copyrighted works such as books because the law is so vague in defining its own borders.

Although the courts are trying to clarify where the legal line is in any particular situation, the problem is that, often, the company suing to protect its copyrights is a large corporation or group and the defendant is either a new small company or even an individual user. Court battles are expensive, and the broad scope of the DMCA essentially prevents "the little guy" from ever making his case, because he cannot afford to fight.

## Note

**In 1998 a law known as the Sonny Bono Copyright Term Extension Act, or CTEA, was passed. This act took the already lengthy copyright protection period (generally 70 years) and extended it by another 20 years, preventing several valuable properties, including film and images of Steamboat Willie (the first Mickey Mouse), from entering the public domain. ■**

From a practical standpoint, what does all this mean to you as a Linux user? Well, it means that if you have to use any trickery to copy MP3s off your CD collection, you could be breaking the law.

Several CD protection schemes used by record companies are designed to prevent digital piracy, but they are very easy to circumvent in many cases. But should you get caught making MP3s off a protected CD, you can be sued and/or arrested (hypothetically speaking). The possibility exists that some of the security on CDs is intentionally weak. It saves development costs and allows the copyright holder to pursue anyone who has ripped the CD because there is no legal means of doing so. But that is just speculation.

Relatively few audio CDs come with protection of any kind, particularly those CDs already owned by the world's audiophiles. If you make fair-use copies of materials you own for your own use, you're not likely to have to worry about anything. If you should decide to transport copyrighted works in a public forum (peer-to-peer networks for example), you are rolling the dice. The RIAA (Recording Industry Association of America) and MPAA (Motion Picture Association of America) have both successfully located and sued users—including children—distributing content illegally online.

## Note

One attempt to allow sharing, remixing, and reusing legally is the Creative Commons Project. As of this writing, the project is nine years old and thousands of items are posted. You can find more information at http://creativecommons.org/.

Two sites worth exploring are Jamendo (www.jamendo.com/en/) and Magnatune (www.magnatune.com). Both are libraries offering free access to music. Jamendo focuses on free distribution of music to help musicians grow their audiences. Magnatune helps musicians by licensing their music to those who would like to use it in commercial ventures (such as films, commercials, Web sites, and so on), while still allowing the musicians to maintain rights to their music. ■

## Exploring codecs

If you want to play a video or audio file, you need the appropriate codec installed and ready for use by your media player. A *codec* is a software-based encoder-decoder used to take existing digital audio/video data and decode the content. Often, codecs use compression technology to reduce the size of the data files while retaining the quality of the output.

If you encounter a media file that you know is a working, playable file and you cannot play the file, you might need to identify and install the proper codec. This often involves installing the proper playback application, such as DivX 5.0.5 for Linux, which installs the MPEG4 codec for video and audio playback.

Many codecs are available, so finding the ones you need is usually not difficult. Advances in codec technology have continued to increase the quality of the encoded content, while reducing file size. Fortunately most widely distributed videos and audio files (from news sites, for example) are created using a few commonly used codecs.

Although some commonly used encoding standards exist, a slew of proprietary codecs are also in use today. This situation is really a battleground of sorts with each vendor/developer trying to produce the superior standard and obtain the spoils of market share that can follow. For the end user, this means you might have to spend time chasing a variety of playback utilities to handle multiple video and audio formats.

Another debate: Can digital media match the quality of analog formats? This hardly seems much of a question anymore because DVD has shown the potential for high-quality digital video, and MPEG codecs have made huge strides in digital audio fidelity. The quality of digital media files is very high and getting better all the time. Some of the key technologies that reflect improvements in how audio and video codecs have improved include

- **Ogg Vorbis**—This audio codec has been developed as a freely available tool—no patents restricting its use. Ogg is the "data container" portion of the codec, and Vorbis is the audio compression scheme. Other compression schemes can be used with Ogg such as Ogg FLAC, which is used for archiving audio in a lossless format, and Ogg Speex, which is used specifically to handle encoding speech.

- **WMA**—Windows Media Audio is used to create high-quality digital audio. WMA is considered a *lossless* codec, which means the audio doesn't lose quality or data as a result of repeated compression-decompression cycles. Among its other benefits is that it's one of the first widely used codecs to support digital surround sound.

- **WMV**—Windows Media Video is used, not surprisingly, to encode and decode video. It is also a very high-quality encoder and is billed to produce a video that is half the size of an MPEG-4 encoded video at a comparable quality level.

- **DivX**—This video codec revolutionized digital video. Extremely high-quality video can be stored with amazingly small file sizes when using this codec. DivX (Digital Video Express) is based on the MPEG-4 video standard and can produce 640 × 480 video about 15 percent of the size of the source DVD material.

Some of these codecs are integral parts of Digital Rights Management (DRM) scenarios. For example, WMA, WMV, and DivX have elements that support DRM. DRM is basically proprietary copy protection.

The term *DRM* applies to a wide range of technologies that use server-based activation, encryption, and other elements to control who can access content and what they can then do with the content after it has been accessed. Although it is very attractive to distributors of audio and video, who are trying to prevent unchecked digital piracy of their content, it can be a real stumbling block for the consumer.

Many DRM solutions require proprietary software and even hardware to work with the protected content. A prime example is the production of some DRM-protected audio CDs, particularly in Europe. Some of these discs will not play in older standalone CD players, some will play only on a computer that supports the DRM application on the CD itself, and (especially frustrating) some will not play on a computer at all. In almost all cases, such DRM solutions do not support Linux. Most support only Windows and a few support Windows and Mac OS X.

Just to make things clear, although the codecs just discussed do not include built-in DRM features, some codecs are specifically designed to integrate with DRM solutions. In other words, all of these codecs can theoretically be used to play encoded content on a Linux system. If the content is protected by a DRM solution, the likelihood that the content is playable on a Linux system is fairly remote. Despite this fact, or perhaps because of it, Linus Torvalds has not excluded the possibility of including support for DRM in Linux. Likewise, several open source projects are working on Linux DRM solutions.

# Playing Music

With an understanding of the challenges and advances in digital media under your belt, let's move on to actually putting digital media to use. This section shows you how to set up your Linux installation for audio playback. It examines the process for getting the hardware up and running and then explores available software options for audio playback.

## Using sound systems in Linux

Several different sound systems have been used to bring audio to your Linux desktop in the past few years. Although sound systems mostly work in the background, the sound system running in Linux can impact the sound mixers and applications you can use. Here is some information related to sound support you might run into when you use Linux:

- **Open Sound System** (www.opensound.com)—Open Sound System (OSS) was the first sound system for Linux and other UNIX systems to unify the sound drivers and sound application interfaces under one framework. OSS was originally available in open source, then was proprietary for several years, but has recently become available in open source again (www.opensound.com/download.cgi). OSS is owned by 4Front Technologies: www.4front-tech.com. Audio applications written for OSS work with both ALSA and PulseAudio sound systems. Because ALSA and PulseAudio are packaged with most desktop Linux systems, OSS is not as commonly used as it once was.

- **Advanced Linux Sound System** (www.alsa-project.org)—Most Linux systems replaced OSS with the Advanced Linux Sound Architecture (ALSA) system for their sound driver and sound interface needs. ALSA also does a good job configuring sound drivers and handling multiple sound devices. ALSA works with both KDE and GNOME desktop systems. Several major Linux distributions have switched to PulseAudio as their default sound system, while still supporting ALSA applications.

- **PulseAudio** (www.pulseaudio.org)—Ubuntu, Fedora, Mandriva, and other Linux distributions have replaced their ALSA sound systems with PulseAudio. Besides adding some features for controlling volume for multiple sound applications and directing audio to PulseAudio servers on other systems, the PulseAudio server will work with many ALSA, aRts, and ESD applications using plug-ins.

- **KDE sound systems**—With KDE 4, the default KDE sound system changed from the analog Real time synthesizer (aRts) to Phonon (http://phonon.kde.org). Although Phonon does consolidate end-user tools for controlling audio, its primary goal is to provide software developers with a multimedia application programming interface that encompasses both audio and video features.

- **GNOME sound systems**—GNOME supports the Enlightened Sound Daemon (ESD) as its sound server. ESD relies on the GStreamer (`www.gstreamer.net`) framework to handle the actual encoding and decoding of multimedia content. You can purchase legal audio and video codecs from a company called Fluendo (`www.fluendo.com`) that work with the GStreamer framework.

Because at least three of the major Linux distributions (Fedora, Ubuntu, and Mandriva) have moved to PulseAudio as their default sound server, the next section focuses on how to use PulseAudio sound tools from your Linux desktop.

## Adjusting sound with PulseAudio

If your Linux desktop has integrated PulseAudio properly, you should be able to use it to work with most sound applications written for Linux. That means that you can not only play lots of audio applications from your desktop, but you can also separately control the volume for each one using the PulseAudio Volume Control.

For example, from the Fedora GNOME desktop, select Applications ➪ Sound & Video ➪ PulseAudio Volume Control. (If you don't see that selection, install the pavucontrol package.) A window similar to the one shown in Figure 4-1 appears.

---

**FIGURE 4-1**

Control volume levels for multiple audio players with PulseAudio.

As audio applications are started, they appear in the Playback tab on the PulseAudio Volume Control window. In Figure 4-1, I opened the ogg123 player to play some music in the background (I moved the sliders to lower the volume). I also opened a YouTube video from my Web browser, which also showed up on the volume control. There's already a slider that lets me adjust system sounds.

If you have multiple audio input and output devices, you can configure volume levels from those devices individually, using the Input Devices and Output Devices tabs. By clicking your mouse on the Input or Output Devices tab, you can change your default audio devices.

Most of the work to configure the plug-ins and devices needed to get your Linux audio applications working should have been set up automatically when you installed your Linux system. However, if you are not able to play some audio applications, refer to the PulseAudio Perfect Setup page (www.pulseaudio.org/wiki/PerfectSetup). It describes how to configure dozens of GNOME, KDE, OSS, ESOUND, GStreamer, Flash, and other sound applications to work with PulseAudio.

## Note

If you are using a Linux system that doesn't have PulseAudio installed, there are other commands you can use to adjust audio levels. The aumix command has a simple way to adjust audio, using command options or a screen-oriented menu. The alsamixer command lets you adjust audio levels for ALSA audio devices. ■

## Setting up audio cards

To start your "quadraphonic wall of sound," you need to have a sound card in your PC. A sound card can be an add-in PCI (or even ISA) card, or it can be integrated on your motherboard. Your card will have a ton of uses—from gaming to audio/video playback. Having a multimedia system just isn't the same without sound.

Fortunately, most modern PCs include a sound card, often of the integrated variety. In the rare case that one isn't included (or the slightly more common case where it isn't supported in Linux), you can add a supported sound card starting for only a few dollars. If you're really pinched, check out eBay, where you probably can get a decent SoundBlaster-compatible card (still *the* standard) for next to nothing.

## Note

If you try the procedures in this book but still don't have a working sound card, visit www.alsa-project.org, home of the Advanced Linux Sound Architecture (ALSA). Another good resource is the ALSA Wiki (http://alsa.opensrc.org). ■

The following list summarizes the basic features that are included in the popular SoundBlaster family of sound cards:

- **Sound recording and playback**—The card can convert analog sound into 8-bit or 16-bit digital numbers. To convert the sound, the board samples the sound in waves from 5 KHz to 48 KHz, or 5,000 to 48,100 times per second. The higher the sampling rate, the better the sound and larger the output files.

- **Full-duplex support**—Full-duplex means that recording and playback occur at the same time. This is particularly useful for bidirectional Internet communication, such as Voice-Over-IP (VOIP) telephony or simultaneous recording and playback.

- **Input/output ports**—Several different ports on the board enable you to connect other input/output devices. These ports include

  - **Line-In (blue)**—Connects an external CD player, cassette deck, synthesizer, MiniDisc, or other device for recording or playback. If you have a television card, you might also patch that card's line out to your sound card's line in.

  - **Microphone (red)**—Connects a microphone for audio recording or communications.

  - **Headphone/Line-Out/Speaker Out (green)**—Connects speakers, headphones, or a stereo amplifier. (On sound cards I've tested, this is marked as Headphone in mixer utilities.)

  - **Joystick/MIDI (15-pin connector)**—Connects a joystick for gaming or MIDI devices. (Some sound cards no longer have these ports because they are now available from most motherboards.)

  - **Digital out (orange)**—A digital out connector can be used to connect a digital audio tape (DAT) device or CD recordable (CD-R) device.

  - **Rear out (black)**—Can be used to deliver audio output to powered speakers or an external amplifier.

  - **Internal CD Audio**—This internal port connects the sound card to your computer's internal CD-ROM drive (this port isn't exposed when the board is installed).

Sound drivers provided in Linux come from many sources. Advanced Linux Sound Architecture (ALSA) sound drivers are integrated into the 2.6 kernel. You may find older Open Sound System (OSS) drivers are useful if ALSA does not support your sound card. You can get OSS drivers for free (recently released as open source) from 4Front Technologies (`www.opensound.com/download.cgi`), which is the company that still maintains OSS.

## Caution

**Before you install a separate sound driver distribution, check to see if your current distribution already has a recent driver. Using the driver that came with the kernel is always a safe bet if you are not experiencing a specific driver-related issue.** ■

At times, a sound application will ask you to identify the device from which to access sound on your system. With the introduction of the Udev feature in the 2.6 kernel, some of the device names are different from those used with the 2.4 kernel. The following are audio device nodes that may be of interest to you as you use sound in Linux:

- `/dev/audio`, `/dev/audio1`—Compatible with Sun workstation audio implementations (audio files with the .au extension). These devices are not recommended for new sound applications.

- `/dev/cdrom`—Represents your first CD-ROM drive. `/dev/cdrom` is usually a symbolic link to the device node, such as `/dev/hdc`, that corresponds to your CD-ROM drive. Additional CD-ROM drives are located at `/dev/cdrom1`, `/dev/cdrom2`, and so on.

- `/dev/dsp`, `/dev/dsp1`—Digital sampling devices, which many audio applications identify to access your sound card.

- `/dev/mixer`, `/dev/mixer1`—Sound-mixing devices.

- `/dev/sequencer`—Provides a low-level interface to MIDI, FM, and GUS.

- `/dev/midi00`—Provides raw access to MIDI ports, if they are available.

For general information about sound in Linux, see the Sound-HOWTO (for tips about sound cards and general sound issues) and the Sound-Playing-HOWTO (for tips on software for playing different types of audio files). You can find Linux HOWTOs at `www.tldp.org`.

## Choosing an audio CD player

Rhythmbox is the default CD player for many GNOME desktop systems. However, a variety of CD players are available for Linux distributions or may be downloaded and installed. Here is a cross-section of choices for playing CDs with Linux:

- **Rhythmbox** (`rhythmbox`)—Import and manage your CD collection with Rhythmbox music management and playback software for GNOME. It uses GStreamer on the audio backend and can rip and compress music using Ogg Vorbis or other audio formats. In addition to enabling you to create playlists of your music library, Rhythmbox also has features for playing Internet radio stations. Free music stores were added to Rhythmbox in recent releases, allowing you to play free music from Jamendo (`www.jamendo.com/en/`) and Magnatune (`www.magnatune.com`), and possibly purchase CDs or license use of that music for commercial projects.

- **KsCD player** (`kscd`)—The KsCD player comes with the KDE desktop. To use it, the kdemultimedia package must be installed. From the main menu on the KDE desktop, select Multimedia ➪ KsCD (or type **kscd** in a Terminal window). This player lets you get title, track, and artist information from the CD database. KsCD, however, also lets you submit information to a CD database (if your CD isn't found there).

- **Grip** (`grip`)—Although Grip is primarily used as a CD ripper, it can also play CDs. Select Multimedia ➪ Grip (or type **grip** in a Terminal window). It includes tools for gathering data from and submitting data to CD databases. It also includes tools for copying (ripping) CD tracks and converting them to different formats (encoding). Naturally, the grip package must be installed to use this command.

- **Amarok** (`amarok`)—With Amarok, you get a nice graphical interface where you can manage music by moving elements around with your mouse. Amarok uses SQLite (or other databases) to store your music. It also supports playlists and streaming audio play-back from online radio stations.

- **X Multimedia System** (xmms)—The XMMS player plays a variety of audio formats but can also play directly from a CD.

### Playing music with Rhythmbox Audio Player

Rhythmbox provides the GNOME music player that lets you play music from CD, local file system, or network location. Rhythmbox is built on the GStreamer framework for developing media players, video editors, and streaming media. You can play music files, import music from CDs, and play Internet radio stations, all from one interface. Other features let you play podcasts and custom radio stations from Last.fm music service. Plug-ins for Rhythmbox let you display album covers, view lyrics, or show visual effects with the music.

The first time you run Rhythmbox, consider setting some Rhythmbox Preferences by selecting Edit Preferences. On the Music tab (see Figure 4-2), you can tell Rhythmbox where you store your music files, and how Rhythmbox should organize and store your music (including how folders are named, songs are titled, and the format in which music is stored).

After you've set up your preferences, you'll see the main music library interface (see Figure 4-3). Rhythmbox makes organizing even large collections of music files easy.

**FIGURE 4-2**

Defining where you store your music

**93**

**FIGURE 4-3**

Viewing a music library with Rhythmbox

## Note

If your distribution does not include support for MP3 playback with Rhythmbox, fear not—there is hope! In Fedora, you can use the ffmpeg-plugin package available from the `rpmfusion.org` repository. For Ubuntu, Freespire, and legacy Linspire Linux distributions, check out support in the Click-N-Run service (`www.cnr.com`). In addition to playing music files, Rhythmbox can easily rip CDs. Just insert the CD you want to rip, right-click the CD when it appears under the Devices heading in the left column, and click the Extract icon on the toolbar. The CD will be ripped and stored with your Rhythmbox music collection folder. ■

Rhythmbox can also play Internet radio stations and podcasts. Without adding more codecs, you can play Ogg Vorbis Internet radio audio streams. Many more streams are available in MP3 format, however. To add an Internet radio station to Rhythmbox, select Radio in the left column and click the New icon. Fill in the Title and Genre of the station. Then choose the Details tab and type in the location of the stream (such as `http://wknc.org:8000/wkncmq.ogg.m3u`).

Adding podcasts can be done the same way. Select Podcasts in the left column and select New. Type the URL for the podcast feed (for example, www.geeknewscentral.com/podcast.xml) into the pop-up that appears. To add an image to your podcast, just download an appropriate image to your computer and drag-and-drop it onto the lower-left corner of the Rhythmbox window while your Podcast is selected. Figure 4-4 shows Rhythmbox playing the Geek News Central podcast.

**FIGURE 4-4**

Rhythmbox playing a podcast feed

## Tip

The site www.di.fm lists a number of free Internet radio channels. ∎

### Playing music with the XMMS multimedia player

The XMMS (X Multimedia System) multimedia player provides a compact, graphical interface for playing music files in MP3, Ogg Vorbis, WAV, and other audio formats. XMMS has some nice extras too, including an equalizer, a playlist editor, and the capability to add more audio plug-ins. One of its greatest attributes is that XMMS is easy to use. If the player looks familiar to you, that's because it is styled after the Windows Winamp program.

To add XMMS to your Fedora system, type **yum install xmms\*** as root user. This command gets you the player and some nice skins to use with it as well. To play MP3 audio with XMMS, you need to add the MPEG Layer 1/2/3 Player plug-in. In Fedora, you can get the xmms-mp3 package from the http://rpmfusion.org free repository.

Start the XMMS audio player by selecting Sound & Video ⇨ Audio Player or by typing **xmms** from a Terminal window. Figure 4-5 shows the XMMS audio player. The skin I selected (right-click XMMS and select Options ⇨ Skin Browser) is called ColderXMMS.

**FIGURE 4-5**

Play Ogg Vorbis and other audio files from the XMMS player.

As noted earlier, you can play several audio file formats. Supported formats include

- MP3 (with added plug-in)
- Ogg Vorbis
- WAV
- AU
- CD Audio
- CIN Movies

## Note

If XMMS is not able to find a configured sound card, it redirects its output to the Disk Writer plug-in. This causes the files you play to be written to hard disk as WAV files. ∎

You can get many more audio plug-ins from www.xmms.org. The XMMS audio player can be used in the following way:

1. Obtain music files by ripping songs from a CD or copying them from the Web so that they are in an accessible directory, or by inserting a music CD in your CD-ROM drive. (XMMS expects the CD to be accessible from /dev/cdrom.)

2. From the Applications menu, select Sound & Video ⇨ Audio Player. The X Multimedia System player appears.

3. Click the Eject button. The Load Files window appears.

4. If you have inserted a CD, the contents of /mnt/cdrom appear in the Files pane. Select the files you want to add to your Playlist and click the Add Selected Files or the Add All

Files in Directory button to add all songs from the current directory. To add audio files from your file system, browse your files and directories and click the same buttons to add the audio files you want. Select Close.

5. Click the Play List button (the tiny button marked PL) on the console. A Playlist Editor window appears.

6. Double-click the music file, and it starts to play.

7. With a file selected and playing, here are a few actions you can take:

   - **Control play**—Buttons for controlling play are what you would expect to see on a standalone CD player. From left to right, the buttons let you go to a previous track, play, pause, stop, go to the next track, and eject the CD. The eject button opens a window, enabling you to load the next file.

   - **Adjust sound**—Use the left slider bar to adjust the volume. Use the right slider bar to change the right-to-left balance.

   - **Display time**—Click in the elapsed time area to toggle between elapsed time and time remaining.

   - **View file information**—Click the button in the upper-left corner of the screen to see the XMMS menu. Then select View File Info. You can often find out a lot of information about the file: title, artist, album, comments, and genre. For an Ogg Vorbis file, you can see specific information about the file itself, such as the format, bit rate, sample rate, frames, file size, and more. You can change or add to the tag information and click Save to keep it.

8. When you are done playing music, click the Stop button to stop the current song. Then click the X in the lower-right corner of the display to close the window.

Special features of the XMMS audio player let you adjust frequencies using a graphic equalizer and gather and play songs using a Playlist Editor. Click the button marked EQ next to the balance bar on the player to open the Equalizer.

### Using the Equalizer

The Equalizer lets you use slider bars to set different levels to different frequencies played. Bars on the left adjust lower frequencies, and those on the right adjust higher frequencies. Click the EQ button to open the Equalizer window. Here are tasks you can perform with the Equalizer:

   - If you like the settings you have for a particular song, you can save them as a Preset. Set each frequency as you like it and click the Preset button. Then choose Save ⇨ Preset. Type a name for the preset and click OK.

   - To reload a preset you created earlier, click the Preset button and select Load ⇨ Preset. Select the preset you want and click OK.

The small window in the center/top of the Equalizer shows the sound wave formed by your settings. You can adjust the Preamp bar on the left to boost different levels in the set range.

### Using the Playlist Editor

The Playlist Editor lets you put together a list of audio files that you want to play. You can add and delete files from this list, save them to a file, and use them again later. Click the PL button in the XMMS window to open the Playlist Editor.

The Playlist Editor enables you to

- **Add files to the playlist**—Click the Add button. The Load Files window appears. Select the directory containing your audio files (it's useful to keep them all in one place) from the left column. Then either select a file from the right column and click Add Selected Files or click Add All Files in the Directory. Click OK. The selected file or files appear(s) in the playlist. You can also add music files by dragging them from the Nautilus file manager onto the playlist window.

- **Select files to play**—To select from the files in the playlist, use the previous track and next track buttons in the main XMMS window. The selected file is highlighted. Click the Play button to play that file. Alternatively, you can double-click any file in the playlist to start it playing.

- **Delete files from the playlist**—To remove files from the playlist, select the file or files you want to remove (use the next track and previous track buttons), right-click the playlist window, and click Remove ➪ Selected. The selected files are removed.

- **Save the playlist**—To save the current playlist, hold the right mouse button down on the List button and then select Playlist ➪ Save List from the pop-up menu. Browse to the directory you want, and then type the name you want to assign to the playlist and click OK. The filename should end with a .m3u extension, such as monkees_hits.m3u.

- **Load the playlist**—To reload a saved playlist, click the List button. Select a playlist from the directory in which you saved it and click OK.

There is also a tiny set of buttons on the bottom of the Playlist Editor screen. These are the same buttons as those on the main screen used for selecting different tracks or playing, pausing, stopping, or ejecting the current track.

One of the most fun aspects to XMMS is that you can change the skin, or the look, of the user interface. XMMS skins allow you to see wildly different interfaces, even though the application remains the same. Not only can you control the looks of XMMS, you can also use skins to adjust for any issues in the XMMS interface. For example, the current song in the playlist window may not be highlighted enough, especially if you have a high-resolution monitor. You can select a skin that provides better highlighting. You can also choose skins that make XMMS look like Winamp on Windows, or like the Mac OS X interface.

XMMS supports Windows .wsz Winamp skins, so you can download those skins and see your favorite musician or animated characters for your music player. Just download and copy the skin to your /usr/share/xmms/Skins directory to add it to your skins list.

## Using MIDI audio players

MIDI (Musical Instrument Digital Interface) files are created from synthesizers and other electronic music devices. They tend to be smaller than other kinds of audio files because instead of storing the complete sounds, they contain information about the notes played, tempo, and articulation. You can think of a MIDI file as electronic sheet music. The MIDI player reproduces the notes to sound like a huge variety of MIDI instruments.

There are lots of sites on the Internet for downloading MIDI files. Try the Ifni MIDI Music site (www.ifnimidi.com), for example, which contains songs by the Beatles, Led Zeppelin, Nirvana, and others organized by album. Most of the MIDI music is pretty simple, but you can have some fun playing with it.

Linux distributions that include the KDE desktop (such as Fedora) often come with the kmid MIDI player. Kmid provides a GUI interface for MIDI music, including the capability to display karaoke lyrics in real time. To start kmid in Fedora, select Sound & Video ➪ KMid (or type **kmid &** from a Terminal window).

## Performing audio file conversion and compression

Many different formats exist for storing and compressing speech and music files. Because music files can be large, they are usually stored in a compressed format. Although MP3 has been the compression format of choice, Ogg Vorbis is quickly becoming the favorite for compressing music in the open source community. Ogg Vorbis has the added benefit of not being encumbered by patents as MP3 is.

Linux tools for converting and compressing audio files include

- **sox** (SoX)—A general-purpose tool for converting audio files among a variety of formats
- **oggenc**—A tool for specifically converting music files to Ogg Vorbis format

### Converting audio files with SoX

If you have a sound file in one format, but you want it to be in another format, Linux offers some conversion tools. The SoX utility can translate to and from any of the audio formats listed in Table 4-1.

## Tip
Type sox -h to see the supported audio types, as well as supported options and effects. ■

**TABLE 4-1**

## Sound Formats Supported by the SoX Utility

| File Extension or Pseudonym | Description | File Extension or Pseudonym | Description |
|---|---|---|---|
| .8svx | 8SVX Amiga musical instrument description format. | .aiff | Apple IIc/IIgs and SGI AIFF files. May require a separate archiver to work with these files. |
| .au, .snd | Sun Microsystems AU audio files. This was once a popular format. (The .snd extension is ambiguous because it's also been used on NeXT format and headerless Mac/PC format.) | .avr | Audio Visual Research format, used on the Mac. |
| .cdr | CD-R files used to master compact discs. | .cvs | Continuously variable slope delta modulation, which is used for voice mail and other speech compression. |
| .dat | Text data files, which contain a text representation of sound data. | .gsm | Lossy Speech Compression (GSM 06.10), used to shrink audio data in voice mail and similar applications. |
| .hcom | Macintosh HCOM files. | .maud | Amiga format used to produce sound that is 8-bit linear, 16-bit linear, a-law, and u-law in mono or stereo. |
| .ogg | Ogg Vorbis compressed audio, which is best used for compressing music and streaming audio. | .ossdsp | Pseudo file, used to open the OSS /dev/dsp file and configure it to use the data type passed to SoX. Used to either play or record. |
| .prc | Psion record.app format, newer than the WVE format. Note that the .prc extension is also used for programs for the Palm handheld devices. | .sf | IRCAM sound files, used by CSound package and MixView sample editor. |
| .sph | Speech audio SPHERE (Speech Header Resources) format from NIST (National Institute of Standards and Technology). | .smp | SampleVision files from Turtle Beach, used to communicate with different MIDI samplers. |

| File Extension or Pseudonym | Description | File Extension or Pseudonym | Description |
|---|---|---|---|
| `.sunau` | Pseudo file, used to open a `/dev/audio` file and set it to use the data type being passed to SoX. | `.txw` | Yamaha TX-16W from a Yamaha sampling keyboard. |
| `.vms` | Used to compress speech audio for voice mail and similar applications. | `.voc` | Sound Blaster VOC file. |
| `.wav` | Microsoft WAV RIFF files. This is the native Microsoft Windows sound format. | `.wve` | 8-bit, a-law, 8 KHz sound files used with Psion Palmtop computers. |
| `.raw` | Raw files (contain no header information, so sample rate, size, and style must be given). | `.ub, .sb, .uw, .sw, .ul, .al, .lu, .la, .sl` | Raw files with set characteristics. `ub` is unsigned byte; `sb` is signed byte; `uw` is unsigned word; `sw` is signed word; and `ul` is `ulaw`. |

If you are not sure about the format of an audio file, you can add the `.auto` extension to the filename. This triggers SoX to guess what kind of audio format is contained in the file. The `.auto` extension can be used only for the input file. If SoX can figure out the content of the input file, it translates the contents to the sound type for the output file you request.

In its most basic form, you can convert one file format (such as a WAV file) to another format (such as an AU file) as follows:

```
$ sox file1.wav file1.au
```

To see what SoX is doing, use the `-V` option. For example:

```
$ sox -V file1.wav file1.voc

sox: Reading Wave file: Microsoft PCM format, 2 channel, 44100 samp/sec
sox: 176400 byte/sec, 4 block align, 16 bits/samp, 50266944 data bytes
sox: Input file: using sample rate 11025
        size bytes, style unsigned, 1 channel
sox: Input file1.wav: comment "file1.wav"

sox: Output file1.voc: using sample rate 44100
        size shorts, encoding signed (2's complement), 2 channels
sox: Output file: comment "file1.wav"
```

You can apply sound effects during the SoX conversion process. The following example shows how to change the sample rate (using the -r option) from 10,000 KHz to 5,000 KHz:

```
$ sox -r 10000 file1.wav -r 5000 file1.voc
```

To reduce the noise, you can send the file through a low-pass filter. Here's an example:

```
$ sox file1.voc file2.voc lowp 2200
```

For more information on SoX and to get the latest download, go to the SoX—Sound eXchange—home page (http://sourceforge.net/projects/sox/).

### Compressing music files with oggenc

The oggenc command takes music or other audio data and converts it from uncompressed formats (such as WAV, RAW, or AIFF) to the compressed Ogg Vorbis format. Using Ogg Vorbis, audio files can be significantly reduced in size without a noticeable loss of sound quality. (I used the default settings in oggenc and reduced a 48MB WAV music file to 4MB.)

In its most basic form, you can use oggenc with one or more WAV or AIFF files following it. For example:

```
$ oggenc *.wav
```

This command would result in all files ending with .wav in the current directory to be converted to Ogg Vorbis format. An OGG file is produced for each WAV file, with oggenc substituting .ogg for .wav as the file suffix for the compressed file. Ogg Vorbis files can be played in many different audio players in Linux, including the XMMS player (described earlier).

In addition, a number of hand-held music players support Ogg Vorbis formats. These include a number of iRiver, Jens of Sweden, MobiBLU, Neuros, and Samsung models. Verify with your product's manual, however, as models and player firmware change often.

## Tip
If you want to rip music files from a CD and compress them, you can use the Grip window (described later in this chapter). Grip enables you to select oggenc as the tool to do the file compression. ■

If you are interested in making a CD jukebox that rips, records, and compresses music CDs using oggenc and other open source software, check out *Linux Toys* by Christopher Negus and Chuck Wolber from Wiley Publishing (2003).

# Recording and Ripping Music

Writable CD-ROM drives are a standard device on computers. Where once you had to settle for a floppy disk (1.44MB) or a Zip disk (100MB) to store personal data, a CD-ROM burner lets you store more than 600MB of data in a format that can be exchanged with most computers. On top of that, you can create CD music discs!

Both graphical and command-line tools exist for creating audio and data CDs on Linux. The cdrecord command enables you to create audio and data CDs from the command line, writing to CD-recordable (CD-R) and CD-rewritable (CD-RW) drives. This command is discussed in the following section.

## Creating an audio CD with cdrecord

You can use the cdrecord command to create either data or music CDs. You can create a data CD by setting up a separate file system and copying the whole image of that file system to CD. Creating an audio CD consists of selecting the audio tracks you want to copy and copying them all at once to the CD.

This section focuses on using cdrecord to create audio CDs. cdrecord can use audio files in .au, .wav, and .cdr formats, automatically translating them when necessary. If you have audio files in other formats, you can convert them to one of the supported formats by using the sox command (described previously in this chapter).

One way to create an audio CD is to use cdda2wav to extract (copy) the music tracks to a directory and then use cdrecord to write them from the directory to the CD. Here's an example:

### Note
If you prefer a graphical tool for copying and burning CDs and DVDs, refer to Appendix A, which describes how to use the K3B CD/DVD Burning Facility for burning CD images. You can also use that tool for copying audio CDs. ■

1. Create a directory to hold the audio files, and change to that directory. (Make sure the directory can hold up to 660MB of data—less if you are burning fewer songs.) For example:

```
# mkdir /tmp/cd
# cd /tmp/cd
```

2. Insert the music CD into your CD-ROM drive. (If a CD player opens on the desktop, close it.)

3. Extract the music tracks you want by using the cdda2wav command. For example:

```
# cdda2wav -D /dev/cdrom -B
```

This reads all the music tracks from the CD-ROM drive. The -B option says to output each track to a separate file. By default, the cdda2wav command outputs the files to the WAV audio format.

Instead of extracting all songs, you can choose a single track or a range of tracks to extract. For example, to extract tracks 3 through 5, add the -t3+5 option. To extract just track 9, add -t9+9. To extract track 7 through the end of the CD, add -t7.

## Note

**If you have a low-quality CD drive or an imperfect CD,** cdda2wav **might not be the best ripping tool. You might try** cdparanoia -B **to extract songs from the CD to hard disk instead.** ∎

4. When cdda2wav is done, remove the music CD and insert a blank CD into your writable CD drive.

5. Use the cdrecord command to write the music tracks to the CD. For example:

```
# cdrecord -v dev=/dev/cdrom -audio *.wav
```

The options to cdrecord tell the command to create an audio CD (-audio) on the writable CD device located at /dev/cdrom. The cdrecord command writes all .wav files from the current directory. The -v option causes verbose output.

6. If you want to change the order of the tracks, you can type their names in the order you want them written (instead of using *.wav). If your CD writer supports higher speeds, you can use the speed option to double (speed=2) or to quadruple (speed=4) the writing speed.

After you have created the music CD, indicate the contents of the CD on its label side. It's now ready to play on any standard music CD player.

## Ripping CDs with Grip

The Grip application (grip package) provides a more graphical method of copying music from CDs to your hard disk so that you can play the songs directly from your hard disk or burn them back onto a blank CD. Besides just ripping music, you can also compress each song as you extract it from the CD.

You can open Grip from the GNOME desktop Applications menu in Ubuntu, Fedora, and other Linux systems by selecting Sound & Video ➪ Grip (or by typing **grip** from a Terminal window). Figure 4-6 shows an example of the Grip window.

To rip audio tracks from a CD with grip, do the following:

1. With the Grip window open, insert a music CD into your CD drive. If you have an active connection to the Internet and the CD is known to the CD database, the title, artist, and track information appear in the window.

2. Click each track that you want to rip (that is, copy to your hard disk). A check mark appears in that track's Rip column.

**FIGURE 4-6**

Rip and play songs from the Grip window.

3. Click the Config tab at the top of the page, and then select Encode.

4. You can choose the type of encoder used to compress the music by clicking the Encoder box and selecting an encoder (by default, `oggenc` compresses files in Ogg Vorbis, assuming that Ogg Vorbis was installed on your Linux distribution). If you have the lame package installed (available from non-free repositories for some Linux distributions), you can encode your music to MP3 format.

5. Click the Rip tab at the top of the page. From the Ripper subtab, indicate the location and format of the ripped files (I use `~/Music/%x/%A/%d/%n.wav` to hold the ripped WAV files in subdirectories of my Music folder.)

6. Click one of the following:

   ● **Rip+Encode**—This rips the selected songs and (if you left in the default oggenc compression in Step 4) compresses them in Ogg Vorbis format. You need an Ogg Vorbis player to play the songs after they have been ripped in this format (many Ogg Vorbis players are available for Linux).

   ● **Rip only**—This rips the selected songs in WAV format. You can use a standard CD player to play these songs. (When I tried this, the same song ripped in WAV was 12 times larger than the Ogg Vorbis file.)

   Songs are copied to the hard disk in the format you selected. By default, the files are copied into a subdirectory of `$HOME/ogg` (such as `/home/jake/ogg`). The subdirectory is named for the artist and CD. For example, if the user jake were ripping the song called "High Life" by the artist Mumbo, the directory containing the ripped songs would be /home/jake/ogg/mumbo/high_life. Each song file is named for the song (for example, fly_fly_fly.wav). Following the earlier example, I would use /home/jake/Music to hold the ripped music, instead of the default ogg directory.

7.  Now you can play any of the files using a player that can play WAV or Ogg files, such as XMMS. Or you can copy the files to a CD using cdrecord. Because the filenames are the song names, they don't appear in the same order as they appear on the CD, so if you want to copy them back to a writable CD in their original order, you may have to type each filename on the cdrecord command line. For example:

```
# cdrecord -v dev=/dev/cdrom -audio fly_fly.wav
big_news.wav about_time.wav
```

The Grip window can also be used to play CDs. Use the buttons on the bottom of the display to play or pause, skip ahead or back, stop, and eject the CD. The toggle track display button lets you shrink the size of the display so it takes up less space on the desktop. Click toggle disc editor to see and change title, artist, and track information.

## Creating CD labels with cdlabelgen

You can use the cdlabelgen command to create tray cards and front cards to fit in CD jewel cases. You gather information about the CD and cdlabelgen produces a PostScript output file that you can send to the printer. The cdlabelgen package also comes with graphics (in /usr/share/cdlabelgen) that you can incorporate into your labels.

Here's an example of a cdlabelgen command line that generates a CD label file in PostScript format (type it all on one line or use backslashes, as shown, to put it on multiple lines):

```
$ cdlabelgen -c cdlabelgen -c "20th Century Collection" \
    -s "Jon Negus" \
    -i "Heart of Mine%20th Century Man%Swing, Swing, Swing%I \
        write the songs%Oh Mistress Mine%Turns%Winter Solstice" \
    -o cover.ps
```

In this example, -c "20th Century Collection" identifies the title of the CD and the -s "Jon Negus" indicates the artist. The tracks are entered after the -i option, with each line separated by a % sign. The output file is sent to the file cover.ps with the -o option. To view and print the results, use the evince command like this:

```
$ evince cover.ps
```

The result of this example is shown in Figure 4-7.

You'll want to edit the cdlabelgen command line to include the title and song names for the CD label and rerun the program a few times to get the label correct. When you are ready to print the label, click Print All to print the label.

**FIGURE 4-7**

Generate CD jewel case labels with cdlabelgen and print them with evince.

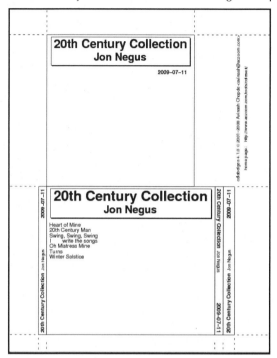

# Working with TV, Video, and Digital Imaging

Getting TV cards, Webcams, and other video devices to play in Linux is still a bit of an adventure. Most manufacturers of TV cards and Webcams are not losing sleep to produce Linux drivers. As a result, most of the drivers that bring video to your Linux desktop have been reverse-engineered (that is, they were created by software engineers who watched what the video device sent and received, rather than seeing the actual code that runs the device).

The first and probably biggest trick is to get a TV card or Webcam that is supported in Linux. After you are getting video output from that device (typically available from /dev/video0), you can try out a couple of applications to begin using it.

This section explores the tvtime program for watching television and the Ekiga program for video conferencing.

# Watching TV with tvtime

The tvtime program (tvtime command) enables you to display video output—television channels, in particular—on your desktop. You can change the channels, adjust volume, and fine-tune your picture. In addition, tvtime sports a slick onscreen display and support for a widescreen display.

The following sections describe how to choose a TV capture card and use tvtime to watch television on your desktop.

## Getting a supported TV card

Video4Linux (V4l/V4I2) is the video interface available for Linux. It supports a variety of TV capture cards and cameras, and is included in some distributions. If your distribution does not include V4l or s/b V4l2, you can install it on your own, although it is not the easiest task to accomplish. For more information about obtaining and installing V4l and the appropriate driver, visit http://linuxtv.org/v4lwiki. The MythTV project offers insight into TV cards for Linux (www.mythtv.org/wiki/Video_capture_card).

Video4Linux is designed to autodetect your TV capture card and load the proper modules to activate it. Install the TV-card hardware (with the appropriate connection to your TV reception), boot Linux, and run the tvtime command as described in the next section. You should see video displayed on your tvtime window.

If your card doesn't appear to be working, here are a few things you can try:

- Check that your TV card was properly seated in its slot and detected by Linux by typing:

```
$ /sbin/lspci | grep -i video
00:09.0 Multimedia video controller: Brooktree Corporation Bt878
    Video Capture (rev 11)
```

  This shows you a list of all valid PCI cards on your computer and displays any containing the word *video*. If your card doesn't show up, you probably have a hardware problem. You can investigate more about which driver and settings are being used by paging through kernel output (type **dmesg | less**).

- Possibly, the card is there but the right card type is not being detected. Improper detection is most likely if you have a card for which there are several revisions, with each requiring a different driver. If you think your card is not being properly detected, find your card in the CARDLIST files. Then add the appropriate line to the /etc/modprobe.conf file. For example, to add a Prolink PV-BT878P, revision 9B card, add the following line to the file:

```
options   bttv   card=72
```

One possible reason that you don't see any video when you try to run tvtime or other video applications is that some other person or video application already has the video driver open. Only one application can use the video driver at a time. Another quirk of Video4Linux is that the first person to open the device on your system becomes the owner. So you might need to open the permissions of the driver to allow people other than the first person to use it to access the Video4Linux driver.

### Running tvtime

To start up the tvtime viewer, simply select TVtime Television Viewer from the Sound & Video or Multimedia menu (depending on your Linux distribution), or type the following from a Terminal window on your desktop:

```
$ tvtime &
```

A video screen should appear in a window on the desktop. Click on the window to see a list of stations. Right-click to see the onscreen Setup menu.

Here are a few things you can now do with your tvtime onscreen display:

- **Configure input**—Change the video source, choose the television standard (which defaults to NTSC for the U.S.), and change the resolution of the input.
- **Set up the picture**—Adjust the brightness, contrast, color, and hue.
- **Adjust the video processing**—Control the attempted frame rate, configure the deinterlacer, or add an input filter.
- **Adjust output**—Control the aspect ratio (for 16:9 output, for example), apply a matte, or set the overscan mode.

## Video conferencing with Ekiga

The Ekiga window lets you communicate with other people over a network through video, audio, and typed messages. Because Ekiga supports the H323 protocol (a standard for multimedia communications), you can use it to communicate with people using other popular videoconferencing clients, such as Microsoft NetMeeting (not including the whiteboard features), Cu-SeeMe, and Intel VideoPhone.

To be able to send video, you need a Webcam supported in Linux—you'll find a few dozen models from which to choose. The following sections show you how to set up your Webcam and use Ekiga for videoconferencing.

## Note

**Ekiga was previously known as GnomeMeeting. Both names may be in use on any given Linux platform.** ∎

### Getting a supported Webcam

As with support for TV capture cards, Webcam support is provided through the Video4Linux interface. To see whether your Webcam is supported, check the /usr/src/linux*/ Documentation directory. A few parallel-port video cameras are described in the video4linux subdirectory; however, the bulk of the supported cameras are listed in the usb directory.

## Tip

**After doing some research, I purchased a Logitech QuickCam Pro 3000. The driver for this Webcam was made for a Philips USB Webcam, but it also works for Webcams from Logitech, Samsung, Creative Labs, and Askey. The pwc driver needed to use these cameras is available with most popular Linux distributions. ∎**

Supported USB cameras should be autodetected, so that when you plug them in, the necessary modules are loaded automatically. Just start up Ekiga (ekiga command), and you should see video from your Webcam on your Linux desktop.

You can check to see that your Webcam is working properly by typing the following:

```
# lsmod
pwc                    79588     0
videodev               30208     3  pwc,tuner,bttv
compat_ioctl32         59072     2  pwc,bttv
```

The output from lsmod shows that the pwc driver is loaded and associated with the videodev module and compat_ioctl32 module.

### Opening your firewall for Ekiga

You need to open a variety of ports in your firewall to use Ekiga. In particular, you need to open TCP port 1720 and TCP port range 30000 to 30010. For UDP ports, you must open ports 5000 through 5007 and ports 5010 through 5013. Examples of exact iptables settings you can use to open these ports are contained in the Ekiga FAQ (www.ekiga.org/faq).

### Running Ekiga

To start Ekiga in most distributions, select Applications ➪ Internet ➪ Ekiga Softphone. To start Ekiga from a Terminal window, type **ekiga &**. If it is not installed, you can get the package for your Linux distribution when you install the GNOME desktop. The first time you run Ekiga, the Ekiga Configuration Assistant starts, enabling you to enter the following information:

- **Personal Data**—Your first name, last name, e-mail address, comment, and location. You can also choose whether you want to be listed in the Ekiga ILS directory.

- **Connection Type**—Indicate the speed of your Internet connection (56K modem, ISDN, DSL/Cable, T1/LAN, or Custom).

After you have entered the data, the Ekiga window opens.

Figure 4-8 shows the Ekiga window with the address book to the right. Select Tools ➪ Address Book to open your GNOME address book. This is the same address book you use for e-mail and other address and telephone information in GNOME. Add ILS servers and friends to that window, and then select the user or server you want to contact and click Contact ➪ Call Contact.

**FIGURE 4-8**

Connect to ILS servers to videoconference with Ekiga.

Use the tabs beneath the video window to adjust your audio levels and video appearance. The History tab shows a log of your activities.

# Watching Movies and Video

Although several fairly high-quality video players are available for Linux, seeing the players included in formal distributions is rare because of legal complications. The issues surrounding the playing of encoded DVD movies in Linux might be responsible for keeping players such as the MPlayer (www.mplayerhq.hu), Ogle (www.dtek.chalmers.se/groups/dvd), and xine (http://www.xine-project.org/) video players out of the main software repositories for common Linux distributions.

By most accounts, however, you can get and use these video players to play a variety of video content for personal use as long as you don't download and use the DeCCS (software for decrypting DVD movies). The following sections provide descriptions of some commonly used video players.

## Watching video with xine

The xine player is an excellent application for playing a variety of video and audio formats. You can get xine from `xine.sourceforge.net` or from software repositories associated with your Linux distribution.

For Fedora, xine-ui is in the main Fedora repository (`yum install xine-ui`). However, you also need to install `xine-lib-extras-freeworld` from the `rpmfusion.org` site. To play commercial DVDs, you also need to get the libdvdcss package (possibly available from the `rpm.livna.org` site). For Ubuntu, you can get xine from non-free repositories (`sudo apt-get install xine-ui libxine1-ffmpeg phonon-backend-xine`).

You can start the xine player by typing **xine&** from a Terminal window. Figure 4-9 shows an example of the xine video player window and controls.

---

**FIGURE 4-9**

Play DVDs, video CDs, MP3s, QuickTime, and other video formats with xine.

## Note

**When you try to install xine, it tells you if you need any additional packages. If your xine player fails to start, see the "xine tips" section later in this chapter.** ∎

Xine supports a bunch of video and audio formats, including

- MPEG (1, 2, and 4)
- QuickTime (see "Xine Tips" if your QuickTime content won't play)
- WMV
- DVDs, CDs, and VCDs
- Motion JPEG
- MPEG audio (MP3)
- AC3 and Dolby Digital audio
- DTS audio
- Commercial movies (libdvdcss package is required)
- Ogg Vorbis audio

Xine understands different file formats that represent a combination of audio and video, including .mpg (MPEG program streams), .ts (MPEG transport streams), .mpv (raw MPEG audio/video streams), .avi (MS AVI format), and .asf (Advanced Streaming format). Although xine can play Video CDs and DVDs, it can't play encrypted DVDs or the Video-on-CD hybrid format (because of legal issues mentioned earlier related to decrypting DVDs).

## Using xine

With xine started, right-click in the xine window to see the controls. The quickest way to play video is to click one of the following buttons, and then click the Play button (right arrow or Play, depending on the skin you are using):

- VCD (for a video CD)
- DVD (for a DVD in /dev/dvd)
- CDA (for a music CD in /dev/cdaudio)

Next, you can use the Pause/Resume, Stop, Play, Fast Motion, Slow Motion, or Eject buttons to work with video. You can also use the Previous and Next buttons to step to different tracks. The controls are very similar to what you would expect on a physical CD or DVD player.

To select individual files, or to put together your own list of content to play, use the Playlist feature.

### Creating playlists with xine

Click the Playlist button on the left side of the xine control window. A Playlist Editor appears, showing the files on your current playlist. You can add and delete content and then save the list to call on later.

xine content is identified as media resource locators (MRLs). Each MRL is identified as a file, DVD, or VCD. Files are in the regular file path (/path/file) or preceded by file:/, fifo:/, or stdin:/. DVDs and VCDs are preceded by dvd and vcd, respectively (for example, vcd://01).

Table 4-2 shows what the xine Playlist Editor buttons do.

**TABLE 4-2**

## Using the xine Playlist Editor

| Button | Description |
|---|---|
| CDA, DVD, or VCD | All content from that CD or DVD is added to the playlist. |
| Add | See the MRL Browser window. From that window, click File to choose a file from your Linux file system, and then click Select to add that file to the Playlist Editor. (MRL stands for Media Resource Locator, which defines the form in which remote and local content are identified.) |
| Move Up Selected MRL Move Down Selected MRL | Move up and down the playlist. |
| Play | Play the contents of the playlist. |
| Delete Selected MRL | Remove the current selection. |
| Delete All Entries | Clear the whole playlist. |
| Save | Save the playlist to your home directory ($HOME/.xine/playlist). |
| Load | Read in your (saved) playlist. |

### xine tips

Getting video and audio to work properly can sometimes be a tricky business. Here are a few quick tips if you are having trouble getting xine to work correctly (or at all):

- **xine won't start.** To work best, xine needs an X driver that supports xvid. If no xvid support exists for your video card in X, xine shuts down immediately when it tries to open the default Xv driver. If this happens to you, try starting xine with the X11 video driver (which is slower, but should work) as follows:

```
$ xine -VXSHM
```

- **xine playback is choppy.** If playback of files from your hard disk is choppy, you can check a couple of settings: 32-bit I/O and DMA, features that, if supported by your hard disk, generally improve hard disk performance. Here's how to check:

## Caution

Improper disk settings can result in destroyed data on your hard disk. Perform this procedure at your own risk. This procedure is for IDE hard drives only (no SCSI)! Also, be sure to have a current backup and no activity on your hard disk if you change DMA or I/O settings as described in this section. ∎

1. Test the speed of hard disk reads. To test the first IDE drive (/dev/hda), type

```
# hdparm -t /dev/hda
Timing buffered disk reads: 64 MB in
      19.31 seconds = 3.31 MB/sec
```

2. To see your current DMA and I/O settings, as root user type

```
# hdparm -c -d /dev/hda
/dev/hda:
 I/O support = 0 (default 16-bit)
 using_dma   = 0 (off)
```

3. This result shows that both 32-bit I/O and DMA are off. To turn them on, type

```
# hdparm -c 1 -d 1 /dev/hda
/dev/hda:
 I/O support = 1 (32-bit)
 using_dma   = 1 (on)
```

4. With both settings on, test the disk again:

```
# hdparm -t /dev/hda
Timing buffered disk reads: 64 MB in
      2.2 seconds = 28.83 MB/sec
```

In this example, buffered disk reads of 64MB went from 19.31 seconds to 2.2 seconds after changing the parameters described. Playback would be much better now.

- **xine won't play particular media.** Messages such as no input plug-in mean that either the file format you are trying to play is not supported or it requires an additional plug-in (as is the case with playing DVDs). If the message is that xyx may be a broken file, the file may be a proprietary version of an otherwise supported format. For example, I had a QuickTime video fail that required an SVQ3 codec (which is currently not supported under Linux), although other QuickTime files played fine.

## Using Totem movie player

The Totem movie player (www.gnome.org/projects/totem) comes with the GNOME desktop environment. In most GNOME desktops, Totem can play video in Theora format with Ogg audio. Totem uses the GStreamer framework (http://gstreamer.freedesktop.org) so it can take advantage of any video codes that work with GStreamer. In particular, free and fee-based codecs that you can purchase from www.fluendo.com for playing a variety of commercial audio/video formats work with Totem.

Totem also supports a xine backend that allows it to play a wide range of video content (in other words, anything xine supports). To play commercial DVD movies, you need to install the totem-xine package available (for Fedora, it's in the rpmfusion.org repository). From that same repository, you can add the libdvdcss, libdvdnav, and xine-lib-extras-nonfree packages (provided the software is legal where you live). Run the totem-xine command instead of totem to play movies.

Besides common controls you would expect with a movie player (play, pause, skip forward, skip backwards, and so on), Totem lets you create playlists, take a snapshot of the current frame, and adjust the volume. You can change preferences, which let you add proprietary plug-ins, select your DVD device, and balance color. Figure 4-10 shows an example of the Totem window.

### FIGURE 4-10

Play movies on the GNOME desktop with Totem.

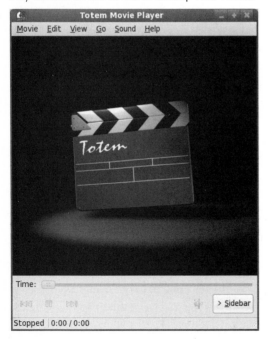

# Using a Digital Camera

With the GNOME Volume Manager, featured in most Linux systems with GNOME desktops, getting images from a digital camera can be as easy in Linux as it is in any desktop operating system. With most digital cameras that can be connected to a USB port on your computer, simply plugging the camera into a USB port (with the camera set to send and receive) causes the GNOME Volume Manager to

- Immediately ask you if you want to download images from your camera.
- Run the gThumb image viewer and browser program so you can look at, manipulate, and download the contents of your digital camera.

Although GNOME Volume Manager opens your camera's contents in an image viewer, you can treat the storage area in your camera much as you would the storage area on a hard disk or a pen drive. I describe how to use your camera to store other data as well.

## Displaying images in gThumb

The GNOME Volume Manager mounts the contents of your USB camera, treating the memory of your camera as it would any file storage device. When I tried it with an Olympus digital camera, my images were available from the `/media/usbdisk/dcim/100olymp` directory. Figure 4-11 shows an example of the gthumb-import window displaying the images from a digital camera.

---

**FIGURE 4-11**

---

Download images from digital cameras with the gThumb image viewer.

---

With your camera connected and the gThumb window open, here are some things you can do with the images on your camera:

- **Download images**—Click a single image or select Edit ➪ Select All to highlight all images from your digital camera. Then select File ➪ Import Photos. From the Import Photos window you can select the destination where you want the images to be downloaded. As an alternative, you can download selected images to a folder on the GNOME desktop.

- **View Slideshow**—Select View ➪ Slide Show. A full-screen slideshow appears on your display, with the images changing every few seconds. The toolbar that appears at the top lets you display information about the photo name, date, and size (click Image Info), go forward and back through the images, and zoom in or out.

- **Manipulate images**—Double-click an image to open it, and select the Image menu. That menu offers a set of tools for enhancing, resizing, cropping, or otherwise transforming the image. You can also adjust the color balance, hue/saturation, and brightness contrast.

- **Assign categories**—With an image selected, click the Categories button. The Categories pop-up window lets you assign the image to a category to help you organize your photos. Assign available categories (such as birthday, family, holidays, or games) or click New and add your own categories.

After images are downloaded to your computer's hard disk, you can continue to work with them using gThumb or use any of a number of tools available for manipulating digital images (GIMP, KView, and Kuickshow, to name a few).

## Note
If your camera saves images to SD or CF cards, you can purchase a USB card reader and view these files from Linux. Some PCs today come with card readers built in. ■

## Using your camera as a storage device

As I noted with my example of an Olympus camera with a USB connector, the GNOME Volume Manager is capable of detecting that camera after it is connected, and mounting its contents as a storage device. With the contents of a digital camera mounted, you can use your camera as a USB mass storage device by

- Opening the mounted directory in a folder window and using any file manager features to work with the images

- Changing to the mounted directory from the shell and using commands to copy, move, rename, or delete digital images

Of course, with your camera mounted as a file system, you are not limited to using it only for digital images. You can use it to store any kind of files you like, essentially using the camera as a storage device. The following list is a partial summary of digital cameras that can be used as a USB storage device:

- **Casio**—Supported models: QV-2400UX, QV-2x00, QV-3x00, QV-4000, and QV-8000
- **Fuji**—FinePix 1300, 1400Zoom, 2300Zoom, 2400Zoom, 2800Zoom, 4200Z, 4500, 4700 Zoom, 4900 Zoom, 6800 Zoom, A101, A201, and S1 Pro
- **HP**—PhotoSmart 315, 318xi, 618, and C912
- **Konica**—KD200Z, KD400Z, and Revio KD300Z
- **Kyocera**—Finecam s3
- **Leica**—Digilux 4.3
- **Minolta**—Dimage 5, Dimage 7, and Dimage X
- **Nikon**—CoolPix 2500, 885, 5000, 775, and 995
- **Olympus**—Brio Zoom D-15, C-100, C-200Z, C-2040, C-220Z, C-2Z, C-3020Z, C-3040Z, C-4040Zoom, C-700, C-700UZ, C-860L, D-510, D-520Z, E-10, and E-20
- **Pentax**—EI2000, Optio 330, and Optio 430
- **Sony**—DSC-F505, DSC-F505V, DSC-F707, DSC-P1, DSC-P20, DSC-P5, DSC-P71, DSC-S30, DSC-S70, DSC-S75, DSC-S85, MVC-CD300, and MVC-FD92
- **Vivitar**—Vivicam 3550
- **Yashica**—Finecam s3

# Summary

Getting up and running with digital media can take some doing, but once it's set up, you can play most audio and video content available today. This chapter takes you through the steps of setting up and troubleshooting your sound card and explains how to find software to play music through that card.

Every desktop Linux distribution comes with one or more ways of playing music from files or CDs. Popular music players include XMMS and Rhythmbox. Tools for ripping and recording CDs include grip and command-line utilities such as cdda2wav and cdrecord.

The chapter also covered playing live video from TV cards and Webcams in the sections on tvtime and Ekiga, respectively. Finally, you saw how to use the xine player to play a variety of video formats and explored the gThumb application for downloading images from a digital camera. If your computer has a CD burner, use the descriptions in this chapter to create your own music CDs and CD labels.

# Working with Words and Images

Writing documents has always been a mainstay of desktop computers. Linux systems have steadily made up ground on Mac and Windows systems when it comes to desktop publishing applications. Now, nearly every feature you would expect for document writing, layout, and publishing (in hard copy and on the Web) is available with Linux systems.

This chapter describes popular Linux office suites (such as OpenOffice. org and KOffice) for creating documents, presentations, and spreadsheets. Scribus is an excellent application for doing page layouts. For working with images, I cover the GNU Image Manipulation Program (The GIMP) and a few image viewers (such as Gwenview and Eye of GNOME). For working with vector graphics, I describe the Inkscape vector graphics editor.

For displaying the content you create, several different viewers are available for displaying output in PDF and PostScript formats. Evince viewer and Adobe Reader are available for PDF. To display PostScript files, there's Ghostview.

To publish on the Web, tools exist for everything from writing basic HTML documents to making Web photo sites to implementing full-blown content management systems. Software that is packaged for Linux to manage your own Web sites include MediaWiki (wiki), WordPress (blogging), Drupal (content management), and Gallery (photo Web site).

# Desktop Publishing in Linux

Whether you are writing a letter, a memo, or a book, you usually begin with a word processor. If your computer doesn't have much power, you might start with a simple text editor or a less demanding word processor such as AbiWord. Most Linux users, however, begin with OpenOffice.org Writer.

## Using text editors and notepads

Before jumping into more complex word processors, here are a few applications you might want to try out if you just want to write some text quickly:

- **GNOME Text Editor (gedit)**—From the GNOME desktop, select Applications ⇨ Accessories ⇨ Text Editor. With the gedit window that opens, you can just type, cut, and paste, and use arrow keys to move around. In addition to creating text documents, gedit has spell check and search tools. Highlight mode (select View ⇨ Highlight Mode), causes different parts of the text you are writing like computer code (such as C or Java) or markup (such as HTML or XML) to be displayed in different colors.

- **KDE Text Editor (kwrite)**—From the KDE desktop, the KWrite application is the default text editor. KWrite includes many of the same text-editing features in gedit, but also has bookmark features and support for multiple language input.

- **Sticky Notes (tomboy)**—Different note-taking applications include KNotes (for KDE) and Tomboy (for GNOME). Tomboy puts a notepad icon in your top panel, from which you can create and manage notes. Create a new note that includes URLs (click to open in a browser) and links to other notes. Spelling is checked as you type. Organize notes in notebooks or do keyword searches to find the note you want. From the desktop, press Alt+F12 to open the Tomboy menu; press Alt+F11 to open the "Start Here" note. Figure 5-1 shows the Tomboy search window and an example of a note.

If you want to move text from your plain text files or sticky notes to a more formal document, you can copy or cut, and then paste the text into one of the word processors described in the next section.

## Using word processors

OpenOffice.org is a powerful open source office suite, available as a download and as part of many Linux distributions. Based on Sun Microsystem's StarOffice productivity suite, OpenOffice. org includes a word processor, spreadsheet program, presentation manager, and other personal productivity tools. In most cases, OpenOffice.org can be used as a drop-in replacement for Microsoft Office.

### Coming from Windows

If you've been using Microsoft Office applications such as Microsoft Word, Excel, and PowerPoint, most files produced in those applications' native formats will work in OpenOffice.org. You can find descriptions of supported office formats later in this chapter. ■

**FIGURE 5-1**

Create, search, and manage notes with Tomboy.

## Using OpenOffice.org Office Suite

Some have called OpenOffice.org the most significant threat to Microsoft's dominance of the desktop market. Thousands in business, education, and government have already migrated their documents, spreadsheets, and presentations from Microsoft Office to OpenOffice.org. Although cost savings are a big reason for using OpenOffice.org, the freedom of not being locked into proprietary formats and forced upgrades may be even more important in the long run.

Many distributions of Linux include the entire OpenOffice.org suite of desktop applications. Some include the StarOffice suite in addition to or in lieu of OpenOffice.org.

Because of its size, the entire OpenOffice.org is usually not included on live CD versions of Linux. However, with an Internet connection, you can usually download and install prepackaged versions of the OpenOffice.org suite. For example, in Fedora, you can install the openoffice.org-calc, openoffice.org-draw, openoffice.org-impress, openoffice.org-writer, and openoffice.org-math packages to get most of the suite.

## Note

**At the time of this writing, the latest version of OpenOffice is 3.1.** ■

OpenOffice.org, which shares its source code with StarOffice, consists of the following office-productivity applications:

- **Writer**—A word-processing application that can work with documents in file formats from Microsoft Word, StarOffice, and several others. Writer also has a full set of features for using templates, working with fonts, navigating your documents (including images and effects), and generating tables of contents.

- **Calc**—A spreadsheet application that lets you incorporate data from Microsoft Excel, StarOffice, dBase, and several other spreadsheet formats. Some nice features in Calc enable you to create charts, set up database ranges (to easily sort data in an area of a spreadsheet), and use the data pilot tool to arrange data in different points of view.

- **Draw**—A drawing application that enables you to create, edit, and align objects; include textures and colors; and work with layers of objects. It lets you incorporate images, vector graphics, AutoCAD, and a variety of other file formats into your drawings. Then, you can save your drawing in the OpenOffice.org Drawing or StarDraw formats.

- **Math**—A calculation program that lets you create mathematical formulas.

- **Impress**—A presentation application that includes a variety of slide effects. You can use Impress to create and save presentations in the Microsoft PowerPoint, StarDraw, and StarImpress formats.

Unlike other applications that were created to work with Microsoft document and data formats, OpenOffice.org (although not perfect) does a very good job of opening and saving those files with few problems. Very basic styles and formatting that open in OpenOffice.org often don't look noticeably different from the way they appear in Microsoft Office. In other cases, such things as bullets, alignment, and indentation can appear quite different in Writer than they do in Word. Also, some Word features, such as macros and scripting features, may not work at all in Writer. For the most part, however, the recent versions of the OpenOffice.org suite handle most Microsoft Office files.

In addition, the OpenOffice.org suite supports the ODF, or Open Document Format, a recently standardized file format for office documents. ODF is becoming more and more important with government and scientific organizations that need to be able to access the documents they create for many years in the future. Using the Microsoft Office formats, for example, locks an organization into paying Microsoft's fee in order to access the organization's data. In the future, that fee could become too high for the organization, or worse yet, Microsoft may choose not to support files created by older versions of the software. Even today, for example, OpenOffice.org supports older versions of Microsoft Word than Word does.

Another nice feature of the OpenOffice.org suite is document signing, so that you can provide better security to shared documents.

To open OpenOffice.org applications, select the Applications menu. In most distributions, there's a folder called Office (or something very similar) located on the Applications menu. Figure 5-2 shows a Microsoft Word document open for editing in OpenOffice.org Writer.

**FIGURE 5-2**

Work with Microsoft Word documents or open document formats in OpenOffice.org Writer.

The controls in Writer are similar to the ones you find in Word. Toolbars include boxes for changing styles, font types, and font sizes. Buttons let you save and print the file, change the text alignment, and cut, copy, and paste text. In other words, Writer includes almost everything you expect in an advanced word processor. In addition, Writer includes a handy PDF button to output a file directly to the PDF format, which is very useful for exchanging documents or placing data on the Internet.

## Other word processors

If your distribution does not include the OpenOffice.org suite, or you just want to try something else, you have some other choices:

- **StarOffice**—The StarOffice productivity suite contains applications for word processing, spreadsheets, presentation graphics, e-mail, news, charting, and graphics.

It was created to run on Linux systems, but it runs in other environments as well. It can import and export a variety of Microsoft file formats. StarOffice is owned by Sun Microsystems, which sells it as a commercial product.

- **AbiWord**—The AbiWord word processor (`abiword` command) is noncommercial software produced by the AbiSource project (`www.abisource.com`). In addition to working with files in its own format (`.abw` and `.zabw`), AbiWord can import files in Microsoft Word and several other formats. Because of its relatively small disk space needs, AbiWord is included on many live CDs that don't include OpenOffice.org.

- **KOffice**—The KOffice package contains a set of office productivity applications designed for the KDE desktop (you must have the KDE desktop environment). The noncommercial software includes a word processor (KWord), spreadsheet (KSpread), presentation creator (KPresenter), and diagram-drawing program (KChart). These applications can be run separately or within a KOffice Workspace.

## Using StarOffice

The StarOffice suite from Sun Microsystems, Inc. (`www.sun.com/software/staroffice`) is a product that runs on Linux, UNIX, and Windows systems. Like its related open source project OpenOffice.org, StarOffice contains many features that make it compatible with Microsoft Office applications. In particular, it includes the capability to import Microsoft Word and Excel files.

StarOffice is probably the most complete integrated office suite for Linux. It includes

- **Writer**—StarOffice's word-processing application. It can import documents from a variety of formats, with special emphasis on Word documents.

- **Calc**—The StarOffice spreadsheet program. You can import spreadsheets from Microsoft Excel and other popular programs.

- **Impress**—Create presentations with this application.

- **Draw**—A vector-oriented drawing program that includes the capability to create 3D objects and to use texturing.

- **Base**—Manage your data sources. You can access a variety of database interfaces.

Other tools in StarOffice enable you to create business graphics, edit raster images, and edit mathematical formulas.

You can download StarOffice for Linux or purchase a boxed set from the StarOffice Web site at `www.sun.com/software/staroffice`. Although StarOffice was once available free for download, the current price to download the software is $34.95. (You can also get a volume discount.) A trial version is available that you can enable (using a license key) if you decide that you like it enough to purchase the product.

One reason to pay for StarOffice when you can get OpenOffice.org software for free is that you get a bunch of extras with StarOffice. The extras include a spell-checker, clip art, many more file converters (although the best ones are for converting Microsoft formats), a database module, and technical support.

## Note

**OpenOffice.org is an open source project sponsored by Sun Microsystems. Sun takes the shared source code used to create OpenOffice.org and combines it with other modules to produce the StarOffice suite. This is very similar to the model used by Red Hat, Inc. where it sponsors the community-driven Fedora project to distribute freely, whereas the Red Hat Enterprise Linux product (based on Fedora) is sold through subscriptions. Although OpenOffice.org is free, you can purchase support programs for OpenOffice.org from Sun Microsystems. ∎**

### Using AbiWord

The AbiWord word processor is a very nice, free word processor from the AbiSource project (www.abisource.com). If you are starting documents from scratch, AbiWord includes many of the basic functions you need to create good-quality documents.

With AbiWord, you can select the type of document the file contains, and select to read the file in the following formats:

- AbiWord (.abw)
- GZipped AbiWord (.zabw)
- Rich Text Format (.rtf)
- Microsoft Word (.doc)
- UTF8 (.utf8)
- Text (.txt)

In addition, AbiWord can import and export ODF, DocBook, and OpenOffice.org files.

AbiWord doesn't yet import all these file types cleanly. Although the recent version supports Word styles, sometimes tables, graphics, and other features don't translate perfectly. If you want to work with a Word document in AbiWord, open it as AbiWord, correct any font problems, and save the document in AbiWord format. AbiWord has vastly improved in the past few releases, but you may still experience problems if you need to exchange files with others who are using Word. (If you want to keep files in the Word format, you'll find that OpenOffice.org and StarOffice work much better, but not perfectly.)

Features recently added to AbiWord such as styles and bullets continue to make it a more useful word-processing tool. It's not yet competitive with comparable commercial products, but its developers continue to improve it.

If you do not have a lot of formatting needs, or if you do not care about Microsoft file formats, AbiWord provides a realistic alternative to larger application suites such as OpenOffice.org. The

AbiWord program is small and executes fast, requiring less system resources such as RAM than OpenOffice.org. The speed and size make it a joy to use.

## Using KOffice

The K Desktop Environment, KDE, provides an office suite along with hundreds of other programs. The KOffice package has the basic applications you would expect in an integrated office suite: a word processor (KWord), spreadsheet program (KSpread), a presentation creator (KPresenter), and a diagram-drawing program (KChart). In Fedora and other Linux systems, installing the koffice-suite package will pull in most of the software you need to use KOffice.

Start by opening the KOffice Workspace (usually from the Office menu or KDE panel menu). In the workspace window that opens, you can select from the different office applications presented in the left column. Open multiple documents in any of the applications, and then click Documents in the left column to choose which one to display at the moment.

Figure 5-3 shows the KOffice Workspace displaying a KWord document.

**FIGURE 5-3**

The KOffice Workspace enables you to work with multiple KDE office applications at once.

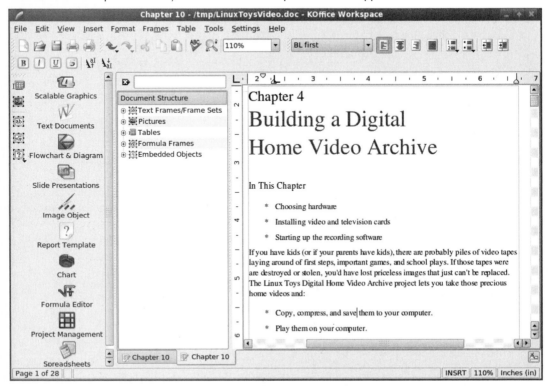

You can work with a variety of document, spreadsheet, and image types. Not many commercial document types are supported yet, so you may need to import documents using other tools before you can read them into KWord. KSpread, however, can open several different spreadsheet styles, including Microsoft Excel and GNUmeric spreadsheets.

# Transitioning documents from Windows

For casual home users, small-office workers, and large corporation personnel alike, moving from Microsoft Office to another Office suite is an experience that can range from simple to harrowing. In general, it is useful to examine this migration in terms of "home use" versus "work use":

- Home users typically have to concern themselves with maintaining access to their own documents. In a personal context, it might be rare for friends and relatives to send Excel spreadsheets, Word documents, and PowerPoint presentations. But over the years you may have accumulated term papers, recipes, letters to the editor, account spreadsheets, and other such documents that you would like to be able to read and print. In most cases, OpenOffice.org applications can handle files in Microsoft formats just fine.

- At work, in addition to the accumulation of documents over time, there is a more pressing issue: Other people will be sharing Microsoft Office documents with you. So while home users need to concern themselves most with access to historical documents, in the workplace you probably need to accommodate new documents as well as your historical information.

Because you can convert your documents, no real challenges exist for migrating simple documents. However, if your Microsoft Office documents include extensive macro, scripting, or embedded object usage, you may find the conversion is not a very clean one. Make sure you attempt conversions using the following options before moving on to the last resort of using multiple applications or re-creating documents.

Using Microsoft Office to convert documents enables you to save your files in an alternative format. For example, Word enables you to save your document files (the Word versions anyway) to a variety of formats, including

- **HTML** (`.htm/.html`)—HTML is a great format for your information if it is basically text and you need only a few formatting options and some embedded images and links. The resulting HTML document will be smaller than the corresponding `.doc` file.

- **Rich Text Format** (`.rtf`)—Another wonderful minimalist format (owned by Microsoft but an open standard nonetheless) that preserves some formatting and graphics, but any scripting or macro usage is lost.

- **Plain Text** (`.txt`)—Works if all you need to save is the text of the file. Everything else is lost.

- **Word Document** (`.doc` or `.docx`)—An alternative format that may save some of the elements you want yet make it more accessible to OpenOffice.org. Using this format may not resolve all the issues you have with converting those hard-to-change documents, but it just might do the trick.

## Note

The default format for Word 2007 files is .docx—Open XML. ∎

Other Microsoft Office applications offer similar functionality. PowerPoint can convert presentations to HTML and general image formats such as JPEG and TIFF. Excel can save tab- and comma-delimited files that are easily importable into a large number of applications.

If you are likely to continue to receive Microsoft Office files and you are concerned about interoperability, here are some options to consider:

- **Run Word in WINE**—Keep a copy of Microsoft Office installed using WINE and the CodeWeavers CrossOver Office plug-in. CrossOver Office lets you run Microsoft Word on a Linux desktop. For more information about CrossOver Office, visit CodeWeavers' Web site at www.codeweavers.com.

- **Use PDF for sharing**—Ask individuals sending you documentation to use a less vendor-specific format, such as Adobe PDF. Document formatting can be exquisitely preserved and will be viewable by anyone capable of installing a PDF viewer, which supports virtually every operating system in widespread use today. Documents posted on Web sites, for example, should be in PDF and not Microsoft Word format for security reasons.

- **Use HTML for forms**—For forms that have user-editable fields, scripting, or complex embedded information, use HTML documents instead. Anyone with a compliant Web browser will be able to interact with the document, and Microsoft Office applications universally support saving files into this format.

- **Use ODF for archiving**—If you will want to access your documents a long time from now, say a few years, consider storing your documents in the Open Document Format, or ODF. ODF, being open and not encumbered by patents, will make it easier for you to access your documents in the future. Remember, Microsoft does not support old versions of Word documents today. Furthermore, Word's latest document format is encumbered by patents, so you may lose the right to access your documents in the future, or you may need to pay any fee required by the vendor. Use ODF.

- **Use SQL to save data**—If you make use of Access to save data, you may want to move data stored in Access's .mdb format into a SQL database. SQL is more scalable, powerful, and virtually platform-independent. Migrating to SQL does preserve your data, but if your .mdb file will not open in OpenOffice.org, you need to re-create any forms for accessing the data that you want to continue using.

## Caution

Before making any wholesale conversion away from Microsoft Office, make sure the files you need to use will work as expected with the new office suite you have selected or that you can construct suitable replacements if needed. Testing things ahead of time enables you to make necessary adjustments without later having to endure the frustration of finding some important document inaccessible or unusable.

Many organizations start their transition away from Microsoft Office by switching to OpenOffice.org on Windows. This way you can have both Office and OpenOffice.org running on the same systems as you gradually work out any conversion issues. After the issues have been resolved, you can migrate to Linux. In any migration effort, follow good practices such as starting with smaller groups to ensure any glitches or problems are properly handled. ■

## Converting documents

Documents can come to you in many different formats. Search just some of the Linux FTP sites on the Internet and you will find files in PostScript, DVI, man, PDF, HTML, and TeX. A variety of graphics formats are also available. Table 5-1 provides a list of common document and graphics conversion utilities.

**TABLE 5-1**

## Document and Graphics Conversion Utilities

| Utility | Converts | To |
|---------|----------|-----|
| dos2unix | DOS text file | UNIX (Linux) text file |
| fax2ps | TIFF facsimile image files | Compressed PostScript format (The PostScript output is optimized to send to a printer on a low-speed line. This format is less efficient for images with a lot of black or continuous tones, for which tiff2ps might be more effective.) |
| fax2tiff | Fax data (Group 3 or Group 4) | TIFF format (The output is either low-resolution or medium-resolution TIFF format.) |
| g32pbm | Group 3 fax file (either digifax or raw) | Portable bitmap |
| gif2tiff | GIF (87) file | TIFF format |
| man2html | Man page | HTML format |
| pal2rgb | TIFF image (palette color) | Full-color RGB image |
| pbm2g3 | Portable bitmap image | Fax file (Group 3) |
| pdf2dsc | PDF file | PostScript document dsc file (The PostScript file conforms to Adobe Document Structuring Conventions. The output enables PostScript readers such as Ghostview to read the PDF file one page at a time.) |
| pdf2ps | PDF file | PostScript file (level 2) |
| pfb2pfa | Type 1 PostScript font (binary MS-DOS ) | ASCII-readable |

*continued*

| **TABLE 5-1** | *(continued)* | |
|---|---|---|
| **Utility** | **Converts** | **To** |
| pk2bm | TeX pkfont font file | Bitmap (ASCII file) |
| ppm2tiff | PPM image file | TIFF format |
| ps2ascii | PostScript or PDF file | ASCII text |
| ps2epsi | PostScript file | Encapsulated PostScript (EPSI) (Some word-processing and graphics programs can read EPSI. Output is often low quality.) |
| ps2pdf | PostScript file | Portable Document Format (PDF) |
| ps2pk | Type 1 PostScript font | TeX pkfont |
| pstotext | PostScript file | ASCII text (pstotext is similar to ps2ascii but handles font encoding and kerning better. It doesn't convert PDFs.) |
| ras2tiff | Sun raster file | TIFF format |
| texi2html | Texinfo file | HTML |
| tiff2bw | RGB or Palette color TIFF image | Grayscale TIFF image |
| tiff2ps | TIFF image | PostScript |
| unix2dos | UNIX (Linux) text file | DOS text file |

Many graphical applications, such as The GIMP, also enable you to save images into several different formats (BMP, JPEG, PNG, TIFF, and so on) through the use of the Save As feature.

## Building structured documents

Documentation projects often need to produce documents that are output in a variety of formats. For example, the same text that describes how to use a software program may need to be output as a printed manual, an HTML page, and a PostScript file. The standards that have been embraced most recently by the Linux community for creating what are referred to as structured documents are SGML and XML. The specific document type definition (DTD) used to produce Linux documentation is called DocBook.

### Understanding SGML and XML

Standard Generalized Markup Language (SGML) was created to provide a standard way of marking text so that it could be output later in a variety of formats. Because SGML markup is done with text tags, you can create SGML documents using any plain-text editor. Documents consist of the text of your document and tags that identify each type of information in the text.

Unlike markup languages such as Groff and TeX, SGML markup is not intended to enforce a particular look when you are creating the document. So, for example, instead of marking a piece of text as being bold or italic, you would identify it as an address, a paragraph, or a name. Later, a style sheet would be applied to the document to assign a look and presentation to the tagged text. HTML is an example of SGML markup.

Because SGML consists of many tags, other projects have cropped up to simplify the production of documents based on SGML and to better focus the ways in which SGML is used. In particular, the Extensible Markup Language (XML) was created to offer a manageable subset of SGML that would be specifically tailored to work well with Web-based publishing.

So far in this description of SGML and XML, I've discussed only the frameworks that are used to produce structured documents. Specific documentation projects need to create and, to some extent, enforce specific markup definitions for the type of documents they need to produce. These definitions are referred to as document type definitions (DTDs). For documentation of Linux itself and other open source projects, DocBook has become the DTD of choice.

## Understanding DocBook

DocBook is a DTD that is well suited for producing computer software documents in a variety of formats. It was originally created by the OASIS Consortium (`www.oasis-open.org`) and is now supported by many different commercial and open source tools.

DocBook's focus is on marking content, instead of indicating a particular look (that is, font type, size, position, and so on). It includes markup that lets you automate the process of creating indices, figure lists, and tables of contents, to name a few.

DocBook is important to the Linux and open source community because many open source projects use it to produce documentation. The following is a list of organizations that use DocBook to create the documents that describe their software:

- Linux Documentation Project
  `www.tldp.org/LDP/LDP-Author-Guide`
- GNOME Documentation
  `http://developer.gnome.org/projects/gdp/handbook/gdp-handbook`
- KDE Documentation Project
  `www.kde.org/documentation`
- FreeBSD Documentation Project
  `www.freebsd.org/docproj/`

If you want to contribute to any of these documentation projects, refer to the Web sites for each organization. In all cases, they publish writers' guides or style guides that describe the DocBook tags that they support.

### Creating DocBook documents

You can create the documents in any text editor, using tags that are similar in appearance to HTML tags (with beginning and end tags appearing between less-than and greater-than signs). Certain word-processing programs also enable you to create DocBook markup.

The following steps show an example of a simple DocBook XML document produced with a plain-text editor and output into HTML using tools that are available in many Linux systems. Install the docbook-utils package (in Fedora and other Linux systems) to get the Docbook utilities you need.

## Note

The DocBook DTD is available in both SGML and XML forms. Of the two, the XML form is actively maintained. ∎

1. Create a directory in your home directory to work in and go to that directory. For example, you can type the following from a Terminal window:

   ```
   $ mkdir $HOME/doctest
   $ cd $HOME/doctest
   ```

2. Open a text editor to hold your DocBook document. For example, you can type:

   ```
   $ gedit cardoc.xml
   ```

3. Enter the tags and text that you want to appear in your document. Most DocBook documents are either <book> type (large, multichapter documents) or <article> type (single-chapter documents). To try out a DocBook document, type the following:

   ```
   <?xml version=""1.0"" ?>
   <article>
     <title>Choosing a new car</title>
     <artheader>
       <abstract>
         In this article, you will learn how to price,
         negotiate for, and purchase an automobile.
       </abstract>
     </artheader>
     <section>
       <title>Getting Started</title>
       <para>
         The first thing you will learn is how to figure out
         what you can afford.
       </para>
     </section>
     <section>
       <title>The Next Step</title>
   ```

```
  <para>
   After you know what you can afford, you can begin
   your search.
  </para>
 </section>
</article>
```

You should notice a few things about this document. The entire document is wrapped in article tags (`<article>` `</article>`). The article title is in title tags (`<title>` `</title>`). The section tags (`<section>` `</section>`) indicate sections of text that each have a title and paragraph. These sections can later be treated separately in the TOC.

**4.** Save the file and exit from the text editor.

**5.** Next, you can try translating the document you just created into several different formats. For example, to create HTML output, you can type the following:

```
$ db2html cardoc.xml
```

The result is a new directory called `cardoc`. The result from `db2html` in the `cardoc` directory is the creation of a stylesheet-images directory, a `t1.html` file, and an `x8.html` file. (You will also see a lot of scary-looking error messages when you run the `db2html` program. For now, you can ignore them. Ideally, the `cardoc.xml` document should have a reference to the DocBook DTD.)

To view the HTML file just created, I typed the following:

```
$ firefox $HOME/doctest/cardoc/t1.html
```

Figure 5-4 shows an example of the output created from the `db2html` command. The screen on the left shows the first page. Click the Next link at the top of the page. The second page that you see is shown on the right. During conversion to HTML, the `db2html` command adds Next/Previous buttons to each page. It also puts the title of each section in a Table of Contents on page 1 and in the browser's title bar.

From this point, you can continue to add content and different types of tags. If you are writing documents for a particular project (such as the Linux projects mentioned earlier), you should get information on the particular tags and other style issues they require.

## Converting DocBook documents

The previous example shows how to create a simple DocBook document and convert it to HTML output. The following utilities convert DocBook to other formats:

- **docbook2dvi**—Device Independent file format
- **docbook2html**—HTML format
- **docbook2man**—Man page format

- **docbook2pdf**—Portable Document Format (PDF)
- **docbook2ps**—PostScript format
- **docbook2rtf**—Rich Text Format (RTF)
- **docbook2texi**—GNU TeXinfo format
- **docbook2txt**—Bare text format

If some of the commands just described are not installed on your system from the docbook-utils package, try installing the docbook-utils-pdf package.

**FIGURE 5-4**

The DocBook file is output in HTML with the db2html command.

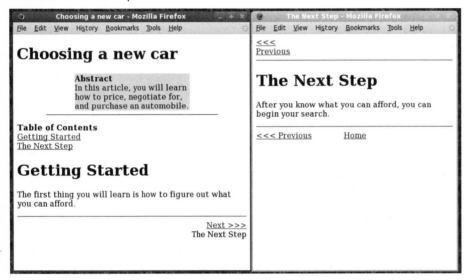

## Doing page layout with Scribus

For brochures, magazines, newsletters, catalogs, and other materials that need more sophisticated layouts than you can do with a word processor, you need a page layout application. The most popular open source page layout application is called Scribus (www.scribus.net).

Although Scribus is intended primarily to produce print publications, you can also use Scribus to produce what are referred to as *intelligent PDFs*. With PDFs you create with Scribus, you can include JavaScript and other features to let others interact with your text (such as by filling in forms).

Scribus is packaged with several different Linux distributions. In Fedora and other distributions, install the scribus package. The package comes with templates and samples you can use to start your own projects with (usually in /usr/share/scribus/).

With the scribus package installed, you can start Scribus from the GNOME desktop by selecting Applications ⇨ Office ⇨ Scribus. Figure 5-5 shows an example of a brochure layout in Scribus.

**FIGURE 5-5**

Produce professional-quality layouts with Scribus.

After Scribus is running on your desktop, you can start by selecting a template (select File ⇨ New from Template). Choose a brochure, newsletter, presentation, or text-based layout to begin with. Here are some steps you can take on the sample layout to get used to using Scribus:

- **Edit text**—Right-click in a text box and select Edit text. In the Story Editor window that appears, change the text, point size, scaling width/height of the text, font, text alignment, color, and other attributes. In that window, select File ⇨ Update Text Frame and Exit to save the changes.

- **Add images**—Right-click an image box and select Get Image. Browse your folders for the image you want. If the image doesn't fit, right-click the image and select Edit Image to open the image in The GIMP to resize or otherwise modify it. Right-click the image and select Adjust Frame to Image to resize the frame to fit your image.

- **Change existing frames**—Right-click in any frame, and then select Is Locked so the check box disappears. After the frame is unlocked, you can do a lot to change it. Grab a corner or side of the frame to resize it. Right-click it and select Sample Text (to fill it with text), or Cut, Copy, or Delete. Grab the frame with your mouse to drag and drop it somewhere else. If you are done changing the frame, select Is Locked to lock the frame in place again.

- **Change document attributes**—Select File ➪ Document Setup. From the Document Setup window that appears, you can change the size and orientation of the page, as well as the type of page (single, double-sided, three-fold, or four-fold). Likewise, you can change all margins. Select topics from the left to add information such as author, title, and keywords. You can also change fonts and hyphenation or add a table of contents.

- **Drawing**—You can do freehand drawing anywhere on your Scribus layout. Select the Insert Freehand Line button (pencil icon) or Insert Bezier Curve button (ink pen icon), and then use the mouse to draw lines on the page. You can also draw boxes, polygons, or lines using buttons on the toolbar. Right-click the drawn element and select Properties. From the Properties window you can adjust the shape, line, and colors of the drawing.

When you are done creating your layout, you can print it by selecting File ➪ Print. The Preflight Verifier window appears within information about the printed document. At the top-right corner of the page, you can select to change PostScript to one of several PDF versions. You can choose now to direct the output to the printer or have it go to a PDF or PostScript file.

# Working with Graphics

Tools for creating and manipulating graphics are becoming both more plentiful and more powerful in Linux systems as a whole. Leading the list is the GNU Image Manipulation Program (GIMP). GIMP enables you to compose and author images as well as retouch photographs. To work with vector graphics (where geometric shapes represent images, instead of just dots), Inkscape is a popular open source application. Other tools for creating graphics include `ksnapshot` (a program for taking screen captures) and `kpaint` (for working with bitmap images).

## Manipulating images with The GIMP

The GIMP is a free software program for manipulating photographs and graphical images. To create images with GIMP, you can either import a drawing, photograph, or 3D image, or you can create one from scratch. You can start GIMP from the system menu by selecting Graphics ➪ GIMP Image Editor or by typing **gimp&** from a Terminal window.

Figure 5-6 shows an example of The GIMP.

**FIGURE 5-6**

The GIMP is a powerful tool for graphic manipulation.

In many ways, GIMP is similar to Adobe Photoshop. Some people feel that GIMP's scripting features are comparable to or even better than Actions in Adobe Photoshop. One capability that GIMP lacks, however, is native support for CMYK (cyan-magenta-yellow-black) separations. If CMYK is not critical for your graphics needs, you will probably find GIMP to be just as powerful and flexible as Photoshop in many ways.

## Tip

See www.blackfiveservices.co.uk/separate.shtml for a CMYK plug-in for GIMP. This plug-in provides only rudimentary support for CMYK, according to its documentation. Even so, that may be enough for your needs. ■

With an image open, you can select tools from the GIMP window to work on the image. When you select a tool, notice that options for that tool appear in tabs below. Figure 5-7 shows the GIMP tools, along with callouts indicating what the tools do.

**FIGURE 5-7**

Use the GIMP window to choose tools for changing images.

The following list describes the tools shown in Figure 5-7:

- **Path tool**—Use the path tool to create special types of rectangle, elliptical, or free-form shapes. Try creating a rectangle, with the final point ending on the first. Hold the Ctrl key and click on the first point to close the box. With the shape complete, select Stroke Path to define the shape with a solid or pattern line.

- **Color picker**—Use the color picker to select any color from your image as your foreground or background color.

- **Magnify**—Select this tool, and then click and drag to choose an area of your image. That area of your image will fill the screen. Or just click to zoom in or Ctrl+click to zoom out on the image.

- **Measure**—With measure selected, click and drag your mouse from one point to another. The status bar shows the distance (in pixels), angle, width, and height you just measured.

- **Select tools**—Use the select tools to select different areas of your image. You can select a rectangle, ellipse, hand-drawn area, a region based on color, an edge of an element, or an area based on foreground objects. Once an area is selected, you can cut, copy, fill, paste, or do other things with it.

- **Text tool**—Select the text tool, click in the image, and begin typing to add text to that point in the image. From the options discussed next, you can change the font, size, color, justification, and other options relating to the text.

- **Paint tools**—Use these tools to add lines and colors to your image. The bucket tool fills a selected area or similar color with the current foreground color, background color, or pattern. The gradient tool lets you shade an area from one color to another. Use the pencil, brush, ink, or airbrush tools to draw lines. Paint over one part of an image from a sample taken from another part of an image or from a selected pattern using the clone tool. Use blur, smudge, and dodge/burn tools to blur and soften selected areas of the image. Erase (to transparency or to the layer below) using the erase tool.

- **Foreground & Background Colors**—The two color boxes show the foreground (upper right) and background (lower left) colors. Click to open a dialog to change either of those colors. Click the swap arrows to switch the two colors.

You can also access the tools just described from the Tools menu. Select the Dialogs menu to see a list of dialog boxes you can display to work with layers, channels, paths, patterns, fonts, and other elements you might need to work on your image.

GIMP also supports a variety of plug-ins. For example, the cartoon plug-in gives an image a cartoon effect, red-eye-removal lets you correct red eye, and cubism lets you convert an image to randomly floating square blobs. Many of these plug-ins are available from the Filters menu in GIMP.

## Tip

If you make a mistake, select Edit ➪ Undo from the GIMP menu, or press the Ctrl+Z key combination to undo the most recent change. You can do multiple undos in this way as well. ■

# Creating vector graphic images with Inkscape

When you need to have maximum flexibility working with graphics and text, a vector graphic editor can let you deal with geometric elements (such as lines, curves, and boxes) instead of dots (as you do with image editors). As a result, you usually get cleaner edges on your fonts and graphics and the ability to bend and shape those elements as you like. Inkscape (www.inkscape.org) is a popular vector graphics editor that is available with most Linux systems.

With Inkscape, you have an application with features similar to those you would find in commercial products such as Adobe Illustrator and CorelDraw. Inkscape creates images in Scalable Vector Graphics (SVG) format—an open standard from the W3C (www.w3.org/Graphics/SVG). Thousands of SVG graphics and clipart elements are available in the public domain or under Creative Commons licenses.

If you are using a Linux distribution such as Fedora, install the inkscape package to get Inkscape. I recommend you also install the openclipart package, which gives you access to hundreds of clipart items to use in your Inkscape creations. With the inkscape and openclipart packages installed, select Applications ➪ Graphics ➪ Inkscape Vector Graphics Editor to open an Inkscape window. Figure 5-8 shows an example of the Inkscape window.

**FIGURE 5-8**

Inkscape enables you to manipulate graphics and text.

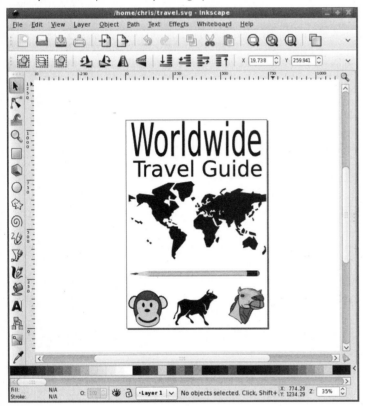

You can start by opening one of the dozens of templates available with Inkscape (select File ➪ New and choose from web banner, business card, DVD cover, or other templates). With the new window open, here are some ways to get started with Inkscape:

- **Add text**—Select the text icon from the toolbar on the left, click on the page, and begin typing. After typing some text, choose the Select icon and click on the text. Use the side or corner arrows to resize the text. Click the text again and use the arrows around the text to slant or rotate the text. Grab the text box with the mouse and drag it where you want it to go. With the text still selected, select Text ➪ Text and Font to see a window where you can choose the font family, font style, layout, and line spacing.

- **Add graphical elements**—From the toolbar on the left, select the rectangle, 3D box, circles, start, or swirls button. Move the mouse cursor to the place where you want the new element, click and hold the mouse on that place, and move the mouse so the new element grows to the size you want. Click the color palette on the bottom of the screen to change the element's color.

- **Add clipart**—If you added the openclipart package, you can import clipart from there. Select File ⇨ Import and browse the /usr/share/clipart/openclipart folder. Choose from hundreds of SVG clipart images in categories such as food, geography, office, recreation, tools, and transportation. After the image imports, use your mouse to select and shape it as you did with the text.

- **Group objects**—Select a text or clipart object, and then hold the Shift key and select other objects. When all the objects you want in the group are selected, choose Object ⇨ Group. You can now move all the grouped objects around together as one unit.

- **Use layers**—Click the Layer button to add, delete, raise, or lower layers.

When you are done creating your vector graphic, you can print that graphic by selecting File ⇨ Print. From the Print window, you can select to have the image in vector or bitmap form from the Rendering tab.

## Acquiring screen captures

Several screen capture tools are available with Linux systems. Using The GIMP program just described, you can take a screen shot by selecting File ⇨ Acquire ⇨ Screenshot. On GNOME desktops, select Applications ⇨ Accessories ⇨ Take Screenshot. From most KDE desktops, select Graphics ⇨ KSnapshot.

Using the example of the GNOME Take Screenshot tool, a dialog box appears that lets you choose to grab the whole desktop or grab the current window. You can set a delay of several seconds, if you need to set up something, such as opening a menu, before you take the shot. Then click Take Screenshot. Figure 5-9 shows an example of the Take Screenshot window after it has captured an image of the current desktop.

**FIGURE 5-9**

Grab a picture of your desktop or selected window with the Take Screenshot utility.

Select a folder to hold the screen shot and type a name for the image. Then click Save to save it.

## Viewing images

If you want to browse through a folder of images and possibly make some simple changes, both KDE and GNOME desktops offer some easy-to-use image viewers. When you open an image from a KDE folder, the Gwenview image viewer opens that image. In GNOME, Eye of GNOME is the default image viewer.

Gwenview does a good job with the basics for managing images if, for example, you are working with a folder of images downloaded from a digital camera. Select the Preview button to preview thumbnails of images in the folder. Zoom in or zoom out to get a better look at each image. If the image is on its side, you can rotate left or right. From the Edit menu, you can also flip, resize, crop, or create a mirror image of the current image. Figure 5-10 shows the Gwenview window.

**FIGURE 5-10**

Go through your images in KDE with Gwenview.

Double-click an image file in a folder window (or right-click on the image and select Open with Image Viewer) to open that image in Eye of GNOME. The Eye of GNOME image viewer doesn't offer as many features for cutting and resizing as does Gwenview. However, you can still rotate and save those changes, if necessary. Select Edit ➪ Properties to view information about the height, width, size, type, and folder for each image. Under the View menu, you can also view Eye of GNOME in Full Screen mode or as a Slideshow.

With Image Collection selected from the View menu (or by pressing the F9 function key), you can step through thumbnails of each image in the current folder. Figure 5-11 shows an example of Eye of GNOME with the Image Collection view selected (notice that the name in the window title bar changes to that of the selected image).

**FIGURE 5-11**

Step through a folder of images and do simple modifications with Eye of GNOME.

# Displaying PDF and PostScript Documents

Document publishing can be very paper-intensive if you send a word-processing document to the printer each time you want to make a change to the document's content or formatting. To save paper and time spent running around, use a print preview program to display your document on the screen as it will appear on the printed page. Likewise, these viewers can be useful to display documents you want to read that are in a read-only format (such as many PDF or PostScript files).

The following sections describe the ghostscript command for displaying PostScript files and the Adobe Reader for displaying Portable Document Format (PDF) files.

## Using the ghostscript and gv commands

To display PostScript or PDF documents in Linux, you can use the ghostscript command. It is a fairly crude interface, intended to let you step through documents and interpret them one line at a time.

You can display any PS or PDF file you happen to have on your computer. For example, if the samba package is installed, you can type the following to display a PDF file (otherwise, you can find your own PDF file to try it):

```
$ ghostscript -sDEVICE=x11 /usr/share/doc/samba-doc*/Samba-HOWTO.pdf
>>showpage, press <return> to continue<<
```

At the prompt, press Enter (or Return) to go through the file one page at a time. When you have reached the end of the document, you can type the name of another PostScript or PDF file and page through that file. When you are done, type **quit**.

You may also see warning or error messages if ghostscript detects problems in the PostScript or PDF file. In most cases, if you can see the document's contents, you can ignore the messages.

The evince command can also be used to display PostScript or PDF files. Simply start the evince command with the ps or pdf file as an argument:

```
$ evince /usr/share/doc/gutenprint-doc/gutenprint-users-manual.pdf
```

## Using Adobe Reader

The Portable Document Format (PDF) provides a way to store documents as they would appear in print. With Adobe Reader, you can view PDF files in a very friendly way. Adobe Reader makes it easy to move around within a PDF file. A PDF file may include hyperlinks, a table of contents, graphics, and a variety of type fonts. Recent versions even enable you to fill in forms or mark up content.

You can get Adobe Reader for Linux from the Adobe Web site (www.adobe.com/products/acrobat/readstep2.html). If you have need for any special forms or editing functions on PDF documents, you should get this reader, as opposed to using an open source PDF viewer such as Evince.

After you install Adobe Reader, select Applications ➪ Office ➪ Adobe Reader to start it. Or you can type the following command to start the program:

```
$ acroread
```

Choose File ➪ Open, and then select the name of a PDF file you want to display. Figure 5-12 shows an example of a PDF file viewed in Adobe Reader.

**FIGURE 5-12**

Display PDF files in the Adobe Reader.

Adobe Acrobat has a lot of nice features. For example, you can display a list of bookmarks alongside the document and click a bookmark to take you to a particular page. You can also display thumbnails of the pages to quickly scroll through and select a page.

Using the menu bar or buttons, you can page through the PDF document, zoom in and out, go to the beginning or end of the document, and display different views of the document (as well as display bookmarks and page thumbnails). To print a copy, choose File ➪ Print.

Other document-viewing programs include Evince and KghostView, a KDE version of the gv, or GhostView, program.

# Using Scanners with SANE

Software for using a scanner with Linux is being driven by an effort called *Scanner Access Now Easy (SANE)*. This effort hopes to standardize how device drivers for equipment such as scanners, digital still cameras, and digital video cameras are created, as well as help simplify the interfaces for applications that use those devices. SANE is now included with a variety of Linux distributions.

Someone wanting to use Linux as a publishing platform is generally interested in two issues about scanners: which scanners are supported and which applications are available to use the scanners. For older scanners, SCSI scanners are generally better supported than parallel scanners. These days, USB scanners are the most popular and best supported scanners.

Because of the ongoing development effort, new scanners are being supported all the time. You can find a current list of supported scanners at `www.sane-project.org/sane-supported-devices.html`, with USB scanners listed at `www.buzzard.me.uk/jonathan/scanners-usb.html`. Epson scanners are often recommended for Linux.

As for scanning applications, some of the more widely used tools available today include

- **xsane**—An X-based graphical front end for SANE scanners, xsane can work as a GIMP plug-in or as a separate application (from most KDE desktops, select Graphics ⇨ Scanning). It supports 8-bit output in JPG, TIFF, PNG, PostScript, and PNM formats. Experimental 16-bit support exists for PNM (ASCII), PNG, and raw formats.

- **scanimage**—Use this command-line interface to obtain scanned images. The command acquires the scanned image, and then directs the data to standard output (so you can send it to a file or pipe it to another program). It supports the same formats as xsane.

In addition to these applications, the OpenOffice.org suite supports SANE.

Because of the architecture of SANE scanner drivers, it is possible to separate scanner drivers from scanner applications. This makes it possible to share scanners across a network.

# Web Publishing

The final destination for your documents and images doesn't have to be paper. Publishing on the Web has become commonplace in the past few years. If you want to control your own Web site for publishing your thoughts and pictures to the world, Linux systems include many software packages to help you do that.

If you are creating simple HTML Web pages, you can build basic HTML documents using word processors such as OpenOffice.org Writer or SeaMonkey composer. If you are really brave, you might even try a plain text editor and add the HTML markup manually. For more complex Web sites, however, there are lots of options.

The following list describes open source software packages that can be used for publishing on the Web. All the software packages described here are packaged for Fedora and Ubuntu, as well as other Linux distributions.

## Caution

**Web servers are constant targets for bad guys on the Internet. If you decide to try some of the software described next, be sure to check with the project site to make sure you get the latest security patches and updates.** ∎

- **Image galleries**—The Gallery project (`http://gallery.menalto.com`) lets you create online photo albums. Gallery makes it easy for you to organize photos into albums, edit your images, tag them, and present them using a variety of themes and colors. In Fedora, install the gallery2 package.

- **Blogging software**—The popular WordPress site (`http://wordpress.com`) uses its own open source WordPress software (`http://wordpress.org`) to offer blogging accounts to others. If you want your own blogging site, you can either sign up for a free account on WordPress.com or you can use that software to set up your own blogging site. Install the wordpress package in Fedora or Ubuntu to get started. Figure 5-13 shows an example of a blog that relies on WordPress software running from WordPress.com.

### FIGURE 5-13

With WordPress, you create your own blogging site.

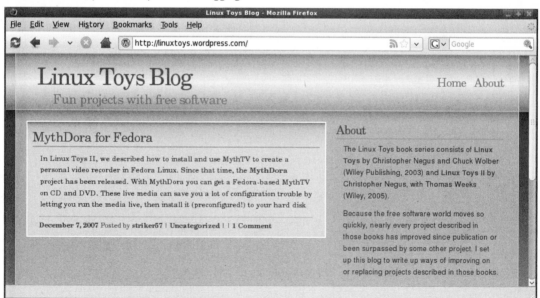

- **Wiki software**—Wikis let you gather and organize large amounts of information online. Instead of having to write everything on a subject by yourself, by creating a wiki you can allow people to sign up for accounts and add and correct articles on your site. Wiki software available to the open source community includes MediaWiki (install the mediawiki package in Fedora or Ubuntu) and MoinMoin (install moin in Fedora or python-moinmoin in Ubuntu). See the MediaWiki.org and MoinMoin.wikiwikiweb.de sites, respectively, for further information.

- **Content management system (CMS) software**—For some Web sites, you might want to offer a range of information. For an active online community you may want to offer articles, forums, online polls, downloads, and other diverse activities. Content management systems (CMS) such as Drupal (install the drupal package) offer a platform for creating and managing those types of activities online. Other open source CMS systems include Plone (http://plone.org) and Zope (www.zope.org). Both Plone and Zope also are packaged for Fedora, Ubuntu, and other Linux systems (plone, zope, or zope3 packages, respectively).

Before installing and making any of these types of Web sites available on the Internet, you should keep in mind that it will take some commitment to stay current with software updates and keep the site maintained. But if you are willing to make that commitment, the open source projects just mentioned can help you produce high-quality sites for publishing on the Internet.

# Summary

Tools available in Linux for publishing words and images on paper and the Web can compete with similar software available commercially. For producing hardcopy documents, you have word processors such as OpenOffice.org Writer, AbiWord and StarOffice. To lay out pages, there is Scribus. To work with photos you have The GIMP, or for vector graphics you can use Inkscape.

Software for publishing content on the Internet is also available now in almost any category you can think of. For blogging, you can create a WordPress site. For image galleries, there is Gallery software. Content management systems include Drupal, Plone, and Zope. To create wikis, there are MediaWiki and Moin Moin.

# E-Mailing and Web Browsing

Web browsers and e-mail clients available with Linux have seen incredible improvements over the past few years. Their features rival those you can get on the most popular Windows clients. Security issues with Outlook mail clients and Internet Explorer browsers have many people taking a fresh look at Linux and open source software for accessing the Internet.

This chapter describes some of the best Web, e-mail, chat, and related tools for accessing the Internet that you can get with the Linux distributions described with this book. If you have never worked with the Internet from Linux, or haven't for a few years, you might be blown away by what's available today.

## Using E-Mail

Any Linux desktop system worth the name *desktop system* will have at least one or two applications for sending, receiving, and working with your personal e-mail. Many users believe that superior tools for managing spam and generally better security mechanisms make Linux a great desktop platform for managing your e-mail.

### Choosing an e-mail client

Choices of e-mail clients range from those that look like clones of popular Windows e-mail programs to those that run in plain text from the shell.

Interfaces vary widely with the e-mail clients that are available with Linux. Here are some different ways in which e-mail clients are integrated into Linux:

- **Standalone**—These days, most e-mail clients are standalone applications in their own right. The primary standalone e-mail application is Mozilla Thunderbird 2 (`www.mozilla.com/en-US/thunderbird/`), although you can find 50 or more choices on Linux such as Sylpheed (`sylpheed.sraoss.jp/en/`).

- **With a Web browser**—Many popular Web browsers include an integrated e-mail client. By configuring the e-mail client that comes with your browser, you are ready to launch a new e-mail message by clicking on a mailto link from a browser window. You can also easily open the e-mail client from your Web browser's toolbar.

  Feature-rich Mozilla SeaMonkey Mail (`www.seamonkey-project.org`) is a popular e-mail client for Linux to come with a Web browser. (At the time of this writing, Seamonkey 2.0 was in beta test, incorporating many new features from Firefox.) Netscape Communicator (`http://netscape.aol.com`) is another Web browser that has its own mail client (although it has been dropped from many Linux distributions because of licensing issues). Most users, however, use the separated clients Thunderbird for e-mail and Firefox for Web browsing.

  The Opera Web browser (`www.opera.com`) also includes an integrated e-mail client. It is perhaps the most elegant of the e-mail clients that comes with a Web browser. Opera is available for personal use without cost.

- **With groupware**—Some e-mail clients have been bundled with other personal productivity applications to form integrated groupware applications. The most popular of these in Linux is Evolution, which is bundled as the default e-mail client with several different Linux distributions. Besides e-mail, Evolution includes a calendar, task list, and contacts directory. Today the GNOME project manages Evolution (`http://projects.gnome.org/evolution/`).

- **From the shell**—Many old school UNIX and Linux power users prefer to use an e-mail client that runs without a graphical desktop. Although not always intuitive to use, text-based e-mail readers run much faster than their graphical counterparts. The `mail` command dates back to the earliest UNIX systems (where there was no GUI). The mutt e-mail client is popular among power users because of its capability to manage large mailboxes, message threads, and attachments efficiently.

Features inside each e-mail client can help you distinguish between them. While most e-mail clients let you get, compose, send, and manage e-mail messages, here are a few extra features you might look for:

- **Filters and spam catchers**—Thunderbird, Evolution, and other mail clients offer message filters and junk mail detectors. You use filters to set up rules to sort incoming mail into different folders, delete certain messages, or otherwise respond to incoming mail. Some e-mail clients also have features that try to automatically detect when junk mail has arrived. If you get a lot of e-mail, these can be invaluable tools for managing your e-mail. (Select the Tools or Message menu from your e-mail client, and then look for a Filters or Junk Mail selection.)

- **Security features**—E-mail clients such as Thunderbird (`www.mozilla.com/en-US/thunderbird/`) enable you to use message encryption, digital signatures, and other security features to keep your e-mail private.

- **Sorting, searching, marking, and displaying**—Again, if you are managing lots of e-mail messages at once (some people manage thousands of messages), the capability to refer back to the one you want can be critical. Some clients let you sort by date, sender, priority, subject, and other items. You might be able to search message contents for text or choose how to display the messages (such as without showing attachments or with source code shown).

- **Mail composition tools**—Most recent mail composers let you include HTML in your messages, which enables you to add images, links, tables, colors, font changes, and other visual enhancements to your messages. One warning: Some mailing lists don't like you to send messages in HTML because some people still use plain-text readers that aren't HTML-aware.

- **Multiple accounts**—Many e-mail clients enable you to configure multiple e-mail accounts to be served by your e-mail reader. Early plain-text e-mail clients pointed to only one mailbox at a time.

- **Performance**—Some lightweight graphical e-mail clients give you much better performance than others. In particular, the Sylpheed e-mail client (which comes with Damn Small Linux) was created to use a minimal amount of memory and processing power, yet still provide a graphical interface. E-mail clients that run from the keyboard, in particular the mutt e-mail client, will run much faster than, say, most full-blown graphical e-mail clients such as Evolution.

## Coming from Windows

**For most home and small business users, Evolution and the standalone Thunderbird are often available from a Linux desktop and will give you much the same experience you would expect from Microsoft Windows mail clients, such as Outlook Express. If you are using the KDE desktop, you can use the KDE groupware client Kontact, which includes KMail (the e-mail client), along with a contact manager, calendar, to-do list application, and more. ■**

Even though the Linux distribution you are using may have only one or two of the e-mail clients described in this section, you can always add a client that interests you.

## Getting here from Windows

To understand how to transition your e-mail client from Windows to Linux, you need to know a bit about your current e-mail setup. Whether you are using Outlook, Outlook Express, or any other e-mail client running in Windows, here are some things you should know:

- **Server type**—Is your e-mail server a POP3 or IMAP server? If it is an IMAP server, all your messages are being stored on the server. Transitioning to a different e-mail server might simply mean pointing the new e-mail client at your server and continuing to use e-mail as you always have. If it is a POP3 server, your messages have probably been downloaded to your local client. To keep your old messages, you need to somehow bring your current mail folders over to your new client, which is a potentially tricky undertaking. (When you sign up for your e-mail account or Internet service, the people providing the service should tell you whether the service is POP3 or IMAP.)

- **Address book**—You need to export your current address book to a format that can be read by your new e-mail client, and import it to your new e-mail client. For example, from the Contacts section of the Evolution e-mail client, you can import address books and/or mailboxes in Berkeley mbox, Evolution, Outlook, Mozilla CVS or tab formats, vCard format, LDAP ldif format, or vCalendar (vcf) or iCalendar (ics) formats.

To transition to Linux, you may want to add a cross-platform e-mail client such as Thunderbird to your Windows systems so that you can get at your resources (addresses, stored mail messages, and so on) during the transition to your new mail client. When you eventually move off Windows altogether, Thunderbird for Linux will work almost exactly as it does in Windows.

If your current e-mail server is a Microsoft Exchange server (2000, 2003, or 2007), you need to get the Evolution Plug-in for Microsoft Exchange to allow Evolution to access information from that server. For Fedora, you need to install the evolution-exchange package then identify your mail server as Microsoft Exchange when you create a new e-mail account.

## Getting started with e-mail

Most Linux systems include an e-mail client that you can select on a panel or by left-clicking on the desktop to bring up a menu. Look for an envelope icon on a panel or a submenu labeled something like Internet. If you want a graphical e-mail reader, you can start by looking for one of these clients: Evolution, Mozilla SeaMonkey Mail, Thunderbird, and KMail.

After you have launched your chosen e-mail client, you need some information to use it. When you first start most graphical e-mail clients, a configuration screen of some sort asks you to set up an account. Here's how to begin setting up a mail account for the e-mail clients described in this chapter:

- **Evolution**—The Evolution Setup Assistant starts the first time each user opens Evolution. After that, select Edit ➪ Preferences from the main Evolution window. Then choose Mail Accounts and double-click the mail account you want to modify or select Add to add a new account.

- **Mozilla SeaMonkey Mail**—An account wizard starts the first time you open SeaMonkey Mail. After that, you can set up or modify accounts from the SeaMonkey Mail window by clicking Edit ➪ Preferences ➪ Mail & Newsgroups.

- **Thunderbird**—This is the next-generation mail client from the people who bring you Firefox and Mozilla (mozilla.org). Now at version 2.0, and with more advanced security features, you might consider Thunderbird. Not only is it faster than SeaMonkey Mail and Evolution, Thunderbird is an ideal complement to Mozilla Firefox Web browser. Firefox and Thunderbird run on a number of operating systems, including Linux, Solaris, Microsoft Windows, and Mac OS X.

- **Sylpheed**—The Sylpheed e-mail client (`http://sylpheed.sraoss.jp/en/`) is used on some mini-desktop distributions, such as Damn Small Linux. Sylpheed is particularly fast and efficient, but still has support for powerful features such as filtering, search, junk mail control, and digital signing and encryption (using GnuPG).

- **KMail**—From the KMail window, select Settings ⇨ Configure KMail. From the Configure KMail window that appears, select the Network icon. From there, you can click Sending or Receiving tabs to configure your outgoing and incoming e-mail settings. KMail is developed by the KDE project (`www.kde.org`).

Initial configuration for text-based e-mail clients is described later in this chapter.

Information you will need to configure your e-mail accounts is much the same for the different graphical e-mail clients covered in this chapter:

- **Name**—Enter your name as you want it to appear on outgoing messages.

- **Email Address**—Enter the e-mail address from which you are sending. You may also be offered the opportunity to supply a different reply-to address, if you want replies to go to an address other than the one you sent from.

- **Mail server type**—Most mail servers are POP3- or IMAP-type servers. (Configuring those types of servers is discussed in Chapter 14.)

- **Server names**—Enter the names of the servers you will use to send outgoing e-mail and receive incoming e-mail. The names can be fully qualified domain names (such as `mail.linuxtoys.net`) or IP addresses. In many cases, the incoming and outgoing mail servers are the same.

- **Username**—Enter the name by which the mail server knows you. For example, if your e-mail address is `chris@linuxtoys.net`, your username to the mail.linuxtoys.net server might simply be chris. However, it's possible that your username on the mail server might be different, so you should find that out from the administrator of your mail server.

- **Account title**—Enter the name that you want to call this mail account so you can refer to it later in your list of mail and newsgroup accounts.

- **Authentication type**—Indicate the type of authentication to use when you get your mail (sometimes authentication is needed to send your mail as well). Password authentication is normal. Usually you can have your e-mail client remember your password if you want. Typically, you are prompted for the password the first time you connect to get your mail.

That is most of the basic information you need to start getting and sending e-mail. However, you may want to further tune how your e-mail client interacts when it gets and sends e-mail.

## Tuning up e-mail

With your basic settings done, you should be ready to start sending and receiving your e-mail. Before you do, however, you should consider some of the other settings that can affect how you use mail:

- **Automatically check messages**—You can set your e-mail client to automatically check and download your messages from the mail server every few minutes.

- **Leave messages on server**—If you turn this feature on for a POP3 server, your e-mail messages remain on the server after you have downloaded them to your e-mail client. People sometimes turn this feature on if they want to check their mail messages while they are on the road yet want to download their messages from their permanent desktop computer later.

- **Certificates**—Your e-mail client may provide a way of using certificates to sign your outgoing messages. For example, Evolution, Thunderbird, and SeaMonkey Mail all have Security tabs for your mail settings that let you enter information about your certificates and indicate that your e-mail be signed. You can also choose to use the certificates for encryption.

Step through your mail account settings because they are slightly different for each e-mail client.

## Reading e-mail with Thunderbird

The Thunderbird e-mail client program is a full-featured mail and newsgroup reader that usually comes with most Linux systems.

### Note

In the past, you may have run the integrated Mozilla suite of applications, now called Mozilla SeaMonkey. The more recent versions of Linux, however, have replaced SeaMonkey with separate e-mail and Web-browsing applications, Thunderbird and Firefox, respectively. If you are used to the older Mozilla suite, you should consider upgrading to Thunderbird. ■

Thunderbird includes features for

- Sending, receiving, reading, and managing e-mail
- Managing multiple mail and newsgroup accounts
- Composing HTML e-mail messages
- Controlling junk e-mail
- Message encryption and signing

### Coming from Windows

Thunderbird runs on Windows as well as Linux, so you can convert your organization to Thunderbird now, and then later migrate to Linux. ■

On most Linux systems, either Thunderbird or Evolution (covered following) will be the primary e-mail client for your Linux distribution. You can launch the e-mail application from the desktop from a menu such as Internet. For example, in Fedora and Ubuntu, you run an e-mail client from the Applications ➪ Internet menu. Fedora defaults to Evolution as the primary e-mail client, so Evolution is listed simply as Email on the Application ➪ Internet menu. Thunderbird is listed as Thunderbird Email (if you install the thunderbird package).

## Setting up an e-mail account

When you launch Thunderbird for the first time, the application presents the New Account Setup dialog, which leads you through setting up an e-mail account (you can create more than one). Figure 6-1 shows this window. Follow these steps to create your e-mail account:

**FIGURE 6-1**

The Thunderbird New Account Setup wizard

1. **Create e-mail account.** To begin setting up an e-mail account, select Email Account and click Next. The Identity screen appears.

2. **Identify yourself.** Type in your name and the e-mail address that you want others to use to send e-mail to you and click Next. The Server Information screen appears.

3. **Enter server settings.** For your incoming mail, indicate whether the mail server is a POP3 or IMAP server. Then type the server name (such as `mail.example.com`). If you want to keep the e-mail from different e-mail accounts separate (as opposed to having all messages stored in a Global Inbox), uncheck this box. Finally, type the name of the

server where your outgoing mail is sent (such as mail.example.com) and then select Next. The User Names screen appears.

4. **Enter usernames.** When you get (incoming) and send (outgoing) e-mail through your mail server, Thunderbird identifies you as a particular username to the server. Usually, that name is the same name used in your e-mail address. For example, if your complete e-mail address were chris@example.com, the incoming and outgoing username would probably be chris. Type in your incoming and outgoing username and click Next. The Account Name screen appears.

5. **Enter account name.** Type a name by which you want to identify the account. This name is only used to help you remember which account it is and doesn't have any effect on what is sent to the server. Thunderbird recommends names such as "Home Account" or "News Account." Click Next to continue.

6. **Finish account setup.** The Congratulations screen appears, which allows you to review your settings and complete the account. Figure 6-2 shows an example of the Congratulations screen. The check box lets you immediately download messages from the server, if you are ready to do that. Click Next to continue.

**FIGURE 6-2**

Before creating your e-mail account, you can confirm all the settings.

Thunderbird is now ready to begin getting and sending mail messages. If you need to change any settings to the account you just set up (change defaults you have not had a chance to change or create another account), Select Edit ➪ Account Settings from the Thunderbird window.

## Tip

With the Junk Mail feature, Thunderbird automatically tags any message it believes to be junk mail with a blue recycle-bin icon. Using the Junk toolbar, you train the Junk Mail feature by telling it when a message is or isn't junk mail. After you have identified which messages are junk mail, you can automatically move incoming junk mail to the Junk folder. ■

### Connecting to the mail server

After you have set up your mail accounts in Thunderbird, you can explicitly ask to download any available mail messages from the server (for POP3 accounts). To do that, click the Get Mail button.

You are prompted for the password for your account on the mail server. Using that password, Thunderbird downloads all your messages from the mail server. It downloads messages again every 10 minutes, or you can click the Get Mail button at any time.

If you want to change how often mail is downloaded, or other features of your account, choose Edit ➪ Account Settings. Under the e-mail account you added are categories to change the setup and behavior of the account. (Click Server Settings to change how often, if at all, new messages are automatically downloaded from the mail server.)

### Managing incoming mail

Select the Inbox title in the left column. It shows how many messages are in your Inbox that have not been read. Your incoming messages appear to the right, with the headers on top and the currently selected message text below it. Figure 6-3 shows Thunderbird displaying some e-mail headers and the current message.

---

**FIGURE 6-3**

Manage incoming mail from the Thunderbird window.

---

Thunderbird offers various ways to store and manage these e-mail messages. Here's a quick rundown of how to manage incoming mail:

- **Mail folders**—Mail messages are stored in folders in the left column. There could be a separate heading for each mail account you have or you might have specified that Thunderbird use a global Inbox where messages from all accounts get placed in the same Inbox folder. For each mail account, incoming messages are stored (by default) in your Inbox folder. You can create additional folders to better keep track of your mail (right-click on Inbox, and select New Folder to add a folder). Other folders contain drafts of messages set aside for a time (Drafts), templates for creating messages (Templates), messages you have sent (Sent), and messages that you have discarded (Trash).

- **Sort messages**—Messages are sorted by date for the folder you select, in the upper-right corner of the display. Click the headings over the messages to sort by subject, sender, date, or priority. The icon on the far right of the Subject header lets you choose what information columns to display for the message headers (such as recipient, size, status, and so on). You can then sort on any of those columns.

- **Read messages**—When you select a message, it appears in the lower-right corner of the display. Click the e-mail address from the sender and a menu enables you to add that address to your address book, compose mail to that address, copy mail to that address, or create a filter from that message.

- **Filter mail**—When Thunderbird grabs your e-mail from the mail server, it drops it into the global Inbox or one associated with your mail account, by default. Thunderbird provides some nice features for checking each message for information you choose, and then acting on that message to move it to another folder, label it, or change its priority. See the "Filtering Mail and Catching Spam" section later in this chapter for details.

- **Search messages**—You can use the search feature to retrieve messages that are in one of your mail folders. With the folder you want to search being the current folder, type a word to search on into the Subject or Sender Contains box. Messages with sender names or subject lines that don't contain that string will disappear from the list of messages. To do more detailed searches, choose Edit ➪ Find ➪ Search Messages.

## Composing and sending mail

To compose e-mail messages, you can either start from scratch or respond to an existing e-mail message. The following are some quick descriptions of how to create outgoing mail:

- **New messages**—To create a new message, choose Message ➪ New Message (or click Write on the toolbar).

- **Reply to messages**—To reply to a mail message, click the message on the right side of your screen and then choose Message ➪ Reply (to reply only to the author of the message) or Message ➪ Reply to All (to reply to everyone listed as a recipient of the message).

- **Forward messages**—To forward a mail message, click the message on the right side of your screen and then choose Message ➪ Forward. You can also forward a message and have it appear in the text (Message ⇨ Forward As ⇨ Inline) or as an attachment (Message ⇨ Forward As ⇨ Attachment).

In each case, a mail Compose window appears, in which you compose your e-mail message. As you compose your message in the Compose window, you can use the following:

- **Address book**—Add e-mail addresses from your personal address book (or from one of several different directory servers) by selecting Tools ⇨ Address Book. Click the Contacts button to select recipients for your missive.

- **Attachments**—Add attachments such as a word processing file, image, or executable program by clicking the Attach button (or choosing File ⇨ Attach ⇨ File) and then selecting a file from your file system to attach. (You can also choose File ⇨ Attach ⇨ Web Page to choose the URL of a Web page that you want to attach.)

- **Certificates**—Add certificates or view security information about your mail message by selecting View ⇨ Message Security Info.

When you are finished composing the message, click Send to send the message. If you prefer, queue the message to be sent later by choosing File ⇨ Send Later. (Send Later is useful if you are not currently online.)

## Tip

If you want to quit and finish the e-mail message later, choose File ⇨ Save As ⇨ Draft, and then click the X in the upper-right corner to close the window. When you are ready to resume work on the message, open the Draft folder in the Thunderbird window and double-click the message. ■

### Filtering mail and catching spam

Thunderbird can do more with incoming messages than just place them in your Inbox. You can set up filters to check each message first and then have Thunderbird take an action you define when a message matches the rules you set up.

For example, your filter can contain a rule that checks the subject, sender, text body, date, priority, status, recipients, or age in days of the message for a particular word, name, or date, as appropriate. If there is a match, you can have Thunderbird put that message in a particular folder, label it with a selected phrase, change its priority, or set its junk mail status. You can add as many rules as you like. For example, you can

- Have all messages sent from a particular address sorted into a separate mail folder. For example, I direct some mailing lists to a separate folder so that important mail doesn't get lost when there's a lot of activity on the mailing lists to which I subscribe.

- Mark incoming messages from important clients as having highest priority.

- Have messages from particular people or places that are being mistakenly marked as spam change their junk status to Not Junk.

To set up filter rules in Thunderbird, select Tools ⇨ Message Filters. The Message Filters pop-up appears. If you have multiple mail accounts, select the account you want to filter. Then click New. From the Filter Rules pop-up window, choose the following:

- **For incoming messages that**—There are different ways to check parts of a message. For example, you can check whether the Sender is in the address book. You can check what the Priority is: low, medium, or high. You can create multiple rules for a filter (click More to add another rule), and then choose whether you want to match all or any of the rules to continue to the action.

- **Perform these actions**—The information in this section describes what to do with a message that matches the rules you've set. You can have the message moved to any existing folder, or label the message. With labels, the message appears in a different color depending on the label: important (red), work (orange), personal (green), to do (blue), or later (purple). You can also change the message priority.

Figure 6-4 shows a rule I created to have a star attached to mail from my friend, Tweeks, when it comes in.

A nice feature of Thunderbird's filtering rules is that you can apply the rules after the fact as well. If you decide you want to move all messages in your Inbox from a particular person to a different folder, for example, you can open the Message Filters window, create a rule to move the selected messages, select Inbox, and click Run Now.

**FIGURE 6-4**

Create filter rules to sort or highlight your e-mail messages.

For junk mail, with a mail message selected, click the Junk button in the toolbar. The message is marked as junk. Your selection helps teach Thunderbird what you think is junk mail. Click Tools ➪ Run Junk Mail Controls on Folder and Thunderbird looks for other messages that look like junk mail. (You can take the junk marker off of any message you think is not junk.) Then select Tools ➪ Delete Mail Marked as Junk in Folder, and the junk mail is deleted. To open a window to configure how you handle junk mail, select Tools ➪ Junk Mail Controls.

## Managing e-mail in Evolution

If you are using Fedora, Ubuntu, or Debian, Evolution is the e-mail client that you can start right from the GNOME desktop (look for the envelope icon on the panel). Evolution is a groupware application, combining several types of applications that help groups of people communicate and work together. The features of Evolution include

- **Mail**—A complete set of features for getting, reading, managing, composing, and sending e-mail on one or more e-mail accounts.
- **Contacts**—Create contact information such as names, addresses, and telephone numbers for friends and associates. A Categories feature helps you remember who gets birthday and anniversary gifts.
- **Calendar**—Create and manage appointments on your personal calendar. You can e-mail appointment information to others and do keyword searches of your calendar.
- **Memos**—Write public, private, or confidential memos.
- **Tasks**—Organize ongoing tasks into folders.

### Coming from Windows

Evolution provides a default interface that looks a lot like that of Microsoft Outlook, making it easy for new users to make a smooth transition to a Linux system. ∎

Additional features recently added to Evolution include improved junk mail handling and Search Folders (for managing multiple physical folders as one folder).

### Receiving, composing, and sending e-mail

Evolution offers a full set of features for sending, receiving, and managing your e-mail. Figure 6-5 shows an example of an Evolution window with the Inbox selected and ready to manage, compose, send, and receive e-mail.

**FIGURE 6-5**

Manage your e-mail from the Evolution Inbox.

Here's a quick rundown of common e-mail tasks:

- **Read e-mail**—Click Inbox in the left column. Your messages appear to the right. Message headers are in the upper right; the current message is displayed in the lower pane. Double-click a message header to display it in a separate window

- **Delete e-mail**—After you have read a message, select it and press the Delete key. Click View ➪ Hide Deleted Messages to toggle whether you can see deleted messages. Click Folder ➪ Expunge to permanently remove all messages marked for deletion in the current folder.

- **Send and receive**—Click the Send/Receive button to send any e-mail queued to be sent and receive any e-mail waiting for you at your mail server. (You may not need to do this if Evolution is configured to download your messages every few minutes. Select Edit ➪ Preferences, and then double-click on your mail account. The Receiving Options tab indicates whether automatic mail checking is being done.)

- **Compose e-mail**—Click New ➪ Mail Message. A Compose a Message window appears. Type your recipient's e-mail address, enter a subject line, and fill in the body of the message. Click Send when you are finished. Buttons on the Compose window enable you to add attachments, cut and paste text, choose a format (HTML or plain text), and sign the message (if you have set up appropriate keys).

- **Use address books**—Click the Contacts button (or View ➪ Window ➪ Contacts menu choice) to see a list of names, addresses, and other contact information for the people in your address book. When you compose a message, click the To or CC buttons to select addresses from the book to add as recipients for your message.

- **Create folders**—If you like to keep old messages, you may want to save them outside your Inbox (so it won't get too junked up). To create a folder in which to keep them, right-click on the Inbox and select New Folder. You can choose to store the new folder as a subfolder to any existing folder. Type a folder name and click OK.

- **Move messages**—With new folders created, you can easily move messages from your Inbox to another folder. The easiest way is to simply drag-and-drop each message (or a set of selected messages) from the message pane to the new folder.

- **Search messages**—Type a keyword in the search box over your e-mail message pane and select whether to search your message subject lines, sender, recipient, or message body. Click Find Now to search for the keyword. After viewing the messages, click Clear to have the other messages reappear.

## Managing e-mail with Search Folders

Managing large amounts of e-mail can become difficult when the messages you want to refer to span several folders, dates, or senders. With Search Folders (also called virtual folders or vFolders), you can identify criteria to group together messages from all your mail folders so you can deal with them in one Search Folder.

# Note

**Where have vFolders gone? Search Folders used to be called vFolders. If you are familiar with older versions of Evolution, note that the name changed to Search Folders. ■**

Here's a procedure for creating a Search Folder:

1. With Evolution open to read mail (click Inbox to get there), select Search ➪ Create Search Folder from Search. A New Search Folder pop-up appears.

2. Type a rule name.

3. Click Add and select criteria for including a message in your Search Folder. At first you should see an entry that says "Message Body contains," after which you can type a term to search on. Otherwise, you can change Message Body to sender, recipient, subject, expression, date sent, or other criteria to search on. Click Add Filter Criteria if you want to add more criteria.

4. If you want to search only specific folders, click Add in the Search Folder Sources box and select the folder you want to search. You can repeat the Add to choose more than

one. Otherwise, you can select to search all local folders, all active remote folders, or all local and active remote folders. Then click OK.

5. Make sure the folder bar is visible (select View ⇨ Layout ⇨ Show Side Bar). The folder you just created is listed under the Search Folders heading. Click that folder to see the messages you gathered with this action.

At this point, you can work with the messages you gathered in the Search Folder. Although it appears that there are multiple versions of each message across your mail folders, there is really only one copy of each. So deleting or moving the message from a Search Folder actually causes it to be deleted or moved from the original folder in which the real message resides.

## Tip

You can also create a Search Folder by performing a search, a sort of query by example. Select the Search ⇨ Create Search Folder from Search menu choice and enter your search criteria. ■

### Filtering e-mail messages

You can take action on an e-mail message before it even lands in your Inbox. Click Message ⇨ Create Rule, and then select the type of filter to create. Evolution shows a Filters window to enable you to add filters to deal with incoming or outgoing messages. Click Add to create criteria and set actions.

For example, you can have all messages from a particular sender, subject, date, status, or size sorted to a selected folder. Or you can have messages matching your criteria deleted or assigned a color, or play a sound clip.

Evolution also supports many common features, such as printing, saving, and viewing e-mail messages in various ways. The help system that comes with Evolution (click the Help button) includes a good manual, FAQ, and service for reporting bugs.

## Reading e-mail with SeaMonkey Mail

The SeaMonkey Mail client program is a full-featured mail and newsgroup reader that comes with the SeaMonkey suite on many Linux systems. In general, the SeaMonkey suite is based on the older Mozilla suite, which was replaced by Thunderbird e-mail and Firefox Web browser clients. Thunderbird and Firefox were split from the large Mozilla suite and each now runs as a separate application. If you are used to the older Mozilla suite, now called SeaMonkey, you should consider upgrading to Thunderbird.

In most respects, SeaMonkey Mail works like Thunderbird, described previously. The major difference is that SeaMonkey Mail, because it is an older application, won't have all the features of the latest Thunderbird. This is a big change. In the last year or so, Thunderbird has all but replaced SeaMonkey Mail.

In many Linux distributions you can simply install the seamonkey package to get the entire SeaMonkey Suite (Web browser, Mail client, Composer, Address Book, and IRC Chat client). If SeaMonkey is not available with your Linux distribution, you can download the Mozilla SeaMonkey suite from `www.mozilla.org/projects/seamonkey/`. Figure 6-6 shows an example of the SeaMonkey mail window.

## FIGURE 6-6

Manage mail and newsgroups with SeaMonkey.

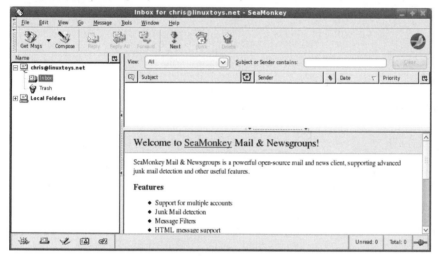

## Working with text-based e-mail readers

The first text-based mail clients could be configured quite simply. Mail clients such as `mutt`, `mail`, or `pine` were often run with the user logged in to the computer that was acting as the mail server. So instead of downloading the messages, using POP3 or IMAP, the mail client would simply open the mailbox (often under the user's name in `/var/spool/mail`) and begin working with mail.

Today, some of these text-based e-mail clients have been enhanced to support more modern features. For example, you can point the `mutt` e-mail client at a remote mail server and access mail from both insecure (`imap` and `pop3`) and secure (`imaps` and `pop3s`) mail access services.

Many text-based mail programs are available for reading, sending, and working with your mail. Many of these programs have been around for a long time, so they are full of features and have been well debugged. As a group, however, they are not very intuitive.

## Tip

Most of these programs use the value of your $MAIL environment variable as your local mailbox, by default. Usually, that location is /var/spool/mail/*user*, where *user* is your username. If you use Thunderbird but want to try out one of the text-based e-mail clients, you can set your $MAIL so that it points to your Thunderbird mailbox. Doing so enables you to use either Thunderbird or a text-based mail program. Add the following line to one of your startup files:

```
export MAIL=$HOME/.thunderbird/*.default/*/Mail/accountname/Inbox
```

Replace *accountname* in the command with the name of an e-mail account you set up. If you usually use Thunderbird for mail, set this variable temporarily to try out some of these mail programs. ∎

Mail readers described in the following sections are text-based and use the entire Terminal window (or other shell display). Although some features are different, menu bars show available options right on the screen.

### Mutt mail reader

The mutt command is a text-based, full-screen mail user agent for reading and sending e-mail. The interface is quick and efficient. Type mutt to start the program. Move arrow keys up and down to select from your listed messages. Press Enter to see a mail message and type i to return to the Main menu.

The menu bar indicates how to mark messages for deletion, undelete them, save messages to a directory, and reply to a message. Type **m** to compose a new message and it opens your default editor (vi, for example) to create the message. Type **y** to send the message. If you want to read mail without having your fingers leave your keyboard, mutt is a nice choice. (It even handles attachments!)

### Pine mail reader

The pine mail reader is another full-screen mail reader, but it offers many more features than does mutt. With pine, you can manage multiple mail folders and newsgroup messages as well as mail messages. As text-based applications go, pine is quite easy to use. It was developed by a group at the University of Washington for use by students on campus, but has become widely used in UNIX and Linux environments.

Start this mail program by typing **pine**. After a brief startup message that invites you to count yourself as a pine user, you should see the following menu, from which you can select items by typing the associated letter or using up and down arrows and pressing Enter:

```
    ?   HELP              - Get help using Pine
    C   COMPOSE MESSAGE   - Compose and send a message
    I   MESSAGE INDEX     - View messages in current folder
    L   FOLDER LIST       - Select a folder to view
    A   ADDRESS BOOK      - Update address book
    S   SETUP             - Configure Pine Options
    Q   QUIT              - Leave the Pine program
```

To read your e-mail, select either I or L. Commands are listed along the bottom of the screen and change to suit the content you are viewing. Use the left (←) and right (→) arrow keys to step backward and forward among the pine screens.

### Mail reader

The `mail` command was the first mail reader for UNIX. It is text-based, but not screen-oriented. Type **mail** to see the messages in your mailbox. You get a prompt after message headings are displayed—you are expected to know what to do next. (You can use the Enter key to step through messages.) Type **?** to see which commands are available.

While in mail, type **h** to see mail headings again. Simply type a message number to see the message. Type **d#** (replacing # with a message number) to delete a message. To create a new message, type **m**. To respond to a message, type **r#** (replacing # with the message number).

# Choosing a Web Browser

Many Web browsers available in Linux are based on the Mozilla Web browser engine, called Gecko. Web browsers that might come with your Linux distribution include

- **Firefox**—This is the leading Web browser for Linux and other open source software systems. There are versions of Firefox available for Linux, Mac OS X, and Windows. Firefox has made inroads into the Mac and Windows worlds as well. This next generation browser from the Mozilla project is designed to be fast, efficient, and safe for Web browsing.

- **SeaMonkey Web Browser**—Offered as part of the SeaMonkey suite, this Web browser is based on Mozilla Navigator, which was once the most popular open source Web browser. Although no longer actively developed by the Mozilla project, the SeaMonkey suite remains available with many Linux systems. Some people still install SeaMonkey for its easy-to-use HTML composer window.

- **Konqueror**—Comes as the default browser with many KDE desktop environments. Konqueror is a file manager as well as a Web browser and helps bring together many features of the KDE desktop. In recent KDE releases, some of Konqueror's file manager features have been moved to the Dolphin file manager, helping to make Konqueror run more efficiently as a Web browser.

- **Opera**—A commercial application that runs on many small devices such as mobile phones or the Nokia Linux–based Internet Tablet, this browser is available for free on Mac OS X, Microsoft Windows, and Linux. Because it is not open source, however, it is not redistributed with most major Linux systems.

- **links, lynx, and w3m**—If you are in a text-based environment (operating from the shell), these are among several text-based Web browsers you can try out.

## Note

Some streamlined Linux versions, such as Damn Small Linux, include a very lightweight Web browser called dillo (www.dillo.org). Although its small size (only about 350KB binary) comes with some limitations (such as limited font and internationalization support), dillo is a good choice for displaying basic HTML on hand-held devices and mini Linux distributions. Another small-footprint browser is minimo (www.mozilla.org/projects/minimo/), short for mini-Mozilla. ■

The following sections describe SeaMonkey, Firefox, and some text-based Web browsers that are available with many Linux systems.

# Exploring the SeaMonkey Suite

During the early 1990s, Netscape Navigator was the most popular Web browser. When it became apparent that Netscape was losing its lead to Microsoft Internet Explorer, its source code was released to the world as open source code.

Mozilla.org (www.mozilla.org) was formed to coordinate the development of a new browser from that code. The result was the Mozilla browser that was included with most Linux distributions. The availability on multiple platforms was great, especially if you must switch between Linux and Windows, for example, using Windows at work and Linux at home. Mozilla looked and acted the same on many platforms.

With the focus of Mozilla project development turning to Firefox and Thunderbird, as mentioned earlier, the suite changed its name to SeaMonkey. In addition to viewing Web pages, you can also manage e-mail, newsgroups, IRC, address books, and even create your own Web pages with SeaMonkey Composer.

## Note

Slackware kept SeaMonkey so that the project could offer the SeaMonkey Composer. The Slackware project noted that SeaMonkey Composer is a WYSIWYG HTML editor that is still used by many open source enthusiasts as an alternative to Microsoft FrontPage for ease-of-use Web page development. ■

In addition to the SeaMonkey browser, the SeaMonkey suite also includes the following features:

- **Mail and Newsgroups**—A full-featured program for sending, receiving, and managing e-mail, as well as for using newsgroups. (The seamonkey RPM or deb package must be installed.) SeaMonkey Mail has mostly been replaced by the Thunderbird application, covered previously.

- **IRC Chat**—An Internet Relay Chat (IRC) window, called ChatZilla, for participating in online, typed conversations. (The mozilla-chat package must be installed.)

- **Composer**—A Web page (HTML) composer application.

- **Address Book**—A feature to manage names, addresses, telephone numbers, and other contact information. This is also part of Thunderbird.

Figure 6-7 shows examples of the Browser and Composer windows available with the SeaMonkey suite.

**FIGURE 6-7**

SeaMonkey includes a browser, composer, and other Internet clients from the old Mozilla suite.

# Using Firefox

Most Linux distributions ship Firefox as the default browser. In many desktop Linux distributions, you start the Firefox Web browser from an icon on the top panel or on an Applications menu. For example, in Debian, select Applications ➪ Internet ➪ Firefox Web Browser. If you don't see it on a menu, you can start Firefox by simply typing **firefox** from a Terminal window.

The current version of Firefox (Firefox 3.5) includes some extraordinary features for ease-of-use, security, and performance. Many of those features are described in the following section. The Firefox project page (`www.mozilla.com/en-US/firefox/`) is shown in a Firefox browser in Figure 6-8.

**FIGURE 6-8**

Firefox is the leading open source Web browser, with thousands of improvements over earlier versions.

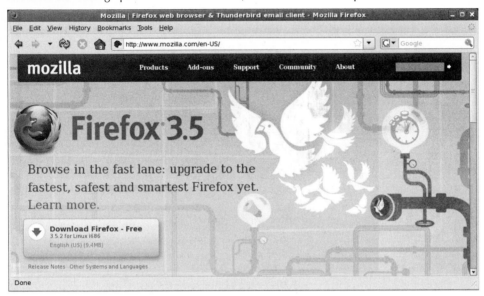

If you have been using Firefox for a while, but are new since Firefox 3, it has many new features you may find interesting. Inside Firefox is the Gecko 1.9 Web rendering platform, with thousands of features to improve performance, rendering, and stability. You should notice improvements in color management and fonts.

One improvement that connects you to several new features in Firefox 3 is the location box. Figure 6-9 shows several location box examples that illustrate new ways of dealing with the Web sites you request.

In Figure 6-9, the left-side example shows what happens when you click on the icon on the left side of the location box when visiting a secured site. You can see that VeriSign verifies the authenticity of the site and that communications are encrypted. In the right-side example, by selecting the star on the right side of the location box, you can work with bookmark information for a page and modify that information. Other icons that might appear in the location box include a variety of security warnings, such as warnings for possible forged or dangerous content.

Firefox has all the basic features you need in a Web browser plus a few special features. The following sections describe how to get the most out of your Firefox Web browser.

## Coming from Windows

**For help transitioning from Internet Explorer to Firefox, see the Firefox site at** `www.mozilla.org/` `products/firefox/switch.html`. ∎

**FIGURE 6-9**

Do site verification and bookmarks from the location box.

# Setting up Firefox

You can do many things to configure Firefox to run like a champ. The following sections describe some ways to customize your browsing experience in Firefox.

## Setting Firefox preferences

You can set your Firefox preferences in the Preferences window (see Figure 6-10). To open Firefox preferences, select Edit ➪ Preferences.

**FIGURE 6-10**

Change settings for navigating the Web from Firefox's Preferences window.

## Tip

If you are upgrading from the Mozilla suite or an earlier Firefox release, you will notice the Preferences window looks completely different. Don't despair, however; the browser preferences have not changed much. The latest Firefox just has a simpler window layout. ∎

The following are some Firefox preferences that you might want to change:

- **Main**—Lets you choose which pages to display when you start Firefox. It also lets you choose how to handle downloads and change add-on preferences.

- **Tabs**—Use these selections to control how Firefox uses tabs, one of the most useful features of this browser.

- **Content**—Set Content preferences to control how Firefox should deal with requests for different types of Web content. These options include

  - **Pop-up windows**—Choose whether or not to block pop-up windows.

  - **Java and JavaScript**—You can control whether these languages are enabled.

  - **Images**—Choose whether or not to load images automatically. (Useful for small screens or low-bandwidth network connections.)

  - **Fonts & Colors**—Select the default font type and size, as well as the colors used for text, background, visited links, and unvisited links.

  - **Language**—For Web pages that can appear in multiple languages, this sets the order in which you would prefer languages to be displayed. For example, you might choose English/United States, English, French, and German. Then Firefox tries to display a Web page you open in each of those languages successively, until one is matched. You can set other advanced features on this tab.

- **Applications**—View, search, and change which applications are used to display different types of content that might be encountered during browsing.

- **Privacy**—Choose how long to store a history of addresses of the sites you have typed in your location bar. (These addresses appear in the History tab on the Firefox sidebar.) Set Privacy preferences to control how Firefox caches private data and allows Web sites to find out information about you in cookies. These preferences include

  - **Cookies**—The Web content you choose can try to open, move, resize, raise, and lower windows. It can request to change your images, status bar text, or bits of information stored in what are called *cookies*. These preferences let you restrict what the content you request can do.

  - **Private Data**—Storing your history of browsing and downloading, forms and searches, visited pages, cookies, passwords, and authenticated sessions can simplify your browsing experience. However, if you are working on someone else's machine or otherwise don't want to leave a record of your browsing behind, you can clear that information with the Clear Now button. You can also select the Settings button to indicate what information you want to clear when Clear Now is selected.

- **Security**—Firefox 3 has a great new feature from the Security preferences tab that lets you select to be warned if a site you are visiting is a suspected attack site or forgery. You can also select to be warned when a site tries to install add-ons. Other settings on this tab let you choose to remember passwords you enter for sites (so you don't have to type them every time you visit) or choose to keep a master password.

- **Advanced**—Several tabs within the Advanced tab include many features that you probably won't use every day. General features let you set accessibility features and browsing features. The Network tab lets you set up special network connections to use with Firefox (such as proxy settings) or configure offline storage cache. From the Update tab you can automatically check for Firefox updates. On the Encryption tab, you can choose the security protocols (SSL and TLS) and personal certificates to use when a site requests that information.

### Adding add-ons and plug-ins

Add-ons extend the features in Firefox to personalize how you use your browser. Dozens of add-ons are available to help you manage and search your Web content more efficiently, handle downloads, work with news feeds, and interact with social networks. Plug-ins are special applications you can add to handle data that Firefox can't work with by default (such as special image or audio files).

To find out about available add-ons and plug-ins, select Tools ➪ Add-ons from the Firefox window to see the Add-ons pop-up window. Figure 6-11 shows an example of that window.

**FIGURE 6-11**

Select add-ons to Firefox to manage content in different ways.

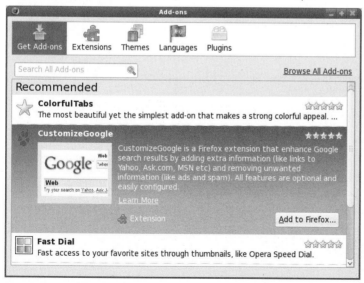

Select the link to see recommended add-ons from the Firefox Add-ons page. You can see reviews of each add-on, ratings, how often they are downloaded, and screenshots of how the add-on appears. Here are a few examples of popular Firefox add-ons:

- **FoxyTunes**—With FoxyTunes (`www.foxytunes.com`) installed, you can use any of more than a dozen music players to play music as you browse the Web. It also helps you find covers, videos, lyrics, biographies, and other information about the artists you play.

- **FireGestures**—With FireGestures, you can map different mouse gestures to launch scripts or perform actions that you set.

- **ColorfulTabs**—The ColorfulTabs add-on lets you set your Firefox browser tabs to different colors. Colors can be set in a variety of ways (such as at random or by domain name). Change settings from the Extensions tab on the Add-on window.

After you have installed an add-on, you need to restart Firefox for it to take effect. In some cases, a change to an extension's option will also require you to restart Firefox. If you want to uninstall an add-on or change an add-on's options, select Tools ➪ Extensions from Firefox. Select the Extensions tab. This displays the add-ons you have installed and offers buttons to disable, uninstall, or change preferences.

Plug-ins are applications you add to your browser to play particular types of content. Usually you do this because either Firefox doesn't include the feature you want or you want to use a different application to play the content (such as your own music player).

Many plug-ins are already packaged by their creators or by third-party repositories for popular Linux distributions. For example, some multimedia plug-ins for Fedora are available from the rpmfusion.org repository, while Ubuntu and Debian might have the same plug-ins packaged in repositories labeled as non-free. The Firefox Plug-ins sidebar describes some popular plug-ins for Firefox.

## Firefox Plug-ins

Many plug-ins are available for use in most Linux versions of Firefox. To see a list of plug-ins that are already installed in your browser, enter **about:plugins** in the address box where you normally type URLs.

Go to `https://addons.mozilla.org/` and select Plugins to view and download the most popular plug-ins, and look at `plugindoc.mozdev.org/linux.html` for links to other plug-ins. Some of the most popular plug-ins are

- **Adobe Reader Plug-in** (`www.adobe.com/support/downloads`)—Displays files in Adobe Systems' PDF (Portable Document Format) format.

- **DjVuLibre Plug-in** (`djvu.sourceforge.net`)—Displays images in DjVu image compression technology. This plug-in is from AT&T.

- **Real Player** (`www.real.com/linux`)—Plays RealAudio and Video content. Real Networks and its open source Helix project have recently made RealVideo codecs available to the Linux community.

- **Adobe Flash Plug-in** (`www.adobe.com/downloads`)—Flash is the most popular player for playing video on the Web. Some Linux systems come with an open source Flash player installed, but most agree that the Adobe version works better so far.

- **CrossOver Plugin** (`www.codeweavers.com`)—Linux plug-ins are not yet available for some of the more interesting and popular plug-ins. QuickTime movies, Shockwave Director multimedia content, and various Microsoft movie, file, and data formats simply will not play natively in Firefox. Using software built on WINE for Linux on x86-based processors, CodeWeavers created the CrossOver Plugin. Although no longer offered as a separate product (you must buy the entire Crossover Linux product for $39.95 US), the CrossOver Plugin lets you play some content that you could not otherwise use in Linux. (Download a demo from `www.codeweavers.com/site/products/download_trial` and choose CrossOver Linux.)

  After you install the CrossOver Plugin, you see a nice Plugin Setup window that lets you selectively install plug-ins for QuickTime, Windows Media Player, Shockwave, Flash, iTunes, and Lotus Notes, as well as Microsoft Word, Excel, and PowerPoint viewers. (Support for later versions of these content formats may be available by the time you read this.) You can also install other multimedia plug-ins, as well as a variety of fonts to use with those plug-ins.

### Changing Firefox themes

Several themes are available for changing the look and feel of your Firefox window. From the Firefox Add-ons site (`http://addons.mozilla.org`), select Themes. When you download a theme for Firefox, it knows that it is a Firefox theme and, on the download window, it gives you the option to install the theme by clicking the Use Theme button.

To change a theme later or get more Themes, select Tools ➪ Add-ons and select the Themes tab. After you have installed a new theme, you need to restart Firefox for the new theme to take effect.

## Securing Firefox

Security has been one of the strongest reasons for people to switch to Firefox. By prohibiting the most unsafe types of content from playing in Firefox, and by warning you of potentially dangerous or annoying content before displaying it, Firefox has become the Web browser of choice for many security-conscious people. Here are some ways that Firefox helps make your Web browsing more secure:

- **ActiveX**—Because of major security flaws found in ActiveX, Firefox will simply not play ActiveX content. Although there have been projects to try to provide ActiveX support in Mozilla, none of those projects are being actively developed.

- **Pop-ups**—When pop-up windows are encountered as you browse with Firefox, a message (by default) tells you that "Firefox prevented this site from opening a popup window." By clicking on that message, you have an opportunity to allow all pop-ups from that site, just allow the requested pop-up, or edit your pop-up settings.

- **Privacy preferences**—From the Privacy window in Firefox (select Edit ➪ Preferences, and then click the Privacy button), you can clear stored private information from your browser in a single click. This is a particularly good feature if you have just used a computer that is not yours to browse the Web. You can select to individually clear your History, information saved in forms you might have filled in, any passwords saved by the browser, history of what you have downloaded, cookies, and cached files. As an alternative, you can click Clear Now and clear all that information from Firefox in one click.

- **Web Forgeries**—The latest Firefox release helps you block forged Web sites by displaying a "Suspected Web Forgery" pop-up message when it encounters a page that has been reported as forged. You can choose to not display the page or ignore the warning. If you suspect a forged page that doesn't display that message, select Help ➪ Report Web Forgery to try to add the page to the Google Web Forgery list.

- **Certificates**—In Firefox, you can install and manage certificates that can be used for validating a Web site and safely performing encryption of communications to that site. Using the Preferences window (select Edit ➪ Preferences and then click the Advanced button), you can manage certificates under the Encryption tab, Certificates heading. Select View Certificates to display a window that lets you import new certificates or view certificates that are already installed. Firefox will check that certificates you encounter are valid (and warn you if they are not).

Along with all the excellent security features built into Firefox, it's important that you incorporate good security practices in your Web browsing. Here are some general tips for safe Web browsing:

- Download and install software only from sites that are secure and known to you to be safe.

- For any online transactions, make sure you are communicating with a secure site (look for the https protocol in the location box and closed lock icon in the lower-right corner of the screen).

- Be careful about being redirected to another Web site when doing a financial transaction. An IP address in the site's address or misspellings on a screen where you enter credit card information are warning signs that you have been directed to an untrustworthy site.

Because new exploits are being discovered all the time, it's important that you keep your Web browser up-to-date. That means that, at the least, you need to get updates of Firefox from the Linux distribution you are using or directly from Mozilla.org. To keep up on the latest security news and information about Firefox and other Mozilla products, refer to the Mozilla Security Center (www.mozilla.org/security/).

## Tips for using Firefox

There are so many nice features in Firefox, it's hard to cover all of them. Just to point you toward a few more fun and useful features, here are some tips for using Firefox:

- **Add smart keywords**—Many Web sites include their own search boxes to enable you to look for information on their sites. With Firefox, you can assign a smart keyword to any search box on the Web, and then use that keyword from the location bar in the Firefox browser to search that site.

  For example, go to the Linux Documentation Project site (`http://tldp.org`). Right-click in the Search/Resources search box. Select Add a Keyword for this Search from the menu that appears. Add a name (Linux Documentation) and a keyword (tldp) and select Add to add the keyword to your Bookmarks.

  After you have added the keyword, you can use it by simply entering the keyword and one or more search terms to the Firefox location box (on the navigation toolbar). For example, I entered `tldp Lego Mindstorms` and came up with a list of HOWTOs for using Lego Mindstorms in Linux.

- **Check config**—Firefox has hundreds of configuration preferences available to set as you please. You can see those options by typing **about:config** into the location box. Casual users should look at these settings, but not change them (because you can do irreparable harm to Firefox if you make a wrong selection).

  If you feel secure about making changes, for true/false options, you can click on the preference name to toggle it between the two values. For other preferences, click the preference to enter a value into a pop-up box. Although many of these values can be changed through the Preferences menu (Edit ➪ Preferences), some technical people prefer to look at settings in a list like the one shown on the about:config page.

- **Multiple home pages**—Instead of just having one home page, you can have a whole set of home pages. When you start Firefox, a separate tab opens in the Firefox window for each address you identify in your home page list. To do this, create multiple tabs (File ➪ New Tab) and enter the address for each page you want in your list of home pages. Then select Edit ➪ Preferences ➪ Main and click the Use Current Pages button. The next time you open Firefox, it will start with the selected tabs open to the home pages you chose. (Clicking the Home icon opens new tabs for all the home pages.) You can also manually enter multiple URLs into the text box. Separate each URL with a pipe character (|).

## Using Firefox controls

If you have used a Web browser before, the Firefox controls are probably as you might expect: location box, forward and back buttons, file and edit menus, and so on. There are a few controls with Firefox, however, that you might not be used to seeing:

- **Display Sidebar**—Select View ➪ Sidebar to toggle the bookmarks or history sidebars on and off. The sidebar is a left column on your Firefox screen for allowing quick access to Bookmarks and History. Use the Bookmarks tab to add your own bookmarks and the History tab to return to pages on your history list.

- **Send Web Content**—You can send an e-mail containing the URL of the current Web page (File ➪ Send Link) to selected recipients. Firefox will load your default e-mail client such as Thunderbird or Evolution to send the e-mail message.

- **Search the Internet**—You can search the Internet for a keyword phrase in many different ways. Choose Tools ➪ Web Search to start a search. Selecting this menu choice moves the mouse cursor to the search box, where you can enter search terms. Click the icon on the left side of this box to choose search engines such as Google, Yahoo!, and others. Select Manage Search Engines to select other search sites to use. Press the Enter key to search.

- **View Web Page Info**—You can view information about the location of a Web page, the location of each of its components, the dates the page was modified, and other information by clicking the right mouse button over a Web page and then choosing View Page Info. In the Page Info window, click the Links tab to see links on that page to other content on the Web. Click the Security tab to see information about verification and encryption used on the page.

## Improving Firefox browsing

Not every Web site you visit with Firefox is going to play well. Some sites don't follow standards: They use unreadable fonts, choose colors that make it hard to see, or demand that you use a particular type of browser to view their content. To improve your browsing experience, there are several things you can add to Firefox.

## Note
If you encounter a problem with Firefox that you can't overcome, I recommend that you refer to the Mozilla Bugzilla database (www.mozilla.org/bugs/). This site is an excellent place to search for bugs others have found (many times you can get workarounds to your problems) or enter a bug report yourself. ■

### Adding a preferences toolbar

Did you ever run into a Web page that required you to use a particular type or version of a browser or had fonts or colors that made a page unreadable? The Firefox preferences toolbar called PrefBar4 enables you to try to spoof Web sites into thinking you are running a different browser. It also lets you choose settings that might improve colors, fonts, and other attributes on difficult-to-read pages.

You can install the neat little toolbar from the Mozdev.org site (http://prefbar.mozdev.org). Click the Install link, and after it is installed, restart Firefox.

The default set of buttons lets you do the following:

- **Colors**—Change between default colors and those set on the Web page.
- **Images**—Toggle between having images loaded or not loaded on pages you display.

- **JavaScript**—Allow or disallow JavaScript content to play in Firefox.
- **Flash**—Allow or refuse all embedded Flash content on the current page.
- **Clear Cache**—Delete all cached content from memory and disk.
- **Save Page**—Save the current page and, optionally, its supporting images and other content, to your hard disk.
- **Real UA**—Choose to have your browser identified as itself (current version of Firefox) or any of the following: Mozilla 1.0 (in Windows 98), Netscape Navigator 4.7 (in Macintosh), Netscape 6.2 (in Linux), Internet Explorer 5.0 (in Macintosh), Internet Explorer 6.0 (in Windows XP), or Lynx (a text-based Web browser).

The user agent (UA) setting is very useful when dealing with Web sites that require Internet Explorer (IE) (and usually IE on Windows, not Mac OS). The IE 6.0 WinXP setting is good enough to allow Firefox to log on to the Microsoft Exchange webmail service, which is usually set up to require IE. If you want to run Linux in a mostly Windows organization, install the Preferences toolbar.

Click the Customize button to add other buttons to the toolbar. You can add buttons to clear your History or Location bar entries. You can even add a Popups button to prevent a page from opening a pop-up window from Firefox.

Many of the preferences take effect immediately. Others may require you to restart Firefox.

## Doing cool things with Firefox

Some neat bells and whistles are built into Firefox that can make your browsing more pleasant. The following sections explore a few of those features.

### Blocking pop-ups

You can block annoying pop-up windows using the Firefox Preferences window. Here's how:

1. Click Edit ➪ Preferences. The Preferences window appears.
2. Click Block Pop-up Windows under the Content category.

By blocking all pop-ups you might keep some Web sites from working properly. Click the Exceptions button to allow pop-ups on certain sites that you choose.

### Using tabbed browsing

If you switch back and forth among several Web pages, you can use the tabbed browsing feature to hold multiple pages in your browser window at once. You can open a new tab for browsing by simply selecting File ➪ New Tab or by pressing Ctrl+T. You can open any link into a new tab by right-clicking over the link and then selecting Open Link in New Tab.

You can also tailor how tabbed browsing works from a Web page or from the Location box. Here's how:

1. Click Edit ⇨ Preferences. The Preferences window appears.
2. Click the Tabs tab.
3. Click the tab-related options you desire.

A tab for each tabbed page appears at the top of the Firefox pane. To close a tab, create a new tab, bookmark a group of tabs, or reload tabs, right-click one of the tabs and choose the function you want from the drop-down menu.

One of the easiest ways to open a link in a tab is to right-click over a link on an HTML page. Select the Open Link in New Tab choice.

### Resizing Web page text

There is a nice keyboard shortcut that lets you quickly resize the text on most Web pages in Firefox. Hold the Ctrl key and press the plus (+) or minus (–) keys. In most cases, the text on the Web page gets larger or smaller, respectively. That page with the insanely small type font is suddenly readable.

There are many more things you can do with Firefox than I have covered in this chapter. If you have questions about Firefox features or you just want to dig up some more cool stuff about Firefox, I recommend checking out the MozillaZine forum for Firefox support:

```
http://forums.mozillazine.org/viewforum.php?f=38
```

This page has a sticky link to Miscellaneous Firefox Tips and a good FAQ post.

# Using Text-Based Web Browsers

If you become a Linux administrator or power user, over time you will inevitably find yourself working on a computer from a remote login or where there is no desktop GUI available. At some point while you are in that state, you will want to check an HTML file or a Web page. To solve the problem, many Linux distributions include several text-based Web browsers.

With text-based Web browsers, any HTML file available from the Web, your local file system, or a computer where you're remotely logged in can be accessed from your shell. There's no need to fire up your GUI or read pages of HTML markup if you just want to take a peek at the contents of a Web page. In addition to enabling you to call up Web pages, move around with those pages, and follow links to other pages, some browsers even display graphics right in a Terminal window!

Which browser you use is a matter of which you are more comfortable with. Browsers that are available include

- **links**—You can open a file or a URL, and then traverse links from the pages you open. Use search forward (/*string*) and back (?*string*) features to find text strings in pages. Use up and down arrows to go forward and back among links. Press Enter to go to the current link. Use the right and left arrow keys to go forward and back among pages you have visited. Press Esc to see a menu bar of features from which to select.

- **lynx**—The lynx browser has a good set of help files (press the ? key). Step through pages using the spacebar. Although lynx can display pages containing frames, it cannot display them in the intended positioning. Use the arrow keys to display the selected link (right arrow), go back to the previous document (left arrow), select the previous link (up arrow), and select the next link (down arrow).

- **w3m**—This browser can display HTML pages containing text, links, frames, and tables. It even tries to display images (although it is a bit shaky). Both English and Japanese help files are available (press H with w3m running). You can also use w3m to page through an HTML document in plain text (for example, `cat index.html | w3m -T text/html`). Use the Page Up and Page Down keys to page through a document. Press Enter on a link to go to that link. Press B to go back to the previous link. Search forward and back for text using the / (slash) and ? (question mark) keys, respectively.

The w3m seems the most sophisticated of these browsers. It features a nice default font selection and seems to handle frames neatly; its use of colors also makes it easy to use. The links browser lets you use the mouse to cut and paste text.

You can start any of these text-based Web browsers by entering a filename, or if you have an active connection to the network, a Web address as an option to the command name. For example, to read the w3m documentation (which is in HTML format) with a w3m browser, type the following from a Terminal window or other shell interface:

```
$ w3m /usr/share/doc/w3m*/MANUAL.html
```

An HTML version of the W3M Manual is displayed. Or you can give w3m a URL to a Web page, such as the following:

```
$ w3m www.handsonhistory.com
```

After a page is open, you can begin viewing the page and moving around to links included in it. Start by using the arrow keys to move around and select links. Use the Page Up and Page Down keys to page through text.

# Summary

A number of high-quality applications are available to fulfill your needs for a Web browser and e-mail client in Linux. Most Web browsers are based on the Mozilla Gecko engine (which came originally from Netscape Navigator). Firefox has become the main Linux Web browser. The combination of security, ease-of-use features, and extensions has made Firefox an extremely popular Web browser for both Linux and Windows users.

Graphical and text-based e-mail clients include Evolution, SeaMonkey Mail, and KMail. Thunderbird has become the next generation e-mail client to replace SeaMonkey Mail. Text-based mail clients include mail, mutt, and pine.

# Gaming with Linux

**E**very type of PC gaming is available now with Linux. Whether you are looking for a solitaire game to fill time or a full-blown online 3D gaming experience, you will have dozens (or hundreds) of choices on the Linux desktop.

Although some companies, such as ID Software (*Quake*) and Epic Games (*Unreal Tournament*) have done work to port their games to Linux, others have used third-party developers (such as RuneSoft) to port commercial games to Linux. Independent games developers, such as Frictional Games (http://frictionalgames.com) and Introversion Software (www.introversion.co.uk) are now producing high-quality gaming experiences in Linux. Linux clients for commercial online gaming, such as EVE Online (www.eve-online.com), are also available.

This chapter provides an overview of the state of Linux gaming today. It describes games that were created specifically to run in Linux, and explains how to find commercial games that run in Linux (either with a Linux version or running a Windows version along with Windows compatibility software, such as Cedega).

## Jumping into Linux Gaming

If you have a Linux system running and want to get started playing a game right now, here are some suggestions:

- **Check the Games menu**—Most Linux desktop systems come with a bunch of games already installed. If you are running either a GNOME or KDE desktop in Linux, select Applications ➪ Games from the panel. You should be able to select a variety of arcade, card, board, tactics, and other games to keep you busy for a while. (KDE and GNOME games are described later in this chapter.)

- **Games packaged for your Linux distribution**—Many of the most popular open source games are packaged to run on your Linux distribution. In Fedora, open the Add/Remove Software (PackageKit) window and select Games to see a list of more than 200 games you can download and play. In Ubuntu, the Add/Remove Applications window shows more than 300 games on the Games menu to download and play.

- **Other open source games**—If the open source game you want is not packaged for your distribution, try going to the game's project site to get the game. There are Internet sites that contain lists of games, and links to each game's site. The Wikipedia Linux Gaming page (en.wikipedia.org/wiki/Linux_gaming) and the Linux Game Tome (http://happypenguin.org) are good places to start.

- **Commercial Windows games**—The latest commercial computer games are not all ported to run in Linux. Boxed commercial games for Linux include *Unreal Tournament 2003* and *2004*, as well as about 50 first-rate commercial games that have been ported to run in Linux. Using Cedega software from Transgaming.com, you can get hundreds more commercial Windows games to run. Commercial Linux games are described in more depth later in this chapter.

Before you can play some of the more demanding 3D games, you need to check that your hardware can handle the games. Some games requiring support for 3D hardware acceleration need more RAM, faster processors, and particular video cards to run in Linux. Issues for setting up a gaming machine in Linux are described later in this chapter.

Here is a quick list of games that are available on Fedora and many other Linux distributions that you can try out. I've listed them in the order of simple-and-addicting to more-complex-and-addicting:

- **Frozen Bubble** (www.frozen-bubble.org)—The Frozen Bubble game is often mentioned as the most addictive Linux game. Shoot frozen bubbles and colored groups of bubbles as they slowly descend on you. Clear bubbles in sets of three or more until they are all gone (or come down and freeze you). The game can be played with multiple players. (Install the frozen-bubble package and select it from the Games menu.)

- **Gweled** (http://sebdelestaing.free.fr/gweled)—In this clone of the popular *Bejeweled* game, exchange two jewels on the board to match three or more jewels (vertically or horizontally). (Install the gweled package and select Gweled from the Games menu.)

- **WarZone 2100** (www.warzone2100.strategyplanet.gamespy.com)—This 1999 real-time strategy game was released in open source in 2004. Build a base from which you design and build vehicles and weapons, set up structures, and research new technologies to fight a global war. (Install the warzone2100 package and select Warzone 2100 from the Games menu.)

- **Quake 3 Arena** (`ftp.idsoftware.com/idstuff/`)—Several first-person shooter games in the *Quake* series are available for download from id Software. In Fedora, install the quake3 package and select Quake 3 Arena. The application that starts up lets you download a demo version of the Quake3 datafiles, which can be freely downloaded. Read and accept the licensing terms to download the data files and begin playing the *Quake 3 Arena* demo.

- **Vega Strike** (`http://vegastrike.sourceforge.net`)—Explore the universe in the 3D action, space simulation game. Accept missions to transport cargo, become a bounty hunter, or patrol space. In this 3D environment you can chat with bartenders or watch news broadcasts to keep up with events in the universe. (To play this game in Fedora, install the vegastrike package and select Vega Strike from the Games menu.)

Figure 7-1 shows small screen shots of the games just described.

**FIGURE 7-1**

Games to install from the Fedora Repository include *Frozen Bubble, Gweled, Warzone 2100, Quake 3 Arena,* and *Vega Strike*.

Frozen Bubble  Gweled  WarZone 2100  Quake 3 Arena  Vega Strike

## Note
**Despite gains in gaming support in Linux, a lot of popular Windows games still don't run in Linux. For that reason, some PC gamers maintain a separate Windows partition on their computers so they can boot to Windows to play particular games.** ■

# Overview of Linux Gaming

Linux is a wonderful platform for both running and, perhaps more especially, developing computer games. Casual gamers have no shortage of fun games to try. Hardcore gamers face a few more challenges with Linux. Here are some of the opportunities and challenges as you approach Linux gaming:

- **3D acceleration**—If you are a more serious gamer, you will almost certainly want a video card that provides hardware acceleration. Open source drivers for some video cards are available from the DRI project. Video cards from NVIDIA and ATI often have binary-only drivers available. Fun open source games, such as *PenguinPlanet Racer, BZFlag,* and others that recommend hardware acceleration, will run much better if you get one of these supported cards and drivers. Some commercial games will not run at all without 3D acceleration support.

- **Gaming servers**—Many commercial computer games that don't have Linux clients available do have Linux game servers associated with them. So Linux is a great operating system for hosting a LAN party or setting up an Internet gaming server.

- **Linux gaming development**—Some of the most advanced tools and application programming interfaces (APIs) for developing computer games run on Linux systems. If you are interested in developing your own games to run in Linux, check out the OpenGL (http://opengl.org) and Simple Directmedia Layer (www.libsdl.org) projects. Blender (www.blender.org) is an open source project for doing animations, 3D models, post-production, and rendering that is being used today in commercial games and movie animations.

Although the development tools available for developing open source games are awesome, a primary goal of this book is to get you up and using Linux as quickly as possible. To that end, I want to give you details on how to get hold of games that already run well in Linux and then show you how to get games working in Linux that are intended for other platforms (particularly Windows and some classic gaming consoles).

# Basic Linux Gaming Information

Many Web sites provide information about the latest games available for Linux, as well as links to download sites. Here are several to get you started:

- **TransGaming Technologies** (www.transgaming.com)—This company's mission is to bring games from other platforms to Linux. It is the provider of Cedega, formerly known as WineX, a powerful tool that enables you to play hundreds of PC games on your Linux system.

- **The Linux Game Tome** (http://happypenguin.org)—Features a database of descriptions and reviews of tons of games that run in Linux. You can do keyword searches for games listed at this site. It also has links to sites where you can get the different games and to other gaming sites.

- **Linuxgames.com** (http://linuxgames.com)—This site can give you some very good insight into the state of Linux gaming. There are links to HOWTOs and Frequently Asked Questions (FAQs), as well as forums for discussing Linux games. There are also links to Web sites that have information about specific games.

- **id Software** (www.idsoftware.com)—Go to the id Software site for information on Linux versions for *Quake* and *Return to Castle Wolfenstein.*

- **Linuxgamepublishing.com** (www.linuxgamepublishing.com)—Linuxgamepublishing.com aims to be a one-stop shopping portal for native Linux games, as well as for ports of games from other platforms. At the time of this writing, it offers about a dozen games. To purchase games from this site, you must create a user account.

- **Loki Entertainment Software** (www.lokigames.com)—Loki provided ports of best-selling games to Linux but went out of business in 2001. Its products included Linux versions of *Civilization: Call to Power, Myth II: Soulblighter, SimCity 3000, Railroad Tycoon II,* and *Quake III Arena.* The Loki Demo Launcher is still available to see demo versions of these games, and some boxed sets are available for very little money. The Loki site also offers a list of commercial resellers for its games, which may or may not still carry those games.

- **Tux Games** (www.tuxgames.com)—The Tux Games Web site is dedicated to the sale of Linux games. In addition to offering Linux gaming news and products, the site lists its top-selling games and includes notices of games that are soon to be released.

- **Wikipedia** (http://en.wikipedia.org)—In the past few years, Wikipedia has become a wonderful resource for information on both commercial and open source games available for Linux. From the Wikipedia Linux games list (http://en.wikipedia.org/wiki/Linux_games) you can find links to free Linux games, Commercial Linux Games, and Professionally Developed Linux Games.

- **Linux Gamers' FAQ** (http://icculus.org/lgfaq)—Contains a wealth of information about free and commercial Linux games. It lists gaming companies that have ported their games to Linux, tells where to get Linux games, and answers queries related to common Linux gaming problems. For a list of Linux games without additional information, see http://icculus.org/lgfaq/gamelist.php.

Although the sites just mentioned provide excellent information on Linux gaming, not all open source games have been packaged specifically for every version of Linux. Even though you can always nudge a game into working on your particular Linux distribution, it's probably easiest to start with games that are ready to run. The following list provides information about where to find out about games packaged for different Linux distributions:

- **Fedora**—Much of the recent increase in Fedora games has come from the Fedora Games SIG (Special Interest Group). You can check out that SIG's activities for information on other games of interest that have not made it into Fedora at http://fedoraproject.org/wiki/SIGs/Games.

- **Debian**—Debian games resources are listed at the Debian wiki. Visit the games section at http://wiki.debian.org/Game.

- **Ubuntu**—The Games Community Ubuntu Documentation page offers some good information about available games and gaming initiatives related to Ubuntu (http://help.ubuntu.com/community/Games).

- **Slackware**—Though GNOME and KDE games run fine in Slackware, not a lot of gaming resources are particular to Slackware. However, because Slackware contains a solid set of libraries and development tools, many open source games will compile and run in Slackware if you are willing to get the source code for the game you want and build it yourself.

# Choosing Gaming Hardware for Linux

In general, you need more RAM, a stronger processor, and a bit more disk space for gaming than you need for most Linux applications. Some of the most demanding commercial PC games will run best with at least 1GB of RAM and a 1 GHz processor. However, the video card is usually the most important piece of hardware.

Because 3D games place extraordinary demands on your video hardware, choosing a good video card and configuring it properly is one of the keys to ensuring a good gaming experience. For advanced gaming, you need to go beyond what an old 64-bit card can do for you.

### Binary-only video card drivers

Most serious Linux gamers have either an NVIDIA or ATI card, so that's the short answer to starting out with serious Linux gaming. Although open source drivers are available from most NVIDIA and ATI cards, those drivers do not support 3D hardware acceleration. Though that's fine for most desktop applications, for gaming you want to get the binary-only drivers for those cards from the following locations:

- **NVIDIA**—To get NVIDIA drivers that run in Linux, go to the Unix Drivers Portal Page (`www.nvidia.com/object/unix.html`).

- **ATI**—To find Linux drivers for ATI video cards, visit the ATI support Knowledge Base page that describes Linux drivers at `http://ati.amd.com/` and click on the Knowledgebase tab.

## Note

The rpm.livna.org site has greatly simplified the process of installing ATI and NVIDIA drivers for Fedora. Refer to the Livna Switcher page (`http://rpm.livna.org/`) to learn how to install RPM packages containing the ATI or NVIDIA drivers you need. (Livna is going to a new site, `RPMfusion.org`. Try `RPMfusion.org` if the drivers you need are no longer at the Livna site.) ∎

When you go to get a binary-only video driver, be sure that you know not only the video card model you are using, but also the name and version of your X server. Type `X -version` to see the version. (XFree86 used to be the most popular, but most Linux distributions now use X.Org.) Resulting video driver modules may be specific to the Linux kernel you are running. So, know that if you upgrade your kernel, you might need to reinstall your video driver as well.

## Caution

If you load a binary-only driver, it does what is referred to as "tainting the kernel." As a result, you won't be able to get support if you run into problems (at least from `kernel.org`) because, lacking the source code, it is hard to debug driver-related problems. Also, binary-only drivers are known to cause obscure problems because they get out of sync with kernel code changes. Similarly, binary-only drivers for some Linux systems aren't updated as frequently as the kernel. Although many people, including myself, use binary-only drivers in special cases, they do have shortcomings that you should be aware of. ∎

## Open source video drivers

If you want to use open source drivers for 3D accelerated gaming, whether you are running the games using Cedega or natively in Linux, look for cards that have drivers that support OpenGL. The DRI project is one initiative that is creating OpenGL driver implementations. Information about the DRI project can be found on its site (http://dri.freedesktop.org/wiki/).

- **ATI Technologies**—You don't have to use binary-only drivers to get 3D acceleration for some ATI video cards with open source drivers. Chip sets from ATI Technologies that support DRI include the Mach64 (Rage Pro), Radeon SDR/DDR, Radeon 7000-9800, Radeon X300-X1250, Radeon X1200-X1950 and Rage 128 (Standard, Pro, Mobility). Cards based on these chip sets include All-in-Wonder 128, Rage Fury, Rage Magnum, Xpert 99, Xpert 128, and Xpert 2000. (ATI is now a subsidiary of AMD.)

- **3dfx**—If you can find a used unit on eBay (3dfx is no longer in business), several 3dfx cards support DRI. In particular, the Voodoo (3, 4, and 5) and Banshee chip sets have drivers that support DRI. Voodoo 5 cards support 16 and 24 bpp. Scan Line Interleaving (SLI), where two or more 3D processors work in parallel (to result in higher frame rates), is not supported for 3dfx cards.

- **3Dlabs**—Graphics cards containing the MX/Gamma chip set from 3Dlabs have drivers available that support DRI in Linux.

- **Intel**—Supported video chip sets from Intel include the i810 (e, e2, and -dc100), i815, i815e, i830G, i845G, i852/855, i865G, i915, i945, i965, G3x, and G4x.

- **Matrox**—The Matrox chip sets that have drivers that support DRI include the G200, G400, G450, and G550. Cards that use these chips include the Millennium G450, Millennium G400, Millennium G200, and Mystique G200.

To find out whether DRI is working on your current video card, type the following:

```
$ glxinfo | grep rendering
direct rendering: Yes
```

This example shows that direct rendering is enabled. If it were not supported, the output would say No instead of Yes. Although DRI can be important, many games implement OpenGL rendering, which is a feature supported by both NVIDIA and ATI video cards. To enable rendering for cards that support it, add the following line to your /etc/X11/xorg.conf file:

```
Load    "render"
```

# Running Open Source Linux Games

A handful of games are delivered with most desktop-oriented Linux distributions. The GNOME and KDE environments, which are available with most desktop Linux distributions (described in Chapter 3), each has a set of games associated with it.

# GNOME games

More than a dozen basic games are delivered with the GNOME desktop. If you are just looking for a game to pass a bit of time, one of the GNOME games will probably work fine for you.

## Coming from Windows

**GNOME games consist of some old card games and a bunch of games that look suspiciously like those you would find on Windows systems. If you are afraid of losing your favorite desktop diversion (such as *Solitaire*, *FreeCell*, and *Minesweeper*) when you leave Windows, have no fear. You can find many of them under GNOME games. ■**

Default installations of Ubuntu, Fedora, and other Linux systems include the gnome-games package. Table 7-1 lists the games included in the gnome-games package. See the GNOME Games site (`http://live.gnome.org/GnomeGames/`) for further details.

**TABLE 7-1**

### GNOME Games

| Game | Description |
|------|-------------|
| *AisleRiot Solitaire* | You can select from among 28 different solitaire card games. |
| *Blackjack* | Card game where you try to get closer to 21 (without going over) than the dealer. |
| *Chess* | Chess game that can be played in 2D or 3D against the computer. |
| *Five or More* | Clone of the color lines game (*glines*). |
| *Four-In-A-Row* | Drop balls to beat the game at making four in a row. |
| *FreeCell Solitaire* | A popular solitaire card game. |
| *GnomeFallingBlocks / Gnometris* | GNOME *Tetris*-like game. |
| *Iagno* | Disk flipping game, similar to *reversi*. |
| *Klotski* | Move pieces around to allow one piece to escape. |
| *Mahjongg* | Classic Asian tile game. |
| *Mines* | *Minesweeper* clone. Click on safe spaces and avoid the bombs. |
| *Nibbles* | Steer a worm around the screen while avoiding walls. |
| *Robots* | Later version of *Gnobots*, which includes movable junk heaps. |
| *Same GNOME* | Eliminate clusters of balls for high score. |
| *Sodoku* | A Japanese logic puzzle where you fill in numbers instead of words. |

| Game | Description |
| --- | --- |
| *Tali* | Yahtzee clone. Roll dice to fill in categories. |
| *Tetravex* | A clone of *Tetravex* from the GNOME project. Move blocks so that numbers on each side align. |

## KDE games

A bunch of games are available for the KDE desktop environment. (In Fedora, Ubuntu, and other versions of Linux that include KDE, these games come in the kdegames package.) Table 7-2 contains a list of KDE games. A different set of games may be included with your Linux distribution.

**TABLE 7-2**

### Games for the KDE Desktop

| Game | Description |
| --- | --- |
| **Arcade Games** | |
| *KAsteroids* | Destroy asteroids in the classic arcade game. |
| *KBounce* | Add walls to block in bouncing balls. |
| *KFoul Eggs* | Squish eggs in this *Tetris*-like game. |
| *Klickety* | Click color groups to erase blocks in this adaptation of *Clickomania*. |
| *Kolf* | Play a round of virtual golf. |
| *KSirtet* | *Tetris* clone. Try to fill in lines of blocks as they drop down. |
| *KSmileTris* | *Tetris* with smiley faces. |
| *KSnakeRace* | Race your snake around a maze. |
| *KSpaceDuel* | Fire at another spaceship as you spin around a planet. |
| **Board Games** | |
| *Atlantik* | Play this Monopoly-like game against other players on the network. |
| *KBackgammon* | Online version of backgammon. |
| *KBlackBox* | Find hidden balls by shooting rays. |
| *Kenolaba* | Move game pieces to push opponents' pieces off the board. |
| *KMahjongg* | Classic oriental tile game. |

*continued*

**TABLE 7-2**    *(continued)*

| Game | Description |
| --- | --- |
| *KReversi* | Flip game pieces to outmaneuver the opponent. |
| *Shisen-Sho* | Tile game similar to Mahjongg. |
| *Kwin4* | Drop colored pieces to get four pieces in a row. |
| **Card Games** | |
| *KPoker* | Video poker clone. Play five-card draw, choosing which cards to hold and which to throw. |
| *Lieutenant Skat* | Play the card game Skat. |
| *Patience* | Choose from nine different solitaire card games. |
| **Tactics and Strategy** | |
| *KAtomic* | Move pieces to create different chemical compounds. |
| *KGoldrunner* | Strategy puzzle game. |
| *KJumping Cube* | Click squares to increase numbers and take over adjacent squares. |
| *KMines* | *Minesweeper* clone. Click safe spaces and avoid the bombs. |
| *Kolor Lines* | Move marbles to form five-in-a-row and score points. |
| *Konquest* | Expand your interstellar empire in this multiplayer game. |
| *Potato Guy* | Build your own potatohead face. |
| *SameGame* | Erase game pieces to score points. |

The games on the KDE menu range from amusing to quite challenging. If you are used to playing games in Windows, *KMines* and *Patience* will seem like old favorites. *KAsteroids* and *KPoker* are good for the mindless game category.

## Games in Fedora

Fedora offers an extensive set of games, resulting from a very active Games special interest group (http://fedoraproject.org/wiki/SIGs/Games). Table 7-3 lists some of the games that are included in the Fedora software repository.

**TABLE 7-3**

## Games from Fedora

| Game | Description |
| --- | --- |
| *Beneath a Steel Sky* (beneath-a-steel-sky) | A popular commercial science fiction adventure game from the early 1990s, set in a repulsive, futuristic city. |
| *BSD Games* (bsd-games) | Text-based card games and adventure games dating back to early UNIX systems of the 1970s and run from the shell. |
| *BZFlag* (bzflag) | 3D multiplayer tank battle game. |
| *Celestia* (celestia) | OpenGL real-time visual space simulation. (Available under the Other menu.) |
| *Flight Gear* (FlightGear) | Flight simulator game. |
| *FooBilliard* (foobilliard) | OpenGL billiard game. |
| *Freeciv* (freeciv) | The Freeciv multiplayer strategy game. |
| *Freedoom* (freedoom) | Data files for Doom game engines (use with prboom package, which provides an open source port of the Doom engine). |
| *Freedroid* (freedroid) | Clone of the C64 game *Paradroid*. |
| *Freedroid* RPG (freedroidrpg) | *Freedroid* theme for role-playing game with Tux as hero. |
| *GL-117* (gl-117) | Action flight simulator. |
| *Chess* (gnuchess) | The GNU chess program. Used with the xboard package to provide a graphical chess game. |
| *Lacewing* (lacewing) | Asteroid game sporting different types of ships. |
| *Lincity* (lincity-ng) | Build simulated cities. |
| *LMarbles* (lmarbles) | *Atomix* clone where you create figures out of marbles. |
| *Maelstrom* (Maelstrom) | A space combat game. |
| *Nexuiz* (nexuiz) | Death match–oriented first-person shooter (multiplayer). |
| *Overgod (overgod)* | Another *Asteroid*-like game. |
| *Powermanga* (powermanga) | Arcade 2D shoot-them-up game. |
| *PPRacer* (ppracer) | 3D racing game featuring Tux. |
| *Rogue* (rogue) | Graphical version of classic adventure game. |

*continued*

| **TABLE 7-3** | *(continued)* |
|---|---|
| **Game** | **Description** |
| *Scorched Earth* (scorched3d) | Game based loosely on the classic DOS game *Scorched Earth*. |
| *Sirius* (sirius) | Othello for GNOME. |
| *Starfighter* (starfighter) | A space arcade game. (Available by typing the `/usr/games/starfighter` command.) |
| *SuperTux* (supertux) | Jump 'n run like game similar to *Mario Bros*. |
| *TORCS* (torcs) | The Open Racing Car Simulator. |
| *The Ur-Quan Masters* (uqm) | A port of the classic game *Star Control II*. |
| *Vega Strike* (vegastrike) | Spaceflight simulator (3D OpenGL). |
| *Virus Killer* (viruskiller) | Frantic shooting game where viruses invade your computer. |
| *Worminator* (worminator) | Multilevel shoot-'em-up game. |
| *Chess* (xboard) | An X Window System graphical chessboard. |
| *X Pilot* (xpilot-ng) | Multiplayer space arcade game. (The xpilot-ng-server is also available.) |
| *xplanet* (xplanet) | Render a planetary image into an X window. (Available by typing the `xplanet` command.) |

The following sections describe two of the more interesting games that you can download directly from the Fedora repository: *Freeciv* and *Extreme Tux Racer*.

### Freeciv

*Freeciv* is a free clone of the popular *Civilization* game series from Atari. With *Freeciv*, you create a civilization that challenges competing civilizations for world dominance.

## Note

**A commercial port of *Civilization* for Linux (*Civilization: Call to Power*) was created a few years ago by Loki Games (described later in this chapter).** ∎

The commonly distributed version of *Freeciv* contains both client software (to play the game) and server software (to connect players together). You can connect to your server and try the game yourself or (with a network connection) play against up to 14 other players on the Internet. To install *Freeciv* if your Linux distribution doesn't offer it, check out the download page on the `http://freeciv.wikia.com` Web site. Choose your language, start downloading, install, and have fun.

You can start *Freeciv* from a Terminal window by typing

```
$ civclient &
```

## Note

If *Freeciv* won't start, you may be logged in as root. You must be logged in as a regular user to run the `civ` command. ∎

You can play a few games by yourself, if you like, to get to know the game before you play against others on the network. Follow these steps to start your first practice *Freeciv* game:

1. Select Start New Game. (In addition to starting the client, this action also starts `civserver`, which allows others to connect to your game, if you like.) You are asked to choose the number of players, skill level, and other game options.

2. Select 2 to play against the computer or more if you want others to join in; then click Start. A What Nation Will You Be? window appears on the client, as shown in Figure 7-2.

---

**FIGURE 7-2**

---

Choose a nation to begin *Freeciv*.

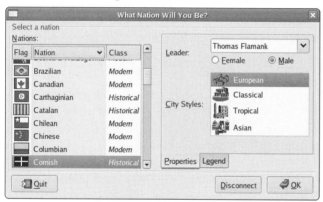

3. Choose a nation, name a leader, select your gender, choose the style of the city, and then click OK. At this point, you should be ready to begin playing *Freeciv*.

### Getting started with Freeciv

Check out the *Freeciv* window before you start playing the game:

- Click the Help button for topical information on many different subjects that will be useful to you as you play. (You can find more help at the *Freeciv* site.)

- The world (by default) is 80 × 50 squares, with 11 × 8 squares visible at a time.

- The active square contains an icon of the active unit (flashing alternatively with the square's terrain).

- Some squares contain special resources. Press and hold the middle mouse button for information on what special resources a square contains. (With a two-button mouse, hold the Ctrl key and click the right mouse button.) Try this a few times to get a feel for the land around you. This action also identifies any units on the terrain, as well as statistics for the unit.

- To see the world outside your 11 × 8 viewing area, click the scroll bars outside the map. At first, the part of the world you haven't explored yet will be black. As units are added, areas closer to those units will be visible. (Press C to return to the active part of your map.)

- An overview map is in the upper-left corner of the *Freeciv* window. As the world becomes more civilized, this provides a good way to get an overview of what is going on. Right-click a spot on the overview map to have your viewport centered there.

- The menu bar contains buttons you can use to play the game:

  - The Game menu enables you to change settings and options, view player data, view messages, and clear your log.

  - The Kingdom menu enables you to change tax rates, find cities, and start revolutions.

  - The View menu enables you to place a grid on the map or center the view.

  - The Orders menu enables you to choose the items you build and the actions you take.

  - The Reports menu enables you to display reports related to cities, military, trade, and science, as well as other special reports.

- A summary of the economy of your civilization appears under the overview map. Information includes number of people, current year, and money in the treasury.

- Ten icons below the overview information represent how money is divided among luxuries (an entertainer), science (a researcher), and taxes (a tax collector). Essentially, these icons represent how much of your resources are placed into improving each of those attributes of your community.

- When you have made all your moves for a turn, click Turn Done. Next to that, a light bulb indicates the progress of your research (increasing at each turn). A sun icon starts clear, but becomes brighter from pollution to warn of possible global warming. A government symbol indicates that you begin with a despotic government. The last icon tells you how much time is left in a turn.

- The Unit box shows information about your current unit. You begin with two Settlers units (covered wagon icons) and one Explorer (a man icon) unit. Click on a Settler, Explorer, city, or other unit to use it or learn about it.

### Building your civilization

Start building your civilization. The *Freeciv* manual makes these suggestions:

- To change the distribution of money, choose Government ➪ Tax Rates. Move the slider bars to redistribute the percentage of assets assigned to luxury, science, and taxes. Try increasing science and reducing taxes to start off.

- Change the current unit to be a settler as follows: Click the stack of units on the map and click one of the Settlers from the menu that appears.

- Begin building a city by clicking Orders ➪ Build City. When prompted, type a name for the city and click OK. The window that appears shows information about the city. It starts with one happy citizen, represented by a single icon (more citizens will appear as the game progresses).

- The Food, Prod, and Trade lines reflect the raw productivity statistics for the city. The first number shows how much is being produced; the second (in parentheses) shows the surplus above what is needed to support the units. The Gold, Luxury, and Science lines indicate the city's trade output. Granary numbers show how much food is stored and the size of the food store. The pollution level begins at zero.

- Close the city window by clicking Close.

### Exploring your world

To begin exploring, move the Settlers and the Explorer:

1. **Using the numeric keypad, press the 9 key three times to begin exploring.** You can move the Explorer up to three times per turn. You begin to see more of the world.

2. **When the next unit (a Settler) begins blinking, move it one square in another direction.** When you have made all the moves you want to make (or all that the game allows), the Turn Done button is highlighted. Click Turn Done to start your next turn. Information for the city is updated. (The city changes and grows, simply through the passage of time reflected in the turns.)

3. **Click the City to see the city window.** Notice that information about the city has been updated. In particular, you should see food storage increase. Close the city window.

4. **Continue exploring and build a road.** With the Explorer flashing, use the numeric keypad to move it another three sections. When the Settler begins blinking, press R to build a road. A small R appears on the square to remind you that the Settler is busy building a road. Click Turn Done.

### Using more controls and actions

Now that you have some understanding of the controls and actions, the game can go in a lot of different directions. Here are a few things that might happen next and things you can do:

- After you take a turn, the computer gets a chance to play. As it plays, its actions are reported to you. You can make decisions on what to do about those actions. Choose Game ⇨ Message Options. The Message Options window appears, containing a listing of different kinds of messages that can come from the server and how they will be presented to you.

- As you explore, you will run into other explorers and eventually other civilizations. Continue exploring by selecting different directions on your numeric keypad.

- Continue to move the Settler one square at a time after it has finished creating the road. The Settler will blink again when it is available. Click Turn Done to continue.

- At this point, you should see a message that your city has finished building Warriors. When buildings and units are complete, you should usually check out what has happened. Click the message associated with the city, and then click Popup City. The city window appears, showing you that it has additional population. The food storage may appear empty, but the new citizens are working to increase the food and trade. You may see an additional Warrior unit.

- A science advisory may also appear to let you choose your city's research goals. Click Change and select Writing as your new research goal. You can then select a different long-term goal as well. Click Close when you are done.

- If your new Warrior is now blinking, press the S key to assign sentry mode to the Warrior.

- Select Reports from time to time to keep track of statistics about your Cities, Units, Economy, Science, and other attributes of your world.

These moves provide familiarity with some of the actions of *Freeciv*. To learn some basic strategies for playing the game, choose Help ⇨ Help Playing.

## Extreme Tux Racer

With *Extreme Tux Racer,* you guide Tux the penguin (the Linux mascot) down a snow-covered hill as fast as you can. *Extreme Tux Racer* is an open source (GPL) version of *TuxRacer,* which was once freeware, but was later made into a commercial game by Sunspire Studios.

To advance in *Extreme Tux Racer,* you need to complete courses in the allotted time while overcoming whatever obstacle is presented (gathering herring or negotiating flags). You move up to try different courses and achieve higher-level cups. Figure 7-3 shows a screenshot of PlanetPenguin Racer.

**FIGURE 7-3**

Race Tux the penguin down a mountain.

# Commercial Linux Games

When Loki Software, Inc. closed its doors a few years ago, the landscape of commercial gaming in Linux changed. Loki produced Linux ports of popular games, including *Myth II* and *Civilization: Call to Power,* to name a couple, and many hoped it would help Linux become the premier gaming platform. Since then, no single company has stepped up to port that wide a range of best-selling games to Linux. However, smaller Linux game publishers and companies porting popular Windows games to Linux have begun to pop up. Also, commercial games that run natively are led by several popular games from id Software (described in the next section) and a few gaming companies that have ported individual titles to Linux.

Some Loki games are still available for purchase on the Web. They sell for a fraction of their original price, but you are on your own if they don't work because Loki Software is no longer there to support them. The Loki Games Demo is still around, if you want to get a feel for a particular Loki game before it disappears completely. (I describe how to find demo and packaged Loki Games later in this chapter.)

Although the state of Linux gaming has improved a great deal in the last few years, Linux is still emerging as a gaming platform. Linux has some of the technology needed to support advanced games, but the technology and developer support have not yet really come together. Most serious gamers still maintain a Windows partition to support their gaming habits.

According to top game developers, significant hurdles—both technological and economic—hinder development of games for Linux. In particular, the relatively small size of the Linux gaming market means that incentives to overcome some technical issues are not particularly strong. However, these limitations are not overwhelming and small Linux gaming developers are beginning to make inroads. As you'll see later in this chapter, even the hardcore game nut can successfully use Linux.

## Getting started with commercial games in Linux

How you get started with Linux gaming depends on how serious you are about it. If all you want to do is play a few games to pass the time, I've already described plenty of diverting X Window games that come with Linux. If you want to play more powerful commercial games, you can choose from the following:

- **Games for Microsoft Windows (Cedega 6.0)**—Many of the most popular commercial games created to run on Microsoft operating systems will run in Linux using Cedega. To get RPM versions of Cedega, you must sign up for a Cedega subscription at www.transgaming.com. Make sure to check in with www.linuxgames.com to see if there is a relevant HOWTO for working with the particular game you have in mind. Many games are covered there including *Half-Life* and *Unreal Tournament*. To see whether your favorite Windows game will run in Linux and Cedega, refer to the TransGaming.Org Games Database at www.cedega.com/gamesdb.

- **Games for Linux (id Software and others)**—Certain popular games have Linux versions available. Most notably, id Software offers its *DOOM* and *Return to Castle Wolfenstein* in Linux versions. Other popular games that run natively in Linux include *Unreal Tournament 2004* and *2005* from Atari (www.unrealtournament.com).

  Commercial games that run in Linux without WINE, Cedega, or some sort of Windows emulation typically come in a boxed version for Windows with some sort of Linux installer included.

- **Independent Linux Game Developers**—Several small companies are currently producing games for Linux. Notable Linux game developers include Introversion Software (introversion.co.uk) and Frictional Games (www.frictionalgames.com). Introversion's games include *Uplink*, *Darwinia*, and *Defcon*. By the time you read this, *Multiwinia* should also be available. Frictional games include *Penumbra: Overture* and *Penumbra: Black Plague*, both of which portray 3D horror stories.

Linux games that were ported directly to Linux from the now defunct company Loki Software, Inc. are still available. Although you cannot purchase the titles directly from Loki, you can go online to one of Loki's resellers at `www.lokigames.com/orders/resellers.php3`. For example, Amazon.com (one of the listed resellers) shows titles, including *Quake III, Myth II: Soulblighter*, and *Heretic II* for Linux.

# Playing commercial Linux games

To get your commercial games running in Linux, you should start from a site such as the Linux Game Tome (`www.happypenguin.org`) or Linux Gamers' FAQ (`http://icculus.org/lgfaq`), which provide information on commercial games that run in Linux and help in getting them to run. In most cases, you need to do the following:

- Purchase a legal copy of the game.
- Go to a Web site that describes how to install, get patches for, and work around any issues related to playing the game in Linux.

Here are examples of a few commercial games that run well in Linux:

- **Duke 3D Atomic Edition for Linux (3D Realms)**—Duke Nukem returns to earth to face aliens and clean up Los Angeles in this third chapter in the *Duke Nukem* series. Visit 3D Realms for official information about *Duke 3D Atomic Edition* (`www.3drealms.com/duke3d`). See the Icculus.org site (`http://icculus.org/duke3d/`) for tips on getting it running.
- **Unreal Tournament 2003 (Epic Games)**—Multiplayer death match set in the future, where warriors face each other with awesome weapons and stuff. Includes a Linux installer. Go to Epic Games (`www.epicgames.com`) or the Unreal Tournament site (`www.unrealtournament.com`) for the official information. Visit the Icculus.org site for tips on installing in Linux (`www.icculus.org/lgfaq#ut2k3_install`).
- **Unreal Tournament 2004 (Epic Games)**—Adds new maps, characters, vehicles, weapons, and modes of play to the 2003 edition.

The following sections describe Linux games from id Software, information about running Windows games using Cedega in Linux, and games from the now-defunct Loki Games still available from other sources today.

# id Software games

Among the most popular games running natively in Linux are *Quake II, Quake III Arena,* and *Return to Castle Wolfenstein* from id Software, Inc. You can purchase Linux versions of these games or download demos of each game before you buy. As noted earlier, *Quake III Arena* demos are available in Fedora and other Linux software repositories.

## Note

If you have trouble getting any id Software games running in Linux, refer to the Linux FAQs available from id Software at `http://zerowing.idsoftware.com/linux`. ∎

### Quake III Arena

*Quake III Arena* is a first-person, shooter-type game where you can choose from lots of weapons (lightning guns, shotguns, grenade launchers, and so on) and pass through scenes with highly detailed 3D surfaces. You can play alone or against your friends. There are multiplayer death-match and capture-the-flag competitions. Standalone play allows you to advance through a tournament structure of skilled AI opponents. This version of the game has a selectable difficulty level, from fairly easy to beat to downright impossible.

If your Linux distribution doesn't already include it, a demo version of *Quake III Arena* for Linux is available from the id Software Web site (click the demo link at `www.idsoftware.com/games/quake/quake3-gold/` and then look for the Linux demo). Because the demo is in the form of a large shell script, to save it you can right-click the link and select Save Link As from your Web browser. Figure 7-4 shows a screenshot from *Quake III Arena*.

**FIGURE 7-4**

*Quake III Arena* is a popular first-person shooter game that runs in Linux.

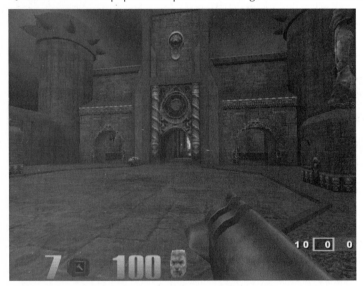

### Return to Castle Wolfenstein

You battle with the Allies to destroy the Third Reich in *Return to Castle Wolfenstein,* which mixes World War II action with creatures conjured up by Nazi scientists. It is based on the *Quake III Arena* engine and offers single-player mode as well as team-based multiplayer mode.

If you purchase *Return to Castle Wolfenstein* for Linux, you actually get the Windows version with an extra Linux installer. If you already have the Windows version, you can download the Linux installer and follow some instructions to get it going. I downloaded the installer called `wolf-linux-1.31.x86.run` from `www.idsoftware.com/games/wolfenstein/rtcw/index.php?game_section=updates`. The `INSTALL` file (in `/usr/local/games/wolfenstein`) describes which files you need to copy from the Windows CD.

To get a demo of *Return to Castle Wolfenstein,* go to `www.idsoftware.com/games/wolfenstein/rtcw/index.php?game_section=overview`. Both single-player and multiplayer demos are available.

### Caution

**You need an NVIDIA card to run *Return to Castle Wolfenstein.*** ∎

Figure 7-5 is a screenshot from *Return to Castle Wolfenstein* running in Linux.

**FIGURE 7-5**

*Return to Castle Wolfenstein* combines strange creatures and World War II battles.

# Playing TransGaming and Cedega games

TransGaming Technologies brings to Linux some of the most popular games that currently run on the Windows platforms. Working with WINE developers, TransGaming is developing Cedega, which enables you to run many different games on Linux that were originally developed for Windows. Although TransGaming is producing a few games that are packaged separately and tuned for Linux, in most cases it sells you a subscription service to Cedega instead of the games. That subscription service lets you stay up-to-date on the continuing development of Cedega so you can run more and more Windows games.

### Coming from Windows

**To get Windows games to run in Linux, Cedega particularly focuses its development on Microsoft DirectX features that are required by many of today's games. Issues related to CD keys and hooks into the Windows operating system also must be overcome (such as requiring Microsoft Active Desktop). A Cedega subscription has value, in part, because it lets you vote on which games you want to see TransGaming work on next.** ∎

A full list of games supported by TransGaming, as well as indications of how popular they are and how well they work, is available from the TransGaming site (`www.cedega.com/gamesdb/`). Browse games by category or alphabetically. An asterisk marks games that are officially supported by TransGaming. On each game description page is a link to a related Wiki Node, when one exists, that gives you details about how well the game works under Cedega and tips for getting it to work better.

## Note

**Depending on your distribution, you may need to get the vanilla kernel from kernel.org and boot that on your system before running games with Cedega. TransGaming has added several new features to the Cedega GUI (formerly called Point2Play). The Cedega GUI provides a graphical window for installing, configuring, and testing Cedega on your computer. This application also lets you install and organize your games so you can launch them graphically. Figure 7-6 shows an example of the TransGaming Cedega window.** ■

**FIGURE 7-6**

Use the Cedega window to launch Windows games in Linux.

Features in the new Cedega GUI window include a new look-and-feel and tools for individually configuring how each game runs under Cedega. (If a game won't run from the GUI, try launching it from a Terminal window.) Here are some games that are known to run well in Cedega:

- *Day of Defeat: Source*
- *World of Warcraft*
- *Planescape*
- *Silkroad Online*
- *Half-Life 2*
- *Call of Duty 2*

To get binary copies (ones that are already compiled to run) of Cedega, you need to subscribe to TransGaming. For details on how to become a "TransGamer," click the Sign Up Today link on the TransGaming home page (www.transgaming.com). Benefits currently include

- Downloads of the latest version of Cedega
- Access to Cedega support forums
- Ability to vote on which games you want TransGaming to support next
- Subscription to the Cedega newsletter

Cedega used to be known as WineX. The source code for WineX may become available in the near future if you want to build your own WineX/Cedega package. To check availability, try the SourceForge.net project site for WineX (sourceforge.net/projects/winex).

## Loki Software game demos

To encourage people to get to know its games, Loki Software, Inc. offered a demo program that let you choose from among more than a dozen of its games to download and try. You can still find some of its games for sale.

### Caution
If you try to download any of the demos described in the following sections, make sure you have enough disk space available. It is common for one of these demos to require several hundred megabytes of disk space. ■

The Loki Demo Launcher page (www.lokigames.com/products/demos.php3) still offers links to FTP sites from which you can download the Demo Launcher. The file that you want to save is loki_demos-full-1.0e-x86.run. Save it to a directory (such as /tmp/loki) and do the following:

1. Change to the directory to which you downloaded the demo. For example:

   ```
   # cd /tmp/loki
   ```

### Note
You may not need to be root user to install these games. However, the paths where the Demo Launcher tries to write by default are accessible only to the root user. ■

2. As root user, run the following command (the program may have a different name if it has been updated):

   ```
   # sh loki_demos-full-1.0e.x86.run
   ```

3. If you have not used the Demo Launcher before, a screen appears asking you to identify the paths used to place the Install Tool. If the default locations shown are okay with you, click Begin Install.

4. Assuming that no problem occurred writing to the install directories, you should see an Install Complete message. Click Exit.

5. The Uninstall Tool window displays. If the paths for holding the Uninstall Tool are okay, click Begin Install. The Install Complete message appears. Click Exit.

6. The next window enables you to set the locations for installing the Demo Pack. If the paths are okay, click Begin Install.

7. A box shows the different demo games available. As you move the cursor over each game, the disk space needed for the game is displayed. Click the games you want to install and then click Continue.

8. A window displays the progress of each download. You may need to click an Update button to complete the update and then click Finish to finish it.

9. The demo should now be ready to start. Either click Play or type **loki_demos** from a Terminal window to start the program.

10. Select to start the game, and you're ready to go.

The following sections describe a few games that may still be available. Again, these games may not be available for long.

### Civilization: Call to Power

You can build online civilizations with *Civilization: Call to Power* (*CCP*). Like earlier versions and public spinoffs (such as the *Freeciv* described earlier in this chapter), *Civilization: Call to Power* for Linux lets you explore the world, build cities, and manage your empire. The last version offered by Loki Games includes multiplayer network competition and extensions that let you extend cities into outer space and under the sea.

If you like *Freeciv*, you will love *CCP*. Engaging game play is improved with enhanced graphics, sound, and animation. English, French, German, Italian, and Spanish versions are available.

## Note

*Freeciv* **is dependent on the Open Sound System for audio support. The Open Sound home page (**www
.opensound.com/osshw.html**) has a list of supported sound cards, mostly older devices. If you do not
have a card that's on the list, you may be unable to enjoy the audio.** ■

The *CCP* demo comes with an excellent tutorial to start you out. If you have never played a civilization game before, the tutorial is a great way to start. Figure 7-7 shows an example scene from the *Civilization: Call to Power* for Linux demo.

### Myth II: Soulblighter

If you like knights and dwarves and storming castles, *Myth II: Soulblighter* for Linux might be for you. In *Myth II,* you are given a mission and some troops with various skills. From there, you need strategy and the desire to shed lots of virtual blood to meet your goal.

**FIGURE 7-7**

Civilization: *Call to Power* features excellent graphics and network play.

*Myth II* was created by Bungie Software (the gaming company known more recently for the *Halo* series) and ported to Linux by Loki Entertainment Software (www.lokigames.com). The Loki port of the popular *Myth* game includes improved graphics and new scenarios. A demo version is available that runs well in most distributions (particularly Fedora/Red Hat). You can get it via the Demo Launcher described earlier. You need at least a modest Pentium 133 MHz, 32MB RAM, 80MB swap space, and 100MB of free disk space. You also need network hardware for multiuser network play (network card or dial-up), and a sound card if you want audio. Figure 7-8 shows a screen in *Myth II*.

**FIGURE 7-8**

Use warriors, archers, and dwarves to battle in *Myth II*.

### Heretic II

Based on the *Quake* engine, *Heretic II* sets you on a path to rid the world of a deadly, magical plague. As the main character, Corvus, you explore dungeons, swamps, and cities to uncover and stop the plague. The graphics are rich, and the game play is quite engaging.

You will experience some crashing problems with *Heretic II* out of the box. Be sure to check for the update to *Heretic II* at `www.updates.lokigames.com`, which should fix most of the problems.

### Neverwinter Nights

BioWare (`www.bioware.com`) dipped its foot into Linux gaming waters with a Linux client for its wildly popular *Neverwinter Nights* game. *Neverwinter Nights* is a classic role-playing game in the swords-and-sorcery mold. You can develop your character and go adventuring or play online with others via a LAN or over the Internet. You can even build your own worlds and host adventures as the Dungeon Master. *Neverwinter Nights* is licensed by Wizards of the Coast to use *Dungeons & Dragons* rules and material.

Of course, to use the *Neverwinter Nights* Linux client, you must purchase the game from BioWare. You must also have access to certain files from a Windows installation of the game. Keep in mind that getting *Neverwinter Nights* running is not a simple process. Important installation instructions and downloadable files are located at `http://nwn.bioware.com/downloads/linux-client.html`. This site includes additional information about expansion packs and updates. If you want the *Neverwinter Nights* experience on your Linux system to be pleasant, I highly recommend reading the instructions thoroughly. And you will need patience in addition to a high-bandwidth Internet connection. Depending on the version of *Neverwinter Nights* to which you have access, you may need to download up to 1.2GB of files.

# Summary

With Linux ports of games such as *Unreal Tournament 2004,* Linux continues to grow as a gaming platform. You can spend plenty of late nights gaming on Linux. Old UNIX games that have made their way to Linux include a variety of basic X Window–based games. Card games, strategy games, and some action games are available for those less inclined to spend 36 hours playing *DOOM 3.*

On the commercial front, *Civilization: Call to Power* for Linux and *Myth II* are available to use on your Linux system. Unfortunately, these will probably disappear because Loki Software (which ported those applications to Linux) went out of business. Fortunately, the future of high-end Linux gaming seems to be in the hands of TransGaming Technologies, which has created Cedega from previous WINE technology to allow Windows games to run in Linux.

Commercial games that run natively in Linux are also available. These include games from id Software, such as *Quake III Arena* and *Return to Castle Wolfenstein.* Smaller Linux game developers have also appeared, including Introversion Software and Frictional Games.

# Part III

# Learning System Administration Skills

# Installing Linux

I f someone hasn't already installed and configured a Linux system for you, this chapter is going to help you get started so you can try out the Linux features described in the rest of the book. Using live CDs and improved installers, several of which are included with this book, getting your hands on a working Linux system is quicker and more solid than ever before.

If you are a first-time Linux user, I recommend that you

- **Try a bootable Linux**—This book's CD and DVD include several bootable Linux systems. The advantage of a bootable Linux is that you can try out Linux without touching the contents of your computer's hard drive. In particular, KNOPPIX is a full-featured Linux system that can give you a good feel for how Linux works. Using the DVD or CD, you can try out several different live CDs, as described in Appendix A. Some of these live CDs also include features for installing Linux to your hard disk. Although live CDs tend to run slower than installed systems and often aren't set up to keep your changes after you reboot, they are good tools for starting out with Linux.

- **Install a desktop Linux system**—Choose one of the Linux distributions and install it on your computer's hard disk. Permanently installing Linux to your hard disk gives you more flexibility for adding and removing software, accessing and saving data to hard disk, and more permanently customizing your system. Installing Linux as a desktop system lets you try out some useful applications and get the feel for Linux before dealing with more complex server issues.

This chapter provides you with an overview of how to choose a Linux distribution, and then describes issues and topics that are common to installing most Linux distributions. Appendix A describes which Linux distributions are included on this book's DVD and CD and how to run them live or use them to install Linux permanently. Each of the other chapters in this part of the book is dedicated to understanding and installing a particular Linux distribution.

After you've installed Linux, you'll want to understand how to get and manage software for your Linux system. These important topics are covered throughout the book, but this chapter describes the major packaging formats and tools to get you going.

# Choosing a Linux Distribution

Dozens of popular Linux distributions are available today. Some are generalized distributions that you can use as a desktop, server, or workstation system; others are specialized for business or computer enthusiasts. One intention of this book is to help you choose which one (or ones) will suit you best.

Using the DVD that comes with this book, you can boot directly to KNOPPIX (or several other live CDs to try out Linux) or run an installer (to install one of several Linux distributions to your computer's hard disk). After you've tried out KNOPPIX and are ready to install Linux on your hard disk, I recommend you try Fedora or Ubuntu.

Using the CD that comes with this book, you can boot directly to Damn Small Linux (or several other smaller bootable Linux distros), Debian, or Gentoo (to do a network install of those distributions to your hard disk). Debian and Damn Small Linux are two distributions that can be set up to work well on computers that are older and less powerful, or have a CD drive but no DVD drive. For Debian and Ubuntu, this book also provides descriptions for setting up Debian as a mail and Web server (see Chapters 13 and 14).

## Linux at work

Because I know a lot of people who use Linux, both informally and at work, I want to share my general impressions of how different Linux distributions are being used in the United States. Many consultants I know who set up small office servers used to use Red Hat Linux. Some have continued to use Red Hat Enterprise Linux (RHEL) whereas others have moved to Fedora, CentOS (built from RHEL source code), Ubuntu, or Debian GNU/Linux. Mandriva Linux (formerly Mandrakelinux) has been popular with people wanting a friendly Linux desktop, but Ubuntu and Fedora are also well-liked. The more technically inclined like to play with Gentoo (highly tunable) or Slackware (Linux in a more basic form).

The agreement between Novell and Microsoft prompted some open source proponents to abandon SUSE. Whether this will result in a migration from SUSE in the enterprise space, however, has yet to play out. However, right now, Red Hat Enterprise Linux offers the best choice in the enterprise realm for those who object to the alliance.

As for the bootable Linuxes, everyone I know thinks they are great fun to try out and a good way to learn about Linux. For a bootable Linux containing desktop software that fits on a full CD (or DVD), KNOPPIX is a good choice, as is Ubuntu; for a bootable mini-CD size Linux, Damn Small Linux works well. However, you can also try out these live CDs from the media that comes with this book: INSERT, Puppy Linux, System Rescue CD, or BackTrack.

This book exposes you to several different Linux distributions. It gives you the advantage of being able to see the strengths and weaknesses of each distribution by actually putting your hands on it. You can also try to connect in to the growing Linux user communities because strong community support results in a more solid software distribution and help when you need it (from such things as forums and online chats).

## Other distributions

There seems to be a new Linux distribution every five minutes and I really have to stop writing this book at some point. To keep the descriptions of Linux distributions to a reasonable size (and actually have the space to describe how to use Linux), several interesting Linux distributions aren't explored in this book.

Notable Linux distributions not included in this book are TurboLinux, Xandros, and CentOS. TurboLinux (`www.turbolinux.com`) is a popular distribution in Asia Pacific countries. Xandros (`www.xandros.com`), designed to operate well in Microsoft Windows environments, has recently entered a patent agreement with Microsoft and seems to be moving from its desktop focus. CentOS has become very popular among consultants who used to use Red Hat Linux. CentOS is a rebuild of the Red Hat Enterprise Linux source code. So, people use it for servers that require longer update cycles than you would get with Fedora. However, because CentOS and Red Hat Enterprise Linux are built from technology developed for Fedora, you can learn a lot about how to use those two distributions by using Fedora. The following sections explain how to look beyond the confines of this book for those and other Linux distributions.

# Getting Your Own Linux Distribution

By packaging a handful of Linux distributions with this book, I hoped to save you the trouble of getting Linux yourself. If you have a DVD drive, perhaps you can use this opportunity to at least try KNOPPIX, so you'll better understand what's being discussed. If you have a CD drive only, at least boot directly to Damn Small Linux from the CD that comes with this book.

If for some reason you can't use the software on the CD or DVD, you may want to get your own Linux distributions to use with the descriptions in this book. Reasons you might want to get your own Linux distributions include

- **No DVD drive**—You need a bootable DVD drive on your computer to use the Linux distributions on the DVD that comes with this book.

- **Later distributions**—You may want a more recent version of a particular distribution than comes with this book.

- **Complete distributions**—Because there's limited space on the CD and DVD and because some distributions require subscriptions or other fees, you may want to obtain your own, more complete distribution with which to work.

Today, there is no shortage of ways to get Linux.

## Finding another Linux distribution

You can go to the Web site of each distribution (such as `http://fedoraproject.org/get-fedora` or `http://slackware.com/getslack`) to get Linux software. Those sites often let you download a complete copy of their distributions and give you the opportunity to purchase a boxed set.

However, one way to get a more complete view of available Linux distributions is to go to a Web site dedicated to spreading information about Linux distributions. Use these sites to connect to forums and download documentation about many Linux distributions. Here are some examples:

- **DistroWatch** (`www.distrowatch.com`)—The first place I go to find Linux distributions is DistroWatch.com. Go to the Major Distributions link to read about the top Linux distributions (most of which are included with this book). Links will take you to download sites, forums, home pages, and other sites related to each distribution.

- **Linux.com Download Directory** (`www.linux.com/directory/Distributions`)—Select Linux distributions from among several categories (desktop, enterprise, live CD, and so on). Descriptions, documentation, and download links are available for each distribution listed.

If you don't want to download and burn the CDs yourself, there are plenty of links on those sites from places willing to sell you Linux CDs or DVDs. Distribution prices are often only a little bit higher than the cost of the media and shipping. If you really like a particular Linux distribution, then purchasing it directly from the organization that makes it is a good idea. Doing so can ensure the health of the distribution into the future.

Books that come with software included can also be a good way to get a Linux distribution. Finding up-to-date documentation can be difficult when you have nothing but a CD to start out with. Standard Linux documentation (such as HOWTOs and man pages) is often out of date with the software. So, I would particularly recommend a book and distribution (such as this one or *Fedora and Red Hat Enterprise Linux Bible* from Wiley Publishing) for first-time Linux users.

## Understanding what you need

The most common media used to install Linux are CDs and DVDs that contain everything you need to complete the install. Another way to start a Linux installation is with a CD that includes an installation boot image and then get the parts of Linux you need live from the network as you install Linux.

The images that are burned onto the CDs are typically stored on the Internet in *software repositories*. You can download the images and burn them to CDs yourself. Alternatively, the software packages are usually also included separately in directories. Those separate software directories enable you to start an install process with a minimal boot disc that can grab packages over the network during the installation process. (Some of the installations I recommend with this book are done that way.)

When you follow links to Linux software repositories, here's what you look for:

- **Download directory**—You often have to step down a few directories from the download link that gets you to a repository. Look for subdirectories that describe the distribution, architecture, release, and medium format. For example, mirrors for the Fedora 12 Linux distribution might be named `fedora/releases/12/Fedora/i386/iso`. Other Linux distributions, such as Gentoo and Debian, have tools that will search out online repositories for you, so you don't have to find a mirror directory on your own. (As an alternative, you can grab the Linux live CD or install images via BitTorrent, as described later.)

- **ISO images**—The software images you are going to burn to CD are typically stored in ISO format. Some repositories include a README file to tell you what images you need (others just assume you know). To install a distribution, you want the set of ISOs containing the Linux distribution's binary files or a single live CD ISO.

## Note
Although an ISO image appears as one file, it's actually like a snapshot of a file system. You can mount that image to see all the files the image contains by using the `loop` feature of the `mount` command. For example, with an image called `abc.iso` in the current directory, create an empty directory (`mkdir myiso`) and, as root, run the mount command: `mount -o loop abc.iso myiso`. Change to the `myiso` directory and you can view the files and directories the ISO image contains. When you are done viewing the contents, leave the directory and unmount the ISO image (`cd .. ; umount myiso`). ∎

- **MD5SUM**—To verify that you got the right CDs completely intact, after you download them look for a file named MD5SUM or ending in `.md5` in the ISO directory. The file contains one or more MD5 (128-bit) checksums, representing the ISO files you want to check. Other distributions publish SHA1 checksums, which does 160-bit checksums. You can use that file to verify the content of each CD (as described later).

## Downloading the distribution

You can download each ISO image by simply clicking the link and downloading it to a directory in your computer when prompted. You can do this on a Windows or Linux system.

If you know the location of the image you want, with a running Linux system, the wget command is a better way to download than just clicking a link in your browser. The advantage of using wget is that you can restart a download that stops in the middle for some reason. A wget command to download a KNOPPIX CD image (starting from the directory you want to download to) might look like this:

```
$ wget -c kernel.org/pub/dist/knoppix/KNOPPIX_V6.0.1CD-2009-02-08-EN.iso
```

If the download stops before it is completed, run the command again. The -c option tells wget to begin where the download left off, so that if you are 690MB into a 696MB download when it stopped, it just adds in the last 6MB.

A more "good citizen" approach to downloading your ISO images is to use a facility called BitTorrent (http://bittorrent.com). BitTorrent enables you to download a file to your computer by grabbing bits of that file from multiple computers on the network that are downloading the file at the same time. For the privilege, you also use your upload capacity to share the same file with others as you are downloading.

During times of heavy demand with a new Linux distribution, BitTorrent can be the best way to go. Some have portrayed BitTorrent as a tool for illegal activities, such as downloading copyrighted materials (movies, music, and so on). Because most Linux distributions contain only software covered under various open source licenses, there is no legal problem with using BitTorrent to distribute Linux distributions. Check out http://linuxtracker.org for a list of Linux distributions that you can download with BitTorrent.

If you are on a dial-up modem, you should strongly consider purchasing Linux CDs (or getting them from a friend) if you don't find what you want on the CD or DVD with this book. You might be able to download an entire 700MB CD in a couple of hours on a fast DSL or cable modem connection. On a dial-up line, you might need an entire day or more per CD. For a large, multi-CD distribution, available disk space can also become a problem (although, with today's large hard disks, it's not as much of a problem as it used to be).

## Burning the distribution to CD

With the CD images copied to your computer, you can proceed to verify their contents and burn them to CD. All you really need is a CD burner on your computer.

With Linux running, you can use the md5sum or sha1sum commands to verify each CD.

## Note

If you are using Windows to validate the contents of the Linux CD, you can get the MD5Summer utility (www.md5summer.org) to verify each CD image. ■

Assuming you downloaded the MD5 file associated with each CD image, and have it in the same directory as your CD images, run the `md5sum` command to verify the image. For example, to verify the KNOPPIX CD shown previously in the `wget` example, you can type the following:

```
$ md5sum KNOPPIX_V6.0.1CD-2009-02-08-EN.iso
d642d524dd2187834a418710001bbf82 KNOPPIX_V5.1.1CD-2007-01-04-EN.iso
```

The MD5SUM file I downloaded previously from the download directory was called `KNOPPIX_V6.0.1CD-2009-02-08-EN.iso`. It contained this content:

```
d642d524dd2187834a418710001bbf82  *KNOPPIX_V6.0.1CD-2009-02-08-EN.iso
```

As you can see, the checksum (first string of characters shown) that is output from the ISO image matches the checksum in the MD5 file, so you know that the image you downloaded is the image they put on the server. If the project uses sha1sum to verify its ISO images, you can test your downloaded images with the `sha1sum` command, as follows:

```
$ sha1sum FC-6-i386-DVD.iso
6722f95b97e5118fa26bafa5b9f622cc7d49530c FC-6-i386-DVD.iso
```

After you have verified the sha1sum or md5sum of the CD or DVD, as long as you got the image from a reliable site, you should be ready to burn the CD or DVD.

With your Linux distribution in hand (either the book's DVD or CD, or the set of CDs you got elsewhere), use commands such as `cdrecord` or `k3b` to burn your CD or DVD images to disk. You can find instructions for installing the distributions from the CD or DVD in individual chapters devoted to each distribution (Chapters 17–28). Before you proceed, however, some information is useful for nearly every Linux system you are installing.

# Exploring Common Installation Topics

Before you begin installing your Linux distribution of choice, you should understand some general Linux information. Reading over this information might help you avoid problems or keep you from getting stuck when you install Linux.

## Knowing your computer hardware

Every Linux distribution will not run on every computer. When installing Linux, most people use a Pentium-class PC. Linux systems exist that are compiled to run on other hardware, such as PowerPCs or x86_64-bit computers. However, the distributions provided with this book run on 32-bit Pentium-class PCs. Note that because new Mac computers are built from standard Intel components, installing Linux on those computers is possible as well (see the "Installing Linux on Intel Macs" sidebar).

# Installing Linux on Intel Macs

Because of the popularity of MacBook and Mac mini-computers, which are based on Intel architecture, several Linux projects have produced procedures for installing their systems to dual-boot with Mac OS X. Most of these procedures involve using the Apple BootCamp software (www.apple.com/support/bootcamp).

To install the Fedora Linux that comes with this book, refer to the Fedora on Mactel page (http://fedoraproject.org/wiki/FedoraOnMactel). For Ubuntu, refer to the Ubuntu MacBook page (https://help.ubuntu.com/community/MacBook).

Minimum hardware requirements from the Fedora Project are pretty good guidelines for most Linux systems:

- **Processor**—The latest version of Fedora recommends that you have at least a Pentium-class processor. For a text-only installation, a 200 MHz Pentium is the minimum, whereas a 400 MHz Pentium II is the minimum for a GUI installation.

## Note

**If you have a 486 machine (at least 100 MHz), consider trying Damn Small Linux or Slackware. The problem is that many machines that old have only floppy disks, so you can't use the CD or DVD that comes with this book. In that case, you can try ZipSlack (www.slackware.com/zipslack), which is a Slackware version that comes on about 30+ floppy disk images or a 100MB Zip disk and can run on a 486 with at least 100MB of disk space. ■**

- **RAM**—You should have at least 64MB of RAM to install most Linux distributions and run it in text mode. Slackware might run on 8MB of RAM, but 16MB is considered the minimum. If you are running in graphical mode, you will probably need at least 192MB. The recommended RAM for graphical mode in Fedora is 512MB. A GNOME environment generally requires a bit less memory to run than a KDE environment. If you are using a more streamlined graphical system (that runs X with a small window manager, such as Blackbox), you might get by with as little as 32MB. In that case, you might try Damn Small Linux or Slackware.

- **DVD or CD drive**—You need to be able to boot up the installation process from a DVD or CD. If you can't boot from a DVD or CD, there are ways to start the installation from a hard disk or USB drive or by using a PXE install. Some distributions such as Slackware let you use floppy disks to boot installation. After the install is booted, the software can sometimes be retrieved from different locations (over the network or from hard disk, for example).

- **Network card**—If you are doing an install of one of the distributions for which we provide a scaled-down boot disk, you might need to have an Ethernet card installed to get the software you need over the network. A dial-up connection won't work for network installs. You don't have to be connected to the Internet necessarily to do a network install. Some people download the necessary software packages to a computer on their LAN, and then use that as an install server.

- **Disk space**—You should have at least 3GB of disk space for an average desktop installation, although installations can range (depending on which packages you choose to install) from 600MB (for a minimal server with no GUI install) to 7GB (to install all packages). You can install the Damn Small Linux live CD to disk with only about 200MB of disk space.

If you're not sure about your computer hardware, there are a few ways to check what you have. If you are running Windows, the System Properties window can show you the processor you have, as well as the amount of RAM that's installed. As an alternative, you can boot KNOPPIX and let it detect and report to you the hardware you have. (See Chapter 11 for instructions on running the `lspci` and `dmseg` commands in Linux to view information about your computer hardware.)

## Upgrading or installing from scratch

If you already have a version of the Linux you are installing on your computer, many Linux distributions offer an upgrade option. This lets you upgrade all packages, for example, from version 1 of the distribution to version 2. Here are a few general rules before performing an upgrade:

- **Back up data**—The possibility exists that after you finish your upgrade, the operating system won't boot. Backing up any critical data and configuration files (in /etc) before doing any major changes to your operating system is always a good idea.

- **Remove extra packages**—If you have software packages you don't need, remove them before you do an upgrade. Upgrade processes typically upgrade only those packages that are on your system. Upgrades generally do more checking and comparing than clean installs do, so any package you can remove saves time during the upgrade process.

- **Check configuration files**—A Linux upgrade procedure often leaves copies of old configuration files. You should check that the new configuration files still work for you.

### Tip
Installing Linux from scratch goes faster than an upgrade. It also results in a cleaner Linux system. So if you have the choice of backing up your data, or just erasing it if you don't need it, a fresh install is usually best. ∎

Some Linux distributions, most notably Gentoo, have taken the approach of ongoing updates. Instead of taking a new release every few months, you simply continuously grab updated packages as they become available and install them on your system.

## Dual booting and virtualization

Having multiple, bootable operating systems on the same computer is possible. You can do this using multiple partitions on a hard disk and/or multiple hard disks, then setting up to boot more than one operating system. You could also create virtual guest operating systems that you can use to run a Linux or other system within your current Linux or Windows system.

## Caution

Although tools for resizing Windows partitions and setting up multiboot systems have improved in recent years, there is still some risk of losing data on Windows/Linux dual-boot systems. Different operating systems often have different views of partition tables and master boot records that can cause your machine to become unbootable (at least temporarily) or lose data permanently. Always back up your data before you try to resize a Windows (NTFS or FAT) file system to make space for Linux. If you have a choice, install Linux on a machine of its own or at least on a separate hard disk. ■

### Setting up for dual booting

If the computer you are using already has a Windows system on it, quite possibly the entire hard disk is devoted to Windows. Although you can run a bootable Linux, such as KNOPPIX or Damn Small Linux, without touching the hard disk, to do a more permanent installation you'll want to find disk space outside of the Windows installation. There are a few ways to do this:

- **Add a hard disk**—Instead of messing with your Windows partition, you can simply add a hard disk and devote it to Linux.
- **Resize your Windows partition**—If you have available space on your Windows partition, you can shrink that partition so free space is available on the disk to devote to Linux. Commercial tools such as Partition Magic from Symantec (`www.symantec.com`) or Acronis Disk Director (`www.acronis.com`) are available to resize your disk partitions and set up a workable boot manager. Some Linux distributions (particularly bootable Linuxes used as rescue CDs) include a tool called QTParted that is an open source clone of Partition Magic (which includes software from the Linux-NTFS project for resizing Windows NTFS partitions).

## Note

GParted is an alternative to QTParted. Type `yum install gparted` **(in Fedora) or** `apt-get install gparted` **(in Ubuntu) to install GParted. Run** `gparted` **as root to start it.** ■

Before you try to resize your Windows partition, you might need to defragment it. To defragment your disk on some Windows systems, so that all of your used space is put in order on the disk, open My Computer, right-click your hard disk icon (typically C:), select Properties, click Tools, and select Defragment Now.

Defragmenting your disk can be a fairly long process. The result of defragmentation is that all the data on your disk are contiguous, creating a lot of contiguous free space at the end of the partition. There are cases where you will have to do the following special tasks to make this true:

- If the Windows swap file is not moved during defragmentation, you must remove it. Then, after you defragment your disk again and resize it, you will need to restore the swap file. To remove the swap file, open the Control Panel, open the System icon, and then click the Performance tab and select Virtual Memory. To disable the swap file, click Disable Virtual Memory.

- If your DOS partition has hidden files that are on the space you are trying to free up, you need to find them. In some cases, you won't be able to delete them. In other cases, such as swap files created by a program, you can safely delete those files. This is a bit tricky because some files should not be deleted, such as DOS system files. You can use the `attrib -s -h` command from the root directory to deal with hidden files.

After your disk is defragmented, you can use commercial tools described earlier (Partition Magic or Acronis Disk Director) to repartition your hard disk to make space for Linux. Or use the open source alternatives QTParted or GParted.

After you have cleared enough disk space to install Linux (see the disk space requirements in the chapter covering the Linux distribution you're installing), you can choose your Linux distribution and install it. As you set up your boot loader during installation, you will be able to identify the Windows, Linux, and any other bootable partitions so that you can select which one to boot when you start your computer.

## Installing Linux to run virtually

Using virtualization technology such as VMWare, VirtualBox, Xen, or KVM, you can configure your computer to run multiple operating systems simultaneously. Typically, you have a host operating system running (such as your Linux or Windows desktop), and then configure guest operating systems to run within that environment.

If you have a Windows system, you can use commercial VMWare products to run Linux on your Windows desktop. Get a trial of VMWare Workstation (`www.vmware.com/tryvmware`) to see if you like it. Then run your installed virtual guests with the free VMWare Player. With a full-blown version of VMWare Workstation you can run multiple distributions at the same time.

Open source virtualization products that are available with Linux systems include VirtualBox (`www.virtualbox.org`), Xen (`www.xen.org`), and KVM (`www.linux-kvm.org`). VirtualBox was developed originally by Sun Microsystems. Xen has been popular with Red Hat systems, but Red Hat has begun moving recently toward KVM technology instead.

## Using installation boot options

Sometimes a Linux installation fails because the computer has some non-functioning or non-supported hardware. Sometimes you can get around those issues by passing options to the install process when it boots up. Those options can do such things as disable selected hardware (`nousb`, `noscsi`, `noide`, and so on) or not probe hardware when you need to select your own driver (`noprobe`).

Although some of these options are distribution-specific, others are simply options that can be passed to an installer environment that works from a Linux kernel. Chapter 21 includes a list of many boot options that you can use with KNOPPIX and other Linux systems.

# Partitioning hard drives

The hard disk (or disks) on your computer provides the permanent storage area for your data files, applications programs, and the operating system itself. Partitioning is the act of dividing a disk into logical areas that can be worked with separately. In Windows, you typically have one partition that consumes the whole hard disk. However, with Linux there are several reasons why you may want to have multiple partitions:

- **Multiple operating systems**—If you install Linux on a PC that already has a Windows operating system, you may want to keep both operating systems on the computer. For all practical purposes, each operating system must exist on a completely separate partition. When your computer boots, you can choose which system to run.

- **Multiple partitions within an operating system**—To protect from having your entire operating system run out of disk space, people often assign separate partitions to different areas of the Linux file system. For example, if /home and /var were assigned to separate partitions, then a gluttonous user who fills up the /home partition wouldn't prevent logging daemons from continuing to write to log files in the /var/log directory.

    Multiple partitions also make doing certain kinds of backups (such as an image backup) easier. For example, an image backup of /home would be much faster (and probably more useful) than an image backup of the root file system (/).

- **Different file system types**—Different kinds of file systems have different structures. File systems of different types must be on their own partitions. In most Linux systems, you need at least one file system type for / (typically ext3 or reiserfs) and one for your swap area. File systems on CD-ROM use the iso9660 file system type.

## Tip

When you create partitions for Linux, you will usually assign the file system type as Linux native (using the ext2 or ext3 type on some Linux systems, and reiserfs on others). Reasons to use other types include needing a file system that allows particularly long filenames, large file sizes, or many inodes (each file consumes an inode).

For example, if you set up a news server, it can use many inodes to store news articles. Another reason for using a different file system type is to copy an image backup tape from another operating system to your local disk (such as one from an OS/2 or Minix operating system). ■

## Coming from Windows

If you have used only Windows operating systems before, you probably had your whole hard disk assigned to C: and never thought about partitions. With many Linux systems, you have the opportunity to view and change the default partitioning based on how you want to use the system. ■

During installation, systems such as openSUSE and Fedora let you partition your hard disk using graphical partitioning tools. The following sections describe how to partition your disk during a Fedora installation or use fdisk to partition your disk. See the section "Tips for Creating Partitions" for some ideas for creating disk partitions.

## Partitioning during Fedora installation

During installation, Fedora gives you the opportunity to change how your hard disk is partitioned. The Disk Setup screen is divided into two sections. The top shows general information about each hard disk. The bottom shows details of each partition. Figure 8-1 shows an example of the Disk Setup window.

**FIGURE 8-1**

Partition your disk during Fedora installation from the disk setup window.

For each of the hard disk partitions, you can see the following:

- **Device**—The device name is the name representing the hard disk partition in the / dev directory. Each disk partition device begins with two letters: sd for SATA or SCSI disks, hd for IDE, ed for ESDI disks, or xd for XT disks. After that is a single letter representing the number of the disk (disk 1 is a, disk 2 is b, disk 3 is c, and so on). So, for example, to refer to the entire first hard disk, use the device name /dev/sda. To refer to a particular partition on that disk, add the partition number (1, 2, 3, and so on). For example, /dev/sda1 represents the first partition on the first SATA hard drive on the computer.

- **Mount Point/Raid/Volume**—The directory where the partition is connected into the Linux file system (if it is). You must assign the root partition (/) to a native Linux partition before you can proceed. If you are using RAID or LVM, the name of the RAID device or LVM volume appears here.

- **Type**—The type of file system that is installed on the disk partition. In many cases, the file system will be Linux (ext3), Win VFAT (vfat), or Linux swap. However, you can also use the previous Linux file system (ext2), logical volume manager physical volume (LVM), or software RAID. If an NTFS partition were shown in Figure 8-1 it would imply that Windows is installed on this computer and this can, therefore, be used as a dual-boot computer with Windows and Linux.

- **Format**—Indicates whether the installation process should format the hard disk partition. Partitions marked with a check are erased! So, on a multi-boot system, be sure your Windows partitions, as well as other partitions containing data you don't want to lose, are not checked!

- **Size (MB)**—The amount of disk space allocated for the partition (in megabytes). If you selected to let the partition grow to fill the existing space, this number may be much larger than the requested amount.

In the top section, you can see each hard disk connected to your computer. The drive name is shown first, followed by the amount of disk space and the model name of the disk.

Before you create any LVM logical volumes, you must create at least one physical LVM partition and assign it to a volume group. To create a RAID array, you must create at least two physical RAID partitions to assign to an array.

### Reasons for partitioning

Different opinions exist as to how to divide up a hard disk. Here are some issues:

- **Do you want to install another operating system?** If you want Windows on your computer along with Linux, you need at least one Windows (Win95 FAT16, VFAT, or NTFS type), one Linux (Linux ext3), and one Linux swap partition.

- **Is it a multiuser system?** If you are using the system yourself, you probably don't need many partitions. One reason for partitioning an operating system is to keep the entire system from running out of disk space at once. That also serves to put boundaries on what an individual can use up in his or her home directory (although disk quotas are good for that as well).

- **Do you have multiple hard disks?** You need at least one partition per hard disk. If your system has two hard disks, you may assign one to / and one to /home (if you have lots of users) or /var (if the computer is a server sharing lots of data). With a separate /home partition, you can install another Linux system in the future without disturbing your home directories (and presumably all or most of your user data).

### Deleting, adding, and editing partitions

Before you can add a partition, some free space must be available on your hard disk. If all space on your hard disk is currently assigned to one partition (as it often is in DOS or Windows), you must delete or resize that partition before you can claim space on another partition. The section "Dual Booting with Windows or Just Linux?" discusses how to add a partition without losing information in your existing single-partition system.

## Caution

**Make sure to back up any data that you want to keep before you delete the partition. When you delete a partition, all of its data is inaccessible.**

Disk Setup is less flexible but more intuitive than the fdisk utility. Disk Setup enables you to delete, add, and edit partitions.

## Tip

**If you create multiple partitions, make sure that you have enough room in the right places to complete the installation. For example, most of the Linux software is installed in the /usr directory (and subdirectories), whereas most user data files are eventually added to the /home or /var directories. ∎**

To delete a partition in Disk Setup, do the following:

1. Select a partition from the list of Current Disk Partitions on the main Disk Setup window (click it or use the arrow keys).
2. To delete the partition, click Delete.
3. When asked to confirm the deletion, click Delete.
4. If you made a mistake, click Reset to return to the partitioning as it was when you started Disk Setup.

To add a partition in Disk Setup, follow these steps from the main Disk Setup window:

1. Select New. A window appears, enabling you to create a new partition.
2. Type the name of the Mount Point (the directory where this partition will connect to the Linux file system). You need at least a root (/) partition and a swap partition.
3. Select the type of file system to be used on the partition. You can select from Linux native (ext2 or preferably ext3), software RAID, Linux swap (swap), physical volume (LVM), or Windows FAT (vfat).

## Tip

**To create a file system type different from those shown, leave the space you want to use free for now. After installation is complete, use fdisk to create a partition of the type you want. ∎**

4. Type the number of megabytes to be used for the partition (in the Size field). If you want this partition to grow to fill the rest of the hard disk, you can put any number in this field (1 will do fine).

5. If you have more than one hard disk, select the disk on which you want to put the partition from the Allowable Drives box.

6. Type the size of the partition (in megabytes) into the Size (MB) box.

7. Select one of the following Additional Size options:

   - **Fixed size**—Click here to use only the number of megabytes you entered into the Size text box when you create the partition.

   - **Fill all space up to (MB)**—If you want to use all remaining space up to a certain number of megabytes, click here and fill in the number. (You may want to do this if you are creating a VFAT partition up to the 2048MB limit that Disk Setup can create.)

   - **Fill to maximum allowable size**—If you want this partition to grow to fill the rest of the disk, click here.

8. Optionally, select Force to Be a Primary Partition if you want to be sure to be able to boot the partition or Check for Bad Blocks if you want to have the partition checked for errors.

9. Click OK if everything is correct. (The changes don't take effect until several steps later when you are asked to begin installing the packages.)

To edit a partition in Disk Setup from the main Disk Setup window, follow these steps:

1. Click the partition you want to edit.

2. Click the Edit button. A window appears, ready to let you edit the partition definition.

3. Change any of the attributes (as described in the add partition procedure). For a new install, you may need to add the mount point (/) for your primary Linux partition.

4. Select OK. (The changes don't take effect until several steps later, when you are asked to begin installing the packages.)

### Partitioning with fdisk

The fdisk utility is available with almost every Linux system for creating and working with disk partitions in Linux. It does the same job as graphical partitioning tools such as Disk Setup, but runs in the shell.

## Tip
During Fedora and other Linux installations that have virtual terminals running, you can switch to a shell (press Ctrl+Alt+F2) and use fdisk manually to partition your hard disk. ∎

The following procedures are performed from the command line as root user.

## Caution

**Remember that any partition commands can easily make your disk inaccessible. Back up critical data before using any tool to change partitions! Then be very careful about the changes you do make. Keeping an emergency boot disk handy is a good idea, too.** ■

The `fdisk` command is available on many different operating systems (although it looks and behaves differently on each). In Linux, `fdisk` is a menu-based command. To use `fdisk` to list all your partitions, type the following (as root user):

```
# fdisk -1
Disk /dev/sda: 40.0 GB, 40020664320 bytes
255 heads, 63 sectors/track, 4865 cylinders
Units = cylinders of 16065 * 512 = 8225280 bytes

   Device Boot    Start      End     Blocks   Id  System
/dev/sda1    *        1       13     104391   83  Linux
/dev/sda2            14     4833   38716650   83  Linux
/dev/sda3          4834     4865     257040   82  Linux swap
```

To see how each partition is being used on your current system, type the following:

```
# df -h
Filesystem        Size  Used  Avail  Use%  Mounted on
/dev/sda2          37G  5.4G    30G   16%  /
/dev/sda1          99M  8.6M    86M   10%  /boot
```

From the output of `df`, you can see that the root of your Linux system (/) is on the `/dev/sda2` partition and that the `/dev/sda1` partition is used for `/boot`.

## Caution

**Before using** `fdisk` **to change your partitions, I strongly recommend running the** `df -h` **command to see how your partitions are currently being defined. This helps reduce the risk of changing or deleting the wrong partition.** ■

To use `fdisk` to change your partitions, you need to identify the hard disk you are partitioning. For example, the first SATA or SCSI hard disk is identified as `/dev/sda`. So, to partition your first hard drive, you can begin (as root user) by typing:

```
# fdisk /dev/sda
```

For different hard drive types or numbers, `/dev/sda` is replaced by the name of the device you want to work with. Table 8-1 shows some of your choices.

| TABLE 8-1 | |
|---|---|

## Disk Device Names

| Device | Description |
|---|---|
| /dev/sda | For the first SATA or SCSI hard disk; sdb, sdc, and so on for other disks. |
| /dev/hda | For the first IDE drive. |

After you have started fdisk, type **m** to see the options. Here is what you can do with fdisk:

- **Delete a partition**—Type **d** and a partition number, and then press Enter. For example, /dev/sda2 would be partition number 2. (The deletion won't take effect until you write the change—you can back out up to that point.)

- **Create a partition**—If you have free space, you can add a new partition. Type **n**; then choose **e** for an extended partition or **p** for a primary partition; then select a partition number from the available range. You can have only four primary partitions. However, after you have three primary partitions, make the fourth an extended partition (consuming all the remaining disk space). Then you can create many more logical partitions from the space in your extended partition.

  Next choose the first cylinder number from those available. (The output from fdisk -l shown earlier will show you cylinders being used under the Start and End columns.)

  After that, enter the cylinder number the partition will end with (or type the specific number of megabytes or kilobytes you want; for example, +50M or +1024K). You just created an ext3 Linux partition. Again, this change isn't permanent until you write the changes.

- **Change the partition type**—Press **t** to choose the type of file system. Enter the partition number of the partition number you want to change. Type the number representing the file system type you want to use in hexadecimal code. (Type **L** at this point to see a list of file system types and codes.) For a Linux file system, use the number 83; for a Linux swap partition, use 82; and for a windows FAT32 file system, use the letter *b*.

- **Display the partition table**—Throughout this process, feel free to type **p** to display (print on the screen) the partition table as it now stands.

- **Quit or save**—Before you write your changes, display the partition table again and make sure that it is what you want it to be. If you don't like a change you made to your partitions, press **q** to exit without saving. Nothing changes on your partition table.

  If your changes are correct, write them to the partition table by pressing **w**. You are warned about how dangerous changing partitions can be, and you must confirm the change.

After you have changed your partition table, you must alert the kernel of the change. To do that, run the partprobe command as root, as follows:

```
# partprobe
```

An alternative to the menu-driven fdisk command is sfdisk, which is a command line–oriented partitioning tool. With sfdisk, you type the full command line to list or change partitions, instead of being taken through a set of prompts (as with fdisk). See the sfdisk man page for details. Linux experts often prefer sfdisk because it can be used in combination with other commands to take and output partitioning information.

## Tips for creating partitions

Changing your disk partitions to handle multiple operating systems can be very tricky, in part because each operating system has its own ideas about how partitioning information should be handled, as well as different tools for doing it. Here are some tips to help you get it right:

- If you are creating a dual-boot system, particularly for Windows XP, try to install the Windows operating system first. Otherwise, the Windows installation may make the Linux partitions inaccessible. Choosing a VFAT instead of NTFS file system for Windows will also make sharing files between your Windows and Linux systems easier and more reliable.

- The fdisk man page recommends that you use partitioning tools that come with an operating system to create partitions for that operating system. For example, the DOS fdisk knows how to create partitions that DOS will like, and the Linux fdisk will happily make your Linux partitions. After your hard disk is set up for dual boot, however, you should probably not go back to Windows-only partitioning tools. Use Linux fdisk or a product made for multi-boot systems (such as Partition Magic).

- You can have up to 63 partitions on an IDE hard disk. A SCSI hard disk can have up to 15 partitions. You typically won't need nearly that many partitions.

If you are using Linux as a desktop system, you probably don't need a lot of different partitions. However, some very good reasons exist for having multiple partitions for Linux systems that are shared by a lot of users or are public Web servers or file servers. Having multiple partitions within Fedora Linux, for example, offers the following advantages:

- **Protection from attacks**—Denial-of-service attacks sometimes take actions that try to fill up your hard disk. If public areas, such as /var, are on separate partitions, a successful attack can fill up a partition without shutting down the whole computer. Because /var is the default location for Web and FTP servers, and expected to hold a lot of data, entire hard disks often are assigned to the /var file system alone.

- **Protection from corrupted file systems**—If you have only one file system (/), its corruption can cause the whole Linux system to be damaged. Corruption of a smaller partition can be easier to fix and often allows the computer to stay in service while the correction is made.

Table 8-2 lists some directories that you may want to consider making into separate file system partitions.

**TABLE 8-2**

### Assigning Partitions to Particular Directories

| Directory | Explanation |
|-----------|-------------|
| /boot | Sometimes the BIOS in older PCs can access only the first 1,024 cylinders of your hard disk. To make sure that the information in your /boot directory is accessible to the BIOS, create a separate disk partition (of about 100MB) for /boot and make sure that it exists below cylinder 1,024. The rest of your Linux system can exist outside of that 1,024-cylinder boundary if you like. Even with several boot images, there is rarely a reason for /boot to be larger than 100MB. (For newer hard disks, you can select the Linear Mode check box during installation. Then the boot partition can be anywhere on the disk.) |
| /usr | This directory structure contains most of the applications and utilities available to Linux users. Having /usr on a separate partition lets you mount that file system as read-only after the operating system has been installed. This prevents attackers from replacing or removing important system applications with their own versions that may cause security problems. A separate /usr partition is also useful if you have diskless workstations on your local network. Using NFS, you can share /usr over the network with those workstations. |
| /var | Your FTP (/var/ftp) and Web server (/var/www) directories are, by default in many Linux systems, stored under /var. Having a separate /var partition can prevent an attack on those facilities from corrupting or filling up your entire hard disk. |
| /home | Because your user account directories are located in this directory, having a separate /home account can prevent a reckless user from filling up the entire hard disk. It also conveniently separates user data from your operating system (for easy backups or new installs). |
| /tmp | Protecting /tmp from the rest of the hard disk by placing it on a separate partition can ensure that applications that need to write to temporary files in /tmp are able to complete their processing, even if the rest of the disk fills up. |

Although people who use Linux systems casually rarely see a need for lots of partitions, those who maintain and occasionally have to recover large systems are thankful when the system they need to fix has several partitions. Multiple partitions can localize deliberate damage (such as denial-of-service attacks), problems from errant users, and accidental file system corruption.

## Using LILO or GRUB boot loaders

A boot loader lets you choose when and how to boot the bootable operating systems installed on your computer's hard disks. Most Linux systems give you the opportunity to use GRUB or LILO boot loaders. The following sections describe both GRUB and LILO boot loaders.

## Note

SYSLINUX is another boot loader you will encounter with Linux systems. The SYSLINUX boot loaders are not typically used for installed Linux systems. However, SYSLINUX is commonly used as the boot loader for Linux CDs and DVDs. SYSLINUX is particularly good for booting ISO9660 CD images and for working on older hardware. ■

### Booting your computer with GRUB

With multiple operating systems installed and several partitions set up, how does your computer know which operating system to start? To select and manage which partition is booted and how it is booted, you need a boot loader. The boot loader that is installed by default with Fedora and other Linux systems is the GRand Unified Boot loader (GRUB).

GRUB is a GNU bootloader (www.gnu.org/software/grub) that replaced LILO as the default boot loader in many Linux systems, including Fedora and Ubuntu. GRUB offers the following features:

- Support for multiple executable formats.
- Support for multi-boot operating systems (such as Fedora, FreeBSD, NetBSD, OpenBSD, and other Linux systems).
- Support for non–multi-boot operating systems (such as Windows 95, Windows 98, Windows NT, Windows ME, Windows XP, and OS/2) via a chain-loading function. Chain-loading is the act of loading another boot loader (presumably one that is specific to the proprietary operating system) from GRUB to start the selected operating system.
- Support for multiple file system types.
- Support for automatic decompression of boot images.
- Support for downloading boot images from a network.

For more information on how GRUB works, type **man grub** or **info grub**. The `info` command contains more details about GRUB.

### Booting with GRUB

When you install Linux, you are typically given the option to configure the information needed to boot your computer (with one or more operating systems) into the default boot loader. With GRUB configured, when you boot your computer, the first thing you see after the BIOS loads is the GRUB boot screen (it says GRUB at the top and lists bootable partitions below it); do one of the following:

- **Default**—If you do nothing, the default operating system will boot automatically after a few seconds. (The timeout is set by the `timeout` value, in seconds, in the `grub.conf` file.)
- **Select an operating system**—Use the up and down arrow keys to select any of the titles, representing operating systems you can boot, that are shown on the screen. Then press Enter to boot that operating system.

- **Edit the boot process**—If you want to change any of the options used during the boot process, use the arrow keys to highlight the operating system you want and type **e** to select it. Follow the next procedure to change your boot options temporarily.

If you want to change your boot options so that they take effect every time you boot your computer, see the section on permanently changing boot options. Changing those options involves editing the /boot/grub/grub.conf file.

## Temporarily changing boot options

From the GRUB boot screen, you can select to change or add boot options for the current boot session. On some Linux systems, the menu is hidden, so you have to press a key (before a few seconds of timeout is exceeded) to see the menu. Then, select the operating system you want (using the arrow keys) and type **e** (as described earlier). A graphical screen appears that looks like the one shown in Figure 8-2.

**FIGURE 8-2**

From the GRUB boot screen, you can select to change boot options.

Three lines in the example of the GRUB editing screen identify the boot process for the operating system you chose. The first line (beginning with root) shows that the entry for the GRUB boot loader is on the fifth partition of the first hard disk (hd0,4). GRUB represents the hard disk as hd, regardless of whether it is a SCSI, IDE, or other type of disk. You just count the drive number and partition number, starting from zero (0).

The second line of the example (beginning with kernel) identifies the boot image (/boot/vmlinuz-2.6.27.24-78.2.53.fc9.i686) and several options. The options identify the partition as initially being loaded ro (read-only) and the location of the root file system on a partition with the label that begins root=UUID. The third line (starting with initrd) identifies the location of the initial RAM disk, which contains the minimum files and directories needed during the boot process.

If you are going to change any of the lines related to the boot process, you would probably change only the second line to add or remove boot options. Here is how you do that:

1. Position the cursor on the `kernel` line and type **e**.

2. Either add or remove options after the name of the boot image. You can use a minimal set of bash shell command-line editing features to edit the line. You can even use command completion (type part of a filename and press Tab to complete it). Here are a few options you may want to add or delete:

   - **Boot to a shell**—If you forgot your root password or if your boot process hangs, you can boot directly to a shell by adding `init=/bin/sh` to the boot line. (The root file system is mounted read-only, so you can copy files out. You need to remount the root file system with read/write permission to be able to change files: `mount -o remount,rw /`)

   - **Select a run level**—If you want to boot to a particular run level, you can add the run level you want to the end of the kernel line. For example, to have Fedora Linux boot to run level 3 (multiuser plus networking mode), add 3 to the end of the kernel line. You can also boot to single-user mode (1), multiuser mode (2), or X GUI mode (5). Level 3 is a good choice if your GUI is temporarily broken. Level 1 is good if you have forgotten your root password.

3. Press Enter to return to the editing screen.

4. Type **b** to boot the computer with the new options. The next time you boot your computer, the new options will not be saved. To add options so they are saved permanently, see the next section.

## Permanently changing boot options

You can change the options that take effect each time you boot your computer by changing the GRUB configuration file. In Fedora and other Linux systems, GRUB configuration centers on the `/boot/grub/grub.conf` file.

The `/boot/grub/grub.conf` file is created when you install Linux. Here's an example of that file for Fedora:

```
# grub.conf generated by anaconda
#boot=/dev/sda
default=0
timeout=10
splashimage=(hd0,4)/boot/grub/splash.xpm.gz
hiddenmenu
title Fedora (2.6.27.24-78.2.53.fc9.i686)
        root (hd0,4)
        kernel /boot/vmlinuz-2.6.27.24-78.2.53.fc9.i686 ro \
```

```
                        root=UUID=eb3834a2-ba78-43c0-908f-d627117696e7 rhgb quiet
                initrd /boot/initrd-2.6.27.24-78.2.53.fc9.i686.img
        title Windows XP
                rootnoverify (hd0,0)
                chainloader +1
```

The default=0 line indicates that the first partition in this list (in this case Fedora) will be the one that is booted by default. The line timeout=10 causes GRUB to pause for 10 seconds before booting the default partition. (That's how much time you have to press **e** if you want to edit the boot line, or to press arrow keys to select a different operating system to boot.)

The splashimage line looks in the seventh partition on the first disk (hd0,4) for the boot partition (in this case /dev/sda5, which is the / partition). GRUB loads splash.xpm.gz as the image on the splash screen (/boot/grub/splash.xpm.gz). The splash screen appears as the background of the boot screen.

## Note

GRUB indicates disk partitions using the following notation: (hd0,0). The first number represents the disk, and the second is the partition on that disk. So, (hd0,1) is the second partition (1) on the first disk (0). ■

The two bootable partitions in this example are Fedora and Windows XP. The title lines for each of those partitions are followed by the name that appears on the boot screen to represent each partition.

For the Fedora Linux system, the root line indicates the location of the boot partition as the second partition on the first disk. So, to find the bootable kernel (vmlinuz-2.6.27.24-78.2.53.fc9.i686) and the initrd initial RAM disk boot image that is loaded (initrd-2.6.27.24-78.2.53.fc9.i686.img), GRUB looks in the root of hd0,4 (which is represented by /dev/sda5 and is mounted as /). Other options on the kernel line set the partition as read-only initially (ro) and set the root file system to the particular UUID set for the root partition.

For the Windows XP partition, the rootnoverify line indicates that GRUB should not try to mount the partition. In this case, Windows XP is on the first partition of the first hard disk (hd0,0) or /dev/sda1. Instead of mounting the partition and passing options to the new operating system, the chainloader +1 indicates to hand control of the booting of the operating system to another boot loader. The +1 indicates that the first sector of the partition is used as the boot loader. (You could similarly set up to boot a Windows Vista or Windows 7 operating system.)

## Note

Microsoft operating systems require that you use the chainloader to boot them from GRUB because GRUB doesn't offer native support for Windows operating systems. ■

If you make any changes to the /boot/grub/grub.conf file, you do *not* need to load those changes. GRUB automatically picks up those changes when you reboot your computer. If you are accustomed to using the LILO boot loader, this may confuse you at first, as LILO requires you to rerun the `lilo` command for the changes to take effect.

## Adding a new GRUB boot image

You may have different boot images for kernels that include different features. In most cases, installing a new kernel package will automatically configure `grub.conf` to use that new kernel. However, if you want to manually add a kernel, here is the procedure for modifying the `grub.conf` file to be able to boot that kernel:

1. Copy the new image from the directory in which it was created (such as `/usr/src/kernels/linux-2.6.25-11/arch/i386/boot`) to the `/boot` directory. Name the file something that reflects its contents, such as `bz-2.6.25-11`. For example:

   ```
   # cp /usr/src/linux-2.6.25-11/arch/i386/boot/bzImage/boot/bz-2.6.25-11
   ```

2. Add several lines to the `/boot/grub/grub.conf` file so that the image can be started at boot time if it is selected. For example:

   ```
   title Fedora (My own IPV6 build)
       root (hd0,4)
       kernel /bz-2.6.25-11 ro root=/dev/sda5
       initrd /initrd-2.6.25-11.img
   ```

3. Reboot your computer.

4. When the GRUB boot screen appears, move your cursor to the title representing the new kernel and press Enter.

The advantage to this approach, as opposed to copying the new boot image over the old one, is that if the kernel fails to boot, you can always go back and restart the old kernel. When you feel confident that the new kernel is working properly, you can use it to replace the old kernel or perhaps just make the new kernel the default boot definition.

## Booting your computer with LILO

LILO stands for LInux LOader. Like other boot loaders, LILO is a program that can stand outside the operating systems installed on the computer so you can choose which system to boot. It also lets you give special options that modify how the operating system is booted. On Slackware and some other Linux systems, LILO is used instead of GRUB as the default boot loader.

If LILO is being used on your computer, it is installed in either the master boot record or the first sector of the root partition. The master boot record is read directly by the computer's BIOS. In general, if LILO is the only loader on your computer, install it in the master boot record. If another boot loader is already in the master boot record, put LILO in the root partition.

# Note

If you are new to Linux and not familiar with boot loaders, it is highly recommended you learn and use GRUB instead of LILO. Support for LILO—and inclusion in distributions—has been reduced in favor of GRUB. ∎

### Using LILO

When your computer boots with the Fedora version of LILO installed in the master boot record, a graphical Fedora screen appears, displaying the bootable partitions on the computer. Use the up and down arrow keys on your keyboard to select the one you want and press Enter. Otherwise, the default partition that you set at installation will boot after a few seconds.

If you want to add any special options when you boot, press Ctrl+X. You will see a text-based boot prompt that appears as follows:

```
boot:
```

LILO pauses for a few seconds and then automatically boots the first image from the default bootable partition. To see the bootable partitions again, quickly press Tab. You may see something similar to the following:

```
LILO boot:
linux linux-up dos
boot:
```

This example shows that three bootable partitions are on your computer, called linux, linux-up, and dos. The first two refer to two different boot images that can boot the Linux partition. The third refers to a bootable DOS partition (presumably containing a Windows operating system). The first bootable partition is loaded if you don't type anything after a few seconds. Or you can use the name of the other partition to have that boot instead.

If you have multiple boot images, press Shift, and LILO asks you which image you want to boot. Available boot images and other options are defined in the /etc/lilo.conf file.

### Setting up the /etc/lilo.conf file

The /etc/lilo.conf file is where LILO gets the information it needs to find and start bootable partitions and images. By adding options to the /etc/lilo.conf file, you can change the behavior of the boot process. The following is an example of some of the contents of the /etc/lilo.conf file:

```
prompt
timeout=50
default=linux
boot=/dev/hda
map=/boot/map
install=/boot/boot.b
message=/boot/message
linear
```

```
image=/boot/vmlinuz-2.6.27.24-78.2.53.fc9.i686
        label=linux
        initrd=/boot/initrd-2.6.27.24-78.2.53.fc9.i686.img
        read-only
        root=/dev/hda5
        append="root=LABEL=/"

other=/dev/hda1
        optional
        label=dos
```

With `prompt` on, the boot prompt appears when the system is booted without requiring that any keys are pressed. The timeout value, in this case 50 tenths of a second (5 seconds), defines how long to wait for keyboard input before booting the default boot image. The boot line indicates that the bootable partition is on the hard disk represented by /dev/hda (the first IDE hard disk).

# Note
**Depending upon the distribution, "hda" may be "sda". If you are using LILO, the odds are good that you are using an older Linux implementation and thus hda is shown in the example and used in this discussion.** ■

The `map` line indicates the location of the map file (/boot/map, by default). The map file contains the name and locations of bootable kernel images. The `install` line indicates that the /boot/boot.b file is used as the new boot sector. The `message` line tells LILO to display the contents of the /boot/message file when booting (which contains the graphical Fedora boot screen). The linear line causes linear sector addresses to be generated (instead of sector/head/cylinder addresses).

The sample file has two bootable partitions. The first (`image=/boot/vmlinuz-2.6.27.24-78.2.53.fc9.i686`) shows an image labeled `linux`. The root file system (/) for that image is on partition /dev/hda5. Read-only indicates that the file system is first mounted read-only, although it is probably mounted as read/write after a file system check. The `initrd` line indicates the location of the initial RAM disk image used to start the system.

The second bootable partition, which is indicated by the word *other* in this example, is on the /dev/hda1 partition. Because it is a Windows system, it is labeled a DOS file system. The table line indicates the device that contains the partition.

Other bootable images are listed in this file, and you can add another boot image yourself (like one you create from reconfiguring your kernel as discussed in the next section) by installing the new image and changing `lilo.conf`.

After you change `lilo.conf`, you then must run the `lilo` command for the changes to take effect. You may have different boot images for kernels that include different features. The following is the procedure for modifying the `lilo.conf` file:

**1.** Copy the new image from the directory in which it was created (such as /usr/src/kernels/2.6.27.24-78.2.53.fc9/arch/i386/boot) to the /boot directory. Name the file something that reflects its contents, such as zImage-2.6.27.24-78.2.53.fc9.img.

2. Add several lines to the /etc/lilo.conf file so that the image can be started at boot time if it is selected. For example:

```
image=/boot/zImage-2.6.27.24-78.2.53.fc9.img
label=new
```

3. Type the **lilo -t** command (as root user) to test that the changes were okay.

4. Type the **lilo** command (with no options) for the changes to be installed.

To boot from this new image, either select new from the graphical boot screen or type **new** and press Enter at the LILO boot prompt. If five seconds is too quick, increase the timeout value (such as 100 for 10 seconds).

Options that you can use in the /etc/lilo.conf file are divided into global options, per-image options, and kernel options. A lot of documentation is available for LILO. For more details on any of the options described here or for other options, you can see the lilo.conf manual page (type **man lilo.conf**) or any of the documents in /usr/share/doc/lilo*/doc.

A few examples follow of global options that you can add to /etc/lilo.conf. Global options apply to LILO as a whole, instead of just to a particular boot image.

You can use the default=*label* option, where *label* is replaced by an image's label name, to indicate that a particular image be used as the default boot image. If that option is excluded, the first image listed in the /etc/lilo.conf file is used as the default. For example, to start the image labeled new by default, add the following line to lilo.conf:

```
default=new
```

Change the delay from 5 seconds to something greater if you want LILO to wait longer before starting the default image. This gives you more time to boot a different image. To change the value from 5 seconds (50) to 15 seconds (150), add the following line:

```
delay=150
```

You can change the message that appears before the LILO prompt by adding that message to a file and changing the message line. For example, you could create a /boot/boot.message file and add the following words to that file: Choose linux, new, or dos. To have that message appear before the boot prompt, add the following line to /etc/lilo.conf:

```
message=/boot/boot.message
```

All per-image options begin with either an image= line (indicating a Linux kernel) or other= (indicating some other kind of operating system, such as a Windows system). The per-image options apply to particular boot images rather than to all images (as global options do). Along with the image or other line is a label= line, which gives a name to that image. The name is what you select at boot time to boot that image. Here are some of the options that you can add to each of those image definitions:

- lock—This enables automatic recording of boot command lines as the defaults for different boot options.

- alias=name—You can replace name with any name. That name becomes an alias for the image name defined in the label option.

- password=password—You can password-protect all images by adding a password option line and replacing password with your own password. The password would have to be entered to boot any of the images.

- restricted—This option is used with the password option. It indicates that a password should be used only if command-line options are given when trying to boot the image.

For Linux kernel images, there are specific options that you can use. These options let you deal with hardware issues that can't be autodetected, or provide information such as how the root file system is mounted. Here are some of the kernel image-specific options:

- append—Add a string of letters and numbers to this option that need to be passed to the kernel. In particular, these can be parameters that need to be passed to better define the hard disk when some aspect of that disk can't be autodetected (for example, append="hd=64,32,202").

- ramdisk—Add the size of the RAM disk that you want to use in order to override the size of the RAM disk built into the kernel.

- read-only—Mount the root file system read-only. It is typically remounted read-write after the disk is checked.

- read-write—Mount the root file system read/write.

### Changing your boot loader

If you don't want to use the GRUB boot loader, or if you tried out LILO and want to switch back to GRUB, then changing to a different boot loader on Linux distributions that support both boot loaders is not hard. To switch your boot loader from GRUB to LILO, do the following:

1. Configure the /etc/lilo.conf file as described in the "Booting Your Computer with LILO" section.

2. As root user from a Terminal window, type the following:

   # lilo

3. The new Master Boot Record is written, including the entries in /etc/lilo.conf.

4. Reboot your computer. You should see the LILO boot screen.

To change your boot loader from LILO to GRUB, do the following:

1. Configure the `/boot/grub/grub.conf` file as described in the "Booting Your Computer with GRUB" section.

2. You need to know the device on which you want to install GRUB. For example, to install GRUB on the master boot record of the first disk, type the following as root user from a Terminal window:

   ```
   # grub-install /dev/hda
   ```
   The new Master Boot Record is written to boot with the GRUB boot loader.

3. Reboot your computer. You should see the GRUB boot screen.

If for some reason you don't see the GRUB boot screen when you reboot, you can use a rescue CD to reboot your computer and fix the problem. When the rescue CD boots up, mount the file system containing the `/boot/grub/grub.conf` file. Then use the `chroot` command to change to the root of that file system. Correct the `grub.conf` file and run `grub-install` again.

## Configuring networking

If you are connecting your computer to an Ethernet LAN that has a DHCP server available, you probably don't need to do anything to start up automatically on your LAN and even be connected to the Internet. However, if no DHCP server is on your LAN and you have to configure your TCP/IP connection manually, here is the information you will probably be prompted for during Linux installation:

- **IP address**—If you set your own IP address, this is the four-part, dot-separated number that represents your computer to the network. Explaining how IP addresses are formed and how you choose them would take more than a few sentences (see Chapter 11 for a more complete description). An example of a private IP address is 192.168.0.1.

- **Netmask**—The netmask is used to determine what part of an IP address represents the network and what part represents a particular host computer. An example of a netmask for a Class C network is 255.255.255.0. If you apply this netmask to an IP address of 192.168.0.1, for example, the network address would be 192.168.0 and the host address 1. Because 0 and 255 can't be assigned to a particular host, that leaves valid host numbers between 1 and 254 available for this local network.

- **Activate on boot**—Some Linux install procedures ask you to indicate whether you want the network to start at boot time (you probably do if you have a LAN).

- **Set the host name**—This is the name identifying your computer within your domain. For example, if your computer were named "baskets" in the `handsonhistory.com` domain, your full host name may be `baskets.handsonhistory.com`. You can either set the domain name yourself (manually) or have it assigned automatically, if that information is being assigned by a DHCP server (automatically via DHCP).

- **Gateway**—This is the IP number of the computer that acts as a gateway to networks outside your LAN. This typically represents a host computer or router that routes packets between your LAN and the Internet.

- **Primary DNS**—This is the IP address of the host that translates computer names you request into IP addresses. It is referred to as a Domain Name System (DNS) server. You may also have Secondary and Tertiary name servers in case the first one can't be reached. (Most ISPs will give you two DNS server addresses.)

## Configuring other administrative features

Depending on which Linux install you are using, you will be asked to enter other types of information. These might involve the following:

- **Firewall**—Most Linux distributions these days use iptables to configure firewalls. Older Linux systems used ipchains. When you configure a default firewall, you typically choose which ports will be open to outside connections on your system (although a firewall can be configured to do many other things as well). The iptables firewall facility is described in Chapter 27.

- **Languages**—Although Linux itself doesn't include support for lots of different languages, some Linux distributions (such as Fedora) and desktop environments (such as KDE) offer support for many different languages. Nearly all Linux distributions will let you configure language-specific keyboards.

- **Root password and additional user**—Every Linux system that uses passwords will have you add at least the root user's password when you install Linux. Some distributions will require that you add at least one additional non-root user as well.

Besides the features just mentioned, every distribution needs to have some initial configuration done before you have a fully functional Linux system. See Chapter 10 for information on basic administrative tasks for Linux.

# Installing from the *Linux Bible* CD or DVD

With the knowledge you've gained in this chapter, you're ready to select a Linux distribution to install. Read the descriptions of Linux distributions in the other chapters in Part V of this book. Each chapter tells you whether the distribution described there is on the CD or DVD included with this book, or if it isn't, where you can get it.

If you need more information about the CD or DVD, Appendix A describes the contents of those discs. It also tells you which Linux distributions you can run live or use to install Linux permanently to your hard disk from those two discs.

# Summary

Although every Linux distribution includes a different installation method, you need to do many common activities, regardless of which Linux system you install. For every Linux system, you need to deal with issues of disk partitioning, network configuration, and boot loaders.

*Linux Bible* includes a DVD and a CD with several different Linux systems you can install. If you prefer, you can instead download and burn your own CDs or DVDs to install Linux. If you go the route of burning your own CDs, this chapter helps you find Linux distributions you can download and describes tools you can use to verify their contents.

# Running Commands from the Shell

**B**efore icons and windows took over computer screens, you typed commands to interact with most computers. On UNIX systems, from which Linux was derived, the program used to interpret and manage commands was referred to as the *shell*.

No matter which Linux distribution you are using, you can always count on one thing being available to you: the shell. It provides a way to create executable script files, run programs, work with file systems, compile computer code, operate a system, and manage the computer. Although the shell is less intuitive than common graphic user interfaces (GUIs), most Linux experts consider the shell to be much more powerful than GUIs. Shells have been around a long time, and many advanced features have been built into them.

The Linux shell illustrated in this chapter is called the *bash shell*, which stands for Bourne Again Shell. The name is derived from the fact that bash is compatible with the one of the earliest UNIX shells: the Bourne shell (named after its creator Stephen Bourne, and represented by the sh command).

Although bash is included with most distributions, and considered a standard, other shells are available. Other popular shells include the C shell (csh), which is popular among BSD UNIX users, and the Korn shell (ksh), which is popular among UNIX System V users. Linux also has a tcsh shell (a C shell look-alike) and an ash shell (another Bourne shell look-alike). Several different shells are introduced in this chapter.

## Tip

The odds are strong that the Linux distribution you are using has more than one shell installed by default and available for your use. ∎

Several major reasons for learning how to use the shell are

- You will know how to get around any Linux or other UNIX-like system. For example, I can log in to my Red Hat Enterprise Linux MySQL server, my bootable floppy router/firewall, or my wife's iMac and explore and use any of those computer systems from a shell.

- Special shell features enable you to gather data input and direct data output between commands and the Linux file system. To save on typing, you can find, edit, and repeat commands from your shell history. Many power users hardly touch a graphical interface, doing most of their work from a shell.

- You can gather commands into a file using programming constructs such as conditional checks, loops, and case statements to quickly do complex operations that would be difficult to retype over and over. Programs consisting of commands that are stored and run from a file are referred to as *shell scripts*. Most Linux system administrators use shell scripts to automate tasks such as backing up data, monitoring log files, or checking system health.

The shell is a command language interpreter. If you have used Microsoft operating systems, you'll see that using a shell in Linux is similar to — but generally much more powerful than — the interpreter used to run commands in DOS or in the CMD command interface. You can happily use Linux from a graphical desktop interface, but as you grow into Linux you will surely need to use the shell at some point to track down a problem or administer some features.

How to use the shell isn't obvious at first, but with the right help you can quickly learn many of the most important shell features. This chapter is your guide to working with the Linux system commands, processes, and file system from the shell. It describes the shell environment and helps you tailor it to your needs. It also explains how to use and move around the file system.

# Starting a Shell

There are several ways to get to a shell interface in Linux. Three of the most common are the shell prompt, Terminal window, and virtual terminal. They're discussed in the following sections.

## Using the shell prompt

If your Linux system has no graphical user interface (or one that isn't working at the moment), you will most likely see a shell prompt after you log in. Typing commands from the shell will probably be your primary means of using the Linux system.

The default prompt for a regular user is simply a dollar sign:

    $

The default prompt for the root user is a pound sign (also called a *hash mark*):

    #

In most Linux systems, the $ and # prompts are preceded by your username, system name, and current directory name. For example, a login prompt for the user named jake on a computer named pine with /tmp as the current directory would appear as

    [jake@pine tmp]$

You can change the prompt to display any characters you like — you can use the current directory, the date, the local computer name, or any string of characters as your prompt, for example. To configure your prompt, see the "Setting your prompt" section later in this chapter.

Although a tremendous number of features are available with the shell, it's easy to begin by just typing a few commands. Try some of the commands shown in the remainder of this section to become familiar with your current shell environment.

In the examples that follow, the dollar ($) and pound (#) symbols indicate a prompt. While a $ indicates that the command can be run by any user, a # typically means you should run the command as the root user — many administrative tools require root permission to be able to run them. The prompt is followed by the command that you type (and then you press Enter or Return, depending on your keyboard). The lines that follow show the output resulting from the command.

## Using a terminal window

With the desktop GUI running, you can open a terminal emulator program (sometimes referred to as a Terminal window) to start a shell. Most Linux distributions make it easy for you to get to a shell from the GUI. Here are two common ways to launch a Terminal window from a Linux desktop:

- **Right-click the desktop.** In the context menu that appears, look for Shells, New Terminal, Terminal Window, Xterm, or some similar item and select it.

- **Click on the panel menu.** Many Linux desktops include a panel at the top or bottom of the screen from which you can launch applications. For example, in some systems that use the GNOME desktop, you can select Applications ➪ System Tools ➪ Terminal to open a Terminal window. For Mandriva, select System ➪ Terminals.

In all cases, you should just be able to type a command as you would from a shell with no GUI. Different terminal emulators are available with Linux. One of the following is likely to be the default used with your Linux system:

- **xterm** — A common terminal emulator for the X Window System. (In fact, I've never seen an X Window System for a major Linux distribution that didn't include xterm.) Although it doesn't provide menus or many special features, it is available with most Linux distributions that support a GUI.

- **gnome-terminal** — The default Terminal emulator window that comes with GNOME. It consumes more system resources than xterm does, and it has useful menus for cutting and pasting, opening new Terminal tabs or windows, and setting terminal profiles.

- **konsole** — The konsole terminal emulator that comes with the KDE desktop environment. With konsole, you can display multilanguage text encoding and text in different colors.

The differences in running commands within a Terminal window have more to do with the shell you are running than the type of Terminal window you are using. Differences in Terminal windows have more to do with the features each supports — for example, how much output is saved that can be scrolled back to; whether you can change font types and sizes, and whether the Terminal window supports features such as transparency or cut and paste.

## Using virtual terminals

Most Linux systems that include a desktop interface start multiple virtual terminals running on the computer. Virtual terminals are a way to have multiple shell sessions open at once outside of the graphical interface you are using.

You can switch between virtual terminals much the same way that you would switch between workspaces on a GUI. Press Ctrl+Alt+F1 (or F2, F3, F4, and so on up to F6 on Fedora and other Linux systems) to display one of six virtual terminals. The next virtual workspace after the virtual terminals is where the GUI is, so if there are six virtual terminals, you can return to the GUI (if one is running) by pressing Ctrl+Alt+F7. (For a system with four virtual terminals, you'd return to the GUI by pressing Ctrl+Alt+F5.)

# Choosing Your Shell

In most Linux systems, your default shell is the bash shell. To find out what your default login shell is, type the following command:

```
$ echo $SHELL
/bin/bash
```

In this example, it's the bash shell. There are many other shells, and you can activate a different one by simply typing the new shell's command (ksh, tcsh, csh, sh, bash, and so forth) from the current shell. For example, to change temporarily to the C shell, type the following command:

```
$ csh
```

## Note

**Most full Linux systems include all the shells described in this section. However, some smaller Linux distributions may include only one or two shells. The best way to find out whether a particular shell is available is to type the command and see whether the shell starts. ■**

You might want to choose a different shell to use because

- You are used to using UNIX System V systems (often ksh by default) or Sun Microsystems and other Berkeley UNIX–based distributions (frequently csh by default), and you are more comfortable using default shells from those environments.

- You want to run shell scripts that were created for a particular shell environment, and you need to run the shell for which they were made so you can test or use those scripts from your current shell.

- You might simply prefer features in one shell over those in another. For example, a member of my Linux Users Group prefers ksh over bash because he doesn't like the way aliases are used with bash.

Although most Linux users have a preference for one shell or another, when you know how to use one shell, you can quickly learn any of the others by occasionally referring to the shell's man page (for example, type **man bash**). Most people use bash just because they don't have a particular reason for using a different shell.

In Chapter 10, you learn how to assign a different default shell for a user. The following sections introduce several of the most common shells available with Linux.

## Using bash (and earlier sh) shells

As mentioned earlier, the name *bash* is an acronym for Bourne Again Shell, acknowledging the roots of bash coming from the Bourne shell (sh command) created by Steve Bourne at AT&T Bell Labs. Brian Fox of the Free Software foundation created bash, under the auspices of the GNU project. Development was later taken over by Chet Ramey at Case Western Reserve University.

Bash includes features originally developed for sh and ksh shells in early UNIX systems, as well as some csh features. Expect bash to be the default shell in whatever Linux system you are using, with the exception of some specialized Linux systems (such as those run on embedded devices or run from a floppy disk) that may require a smaller shell that needs less memory and entails fewer features. Most of the examples in this chapter are based on the bash shell.

## Tip

**The bash shell is worth knowing not only because it is the default in most installations, but because it is the one you will use with most Linux certification exams. ■**

Bash can be run in various compatibility modes so that it behaves like different shells. It can be run to behave as a Bourne shell (bash +B) or as a POSIX-compliant shell (type bash --posix), for example, enabling it to read configuration files that are specific to those shells and run initialization shell scripts written directly for those shells, with a greater chance of success.

All the Linux distributions included with this book use bash as the default shell, with the exception of some bootable Linux distributions, which use the ash shell instead.

## Using tcsh (and earlier csh) shells

The tcsh shell is the open source version of the C shell (csh). The csh shell was created by Bill Joy and used with most Berkeley UNIX systems (such as those produced by Sun Microsystems) as the default shell. Features from the TENEX and TOPS-20 operating systems (used on PDP-11s in the 1970s) that are included in this shell are responsible for the T in tcsh.

Many features of the original csh shell, such as command-line editing and its history mechanism, are included in tcsh as well as in other shells. Although you can run both csh and tcsh on most Linux systems, both commands actually point to the same executable file. In other words, starting csh actually runs the tcsh shell in csh compatibility mode.

## Using ash

The ash shell is a lightweight version of the Berkeley UNIX sh shell. It doesn't include many of the sh shell's basic features, and is missing such features as command histories. Kenneth Almquist created the ash shell used with NetBSD. A port of ash called dash is available in Debian systems.

The ash shell is a good shell for embedded systems that have fewer system resources available. The ash shell is about one-seventh the size of bash (about 92K versus 724K for bash). Because of cheaper memory prices these days, however, many embedded and small bootable Linux systems have enough space to include the full bash shell.

## Using ksh

The ksh shell was created by David Korn at AT&T Bell Labs and is the successor to the sh shell. It became the default and most commonly used shell with UNIX System V systems. The open source version of ksh was originally available in many rpm-based systems (such as Fedora and Red Hat Enterprise Linux) as part of the pdksh package. Now, however, David Korn has released the original ksh shell as open source, so you can look for it as part of a ksh software package in most Linux systems (see www.kornshell.com).

## Using zsh

The zsh shell is another clone of the sh shell. It is POSIX-compliant (as is bash), but includes some different features, such as spell-checking and a different approach to command editing. The first Mac OS X systems used zsh as the default shell, although now bash is used by default.

# Exploring the Shell

After you have access to a shell in Linux, you can begin by typing some simple commands. The "Using the Shell in Linux" section later in this chapter provides more details about options, arguments, and environment variables. For the time being, the following sections can help you poke around the shell a bit.

## Note

**If you don't like your default shell, simply type the name of the shell you want to try out temporarily. To change your shell permanently, use the** usermod **command. For example, to change to the csh shell for the user named chris, type the following as root user from a shell:**

```
# usermod -s /bin/csh chris ■
```

## Checking your login session

When you log in to a Linux system, Linux views you as having a particular identity, which includes your username, group name, user ID, and group ID. Linux also keeps track of your login session: It knows when you logged in, how long you have been idle, and where you logged in from.

To find out information about your identity, use the id command as follows:

```
$ id
uid=501(chris) gid=105(sales) groups=105(sales),4(adm),7(lp)
```

In this example, the username is chris, which is represented by the numeric user ID (uid) 501. The primary group for chris is called sales, which has a group ID (gid) of 105. The user chris also belongs to other groups called adm (gid 4) and lp (gid 7). These names and numbers represent the permissions that chris has to access computer resources. (Permissions are described in the "Understanding file permissions" section later in this chapter.)

## Note

**Based on the distribution you are using, the uid numbering may be in the thousands. ■**

You can see information about your current login session by using the who command. In the following example, the -u option says to add information about idle time and the process ID and -H asks that a header be printed:

```
$ who -uH
NAME     LINE   TIME          IDLE   PID   COMMENT
chris    tty1   Jan 13 20:57   .     2013
```

The output from this who command shows that the user chris is logged in on tty1 (which is the monitor connected to the computer), and his login session began at 20:57 on January 13. The IDLE time shows how long the shell has been open without any command being typed (the dot indicates that it is currently active). PID shows the process ID of the user's login shell. COMMENT would show the name of the remote computer the user had logged in from, if that user had logged in from another computer on the network, or the name of the local X display if you were using a Terminal window (such as :0.0).

# Checking directories and permissions

Associated with each shell is a location in the Linux file system known as the *current* or *working directory*. Each user has a directory that is identified as the user's home directory. When you first log in to Linux, you begin with your home directory as the current directory.

When you request to open or save a file, your shell uses the current directory as the point of reference. Simply provide a filename when you save a file, and it is placed in the current directory. Alternatively, you can identify a file by its relation to the current directory (relative path), or you can ignore the current directory and identify a file by the full directory hierarchy that locates it (absolute path). The structure and use of the file system is described in detail later in this chapter.

To find out what your current directory (the present working directory) is, type the pwd command:

```
$ pwd
/usr/bin
```

In this example, the current/working directory is /usr/bin. To find out the name of your home directory, type the echo command, followed by the $HOME variable:

```
$ echo $HOME
/home/chris
```

Here the home directory is /home/chris. To get back to your home directory, just type the change directory (cd) command. (Although cd followed by a directory name changes the current directory to the directory that you choose, simply typing **cd** with no directory name takes you to your home directory):

```
$ cd
```

## Note
Instead of typing $HOME, you can use the tilde (~) to refer to your home directory. So, to see your home directory, you could simply type **echo ~**. ■

To list the contents of your home directory with the ls command, either type the full path to your home directory, or use the ls command without a directory name. Using the -a option to ls enables you to view the hidden files (known as *dot files* because they start with the dot character) as well as all other files. With the -l option, you can see a long, detailed list of information on each file. (You can put multiple single-letter options together after a single dash; for example, -la.)

```
$ ls -la /home/chris
total 158
drwxrwxrwx    2   chris    sales    4096  May 12 13:55  .
```

```
drwxr-xr-x    3  root    root      4096  May 10 01:49  ..
-rw-------    1  chris   sales     2204  May 18 21:30  .bash_history
-rw-r--r--    1  chris   sales       24  May 10 01:50  .bash_logout
-rw-r--r--    1  chris   sales      230  May 10 01:50  .bash_profile
-rw-r--r--    1  chris   sales      124  May 10 01:50  .bashrc
drw-r--r--    1  chris   sales     4096  May 10 01:50  .kde
-rw-rw-r--    1  chris   sales   149872  May 11 22:49  letter

      ^          ^       ^          ^        ^             ^
    col 1      col 2   col 3     col 4    col 5        col 6        col 7
```

Displaying a long list (-l option) of the contents of your home directory shows you more about file sizes and directories. The `total` line shows the total amount of disk space used by the files in the list (158 kilobytes in this example). Directories such as the current directory (.) and the parent directory (..) — the directory above the current directory — are noted as directories by the letter d at the beginning of each entry (each directory begins with a d and each file begins with a -).

The file and directory names are shown in column 7. In this example, a dot (.) represents /home/chris and two dots (..) represents /home — the parent directory of /chris. Most of the files in this example are dot (.) files that are used to store GUI properties (.kde directory) or shell properties (.bash files). The only non-dot file in this list is the one named letter. Column 3 shows the directory or file owner. The /home directory is owned by root, and everything else is owned by the user chris, who belongs to the sales group (groups are listed in column 4).

In addition to the d or -, column 1 on each line contains the permissions set for that file or directory. (Permissions and configuring shell property files are described later in this chapter.) Other information in the listing includes the number of hard links to the item (column 2) the size of each file in bytes (column 5) and the date and time each file was most recently modified (column 6).

Here are a few other items related to file and directory listings:

- The number of characters shown for a directory (4096 bytes in these examples) reflects the size of the file containing information about the directory. Although this number can grow above 4096 bytes for a directory that contains a lot of files, this number doesn't reflect the size of files contained in that directory.

- The format of the time and date column can vary. Instead of displaying "May 12," the display can be "2009-05-12" depending upon the distribution.

- On occasion, instead of seeing the execute bit (x) set on an executable file, you may see an s in that spot instead. With an s appearing within either the owner (-rwsr-xr-x) or group (-rwxr-sr-x) permissions, or both (-rwsr-sr-x), the application can be run by any user, but ownership of the running process is assigned to the application's user/group instead of that of the user launching the command. This is referred to as a *set UID* or *set GID* program, respectively. For example, the mount command has permissions set as -rwsr-xr-x. This allows any user to run mount to list mounted file systems (although you still have to be root to use mount to actually mount file systems, in most cases).

- If a t appears at the end of a directory, it indicates that the sticky bit is set for that directory (for example, drwxrwxr-t). By setting the sticky bit on a directory, the directory's owner can allow other users and groups to add files to the directory, but prevents users from deleting each other's files in that directory. With a set GID assigned to a directory, any files created in that directory are assigned the same group as the directory's group.

## Checking system activity

In addition to being a multiuser operating system, Linux is also a multitasking system. *Multitasking* means that many programs can be running at the same time. An instance of a running program is referred to as a *process*. Linux provides tools for listing running processes, monitoring system usage, and stopping (or killing) processes when necessary.

The most common utility for checking running processes is the ps command. Use it to see which programs are running, the resources they are using, and who is running them. Here's an example of the ps command:

```
$ ps u
USER     PID %CPU %MEM  VSZ    RSS   TTY    STAT START  TIME COMMAND
jake    2147 0.0  0.7 1836   1020   tty1   S+   14:50  0:00 -bash
jake    2310 0.0  0.7 2592    912   tty1   R+   18:22  0:00 ps u
```

In this example, the u option asks that usernames be shown, as well as other information such as the time the process started and memory and CPU usage for processes associated with the current user. The processes shown are associated with the current terminal (tty1). The concept of a terminal comes from the old days, when people worked exclusively from character terminals, so a terminal typically represented a single person at a single screen. Now you can have many "terminals" on one screen by opening multiple virtual terminals or Terminal windows on the desktop.

On this shell session, there isn't much happening. The first process shows that the user named jake opened a bash shell after logging in. The next process shows that jake has run the ps u command. The terminal device tty1 is being used for the login session. The STAT column represents the state of the process, with R indicating a currently running process and S representing a sleeping process.

## Note

Several other values can appear under the STAT column. For example, a plus sign (+) indicates that the process is associated with the foreground operations. ■

The USER column shows the name of the user who started the process. Each process is represented by a unique ID number referred to as a process ID (PID). (You can use the PID if you ever need to kill a runaway process or send another kind of signal to a process.) The %CPU and %MEM columns show the percentages of the processor and random access memory, respectively, that the process is consuming. VSZ (virtual set size) shows the size of the image process (in kilobytes), and RSS (resident set size) shows the size of the program in memory. START shows the time the process began running, and TIME shows the cumulative system time used. (Many commands consume very little CPU time, as is reflected by 0:00 for processes that haven't even used a whole second of CPU time.)

Many processes running on a computer are not associated with a terminal. A normal Linux system has many processes running in the background. Background system processes perform such tasks as logging system activity or listening for data coming in from the network. They are often started when Linux boots up and run continuously until it shuts down. To page through all the processes running on your Linux system for the current user, add the pipe (|) and the less command to ps ux, like this:

```
$ ps ux | less
```

To page through all processes running for all users on your system, use the ps aux command as follows:

```
$ ps aux | less
```

A pipe (above the backslash character on the keyboard) enables you to direct the output of one command to be the input of the next command. In this example, the output of the ps command (a list of processes) is directed to the less command, which lets you page through that information. Use the spacebar to page through and type **q** to end the list. You can also use the arrow keys to move one line at a time through the output.

## Exiting the shell

To exit the shell when you are done, type **exit** or press Ctrl+D.

You've just seen a few commands that can help you quickly familiarize yourself with your Linux system. There are hundreds of other commands that you can try. You'll find many in the /bin and /usr/bin directories, and you can use ls to see a directory's command list: ls /bin, for example, results in a list of commands in the /bin. Then use the man command (for example, man hostname to see what each command does. Administrative commands are also in /sbin or / usr/sbin directories.

# Using the Shell in Linux

When you type a command in a shell, you can include other characters that change or add to how the command works. In addition to the command itself, these are some of the other items that you can type on a shell command line:

- **Options** — Most commands have one or more options you can add to change their behavior. Options typically consist of a single letter, preceded by a dash. You can also often combine several options after a single dash. For example, the command ls -la lists the contents of the current directory. The -l asks for a detailed (long) list of information, and the -a asks that files beginning with a dot (.) also be listed. When a single option consists of a word, it is usually preceded by a double dash (--). For example, to use the help option on many commands, you enter --help on the command line.

## Note

You can use the `--help` option with most commands to see the options and arguments that they support. For example, `hostname --help`. ∎

- **Arguments** — Many commands also accept *arguments* after certain options are entered or at the end of the entire command line. An argument is an extra piece of information, such as a filename, that can be used by the command. For example, `cat /etc/passwd` displays the contents of the `/etc/passwd` file on your screen. In this case, `/etc/passwd` is the argument.

- **Environment variables** — The shell itself stores information that may be useful to the user's shell session in what are called *environment variables*. Examples of environment variables include `$SHELL` (which identifies the shell you are using), `$PS1` (which defines your shell prompt), and `$MAIL` (which identifies the location of your mailbox). See the "Using shell environment variables" section later in this chapter for more information.

## Tip

You can check your environment variables at any time. Type declare to list the current environment variables. Or you can type **echo $VALUE**, where **VALUE** is replaced by the name of a particular environment variable you want to list. And because there are always multiple ways to do anything in Linux, you can also type **env** to get a succinct list of the current environment variables and their values. ∎

- **Metacharacters** — These characters have special meaning to the shell. They can be used to direct the output of a command to a file (>), pipe the output to another command (|), and run a command in the background (&), to name a few. Metacharacters are discussed later in this chapter.

To save you some typing, there are shell features that let you store commands you want to reuse, recall previous commands, and edit commands. You can create aliases that enable you to type a short command to run a longer one. The shell stores previously entered commands in a history list, which you can display and from which you can recall commands. You'll see how this works a little later in the chapter.

Unless you specifically change to another shell, the bash shell is the one you use with most Linux systems. The bash shell contains most of the powerful features available in other shells. Although the description in this chapter steps you through many bash shell features, you can learn more about the bash shell by typing `man bash`, and the sidebar "Getting Help Using the Shell" shows you a few other ways to learn about using the shell.

## Locating commands

If you know the directory that contains the command you want to run, one way to run it is to type the full, or absolute, path to that command. For example, you run the `date` command from the `/bin` directory by typing

```
$ /bin/date
```

Of course, this can be inconvenient, especially if the command resides in a directory with a long path name. The better way is to have commands stored in well-known directories, and then add those directories to your shell's PATH environment variable. The path consists of a list of directories that are checked sequentially for the commands you enter. To see your current path, type the following:

```
$ echo $PATH
/usr/local/bin:/bin:/usr/bin:/usr/X11R6/bin:/home/chris/bin
```

The results show a common default path for a regular Linux user. Directories in the path list are separated by colons. Most user commands that come with Linux are stored in the /bin, /usr/bin, or /usr/local/bin directories. Although many graphical commands (that are used with GUIs) are contained in /usr/bin, some special X commands are in the /usr/X11R6/bin directory. The last directory shown is the bin directory in the user's home directory.

## Tip

**If you want to add your own commands or shell scripts, place them in the bin directory in your home directory (such as /home/chris/bin for the user named chris). This directory is automatically added to your path in some Linux systems, although you may need to create that directory or add it to your PATH on other Linux systems. So, as long as you add the command to your bin with execute permission (described in the "Understanding file permissions" section), you can begin using it by simply typing the command name at your shell prompt. To make commands available to all users, add them to /usr/local/bin. ■**

Unlike some other operating systems, Linux does not, by default, check the current directory for an executable before searching the path. It immediately begins searching the path, and executables in the current directory are run only if they are in the PATH variable or you give their absolute address.

# Getting Help Using the Shell

When you first start using the shell, it can be intimidating. All you see is a prompt. How do you know which commands are available, which options they use, or how to use advanced features? Fortunately, lots of help is available. Here are some places you can look to supplement what you learn in this chapter:

- Check the PATH — Type **echo $PATH**. You see a list of the directories containing commands that are immediately accessible to you. Listing the contents of those directories displays most standard Linux commands.

- Use the help command — Some commands are built into the shell, so they do not appear in a directory. The help command lists those commands and shows options available with each of them. (Type **help | less** to page through the list.) For help with a particular built-in command, type **help command**, replacing command with the name that interests you. The help command works with the bash shell only.

*continued*

*continued*

- Use `--help` with the command — Many commands include a `--help` option that you can use to get information about how the command is used. For example, type **date --help | less**. The output shows not only options, but also time formats you can use with the date command.

- Use the `man` command — To learn more about a particular command, type **man *command***. (Replace ***command*** with the command name you want.) A description of the command and its options appears on the screen.

- Use the `info` command — The `info` command is another tool for displaying information about commands from the shell. The `info` command can move among a hierarchy of nodes to find information about commands and other items. Not all commands have information available in the info database, but sometimes more information can be found there than on a man page.

The path directory order is important. Directories are checked from left to right. So, in this example, if there is a command called `foo` located in both the `/bin` and `/usr/bin` directories, the one in `/bin` is executed. To have the other `foo` command run, you either type the full path to the command or change your PATH variable. If you are the root user, directories containing administrative commands are also in your path. These directories include `/sbin` and `/usr/sbin`. (Changing your PATH and adding directories to it are described later in this chapter.)

Not all the commands that you run are located in directories in your PATH variable. Some commands are built into the shell. Other commands can be overridden by creating aliases that define any commands and options that you want the command to run. There are also ways of defining a function that consists of a stored series of commands. Here is the order in which the shell checks for the commands you type

1. **Aliases** — Names set by the `alias` command that represent a particular command and a set of options. (Type **alias** to see what aliases are set.) Often, aliases enable you to define a short name for a long, complicated command.

2. **Shell reserved word** — Words reserved by the shell for special use. Many of these are words that you would use in programming-type functions, such as `do`, `while`, `case`, and `else`.

3. **Function** — A set of commands that are executed together within the current shell.

4. **Built-in command** — A command built into the shell. As a result, there is no representation of the command in the file system. Some of the most common commands you will use are shell built-in commands, such as `cd` (to change directories), `echo` (to echo text to the screen), `exit` (to exit from a shell), `fg` (to bring a command running in the background to the foreground), `history` (to see a list of commands that were previously run), `pwd` (to list the present working directory), `set` (to set shell options), and `type` (to show the location of a command).

5. **File system command** — This command is stored in and executed from the computer's file system. (These are the commands that are indicated by the value of the PATH variable.)

To find out where a particular command is taken from, you can use the `type` command. (If you are using a shell other than `bash`, use the `which` command instead.) For example, to find out where the bash shell command is located, type the following:

```
$ type bash
bash is /bin/bash
```

Try these few words with the `type` command to see other locations of commands: `which`, `case`, and `return`. If a command resides in several locations, you can add the `-a` option to have all the known locations of the command printed.

## Tip

Sometimes you run a command and receive an error message that the command was not found or that permission to run the command was denied. In the first case, check that you spelled the command correctly and that it is located in your PATH variable. In the second case, the command may be in the PATH variable, but may not be executable. Adding execute permissions to a command is described later in this chapter. Also remember that case is important, so typing CAT or Cat will not find the cat command. ■

# Rerunning commands

After typing a long or complex command line, learning that you mistyped something is annoying. Fortunately, some shell features let you recall previous command lines, edit those lines, or complete a partially typed command line.

The *shell history* is a list of the commands that you have entered before. Using the `history` command in a `bash` shell, you can view your previous commands. Then, using various shell features, you can recall individual command lines from that list and change them however you please.

The rest of this section describes how to do command-line editing, how to complete parts of command lines, and how to recall and work with the history list.

## Command-line editing

If you type something wrong on a command line, the bash shell ensures that you don't have to delete the entire line and start over. Likewise, you can recall a previous command line and change the elements to make a new command.

By default, the bash shell uses command-line editing that is based on the emacs text editor. (Type **man emacs** to read about it, if you care to.) If you are familiar with emacs, you probably already know most of the keystrokes described here.

## Tip

If you prefer the `vi` command for editing shell command lines, you can easily make that happen. Add the line:

```
set -o vi
```

to the `.bashrc` file in your home directory. The next time you open a shell, you can use `vi` commands (as described in the tutorial later in this chapter) to edit your command lines. ∎

To do the editing, you can use a combination of control keys, meta keys, and arrow keys. For example, Ctrl+F means to hold the Ctrl key and type **f**. Alt+F means to hold the Alt key and type **f**. (Instead of the Alt key, your keyboard may use a Meta key or the Esc key. On a Windows keyboard, you can use the Windows key.)

To try out a bit of command-line editing, type the following:

```
$ ls /usr/bin | sort -f | less
```

This command lists the contents of the /usr/bin directory, sorts the contents in alphabetical order (regardless of case), and pipes the output to less. The less command displays the first page of output, after which you can go through the rest of the output a line (press Enter) or a page (press spacebar) at a time (press q when you are done). Now, suppose you want to change /usr/ bin to /bin. You can use the following steps to change the command:

1. Press the up arrow to recall the line.
2. Press Ctrl+A. This moves the cursor to the beginning of the command line.
3. Press Ctrl+F or the right arrow (→) key. Repeat this command a few times to position the cursor under the first slash (/).
4. Press Ctrl+D. Type this command four times to delete /usr from the line.
5. Press Enter. This executes the command line.

As you edit a command line, at any point you can type regular characters to add those characters to the command line. The characters appear at the location of your cursor. You can use right (→) and left (←) arrows to move the cursor from one end to the other on the command line. You can also press the up (↑) and down (↓) arrow keys to step through previous commands in the history list to select a command line for editing. (See the discussion on command recall for details on how to recall commands from the history list.)

There are many keystrokes you can use to edit your command lines. Table 9-1 lists the keystrokes that you can use to move around the command line.

**TABLE 9-1**

## Keystrokes for Navigating Command Lines

| Keystroke | Full Name | Meaning |
|-----------|-----------|---------|
| Ctrl+F | Character forward | Go forward one character. |
| Ctrl+B | Character backward | Go backward one character. |
| Alt+F | Word forward | Go forward one word. |
| Alt+B | Word backward | Go backward one word. |
| Ctrl+A | Beginning of line | Go to the beginning of the current line. |
| Ctrl+E | End of line | Go to the end of the line. |
| Ctrl+L | Clear screen | Clear screen and leave line at the top of the screen. |

The keystrokes in Table 9-2 can be used to edit command lines.

**TABLE 9-2**

## Keystrokes for Editing Command Lines

| Keystroke | Full Name | Meaning |
|-----------|-----------|---------|
| Ctrl+D | Delete current | Delete the current character. |
| Backspace | Delete previous | Delete the previous character. |
| Ctrl+T | Transpose character | Switch positions of current and previous characters. |
| Alt+T | Transpose words | Switch positions of current and previous words. |
| Alt+U | Uppercase word | Change the current word to uppercase. |
| Alt+L | Lowercase word | Change the current word to lowercase. |
| Alt+C | Capitalize word | Change the current word to an initial capital. |
| Ctrl+V | Insert special character | Add a special character. For example, to add a Tab character, press Ctrl+V+Tab. |

Use the keystrokes in Table 9-3 to cut and paste text on a command line.

**TABLE 9-3**

### Keystrokes for Cutting and Pasting Text in Command Lines

| Keystroke | Full Name | Meaning |
|-----------|-----------|---------|
| Ctrl+K | Cut end of line | Cut text to the end of the line. |
| Ctrl+U | Cut beginning of line | Cut text to the beginning of the line. |
| Ctrl+W | Cut previous word | Cut the word located behind the cursor. |
| Alt+D | Cut next word | Cut the word following the cursor. |
| Ctrl+Y | Paste recent text | Paste most recently cut text. |
| Alt+Y | Paste earlier text | Rotate back to previously cut text and paste it. |
| Ctrl+C | Delete whole line | Delete the entire line. |

### Command-line completion

To save you a few keystrokes, the bash shell offers several different ways of completing partially typed values. To attempt to complete a value, type the first few characters, and then press Tab. Here are some of the values you can type partially:

- **Environment variable** — If the text you type begins with a dollar sign ($), the shell completes the text with an environment variable from the current shell.

- **Username** — If the text you type begins with a tilde (~), the shell completes the text with a username.

- **Command, alias, or function** — If the text you type begins with regular characters, the shell tries to complete the text with a command, alias, or function name.

- **Hostname** — If the text you type begins with an at (@) sign, the shell completes the text with a hostname taken from the /etc/hosts file.

### Tip

**To add hostnames from an additional file, you can set the HOSTFILE variable to the name of that file. The file must be in the same format as** /etc/hosts. ■

Here are a few examples of command completion. (When you see *<Tab>*, it means to press the Tab key on your keyboard.) Type the following:

```
$ echo $OS<Tab>
$ cd ~ro<Tab>
$ fing<Tab>
```

The first example causes $0S to expand to the $0STYPE variable. In the next example, ~ro expands to the root user's home directory (~root/). Next, fing expands to the finger command.

Pressing Tab twice offers some wonderful possibilities. There are times when several possible completions for the string of characters you have entered are available. In those cases, you can check the possible ways text can be expanded by pressing Tab twice at the point where you want to do completion.

This shows the result you would get if you checked for possible completions on $P.

```
$ echo $P<Tab><Tab>
$PATH $PPID $PS1 $PS2 $PS4 $PWD
$ echo $P
```

In this case, there are six possible variables that begin with $P. After possibilities are displayed, the original command line returns, ready for you to complete it as you choose.

## Command-line recall

After you type a command line, that entire command line is saved in your shell's history list. The list is stored in a history file, from which any command can be recalled to run again. After it is recalled, you can modify the command line, as described earlier.

To view your history list, use the history command. Type the command without options or followed by a number to list that many of the most recent commands. For example:

```
$ history 8
382 date
383 ls /usr/bin | sort -a | more
384 man sort
385 cd /usr/local/bin
386 man more
387 useradd -m /home/chris -u 101 chris
388 passwd chris
389 history 8
```

A number precedes each command line in the list. You can recall one of those commands using an exclamation point (!). Keep in mind that when using an exclamation point, the command runs blind, without presenting an opportunity to confirm the command you're referencing. There are several ways to run a command immediately from this list, including the following:

- !n — Run command number. Replace the *n* with the number of the command line, and that line is run. For example, here's how to repeat the date command shown as command number 382 in the preceding history listing:

```
$ !382
date
Thu Oct 29 21:30:06 PDT 2010
```

- !! — Run previous command. Runs the previous command line. Here's how you would immediately run that same date command:

```
$ !!
date
Thu Oct 29 21:30:39 PDT 2010
```

- !?string? — Run command containing string. This runs the most recent command that contains a particular *string* of characters. For example, you can run the date command again by just searching for part of that command line as follows:

```
$ !?dat?
date
Thu Oct 29 21:32:41 PDT 2010
```

Instead of just running a history command line immediately, you can recall a particular line and edit it. You can use the following keys or key combinations to do that, as shown in Table 9-4.

**TABLE 9-4**

## Key Strokes for Using Command History

| Key(s) | Function Name | Description |
|--------|---------------|-------------|
| Arrow Keys (↑ and ↓) | Step | Press the up and down arrow keys to step through each command line in your history list to arrive at the one you want. (Ctrl+P and Ctrl+N do the same functions, respectively.) |
| Ctrl+R | Reverse Incremental Search | After you press these keys, you enter a search string to do a reverse search. As you type the string, a matching command line appears that you can run or edit. |
| Ctrl+S | Forward Incremental Search | Same as the preceding function but for forward search. |
| Alt+P | Reverse Search | After you press these keys, you enter a string to do a reverse search. Type a string and press Enter to see the most recent command line that includes that string. |
| Alt+N | Forward Search | Same as the preceding function but for forward search. |

Another way to work with your history list is to use the `fc` command. Type **fc** followed by a history line number, and that command line is opened in a text editor. Make the changes that you want. When you exit the editor, the command runs. You can also give a range of line numbers (for example, `fc 100 105`). All the commands open in your text editor, and then run one after the other when you exit the editor.

The history list is stored in the `.bash_history` file in your home directory. Up to 1,000 history commands are stored for you by default.

## Note

**Some people disable the history feature for the root user by setting the** `HISTFILE` **to** `/dev/null` **or simply leaving** `HISTSIZE` **blank. This prevents information about the root user's activities from potentially being exploited. If you are an administrative user with root privileges, you may want to consider emptying your file upon exiting as well for the same reasons.** ■

## Connecting and expanding commands

A truly powerful feature of the shell is the capability to redirect the input and output of commands to and from other commands and files. To allow commands to be strung together, the shell uses metacharacters. As noted earlier, a metacharacter is a typed character that has special meaning to the shell for connecting commands or requesting expansion.

### Piping commands

The pipe (|) metacharacter connects the output from one command to the input of another command. This lets you have one command work on some data, and then have the next command deal with the results. Here is an example of a command line that includes pipes:

```
$ cat /etc/passwd | sort | less
```

This command lists the contents of the `/etc/passwd` file and pipes the output to the `sort` command. The `sort` command takes the usernames that begin each line of the `/etc/passwd` file, sorts them alphabetically, and pipes the output to the `less` command (to page through the output).

Pipes are an excellent illustration of how UNIX, the predecessor of Linux, was created as an operating system made up of building blocks. A standard practice in UNIX was to connect utilities in different ways to get different jobs done. For example, before the days of graphical word processors, users created plain-text files that included macros to indicate formatting. To see how the document really appeared, they would use a command such as the following:

```
$ gunzip < /usr/share/man/man1/grep.1.gz | nroff -c -man | less
```

In this example, the contents of the `grep` man page (`grep.1.gz`) are directed to the `gunzip` command to be unzipped. The output from `gunzip` is piped to the `nroff` command to format the man page using the manual macro (`-man`). The output is piped to the `less` command to display the output. Because the file being displayed is in plain text, you could have substituted any number of options to work with the text before displaying it. You could sort the contents, change or delete some of the content, or bring in text from other documents. The key is that, instead of all those features being in one program, you get results from piping and redirecting input and output between multiple commands.

## Sequential commands

Sometimes you may want a sequence of commands to run, with one command completing before the next command begins. You can do this by typing several commands on the same command line and separating them with semicolons (;):

```
$ date ; troff -me verylargedocument | lpr ; date
```

In this example, I was formatting a huge document and wanted to know how long it would take. The first command (date) showed the date and time before the formatting started. The troff command formatted the document and then piped the output to the printer. When the formatting was done, the date and time were printed again (so I knew how long the troff command took to complete).

Another useful command to add to the end of a long command line is the mail command. You could add

```
; mail -s "Finished the long command" chris@example.com
```

to the end of a command line. Then, for example, a mail message is sent to the user you choose after the command completes.

## Background commands

Some commands can take a while to complete. Sometimes you may not want to tie up your shell waiting for a command to finish. In those cases, you can have the commands run in the background by using the ampersand (&).

Text formatting commands (such as nroff and troff, described earlier) are examples of commands that are often run in the background to format a large document. You also might want to create your own shell scripts that run in the background to check continuously for certain events to occur, such as the hard disk filling up or particular users logging in.

Here is an example of a command being run in the background:

```
$ troff -me verylargedocument | lpr &
```

Other ways to manage background and foreground processes are described in the "Managing background and foreground processes" section later in this chapter.

## Expanding commands

With command substitution, you can have the output of a command interpreted by the shell instead of by the command itself. In this way, you can have the standard output of a command become an argument for another command. The two forms of command substitution are `$(command)` and `` `command` `` (backticks, not single quotes).

The command in this case can include options, metacharacters, and arguments. Here is an example of using command substitution:

```
$ vi $(find /home | grep xyzzy)
```

In this example, the command substitution is done before the `vi` command is run. First, the `find` command starts at the `/home` directory and prints out all files and directories below that point in the file system. The output is piped to the `grep` command, which filters out all files except for those that include the string `xyzzy` in the filename. Finally, the `vi` command opens all filenames for editing (one at a time) that include `xyzzy`.

This particular example is useful if you want to edit a file for which you know the name but not the location. As long as the string is uncommon, you can find and open every instance of a filename existing beneath a point you choose in the file system. (In other words, don't use `grep` from the root file system or you'll match and try to edit several thousand files.)

## Expanding arithmetic expressions

There may be times when you want to pass arithmetic results to a command. There are two forms you can use to expand an arithmetic expression and pass it to the shell: `$[expression]` or `$(expression)`. Here is an example:

```
$ echo "I am $[2010 - 1957] years old."
I am 53 years old.
```

The shell interprets the arithmetic expression first (2010 - 1957), and then passes that information to the `echo` command. The `echo` command displays the text, with the results of the arithmetic (53) inserted.

Here's an example of the other form:

```
$ echo "There are $(ls | wc -w) files in this directory."
There are 14 files in this directory.
```

This lists the contents of the current directory (`ls`) and runs the word count command to count the number of files found (`wc -w`). The resulting number (14 in this case) is echoed back with the rest of the sentence shown.

## Expanding environment variables

Environment variables that store information within the shell can be expanded using the dollar sign ($) metacharacter. When you expand an environment variable on a command line, the value of the variable is printed instead of the variable name itself, as follows:

```
$ ls -l $BASH
-rwxr-xr-x 1 root   root   625516 Dec 5 11:13 /bin/bash
```

Using $BASH as an argument to ls -l causes a long listing of the bash command to be printed. The following section discusses shell environment variables.

# Creating Your Shell Environment

You can tune your shell to help you work more efficiently. Your prompt can provide pertinent information each time you press Enter. You can set aliases to save your keystrokes and permanently set environment variables to suit your needs. To make each change occur when you start a shell, add this information to your shell configuration files.

## Configuring your shell

Several configuration files support how your shell behaves. Some of the files are executed for every user and every shell, whereas others are specific to the user who creates the configuration file. Table 9-5 shows the files that are of interest to anyone using the bash shell in Linux.

**TABLE 9-5**

### Bash Configuration Files

| File | Description |
| --- | --- |
| /etc/profile | Sets up user environment information for every user. It is executed when you first log in. This file provides values for your path, as well as setting environment variables for such things as the location of your mailbox and the size of your history files. Finally, /etc/profile gathers shell settings from configuration files in the /etc/profile.d directory. |
| /etc/bashrc | Executes for every user who runs the bash shell, each time a bash shell is opened. It sets the default prompt and may add one or more aliases. Values in this file can be overridden by information in each user's ~/.bashrc file. |
| ~/.bash_profile | Used by each user to enter information that is specific to his or her own use of the shell. It is executed only once, when the user logs in. By default, it sets a few environment variables and executes the user's .bashrc file. |
| ~/.bashrc | Contains the information that is specific to your bash shells. It is read when you log in and also each time you open a new bash shell. This is the best location to add environment variables and aliases so that your shell picks them up. |
| ~/.bash_logout | Executes each time you log out (exit the last bash shell). By default, it simply clears your screen. |

To change the /etc/profile or /etc/bashrc files, you must be the root user. Users can change the information in the $HOME/.bash_profile, $HOME/.bashrc, and $HOME/.bash_logout files in their own home directories.

The following sections provide ideas about items to add to your shell configuration files. In most cases, you add these values to the .bashrc file in your home directory. However, if you administer a system, you may want to set some of these values as defaults for all of your Linux system's users.

### Setting your prompt

Your prompt consists of a set of characters that appear each time the shell is ready to accept a command. The PS1 environment variable sets what the prompt contains and is what you interact with most of the time. If your shell requires additional input, it uses the values of PS2, PS3, and PS4.

When your Linux system is installed, often a prompt is set to contain more than just a dollar sign or pound sign. For example, in Fedora or Red Hat Enterprise Linux, your prompt is set to include the following information: your username, your hostname, and the base name of your current working directory. That information is surrounded by brackets and followed by a dollar sign (for regular users) or a pound sign (for the root user). Here is an example of that prompt:

```
[chris@myhost bin]$
```

If you change directories, the bin name would change to the name of the new directory. Likewise, if you were to log in as a different user or to a different host, that information would change.

You can use several special characters (indicated by adding a backslash to a variety of letters) to include different information in your prompt. These can include your terminal number, the date, and the time, as well as other pieces of information. Table 9-6 provides some examples (you can find more on the bash man page).

**TABLE 9-6**

## Characters to Add Information to bash Prompt

| Special Character | Description |
|---|---|
| \! | Shows the current command history number. This includes all previous commands stored for your username. |
| \# | Shows the command number of the current command. This includes only the commands for the active shell. |
| \$ | Shows the user prompt ($) or root prompt (#), depending on which user you are. |
| \W | Shows only the current working directory base name. For example, if the current working directory was /var/spool/mail, this value simply appears as mail. |
| \[ | Precedes a sequence of nonprinting characters. This can be used to add a terminal control sequence into the prompt for such things as changing colors, adding blink effects, or making characters bold. (Your terminal determines the exact sequences available.) |

*continued*

| **TABLE 9-6** | *(continued)* |
|---|---|
| **Special Character** | **Description** |
| \] | Follows a sequence of nonprinting characters. |
| \\ | Shows a backslash. |
| \d | Displays the day name, month, and day number of the current date. For example: Sat Jan 23. |
| \h | Shows the hostname of the computer running the shell. |
| \n | Causes a newline to occur. |
| \nnn | Shows the character that relates to the octal number replacing *nnn*. |
| \s | Displays the current shell name. For the bash shell, the value would be bash. |
| \t | Prints the current time in hours, minutes, and seconds (for example, 10:14:39). |
| \u | Prints your current username. |
| \w | Displays the full path to the current working directory. |

## Tip

**If you are setting your prompt temporarily by typing at the shell, you should put the value of** PS1 **in quotes. For example, you could type export PS1="[\t \w]\$ " to see a prompt that looks like this:** [20:26:32 /var/spool]$. ∎

To make a change to your prompt permanent, add the value of PS1 to your .bashrc file in your home directory (assuming that you are using the bash shell). There may already be a PS1 value in that file that you can modify. Refer to the Bash Prompt HOWTO (www.tldp.org/HOWTO/Bash-Prompt-HOWTO) for information on changing colors, commands, and other features of your bash shell prompt.

### Adding environment variables

You may consider adding a few environment variables to your .bashrc file. These can help make working with the shell more efficient and effective:

- TMOUT — Sets how long the shell can be inactive before bash automatically exits. The value is the number of seconds for which the shell has not received input. This can be a nice security feature, in case you leave your desk while you are still logged in to Linux. So as not to be logged off while you are working, you may want to set the value to something like TMOUT=1800 (to allow 30 minutes of idle time). You can use any terminal session to close the current shell after a set number of seconds, for example TMOUT=30.

- PATH — As described earlier, the PATH variable sets the directories that are searched for commands you use. If you often use directories of commands that are not in your PATH, you can permanently add them. To do this, add a PATH variable to your .bashrc file. For example, to add a directory called /getstuff/bin, add the following:

```
PATH=$PATH:/getstuff/bin ; export PATH
```

This example first reads all the current path directories into the new PATH ($PATH), adds the /getstuff/bin directory, and then exports the new PATH.

## Caution

**Some people add the current directory to their PATH by adding a directory identified simply as a dot (.), as follows:**

```
PATH=.:$PATH ; export PATH
```

**This enables you always to run commands in your current directory before evaluating any other command in the path (which people may be used to if they have used DOS). However, the security risk with this procedure is that you could be in a directory that contains a command that you don't intend to run from that directory. For example, a malicious person could put an ls command in a directory that, instead of listing the content of your directory, does something devious. Because of this, the practice of adding the dot to your path is highly discouraged.** ■

- WHATEVER — You can create your own environment variables to provide shortcuts in your work. Choose any name that is not being used and assign a useful value to it. For example, if you do a lot of work with files in the /work/time/files/info/memos directory, you could set the following variable:

  ```
  M=/work/time/files/info/memos ; export M
  ```

  You could make that your current directory by typing cd $M. You could run a program from that directory called hotdog by typing $M/hotdog. You could edit a file from there called bun by typing vi $M/bun.

### Adding aliases

Setting aliases can save you even more typing than setting environment variables. With aliases, you can have a string of characters execute an entire command line. You can add and list aliases with the alias command. Here are some examples of using alias from a bash shell:

```
alias p='pwd ; ls -CF'
alias rm='rm -i'
```

In the first example, the letter p is assigned to run the command pwd, and then to run ls -CF to print the current working directory and list its contents in column form. The second runs the rm command with the -i option each time you simply type rm. (This is an alias that is often set automatically for the root user. Instead of just removing files, you are prompted for each individual file removal. This prevents you from automatically removing all the files in a directory by mistakenly typing something such as rm *.)

While you are in the shell, you can check which aliases are set by typing the alias command. If you want to remove an alias, type unalias. (Remember that if the alias is set in a configuration file, it will be set again when you open another shell.)

# Using shell environment variables

Every active shell stores pieces of information that it needs to use in what are called *environment variables*. An environment variable can store things such as locations of configuration files, mailboxes, and path directories. They can also store values for your shell prompts, the size of your history list, and type of operating system.

To see the environment variables currently assigned to your shell, type the declare command. (It will probably fill more than one screen, so type **declare | more**. The declare command also shows functions as well as environment variables.) You can refer to the value of any of those variables by preceding it with a dollar sign ($) and placing it anywhere on a command line. For example:

```
$ echo $USER
chris
```

This command prints the value of the USER variable, which holds your username (chris). Substitute any other value for USER to print its value instead.

## Common shell environment variables

When you start a shell (by logging in or opening a Terminal window), a lot of environment variables are already set. Table 9-7 shows some variables that are either set when you use a bash shell or that can be set by you to use with different features.

**TABLE 9-7**

### Common Shell Environment Variables

| Variable | Description |
|---|---|
| BASH | Contains the full path name of the bash command. This is usually /bin/bash. |
| BASH_VERSION | A number representing the current version of the bash command. |
| EUID | This is the effective user ID number of the current user. It is assigned when the shell starts, based on the user's entry in the /etc/passwd file. |
| FCEDIT | If set, this variable indicates the text editor used by the fc command to edit history commands. If this variable isn't set, the vi command is used. |

| Variable | Description |
|---|---|
| HISTFILE | The location of your history file. It is typically located at $HOME/.bash_history. |
| HISTFILESIZE | The number of history entries that can be stored. After this number is reached, the oldest commands are discarded. The default value is 1000. |
| HISTCMD | This returns the number of the current command in the history list. |
| HOME | This is your home directory. It is your current working directory each time you log in or type the cd command with any options. |
| HOSTTYPE | A value that describes the computer architecture on which the Linux system is running. For Intel-compatible PCs, the value is i386, i486, i586, i686, or something like i386-linux. For AMD 64-bit machines, the value is x86_64. |
| MAIL | This is the location of your mailbox file. The file is typically your username in the /var/spool/mail directory. |
| OLDPWD | The directory that was the working directory before you changed to the current working directory. |
| OSTYPE | A name identifying the current operating system. For Fedora Linux, the OSTYPE value is either linux or linux-gnu, depending on the type of shell you are using. (Bash can run on other operating systems as well.) |
| PATH | The colon-separated list of directories used to find commands that you type. The default value for regular users varies for different distributions, but typically includes the following: /bin:/usr/bin:/usr/local/bin:/usr/bin/X11:/usr/X11R6/bin:~/bin. You need to type the full path or a relative path to a command you want to run that is not in your PATH. For the root user, the value also includes /sbin, /usr/sbin, and /usr/local/sbin. |
| PPID | The process ID of the command that started the current shell (for example, the Terminal window containing the shell). |
| PROMPT_COMMAND | Can be set to a command name that is run each time before your shell prompt is displayed. Setting PROMPT_COMMAND=date lists the current date/time before the prompt appears. |
| PS1 | Sets the value of your shell prompt. There are many items that you can read into your prompt (date, time, username, hostname, and so on). Sometimes a command requires additional prompts, which you can set with the variables PS2, PS3, and so on. |
| PWD | This is the directory that is assigned as your current directory. This value changes each time you change directories using the cd command. |
| RANDOM | Accessing this variable causes a random number to be generated. The number is between 0 and 99999. |

*continued*

| **TABLE 9-7** | *(continued)* |
| Variable | Description |
| --- | --- |
| SECONDS | The number of seconds since the time the shell was started. |
| SHLVL | The number of shell levels associated with the current shell session. When you log in to the shell, the SHLVL is 1. Each time you start a new bash command (by, for example, using su to become a new user, or by simply typing bash), this number is incremented. |
| TMOUT | Can be set to a number representing the number of seconds the shell can be idle without receiving input. After the number of seconds is reached, the shell exits. This security feature makes it less likely for unattended shells to be accessed by unauthorized people. (This must be set in the login shell for it to actually cause the shell to log out the user.) |
| UID | The user ID number assigned to your username. The user ID number is stored in the /etc/passwd file. |

### Set your own environment variables

Environment variables can provide a handy way to store bits of information that you use often from the shell. You can create any variables that you want (avoiding those that are already in use) so that you can read in the values of those variables as you use the shell. (The bash man page lists variables already in use.)

To set an environment variable temporarily, you can simply type a variable name and assign it to a value. Here's an example:

```
$ AB=/usr/dog/contagious/ringbearer/grind ; export AB
```

This example causes a long directory path to be assigned to the AB variable. The export AB command says to export the value to the shell so that it can be propagated to other shells you may open. With AB set, you go to the directory by typing the following:

```
$ cd $AB
```

The problem with setting environment variables in this way is that as soon as you exit the shell in which you set the variable, the setting is lost. To set variables permanently, add variable settings to a bash configuration file, as described later in this section.

## Note

**Another option to add the settings to the bash configuration file is to create an executable script file that contains these settings. This is useful when you don't use the settings all the time, but need to use them occasionally. They are there only for the life of the session after the script file has run. ∎**

If you want to have other text right up against the output from an environment variable, you can surround the variable in braces. This protects the variable name from being misunderstood. For example, if you want to add a command name to the AB variable shown earlier, you can type the following:

```
$ echo ${AB}/adventure
/usr/dog/contagious/ringbearer/grind/adventure
```

Remember that you must export the variable so that it can be picked up by other shell commands. You must add the export line to a shell configuration file for it to take effect the next time you log in. The export command is fairly flexible. Instead of running the export command after you set the variable, you can do it all in one step, as follows:

```
$ export XYZ=/home/xyz/bin
```

You can override the value of any environment variable. This can be temporary, by simply typing the new value, or you can add the new export line to your $HOME/.bashrc file. One useful variable to update is PATH:

```
$ export PATH=$PATH:/home/xyz/bin
```

In this example, the /home/xyz/bin directory is added to the PATH, a useful technique if you want to run a bunch of commands from a directory that is not normally in your PATH, without typing the full or relative path each time.

If you decide that you no longer want a variable to be set, you can use the unset command to erase its value. For example, you can type unset XYZ, which causes XYZ to have no value set. (Remember to remove the export from the $HOME/.bashrc file — if you added it there — or it will return the next time you open a shell.)

## Managing background and foreground processes

If you are using Linux over a network or from a *dumb* terminal (a monitor that allows only text input with no GUI support), your shell may be all that you have. You may be used to a graphical environment where you have a lot of programs active at the same time so that you can switch among them as needed. This shell thing can seem pretty limited.

Although the bash shell doesn't include a GUI for running many programs, it does let you move active programs between the background and foreground. In this way, you can have a lot of stuff running, while selectively choosing the one you want to deal with at the moment.

There are several ways to place an active program in the background. One mentioned earlier is to add an ampersand (&) to the end of a command line. Another way is to use the at command to run commands in a way in which they are not connected to the shell.

To stop a running command and put it in the background, press Ctrl+Z. After the command is stopped, you can either bring it back into the foreground to run (the fg command) or start it running in the background (the bg command). Keep in mind that any command running in the background might spew output during commands that you run subsequently from that shell. For example, if output appears from a command running in the background during a vi session, simply press Ctrl+L to redraw the screen to get rid of the output.

## Tip

**To avoid having the output appear, you should have any process running in the background send its output to a file or to null. ■**

### Starting background processes

If you have programs that you want to run while you continue to work in the shell, you can place the programs in the background. To place a program in the background at the time you run the program, type an ampersand (&) at the end of the command line, like this:

```
$ find /usr > /tmp/allusrfiles &
```

This example command finds all files on your Linux system (starting from /usr), prints those filenames, and puts those names in the file /tmp/allusrfiles. The ampersand (&) runs that command line in the background. To check which commands you have running in the background, use the jobs command, as follows:

```
$ jobs
[1]  Stopped (tty output)  vi /tmp/myfile
[2]  Running               find /usr -print > /tmp/allusrfiles &
[3]  Running               nroff -man /usr/man2/* >/tmp/man2 &
[4]- Running               nroff -man /usr/man3/* >/tmp/man3 &
[5]+ Stopped               nroff -man /usr/man4/* >/tmp/man4
```

The first job shows a text-editing command (vi) that I placed in the background and stopped by pressing Ctrl+Z while I was editing. Job 2 shows the find command I just ran. Jobs 3 and 4 show nroff commands currently running in the background. Job 5 had been running in the shell (foreground) until I decided too many processes were running and pressed Ctrl+Z to stop job 5 until a few processes had completed.

The plus sign (+) next to number 5 shows that it was most recently placed in the background. The minus sign (-) next to number 4 shows that it was placed in the background just before the most recent background job. Because job 1 requires terminal input, it cannot run in the background. As a result, it is Stopped until it is brought to the foreground again.

## Tip

**To see the process ID for the background job, add a -l (the lowercase letter L) option to the jobs command. If you type ps, you can use the process ID to figure out which command is for a particular background job. ■**

### Using foreground and background commands

Continuing with the example, you can bring any of the commands on the jobs list to the foreground. For example, to edit myfile again, type

```
$ fg %1
```

As a result, the vi command opens again, with all text as it was when you stopped the vi job.

## Caution

**Before you put a text processor, word processor, or similar program in the background, make sure you save your file. It's easy to forget you have a program in the background and you will lose your data if you log out or the computer reboots later on. ∎**

To refer to a background job (to cancel or bring it to the foreground), use a percent sign (%) followed by the job number. You can also use the following to refer to a background job:

- % — Refers to the most recent command put into the background (indicated by the plus sign when you type the jobs command). This action brings the command to the foreground.

- %string — Refers to a job where the command begins with a particular string of characters. The string must be unambiguous. (In other words, typing %vi when there are two vi commands in the background results in an error message.)

- %?string — Refers to a job where the command line contains a string at any point. The string must be unambiguous or the match will fail.

- %-- — Refers to the previous job stopped before the one most recently stopped.

If a command is stopped, you can start it running again in the background using the bg command. For example, take job 5 from the jobs list in the previous example:

```
[5]+ Stopped              nroff -man man4/* >/tmp/man4
```

Type the following:

```
$ bg %5
```

After that, the job runs in the background. Its jobs entry appears as follows:

```
[5]  Running              nroff -man man4/* >/tmp/man4 &
```

# Working with the Linux File System

The Linux file system is the structure in which all the information on your computer is stored. Files are organized within a hierarchy of directories. Each directory can contain files, as well as other directories.

If you were to map out the files and directories in Linux, it would look like an upside-down tree. At the top is the root directory, which is represented by a single slash (/). Below that is a set of common directories in the Linux system, such as bin, dev, home, lib, and tmp, to name a few. Each of those directories, as well as directories added to the root, can contain subdirectories.

Figure 9-1 illustrates how the Linux file system is organized as a hierarchy. To demonstrate how directories are connected, the figure shows a /home directory that contains subdirectories for three users: chris, mary, and tom. Within the chris directory are subdirectories: briefs, memos, and personal. To refer to a file called inventory in the chris/memos directory, you can type the full path of /home/chris/memos/inventory. If your current directory is /home/chris/memos, you can refer to the file as simply inventory.

**FIGURE 9-1**

The Linux file system is organized as a hierarchy of directories.

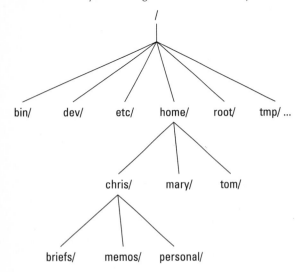

Some of the Linux directories that may interest you include the following:

- /bin — Contains common Linux user commands, such as ls, sort, date, and chmod.
- /boot — Has the bootable Linux kernel and boot loader configuration files (GRUB).
- /dev — Contains files representing access points to devices on your systems. These include terminal devices (tty*), floppy disks (fd*), hard disks (hd*), RAM (ram*), and CD-ROM (cd*). (Users typically access these devices directly through the device files.)
- /etc — Contains administrative configuration files.
- /home — Contains directories assigned to each user with a login account (with the exception of root).
- /media — Provides a standard location for mounting and automounting devices, such as remote file systems and removable media (with directory names of cdrecorder, floppy, and so on).
- /mnt — A common mount point for many devices before it was supplanted by the standard /media directory. Some bootable Linux systems still used this directory to mount hard disk partitions and remote file systems.

- `/proc` — Contains information about system resources.

- `/root` — Represents the root user's home directory. The home directory for root does not reside beneath `/home` for security reasons.

- `/sbin` — Contains administrative commands and daemon processes.

- `/sys` — A `/proc`-like file system, new in the Linux 2.6 kernel and intended to contain files for getting hardware status and reflecting the system's device tree as it is seen by the kernel. It pulls many of its functions from `/proc`.

- `/tmp` — Contains temporary files used by applications.

- `/usr` — Contains user documentation, games, graphical files (X11), libraries (lib), and a variety of other user and administrative commands and files.

- `/var` — Contains directories of data used by various applications. In particular, this is where you would place files that you share as an FTP server (`/var/ftp`) or a Web server (`/var/www`). It also contains all system log files (`/var/log`) and spool files in `/var/spool` (such as `mail`, `cups`, and `news`).

The file systems in the DOS or Microsoft Windows operating systems differ from Linux's file structure, as the "Linux File Systems Versus Windows-Based File Systems" sidebar explains.

# Linux File Systems Versus Windows-Based File Systems

Although similar in many ways, the Linux file system has some striking differences from file systems used in MS-DOS and Windows operating systems. Here are a few:

- In MS-DOS and Windows file systems, drive letters represent different storage devices (for example, A: is a floppy drive and C: is a hard disk). In Linux, all storage devices are fit into the file system hierarchy. So, the fact that all of `/usr` may be on a separate hard disk or that `/mnt/rem1` is a file system from another computer is invisible to the user.

- Slashes, rather than backslashes, are used to separate directory names in Linux. So, `C:\home\chris` in an MS system is `/home/chris` in a Linux system.

- Filenames almost always have suffixes in DOS (such as .txt for text files or .doc for word-processing files). Although at times you can use that convention in Linux, three-character suffixes have no required meaning in Linux. They can be useful for identifying a file type. Many Linux applications and desktop environments use file suffixes to determine the contents of a file. In Linux, however, DOS command extensions such as .com, .exe, and .bat don't necessarily signify an executable (permission flags make Linux files executable).

- Every file and directory in a Linux system has permissions and ownership associated with it. Security varies among Microsoft systems. Because DOS and MS Windows began as single-user systems, file ownership was not built into those systems when they were designed. Later releases added features such as file and folder attributes to address this problem.

# Creating files and directories

As a Linux user, most of the files you save and work with will probably be in your home directory. Table 9-8 shows commands to create and use files and directories.

**TABLE 9-8**

## Commands to Create and Use Files

| Command | Result |
|---------|--------|
| cd | Change to another directory. |
| pwd | Print the name of the current (or present) working directory. |
| mkdir | Create a directory. |
| chmod | Change the permission on a file or directory. |
| ls | List the contents of a directory. |

The following steps lead you through creating directories within your home directory and moving among your directories, with a mention of setting appropriate file permissions:

1. Go to your home directory. To do this, simply type **cd**. (For other ways of referring to your home directory, see the "Identifying Directories" sidebar.)

2. To make sure that you're in your home directory, type **pwd**. When I do this, I get the following response (yours will reflect your home directory):

```
$ pwd
/home/chris
```

3. Create a new directory called test in your home directory, as follows:

```
$ mkdir test
```

4. Check the permissions of the directory:

```
$ ls -ld test
drwxr-xr-x  2 chris  sales   1024  Jan 24 12:17 test
```

This listing shows that test is a directory (d). The d is followed by the permissions (rwxr-xr-x), which are explained later in the "Understanding file permissions" section. The rest of the information indicates the owner (chris), the group (sales), and the date that the files in the directory were most recently modified (Jan. 24 at 12:17 p.m.).

## Note

In some Linux systems, such as Fedora, when you add a new user, the user is assigned to a group of the same name by default. For example, in the preceding text, the user `chris` would be assigned to the group `chris`. This approach to assigning groups is referred to as the user private group scheme. ■

For now, type the following:

```
$ chmod 700 test
```

This step changes the permissions of the directory to give you complete access and everyone else no access at all. (The new permissions should read `rwx------`.)

5. Make the test directory your current directory as follows:

```
$ cd test
```

## Identifying Directories

When you need to identify your home directory on a shell command line, you can use the following:

- `$HOME` — This environment variable stores your home directory name.
- `~` — The tilde (~) represents your home directory on the command line.

You can also use the tilde to identify someone else's home directory. For example, `~chris` would be expanded to the `chris` home directory (probably `/home/chris`).

Other special ways of identifying directories in the shell include the following:

- `.` — A single dot (.) refers to the current directory.
- `..` — Two dots (..) refer to a directory directly above the current directory.
- `$PWD` — This environment variable refers to the current working directory.
- `$OLDPWD` — This environment variable refers to the previous working directory before you changed to the current one.

### Using metacharacters and operators

To make efficient use of your shell, the bash shell lets you use certain special characters, referred to as metacharacters and operators. Metacharacters can help you match one or more files without typing each file completely. Operators enable you to direct information from one command or file to another command or file.

## Using file-matching metacharacters

To save you some keystrokes and to be able to refer easily to a group of files, the bash shell lets you use metacharacters. Anytime you need to refer to a file or directory, such as to list it, open it, or remove it, you can use metacharacters to match the files you want. Here are some useful metacharacters for matching filenames:

- * — Matches any number of characters.
- ? — Matches any one character.
- [...] — Matches any one of the characters between the brackets, which can include a dash-separated range of letters or numbers.

Try out some of these file-matching metacharacters by first going to an empty directory (such as the test directory described in the previous section) and creating some empty files:

```
$ touch apple banana grape grapefruit watermelon
```

The touch command creates empty files. The next few commands show you how to use shell metacharacters with the ls command to match filenames. Try the following commands to see whether you get the same responses:

```
$ ls a*
apple
$ ls g*
grape
grapefruit
$ ls g*t
grapefruit
$ ls *e*
apple grape grapefruit watermelon
$ ls *n*
banana watermelon
```

The first example matches any file that begins with an a (apple). The next example matches any files that begin with g (grape, grapefruit). Next, files beginning with g and ending in t are matched (grapefruit). Next, any file that contains an e in the name is matched (apple, grape, grapefruit, watermelon). Finally, any file that contains an n is matched (banana, watermelon).

Here are a few examples of pattern matching with the question mark (?):

```
$ ls ????e
apple grape
$ ls g???e*
grape grapefruit
```

The first example matches any five-character file that ends in e (apple, grape). The second matches any file that begins with g and has e as its fifth character (grape, grapefruit).

Here are a couple of examples using braces to do pattern matching:

```
$ ls [abw]*
apple banana watermelon
$ ls [agw]*[ne]
apple grape watermelon
```

In the first example, any file beginning with a, b, or w is matched. In the second, any file that begins with a, g, or w and also ends with either n or e is matched. You can also include ranges within brackets. For example:

```
$ ls [a-g]*
apple banana grape grapefruit
```

Here, any filenames beginning with a letter from a through g is matched.

## Using file-redirection metacharacters

Commands receive data from standard input and send it to standard output. Using pipes (described earlier), you can direct standard output from one command to the standard input of another. With files, you can use less than (<) and greater than (>) signs to direct data to and from files. Here are the file-redirection characters:

- < — Directs the contents of a file to the command. In most cases, this is the default action expected by the command and the use of the character is optional; using `more bigfile` is the same as `more < bigfile`.

- > — Directs the standard output of a command to a file, deleting the existing file.

- 2> — Directs standard error (error messages) to the file.

- &> — Directs both standard output and standard error to the file.

- >> — Directs the output of a command to a file, adding the output to the end of the existing file.

Here are some examples of command lines where information is directed to and from files:

```
$ mail root < ~/.bashrc
$ man chmod | col -b > /tmp/chmod
$ echo "I finished the project on $(date)" >> ~/projects
```

In the first example, the contents of the .bashrc file in the home directory are sent in a mail message to the computer's root user. The second command line formats the chmod man page (using the man command), removes extra back spaces (col -b), and sends the output to the file /tmp/chmod (erasing the previous /tmp/chmod file, if it exists). The final command results in the following text being added to the user's project file:

```
I finished the project on Sat Jan 23 13:46:49 PST 2010
```

Another type of redirection referred to as *here documents* lets you type text that can be used as standard input for a command. Here documents involve entering two less-than characters (<<), after a command, followed by a word. All typing following that word is taken as user input until the word is repeated. Here is an example:

```
$ mail root cnegus rjones bdecker <<thetext
> I want to tell everyone that there will be a 10 am
> meeting in conference room B. Everyone should attend.
>
> -- James
> thetext
$
```

The example just shown sends a mail message to root, cnegus, rjones, and bdecker usernames. The text entered between <<thetext and thetext become the contents of the message. A common use of a here document is to use it with a text editor to create or add to a file from within a script:

```
/bin/ed /etc/resolv.conf <<resendit
a
nameserver 100.100.100.100
.
w
q
resendit
```

With these lines added to a script run by the root user, the ed text editor adds the IP address of a DNS server to the /etc/resolv.conf file.

### Understanding file permissions

After you've worked with Linux for a while, you are almost sure to get a Permission denied message. Permissions associated with files and directories in Linux were designed to keep users from accessing other users' private files and to protect important system files.

The nine bits assigned to each file for permissions define the access that you and others have to your file. Permission bits for a regular file appear as -rwxrwxrwx.

## Note

For a regular file, a dash appears in front of the nine-bit permissions indicator. Instead of a dash, you might see a d (for a directory), l (for a link), b (for a block device), or c (for a character device). ■

Of the nine-bit permissions, the first three bits apply to the owner's permission, the next three apply to the group assigned to the file, and the last three apply to all others. The r stands for read, the w stands for write, and the x stands for execute permissions. If a dash appears instead of the letter, it means that permission is turned off for that associated read, write, or execute.

Because files and directories are different types of elements, read, write, and execute permissions on files and directories mean different things. Table 9-9 explains what you can do with each of them.

**TABLE 9-9**

## Setting Read, Write, and Execute Permissions

| Permission | File | Directory |
|---|---|---|
| Read | View what's in the file. | See what files and subdirectories it contains. |
| Write | Change the file's content, rename it, or delete it. | Add files or subdirectories to the directory. |
| Execute | Run the file as a program. | Change to that directory as the current directory, search through the directory, or execute a program from the directory. |

You can see the permission for any file or directory by typing the `ls -ld` command. The named file or directory appears as those shown in this example:

```
$ ls -ld ch3 test
-rw-rw-r--  1 chris   sales    4983  Jan 18 22:13 ch3
drwxr-xr-x  2 chris   sales    1024  Jan 24 13:47 test
```

The first line shows that the ch3 file has read and write permission for the owner and the group. All other users have read permission, which means they can view the file but cannot change its contents or remove it. The second line shows the test directory (indicated by the letter d before the permission bits). The owner has read, write, and execute permissions while the group and other users have only read and execute permissions. As a result, the owner can add, change, or delete files in that directory, and everyone else can only read the contents, change to that directory, and list the contents of the directory.

If you own a file, you can use the chmod command to change the permission on it as you please. In one method of doing this, each permission (read, write, and execute) is assigned a number — r=4, w=2, and x=1 — and you use each set's total number to establish the permission. For example, to make permissions wide open for yourself as owner, you would set the first number to 7 (4+2+1), and then you would give the group and others read-only permission by setting both the second and third numbers to 4 (4+0+0), so that the final number is 744. Any combination of permissions can result from 0 (no permission) through 7 (full permission).

Here are some examples of how to change permission on a file (named file) and what the resulting permission would be:

```
# chmod 777 file    rwxrwxrwx
# chmod 755 file    rwxr-xr-x
# chmod 644 file    rw-r--r-
# chmod 000 file    ---------
```

You can also turn file permissions on and off using plus (+) and minus (-) signs, respectively. This can be done for the owner user (u), owner group (g), others (o), and all users (a). For example, start with a file that has all permissions open (rwxrwxrwx). Run the following chmod commands using minus sign options. The resulting permissions are shown to the right of each command:

```
chmod a-w file          r-xr-xr-x
chmod o-x file          rwxrwxrw-
chmod go-rwx file       rwx------
```

Likewise, here are some examples, starting with all permissions closed (---------) where the plus sign is used with chmod to turn permissions on:

```
chmod u+rw files        rw-------
chmod a+x files         --x--x--x
chmod ug+rx files       r-xr-x---
```

When you create a file, it's given the permission rw-r--r-- by default. A directory is given the permission rwxr-xr-x. These default values are determined by the value of umask. Type **umask** to see what your umask value is. For example:

```
$ umask
022
```

The umask value masks the permissions value of 666 for a file and 777 for a directory. The umask value of 022 results in permission for a directory of 755 (rwxr-xr-x). That same umask results in a file permission of 644 (rw-r--r--). (Execute permissions are off by default for regular files.)

## Tip

Time saver: Use the -R options of chmod, to change the permission for all the files and directories within a directory structure at once. For example, if you wanted to open permissions completely to all files and directories in the /tmp/test directory, you could type the following:

```
$ chmod -R 777 /tmp/test
```

This command line runs chmod recursively (-R) for the /tmp/test directory, as well as any files or directories that exist below that point in the file system (for example, /tmp/test/hat, /tmp/test/hat/caps, and so on). All would be set to 777 (full read/write/execute permissions). This is not something you would do on an important directory on a read/write file system. However, you might do this before you create a directory structure on a CD-ROM that you want to be fully readable and executable to someone using the CD-ROM later. ■

## Caution

The -R option of chmod works best if you are opening permissions completely or adding execute permission (as well as the appropriate read/write permission). The reason is that if you turn off execute permission recursively, you close off your capability to change to any directory in that structure. For example, chmod -R 644 /tmp/test turns off execute permission for the /tmp/test directory, and then fails to change any files or directories below that point. Execute permissions must be on for a directory to be able to change to that directory. ■

## Moving, copying, and deleting files

Commands for moving, copying, and deleting files are fairly straightforward. To change the location of a file, use the mv command. To copy a file from one location to another, use the cp command. To remove a file, use the rm command. Here are some examples:

```
$ mv abc def
$ mv abc ~
$ cp abc def
$ cp abc ~
$ rm abc
$ rm *
```

Of the two move (mv) commands, the first moves the file abc to the file def in the same directory (essentially renaming it), whereas the second moves the file abc to your home directory (~). The first copy command (cp) copies abc to the file def in the same directory, whereas the second copies abc to your home directory (~). The first remove command (rm) deletes the abc file; the second removes all the files in the current directory (except those that start with a dot).

### Note

For the root user, the mv, cp, and rm commands are aliased to each be run with the -i option. This causes a prompt to appear asking you to confirm each move, copy, and removal, one file at a time, and is done to prevent the root user from messing up a large group of files by mistake.

Another alternative with mv is to use the -b option. With -b, if a file of the same name exists at the destination, a backup copy of the old file is made before the new file is moved there. ∎

# Using the vi Text Editor

It's almost impossible to use Linux for any period of time and not need to use a text editor. This is because most Linux configuration files are plain text files that you will almost certainly need to change manually at some point.

If you are using a GUI, you can run gedit, which is fairly intuitive for editing text. There's also a simple text editor you can run from the shell called nano. However, most Linux shell users will use either the vi or emacs command to edit text files. The advantage of vi or emacs over a graphical editor is that you can use it from any shell, a character terminal, or a character-based connection over a network (using telnet or ssh, for example) — no GUI is required. They also each contain tons of features, so you can continue to grow with them.

This section provides a brief tutorial on the vi text editor, which you can use to manually edit a configuration file from any shell. (If vi doesn't suit you, see the "Exploring Other Text Editors" sidebar for other options.)

The vi editor is difficult to learn at first, but once you know it, you never have to use a mouse or a function key — you can edit and move around quickly and efficiently within files just by using the keyboard.

# Exploring Other Text Editors

Dozens of text editors are available for use with Linux. Here are a few that might be in your Linux distribution, which you can try out if you find vi to be too taxing.

| Text Editor | Description |
| --- | --- |
| nano | A popular, streamlined text editor that is used with many bootable Linuxes and other limited-space Linux environments. For example, nano is available to edit text files during a Gentoo Linux install process. |
| gedit | The GNOME text editor that runs in the GUI. |
| jed | This screen-oriented editor was made for programmers. Using colors, jed can highlight code you create so you can easily read the code and spot syntax errors. Use the Alt key to select menus to manipulate your text. |
| joe | The joe editor is similar to many PC text editors. Use control and arrow keys to move around. Press Ctrl+C to exit with no save or Ctrl+X to save and exit. |
| kate | A nice-looking editor that comes in the kdebase package. It has lots of bells and whistles, such as highlighting for different types of programming languages and controls for managing word wrap. |
| kedit | A GUI-based text editor that comes with the KDE desktop. |
| mcedit | With mcedit, function keys help you get around, save, copy, move, and delete text. Like jed and joe, mcedit is screen-oriented. |
| nedit | An excellent programmer's editor. You need to install the optional nedit package to get this editor. |

If you use ssh to log in to other Linux computers on your network, you can use any editor to edit files. A GUI-based editor will pop up on your screen. When no GUI is available, you will need a text editor that runs in the shell, such as vi, jed, or joe.

## Starting with vi

Most often, you start vi to open a particular file. For example, to open a file called /tmp/test, type the following command:

```
$ vi /tmp/test
```

If this is a new file, you should see something similar to the following:

```
~
~
~
~
~
"/tmp/test" [New File]
```

The box at the top represents where your cursor is. The bottom line keeps you informed about what is going on with your editing (here you just opened a new file). In between, there are tildes (~) as filler because there is no text in the file yet. Now here's the intimidating part: There are no hints, menus, or icons to tell you what to do. On top of that, you can't just start typing. If you do, the computer is likely to beep at you. And some people complain that Linux isn't friendly.

The first things you need to know are the different operating modes: command and input. The vi editor always starts in command mode. Before you can add or change text in the file, you have to type a command (one or two letters and an optional number) to tell vi what you want to do. Case is important, so use uppercase and lowercase exactly as shown in the examples! To get into input mode, type an input command. To start out, type either of the following:

- **a** — The add command. After it, you can input text that starts to the *right* of the cursor.
- **i** — The insert command. After it, you can input text that starts to the *left* of the cursor.

## Tip
When you are in insert mode, `-- INSERT --` will appear at the bottom of the screen. ∎

Type a few words and then press Enter. Repeat that a few times until you have a few lines of text. When you're finished typing, press Esc to return to command mode. Now that you have a file with some text in it, try moving around in your text with the following keys or letters:

## Tip
Remember the Esc key! It always places you back into command mode. ∎

- **Arrow keys** — Move the cursor up, down, left, or right in the file one character at a time. To move left and right, you can also use Backspace and the spacebar, respectively. If you prefer to keep your fingers on the keyboard, move the cursor with h (left), l (right), j (down), or k (up).
- **w** — Moves the cursor to the beginning of the next word.
- **b** — Moves the cursor to the beginning of the previous word.
- **0** (zero) — Moves the cursor to the beginning of the current line.
- **$** — Moves the cursor to the end of the current line.
- **H** — Moves the cursor to the upper-left corner of the screen (first line on the screen).
- **M** — Moves the cursor to the first character of the middle line on the screen.
- **L** — Moves the cursor to the lower-left corner of the screen (last line on the screen).

The only other editing you need to know is how to delete text. Here are a few vi commands for deleting text:

- **x** — Deletes the character under the cursor.
- **X** — Deletes the character directly before the cursor.
- **dw** — Deletes from the current character to the end of the current word.
- **d$** — Deletes from the current character to the end of the current line.
- **d0** — Deletes from the previous character to the beginning of the current line.

To wrap things up, use the following keystrokes for saving and quitting the file:

- **ZZ** — Save the current changes to the file and exit from vi.
- **:w** — Save the current file but continue editing.
- **:wq** — Same as ZZ.
- **:q** — Quit the current file. This works only if you don't have any unsaved changes.
- **:q!** — Quit the current file and *don't* save the changes you just made to the file.

## Tip

If you've really trashed the file by mistake, the :q! command is the best way to exit and abandon your changes. The file reverts to the most recently changed version. So, if you just did a :w, you are stuck with the changes up to that point. If you just want to undo a few bad edits, press u to back out of changes. ∎

You have learned a few vi editing commands. I describe more commands in the following sections. First, however, here are a few tips to smooth out your first trials with vi:

- **Esc** — Remember that Esc gets you back to command mode. (I've watched people press every key on the keyboard trying to get out of a file.) Esc followed by ZZ gets you out of command mode, saves the file, and exits.
- **u** — Press u to undo the previous change you made. Continue to press u to undo the change before that, and the one before that.
- **Ctrl+R** — If you decide you didn't want to undo the previous command, use Ctrl+R for Redo. Essentially, this command undoes your undo.
- **Caps Lock** — Beware of hitting Caps Lock by mistake. Everything you type in vi has a different meaning when the letters are capitalized. You don't get a warning that you are typing capitals — things just start acting weird.
- **:! *command*** — You can run a command while you are in vi using :! followed by a command name. For example, type **:!date** to see the current date and time, type **:!pwd** to see what your current directory is, or type **:!jobs** to see whether you have any jobs running in the background. When the command completes, press Enter and you are back to editing the file. You could even use this technique to launch a shell (**:!bash**) from vi,

run a few commands from that shell, and then type **exit** to return to vi. (I recommend doing a save before escaping to the shell, just in case you forget to go back to vi.)

- **Ctrl+G** — If you forget what you are editing, pressing these keys displays the name of the file that you are editing and the current line that you are on at the bottom of the screen. It also displays the total number of lines in the file, the percentage of how far you are through the file, and the column number the cursor is on. This just helps you get your bearings after you've stopped for a cup of coffee at 3 a.m.

## Moving around the file

Besides the few movement commands described earlier, there are other ways of moving around a vi file. To try these out, open a large file that you can't do much damage to. (Try copying /var/log/messages to /tmp and opening it in vi.) Here are some movement commands you can use:

- **Ctrl+F** — Page ahead, one page at a time.
- **Ctrl+B** — Page back, one page at a time.
- **Ctrl+D** — Page ahead one-half page at a time.
- **Ctrl+U** — Page back one-half page at a time.
- **G** — Go to the last line of the file.
- **1G** — Go to the first line of the file. (Use any number to go to that line in the file.)

## Searching for text

To search for the next occurrence of text in the file, use either the slash (/) or the question mark (?) character. Follow the slash or question mark with a pattern (string of text) to search forward or backward, respectively, for that pattern. Within the search, you can also use metacharacters. Here are some examples:

- /hello — Searches forward for the word hello.
- ?goodbye — Searches backward for the word goodbye.
- /The.*foot — Searches forward for a line that has the word The in it and also, after that at some point, the word foot.
- ?[pP]rint — Searches backward for either print or Print. Remember that case matters in Linux, so make use of brackets to search for words that could have different capitalization.

After you have entered a search term, simply type / or ? to search forward or backward for the same term again, respectively.

The vi editor was originally based on the ex editor, which didn't let you work in full-screen mode. However, it did enable you to run commands that let you find and change text on one or more lines at a time. When you type a colon and the cursor goes to the bottom of the screen, you are essentially in ex mode. Here is an example of some of those ex commands for searching for and changing text. (I chose the words Local and Remote to search for, but you can use any appropriate words.)

- :g/Local — Searches for the word Local and prints every occurrence of that line from the file. (If there is more than a screenful, the output is piped to the more command.)
- :s/Local/Remote — Substitutes Remote for the word Local on the current line.
- :g/Local/s//Remote — Substitutes the first occurrence of the word Local on every line of the file with the word Remote.
- :g/Local/s//Remote/g — Substitutes every occurrence of the word Local with the word Remote in the entire file.
- :g/Local/s//Remote/gp — Substitutes every occurrence of the word Local with the word Remote in the entire file, and then prints each line so that you can see the changes (piping it through more if output fills more than one page).

## Using numbers with commands

You can precede most vi commands with numbers to have the command repeated that number of times. This is a handy way to deal with several lines, words, or characters at a time. Here are some examples:

- 3dw — Deletes the next three words.
- 5cl — Changes the next five letters (that is, removes the letters and enters input mode).
- 12j — Moves down 12 lines.

Putting a number in front of most commands just repeats those commands. At this point, you should be fairly proficient at using the vi command. After you get used to using vi, you will probably find other text editors less efficient to use.

## Note

When you invoke vi in many Linux systems, you're actually invoking the vim text editor, which runs in vi compatibility mode. Those who do a lot of programming might prefer vim because it shows different levels of code in different colors. vim has other useful features, such as the capability to open a document with the cursor at the same place as it was when you last exited that file. ■

# Summary

Working from a shell command line within Linux may not be as simple as using a GUI, but it offers many powerful and flexible features. This chapter explains how to find your way around the shell in Linux and provides examples of running commands, including recalling commands from a history list, completing commands, and joining commands.

The chapter describes how shell environment variables can be used to store and recall important pieces of information. It also teaches you how to modify shell configuration files to tailor the shell to suit your needs. Finally, this chapter shows you how to use the Linux file system to create files and directories, use permissions, and work with files (moving, copying, and removing them), and how to edit text files from the shell using the vi command.

# Learning Basic Administration

L inux, like other UNIX-based systems, was intended for use by more than one person at a time. *Multiuser* features enable many people to have accounts on a single Linux system, with their data kept secure from others. *Multitasking* enables many people to run many programs on the computer at the same time, with each person able to run more than one program. Sophisticated networking protocols and applications make it possible for a Linux system to extend its capabilities to network users and computers around the world. The person assigned to manage all of this stuff is called the *system administrator*.

Even if you are the only person using a Linux system, system administration is still set up to be separate from other computer use. To do most administrative tasks, you need to be logged in as the root user (also called the *superuser*) or temporarily get root permission. Users other than root cannot change, or in some cases even see, some of the configuration information for a Linux system. In particular, security features such as stored passwords are protected from general view.

Because Linux system administration is such a huge topic, this chapter focuses on the general principles of Linux system administration. In particular, it examines some of the basic tools you need to administer a Linux system for a personal desktop or on a small LAN. Beyond the basics, this chapter also teaches you how to work with file systems and monitor the setup and performance of your Linux system.

# Graphical Administration Tools

Many Linux systems come with simplified graphical tools for administering Linux. If you are a casual user, these tools often let you do everything you need to administer your system without editing configuration files or running shell commands.

Let's examine some of the Web-based administration tools available to use with most Linux systems.

## Using Web-based administration

Web-based administration tools are available with many open source projects to make those projects more accessible to casual users. Often all you need to use those tools is a Web browser (such as Firefox), the port number of the service, and the root password. Projects such as Samba and CUPS come with their own Web administration tools. Webmin is a general-purpose tool for administering a variety of Linux system services from your Web browser.

The advantages of Web-based administration tools are that you can operate them from a familiar interface (your Web browser) and you can access them remotely. Webmin includes graphical interfaces for configuring Apache Web server, Sendmail mail server, and SSH server.

## Note
Some Linux distributions come with their own set of graphical administration tools (such as SUSE's YaST or Red Hat's system-config tools). You should generally use those instead of any Web-based interface that comes with a project because a distribution's own tools are usually better integrated with its features for starting and stopping services. ■

### Open source projects offering Web administration

Several major open source projects come with Web-based interfaces for configuring those projects. Regardless of which Linux you are using, you can use your Web browser to configure the following projects:

- **Samba**—To set up Samba for doing file and printer sharing with Microsoft Windows systems on your LAN, use the Samba SWAT Web-based administration tools from any Web browser. With SWAT installed and running, you can access your Samba server configuration from your Web browser by typing the following URL in the location box:

    ```
    http://localhost:901
    ```

## Note
If you get an `Unable to Connect` message, it may be because Samba or SWAT is not running. Or your firewall may be blocking access. ■

The Samba project also offers other graphical tools for administering Samba. You can check them out at `http://samba.org/samba/GUI`. For descriptions of these tools, see Chapters 15 and 16.

- **CUPS**—The Common UNIX Printing Service (CUPS) has its own Web administration tool. With CUPS installed and configured, you can typically use CUPS Web administration by typing the following URL in your Web browser's location box:

    `http://localhost:631`

    You use the CUPS administration tool to manage printers and classes and do a variety of administration tasks. CUPS is described in Chapter 15.

Samba and CUPS are included with many Linux distributions. Other projects that offer Web-based administration that may or may not be in your Linux distribution include SquirrelMail (a Webmail interface) and Mailman (a mailing list facility).

Because many Web browser administrative interfaces send data in clear text, they are most appropriate for use on the local system. However, because they are Web-based, you can also use these interfaces from your LAN or other network. If you plan to expose these administrative interfaces to an untrusted network, however, you should consider encrypting your communications (for example, by using Web-based administration tools over an SSH tunnel, as described later in this chapter).

## The Webmin administration tool

The Webmin facility (`www.webmin.com`) offers more complete Web-based Linux and UNIX administration features. Although Webmin isn't delivered with some Linux systems that offer their own graphical administration tools (such as Fedora and RHEL), the Webmin project has ported Webmin to run on more than 70 different operating systems. Supported Linux distributions include SUSE, Red Hat (Fedora and RHEL), Debian, Ubuntu, Gentoo, Slackware, Mandriva, Yellow Dog, and others (see `www.webmin.com/support.html` for a complete list).

After you get Webmin from Webmin.com and install it, you can use Webmin from your Web browser. To start the Webmin interface, type the following in the Web browser's location box:

    `http://localhost:10000`

After you log in as root user, the main Webmin page displays, as shown in Figure 10-1.

**FIGURE 10-1**

Webmin offers a Web browser interface for administering Linux.

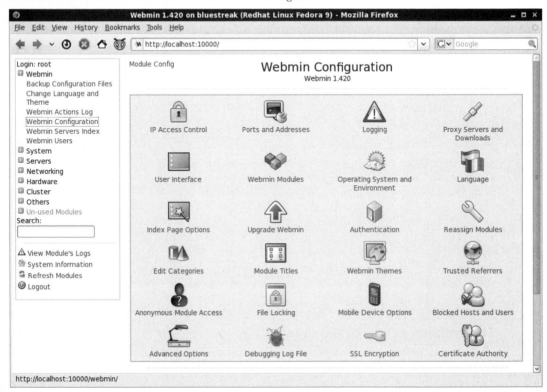

## Graphical administration with different distributions

Some people fear that after they've left the familiar confines of their Microsoft Windows system for Linux, they'll be stuck doing everything from a command line. To gain a wider audience, commercial Linux distributions such as Red Hat Enterprise Linux and SUSE have their own sets of graphical tools to provide an easy entry point for new Linux users. The following sections describe the Fedora and Red Hat Enterprise Linux system-config and SUSE's YaST graphical administration tools.

### Fedora/RHEL config tools

A set of graphical tools that comes with Fedora and Red Hat Enterprise Linux systems can be launched from the Administration submenu of the System menu or from the command line. Most of the Fedora and RHEL tools that launch from the command line begin with the system-

`config` string (such as `system-config-network`). These administrative tasks require root permission; if you are logged in as a regular user, you must enter the root password before the GUI application's window opens. Once you have typed the password, look for a yellow badge icon in the upper-right corner of the panel, indicating that you have root authorization. Click the badge to open a pop-up window that enables you to remove authorization. Otherwise, authorization goes away after a few minutes. While the badge is displayed, you can open any administrative GUI application without having to enter the password again.

The following list describes many of the graphical tools you can use to administer a Fedora or Red Hat Enterprise Linux system. Start these windows from the Administration submenu on the System menu. The name of the package that must be installed to get the feature is shown in parentheses:

## Note
**The availability of the selections described in the following list depends on which features you have installed.** ■

- **Add/Remove Software (PackageKit)**—Launch the Add/Remove Software window for finding, adding, and removing software associated with software repositories configured for your system.

- **Server Settings**—Access the following server configuration windows from this submenu:

  - **Domain Name System (system-config-bind)**—Create and configure zones if your computer is acting as a DNS server.

  - **HTTP (system-config-httpd)**—Configure your computer as an Apache Web server.

  - **NFS (system-config-nfs)**—Set up directories from your system to be shared with other computers on your network using the NFS service.

  - **Samba NFS (system-config-samba)**—Configure Windows (SMB) file sharing. (To configure other Samba features, you can use the SWAT window.)

  - **Services (system-config-services)**—Display and change which services are running on your Fedora system at different run levels from the Service Configuration window.

- **Authentication (authconfig-gtk)**—Change how users are authenticated on your system. Usually, Shadow Passwords and MD5 Passwords are selected. However, if your network supports LDAP, Kerberos, SMB, NIS, or Hesiod authentication, you can select to use any of those authentication types.

- **Bootloader (system-config-boot)**—If you have multiple operating systems on your computer, or multiple Linux kernels available to boot in Linux, you can use the Boot Configuration screen to choose which to boot by default. For example, you might have Fedora Linux, SUSE, and Windows XP all on the same hard disk. You could choose which would start automatically (after a set number of seconds), if one wasn't selected explicitly.

- **Date & Time (system-config-date)**—Set the date and time or choose to have an NTP server keep system time in sync.

- **Display (system-config-display)**—Change the settings for your X desktop, including color depth and resolution for your display. You can also choose settings for your video card and monitor.

- **Firewall and SELinux (system-config-firewall)**—Configure your firewall to allow or deny services to computers from the network.

- **Language (system-config-language)**—Select the default language used for the system.

- **Logical Volume Management (system-config-lvm)**—Manage your LVM partitions.

- **Network (system-config-network)**—Manage your current network interfaces and add interfaces.

- **Printing (system-config-printer)**—Configure local and network printers.

- **Root Password (system-config-rootpassword)**—Change the root password.

- **SELinux Management (system-config-selinux)**—Set SELinux enforcing modes and default policy.

- **SELinux Troubleshooter (setroubleshoot-server)**—Monitor and diagnose SELinux AVC denials.

- **Users & Groups (system-config-users)**—Add, display, and change user and group accounts for your Fedora system.

Other administrative utilities are available from the Applications menu on the top panel. Select the System Tools submenu to see some of the following options:

- **Configuration Editor (gconf-editor)**—Directly edit the GNOME configuration database.

- **Disk Usage Analyzer (gnome-utils)**—Display detailed information about your hard disks and removable storage devices.

- **Kickstart (system-config-kickstart)**—Create a kickstart configuration file that can be used to install multiple Fedora systems without user interaction.

Other applications that you add to Fedora or RHEL may also include administrative utilities that will appear in the System Tools submenu.

## SUSE YaST tools

The YaST administrative interface is one of the strongest features of SUSE Linux. From a SUSE desktop, open the YaST Control Center by selecting YaST from the Computer menu. Figure 10-2 shows an example of the YaST Control Center that appears.

**FIGURE 10-2**

Use the YaST Control Center to administer SUSE systems.

YaST has some useful tools in its Hardware section that enable you to probe your computer hardware. Selecting Hardware Information on my system, for example, enabled me to see that the CD-ROM drive that YaST detected was available through device /dev/cdrom and that it supported CD-R, CD-RW, and DVD media. I could also see detailed information about my CPU, network card, PCI devices, sound card, and various storage media.

YaST also offers interfaces for configuring and starting network devices, as well as a variety of services to run on those devices. In addition, you can use YaST to configure your computer as a client for file sharing (Samba and NFS), mail transfer agent (sendmail), and a variety of network services.

SUSE Linux Enterprise Server comes with a wider range of configuration tools that are specifically geared toward server setup, including tools for configuring a mail server, VPN tunnels, and full Samba 3. Although other distributions may include proprietary tools, YaST is in a class of its own.

# Using the root Login

Every Linux system starts out with at least one administrative user account (the root user) and possibly one or more regular user accounts (given a name that you choose, or a name assigned by your Linux distribution). In most cases, you log in as a regular user and become the root user to do an administrative task.

The root user has complete control of the operation of your Linux system. That user can open any file or run any program. The root user also installs software packages and adds accounts for other people who use the system.

## Tip

**Think of the root user in Linux as similar to the Administrator user in Windows.** ■

When you first install most Linux systems, you add a password for the root user. You must remember and protect this password—you will need it to log in as root or to obtain root permission while you are logged in as some other user. Other Linux systems (such as KNOPPIX) start you without an available root password, so you may want to add one when you first start up by typing the following from a Terminal window or other shell:

```
# passwd root
Changing password for user root.
New UNIX password: ********
Retype new UNIX password: ********
```

## Note

**Some bootable Linux distributions give you (as a regular user) the power to run commands as root. You simply have to ask for the privilege using the** sudo **command. For example, from a Terminal window, to open a shell as root, type the following:** ■

```
$ sudo su -
#
```

You'll find out more about the sudo command later in this chapter.

The home directory for the root user is typically /root. The home directory and other information associated with the root user account are located in the /etc/passwd file. Here's what the root entry looks like in the /etc/passwd file:

```
root:x:0:0:root:/root:/bin/bash
```

This shows that for the user named root the user ID is set to 0 (root user), the group ID is set to 0 (root group), the home directory is /root, and the shell for that user is /bin/bash. (We're using a shadow password file to store encrypted password data, so the password field here contains an *x*.) You can change the home directory or the shell used by editing the values in this file. A better way to change these values, however, is to use the usermod command (see the "Modifying Users with usermod" section later in this chapter).

**Note**

By default, the root account is disabled in Ubuntu. This means that even though the account exists, you cannot log in using it or use su to become the root user. This adds an additional level of security to Ubuntu, and requires you to use sudo before each command you want to execute as the root user. ∎

# Becoming root from the shell (su command)

Although you can become the superuser by logging in as root, sometimes that is not convenient. For example, you may be logged in to a regular user account and just want to make a quick administrative change to your system without having to log out and log back in. Or, you may need to log in over the network to make a change to a Linux system but find that the system doesn't allow root users in from over the network (a common practice in the days before secure shells were available).

The solution is to use the su command. From any Terminal window or shell, you can simply type the following:

```
$ su
Password: ******
#
```

When you are prompted, type in the root user's password. The prompt for the regular user ($) changes to the superuser prompt (#). At this point, you have full permission to run any command and use any file on the system. However, one thing that the su command doesn't do when used this way is read in the root user's environment. As a result, you may type a command that you know is available and get the message Command Not Found. To fix this problem, use the su command with the dash (-) option instead, like this:

```
$ su -
Password: ******
#
```

You still need to type the password, but after that, everything that normally happens at login for the root user happens after the su command is completed. Your current directory will be root's home directory (probably /root), and things such as the root user's PATH variable will be used. If you become the root user by just typing su, rather than su -, you won't change directories or the environment of the current login session.

You can also use the su command to become a user other than root. This is useful for troubleshooting a problem that is being experienced by a particular user, but not by others on the computer (such as an inability to print or send e-mail). For example, to have the permissions of a user named jsmith, you'd type the following:

```
$ su - jsmith
```

Even if you were root user before you typed this command, afterward you would have only the permissions to open files and run programs that are available to jsmith. As root user, however, after you type the su command to become another user, you don't need a password to continue. If you type that command as a regular user, you must type the new user's password.

When you are finished using superuser permissions, return to the previous shell by exiting the current shell. Do this by pressing Ctrl+D or by typing **exit**. If you are the administrator for a computer that is accessible to multiple users, don't leave a root shell open on someone else's screen—unless you want to let that person do anything he wants to the computer!

## Allowing limited administrative access

As mentioned earlier, when you run GUI tools as a regular user (from Fedora, SUSE, or some other Linux systems), you are prompted for the root password before you are able to access the tool. By entering the root password, you are given root privilege for that task. In the case of Fedora, after you enter the password a yellow badge icon appears in the top panel, indicating that root authorization is still available for other GUI tools to run from that desktop session. A particular user can also be given administrative permissions for particular tasks without being given the root password. For example, a system administrator can add a user to particular groups, such as modem, disk, users, cdrom, ftp, mail, or www, and then open group permission to use those services. Or, an administrator can add a user to the wheel group and add entries to the /etc/ sudoers file to allow that user to use the sudo command to run individual commands as root. (See the description of sudo later in this chapter.)

## Note

The wheel group does not exist in all distributions. In Ubuntu, for example, wheel is not created automatically. ■

A feature available in some Linux distributions that adds an additional level of security is Security Enhanced Linux (SELinux). With SELinux, instead of one all-powerful root user account, multiple roles can be defined to protect selected files and services. In that way, for example, if someone cracks your Web server, he does not automatically have access to your mail server, user passwords, or other services running on the computer.

# Exploring Administrative Commands, Configuration Files, and Log Files

You can expect to find many commands, configuration files, and log files in the same places in the file system, regardless of which Linux distribution you are using. The following sections give you some pointers on where to look for these important elements.

## Coming from Windows

If GUI administrative tools for Linux have become so good, why do you need to know about administrative files? For one thing, while GUI tools differ among Linux versions, many underlying configuration files are the same. So, if you learn to work with them, you can work with almost any Linux system. Also, if a feature is broken or if you need to do something that's not supported by the GUI, when you ask for help, Linux experts almost always tell you how to change the configuration file directly. ■

# Administrative commands

Only the root user is intended to use many administrative commands. When you log in as root (or use su - from the shell to become root), your $PATH variable is set to include some directories that contain commands for the root user. These include the following:

- /sbin—Contains commands for modifying your disk partitions (such as fdisk), checking file systems (fsck), and changing system states (init).

- /usr/sbin—Contains commands for managing user accounts (such as useradd) and adding mount points for automounting file systems (automount). Commands that run as daemon processes are also contained in this directory. (Look for commands that end in d, such as sshd, pppd, and cupsd.)

Some administrative commands are contained in regular user directories (such as /bin and /usr/bin). This is especially true of commands that have some options available to everyone. An example is the /bin/mount command, which anyone can use to list mounted file systems, but only root can use to mount file systems. (Some desktops, however, are configured to let regular users use mount to mount CDs, DVDs, or other removable media by adding keywords to the /etc/fstab file.)

## Note

See the section "Mounting File Systems" later in this chapter for instructions on how to mount a file system. ■

To find commands intended primarily for the system administrator, check out the section 8 manual pages (usually in /usr/share/man/man8). They contain descriptions and options for most Linux administrative commands.

Some third-party applications add administrative commands to directories that are not in your PATH. For example, an application may put commands in /usr/local/bin, /opt/bin, or /usr/local/sbin. Some Linux distributions automatically add those directories to your PATH, usually before your standard bin and sbin directories. In that way, commands installed to those directories are not only accessible, but can also override commands of the same name in other directories.

## Administrative configuration files

Configuration files are another mainstay of Linux administration. Almost everything you set up for your particular computer—user accounts, network addresses, or GUI preferences—is stored in plain-text files. This has some advantages and some disadvantages.

The advantage of plain-text files is that it's easy to read and change them. Any text editor will do. The downside, however, is that as you edit configuration files, no error checking is going on. You have to run the program that reads these files (such as a network daemon or the X desktop) to find out whether you set up the files correctly. There are no standards for the structure of configuration files, so you need to learn the format of each file individually. A comma or a quote in the wrong place can sometimes cause a whole interface to fail.

## Note

Some software packages offer a command to test the sanity of the configuration file tied to a package before you start a service. For example, the testparm command is used with Samba to check the sanity of your smb.conf file. Other times, the daemon process providing a service offers an option for checking your config file. For example, run httpd -t to check your Apache Web server configuration before starting your Web server. ■

Throughout this book you'll find descriptions of the configuration files you need to set up the different features that make up Linux systems. The two major locations of configuration files are your home directory (where your personal configuration files are kept) and the /etc directory (which holds systemwide configuration files).

Following are descriptions of directories (and subdirectories) that contain useful configuration files. (Refer to Table 10-1 for some individual configuration files in /etc that are of particular interest.) Viewing the contents of Linux configuration files can teach you a lot about administering Linux systems.

- $HOME—All users store information in their home directories that directs how their login accounts behave. Most configuration files in $HOME begin with a dot (.), so they don't appear in a user's directory when you use a standard ls command (you need to type ls -a to see them). Likewise, dot files and directories won't show up in most file manager windows by default. There are dot files that define how each user's shell behaves, the desktop look-and-feel, and options used with your text editor. There are even files such as .ssh/* and .rhosts that configure network permissions for each user. (To see the name of your home directory, type echo $HOME from a shell.)
- /etc—This directory contains most of the basic Linux system-configuration files. Table 10-1 shows some /etc configuration files of interest.
- /etc/cron*—Directories in this set contain files that define how the crond utility runs applications on a daily (cron.daily), hourly (cron.hourly), monthly (cron.monthly), or weekly (cron.weekly) schedule.
- /etc/cups—Contains files used to configure the CUPS printing service.

- /etc/default—Contains files that set default values for various utilities. For example, the file for the useradd command defines the default group number, home directory, password expiration date, shell, and skeleton directory (/etc/skel) that are used when creating a new user account.

- /etc/httpd—Contains a variety of files used to configure the behavior of your Apache Web server (specifically, the httpd daemon process). (On some Linux systems, /etc/apache or /etc/apache2 is used instead.)

- /etc/init.d—Contains the permanent copies of System V–style run-level scripts. These scripts are often linked from the /etc/rc?.d directories to have each service associated with a script started or stopped for the particular run level. The ? is replaced by the run-level number (0 through 6). (Slackware puts its run-level scripts in the /etc/rc.d directory.)

- /etc/mail—Contains files used to configure your sendmail mail service.

- /etc/pcmcia—Contains configuration files that allow you to have a variety of PCMCIA cards configured for your computer. (PCMCIA slots are those openings on your laptop that enable you to have credit card–sized cards attached to your computer. You can attach devices such as modems and external CD-ROMs.)

- /etc/postfix—Contains configuration files for the postfix mail transport agent.

- /etc/ppp—Contains several configuration files used to set up Point-to-Point Protocol (PPP) so that you can have your computer dial out to the Internet.

- /etc/rc?.d—There is a separate rc?.d directory for each valid system state: rc0.d (shutdown state), rc1.d (single-user state), rc2.d (multiuser state), rc3.d (multiuser plus networking state), rc4.d (user-defined state), rc5.d (multiuser, networking, plus GUI login state), and rc6.d (reboot state). Some Linux distros, such as Slackware, put most of the start-up scripts directly in /etc/rc.d, without the run-level notation.

- /etc/security—Contains files that set a variety of default security conditions for your computer. These files are part of the pam (pluggable authentication modules) package.

- /etc/skel—Any files contained in this directory are automatically copied to a user's home directory when that user is added to the system. By default, most of these files are dot (.) files, such as .kde (a directory for setting KDE desktop defaults) and .bashrc (for setting default values used with the bash shell).

- /etc/sysconfig—Contains important system configuration files that are created and maintained by various services (including iptables, samba, and most networking services). These files are critical for Linux distributions that use GUI administration tools but are not used on other Linux systems at all.

- /etc/xinetd.d—Contains a set of files, each of which defines a network service that the xinetd daemon listens for on a particular port. When the xinetd daemon process receives a request for a service, it uses the information in these files to determine which daemon processes to start to handle the request.

**TABLE 10-1**

## /etc Configuration Files of Interest

| File | Description |
| --- | --- |
| aliases | Can contain distribution lists used by the Linux mail service. (This file may be located in /etc/mail.) |
| bashrc | Sets system-wide defaults for bash shell users. (This may be called bash.bashrc on some Linux distributions.) |
| crontab | Sets cron environment and times for running automated tasks. |
| csh.cshrc (or cshrc) | Sets system-wide defaults for csh (C shell) users. |
| exports | Contains a list of local directories that are available to be shared by remote computers using the Network File System (NFS). |
| fstab | Identifies the devices for common storage media (hard disk, floppy, CD-ROM, and so on) and locations where they are mounted in the Linux system. This is used by the mount command to choose which file systems to mount when the system first boots. |
| group | Identifies group names and group IDs (GIDs) that are defined on the system. Group permissions in Linux are defined by the second of three sets of rwx (read, write, execute) bits associated with each file and directory. |
| gshadow | Contains shadow passwords for groups. |
| host.conf | Sets the locations in which domain names (for example, redhat.com) are searched for on TCP/IP networks (such as the Internet). By default, the local hosts file is searched and then any name server entries in resolv.conf. |
| hosts | Contains IP addresses and host names that you can reach from your computer. (Usually this file is used just to store names of computers on your LAN or small private network.) |
| hosts.allow | Lists host computers that are allowed to use certain TCP/IP services from the local computer. |
| hosts.deny | Lists host computers that are *not* allowed to use certain TCP/IP services from the local computer (although this file will be used if you create it, it doesn't exist by default). |
| inittab | Contains information that defines which programs start and stop when Linux boots, shuts down, or goes into different states in between. This is the most basic configuration file for starting Linux. |
| lilo.conf | Sets Linux boot loader (lilo) parameters to boot the computer. In particular, it lists information about bootable partitions on your computer. (If your distribution uses the GRUB boot loader, you may not see this file.) |
| modules.conf | Contains aliases and options related to loadable kernel modules used by your computer. |

| File | Description |
|------|-------------|
| mtab | Contains a list of file systems that are currently mounted. |
| mtools.conf | Contains settings used by DOS tools in Linux. |
| named.conf | Contains DNS settings if you are running your own DNS server. |
| ntp.conf | Includes information needed to run the Network Time Protocol (NTP). |
| passwd | Stores account information for all valid users for the system. Also includes other information, such as the home directory and default shell. (Rarely includes the user passwords themselves, which are typically stored in the /etc/shadow file.) |
| printcap | Contains definitions for the printers configured for your computer. (If the printcap file doesn't exist, look for printer information in the /etc/cups directory.) |
| profile | Sets system-wide environment and startup programs for all users. This file is read when the user logs in. |
| protocols | Sets protocol numbers and names for a variety of Internet services. |
| resolv.conf | Identifies the locations of DNS name server computers that are used by TCP/IP to translate Internet *host.domain* names into IP addresses. (When a Web browser or mail client looks for an Internet site, it checks servers listed in this file to locate the site.) |
| rpc | Defines remote procedure call names and numbers. |
| services | Defines TCP/IP and UDP services and their port assignments. |
| shadow | Contains encrypted passwords for users who are defined in the passwd file. (This is viewed as a more secure way to store passwords than the original encrypted password in the passwd file. The passwd file needs to be publicly readable, whereas the shadow file can be unreadable by all but the root user.) |
| shells | Lists the shell command-line interpreters (bash, sh, csh, and so on) that are available on the system, as well as their locations. |
| sudoers | Sets commands that can be run by users, who may not otherwise have permission to run the command, using the sudo command. In particular, this file is used to provide selected users with root permission. |
| syslog.conf | Defines what logging messages are gathered by the syslogd daemon and what files they are stored in. (Typically, log messages are stored in files contained in the /var/log directory.) |
| termcap | Lists definitions for character terminals, so that character-based applications know what features are supported by a given terminal. Graphical terminals and applications have made this file obsolete to most people. (Termcap was the BSD UNIX way of storing terminal information; UNIX System V used definitions in /usr/share/terminfo files.) |
| xinetd.conf | Contains simple configuration information used by the xinetd daemon process. This file mostly points to the /etc/xinetd.d directory for information about individual services. (Some systems use the inetd.conf file and the inetd daemon instead.) |

Another directory, /etc/X11, includes subdirectories that each contain system-wide configuration files used by X and different X window managers available for Linux. The xorg.conf file (which makes your computer and monitor usable with X) and configuration directories containing files used by xdm and xinit to start X are in here.

Directories relating to window managers contain files that include the default values that a user will get if that user starts one of these window managers on your system. Window managers that may have system-wide configuration files in these directories include Twm (twm/) and Xfce (xdg/).

## Note

Some files and directories in /etc/X11 are linked to locations in the /usr/X11R6 directory. ∎

## Administrative log files

One of the things that Linux does well is keep track of itself. This is a good thing, when you consider how much is going on in a complex operating system. Sometimes you are trying to get a new facility to work and it fails without giving you the foggiest reason why. Other times you want to monitor your system to see whether people are trying to access your computer illegally. In any of those cases, you can use log files to help track down the problem.

The main utilities for logging error and debugging messages for Linux are the syslogd and klogd daemons. General system logging is done by syslogd. Logging that is specific to kernel activity is done by klogd. Logging is done according to information in the /etc/syslog.conf file. Messages are typically directed to log files that are usually in the /var/log directory. Here are a few common log files:

- boot.log—Contains boot messages about services as they start up.
- messages—Contains many general informational messages about the system.
- secure—Contains security-related messages, such as login activity.
- XFree86.0.log or Xorg.0.log—Depending on which X server you are using, contains messages about your video card, mouse, and monitor configuration.

If you are using a Fedora or Ubuntu systems, the System Log Viewer utility is a good way to step through your system's log files. From the Applications menu, select System ➪ Administration ➪ Log File Viewer. You not only can view boot, kernel, mail, security, and other system logs, but you can also use the viewing pane to select log messages from a particular date.

## Using sudo and Other Administrative Logins

You don't hear much about other administrative logins (besides root) being used with Linux. It was a fairly common practice in UNIX systems to have several different administrative logins that allowed administrative tasks to be split among several users. For example, people sitting near a printer could have lp permissions to move print jobs to another printer if they knew a printer wasn't working.

In any case, administrative logins are available with Linux; however, logging in directly as those users is disabled by default. The accounts are maintained primarily to provide ownership for files and processes associated with particular services. Here are some examples:

- **lp**—This user account owns such things as the /var/log/cups printing log file and various printing cache and spool files. The home directory for lp is /var/spool/lpd.

- **uucp**—User owns various uucp commands (once used as the primary method for dial-up serial communications) as well as log files in /var/log/uucp, spool files in /var/spool, administrative commands (such as uuchk, uucico, uuconv, and uuxqt) in /usr/sbin, and user commands (uucp, cu, uuname, uustat, and uux) in /usr/bin. The home directory for uucp is /var/spool/uucp.

- **bin**—User owns many commands in /bin in traditional UNIX systems. This is not the case in some Linux systems (such as Fedora and Gentoo) because root owns most executable files. The home directory of bin is /bin.

- **news**—User could do administration of Internet news services, depending on how you set permission for /var/spool/news and other news-related resources. The home directory for news is /etc/news.

By default, the administrative logins in the preceding list are disabled. You would need to change the default shell from its current setting (usually /sbin/nologin or /bin/false) to a real shell (typically /bin/bash) to be able to log in as these users.

One way to give full or limited root privileges to any nonroot user is to set up the sudo facility, which simply entails adding the user to /etc/sudoers and defining what privilege you want that user to have. Then the user can run any command he or she is privileged to use by preceding that command with the sudo command.

Here's an example of how to use the sudo facility to cause any users that are added to the wheel group to have full root privileges.

**1.** As the root user, edit the /etc/sudoers file by running the visudo command:

```
# /usr/sbin/visudo
```

By default, the file opens in vi, unless your EDITOR variable happens to be set to some other editor acceptable to visudo (for example, export EDITOR=gedit). The reason for using visudo is that the command locks the /etc/sudoers file and does some basic sanity checking of the file to ensure it has been edited correctly.

## Note
If you are stuck here, refer to the vi tutorial in Chapter 9 for information on using the vi editor. ∎

2. Uncomment the following line to allow users in the wheel group to have full root privileges on the computer:

```
%wheel       ALL=(ALL)       ALL
```

## Tip

If you look at the `sudoers` file in Ubuntu, you will see that this privilege exists, by default, for the admin group members. ∎

This `line` causes users in the `wheel` group to provide a password (their own password, not the root password) in order to use administrative commands. To allow users in the wheel group to have that privilege without using a password, uncomment the following line instead:

```
%wheel       ALL=(ALL)       NOPASSWD: ALL
```

3. Save the changes to the `/etc/sudoers` file (in vi, type **Esc**, and then **ZZ**).
4. Still as root user, open the `/etc/group` file using the `vigr` command and add to the `wheel` line any users you want to have root privilege. For example, if you were to add the users mary and jake to the wheel group, the line would appear as follows:

```
wheel:x:10:root,mary,jake
```

Now users mary and jake can run the `sudo` command to run commands, or parts of commands, that are normally restricted to the root user. The following is an example of a session by the user jake after he has been assigned `sudo` privileges:

```
[jake]$ sudo umount /mnt/win

    We trust you have received the usual lecture
    from the local System Administrator. It usually
    boils down to these two things:

        #1) Respect the privacy of others.
        #2) Think before you type.

Password: *********
 [jake]$ umount /mnt/win
mount: only root can mount /dev/sda1 on /mnt/win
[jake]$ sudo umount /mnt/win
[jake]$
```

In this session, the user jake runs the `sudo` command to unmount the `/mnt/win` file system (using the `umount` command). He is given a warning and asked to provide his password (this is jake's password, *not* the root password).

Even after jake has given the password, he must still use the sudo command to run subsequent administrative commands as root (the umount fails, but the sudo umount succeeds). Notice that he is not prompted for a password for the second sudo. That's because after entering his password successfully, he can enter as many sudo commands as he wants for the next 5 minutes without having to enter it again. (You can change the timeout value from 5 minutes to however long you want by setting the passwd_timeout value in the /etc/sudoers file.)

The preceding example grants a simple all-or-nothing administrative privilege to everyone you put in the wheel group. However, the /etc/sudoers file gives you an incredible amount of flexibility in permitting individual users and groups to use individual applications or groups of applications. Refer to the sudoers and sudo man pages for information about how to tune your sudo facility. Refer to the pam_wheel man page to see how the PAM facility affects members of the wheel group.

# Administering Your Linux System

Your system administrator duties don't end after you have installed Linux. If multiple people are using your Linux system, you, as administrator, must give each person his own login account. You'll use useradd and related commands to add, modify, and delete user accounts.

Configuring hardware is also on your duty list. When you add hardware to your Linux computer, that hardware is often detected and configured automatically. In some cases, however, the hardware may not have been set up properly, and you will use commands such as lsmod, modprobe, insmod, and rmmod to configure the right modules to get the hardware working.

## Note
A *device driver* is the code permanently built into the kernel to allow application programs to talk to a particular piece of hardware. A *module* is like a driver, but it is loaded on demand. The "Configuring Hardware" section later in this chapter includes information about using these commands to configure modules. ∎

Managing file systems and disk space is your responsibility, too. You must keep track of the disk space being consumed, especially if your Linux system is shared by multiple users. At some point, you may need to add a hard disk or track down what is eating up your disk space (you use commands such as find to do this).

Your duties also include monitoring system performance. You may have a runaway process on your system or you may just be experiencing slow performance. Tools that come with Linux can help you determine how much of your CPU and memory are being consumed.

These tasks are explored in the rest of this chapter.

# Creating User Accounts

Every person who uses your Linux system should have a separate user account. Having a user account provides each person with an area in which to securely store files, as well as a means of tailoring his or her user interface (GUI, path, environment variables, and so on) to suit the way that he or she uses the computer.

You can add user accounts to most Linux systems in several ways—Fedora and Red Hat Enterprise Linux systems use the system-config-users utility, for example, and SUSE offers a user setup module in YaST. This chapter describes how to add user accounts from the command line with useradd because most Linux systems include that command. (In some cases a Linux system will have a similar command called adduser.)

## Adding users with useradd

The most straightforward method for creating a new user from the shell is with the useradd command. After opening a Terminal window with root permission, you simply invoke useradd at the command prompt, with details of the new account as parameters.

The only required parameter is the login name of the user, but you probably want to include some additional information ahead of it. Each item of account information is preceded by a single letter option code with a dash in front of it. Table 10-2 lists the options available with useradd.

**TABLE 10-2**

### useradd Command Options

| Option | Description |
| --- | --- |
| -c comment<br>-c "comment here" | Provide a description of the new user account. Often the person's full name. Replace comment with the name of the user account (-c jake). Use quotes to enter multiple words (-c "jake jackson"). |
| -d home_dir | Set the home directory to use for the account. The default is to name it the same as the login name and to place it in /home. Replace home_dir with the directory name to use (for example, -d /mnt/homes/jake). |
| -D | Rather than create a new account, save the supplied information as the new default settings for any new accounts that are created. |
| -e expire_date | Assign the expiration date for the account in MM/DD/YYYY format. Replace expire_date with a date you want to use (-e 05/06/2010). |
| -f -1 | Set the number of days after a password expires until the account is permanently disabled. The default, -1, disables the option. Setting this to 0 disables the account immediately after the password has expired. Replace -1 with the number to use. |

| Option | Description |
| --- | --- |
| `-g group` | Set the primary group (as listed in the `/etc/group` file) the new user will be in. Replace `group` with the group name (`-g wheel`). |
| `-G grouplist` | Add the new user to the supplied comma-separated list of groups (`-G wheel,sales,tech,lunch`). |
| `-k skel_dir` | Set the skeleton directory containing initial configuration files and login scripts that should be copied to a new user's home directory. This parameter can be used only in conjunction with the `-m` option. Replace `skel_dir` with the directory name to use. (Without this option, the `/etc/skel` directory is used.) |
| `-m` | Automatically create the user's home directory and copy the files in the skeleton directory (`/etc/skel`) to it. |
| `-M` | Do not create the new user's home directory, even if the default behavior is set to create it. |
| `-n` | Turn off the default behavior of creating a new group that matches the name and user ID of the new user. This option is available with Red Hat Linux systems. Other Linux systems often assign a new user to the group named `users` instead. |
| `-o` | Use with `-u uid` to create a user account that has the same UID as another username. (This effectively lets you have two different usernames with authority over the same set of files and directories.) |
| `-p passwd` | Enter a password for the account you are adding. This must be an encrypted password. Instead of adding an encrypted password here, you can simply use the `passwd user` command later to add a password for `user`. |
| `-s shell` | Specify the command shell to use for this account. Replace `shell` with the command shell (`-s bash`). |
| `-u user_id` | Specify the user ID number for the account (`-u 474`). Without the `-u` option, the default behavior is to automatically assign the next available number. Replace `user_id` with the ID number (`-u`). |

For example, let's create an account for a new user named Mary Smith with a login name of mary. First, log in as root, and then type the following command:

```
# useradd -c "Mary Smith" mary
```

# Tip

When you choose a username, don't begin with a number (for example, 26jsmith). Also, it's best to use all lowercase letters, no control characters or spaces, and a maximum of 8 characters. The `useradd` command allows up to 32 characters, but some applications can't deal with usernames that long. Tools such as `ps` display UIDs instead of names if names are too long. Having users named Jsmith and jsmith can cause confusion with programs (such as sendmail) that don't distinguish case. ■

Next, set Mary's initial password using the passwd command. You're prompted to type the password twice:

```
# passwd mary
Changing password for user mary.
New password: *******
Retype new password: *******
```

## Note

**Asterisks in this example represent the password you type. Nothing is actually displayed when you type the password. Also keep in mind that running** passwd **as root user lets you add short or blank passwords that regular users cannot add themselves.** ∎

In creating the account for Mary, the useradd command performs several actions:

- Reads the /etc/login.defs file to get default values to use when creating accounts.
- Checks command-line parameters to find out which default values to override.
- Creates a new user entry in the /etc/passwd and /etc/shadow files based on the default values and command-line parameters.
- Creates any new group entries in the /etc/group file. (Fedora creates a group using the new user's name; Gentoo adds the user to the users group; and SUSE adds it to every group you set for new users, such as dialout, audio, video, and other services.)
- Creates a home directory, based on the user's name, in the /home directory.
- Copies any files located within the /etc/skel directory to the new home directory. This usually includes login and application startup scripts.

The preceding example uses only a few of the available useradd options. Most account settings are assigned using default values. You can set more values explicitly, if you want to; here's an example that uses a few more options to do so:

```
# useradd -g users -G wheel,apache -s /bin/tcsh -c "Mary Smith" mary
```

In this case, useradd is told to make users the primary group mary belongs to (-g), add her to the wheel and apache groups, and assign tcsh as her primary command shell (-s). A home directory in /home under the user's name (/home/mary) is created by default. This command line results in a line similar to the following being added to the /etc/passwd file:

```
mary:x:502:100:Mary Smith:/home/mary:/bin/tcsh
```

Each line in the /etc/passwd file represents a single user account record. Each field is separated from the next by a colon (:) character. The field's position in the sequence determines what it is. As you can see, the login name is first. Again, the password field contains an *x* because we are using a shadow password file to store encrypted password data. The user ID selected by useradd is 502. The primary group ID is 100, which corresponds to the users group in the /etc/group file. The comment field was correctly set to Mary Smith, the home directory was automatically assigned as /home/mary, and the command shell was assigned as /bin/tcsh, exactly as specified with the useradd options.

By leaving out many of the options (as I did in the first useradd example), defaults are assigned in most cases. For example, by not using -g users or -G wheel,apache, in Fedora a group named mary would have been created and assigned to the new user. Other Linux systems assign users as the group name by default. Likewise, excluding -s /bin/tcsh causes /bin/bash to be assigned as the default shell.

The /etc/group file holds information about the different groups on your Linux system and the users who belong to them. Groups are useful for enabling multiple users to share access to the same files while denying access to others. Peek at the /etc/group file, and you find something similar to this:

```
bin:x:1:root,bin,daemon
daemon:x:2:root,bin,daemon
sys:x:3:root,bin,adm
adm:x:4:root,adm,daemon
tty:x:5:
disk:x:6:root
lp:x:7:daemon,lp
mem:x:8:
kmem:x:9:
wheel:x:10:root,joe,mary
apache:x:48:mary
     .
     .
     .
nobody:x:99:
users:x:100:
chris:x:500
sheree:x:501
```

Each line in the group file contains the name of a group, the group ID number associated with it, and a list of users in that group. By default, each user is added to his or her own group, beginning with GID 500. Note that mary was added to the wheel and apache groups instead of having her own group.

It is actually rather significant that mary was added to the wheel group. By doing this, you grant her the capability to use the sudo command to run commands as the root user (provided that sudo is configured as described earlier in this chapter).

## Setting user defaults

The useradd command determines the default values for new accounts by reading the /etc/login.defs file. You can modify those defaults by either editing that file manually with a standard text editor or by running the useradd command with the -D option. Although login.

defs is different on different Linux systems, here is an example containing many of the settings you might find in a login.defs file:

```
PASS_MAX_DAYS    99999
PASS_MIN_DAYS    0
PASS_MIN_LEN     5
PASS_WARN_AGE    7

UID_MIN                 500
UID_MAX               60000
GID_MIN                 500
GID_MAX               60000

CREATE_HOME yes
```

All uncommented lines contain keyword/value pairs. For example, the keyword PASS_MIN_LEN is followed by some white space and the value 5. This tells useradd that the user password must be at least five characters. Other lines let you customize the valid range of automatically assigned user ID numbers or group ID numbers. (Fedora starts at UID 500; other Linuxes start with UID 100.) A comment section that explains that keyword's purpose precedes each keyword (which I edited out here to save space). Altering a default value is as simple as editing the value associated with a keyword and then saving the file.

If you want to view the defaults, type the useradd command with the -D option, as follows:

```
# useradd -D
GROUP=100
HOME=/home
INACTIVE=-1
EXPIRE=
SHELL=/bin/bash
SKEL=/etc/skel
```

You can also use the -D option to change defaults. When run with this flag, useradd refrains from actually creating a new user account; instead, it saves any additionally supplied options as the new default values in /etc/login.defs. Not all useradd options can be used in conjunction with the -D option. You can use only the five options listed in Table 10-3.

**TABLE 10-3**

## useradd Options for Changing User Defaults

| Options | Description |
| --- | --- |
| -b *default_home* | Set the default directory in which user home directories are created. Replace *default_home* with the directory name to use (-b /garage). Usually this is /home. |

| Options | Description |
|---------|-------------|
| -e *default_expire_date* | Set the default expiration date on which the user account is disabled. The *default_expire_date* value should be replaced with a date in the form MM/DD/YYYY (-e 10/15/2009). |
| -f *default_inactive* | Set the number of days after a password has expired before the account is disabled. Replace *default_inactive* with a number representing the number of days (-f 7). |
| -g *default_group* | Set the default group that new users will be placed in. Normally useradd creates a new group with the same name and ID number as the user. Replace *default_group* with the group name to use (-g bears). |
| -s *default_shell* | Set the default shell for new users. Normally this is /bin/bash. Replace *default_shell* with the full path to the shell that you want as the default for new users (-s /bin/ash). |

To set any of the defaults, give the -D option first, and then add the defaults you want to set. For example, to set the default home directory location to /home/everyone and the default shell to /bin/tcsh, type the following:

```
# useradd -D -b /home/everyone -s /bin/tcsh
```

Besides setting up user defaults, an administrator can create default files that are copied to each user's home directory for use. These files can include login scripts and shell configuration files (such as .bashrc).

Other commands that are useful for working with user accounts include usermod (to modify settings for an existing account) and userdel (to delete an existing user account).

## Modifying users with usermod

The usermod command provides a simple and straightforward method for changing account parameters. Many of the options available with it mirror those found in useradd. Table 10-4 lists the options that can be used with this command.

---

**TABLE 10-4**

### usermod Options

| Option | Description |
| --- | --- |
| -c *username* | Change the description associated with the user account. Replace *username* with the name of the user account (-c jake). Use quotes to enter multiple words (-c "jake jackson"). |
| -d *home_dir* | Change the home directory to use for the account. The default is to name it the same as the login name and to place it in /home. Replace *home_dir* with the directory name to use (for example, -d /mnt/homes/jake). |
| -e *expire_date* | Assign a new expiration date for the account in MM/DD/YYYY format. Replace *expire_date* with a date you want to use (-e 05/06/2010). |
| -f *-1* | Change the number of days after a password expires until the account is permanently disabled. The default, -1, disables the option. Setting this to 0 disables the account immediately after the password has expired. Replace *-1* with the number to use. |
| -g *group* | Change the primary group (as listed in the /etc/group file) the user will be in. Replace *group* with the group name (-g wheel). |
| -G *grouplist* | Add the user to the supplied comma-separated list of groups (-G wheel,sales,tech,lunch). |
| -l *login_name* | Change the login name of the account. |
| -m | Available only when -d is used, this causes the contents of the user's home directory to be copied to the new directory. |
| -o | Use only with -u uid to remove the restriction that UIDs must be unique. |
| -s *shell* | Specify a different command shell to use for this account. Replace *shell* with the command shell (-s bash). |
| -u *user_id* | Change the user ID number for the account. Replace *user_id* with the ID number (-u 474). |

As an example, to change the shell to the csh shell for the user named chris, type the following as root user from a shell:

```
# usermod -s /bin/csh chris
```

## Deleting users with userdel

Just as usermod is used to modify user settings and useradd is used to create users, userdel is used to remove users. The following command will remove the user chris:

```
# userdel chris
```

The only option available with this utility is -r, which is used to remove not only the user, but also their home directory:

```
# userdel -r chris
```

# Configuring Hardware

In a perfect world, after installing and booting Linux, all of your hardware is detected and available for access. Although many Linux systems are rapidly moving closer to that world, there are times when you must take special steps to get your computer hardware working. Also, the growing use of removable USB and FireWire devices (CDs, DVDs, flash drives, digital cameras, and removable hard drives) has made it important for Linux to

- Efficiently manage hardware that comes and goes
- Look at the same piece of hardware in different ways (for example, be able to see a printer as a fax machine, scanner, and storage device, as well as a printer)

If you are using a Linux system that includes the 2.6 kernel (as the latest versions of most major Linux systems do), new kernel features have made it possible to change drastically the way hardware devices are detected and managed. Features in, or closely related to, the kernel include Udev (to dynamically name and create devices as hardware comes and goes) and Hotplug and HAL (to pass information about hardware changes to user space).

If all this sounds a bit confusing, don't worry. It's actually designed to make your life as a Linux user much easier. The end result of features built on the 2.6 kernel is that device handling in Linux has become

- **More automatic**—For most common hardware, when a hardware device is connected or disconnected, it is automatically detected and identified. Interfaces to access the hardware are added, so it is accessible to Linux. Then the fact that the hardware is present (or removed) is passed to the user level, where applications listening for hardware changes are ready to mount the hardware and/or launch an application (such as an image viewer or music player).
- **More flexible**—If you don't like what happens automatically when a hardware item is connected or disconnected, you can change it. For example, features built into GNOME and KDE desktops let you choose what happens when a music CD or movie DVD is inserted, or when a digital camera is connected. If you prefer a different program be launched to handle it, you can easily make that change.

This section covers several issues relating to getting your hardware working properly in Linux. First, it describes how to configure Linux to deal with removable media. Then it tells how to use tools for manually loading and working with drivers for hardware that is not detected and loaded properly.

# Managing removable hardware

Linux systems such as SUSE, RHEL, Fedora, and others that support full KDE and GNOME desktop environments include simple graphical tools for configuring what happens when you attach popular removable devices to the computer. So, with a KDE or GNOME desktop running, you simply plug in a USB device or insert a CD or DVD and a window may pop up to deal with that device.

Although different desktop environments share many of the same underlying mechanisms (in particular, Udev) to detect and name removable hardware, they offer different tools for configuring how they are mounted or used. Udev (using the udevd daemon) creates and removes devices (/dev directory) as hardware is added and removed from the computer. The Hardware Abstraction layer (HAL) provides the overall platform for discovering and configuring hardware. Settings that are of interest to someone using a desktop Linux system, however, can be configured with easy-to-use desktop tools.

The following sections describe how removable hardware and media are configured, using a GNOME desktop in Fedora and a KDE desktop in SUSE.

## Removable media on a GNOME desktop

The Nautilus file manager used with the GNOME desktop lets you define what happens when you attach removable devices or insert removable media into the computer from the File Management Preferences window. The descriptions in this section are based on GNOME 2.24.

From a Nautilus file manager window, select Edit ➪ Preferences, and then select the Media tab to see how your system is configured to handle removable media. Figure 10-3 shows an example of that window.

The following settings are available from the Media tab on the File Management Preferences window. These settings relate to how removable media are handled when they are inserted or plugged in. In most cases, you are prompted how to handle a medium that is inserted or connected.

- **CD Audio**—When an audio CD is inserted, you can choose to be prompted for what to do (default), do nothing, open the contents in a folder window, or select from various audio CD players to be launched to play the content. Rhythmbox music player and Sound Juicer CD ripper are among the choices you have for handling an inserted audio CD.

- **DVD Video**—When a commercial video DVD is inserted, you are prompted for what to do with that DVD. You can change that default to launch Movie Player (Totem) or another media player you have installed (such as MPlayer).

- **Music Player**—When inserted media contains audio files, you are asked what to do. You can select to have Rhythmbox or some other music player begin playing the files by selecting that player from this box.

**FIGURE 10-3**

Change removable media settings in Nautilus.

- **Photos**—When inserted media (such as a memory card from a digital camera) contains digital images, you are asked what to do with those images. You can select to do nothing. Or you can select to have the images opened in gThumb image viewer or F-Spot photo manager.

- **Software**—When inserted media contains an autorun application, an autorun prompt will open. To change that behavior (to do nothing or open the media contents in a folder), you can select that from this box.

- **Other Media Type**—Select the Type box under the Other Media heading to select how less commonly used media are handled. For example, you can select what actions are taken to handle blank Blu-Ray discs, CDs, or DVDs. You can select what applications to launch for Blu-Ray video, DVD audio, HD DVD videos, picture CDs, super video CDs, and video CDs.

Note that the settings described here are only in effect for the user who is currently logged in. If multiple users have login accounts, each can have his or her own way of handling removable media.

## Note

The Totem movie player will not play movie DVDs unless you add extra software to decrypt the DVD. There are legal issues and other movie player options you should look into if you want to play commercial DVD movies from Linux. See Chapter 4 for more information about video players in Linux. ∎

If you have an earlier version of GNOME, you may see a Portable Music Players entry. A music player is started in Linux to play files from your portable iPod or other music player, if that is selected and you enter a player to use. The banshee project (http://banshee-project.org) includes software for playing music from iPods in Linux. (From Fedora, type **yum install banshee** to install the software from the Fedora repository. Then add **ipod %d** to this field to use the player.) Other players with iPod support include gPodder (http://gpodder.berlios.de/) and gtkpod (http://www.gtkpod.org/).

### Removable media on a SUSE KDE desktop

When you insert a removable medium (CD or DVD) or plug in a removable device (digital camera or USB flash drive) from a KDE desktop in SUSE, a window opens to let you choose the type of action to take on it. If you want to add a different action, or change an existing action, click the Configure button.

Figure 10-4 shows an example of the window that appears when a 32MB USB flash drive is inserted, as well as the KDE Control Module that appears when Configure is selected.

**FIGURE 10-4**

Use the KDE Control Module to set how to respond to inserted media.

From the KDE Control Module, select the media type you want to change (in this case, Mounted Removable Medium). Click Add, and then select the type of action you would like to add as an option when that type of media is detected.

# Working with loadable modules

If you have added hardware to your computer that isn't properly detected, you might need to manually load a module for that hardware. Linux comes with a set of commands for loading, unloading, and getting information about hardware modules.

If you have installed the Linux kernel source code, source code files for available drivers are stored in subdirectories of the /usr/src/linux*/drivers directory. You can find information about these drivers in a couple of ways:

- make xconfig—With /usr/src/linux* as your current directory (and Linux kernel source code installed), type **make xconfig** from a Terminal window on the desktop. Select the category of module you want and then click Help next to the driver that interests you. The help information that appears includes a description of the driver. (If your system is missing graphical libraries needed to run make xconfig, try make menuconfig instead.)

- **Documentation**—The /usr/src/linux*/Documentation directory contains lots of plain-text files describing different aspects of the kernel and related drivers.

After modules have been built, they are installed in the /lib/modules/ subdirectories. The name of the directory is based on the release number of the kernel that the modules were compiled for. Modules that are in that directory can then be loaded and unloaded as they are needed. Before building modules for a new kernel, or more important, a current kernel, it may be wise to add your initials to the kernel Makefile under the variable EXTRAVERSION at the top of the Makefile. This installs your new modules under /lib/modules/*kernel-version* with the EXTRAVERSION suffixed to the directory. If you completely wreck the module build, you haven't overwritten the current modules you may be running. It also makes it easier to identify custom kernel modules when debugging. To see your current kernel version, type

```
$ uname -r
```

## Listing loaded modules

To see which modules are currently loaded into the running kernel on your computer, use the lsmod command. Here's an example:

```
# lsmod
Module                  Size  Used by
snd_seq_oss            38912  0
snd_seq_midi_event      9344  1 snd_seq_oss
snd_seq                67728  4
snd_seq_oss,snd_seq_midi_event
```

```
snd_seq_device          8328   2 snd_seq_oss,snd_seq
.
.
.
autofs                 16512   0
ne2k_pci                9056   0
8390                   13568   1 ne2k_pci
ohci1394               41860   0
ieee1394              284464   1 ohci1394
floppy                 65712   0
sg                     36120   0
scsi_mod              124600   1 sg
parport_pc             39724   0
parport                47336   1 parport_pc
ext3                  128424   2
jbd                    86040   1 ext3
```

## Note

If you don't have a Linux system installed yet, try booting KNOPPIX and using lsmod to list your loaded modules. If all your hardware is working properly, write down the list of modules. Later, when you permanently install Fedora or some other Linux system, if your CD drive, modem, video card, or other hardware doesn't work properly, you can use your list of modules to determine which module should have been used and load it, as described in the next section. ■

This output shows a variety of modules that have been loaded on a Linux system, including several to support the ALSA sound system, some of which provide OSS compatibility (snd_seq_oss).

To find information about any of the loaded modules, use the modinfo command. For example, you could type the following:

```
# /sbin/modinfo -d snd-seq-oss
"OSS-compatible sequencer module"
```

Not all modules have descriptions available and if nothing is available, no data will be returned. In this case, however, the snd-seq-oss module is described as an OSS-compatible sequencer module. You can also use the -a option to see the author of the module, or -n to see the object file representing the module. The author information often has the e-mail address of the driver's creator, so you can contact the author if you have problems or questions about it.

### Loading modules

You can load any module that has been compiled and installed (to a /lib/modules subdirectory) into your running kernel using the modprobe command. A common reason for loading a module is to use a feature temporarily (such as loading a module to support a special file system on a floppy you want to access). Another reason is to identify a module that will be used by a particular piece of hardware that could not be autodetected.

Here is an example of the modprobe command being used to load the parport module, which provides the core functions to share parallel ports with multiple devices:

```
# modprobe parport
```

After parport is loaded, you can load the parport_pc module to define the PC-style ports available through the interface. The parport_pc module lets you optionally define the addresses and IRQ numbers associated with each device sharing the parallel port. For example:

```
# modprobe parport_pc io=0x3bc irq=auto
```

In this example, a device is identified as having an address of 0x3bc, and the IRQ for the device is autodetected.

The modprobe command loads modules temporarily—they disappear at the next reboot. To permanently add the module to your system, add the modprobe command line to one of the startup scripts run at boot time. You can also add modules to the /etc/modules file to have them loaded at startup.

## Note

An alternative to modprobe is the insmod command. The advantage of using modprobe, however, is that insmod loads only the module you request, whereas modprobe tries to load other modules that the one you requested is dependent on. ■

### Removing modules

Use the rmmod command to remove a module from a running kernel. For example, to remove the module parport_pc from the current kernel, type the following:

```
# rmmod parport_pc
```

If it is not currently busy, the parport_pc module is removed from the running kernel. If it is busy, try killing any process that might be using the device. Then run rmmod again. Sometimes, the module you are trying to remove depends on other modules that may be loaded. For instance, the usbcore module cannot be unloaded while the USB printer module (usblp) is loaded, as shown here:

```
# rmmod usbcore
ERROR: Module usbcore is in use by wacom,usblp,ehci_hcd,ohci_hcd
```

# Managing File Systems and Disk Space

File systems in Linux are organized in a hierarchy, beginning from root (/) and continuing downward in a structure of directories and subdirectories. As an administrator of a Linux system, it's your duty to make sure that all the disk drives that represent your file system are available to the users of the computer. It is also your job to make sure there is enough disk space in the right places in the file system for users to store what they need.

## Coming from Windows

**File systems are organized differently in Linux than they are in Microsoft Windows operating systems. Instead of drive letters (for example, A:, B:, C:) for each local disk, network file system, CD-ROM, or other type of storage medium, everything fits neatly into the directory structure.**

**Some drives are connected (mounted) automatically into the file system. For example, a CD might be mounted on /media/cdrom. If the drive isn't mounted automatically, it is up to an administrator to create a mount point in the file system and then connect the disk to that point. ∎**

The organization of your file system begins when you install Linux. Part of the installation process is to divide your hard disk (or disks) into partitions. Those partitions can then be assigned to

- A part of the Linux file system
- Swap space for Linux
- Other file system types (perhaps containing other bootable operating systems)
- Free space (you can leave space unassigned so you can format it later as you need it)

This chapter focuses on partitions that are used for the Linux file system. To see what partitions are currently set up on partitions that the Linux kernel has detected, use the fdisk command:

```
# /sbin/fdisk -1
Disk /dev/sda:  40.0 GB, 40020664320 bytes
255 heads, 63 sectors/track, 4825 cylinders
Units = cylinders of 16065 * 512 bytes = 8225280 bytes

   Device Boot    Start      End     Blocks   Id  System
/dev/sda1    *        1       13        104    b  Win95 FAT32
/dev/sda2            84       89      48195   83  Linux
/dev/sda3            90      522   3478072+   83  Linux
/dev/sda4           523      554     257040    5  Extended
/dev/sda5           523      554    257008+   82  Linux swap
```

This output shows the disk partitioning for a computer capable of running both Linux and Microsoft Windows. You can see that the Linux partition on /dev/sda3 has most of the space available for data. There is a Windows partition (/dev/sda1) and a Linux swap partition (/dev/sda5). There is also a small /boot partition (46MB) on /dev/sda2. In this case, the root partition for Linux has 3.3GB of disk space and resides on /dev/sda3. The fdisk -1 command uses partition information found in /proc/partitions unless explicitly given on the command line.

Next use the mount command (with no options) to see what partitions are actually being used for your Linux system (which available disk partitions are actually mounted and where they are mounted):

```
# mount
/dev/sda3 on / type ext3 (rw)
/dev/sda2 on /boot type ext3 (rw)
/dev/sda1 on /mnt/win type vfat (rw)
/dev/proc on /proc type proc (rw)
/dev/sys on /sys type sysfs (rw)
/dev/devpts on /dev/pts type devpts (rw,gid=5,mode=620)
/dev/shm on /dev/shm type tmpfs (rw)
none on /proc/sys/fs/binfmt_misc type binfmt_misc (rw)
/dev/cdrom on /media/cdrecorder type iso9660 (ro,nosuid,nodev)
```

Although some of the file systems shown as mounted are for special purposes (/sys, /proc, and others), our concern here is with disk partition (/dev/hd*, /dev/sd*, and so on). The mounted Linux partitions in this case are /dev/sda2, which provides space for the /boot directory (contains data for booting Linux), and /dev/sda3, which provides space for the rest of the Linux file system beginning from the root directory (/).

This particular system also contains a Windows partition that was mounted in the /mnt/win directory and a CD that was mounted in /media/cdrecorder. (With most GUI interfaces, the CD is typically mounted automatically when you insert it. For 2.6 kernels, look in the /media directory; for 2.4 kernels the /mnt directory is often used.)

After the word type, you can see the type of file system contained on the device. (See the description of different file system types in Table 10-5 in the following section.) Particularly on larger Linux systems, you may have multiple partitions for several reasons:

- **Multiple hard disks**—You may have several hard disks available to your users. In that case you would have to mount each disk (and possibly several partitions from each disk) in different locations in your file system.

- **Protecting different parts of the file system**—If the users on a system consume all the file system space, the entire system can fail. For example, there may be no place for temporary files to be copied (so the programs writing to temporary files fail), and incoming mail may fail to be written to mail boxes. With multiple mounted partitions, if one partition runs out of space, the others can continue to work.

- **Multiple operating systems**—You can configure your disk to contain multiple partitions that can each be used to hold a different operating system type. For example, if you started with a computer that had Windows on the hard disk, you could put Linux on a separate partition, and then set up the computer to boot either operating system.

- **Backups**—Some fast ways exist to back up data from your computer that involve copying the entire image of a disk or partition. If you want to restore that partition later, you can simply copy it back (bit by bit) to a hard disk. With smaller partitions, this approach can be done fairly efficiently.

- **Protecting from disk failure**—If one disk (or part of one disk) fails, having multiple partitions mounted on your file system may let you continue working and just fix the one disk that fails. Ghost for Linux (`http://freshmeat.net/projects/g4l`) is an example of a tool for backing up a hard disk partition in Linux.

When a disk partition is mounted on the Linux file system, all directories and subdirectories below that mount point are stored on that partition. So, for example, if you were to mount one partition on / and one on /usr, everything below the /usr mount point would be stored on the second partition while everything else would be stored on the first partition. If you then mounted another partition on /usr/local, everything below that mount point would be on the third partition, while everything else below /usr would be on the second partition.

## Tip

**What happens if a remote file system is unmounted from your computer, and you go to save a file in that mount point directory? You will write the file to that directory and it will be stored on your local hard disk. When the remote file system is remounted, however, the file you saved will seem to disappear. To get the file back, you'll have to unmount the remote file system (causing the file to reappear), move the file to another location, remount the file system, and copy the file back there. ■**

Mount points often mentioned as being candidates for separate partitions include /, /boot, /home, /usr, and /var. The root file system (/) is the catchall for directories that aren't in other mount points. The root file system's mount point (/) is the only one that is required. The /boot directory holds the images needed to boot the operating system. The /home file system is where all the user accounts are typically stored. Applications and documentation are stored in /usr. Below the /var mount point is where log files, temporary files, server files (Web, FTP, and so on), and lock files are stored (that is, items that need disk space for your computer's applications to keep running).

The fact that multiple partitions are mounted on your file system is invisible to people using your Linux system. It is an issue only when a partition runs out of space or if users need to save or use information from a particular device (such as a floppy disk or remote file system) that isn't mounted. Of course, any user can check this by typing the mount command.

## Mounting file systems

Most of your hard disk partitions are mounted automatically for you. When you install Fedora, Ubuntu, SUSE, and some other Linux systems, you are asked to create partitions and indicate the mount points for those partitions. (Other Linux installation procedures will expect you to know that you have to partition before beginning.) When you boot Linux, all Linux partitions residing on hard disk that are listed in your /etc/fstab file are typically mounted. For that reason, this section focuses mostly on how to mount other types of devices so that they become part of your Linux file system.

The mount command is used not only to mount devices but also to mount other kinds of file systems on your Linux system. This means that you can store files from other operating systems or use file systems that are appropriate for certain kinds of activities (such as writing large block sizes). The most common use of this feature for the average Linux user, however, is to enable that user to obtain and work with files from floppy disks, CD-ROMs, or other removable media.

## Note

With the addition of automatic mounting features and changes in how removable media are identified with the Linux 2.6 kernel (see descriptions of Udev and HAL earlier in this chapter), you no longer need to manually mount removable media for many Linux desktop systems. Understanding how to manually mount and unmount file systems on a Linux server, however, can be a very useful skill. ■

### Supported file systems

To see file system types that are currently available to be used on your system, type `cat /proc/filesystems`. Table 10-5 shows the file system types that are supported in Linux, although they may not be in use at the moment or they may not be built into your current kernel (so they may need to be loaded as modules).

**TABLE 10-5**

## Supported File System Types

| Type | Description |
| --- | --- |
| adfs | Acorn disk file system, which is the standard file system used on RiscOS operating systems. |
| befs | File system used by the BeOS operating system. |
| cifs | Common Internet File System (CIFS), the virtual file system used to access servers that comply with the SNIA CIFS specification. CIFS is an attempt to refine and standardize the SMB protocol used by Samba and Windows file sharing. |
| ext4 | Successor to the popular ext3 file system. It includes many improvements over ext3, such as support for volumes up to 1 exbibyte and file sizes up to 16 tebibytes. (This has replaced ext3 as the default file system used in Fedora.) |
| ext3 | Ext file systems are the most common in most Linux systems. The ext3 file system, also called the Third Extended file system, includes journaling features that, compared to ext2, improve a file system's capability to recover from crashes. |
| ext2 | The default file system type for earlier Linux systems. Features are the same as ext3, except that ext2 doesn't include journaling features. |
| ext | This is the first version of ext3. It is not used very often anymore. |
| iso9660 | Evolved from the High Sierra file system (the original standard for CD-ROMs). Extensions to the High Sierra standard (called Rock Ridge extensions) allow iso9660 file systems to support long filenames and UNIX-style information (such as file permissions, ownership, and links). Data CD-ROMs typically use this file system type. |

*continued*

| TABLE 10-5 | *(continued)* |
|---|---|
| **Type** | **Description** |
| kafs | AFS client file system. Used in distributed computing environments to share files with Linux, Windows, and Macintosh clients. |
| minix | Minix file system type, used originally with the Minix version of UNIX. It supports filenames of up to only 30 characters. |
| msdos | An MS-DOS file system. You can use this type to mount floppy disks that come from Microsoft operating systems. |
| vfat | Microsoft extended FAT (VFAT) file system. |
| umsdos | An MS-DOS file system with extensions to allow features that are similar to UNIX (including long filenames). |
| proc | Not a real file system, but rather a file system interface to the Linux kernel. You probably won't do anything special to set up a proc file system. However, the /proc mount point should be a proc file system. Many utilities rely on /proc to gain access to Linux kernel information. |
| reiserfs | ReiserFS journaled file system. ReiserFS was once a common default file system type for several Linux distributions. However, ext3 is now by far the most common file system type used with Linux today. |
| swap | Used for swap partitions. Swap areas are used to hold data temporarily when RAM is currently used up. Data is swapped to the swap area and then returned to RAM when it is needed again. |
| squashfs | Compressed, read-only file system type. Squashfs is popular on live CDs, where there is limited space and a read-only medium (such as a CD or DVD). |
| nfs | Network File System (NFS) type of file system. NFS is used to mount file systems on other Linux or UNIX computers. |
| hpfs | File system is used to do read-only mounts of an OS/2 HPFS file system. |
| ncpfs | This relates to Novell NetWare file systems. NetWare file systems can be mounted over a network. |
| ntfs | Windows NT file system. Depending upon the distribution you have, it may be supported as a read-only file system (so that you can mount and copy files from it). |
| affs | File system is used with Amiga computers. |
| ufs | File system popular on Sun Microsystems operating systems (that is, Solaris and SunOS). |

If you want to use a file system type that is not currently shown as available on your system (when you type cat /proc/filesystems), try using modprobe to load the module for that file systems. For example, modprobe ufs adds the UFS file system type to the running kernel. Type man fs to see descriptions of Linux file systems.

### Using the fstab file to define mountable file systems

The hard disk partitions on your local computer and the remote file systems you use every day are probably set up to automatically mount when you boot Linux. The /etc/fstab file contains definitions for each partition, along with options describing how the partition is mounted. Here's an example of an /etc/fstab file:

```
LABEL=/         /               ext3        defaults                1 1
LABEL=/boot     /boot           ext3        defaults                1 2
/dev/devpts     /dev/pts        devpts      gid=5,mode=620          0 0
/dev/shm        /dev/shm        tmpfs       defaults                0 0
/dev/proc       /proc           proc        defaults                0 0
/dev/sys        /sys            sysfs       defaults                0 0
/dev/sda5       swap            swap        defaults                0 0
/dev/cdrom      /media/cdrecorder udf,iso9660 exec,noauto,managed   0 0
/dev/sda1       /mnt/win        vfat        noauto                  0 0
/dev/fd0        /mnt/floppy     auto        noauto,owner            0 0
```

All partitions listed in this file are mounted at boot time, except for those set to noauto in the fourth field. In this example, the root (/) and boot (/boot) hard disk partitions are mounted at boot time, along with the /dev/pts, /dev/shm, /dev/sys, /dev/shm, and /proc file systems (which are not associated with particular storage devices). The CD drive (/dev/cdrom) and floppy disk (/dev/fd0) drives are not mounted at boot time. Definitions are put in the fstab file for floppy and CD drives so that they can be mounted in the future (as described later).

I also added one line for /dev/sda1, which enables me to mount the Windows (vfat) partition on my computer so I don't have to always boot Windows to get at the files on my Windows partition.

## Coming from Windows

**Most Windows systems today use the NTFS file system. Support for this system, however, is not delivered with every Linux system. NTFS support was added to the Fedora repository in Fedora 7 with the ntfs-3g package. Other NTFS support is available from the Linux-NTFS project (**www.linux-ntfs.org/)**.**

**If your computer is configured to dual boot Linux and Windows, you can mount your Windows file system to make it available in Linux. To access your Windows partition, you must first create the mount point (in this example, by typing mkdir /mnt/win). Then you can mount it when you choose by typing (as root) mount / mnt/win. ∎**

Different Linux distributions will set up their fstab file differently. Some don't use labels and many others don't use a separate /boot partition by default. They will just have a swap partition and have all user data under the root partition (/).

Here is what's in each field of the fstab file:

- Field 1—The name of the device representing the file system. This field can include the LABEL option, with which you can indicate a universally unique identifier (UUID) or volume label instead of a device name. The advantage to this approach is that because the partition is identified by volume name, you can move a volume to a different device name and not have to change the fstab file.

- **Field 2**—The mount point in the file system. The file system contains all data from the mount point down the directory tree structure unless another file system is mounted at some point beneath it.

- **Field 3**—The file system type. Valid file system types are described in the "Supported File Systems" section earlier in this chapter.

- **Field 4**—Options to the mount command. In the preceding example, the noauto option prevents the indicated file system from being mounted at boot time, and ro says to mount the file system read-only (which is reasonable for a CD drive). Commas must separate options. See the mount command manual page (under the -o option) for information on other supported options.

## Tip

Normally, only the root user is allowed to mount a file system using the mount command. However, to allow any user to mount a file system (such as a file system on a floppy disk), you could add the user option to Field 4 of /etc/fstab. In openSUSE, read/write permissions are given to specific devices (such as disk or audio devices) by specific groups (such as the disk or audio group) so that users assigned to those groups can mount or otherwise access those devices. In the YaST Control Center, choose the Security and Users ➪ User Management ➪ Expert Options ➪ Defaults for New Users. The Secondary Groups box indicates which of these additional groups each user is assigned to. ■

- **Field 5**—The number in this field indicates whether the indicated file system needs to be dumped (that is, have its data backed up). A 1 means that the file system needs to be dumped, and a 0 means that it doesn't. (I don't think this field is useful anymore because many Linux systems no longer include the dump command. Most often, a 0 is used.)

- **Field 6**—The number in this field indicates whether the indicated file system needs to be checked with fsck: 1 means it needs to be checked first, 2 means to check after all those indicated by 1 have already been checked and 0 means don't check it.

If you want to add an additional local disk or partition, you can create an entry for it in the /etc/fstab file. See Chapter 16 for information on mounting Samba, NFS, and other remount file systems from /etc/fstab.

### Using the mount command to mount file systems

Linux systems automatically run mount -a (mount all file systems) each time you boot. For that reason, you generally use the mount command only for special situations. In particular, the average user or administrator uses mount in two ways:

- To display the disks, partitions, and remote file systems currently mounted
- To temporarily mount a file system

Any user can type mount (with no options) to see what file systems are currently mounted on the local Linux system. The following is an example of the mount command. It shows a single hard disk partition (/dev/sda1) containing the root (/) file system, and proc and devpts file system types mounted on /proc and /dev, respectively. The last entry shows a floppy disk, formatted with a standard Linux file system (ext3) mounted on the /mnt/floppy directory.

```
$ mount
/dev/sda3 on / type ext3 (rw)
/dev/sda2 on /boot type ext3 (rw)
/dev/sda1 on /mnt/win type vfat (rw)
/dev/proc on /proc type proc (rw)
/dev/sys on /sys type sysfs (rw)
/dev/devpts on /dev/pts type devpts (rw,gid=5,mode=620)
/dev/shm on /dev/shm type tmpfs (rw)
none on /proc/sys/fs/binfmt_misc type binfmt_misc (rw)
/dev/cdrom on /media/cdrecorder type iso9660 (ro,nosuid,nodev)
/dev/fd0 on /mnt/floppy type ext3 (rw)
```

Traditionally, the most common devices to mount by hand are your floppy disk and your CD drive. However, depending on the type of desktop you are using, CDs and floppy disks may be mounted for you automatically when you insert them. (In some cases, the autorun program may also run automatically. For example, autorun may start a CD music player or software package installer to handle the data on the medium.)

## Mounting removable media

If you want to mount a file system manually, the /etc/fstab file helps make it simple to mount a floppy disk or a CD. In some cases, you can use the mount command with a single option to indicate what you want to mount, and information is taken from the /etc/fstab file to fill in the other options. Entries might already exist in your /etc/fstab file to let you do these quick mounts in the following two cases:

- **CD**—If you are mounting a CD that is in the standard ISO 9960 format (as most software CD-ROMs are), assuming there's an entry in the /etc/fstab file for that CD drive, you can mount that CD by placing it in your CD-ROM drive and typing one of the following:

```
# mount /media/cd*
# mount /mnt/cdrom
```

By default, a CD is usually mounted on the /mnt/cdrom directory (Linux 2.4 kernels) or a subdirectory of /media (Linux 2.6 kernels). (The file system type, device name, and other options are filled in automatically.) To see the contents, type **cd /mnt/cdrom** or **cd /media/disk**, and then type **ls**. Files from the CD's root directory will be displayed. (With newer desktop features such as Udev and HAL, often CDs and DVDs are mounted automatically, so there is no need to manually run the mount command. Also, if the media has a volume name associated with it, that volume name is used as the directory name in /media on which the CD is mounted.)

- **Floppy disk**—If you want to mount a floppy in the Linux ext3 file system format (ext3), or in some cases a format that can be autodetected, mount that floppy disk by inserting it in your floppy drive and typing one of the following:

```
# mount /media/floppy*
# mount /mnt/floppy
```

The file system type (ext3), device (/dev/fd0), and mount options are filled in from the /etc/fstab file. You should be able to change to the floppy disk directory (cd /mnt/floppy or cd /media/floppy*) and list the contents of the floppy's top directory (ls).

# Note

**In both of these cases, you could give the device name (which is something like** /dev/cdrom **or** /dev/fd0**) instead of the mount point directory to get the same results.** ∎

Of course, it is possible that you may get floppy disks you want to use that are in different formats. Someone may give you a floppy containing files from an older Microsoft operating system (in MS-DOS format). Or you may get a file from another UNIX system. In those cases, you can fill in your own options instead of relying on options from the /etc/fstab file. In some cases, Linux autodetects that the floppy disk contains an MS-DOS (or Windows vfat) file system and mounts it properly without additional arguments. If it doesn't, here's an example of how to mount a floppy containing MS-DOS files:

```
# mkdir /mnt/floppy
# mount -t msdos /dev/fd0 /mnt/floppy
```

This shows the basic format of the mount command you would use to mount a floppy disk. You can change msdos to any other supported file system type (described earlier in this chapter) to mount a floppy of that type. Instead of using floppy drive A: (/dev/fd0), you could use drive B: (/dev/fd1) or any other accessible drive. Instead of mounting on /mnt/floppy, you could create any other directory and mount the floppy there.

Here are some other useful options you could add to the mount command:

- **-t auto**—If you aren't sure exactly what type of file system is contained on the floppy disk (or other medium you are mounting), use this option to indicate the file system type. The mount command will query the disk to try to ascertain what type of file system it contains.
- **-r**—If you don't want to make changes to the mounted file system (or can't because it is a read-only medium), use this option to mount it read-only.

- -w—This mounts the file system with read/write permission.
- -remount—This option remounts the file system while that file system is still in use. This is a great tool for remounting a read-only file system as read-write. For example:

```
# mount -o remount,rw /mnt/mydisk
```

### Mounting a disk image in loopback

Another valuable way to use the mount command has to do with disk images. If you download a CD or floppy disk image from the Internet and you want to see what it contains, you can do so without burning it to CD or floppy. With the image on your hard disk, create a mount point and use the -o loop option to mount it locally. Here's an example:

```
# mkdir /mnt/mycdimage
# mount -o loop whatever-i386-disc1.iso /mnt/mycdimage
```

In this example, the /mnt/mycdimage directory is created, and then the disk image file (whatever-i386-disc1.iso) residing in the current directory is mounted on it. You can now cd to that directory, view the contents of it, and copy or use any of its contents. This is useful for downloaded CD images from which you want to install software without having to burn the image to CD. You could also share that mountpoint over NFS, so you could install the software from another computer. When you are done, just type **umount /mnt/mycdimage** to unmount it.

Other options to mount are available only for specific file system types. See the mount manual page for those and other useful options.

## Using the umount command

When you are done using a temporary file system, or you want to unmount a permanent file system temporarily, use the umount command. This command detaches the file system from its mount point in your Linux file system. To use umount, you can give it either a directory name or a device name. For example:

```
# umount /mnt/floppy
```

This unmounts the device (probably /dev/fd0) from the mount point /mnt/floppy. You can also unmount using the form

```
# umount /dev/fd0
```

In general, it's better to use the directory name (/mnt/floppy) because the umount command will fail if the device is mounted in more than one location. (Device names all begin with /dev.)

If you get the message device is busy, the umount request has failed because either a process has a file open on the device or you have a shell open with a directory on the device as a current directory. Stop the processes or change to a directory outside the device you are trying to unmount for the umount request to succeed.

An alternative for unmounting a busy device is the -1 option. With umount -1 (a lazy unmount), the unmount happens as soon as the device is no longer busy. To unmount a remote NFS file system that's no longer available (for example, the server went down), you can use the umount -f option to forcibly unmount the NFS file system.

## Tip

A really useful tool for discovering what's holding open a device you want to unmount is the lsof command. Type lsof with the name of the partition you want to unmount (such as lsof /mnt/floppy). The output shows you what commands are holding files open on that partition. The fuser command can be used in the same way. ∎

## Using the mkfs command to create a file system

You can create a file system for any supported file system type on a disk or partition that you choose. You do so with the mkfs command. Although this is most useful for creating file systems on hard-disk partitions, you can create file systems on USB flash drives, floppy disks, or rewritable CDs as well.

Before you create a new file system, make sure:

- You have partitioned the disk as you want (using the fdisk command, as described in the "Adding a Hard Disk" section that follows).

- You get the device name correct, or you may end up overwriting your hard disk by mistake. For example, the first partition on the second SCSI or USB disk on your system would be /dev/sdb1 and the third would be /dev/sdc1.

- To unmount the partition if it's mounted before creating the file system.

Here is an example of using mkfs to create a file system on the first (and only) partition on a 2GB USB flash drive located as the third SCSI disk (/dev/sdc1):

```
# mkfs -t ext3 /dev/sdc1
mke2fs 1.40.8 (13-Mar-2008)
Warning: 256-byte inodes not usable on older systems
Filesystem label=
OS type: Linux
Block size=4096 (log=2)
Fragment size=4096 (log=2)
122160 inodes, 487699 blocks
24384 blocks (5.00%) reserved for the super user
First data block=0
Maximum filesystem blocks=503316480
15 block groups
32768 blocks per group, 32768 fragments per group
8144 inodes per group
Superblock backups stored on blocks:
        32768, 98304, 163840, 229376, 294912
```

```
Writing inode tables: done
Creating journal (8192 blocks): done
Writing superblocks and filesystem accounting information: done

This filesystem will be automatically checked every 39 mounts or
180 days, whichever comes first.  Use tune2fs -c or -i to override.
```

You can see the statistics that are output with the formatting done by the mkfs command. The number of inodes and blocks created are output, as are the number of blocks per group and fragments per group. You could now mount this file system (mkdir /mnt/myusb ; mount /mnt/myusb), change to it as your current directory (cd /mnt/myusb), and create files on it as you please.

## Adding a hard disk

Adding a new hard disk to your computer so that it can be used by Linux requires a combination of steps described in previous sections. Here's the general procedure:

1. Install the new hard disk hardware.
2. Identify the partitions on the new disk.
3. Create the file systems on the new disk.
4. Mount the file systems.

The easiest way to add a hard disk to Linux is to have the entire disk devoted to a single Linux partition. You can have multiple partitions, however, and assign them each to different types of file systems and different mount points, if you like. The following process takes you through adding a hard disk containing a single Linux partition. Along the way, it also notes which steps you need to repeat to have multiple file systems with multiple mount points.

## Note

This procedure assumes that Linux is already installed and working on the computer. If this is not the case, follow the instructions for adding a hard disk on your current operating system. Later, when you install Linux, you can identify this disk when you are asked to partition your hard disk(s). ■

1. Follow the manufacturer's instructions for physically installing and connecting the new hard disk in your computer. If, presumably, this is a second hard disk, you may need to change jumpers on the hard disk unit itself to have it operate as a slave hard disk (if it's on the same cable as your first hard disk). You may also need to change the BIOS settings.
2. Boot your computer to Linux.
3. Determine the device name for the hard disk. As root user from a shell, type:

```
# dmesg | less
```

4. From the output, look for an indication that the new disk was found. For example, if it's a second IDE hard disk, you should see hdb: in the output. For a second SCSI drive, you should see sdb: instead. (The hd? and sd? drive letters are incremented as they are found by the kernel.) Be sure you identify the correct disk, or you will erase all the data from disks you probably want to keep!

5. Use the fdisk command to create partitions on the new disk. For example, if you are formatting the second IDE disk (hdb), you can type the following:

```
# fdisk /dev/hdb
```

Now you are in fdisk command mode, where you can use the fdisk single-letter command set to work with your partitions. If the disk had existing partitions on it, you can change or delete those partitions now. Or, you can simply reformat the whole disk to blow everything away. Use p to view all partitions and d to delete a partition.

6. To create a new partition, type the letter **n**.

7. Choose an extended (e) or primary partition (p). To choose a primary partition, type the letter **p**.

8. Type in the partition number. If you are creating the first partition (or for only one partition), type the number **1**.

   Enter the first cylinder number (1 is the default). A range of cylinder numbers is displayed (for example, 1–4865 is the number of cylinders that appears for my 40GB hard drive).

9. To assign the new partition to begin at the first cylinder on the new hard disk, type the number **1**.

10. Enter the last cylinder number. If you are using the entire hard disk, use the last cylinder number shown. Otherwise, choose the ending cylinder number or indicate how many megabytes the partition should have.

11. To create more partitions on the hard disk, repeat Steps 6 through 10 for each partition (possibly changing the file system types as needed).

12. Type **w** to write changes to the hard disk and exit from the fdisk command. At this point, you should be back at the shell.

13. To create a file system on the new disk partition, use the mkfs command. By default, this command creates an ext2 file system, which is usable by Linux. However, in most cases you will want to use a journaling file system (such as ext3 or reiserfs). To create an ext3 file system on the first partition of the second hard disk, type the following:

```
# mkfs -t ext3 /dev/hdb1
```

If you created multiple partitions, repeat this step for each partition (such as /dev/hdb2, /dev/hdb3, and so on).

## Tip

If you don't use `-t ext3`, an ext2 file system is created by default. Use other commands, or options to this command, to create other file system types. For example, use `mkfs.vfat` to create a VFAT file system, `mkfs.msdos` for DOS, or `mkfs.reiserfs` for Reiser file system type. The `tune2fs` command, described later in this section, can be used to change an ext2 file system to an ext3 file system. ∎

14. After the file system is created, you can have the partition permanently mounted by editing the /etc/fstab and adding the new partition. Here is an example of a line you might add to that file:

    ```
    /dev/hdb1      /abc          ext3      defaults       1 1
    ```

    In this example, the partition (/dev/hdb1) is mounted on the /abc directory as an ext3 file system. The `defaults` keyword causes the partition to be mounted at boot time. The numbers 1 1 cause the disk to be checked for errors. Add one line like this example for each partition you created.

15. Create the mount point. For example, to mount the partition on /abc (as shown in the previous step), type the following:

    ```
    # mkdir /abc
    ```

16. Create your other mount points if you created multiple partitions. The next time you boot Linux, the new partition(s) will be automatically mounted on the /abc directory.

After you have created the file systems on your partitions, a nice tool for adjusting those file systems is the `tune2fs` command. You can use it to change volume labels, how often the file system is checked, and error behavior. You can also use it to change an ext2 file system to an ext3 file system so the file system can use journaling. For example:

```
# tune2fs -j /dev/hdb1
tune2fs 1.40.4 (29-May-2008)
Creating journal inode: done
This filesystem will be automatically checked every 38 mounts or
180 days, whichever comes first. Use tune2fs -c or -i to override.
```

By adding the `-j` option to `tune2fs`, you can change either the journal size or attach the file system to an external journal block device (essentially turning a nonjournaling ext2 file system into a journaling ext3 file system). After you use `tune2fs` to change your file system type, you probably need to correct your /etc/fstab file to include the file type change (from ext2 to ext3). To see the current settings for your ext2/ext3 file system, type the following command:

```
# tune2fs -l /dev/hdb1
```

## Checking system space

Running out of disk space on your computer is not a happy situation. You can use tools that come with Linux to keep track of how much disk space has been used on your computer, and you can keep an eye on users who consume a lot of disk space.

### Displaying system space with df

You can display the space available in your file systems using the df command. To see the amount of space available on all the mounted file systems on your Linux computer, type **df** with no options:

```
$ df
Filesystem   1k-blocks      Used   Available   Use%   Mounted on
/dev/sda1     30645460   2958356    26130408    11%   /
/dev/sda2        46668      8340       35919    19%   /boot
/dev/fd0          1412        13        1327     1%   /mnt/floppy
```

This example output shows the space available on the hard disk partition mounted on the / (root) partition (/dev/sda1) and /boot partition (/dev/sda2), and the floppy disk mounted on the /mnt/floppy directory (/dev/fd0). Disk space is shown in 1K blocks. To produce output in a more human-readable form, use the -h option:

```
$ df -h
Filesystem      Size   Used   Avail   Use%   Mounted on
/dev/sda1        29G   2.9G     24G    11%   /
/dev/sda2        46M   8.2M     25M    19%   /boot
/dev/fd0        1.4M    13k    1.2M     1%   /mnt/floppy
```

With the df -h option, output appears in a friendlier megabyte or gigabyte listing. Other options with df enable you to do the following:

- Print only file systems of a particular type (-t type)
- Exclude file systems of a particular type (-x type)
- Include file systems that have no space, such as /proc and /dev/pts (-a)
- List only available and used inodes (-i)
- Display disk space in certain block sizes (--block-size=#)

### Checking disk usage with du

To find out how much space is being consumed by a particular directory (and its subdirectories), use the du command. With no options, du lists all directories below the current directory, along with the space consumed by each directory. At the end, du produces total disk space used within that directory structure.

The du command is a good way to check how much space is being used by a particular user (du /home/user1) or in a particular file system partition (du /var). By default, disk space is displayed in 1K block sizes. To make the output friendlier (in kilobytes, megabytes, and gigabytes), use the -h option as follows:

```
$ du -h /home/jake
114k    /home/jake/httpd/stuff
234k    /home/jake/httpd
137k    /home/jake/uucp/data
701k    /home/jake/uucp
1.0M    /home/jake
```

The output shows the disk space used in each directory under the home directory of the user named jake (/home/jake). Disk space consumed is shown in kilobytes (k) and megabytes (M). The total space consumed by /home/jake is shown on the last line. Add the -s option to see total disk space used for a directory and its subdirectories.

### Finding disk consumption with find

The find command is a great way to find file consumption of your hard disk using a variety of criteria. You can get a good idea of where disk space can be recovered by finding files that are over a certain size or were created by a particular person.

## Note

You must be root user to run this command effectively, unless you are just checking your personal files. If you are not root user, there will be many places in the file system that you will not have permission to check. Regular users can usually check their own home directories but not those of others. ∎

In the following example, the find command searches the root file system (/) for any files owned by the user named jake (-user jake) and prints the filenames. The output of the find command is organized in a long listing in size order (ls -ldS). Finally, that output is sent to the file /tmp/jake. When you view the file /tmp/jake (for example, less /tmp/jake), you will find all the files that are owned by the user jake listed in size order. Here is the command line:

```
# find / -xdev -user jake -print | xargs ls -ldS > /tmp/jake
```

## Tip

The -xdev option prevents file systems other than the selected file system from being searched. This is a good way to cut out a lot of junk that may be output from the /proc file system. It can also keep large remotely mounted file systems from being searched. ∎

Here's another example, except that instead of looking for a user's files, we're looking for files larger than 100 kilobytes (-size +100k):

```
# find / -xdev -size +100k -print | xargs ls -ldS > /tmp/size
```

You can save yourself a lot of disk space by just removing some of the largest files that are no longer needed. In this example, you can see large files are sorted by size in the /tmp/size file.

# Monitoring System Performance

If your Linux system is a multiuser computer, sharing the processing power of that computer can be a major issue. Likewise, any time you can stop a runaway process or reduce the overhead of an unnecessary program running, your Linux server can do a better job serving files, Web pages, or e-mail to the people who rely on it.

Some distributions of Linux include graphical utilities to simplify administration, such as System Monitor in Ubuntu (shown in Figure 10-5).

**FIGURE 10-5**

System Monitor, in Ubuntu, allows you to view processes, resources, and devices.

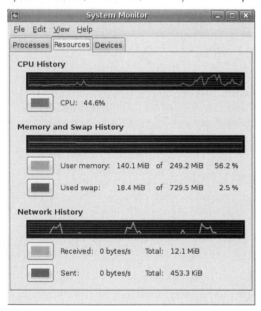

All Linux distributions include utilities that can help you monitor the performance of your Linux system. The kinds of features you want to monitor in Linux include CPU usage, memory usage (RAM and swap space), and overall load on the system. A popular tool for monitoring that information in Linux is the top command.

To start the top utility in a Terminal window, type **top**. The `top` command determines the largest CPU-consuming processes on your computer, displays them in descending order on your screen, and updates the list every five seconds.

By adding the `-S` option to `top`, the display shows you the cumulative CPU time for each process, as well as any child processes that may already have exited. If you want to change how often the screen is updated, you can add the `-d secs` option, where *secs* is replaced by the number of seconds between updates.

By default, processes are sorted by CPU usage. You can sort processes numerically by PID (press N), by age (press A), by resident memory usage (press M), or by time (press T). To return to CPU usage, press P. To terminate a process, type **k** and enter the PID of the process you want to kill (listed in the left column). Be careful to kill only processes you are sure you don't need or want.

# Doing Remote System Administration

Linux offers dozens of tools for administering remote systems. Among the most popular tools for doing remote system administration are those that come from the OpenSSH project. These include

- `ssh`—Command for doing remote login and remote execution
- `scp`—Command for copying files and directories to remote systems
- `sftp`—Command that includes an ftp client type of interface for traversing remote file systems and getting and putting files across the network connection

Although login commands such as `telnet` and `rlogin` and `rsh` remote execution command have been around much longer, the `ssh` command is the preferred tool for remote logins and executions. The reason is that `ssh` provides encrypted communication so you can use it securely over insecure, public networks between hosts that don't know each other.

Here is an example of `ssh` being used to log in to a computer named `test.example.com`. Because no user is specified, `ssh` tries to log in as the current user (which is the root user in this case).

```
# ssh test.example.com
root@test's password:
```

To log in as a different user, you could use the `-l` option. For example, to log in to the computer named test as the user named jake, you could type the following:

```
# ssh jake@test.example.com
jake@test's password:
```

The ssh command can also be used to execute a command on the remote computer. For example, if you wanted to monitor the messages file on a remote computer for a minute, you could type the following command:

```
# ssh root@test.example.com "tail -f /var/log/messages"
root@test's password:
```

After you type the password, the last several lines of the /var/log/messages file on the remote computer are displayed. As messages are received, they continue to be displayed until you decide to exit (press Ctrl+C to exit the tail command).

A wonderful way to use remote ssh for remote execution is with the -X option. Using -X, ssh opens a tunnel to the remote system in which you can launch X Window system clients. So, for example, to log in to a remote system and launch a GUI tool for editing the remote system's network configurations, you could type the following:

```
# ssh -X root@test.example.com
root@test's password:
# system-config-network
```

The remote system's Network Configuration menu tool opens on your local desktop, ready to let you configure the remote system. In this same way, you can launch any remote X client to your local desktop.

The scp command is a simple yet secure way of copying files among Linux systems. It uses the underlying ssh facility, so if ssh is enabled, so is scp. Here is an example of using scp to copy a file from one computer to another:

```
# scp myfile toys.linuxtoys.net:/home/chris
root@toys.linuxtoys.net's password: ******
```

In this example, the file myfile is copied to the computer named toys.linuxtoys.net in the /home/chris directory. If you don't provide a user name, scp assumes you are using the current user name. Instead of myfile, you could indicate a directory name and add the -r option to recursively copy all files from that directory (and its subdirectories) to the remote system.

Unlike some tools that provide remote login, scp and ssh do allow you to log in as root user over the network, by default. (Many people turn off this feature for security reasons.)

The sftp command, which also communicates using secure ssh protocols, is a command for copying files from an FTP server. It is considered a more secure way of getting files from a remote system that has an sshd server running. The sftp command can be disabled on the server by commenting out the sftp line in the sshd_config directory.

If the sshd service doesn't seem to be running on a remote system, you may need to start the sshd daemon. In systems such as Fedora and RHEL, you could type the following:

```
# service sshd start
# chkconfig sshd on
```

# Summary

Although you may be using Linux as a single-user system, many of the tasks you must perform to keep your computer running are defined as administrator tasks. A special user account called the root user is needed to do many of the things necessary to keep Linux working as you would like it to. If you are administering a Linux system used by lots of people, the task of administration becomes even larger. You must be able to add and support users, maintain the file systems, and ensure that system performance serves your users well.

To help the administrator, Linux comes with a variety of command-line utilities and graphical windows for configuring and maintaining your system. Commands such as mkfs and mount let you create and mount file systems, respectively. Tools such as top let you monitor system performance. Commands such as ssh and scp let you administer your system remotely.

# Getting on the Internet

You won't tap into the real power of Linux until you have connected it to a network—in particular, the Internet. Your computer probably has an Ethernet interface built in, so you can just plug a LAN (local area network) cable into it to connect to a LAN (hub or switch), DSL bridge or router, or cable modem. Some computers, particularly laptops, may have wireless Ethernet hardware built in.

Your computer also may have a dial-up modem. Although much more rare these days, there are still cases where someone may have an older computer that has no Ethernet card. Or you may be in a situation in which you need to dial out over regular phone lines to reach your Internet service provider (ISP), and need to use this modem to get on the Internet.

This chapter describes how to connect your Linux system to the Internet. With broadband and wireless networks becoming more prevalent, Ethernet connections are becoming the most common means of connecting to the Internet. For dial-up connections, you'll see how to use kppp (a dialer GUI that is often packaged with KDE desktops).

Sharing Internet connections with multiple desktop systems or even your own mail or Web server is not that difficult to do from a hardware perspective. However, you need to consider some security and configuration issues when you set out to expand how you use your Internet connection. Most Linux systems include software that lets you configure them as firewalls, routers, and a variety of server types to help you get this done.

# Connecting to the Network

Linux supports a wide range of wired and wireless network devices, as well as a dizzying array of network protocols to communicate over that media. As a home or small office Linux user, you can start evaluating how to configure your connection to the Internet from Linux by considering

- The type of Internet account you have with your ISP (dial-up or broadband)
- Whether you are connecting a single computer, a bunch of desktops, and/or one or more server machines to the Internet

## Connecting via dial-up service

A few years ago, dial-up was the most common method for an individual to get on to the Internet. Many computers had dial-up modems built into the motherboard or had serial ports where a modem could easily be connected. Many computers today do not include modems, but serial or USB modems can be purchased for just a few dollars if you need to use dial-up.

After you have a modem (56 Kbps speed is the standard today), the only other equipment you need is a regular telephone line. Essentially, you can use a dial-up modem anywhere you can connect to a phone line. Linux contains the tools you need to configure and complete a dial-up connection. Figure 11-1 shows the setup for the connection.

**FIGURE 11-1**

Connect a modem to a serial or USB port and dial out over regular phone lines.

One difficulty with using modems in Linux is that many computers with built-in modems (especially laptops) come with what are referred to as *Winmodems*. With Winmodems, some of the processing normally done on the modem is actually implemented within the Windows system. Winmodems don't always look like real modems to Linux systems because, without the code that's inside Windows, they don't behave like real modems when they are connected to Linux systems.

Some Winmodems are supported in Linux, and those are sometimes referred to as *Linmodems*. If you find that Linux fails to detect your modem, check out the Linmodems Support Page (`http://linmodems.technion.ac.il`) or the LinModems.org page (`www.linmodems.org`). These pages can help you determine whether you have a Winmodem and, if so, help you find the right Linmodem driver (if one is available).

## Tip

**If you find that you have a Winmodem, you are usually better off getting a real modem instead. An inexpensive external serial modem can save you the trouble of getting and loading a Linmodem driver that may or may not work. Most external modems or internal PCI modems described as being "controller-based" work well in Linux. ■**

# Connecting a single wired Ethernet card

Increasingly, individuals have the option of signing up for broadband Internet service with cable television providers or local telephone companies. These connections typically provide transmission speeds rated at least five times greater than you can get with a dial-up connection.

To make broadband connections from your home or small office, you typically need a cable modem or Digital Subscriber Line (DSL) modem. Cable modems share the bandwidth of the cable television line coming into your location. DSL uses existing house or office phone wires to connect to the Internet, sharing the wires with your phone service.

Because there are many ways that your ISP may be providing your Internet service, you should check with it to get the right hardware you need to connect. In particular, you should know that several incompatible DSL standards exist (ADSL, CDSL, HDSL, SDSL, and so on), so you can't just go out and buy DSL equipment without some guidance.

If you are using an external DSL or cable modem, chances are that a single connection from your Linux machine to that equipment requires only

- An Ethernet port on your computer
- A LAN cable (often provided with the ISP equipment)
- The DSL router/bridge or cable modem (often provided by ISP)

Figure 11-2 illustrates a Linux computer connected to a broadband cable modem.

Broadband equipment often supplies a service called Dynamic Host Configuration Protocol (DHCP). DHCP provides the Internet addresses and other information that a client computer needs to connect to the network. With the cable/DSL modem acting as a DHCP server, you can literally start using the Internet without doing any special configuration in Linux. Just plug in, boot Linux, and start browsing the Web.

**FIGURE 11-2**

Connect an Ethernet card to broadband and start surfing.

## Note

The DSL or cable modem often acts as a router between the ISP and your computer. Usually that device also includes a firewall configured to do network address translation. Alternatively, some broadband equipment operates in a "bridging mode," in which it doesn't do routing, but simply passes data through as if your computer were on the same LAN as that of the ISP. In this setup, the public IP address is assigned to your computer instead of the DSL or cable modem. Because bridging mode exposes the IP addresses behind your firewall to the Internet, in most cases you should not set your DSL or cable modem to bridging mode. ■

# Sharing a network connection with other computers

Instead of connecting your Linux computer directly to the cable modem or DSL equipment, you can join your machines together on a LAN, and then connect the LAN to your ISP equipment so that everyone in the house or office can share the broadband connection. It's fairly simple—you just connect your cable/DSL modem to your LAN instead of directly to your Linux box. In this configuration, however, you should consider adding a firewall/router as a buffer between your LAN and the outside world. That machine would perform such duties as

- **Blocking access**—A well-configured firewall blocks access to all ports except those that you need to access the Internet the way you want, thereby minimizing the risks of intruders getting into your LAN.

- **NAT or IP Masquerading**—For the most part, you want the computers behind your firewall that are simply desktop systems to not be accessible to others from the Internet. By configuring your firewall to do NAT or IP Masquerading, your computers can be assigned private IP addresses. Your firewall then handles forwarding of messages between your LAN and the Internet. This is a good arrangement for several reasons. For one thing, the IP addresses of your private computers are not exposed to the outside world. Also, you can save the cost of paying your ISP for permanent IP addresses.

- **DHCP service**—Many firewall systems can act as a DHCP server. Those private IP addresses you can use with a NAT firewall can be assigned from the DHCP service running on your firewall system. When the client computer on your LAN starts up, besides its IP address, your DHCP service can tell the client the location of its DNS server, gateway to the Internet, or other information.

- **Routing**—In the home and small-office LAN environment illustrated in Figure 11-3, the firewall computer often has two Ethernet interfaces: one connected to the LAN and the other to the DSL or cable modem that leads to the ISP. Because the Ethernet interfaces are viewed as being on separate subnetworks, the firewall/router must be configured to forward packets across the two interfaces. It's not a big deal, but it does require a separate step to tell the firewall system that you want it to forward packets between the two subnetworks.

## Cross-Reference

**Chapter 27 discusses setting up a firewall/router, using a Linux distribution designed specifically for the task. ■**

FIGURE 11-3

A firewall provides a safeguard between your LAN and the Internet.

In this example, the equipment you need includes

- An Ethernet network interface card (NIC) on each computer and at least two NICs on the firewall/router

- A LAN cable for each computer

- A hub or a switch

- A low-end PC (a PC with as little power as a 486 might do) running as a Linux firewall/router
- The DSL or cable modem

An alternative to this wired configuration is to replace the hub or switch with a wireless access point. Then each computer equipped with a wireless LAN card can get on the network without wires.

## Connecting servers

So far you've seen configurations that let one or more computers from your home or small business browse the Web. Allowing someone from the Internet to request services (Web pages, file transfers, and so forth) from your computers requires some extra thought.

After you have TCP/IP (the primary set of protocols used on the Internet) configured to connect to your ISP, requests for data can pass in either direction between your computers and the Internet unless you use a firewall to restrict traffic. So the same connection you use for Internet browsing can be used to offer services to the Internet, with a few caveats:

- **Permanent IP address**—Each time you reboot your computer, your ISP's DHCP server dynamically assigns your DSL/cable modem's IP address. For that reason, your IP address could change at each reboot. If you want your servers to be reachable on a permanent basis, you usually need at least one permanent IP address at which people can reach your servers. You will have to ask your ISP about a permanent IP address, and it might cost you extra money to have one.

## Note
A service called Dynamic DNS can be used in place of paying for a permanent IP address. With Dynamic DNS, you hire a service to constantly check whether your IP address has changed and assign your DNS host name to the new address if it does. You can search the Web for "Dynamic DNS" to find companies that offer that service. ■

- **ISP acceptable use policy**—Check that you are allowed to have incoming connections. Some ISPs, especially for inexpensive, home-use broadband service, will block incoming connections to Web servers or mail servers.
- **DNS hostname**—Although typing an IP address into a browser location box works just fine, most people prefer to use names (such as www.linuxtoys.net) to reach a server. That requires you to purchase a DNS domain name and have an entry set up in a DNS server to resolve the name to the IP address of your server.

Although there is nothing magical about setting up an Internet server, given the few issues just mentioned, creating a public server can be a lot like opening up the doors of your house so that strangers can wander in. You want some policies in place to restrict where the strangers can go and what they can do.

For home or small-office locations that have a single Internet connection (represented by one public IP address), servers can be more exposed to the Internet than desktop systems by keeping them in one area that's referred to as the DMZ (demilitarized zone). In this configuration (illustrated in Figure 11-4), servers are directly behind the outside firewall. Desktop systems (that aren't to be accessible by people from the Internet) are behind a second, more restrictive firewall.

### FIGURE 11-4

Add servers to a DMZ where they can be more publicly accessible than your desktop systems.

Whether you use Linux or dedicated firewall devices to provide firewall service, the outside firewall allows requests in for Web services (port 80), FTP services (ports 20 and 21), simple mail transfer protocol (port 25), and possibly other services. The internal firewall blocks any requests for services from the outside and allows only Internet communications that were initiated from computers behind the inside firewall.

## Cross-Reference

Chapters 13 through 16 explain how to configure different server types, and Chapter 27 describes how to set up Linux as a router/firewall. Chapter 27 includes details on how to configure features such as IP masquerading, NAT, and packet forwarding. ∎

## Connecting other equipment

Although I've focused on basic Ethernet equipment and dial-up modems for configuring network connections, Linux supports many other types of network equipment as well as different protocols for communicating over that equipment. Here are a few examples:

- **ISDN**—Integrated Services Digital Network (ISDN) lines were the preferred method of high-speed data lines to small businesses in the United States before DSL became widespread. It is still popular in Europe, but is being supplanted by more affordable DSL equipment. ISDN4LINUX drivers and tools (`www.isdn4linux.de`) are available in many Linux systems for connecting to ISDN networks.

- **USB cable modem**—Most cable modems offer an Ethernet port that you can connect to directly from your computer's own Ethernet port. However, if you don't have an Ethernet port, often you can connect to the cable modem through one of your USB ports. (You may need to manually load usbnet and cdc_ether drivers to get this to work.)

- **Token ring**—Although rarely used now, token ring network cards are still supported. Support for token ring network cards is included in most Linux systems, although token rings are rarely used now. They were once popular at locations that had many IBM systems.

- **PLIP**—It's possible to connect two computers together from their parallel ports so that they can communicate using TCP/IP protocols. Parallel Line Internet Protocol (PLIP) requires only a special type of null modem cable (for the specs for that cable, refer to `http://tldp.org/HOWTO/NET3-4-HOWTO-9.html`). Most Linux systems have built-in software that enables you to log in, transfer files, and perform other activities over that connection.

If your system has Linux source code installed, you can read about supported hardware devices in the documentation that comes with that source code. On Fedora and some other Linux systems, the location of kernel documentation for various networking hardware is `/usr/src/linux*/Documentation/networking`.

# Using Ethernet Connections to the Internet

Most Linux systems today will either automatically detect or allow you to set up your Internet connection when you install Linux. Here's the general (default) way that a network connection on a desktop system, with Linux installed, is started up:

1. Check whether you have an Ethernet port on your computer (most recent computers have one). If so, connect your Ethernet card to the equipment that gets you to the Internet (cable modem, DSL router/bridge, or network hub/switch). If not, you can purchase an Ethernet card at any retailer that sells computer hardware.

2. Ensure that appropriate drivers are available for the card and bring up the interface (typically, the first wired Ethernet card is assigned to the eth0 interface). Usually, simply starting the computer causes the card to be detected and the appropriate driver loaded.

3. Get an IP address using DHCP if a DHCP server is available through the interface. Most ISPs and businesses expect you to connect to their networks using DHCP, so they will have provided a DHCP server to the equipment where you connect your computer to the network.

As long as your desktop system is connected to a network that has a DHCP server willing to give it an IP address, you can be up and browsing the Web in no time.

If you find that the automatic method (DHCP) of connecting to your network doesn't work, then connecting to the Internet gets a bit trickier. Different Linux distributions offer different tools for manually configuring your Internet connection. The following sections describe a few graphical tools and some command-line and configuration-file approaches to configuring wired and wireless network connections.

## Configuring Ethernet during installation

Many Linux install processes ask you whether you want to configure your network connection for your Ethernet cards. This is typically just for your Ethernet cards and not for dial-up modems or other networking equipment. Information about what you'll need for that process (IP address, gateway, DNS server, and so on) is explained in Chapter 8.

When you boot Linux, you can check whether you have access to the Internet by opening a Web browser (such as Firefox or Konqueror) and typing in a Web address. If the Web site doesn't appear in your browser, you'll need to do some troubleshooting. The "Understanding Your Internet Connection" section later in this chapter provides information on how to track down problems with your Internet connection.

## Configuring Ethernet from the desktop

Most major Linux distributions offer graphical tools for configuring network interfaces. These tools step you through the information you need to enter, and then start up the network interface (if you choose) to begin browsing the Web.

Here is a list of tools for configuring network interfaces in a few different Linux distributions. Some of these are graphical tools, and some are menu-based:

- **Red Hat Enterprise Linux/Fedora**—The Network Configuration window lets you configure network connection using Ethernet, ISDN, modem, Token Ring, Wireless, and xDSL hardware. Start the Network Configuration window from the System menu by selecting Administration ⇨ Network or by typing **system-config-network** and entering the root password when prompted. (On older Red Hat Linux systems, the command was redhat-config-network.) The new NetworkManager feature is also available to let you detect and choose wired and wireless interfaces in Fedora.

- **SUSE Linux**—The YaST Control Center that comes with SUSE contains features for configuring your network. The YaST Control Center lets you configure a DSL, ISDN, Modem, or Network Card interface to the network. Select Network Card to configure your wired Ethernet Interface to the Internet.

- **Gentoo Linux**—From a shell (as root user), type **net-setup eth0** to start a menu-driven interface to configure the network connection from your first Ethernet card (eth0). Use this tool to set each network interface to use DHCP or a static IP address you provide yourself.

- **Ubuntu Linux**—In Ubuntu, you are encouraged to use the Network Connections window for NetworkManager. Right-click the NetworkManager icon in your top panel and select Edit Connections. From the dialog box that appears, select the interface you are interested in and choose Edit, as shown in Figure 11-5.

**FIGURE 11-5**

Configuring an interface in Ubuntu

- **KNOPPIX**—Select the squished penguin icon in the panel on the KNOPPIX desktop, and choose Networking/Internet from the menu. Select the Network card configuration menu entry to configure your network card. Or select from several other network equipment types instead (ADSL, GPRS, ISDN, Modem, or Wavelan).

## Using Network Configuration GUI in Fedora

An example of a graphical tool for configuring your Ethernet interface is the Network Configuration GUI that comes with Fedora and Red Hat Enterprise Linux systems. If you did not configure your LAN connection during installation of Fedora or RHEL, you can do so at any time using the Network Configuration window. The IP address and hostnames can be assigned statically to an Ethernet interface or retrieved dynamically at boot time from a DHCP server.

## Note

A computer can have more than one IP address because it can have multiple network interfaces. Each network interface must have an IP address to connect to a network (even if the address is assigned temporarily). So, if you have two Ethernet cards (eth0 and eth1), each needs its own IP address. Also, the address 127.0.0.1 represents the local host so that users on the local computer can access services without those requests going out on the network. ■

Here's how to define the IP address for your Ethernet interface in Fedora or RHEL:

1. From the System menu, choose System ⇨ Administration ⇨ Network or, as root user from a Terminal window, type **system-config-network**. (If prompted, type the root password.) The Network Configuration window appears.

2. Click the Devices tab. A listing of your existing network interfaces appears.

3. Double-click the eth0 interface (representing your first Ethernet card). A pop-up window titled Ethernet Device appears (see Figure 11-6), enabling you to configure your eth0 interface.

### FIGURE 11-6

Configure and activate Ethernet devices in Fedora.

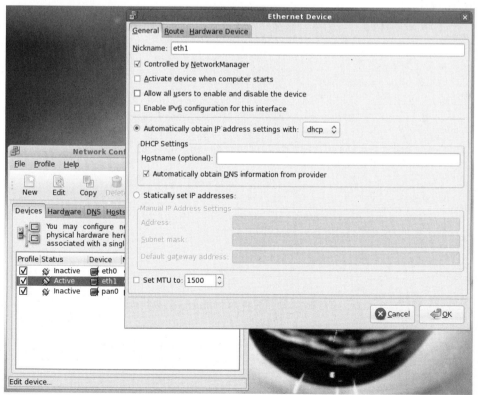

4. Select your preferences:

   - **Controlled by NetworkManager**—In the most recent versions of Fedora, NetworkManager controls your network interfaces. Unselect this box to manage your interfaces directly with the Network Configuration window.

   - **Activate device when computer starts**—Check here to have eth0 start at boot time.

   - **Allow all users to enable and disable the device**—Check to let non-root users enable and disable the network interface.

   - **Enable IPv6 configuration for this interface**—Check here if you are connected to an IPV6 network. (Most networks are still IPV4.)

5. You also must choose whether to get your IP addresses from another computer at boot time or enter the addresses yourself:

   - **Automatically obtain IP address settings with**—Select this box if you have a DHCP or BOOTP server on the network from which you can obtain your computer's IP address, netmask, and gateway. DHCP is recommended if you have more than just a couple of computers on your LAN. Optionally, you can set your own hostname, which can be just a name (such as `jukebox`) or a fully qualified domain name (such as `jukebox.linuxtoys.net`).

   - **Statically set IP addresses**—If no DHCP or other boot server exists on your LAN, add necessary IP address information statically by selecting this option and following these steps:

     a. Type the IP address of the computer into the Address box. This number must be unique on your network. For your private LAN, you can use private IP addresses.

     b. Enter the netmask in the Subnet Mask box. The netmask indicates the part of the IP address that represents the network.

     c. Type the IP address of the computer into the Default Gateway Address box if a computer or router connected to your LAN provides routing functions to the Internet or other network. (Chapter 27 describes how to use NAT or IP Masquerading and how to use Linux as a router.)

6. Click OK in the Ethernet Device window to save the configuration and close the window.

7. Click File ➪ Save to save the information you entered.

8. Click Activate in the Network Configuration window to start your connection to the LAN.

## Identifying other computers (hosts and DNS)

Each time you use a name to identify a computer, such as when browsing the Web or using an e-mail address, the computer name must be translated into an IP address. To resolve names to IP addresses, Linux goes through a search order (usually based on the contents of three files in the /etc directory: `resolv.conf, nsswitch.conf,` and `host.conf`). By default, it checks hostnames you add yourself (which end up in the /etc/hosts file), hosts available via NIS, and host names available via DNS.

Again, for RHEL and Fedora systems, you can use the Network Configuration window to add

- **Hostnames**—You might do this to identify hosts on your LAN that are not configured on a DNS server.

- **DNS search path**—By adding domain names to a search path (such as linuxtoys. net), you can browse to a site by its host name (such as jukebox), and have Linux search the domains you added to the search path to find the host you are looking for (such as jukebox.linuxtoys.net).

- **DNS name servers**—A DNS server can resolve addresses for the domains it serves and contact other DNS servers to get addresses for all other DNS domains.

## Note

If you are configuring a DNS server, you can use that server to centrally store names and IP addresses for your LAN. This saves you the trouble of updating every computer's /etc/hosts file every time you add or change a computer on your LAN. ∎

To add hostnames, IP addresses, search paths, and DNS servers in Fedora, do the following:

1. Start the Network Configuration. As root user from a Terminal window, type **system-config-network** or from the top panel, click System ➪ Administration ➪ Network. The Network Configuration window appears.

2. Click the Hosts tab. A list of IP addresses, hostnames, and aliases appears.

3. Click New. An Add/Edit Hosts Entry pop-up window appears.

4. Type in the IP address number, hostname, and, optionally, the host alias.

5. Click OK.

6. Repeat this process until you have added every computer on your LAN that cannot be reached by DNS.

7. Click the DNS tab.

8. Type the IP address of the computers that serve as your Primary and Secondary DNS servers. (You get these IP addresses from your ISP or, if you created your own DNS server, you can enter that server's IP address.)

9. Type the name of the domain (probably the name of your local domain) to be searched for host names into the DNS Search Path box.

10. Click File ➪ Save to save the changes.

11. Click File ➪ Quit to exit.

Now, when you use programs such as sftp, ssh, or other TCP/IP utilities, you can use any hostname that is identified on your local computer, exists in your search path domain, or can be resolved from the public Internet DNS servers. (Strictly speaking, you don't have to set up your

/etc/hosts file. You could use IP addresses as arguments to TCP/IP commands. But names are easier to work with.)

## Understanding your Internet connection

If your Ethernet interface to the Internet is not working, there are ways to check what's happening that will work on many Linux distributions. Use the following procedure to find out how your network interfaces are working:

1. Open a shell (if you are using a graphical interface, open a Terminal window).

2. Type the following right after you boot your computer to verify whether Linux found your card and installed the Ethernet interface properly:

   ```
   dmesg | grep eth | less
   ```

   The dmesg command lists all the messages that were output by Linux at boot time. The grep eth command causes only those lines that contain the word *eth* to be printed. Here are a couple of examples:

   ```
   eth0: VIA Rhine II at 0xee001000, 00:0d:61:25:d4:17, IRQ 185.
   eth0: MII PHY found at address 1, status 0x786d advertising
   01e1 Link 45e1.
   eth0: link up, 100Mbps, full-duplex, lpa 0x45E1
   eth0: no IPv6 routers present
   ```

   The first message appeared on my desktop computer with a VIA Rhine Ethernet controller. It shows that a card was found at software IRQ 185 with a port address of 0xee001000 and an Ethernet hardware address (MAC address) of 00:0d:61:25:d4:17. The other lines indicate that the link is up on the eth0 interface and running at 100 Mbps in full-duplex. In this case, IPv6 routing is not enabled.

## Note

If the eth0 interface is not found, but you know that you have a supported Ethernet card, type **lspci -vv |** **grep -i eth** to see whether the Ethernet card is detected on the PCI bus. If it doesn't appear, check that your Ethernet card is properly seated in its slot. Here's what appeared for the preceding example:

```
00:12.0 Ethernet controller: VIA Technologies, Inc.
VT6102 [Rhine-II] (rev 74) ∎
```

3. To view which network interfaces are up and running, type the following:

   ```
   $ /sbin/ifconfig -a
   eth0      Link encap:Ethernet  HWaddr 00:0D:61:25:D4:17
             inet addr:10.0.0.5  Bcast:10.0.0.255  Mask:255.255.255.0
             UP BROADCAST RUNNING MULTICAST  MTU:1500  Metric:1
             RX packets:326100 errors:0 dropped:0 overruns:0 frame:0
   ```

```
             TX packets:215931 errors:0 dropped:0 overruns:0 carrier:0
             collisions:5919 txqueuelen: 1000
             RX bytes:168378315 (160.5 Mb)  TX bytes:40853243 (38.9 Mb)

lo           Link encap:Local Loopback
             inet addr:127.0.0.1  Mask:255.0.0.0
             UP LOOPBACK RUNNING  MTU:16436  Metric:1
             RX packets:37435 errors:0 dropped:0 overruns:0 frame:0
             TX packets:37435 errors:0 dropped:0 overruns:0 carrier:0
             collisions:0 txqueuelen: 0
             RX bytes:2353172 (2.2 Mb)  TX bytes:2353172 (2.2 Mb)
```

The output shows a loopback interface (lo) and one Ethernet card (eth0). The Ethernet interface (eth0) is assigned the IP address of 10.0.0.5. Again, notice that the MAC address, which is a unique address related to the Ethernet card hardware, is noted after the HWaddr indicator (00:0D:61:25:D4:17).

**4.** Communicate with another computer on the LAN. The ping command can be used to send a packet to another computer and to ask for a packet in return. You can give ping either a hostname (butch) or an IP address (10.0.0.10). For example, to ping a computer on the network called butch, type the following command:

```
# ping butch
```

If the computer can be reached, the output will look similar to the following:

```
PING butch (10.0.0.10): 56(84) data bytes
64 bytes from butch (10.0.0.10): icmp_seq=1 ttl=255 time=0.351 ms
64 bytes from butch (10.0.0.10): icmp_seq=2 ttl=255 time=0.445 ms
64 bytes from butch (10.0.0.10): icmp_seq=3 ttl=255 time=0.409 ms
64 bytes from butch (10.0.0.10): icmp_seq=4 ttl=255 time=0.457 ms
64 bytes from butch (10.0.0.10): icmp_seq=5 ttl=255 time=0.401 ms
64 bytes from butch (10.0.0.10): icmp_seq=6 ttl=255 time=0.405 ms
64 bytes from butch (10.0.0.10): icmp_seq=7 ttl=255 time=0.443 ms
64 bytes from butch (10.0.0.10): icmp_seq=8 ttl=255 time=0.384 ms
64 bytes from butch (10.0.0.10): icmp_seq=9 ttl=255 time=0.365 ms
64 bytes from butch (10.0.0.10): icmp_seq=10 ttl=255 time=0.367 ms

--- butch statistics ---
10 packets transmitted, 10 packets received, 0% packet loss, time 9011ms
rtt min/avg/max/mdev = 0.351/0.402/0.457/0.042 ms
```

A line of output is printed each time a packet is sent and received in return. It shows how much data was sent and how long it took for each package to be received. Watch this for a while, and then press Ctrl+C to stop ping; you'll see statistics on how many packets were transmitted, received, and lost.

If the output doesn't show that packets have been received, there's no contact with the other computer. Verify that the names and addresses of the computers that you want to reach are in your /etc/hosts file or that your DNS server is accessible. Next, confirm that the names and IP addresses you have for the other computers you are trying to reach are correct (the IP addresses are the most critical).

5. If you are able to reach an IP address on your LAN with ping, but are unable to ping a host computer by name, you may not be communicating with your DNS server. Repeat the ping command with the IP address of your DNS server to see whether it is up and that you are able to communicate with it.

# Using Dial-Up Connections to the Internet

On the rare occasion that broadband is not available, you can still connect to the Internet using modems and telephone lines. The modem connects to a serial port (COM1, COM2, and so on) on your computer and then into a telephone jack. Your computer dials a modem at your Internet service provider or business that has a connection to the Internet.

The most common protocol for making dial-up connections to the Internet (or other TCP/IP network) is Point-to-Point Protocol (PPP). Let's look at how to use PPP to connect to the Internet.

## Cross-Reference
See Chapter 19 for information on configuring a dial-up connection that is specific to Debian. ■

## Getting information

To establish a PPP connection, you need to get some information from the administrator of the network to which you are connecting. This is either your Internet service provider (ISP) when you sign up for Internet service, or the person in your workplace who walks around carrying cables, two or more cellular phones, and a couple of beepers (when a network goes down, these people are in demand!). Here is the kind of information you need to set up your PPP connection:

- **Telephone number**—Gives you access to the modem (or pool of modems) at the ISP. If it is a national ISP, make sure that you get a local or toll-free telephone number (otherwise, you'll rack up long-distance fees on top of your ISP fees).

- **Account name and password**—Used to verify that you have an Internet account with the ISP. This is an account name when you connect to Linux or other UNIX system, but may be referred to as a system name when you connect to an NT server.

- **An IP address**—Most ISPs use Dynamic IP numbers, which means that you are assigned an IP number temporarily when you are connected. Your ISP assigns a permanent IP number if it uses Static IP addresses. If your computer or all the computers on your LAN need to have a more permanent presence on the network, you may be given one Static IP number or a set of Static IP addresses to use.

- **DNS Server IP addresses**—Your computer translates Internet hostnames to IP addresses by querying a domain name system (DNS) server. Your ISP should give you at least one IP address for a preferred (and possibly alternate) DNS server.

- **PAP or CHAP secrets**—You may need a PAP (Password Authentication Protocol) ID or CHAP (Challenge Handshake Authentication Protocol) ID and a secret, instead of a username and password when connecting to a Windows NT system. These features are used with authentication on Microsoft and some other operating systems. Linux and other UNIX servers don't typically use this type of authentication, although they support PAP and CHAP on the client side. Your ISP will tell you whether you are using PAP or CHAP.

Your ISP typically provides services such as news and mail servers for use with your Internet connection. To configure these useful services, you need the following information:

- **Mail server**—If your ISP is providing you with an e-mail account, you must know the address of the mail server, the type of mail service (such as POP3—Post Office Protocol; or IMAP—Internet Message Access Protocol), and the authentication password for the mail server so you can get your e-mail.

- **News server**—If your ISP provides the name of a news server so that you can participate in newsgroups, the server may require you to log on, so you need a password. The ISP provides that password, if required.

After you've gathered this information, you're ready to set up your connection to the Internet. To configure Linux to connect to your ISP, read on.

## Setting up dial-up PPP

PPP is used to create IP connections over serial lines. Most often, the serial connection is established over a modem; however, it also works over serial cables (null modem cables) or digital lines (including ISDN and DSL).

Although one side must dial out and the other side must receive the call to create the PPP connection over a modem, after the connection is established, information can flow in both directions. For the sake of clarity, however, I refer to the computer placing the call as the client and the computer receiving the call as the server.

To simplify the process of configuring PPP (and other network interfaces), most Linux systems include graphical tools to configure dial-up. Two such tools, available with Fedora and RHEL, are

- **Network Configuration Window**—The same utility used to configure Ethernet cards can be used to configure modems. From the GNOME top panel in Fedora and RHEL systems, choose System ➪ Administration ➪ Network. When that window appears, select New. The Select Device Type pop-up that appears enables you to configure and test your modem for a dial-up PPP connection.

- **KDE PPP (KPPP) Window**—From the KDE desktop, select Internet ⇨ KPPP, or from a Terminal window run the kppp command. From the KPPP window, you can set up and launch a PPP dial-up connection.

Before you begin either of these procedures, physically connect your modem to your computer, plug it in, and connect it to your telephone line. If you have an internal modem, you will probably see a telephone port on the back of your computer to which you need to connect. If your modem isn't detected, you can reboot your computer or run wvdialconf create (as described later in this chapter) to have it detected.

## Creating a dial-up connection with the Internet Configuration Wizard

If you are using a Fedora or RHEL system, you could use the Internet Configuration Wizard to set up dial-up networking. Here's how:

1. **Choose System ⇨ Administration ⇨ Network.** When the window appears, select New. (Type the root password, if prompted.) An Add New Device Type window appears (see Figure 11-7).

**FIGURE 11-7**

The Internet Configuration Wizard helps you set up a PPP Internet connection.

2. **Select Modem connection and click Forward.** The wizard searches for a modem and then the Select Modem window appears.

3. **Select the following modem properties:**

   - **Modem Device**—If the modem is connected to your first serial port (COM1) you can select /dev/ttyS0; for the second serial port (COM2) choose /dev/ttyS1. (By convention, the device is often linked to /dev/modem. Type **ls –l /dev/modem** to see whether it is linked to /dev/ttyS0, /dev/ttyS1, or another tty device.)

   - **Baud Rate**—The rate at which the computer talks to the modem (which is typically considerably faster than the modem can talk over the phone lines). The default is 115,200 bits per second, which is probably fine for dial-up connections.

   - **Flow Control**—Check the modem documentation to see whether the modem supports hardware flow control (CRTSCTS). If it doesn't, select software flow control (XON/XOFF). Flow control prevents more data than the modem can handle from being sent to it.

   - **Modem Volume**—This is off by default because the noise can be annoying, but if you select medium while you're setting up the modem, the sound can give you a sense of where things are stopping if you can't get a connection. You can turn it off after everything's working.

   - **Use Touch Tone Dialing**—Leave this check box selected in most cases. If for some reason your phone system doesn't support touch-tone dialing, you can turn it off.

4. **Click Forward. The Select Provider window appears.** Enter the following provider information:

   - **Internet Provider**—If you are using Internet service in any of the countries shown in the Internet Provider window, select the plus sign next to that country name. If your Internet service provider appears in the National list, select it. Information is automatically filled in for that provider. Otherwise, you need to fill in the rest of the dialog window.

   - **Phone Number**—The telephone number of the ISP you want to dial in to. (An optional prefix is available in case you need to dial 9 or some other number to get an outside dial tone.)

   - **Provider Name**—The name of the Internet service provider. If there is only one ISP, I recommend you use it as the ppp0 provider name.

   - **Login Name**—The login name assigned to you by the ISP. The ISP may have called the login name a login ID or something similar.

   - **Password**—The password associated with the login name.

5. **Click Forward. The IP Settings window appears.** With a dial-up connection, you would typically select Automatically Obtain IP Address Settings. However, if the ISP has assigned a static IP address that you can use, select the Statically Set IP Addresses check box, and then enter your IP address, subnet mask, and default gateway address in the

appropriate fields. Click Forward to continue. The Create Dialup Connection window appears, displaying the information you just entered.

6. **If all the information looks correct, click Apply** (otherwise, click the Back button, correct your information, and click Forward again to return to this window). The Network Configuration window appears, ideally with a new PPP connection of modem type appearing in the window.

7. **If the Network Configuration window doesn't appear, select System Settings ➪ Network.**

8. **Select the new dial-up entry (so it is highlighted), and choose File ➪ Save. This saves its new dial-up configuration.**

Now select the PPP device name and click the Activate button. The Internet dialer starts up and dials your ISP. (If you have sound turned on, you should hear your modem dialing out.) If everything is working properly, your login and password are accepted and the PPP connection completed.

Try opening Firefox or another Web browser to see whether you can access a Web site on the Internet. If this doesn't work the first time, don't be discouraged. There are things to check to get your dial-up PPP connection working. Skip ahead to the "Checking Your PPP Connection" section.

## Launching your PPP connection

Your dial-up connection is now configured, but it is not set to connect automatically. One way to start the connection is to set it up to launch manually from the desktop panel. The following steps show you how.

From the GNOME desktop:

1. Right-click the panel, and choose Add to Panel ➪ Modem Lights, and then select Add. A Modem Lights icon appears on the panel.

2. Select the new icon from the panel. You are asked whether you want to start a connection with your modem.

3. Select Connect to start the connection.

From the KDE desktop:

1. Right-click the panel and then choose Add Application to Panel ➪ Internet ➪ KPPP.

2. Select the new icon from the panel (type the root password, if prompted). A KPPP window appears.

3. Select the dial-up interface you added (probably ppp0) and click Connect to connect.

From this point forward, icons appear on your desktop that you can select to immediately connect to your ISP over the dial-up connection you configured.

## Launching your PPP connection on demand

Instead of starting a dial-up PPP connection manually each time you want to contact the Internet, you can set your dial-up connection to start automatically when an application (such as a Web browser or e-mail program) tries to use the connection. On-demand dialing is particularly useful if

- The dial-up connection on your Linux system is acting as the gateway for other computers in your home or office. You don't have to run over to your Linux box to start the connection when another computer needs the dial-up connection.

- Programs that you run during off hours, such as remote backups, require an Internet connection.

- You don't want to be bothered clicking an extra icon when you just want to browse the Web a bit.

The risk of on-demand dialing is that because it gets going automatically, the dial-up connection can start up when you don't want it to. (Some people get worried when their computers start dialing by themselves in the middle of the night.)

For RHEL and Fedora systems, here is an example of settings you can add to your dial-up configuration file (probably /etc/sysconfig/network-scripts/ifcfg-ppp0) to configure on-demand dialing:

```
ONBOOT=yes
DEMAND=yes
IDLETIMEOUT=600
RETRYTIMEOUT=30
```

The ONBOOT=yes starts the pppd daemon (but doesn't immediately begin dialing because DEMAND is set to yes). Also, because of the setting DEMAND=yes, a dial-up connection attempt is made any time traffic tries to use your dial-up connection. With IDLETIMEOUT set to 600, the connection is dropped after 600 seconds (10 minutes) with no traffic on the connection. With RETRYTIMEOUT set to 30, a dropped connection is retried after 30 seconds (unless the connection was dropped by an idle timeout, in which case there is no retry). You can change the timeout values as it suits you.

## Note
Because establishing dial-up connections can take a bit of time, operations may fail while dialing occurs. In particular, DNS requests can time out in 30 seconds, which may not be long enough to establish a dial-up connection. If you have three DNS servers configured for each client, you have a 90-second timeout period. As a result, the modem connection may be running before the request fails. ∎

## Checking your PPP connection

To debug your PPP connection or simply to better understand how it works, you can run through the following steps. They can help you understand where information is being stored and how to use tools to track this information.

## Checking that your modem was detected

It is possible that your modem is not supported under Linux. If that is the case, your PPP connection might be failing because the modem was not detected at all. To scan your serial ports to see where your modem might be, type the following (as root user):

```
$ wvdialconf /etc/wvdial.conf.new
```

The wvdialconf command builds a configuration file (in this example, the /etc/wvdial. conf.new file) that is used by the dialer command (wvdial). (You need this file only if you use wvdial to do your dial-up.) Its first action, however, is to scan the serial ports on your computer and report where it finds modems. If it tells you that no modem was detected, it's likely that either your modem isn't connected properly or no driver is available to support the modem.

If the modem wasn't detected, you should determine whether it is a modem supported in Linux. You can do this by finding out what type of chip set is used in the modem. This is even more important than finding out the manufacturer of the modem because the same manufacturer can use chips from different companies. (This applies primarily to internal modems because most external serial modems and many USB modems are supported in Linux.)

After you have determined the chip set being used, check the Linmodems.org Web site (www. linmodems.org). Search for the chip set on your modem from this site. In many cases, the site can tell you whether a driver is available for your modem.

A nice tool for determining what type of Winmodem you have and how to get it working is scan-Modem. If you have access to the Internet from another machine, you can download scanModem from this address:

```
http://linmodems.technion.ac.il/packages/scanModem.gz
```

Because you probably don't have a working Internet connection yet, find a way to copy scan-Modem.gz to your Linux system (maybe copy it to a flash drive or burn it to a CD). As root user from a Terminal window, type these commands, with that file in the current directory:

```
# gunzip scanModem.gz
# chmod 755 scanModem
# ./scanModem
```

The result is a Modem directory containing text files describing your modem and what you can do to configure it.

## Note

If you are a new Linux user with a Winmodem and you are still baffled after referring to the `linmodems.org` site, you might consider getting a serial or USB modem. To get your Winmodem working, you might need to download, compile, and load a modem driver. Especially with some older Winmodems, drivers have not all been updated to work with the latest kernels. Picking up a cheap hardware modem (under $20), that you can connect to a serial port, from a used computer store can save hours of frustration with a Winmodem that may ultimately not work anyway. ■

# Connecting to the Internet with Wireless

Setting up a wireless network connection used to be one of the more challenging features to get working in Linux. In recent releases of Ubuntu, Fedora, and other major Linux distributions, that situation has changed for several major reasons:

- **Wireless drivers**—Because most wireless card manufacturers did not make source code available with their drivers, most Linux distributions resisted including those drivers in their distributions. Recently, most distributions have relented and included those drivers.

- **NetworkManager**—To use NetworkManager as the default tool for managing network interfaces in Fedora, Ubuntu, and others, simply click the NetworkManager icon on the top panel. This shows you a list of all wireless networks detected in your area.

As a result of the issues just described, in most cases Linux laptop or desktop users can simply log in to their systems and select the NetworkManager icon in the panel. From the menu that appears, the person can choose the desired wireless network interface from a list that appears and type any user and password information required to connect to that interface.

However, if your Linux system doesn't include the wireless drivers you need and isn't configured to automatically detect your network interfaces, here are a few open source projects you can look into to help get wireless working:

- **ndiswrappers** (`http://ndiswrapper.sourceforge.net`)—This project lets you use wireless drivers in Linux that were created to run in Windows.

- **madwifi** (`http://madwifi.org`)—Supports drivers for wireless chip sets from Atheros (`www.atheros.com`).

- **Intel PRO/Wireless for Linux** (`http://ipw2100.sourceforge.net`)— Several wireless driver projects support drivers for Intel PRO/Wireless hardware.

## Note

If you are using Red Hat Enterprise Linux and your wireless card isn't working, check the Drivers disc that comes with your RHEL boxed set. Many wireless drivers are included on that disc. ■

After the proper driver for your wireless card is installed and activated, different tools are available for configuring your wireless cards in different Linux releases. Here are examples:

- **Wireless in Fedora**—In Fedora, use the NetworkManager to configure your wireless network cards. It should be on by default. If it's not, however, as root you can type the following: `service NetworkManager on`. Then configure your wireless connection from a network icon that appears in the panel.

- **Wireless in KNOPPIX**—In KNOPPIX, try KWiFiManager. From the KDE menu, select KNOPPIX ➪ Network/Internet ➪ KWiFiManager.

For further information on configuring wireless devices in Linux, refer to the Wireless LAN resources for Linux page:

```
http://hpl.hp.com/personal/Jean_Tourrilhes/Linux/Wireless.html
```

If you find that you are unable to get the driver for your particular wireless card working at all, determine the type of card you have, using one of the following commands:

```
# dmesg |grep -i wireless
# lspci -vv |grep -i wireless
```

Then use some search tool, such as Google, to search for the name and model of your wireless card, along with the word *Linux* or the particular distribution of Linux you are using. Chances are, if your wireless device is at all popular, someone else has tried to get it working in Linux and has probably shared his or her experiences somewhere online.

# Summary

Many different tools exist for configuring network connections in the various Linux distributions. Fedora and other Red Hat Enterprise Linux systems use a graphical Network Configuration. SUSE Linux uses its YaST administrative interface to configure network equipment. For dial-up networks, the KDE desktop includes the kppp GUI tool for configuring modems. If your network connection doesn't start up automatically (as it does in many cases), this chapter explains how to use some of these network configuration tools to configure it manually.

By adding your computer to a public network, such as the Internet, you open it to possible intruders. The next chapter describes ways in which you can secure your computer from unwanted access.

# Securing Linux

S ince the dawn of interconnected networks, some users have been trying to break into other users' systems. As the Internet has grown and broadband Internet access has spread, the problem has only become more severe. A home computer running an insecure configuration can be used as a powerful mail relay, provide storage for traffic in pirated data, allow the user's personal information to become compromised, or any number of other such horrors.

Once upon a time network attacks required some effort and skill on the part of the attacker. Today, automated tools can get even the most novice user up and running trying to compromise network-attached systems in an alarmingly short time. Additionally, worms have the capability to turn large numbers of insecure systems into an army of "zombies" usable for massive, coordinated, distributed denial-of-service (DDoS) attacks.

Why should you care about security? According to the Internet Storm Center (`http://isc.sans.org`), a computer connected to the Internet has an average of 16 minutes before it falls under some form of attack. Securing any computer system is not hugely difficult; it simply requires some common sense and careful application of good security practices.

In many cases, good practices for setting and protecting passwords, monitoring log files, and creating good firewalls will keep out many would-be intruders. Sometimes, more proactive approaches are needed to respond to break-ins.

Many tasks associated with securing your Linux system are common to desktop and server systems. However, because servers allow some level of access by outside clients, there are special considerations for protecting servers.

This chapter describes general tasks for securing Linux systems and techniques for securing desktop and server systems. It then describes some tools you can try out from a bootable Linux system to troubleshoot your computer and network.

# Linux Security Checklist

Although most Linux systems offer all the tools you need to secure your computer, if you are reckless, someone can (and probably will) harm your system, take it over, or try to steal your data. Keep in mind that no security measures are 100 percent reliable and that, given physical access to a computer or an unlimited amount of time to try to break in, a skilled and determined cracker can break into any computer.

That said, however, you can take many safeguards to improve your chances of keeping your Linux system safe. The following checklist covers a range of security features to protect your Linux desktop or server.

- **Control physical access**—Keeping your computer behind locked doors is a good idea, especially if it contains critical data. You can limit what a person can do to your computer with physical access by enabling passwords in the BIOS (to prevent the computer from booting at all) and in the GRUB or LILO boot loader. You can also limit which devices can be booted in the BIOS.

- **Add users and passwords**—Creating separate user accounts (each with a good password) is your first line of defense in keeping your data secure. Users are protected from each other, as well as from an outsider who takes over one user account. Setting up group accounts can extend the concept of ownership to multiple users. See Chapter 10 for more on setting up user accounts and also see "Using password protection" later in this chapter.

- **Set read, write, and execute permissions**—Every item in a Linux system (including files, directories, applications, and devices) can be restricted by read, write, and execute permissions for that item's owner and group, as well as by all others. In this way, for example, you can let other users run a command or open a file, without allowing them to change it. See Chapter 9 for information on setting file and directory permissions.

- **Protect the root user**—In standard Linux systems, the root user (as well as other administrative user accounts such as apache) has special abilities to use and change your Linux system. Protect the root account's password and don't use the root account when you don't need to. An open shell or desktop owned by the root user can be a target for attack. Running graphical administration windows as a regular user (then entering the root password as prompted) and running administrative commands using sudo can reduce exposure to attacks on your root account. See Chapter 10 for information on handling the root user account.

## Note
**Some distributions, such as Ubuntu, simplify the protection of the root account by automatically disabling it.** ■

- **Use trusted software**—Although no guarantees come with open source software, you have a better chance of avoiding compromised software by using an established Linux distribution (such as Fedora, Debian, or SUSE). Software repositories where you get add-on packages or updates should likewise be scrutinized. Using valid GPG public keys can help ensure that the software you install comes from a valid vendor. And, of course, always be sure of the source of data files you receive before opening them in a Linux application. If you download full ISO images of a distribution, check their integrity using MD5 or SHA1 checksums provided from their creator.

- **Get software updates**—As vulnerabilities and bugs are discovered in software packages, every major Linux distribution (including Debian, SUSE, Gentoo, and Red Hat distributions) offers tools for getting and installing those updates. Be sure to get those updates, especially if you are using Linux as a server. These tools include apt, yum, and emerge.

- **Use secure applications**—Even with software that is valid and working, some applications offer better protection from attack or invasion than others. For example, if you want to log in to a computer over the Internet, the secure shell service (ssh) is considered more secure than rlogin or telnet services (which pass clear-text passwords). Also, some services that are thought to be insecure if you expose them on the Internet (such as Samba and NFS) can be used more securely over the Internet through VPN tunnels (such as IPSec or CIPE).

- **Use restrictive firewalls**—A primary job of a firewall is to accept requests for services from a network that you want to allow and turn away requests that you don't (based primarily on port numbers requested). A desktop system should refuse requests that come in on most ports. A server system should allow requests for a controlled set of ports. See Chapter 27 for information on how to set up a firewall using iptables.

- **Enable only services you need**—To offer services in Linux (such as Web, file, or mail services), a daemon process will listen on a particular port number. Don't enable services you don't need.

## Note

A program that runs quietly in the background handling service requests (such as sendmail) is called a *daemon*. Usually, daemons are started automatically when your system boots up and they keep running until your system is shut down. Daemons may also be started on an as-needed basis by xinetd, a special daemon that listens on a large number of port numbers and then launches the requested process. ∎

- **Limit access to services**—You can restrict access to a service you want to have on by allowing access only from a particular host computer, domain, or network interface. For example, a computer with interfaces to both the Internet and a local LAN might limit access to a service such as NFS to computers on the LAN, but not offer those same services to the Internet. Services may limit access in their own configuration files or using TCP/IP wrappers (described later in this chapter).

- **Check your system**—Linux has tons of tools available for checking the security of your system. After you install Linux, you can check access to its ports using nmap or watch network traffic using Wireshark. You can also add popular security tools such as Nessus, to get a more complete view of your system security. Security tools included on the CD and DVD with this book are described in this chapter.

- **Monitor your system**—You can log almost every type of activity on your Linux system. System log files, using the syslogd and klogd facilities, can be configured to track as much or as little of your system activity as you choose. Utilities such as logwatch provide easy ways to have the potential problem messages forwarded to your administrative e-mail account. Linux logging features are described later in this chapter.

## Note

Remember that monitoring your system does not mean that you simply turn on logging—you must also carefully monitor those logs and react to what they tell you. ∎

- **Use SELinux**—Security Enhanced Linux (SELinux) is an extraordinarily rich (and complex) facility that you can use to manage access to nearly every aspect of a Linux system. Red Hat systems offer a useful, limited set of SELinux policies that are turned on by default in Fedora and Red Hat Enterprise Linux systems. Other Linux distributions, such as openSUSE, are working on and including SELinux implementations as well. Figure 12-1 shows an example of the SELinux Administration tool included with Fedora (select System ➪ Administration ➪ SELinux Management), and Figure 12-2 shows the SELinux Troubleshooter (select Applications ➪ System Tools ➪ SELinux Troubleshooter).

### FIGURE 12-1

SELinux utilities are included with Fedora.

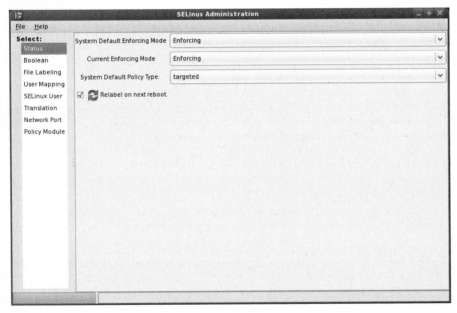

**FIGURE 12-2**

The SELinux Troubleshooter can identify areas of concern.

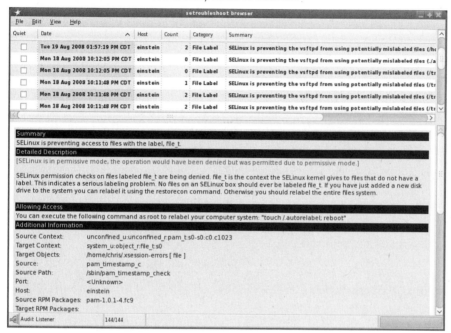

## Finding distribution-specific security resources

Most major Linux distributions have resources devoted to helping you secure Linux and keep up with security information that is specific to that version of Linux. Here are a few online resources that focus on security for several Linux distributions:

- **Red Hat Enterprise Linux and Fedora security**—Check the Red Hat Security site (www.redhat.com/security) for RHEL security issues (that typically relate to Fedora systems as well). From here you can look for and read about available updates. You can also get information on security training and consulting from Red Hat, Inc. For Fedora security issues, see the Fedora Wiki (http://fedoraproject.org/wiki/Security/Features).

  Refer to the Red Hat Enterprise Linux 4 Security Guide for an in-depth look at Linux security for Red Hat systems. You can access this guide online from the following address:

  www.redhat.com/docs/manuals/enterprise/RHEL-4-Manual/en-US/Security_Guide

- **Debian security**—The Debian Security Information page (`www.debian.org/security`) provides a central point for finding security advisories, answers to common Debian security questions, and links to security documents. You can find the Securing Debian online manual here:

  `www.debian.org/doc/manuals/securing-debian-howto`

- **Ubuntu security**—Find security guides and tools for Ubuntu on the Ubuntu security page (`https://help.ubuntu.com/community/Security`).

- **Gentoo security**—Included on the Gentoo Linux Security page (`www.gentoo.org/security`) are tools, announcements, and links to security policy and project documents associated with securing Gentoo systems. Find the Gentoo security handbook here:

  `www.gentoo.org/doc/en/security`

- **Slackware security**—To keep up with Slackware security issues, refer to the Slackware Security Advisories (`www.slackware.com/security`). You can also join the security mailing list (`www.slackware.com/lists`) for Slackware.

- **SUSE security**—Online security support for SUSE is provided by SUSE's parent company, Novell. Find links to a variety of SUSE security topics from this site:

  `www.novell.com/linux/security/securitysupport.html`

  For openSUSE visit this site:

  `www.novell.com/products/opensuse/security.html`

## Finding general security resources

Many computer security Web resources now offer information that is particularly useful to Linux system administrators. Here are a few sites you can check out:

- **CERT** (`www.cert.org`)—The CERT Coordination center follows computer security issues. Check its home page for the latest vulnerability issues. The site has many tips, including recommendations on what you should do if your computer has been compromised (`www.cert.org/tech_tips`).

- **SecurityFocus** (`www.securityfocus.com`)—In addition to offering news and information on general computer security topics, SecurityFocus also offers several Linux-specific resources. In particular, you can subscribe to receive a weekly Linux Security News newsletter.

- **LinuxSecurity** (`www.linuxsecurity.com`)—This site contains many news articles and features related to Linux security. It also tracks security advisories for more than a dozen Linux distributions.

# Using Linux Securely

Getting and keeping your Linux systems secure means not only making good decisions about how you initially set up your system but also how you use it going forward. Whether you are using your Linux system as a desktop or server system, good security practices related to passwords, using secure applications, and monitoring log files are always important.

Setting up a secure firewall (as described in Chapter 27) is critical to having a secure Linux system. There are also other security measures you should apply to Linux. This section describes some good practices for using passwords, keeping track of system activity by watching log files, and communicating with other systems using secure shell (ssh) applications.

## Using password protection

Passwords are the most fundamental security tool of any modern operating system and consequently, the most commonly attacked security feature. It is natural to want to choose a password that is easy to remember, but very often this means choosing a password that is also easy to guess. Crackers know that on any system with more than a few users, at least one person is likely to have an easily guessed password.

By using the "brute force" method of attempting to log in to every account on the system and trying the most common passwords on each of these accounts, a persistent cracker has a good shot of finding a way in. Remember that a cracker will automate this attack, so thousands of login attempts are not out of the question. Obviously, choosing good passwords is the first and most important step to having a secure system.

Here are some things to avoid when choosing a password:

- Do not use any variation of your login name or your full name. Even if you use varied case, append or prepend numbers or punctuation, or type it backwards, this will still be an easily guessed password.
- Do not use a dictionary word, even if you add numbers or punctuation to it.
- Do not use proper names of any kind.
- Do not use any contiguous line of letters or numbers on the keyboard (such as "qwerty" or "asdfg").

## Choosing good passwords

A good way to choose a strong password is to take the first letter from each word of an easily remembered sentence. The password can be made even better by adding numbers, punctuation, and varied case. The sentence you choose should have meaning only to you, and should not be publicly available (choosing a sentence on your personal Web page is a bad idea). Table 12-1 lists examples of strong passwords and the tricks used to remember them.

**TABLE 12-1**

### Ideas for Good Passwords

| Password | How to Remember It |
|----------|--------------------|
| Mrci7yo! | My rusty car is 7 years old! |
| 2emBp1ib | 2 elephants make BAD pets, 1 is better |
| ItMc?Gib | Is that MY coat? Give it back |

The passwords look like gibberish but are actually rather easy to remember. As you can see, I can place emphasis on words that stand for capital letters in the password. You set your password using the passwd command. Type the passwd command within a command shell, and it will enable you to change your password. First, it prompts you to enter your old password. To protect against someone "shoulder surfing" and learning your password, the password will not be displayed as you type.

## Note

**Several distributions include random password generators that can be used to conjure up secure passwords. Figure 12-3, for example, shows a password generator in the Users and Groups tool available in Ubuntu.** ■

**FIGURE 12-3**

Generating random passwords

Assuming you type your old password correctly, the passwd command will prompt you for the new password. When you type in your new password, the passwd command checks the password against cracklib to determine whether it is a *good* or *bad* password. Non-root users will be required to try a different password if the one they have chosen is not a good password.

The root user is the only user who is permitted to assign *bad* passwords. After the password has been accepted by cracklib, the passwd command asks you to enter the new password a second time to make sure there are no typos (which are hard to detect when you can't see what you are typing). When running as root, changing a user's password is possible by supplying that user's login name as a parameter to the passwd command. For example

```
# passwd joe
Changing password for user joe.
New UNIX password: ********
Retype new UNIX password: ********
passwd: all authentication tokens updated successfully.
```

Here the passwd command prompts you twice to enter a new password for joe. It does not prompt you for his old password in this case. This allows root to reset a user's password when that user has forgotten it (an event that happens all too often).

## Note

**Many Linux systems incorporate the pluggable authentication modules (PAM) facility for controlling authentication. By modifying the /etc/pam.d/system-auth file you can change how utilities on your system authenticate user logins. For example, you can change how many failed password attempts would be permitted and what to do if that number is reached. (Be careful modifying PAM files, however, because a misconfigured PAM facility can lock out all user login attempts.) ∎**

## Using a shadow password file

In early versions of UNIX, all user account and password information was stored in a file that all users could read (although only root could write to it). This was generally not a problem because the password information was encrypted. The password was encrypted using a *trapdoor algorithm*, meaning the unencoded password could be encoded into a scrambled string of characters, but the string could not be translated back to the non-encoded password. In other words, the trapdoor implies that encryption only goes in one direction, so the encrypted password can't be used to go back to the unencoded password.

How does the system check your password in this case? When you log in, the system encodes the password you entered, compares the resulting scrambled string with the scrambled string that is stored in the password file, and grants you access only if the two match. Have you ever asked a system administrator what the password on your account is only to hear, "I don't know" in response? If so, this is why: The administrator really doesn't have the password, only the encrypted version. The unencoded password exists only at the moment you type it.

### Breaking encrypted passwords

There is a problem with people being able to see encrypted passwords, however. Although reversing the encryption of a trapdoor algorithm may be difficult (or even impossible), encoding a large number of password guesses and comparing them to the encoded passwords in the password file is very easy. This is, in order of magnitude, more efficient than trying actual login attempts for each user name and password. If a cracker can get a copy of your password file, the cracker has a much better chance of breaking into your system.

Fortunately, Linux and all modern UNIX systems support a shadow password file by default. The shadow file is a special version of the passwd file that only root can read. It contains the encrypted password information, so passwords can be left out of the passwd file, which any user on the system can read. Linux supports the older, single password file method as well as the newer shadow password file. You should always use the shadow password file (it is used by default).

### Checking for the shadow password file

The password file is named passwd and is found in the /etc directory. The shadow password file is named shadow and is also located in /etc. If your /etc/shadow file is missing, it is likely that your Linux system is storing the password information in the /etc/passwd file instead. Verify this by displaying the file with the less command.

```
# less /etc/passwd
```

Something similar to the following should be displayed:

```
root:DkkS6Uke799fQ:0:0:root:/root:/bin/bash
bin:x:1:1:bin:/bin:
daemon:x:2:2:daemon:/sbin:/bin/sh
    .
    .
    .
mary:KpRUp2ozmY5TA:500:100:Mary Smith:/home/mary:/bin/bash
joe:OsXrzvKnQaksI:501:100:Joe Johnson:/home/joe:/bin/bash
jane:ptNoiueYEjwX.:502:100:Jane Anderson:/home/jane:/bin/bash
bob:Ju2vY7AOX6Kzw:503:100:Bob Reynolds:/home/bob:/bin/bash
```

Each line in this listing corresponds to a single user account on the Linux system. Each line is made up of seven fields separated by colon (:) characters. From left to right the fields are the login name, the encrypted password, the user ID, the group ID, the description, the home directory, and the default shell. Looking at the first line, you see that it is for the root account and has an encrypted password of DkkS6Uke799fQ. You can also see that root has a user ID of zero, a group ID of zero, and a home directory of /root, and root's default shell is /bin/bash.

All of these values are quite normal for a root account, but seeing that encrypted password should set off alarm bells in your head. It confirms that your system is not using the shadow password file. At this point, you should immediately convert your password file so that it uses /etc/shadow to store the password information. You do this by using the pwconv command. Simply log in as root (or use the su command to become root) and enter the pwconv command at a prompt. It will print no messages, but when your shell prompt returns, you should have a `/etc/shadow` file and your `/etc/passwd` file should now look like this:

```
root:x:0:0:root:/root:/bin/bash
bin:x:1:1:bin:/bin:
daemon:x:2:2:daemon:/sbin:
        .
        .
        .
mary:x:500:100:Mary Smith:/home/mary:/bin/bash
joe:x:501:100:Joe Johnson:/home/joe:/bin/bash
jane:x:502:100:Jane Anderson:/home/jane:/bin/bash
bob:x:503:100:Bob Reynolds:/home/bob:/bin/bash
```

Encrypted password data is replaced with an `x`. Password data has been moved to `/etc/shadow`.

You can also use an Authentication Configuration utility (available with Fedora and RHEL systems) to manage shadow passwords and other system authentication information. By default, this tool is enabled to work with MD5 passwords. However, you can also configure it to obtain user and password information from LDAP, NIS, or Kerberos 5 facilities. Select System ⇨ Administration ⇨ Authentication, and step through the screens to use it.

To work with passwords for groups, you can use the `grpconv` command to convert passwords in `/etc/groups` to shadowed group passwords in `/etc/gshadow`. If you change `passwd` or group passwords and something breaks (you are unable to log in to the accounts), you can use the `pwunconv` and `grpunconv` commands, respectively, to reverse password conversion.

So, now you are using the shadow password file and picking good passwords. You have made a great start toward securing your system. You may also have noticed by now that security is not just a one-time job. It is an ongoing process, as much about policies as programs. Keep reading to learn more.

# Using Log Files

If you make use of good firewalling practices as described in Chapter 27, you will be well prepared to mitigate and prevent most cracker attacks. If your firewall should fail to stop an intrusion, you must be able to recognize the attack when it is occurring. Understanding the various (and numerous) log files in which Linux records important events is critical to this goal. The log files for your Linux system are in the `/var/log` directory.

Most Linux systems make use of log-viewing tools, either provided with the desktop environment (such as GNOME) or as a command you can execute from a Terminal window. GNOME-based desktops often include a System Log Viewer window (`gnome-system-log` command) that you can use to view and search critical system log files from the GUI. To open the System Log Viewer window from the top panel in a Fedora GNOME desktop, select Applications ⇨ System Tools ⇨ Log File Viewer. Figure 12-4 shows an example of the System Log Viewer window.

**FIGURE 12-4**

Display system log files in the System Log Viewer window.

To view a particular log file, click the log name in the left column. Then scroll through the contents of that log.

Table 12-2 contains a listing of log files displayed in the System Log Viewer window, along with other files in the /var/log directory that may interest you. (Select File ⇨ Open to open a log file that doesn't appear in the left column.) Many of these files are included with most Linux systems and are viewable only by root. Also, some Linux systems may use different file or directory names (for example, /etc/httpd is /etc/apache on some Linux systems).

Because these logs are stored in plain-text files, you can view them using any text editor (such as vi or gedit) or paging command (such as the less command).

**TABLE 12-2**

## Log Files in the /var/log Directory

| System Log Name | Filename | Description |
|---|---|---|
| Boot Log | boot.log | Contains messages indicating which systems services have started and shut down successfully and which (if any) have failed to start or stop. The most recent bootup messages are listed near the end of the file. |
| Cron Log | cron | Contains status messages from the crond, a daemon that periodically runs scheduled jobs, such as backups and log file rotation. |

| System Log Name | Filename | Description |
| --- | --- | --- |
| Kernel Startup Log | dmesg | A recording of messages printed by the kernel when the system boots. |
| FTP Log | xferlog | Contains information about files transferred using the FTP service. |
| Apache Access Log | httpd/ access_log | Logs requests for information from your Apache Web server. |
| Apache Error Log | httpd/ error_log | Logs errors encountered from clients trying to access data on your Apache Web server. |
| Mail Log | maillog | Contains information about addresses to which and from which e-mail was sent. Useful for detecting spamming. |
| MySQL Server Log | mysqld.log | Includes information related to activities of the MySQL database server (mysqld). |
| News Log | spooler | Directory containing logs of messages from the Usenet News server if you are running one. |
| RPM Packages | rpmpkgs | Contains a listing of RPM packages that are installed on your system. (For systems that are not based on RPM packaging, look for a debian-installer or packages directory to find lists of installed packages.) |
| Security Log | secure | Records the date, time, and duration of login attempts and sessions. |
| System Log | messages | A general-purpose log file to which many programs record messages. |
| X.Org X11 Log | Xorg.0.log | Includes messages output by the X.Org X server. |
| * | gdm/:0.log | Holds messages related to the login screen (GNOME display manager). |
| * | samba/log. smbd | Shows messages from the Samba SMB file service daemon. |
| * | squid/ access.log | Contains messages related to the squid proxy/caching server. |
| * | vsftpd.log | Contains messages relating to transfers made using the vsFTPd daemon (FTP server). |
| * | sendmail | Shows error messages recorded by the sendmail daemon. |
| * | uucp | Shows status messages from the UNIX to UNIX Copy Protocol daemon. |

* Indicates a log file that is not contained in the System Log Viewer window. Access these files directly from /var/log.

**Note**

The GNOME desktop also includes Seahorse—a front-end to GNU Privacy Guard. Seahorse allows you to digitally sign or authenticate documents and works with OpenPGP and SSH keys. You can find more information at www.gnome.org/projects/seahorse/index.html. ∎

## The role of syslogd

Most of the files in the /var/log directory are maintained by the syslogd service. The syslogd daemon is the system logging daemon. It accepts log messages from a variety of other programs and writes them to the appropriate log files. This is better than having every program write directly to its own log file because it enables you to centrally manage how log files are handled. Configuring syslogd to record varying levels of detail in the log files is possible. It can be told to ignore all but the most critical messages, or it can record every detail.

**Note**

Fedora now uses a multithreaded version of syslogd called rsyslogd. Although syslogd and rsyslogd are mostly compatible, the names of the daemon process (rsyslogd), configuration file (/etc/rsyslogd), and sysconfig file (/etc/sysconfig/rsyslog) are different. See www.rsyslog.com for details. ∎

The syslogd daemon can even accept messages from other computers on your network. This feature is particularly handy because it enables you to centralize the management and reviewing of the log files from many systems on your network. There is also a major security benefit to this practice.

If a system on your network is broken into, the cracker cannot delete or modify the log files because those files are stored on a separate computer. It is important to remember, however, that those log messages are not, by default, encrypted. Anyone tapping into your local network can eavesdrop on those messages as they pass from one machine to another. Also, although the cracker may not be able to change old log entries, he can affect the system such that any new log messages should not be trusted.

Running a dedicated loghost, a computer that serves no other purpose than to record log messages from other computers on the network, is not uncommon. Because this system runs no other services, it is unlikely that it will be broken into. This makes it nearly impossible for a cracker to erase his or her tracks, but it does not mean that all the log entries are accurate after a cracker has broken into a machine on your network.

## Redirecting logs to a loghost with syslogd

To redirect your computer's log files to another computer's syslogd, you must make some changes to your local syslogd's configuration file, /etc/syslog.conf. Become root using the su - command and then open the /etc/syslog.conf file in a text editor (such as vi). You should see something similar to this:

```
# Log all kernel messages to the console.
# Logging much else clutters up the screen.
```

```
#kern.*                                      /dev/console

# Log anything (except mail) of level info or higher.
# Don't log private authentication messages!
*.info;mail.none;news.none;authpriv.none;cron.none  /var/log/messages

# The authpriv file has restricted access.
authpriv.*                                   /var/log/secure

# Log all the mail messages in one place.
mail.*                                       /var/log/maillog

# Log cron stuff
cron.*                                       /var/log/cron

# Everybody gets emergency messages
*.emerg                                          *

# Save news errors of level crit and higher in a special file.
uucp,news.crit                               /var/log/spooler

# Save boot messages also to boot.log
local7.*                                     /var/log/boot.log

#
# INN
#
news.=crit                                   /var/log/news/news.crit
news.=err                                    /var/log/news/news.err
news.notice                                  /var/log/news/news.notice
```

The lines beginning with a # character are comments. Other lines contain two columns of information. The left field is a semicolon-separated list (spaces won't work) of message types and message priorities. The right field is the log file to which those messages should be written.

To send the messages to another computer (the loghost) instead of a file, start by replacing the log filename with the @ character followed by the name of the loghost. For example, to redirect the output normally sent to the messages, secure, and maillog log files, make these changes to the preceding file:

```
# Log anything (except mail) of level info or higher.
# Don't log private authentication messages!
*.info;mail.none;news.none;authpriv.none;cron.none  @loghost

# The authpriv file has restricted access.
authpriv.*                                   @loghost

# Log all the mail messages in one place.
mail.*                                       @loghost
```

The messages will now be sent to the `syslogd` running on the computer named loghost. The name *loghost* was not an arbitrary choice. Creating such a host name and making it an alias to the actual system acting as the loghost is customary. That way, if you ever need to switch the loghost duties to a different machine, you need to change only the loghost alias; you do not need to re-edit the `syslog.conf` file on every computer.

On the loghost side, that machine must run `syslogd` with the `-r` option, so it will listen on the network for log messages from other machines. In Fedora systems, that means adding a `-r` option to the `SYSLOGD_OPTIONS` variable in the `/etc/sysconfig/syslog` file and restarting the syslog service (`service syslog restart`). The loghost must also have UDP port 514 accessible to be used by `syslogd` (check the `/etc/services` file), so you might need to add a firewall rule to allow that.

## Understanding the messages log file

Because of the many programs and services that record information to the `messages` log file, understanding the format of this file is important. You can get a good early warning of problems developing on your system by examining this file. Each line in the file is a single message recorded by some program or service. Here is a snippet of an actual `messages` log file:

```
Feb 25 11:04:32 toys network: Bringing up loopback interface:  succeeded
Feb 25 11:04:35 toys network: Bringing up interface eth0:  succeeded
Feb 25 13:01:14 toys vsftpd(pam_unix)[10565]: authentication failure;
     logname= uid=0 euid=0 tty= ruser= rhost=10.0.0.5  user=chris
Feb 25 14:44:24 toys su(pam_unix)[11439]: session opened for
     user root by chris(uid=500)
```

This is really very simple when you know what to look for. Each message is divided into five main parts. From left to right, they are

- The date and time that the message was logged

- The name of the computer from which the message came

- The program or service name to which the message pertains

- The process number (enclosed in square brackets) of the program sending the message

- The actual text message

Take another look at the preceding file snippet. In the first two lines, you can see that the network was restarted. The next line shows that the user named chris tried and failed to get to the FTP server on this system from a computer at address `10.0.0.5` (he typed the wrong password and authentication failed). The last line shows chris using the `su` command to become root user.

By occasionally reviewing the `messages` and `secure` files, it's possible to catch a cracking attempt before it is successful. If you see an excessive number of connection attempts for a particular service, especially if they are coming from systems on the Internet, you may be under attack.

# Using Secure Shell Tools

The Secure Shell (ssh) tools are a set of client and server applications that allow you to do basic communications (remote login, remote copy, remote execution, and so on) between remote computers and your Linux system. Because communication is encrypted between the server (typically the sshd daemon process) and clients (such as `ssh`, `scp`, and `sftp`), these tools are inherently more secure than similar, older UNIX tools such as `telnet`, `rsh`, `rcp`, and `rlogin`.

Most Linux systems include secure shell clients, while many include the sshd server as well. If you are using the Fedora or Red Hat Enterprise Linux distributions, for example, the following client and server software packages include the ssh software: openssh, openssh-clients, and openssh-server packages.

## Starting the ssh service

Linux systems that come with the ssh service already installed often are configured for it to start automatically. In Fedora and RHEL systems, the sshd daemon is started from the `/etc/init.d/sshd` startup script. To make sure the service is set up to start automatically in Fedora, RHEL, and other RPM-based Linux systems, type the following (as root user):

```
# chkconfig --list sshd
sshd      0:off   1:off   2:on   3:on   4:on   5:on   6:off
```

This shows that the `sshd` service is set to run in system states 2, 3, 4, and 5 (normal bootup states) and set to be off in all other states. You can turn on the SSH service, if it is off, for your default run state, by typing the following as root user:

```
# chkconfig sshd on
```

This line turns on the ssh service when you enter run levels 2, 3, 4, or 5. To start the service immediately, type the following:

```
# service sshd start
```

Other Linux distributions may simply start the sshd daemon from an entry in the `/etc/rc.d` directory from a file named something like `rc.sshd`. In any case, you can find out whether the sshd daemon is currently running on your system by typing the following:

```
$ ps ax | grep sshd
1996 ?      Ss   0:00 /usr/sbin/sshd
```

The preceding example shows that the sshd daemon is running. If that is the case, and your firewall allows secure shell service (with TCP port 22 open), you should be able to use ssh client commands to access your system. (Any further configuration you want to do to restrict what the sshd daemon will allow is typically done in the `/etc/ssh/sshd_config` file.)

# Using the ssh, sftp, and scp commands

Three commands you can use with the SSH service are ssh, sftp, and scp. Remote users use the ssh command to log in to your system securely or remotely execute a command on your system. The scp command lets remote users copy files to and from a system. The sftp command provides a safe way to access FTP sites through the SSH service (for sites that offer SSH access to their FTP content).

As with the normal remote shell services, secure shell looks in the /etc/hosts.equiv file and in a user's .rhost file to determine whether it should allow a connection. It also looks in the ssh-specific files /etc/shosts.equiv and .shosts. Using the shosts.equiv and the .shosts files is preferable because it avoids granting access to the unencrypted remote shell services. The /etc/shosts.equiv and .shosts files are functionally equivalent to the traditional hosts.equiv and .rhosts files, so the same instructions and rules apply.

Now you are ready to test the SSH service. From another computer on which SSH has been installed (or even from the same computer if another is not available), type the ssh command followed by a space and the name of the user and system you are connecting to. For example, to connect to the system ratbert.glaci.com, type:

```
# ssh jake@ratbert.glaci.com
```

If this is the first time ever you have logged in to that system using the ssh command, the system will ask you to confirm that you really want to connect. Type **yes** and press Enter when it asks this:

```
The authenticity of host 'ratbert.glaci.com (199.170.177.18)' can't be
established.
RSA key fingerprint is xx:xx:xx:xx:xx:xx:xx:xx:xx:xx:xx:xx:xx:xx:xx:xx.
Are you sure you want to continue connecting (yes/no)?
```

It should then prompt you for a password in the normal way. (If you don't type a username, it will assume you want to log in using your local username.) The connection will then function like a normal remote login connection (in other words, you can begin typing shell commands). The only difference is that the information is encrypted as it travels over the network. You should now also be able to use the ssh command to run remote commands from a shell on the remote system.

The scp command is similar to the rcp command for copying files to and from Linux systems. Here is an example of using the scp command to copy a file called memo from the home directory of the user named jake to the /tmp directory on a computer called maple:

```
$ scp /home/jake/memo jake@maple:/tmp
jake@maple's password: ********
memo          100%|****************|   153    0:00
```

Enter the password for your username (if a password is requested). If the password is accepted, the remote system indicates that the file has been copied successfully.

Similarly, the sftp command starts an interactive FTP-style session with a server that supports SSH connections (not an FTP server). Many security-conscious people prefer sftp to other ftp clients because it provides a secure connection between you and the remote host. Here's an example:

```
$ sftp jake@ftp.handsonhistory.com
Connecting to ftp.handsonhistory.com
jake@ftp.handsonhistory.com's password: ********
sftp>
```

At this point you can begin an interactive FTP session. You can use get and put commands on files as you would using any FTP client, but with the comfort of knowing that you are working on a secure connection.

## Tip

The sftp **command, as with** ssh **and** scp, **requires that the SSH service be running on the server. If you can't connect to a server using** sftp, **the SSH service may not be available.** ■

## Using ssh, scp, and sftp without passwords

For machines that you use a great deal (particularly machines behind a firewall on your LAN), setting them up so that you do not have to use a password to log in is often helpful. The following procedure shows you how to do that.

These steps take you through setting up password-less authentication from one machine to another. In this example, the local user is named chester on a computer named host1. The remote user is also chester on a computer named host2.

1. Log in to the local computer (in this example, I log in as chester to host1).

## Note

Run Step 2 only once as local user on your local workstation. Do not run it again unless you lose your ssh keys. When configuring subsequent remote servers, skip right to Step 3. ■

2. Type the following to generate the ssh key:

```
$ ssh-keygen -t dsa
Generating public/private dsa key pair.
Enter file in which to save the key
(/home/chester/.ssh/id_dsa): <Enter>
Enter passphrase (empty for no passphrase): <Enter>
Enter same passphrase again: <Enter>
Your identification has been saved in /home/chester/.ssh/id_dsa.
Your public key has been saved in /home/chester/.ssh/id_dsa.pub.
The key fingerprint is:
3b:c0:2f:63:a5:65:70:b7:4b:f0:2a:c4:18:24:47:69 chester@host1
```

As shown in the example, press Enter to accept the filename where the key is stored. Then press Enter twice to accept a blank passphrase. (If you enter a passphrase, you will be prompted for that passphrase and won't be able to log in without it.)

3. You must secure the permissions of your authentication keys by closing permissions to your home directory, .ssh directory, and authentication files as follows:

```
$ chmod 700 $HOME $HOME/.ssh
$ chmod go-rwx $HOME/.ssh/*
```

4. Type the following to copy the key to the remote server (replace chester with the remote username and host2 with the remote host name):

```
$ ssh-copy-id -i ~/.ssh/id_dsa.pub chester@host2
chester@host2's password: ******
```

5. For the sshd daemon to accept the key you copied to host2, the home directory and the authorized_keys file itself must have secure permissions. To secure that file and those directories, type the following:

```
$ ssh chester@host2 chmod 700 $HOME $HOME/.ssh
$ ssh chester@host2 chmod 600 $HOME/.ssh/authorized_keys2
```

It is important to note that after you have this working, it will work regardless of how many times the IP address changes on your local computer. The IP address has nothing to do with this form of authentication.

# Securing Linux Servers

Opening up your Linux system as a server on a public network creates a whole new set of challenges when it comes to security. Instead of just turning away nearly all incoming requests, your computer will be expected to respond to requests for supported services (such as Web, FTP, or mail service) by supplying information or possibly running scripts that take in data.

Entire books have been filled with information on how to go about securing your servers. Many businesses that rely on Internet servers assign full-time administrators to watch over the security of their servers. So, think of this section as an overview of some of the kinds of attacks to look out for and some tools available to secure your Linux server.

## Controlling access to services with TCP wrappers

Completely disabling an unused service is fine, but what about the services that you really need? How can you selectively grant and deny access to these services? For Linux systems that incorporate TCP wrapper support, the /etc/hosts.allow and /etc/hosts.deny files determine when a particular connection should be granted or refused for services such as sshd, vsftpd, rlogin, rsh, telnet, finger, and talk.

Most Linux systems that implement TCP wrappers do so for a set of services that are monitored by a single listening process called the Internet super server. For Fedora and RHEL systems, that server is the xinetd daemon, whereas in other systems (such as Debian) the inetd daemon is used. When a service that relies on TCP wrappers is requested from the server process, the hosts. allow and hosts.deny files are scanned and checked for an entry that matches the IP address of the connecting machine. These checks are made when connection attempts occur:

- If the address is listed in the hosts.allow file, the connection is allowed and hosts. deny is not checked.

- If the address is not matched in hosts.allow, but is in hosts.deny, the connection is denied.

- If the address is in neither file, the connection is allowed.

The service names you list refer to the daemon names (as opposed to the service name listed in the /etc/init.d directory, which may be different). To check whether or not a daemon is enabled to use TCP wrappers, run the strings or ldd command on the daemon and check for hosts_access or libwrap, respectively:

```
$ strings /usr/sbin/vsftpd |grep hosts
hosts_access
$ ldd /usr/sbin/sshd |grep libwrap
libwrap.so.0 => /lib/libwrap.so.0 (0x0012f000)
```

Keep in mind that the order in which hosts are evaluated is important. For example, you cannot deny access to a host in the hosts.deny file that has already been given access in the hosts. allow file.

Listing every single address that may try to connect to your computer is not necessary (or even possible). The hosts.allow and hosts.deny files enable you to specify entire subnets and groups of addresses. You can even use the keyword ALL to specify all possible addresses. You can also restrict specific entries in these files so they apply only to specific network services. Look at an example of a typical pair of hosts.allow and hosts.deny files. Here's the /etc/hosts. allow file:

```
#
# hosts.allow  This file describes the names of the hosts that are
#              allowed to use the local INET services, as decided
#              by the '/usr/sbin/tcpd' server.
#

sshd: 199.170.177.
in.telnetd: 199.170.177., .linuxtoys.net
vsftpd: ALL
```

Here's the /etc/hosts.deny file:

```
#
# hosts.deny This file describes names of the hosts which are
#            *not* allowed to use the local INET services, as
#            decided by the '/usr/sbin/tcpd' server.
#

ALL: ALL
```

The preceding example is a rather restrictive configuration. It allows connections to the sshd and telnet services from certain hosts, but then denies all other connections. It also allows connections to the FTP service (vsftp) to all hosts. Let's examine the files in detail.

As usual, lines beginning with a # character are comments and are ignored by xinetd or inetd when it parses the file. Each noncomment line consists of a comma-separated list of daemons followed by a colon (:) character and then a comma-separated list of client addresses to check. In this context, a client is any computer that attempts to access a network service on your system.

A client entry can be a numeric IP address (such as 199.170.177.25) or a host name (such as jukebox.linuxtoys.net), but is more often a wildcard variation that specifies an entire range of addresses. A client entry can take four different forms. The online manual page for the hosts.allow file describes them as follows:

- A string that begins with a dot (.) character. A host name is matched if the last components of its name match the specified pattern. For example, the pattern .tue.nl matches the host name wzv.win.tue.nl.

- A string that ends with a dot (.) character. A host address is matched if its first numeric fields match the given string. For example, the pattern 131.155. matches the address of (almost) every host on the Eindhoven University network (131.155.x.x).

- A string that begins with an at (@) sign is treated as an NIS netgroup name. A host name is matched if it is a host member of the specified netgroup. Netgroup matches are not supported for daemon process names or for client usernames.

- An expression of the form n.n.n.n/m.m.m.m is interpreted as a *net/mask* pair. A host address is matched if *net* is equal to the bitwise *and* of the address and the mask. For example, the net/mask pattern 131.155.72.0/255.255.254.0 matches every address in the range 131.155.72.0 through 131.155.73.255.

The example host.allow contains the first two types of client specification. The entry 199.170.177. will match any IP address that begins with that string, such as 199.170.177.25. The client entry .linuxtoys.net will match host names such as jukebox.linuxtoys.net or picframe.linuxtoys.net.

Let's examine what happens when a host named `jukebox.linuxtoys.net` (with IP address `199.170.179.18`) connects to your Linux system using the Telnet protocol. In this case, the Linux system is Fedora, which uses the xinetd daemon to listen for service requests associated with TCP wrappers:

1. `xinetd` receives the connection request.

2. `xinetd` begins comparing the address and name of `jukebox.linuxtoys.net` to the rules listed in `/etc/hosts.allow`. It starts at the top of the file and works its way down the file until finding a match. Both the daemon (the program handling the network service on your Fedora box) and the connecting client's IP address or name must match the information in the `hosts.allow` file. In this case, the second rule that is encountered matches the request:

   ```
   in.telnetd: 199.170.177., .linuxtoys.net
   ```

3. The `jukebox` host is not in the `199.170.177` subnet, but it is in the `linuxtoys.net` domain. `xinetd` stops searching the file as soon as it finds this match.

How about if `jukebox` connects to your box using the CUPS-lpd protocol? In this case, it matches none of the rules in `hosts.allow`; the only line that refers to the lpd daemon does not refer to the `199.170.179` subnet or to the `linuxtoys.net` domain. `xinetd` continues on to the `hosts.deny` file. The entry `ALL: ALL` matches anything, so `tcpd` denies the connection.

The `ALL` wildcard was also used in the `hosts.allow` file. In this case, we are telling `xinetd` to permit absolutely any host to connect to the FTP service on the Linux box. This is appropriate for running an anonymous FTP server that anyone on the Internet can access. If you are not running an anonymous FTP site, you probably should not use the `ALL` flag.

A good general rule is to make your `hosts.allow` and `hosts.deny` files as restrictive as possible and then explicitly enable only those services that you really need. Also, grant access only to those systems that really need access. Using the `ALL` flag to grant universal access to a particular service may be easier than typing a long list of subnets or domains, but better a few minutes spent on proper security measures than many hours recovering from a break-in.

## Tip

For Linux systems that use the xinetd service, you can further restrict access to services using various options within the `/etc/xinetd.conf` file, even to the point of limiting access to certain services to specific times of the day. Read the manual page for `xinetd` (by typing **man xinetd** at a command prompt) to learn more about these options. ∎

## Understanding attack techniques

Attacks on computing systems take on different forms, depending on the goal and resources of the attacker. Some attackers want to be disruptive, whereas others want to infiltrate your machines and utilize the resources for their own nefarious purposes. Still others are targeting your data for financial gain or blackmail. Here are three major categories of attacks:

- **Denial-of-Service (DoS)**—The easiest attacks to perpetrate are denial-of-service attacks. The primary purpose of these attacks is to disrupt the activities of a remote site by overloading it with irrelevant data. DoS attacks can be as simple as sending thousands of page requests per second at a Web site. These types of attacks are easy to perpetrate and easy to protect against. After you have a handle on where the attack is coming from, a simple phone call to the perpetrator's ISP will get the problem solved.

- **Distributed Denial-of-Service (DDoS)**—More advanced DoS attacks are called distributed denial-of-service attacks. DDoS attacks are much harder to perpetrate and nearly impossible to stop. In this form of attack, an attacker takes control of hundreds or even thousands of weakly secured Internet-connected computers. The attacker then directs them in unison to send a stream of irrelevant data to a single Internet host. The result is that the power of one attacker is magnified thousands of times. Instead of an attack coming from one direction, as is the case in a normal DoS, it comes from thousands of directions at once. The best defense against a DDoS attack is to contact your ISP to see whether or not it can filter traffic at its border routers.

  Many people use the excuse, "I have nothing on my machine anyone would want" to avoid having to consider security. The problem with this argument is that attackers have a lot of reasons to use your machine. The attacker can turn your machine into an agent for later use in a DDoS attack. More than once, authorities have shown up at the door of a dumbfounded computer user asking questions about threats originating from their computer. By ignoring security, the owners have opened themselves up to a great deal of liability.

- **Intrusion attacks**—To remotely use the resources of a target machine, attackers must first look for an opening to exploit. In the absence of inside information such as passwords or encryption keys, they must scan the target machine to see what services are offered. Perhaps one of the services is weakly secured and the attacker can use some known exploit to finagle his or her way in.

  A tool called nmap is generally considered the best way to scan a host for services (note that nmap is a tool that can be used for good and evil). When the attacker has a list of the available services running on his target, he needs to find a way to trick one of those services into letting him have privileged access to the system. Usually, this is done with a program called an *exploit*.

Although DoS attacks are disruptive, intrusion attacks are the most damaging. The reasons are varied, but the result is always the same. An uninvited guest is now taking up residence on your machine and is using it in a way you have no control over.

## Protecting against denial-of-service attacks

As explained earlier, a denial-of-service attack attempts to crash your computer or at least degrade its performance to an unusable level. A variety of denial-of-service exploits exist.

Most try to overload some system resource, such as your available disk space or your Internet connection. Some common attacks and defenses are discussed in the following sections.

## Mailbombing

*Mailbombing* is the practice of sending so much e-mail to a particular user or system that the computer's hard drive becomes full. You have several ways to protect yourself from mailbombing, as described in the following sections. You can use the Procmail e-mail-filtering tool or, if you are using sendmail as your mail transport agent, configure your sendmail daemon.

### Blocking mail with Procmail

The Procmail e-mail-filtering tool, installed by default with Fedora, RHEL, and many other Linux systems, is tightly integrated with the sendmail e-mail daemon; thus, it can be used to selectively block or filter out specific types of e-mail. You can learn more about Procmail at the Procmail Web site: www.procmail.org.

To enable Procmail for your user account, create a .procmailrc file in your home directory. The file should be mode 0600 (readable by you but nobody else). Type the following, replacing *evil-mailer* with the actual e-mail address that is mailbombing you.

```
# Delete mail from evilmailer
:0
* ^From.*evilmailer
/dev/null
```

The Procmail recipe looks for the From line at the start of each e-mail to see if it includes the string evilmailer. If it does, the message is sent to /dev/null (effectively throwing it away).

### Blocking mail with sendmail

The Procmail e-mail tool works quite well when only one user is being mailbombed. If, however, the mailbombing affects many users, you should probably configure your sendmail daemon to block all e-mail from the mailbomber. Do this by adding the mailbomber's e-mail address or system name to the access file located in the /etc/mail directory.

Each line of the access file contains an e-mail address, host name, domain, or IP address followed by a tab and then a keyword specifying what action to take when that entity sends you a message. Valid keywords are OK, RELAY, REJECT, DISCARD, and ERROR. Using the REJECT keyword will cause a sender's e-mail to be bounced back with an error message. The keyword DISCARD will cause the message to be silently dropped without sending an error back. You can even return a custom error message by using the ERROR keyword.

Thus, an example /etc/mail/access file may look similar to this:

```
# Check the /usr/share/doc/sendmail/README.cf file for a description
# of the format of this file. (search for access_db in that file)
# The /usr/share/doc/sendmail/README.cf is part of the sendmail-doc
# package.
```

```
#
# by default we allow relaying from localhost...
localhost.localdomain              RELAY
localhost                          RELAY
127.0.0.1                          RELAY
#
# Senders we want to Block
#
evilmailer@yahoo.com    REJECT
stimpy.glaci.com        REJECT
cyberpromo.com          DISCARD
199.170.176.99          ERROR:"550 Die Spammer Scum!"
199.170.177             ERROR:"550 Email Refused"
```

As with most Linux configuration files, lines that begin with a pound (#) sign are comments. The list of blocked spammers is at the end of this example file. Note that the address to block can be a complete e-mail address, a full host name, a domain only, an IP address, or a subnet.

To block a particular e-mail address or host from mailbombing you, log in to your system as root, edit the /etc/mail/access file, and add a line to DISCARD mail from the offending sender.

After saving the file and exiting the editor, you must convert the access file into a hash-indexed database called access.db. The database is updated automatically the next time sendmail starts. On Fedora and other Red Hat systems, you can convert the database immediately, as follows:

```
# cd /etc/mail
# make
```

Sendmail should now discard e-mail from the addresses you added.

### Spam relaying

Your e-mail services can also be abused by having your system used as a spam relay. *Spam* refers to the unsolicited junk e-mail that has become a common occurrence on the Internet. *Relay* refers to the mail server feature that causes it to send mail it receives to another server. (Normally, only users with valid e-mail accounts on the server are allowed to use a mail server to relay messages in their behalf. A mail server configured as an open relay will allow anyone to forward e-mail messages through it and is, therefore, considered to be a very bad practice.)

Spammers often deliver their annoying messages from a normal dial-up Internet account. They need some kind of high-capacity e-mail server to accept and buffer the payload of messages. They deliver the spam to the server all in one huge batch and then log off, letting the server do the work of delivering the messages to the many victims.

Naturally, no self-respecting Internet service provider will cooperate with this action, so spammers resort to hijacking servers at another ISP to do the dirty work. Having your mailserver hijacked to act as a spam relay can have a devastating effect on your system and your reputation. Fortunately, open mail relaying is deactivated by default on Fedora and Red Hat Enterprise Linux installations. Open mail relaying is one security issue that you will not have to worry about.

You can allow specific hosts or domains to relay mail through your system by adding those senders to your /etc/mail/access file with keyword RELAY. By default, relaying is allowed from the local host only.

## Tip
**One package you might consider using to filter out spam on your mail server is SpamAssassin. SpamAssassin examines the text of incoming mail messages and attempts to filter out messages that are determined to be spam. SpamAssassin is described in Chapter 14. ■**

### Smurf amplification attack

*Smurfing* refers to a particular type of denial-of-service attack aimed at flooding your Internet connection. It can be a difficult attack to defend against because tracing the attack to the attacker is not easy. Here is how smurfing works.

The attack makes use of the ICMP protocol, a service intended for checking the speed and availability of network connections. Using the ping command, you can send a network packet from your computer to another computer on the Internet. The remote computer will recognize the packet as an ICMP request and echo a reply packet to your computer. Your computer can then print a message revealing that the remote system is up and telling you how long it took to reply to the ping.

A smurfing attack uses a malformed ICMP request to bury your computer in network traffic. The attacker does this by bouncing a ping request off an unwitting third party in such a way that the reply is duplicated dozens or even hundreds of times. An organization with a fast Internet connection and a large number of computers is used as the relay. The destination address of the ping is set to an entire subnet instead of a single host. The return address is forged to be your machine's address instead of the actual sender. When the ICMP packet arrives at the unwitting relay's network, every host on that subnet replies to the ping! Furthermore, they reply to your computer instead of to the actual sender. If the relay's network has hundreds of computers, your Internet connection can be quickly flooded.

The best fix is to contact the organization being used as a relay and inform it of the abuse. Usually, they need only to reconfigure their Internet router to stop any future attacks. If the organization is uncooperative, you can minimize the effect of the attack by blocking the ICMP protocol on your router. This will at least keep the traffic off your internal network. If you can convince your ISP to block ICMP packets aimed at your network, it will help even more. (Note that some debate exists about whether or not blocking ICMP packets is a good idea because ICMP services can be useful for various administrative purposes.)

## Protecting against distributed DoS attacks

DDoS attacks are much harder to initiate and extremely difficult to stop. A DDoS attack begins with the penetration of hundreds or even thousands of weakly secured machines. These machines can then be directed to attack a single host based on the whims of the attacker.

With the advent of DSL and cable modem, millions of people are enjoying Internet access with virtually no speed restrictions. In their rush to get online, many of those people neglect even the most basic security. Because the vast majority of these people run Microsoft operating systems, they tend to get hit with worms and viruses rather quickly. After the machine has been infiltrated, quite often the worm or virus installs a program on the victim's machine that instructs it to quietly *call home* and announce that it is now ready to do *the master's bidding*.

At the whim of the master, the infected machines can now be used to focus a concentrated stream of garbage data at a selected host. In concert with thousands of other infected machines, a *script kiddie* now has the power to take down nearly any site on the Internet.

Detecting a DDoS is similar to detecting a DoS attack. One or more of the following signs are likely to be present:

- Sustained saturated data link
- No reduction in link saturation during off-peak hours
- Hundreds or even thousands of simultaneous network connections
- Extremely slow system performance

To determine if your data link is saturated, the act of pinging an outside host can tell much of the story. Much higher than usual latency is a dead giveaway. Normal ping latency (that is, the time it takes for a ping response to come back from a remote host) looks like the following:

```
# ping www.example.com
PING www.example.com (192.0.34.166) from 10.0.0.11: 56(84) bytes of data
64 bytes from 192.0.34.166: icmp_seq=1 ttl=49 time=40.1 ms
64 bytes from 192.0.34.166: icmp_seq=2 ttl=49 time=42.5 ms
64 bytes from 192.0.34.166: icmp_seq=3 ttl=49 time=39.5 ms
64 bytes from 192.0.34.166: icmp_seq=4 ttl=49 time=38.4 ms
64 bytes from 192.0.34.166: icmp_seq=5 ttl=49 time=39.0 ms

--- www.example.com ping statistics ---
5 packets transmitted, 5 received, 0% loss, time 4035ms
rtt min/avg/max/mdev = 38.472/39.971/42.584/1.432 ms
```

In the preceding example, the average time for a ping packet to make the roundtrip was about 39 thousandths of a second.

A ping to a nearly saturated link looks like the following:

```
# ping www.example.com
PING www.example.com (192.0.34.166): from 10.0.0.11: 56(84)bytes of data
64 bytes from 192.0.34.166: icmp_seq=1 ttl=62 time=1252 ms
64 bytes from 192.0.34.166: icmp_seq=2 ttl=62 time=1218 ms
64 bytes from 192.0.34.166: icmp_seq=3 ttl=62 time=1290 ms
64 bytes from 192.0.34.166: icmp_seq=4 ttl=62 time=1288 ms
64 bytes from 192.0.34.166: icmp_seq=5 ttl=62 time=1241 ms

--- www.example.com ping statistics ---
5 packets transmitted, 5 received, 0% loss, time 5032ms
rtt min/avg/max/mdev = 1218.059/1258.384/1290.861/28.000 ms
```

In this example, a ping packet took, on average, 1.3 seconds to make the roundtrip. From the first example to the second example, latency increased by a factor of 31! A data link that goes from working normally to slowing down by a factor of 31 is a clear sign that link utilization should be investigated.

For a more accurate measure of data throughput, you can use a tool such as ttcp. To test your connection with ttcp you must have installed the ttcp package on machines inside *and* outside of your network. (The ttcp package is available with Fedora and other Linux systems.) If you are not sure whether the package is installed, simply type **ttcp** at a command prompt. You should see something like the following:

```
# ttcp
Usage: ttcp -t [-options] host [ < in ]
       ttcp -r [-options > out]
Common options:
        -l ##    length of bufs read from or written to network (default 8192)
        -u       use UDP instead of TCP
        -p ##    port number to send to or listen at (default 5001)
        -s       -t: source a pattern to network
                 -r: sink (discard) all data from network
        -A       align the start of buffers to this modulus (default 16384)
        -O       start buffers at this offset from the modulus (default 0)
        -v       verbose: print more statistics
        -d       set SO_DEBUG socket option
        -b ##    set socket buffer size (if supported)
        -f X     format for rate: k,K = kilo{bit,byte}; m,M = mega; g,G = giga
Options specific to -t:
        -n##     number of source bufs written to network (default 2048)
        -D       don't buffer TCP writes (sets TCP_NODELAY socket option)
     -w ## number of microseconds to wait between each write
Options specific to -r:
        -B       for -s, only output full blocks as specified by -l (for TAR)
        -T       "touch": access each byte as it's read
     -I if Specify the network interface (e.g. eth0) to use
```

The first step is to start up a receiver process on the server machine:

```
# ttcp -rs
ttcp-r: buflen=8192, nbuf=2048, align=16384/0, port=5001  tcp
ttcp-r: socket
```

The -r flag denotes that the server machine will be the receiver. The -s flag, in conjunction with the -r flag, tells ttcp that we want to ignore any received data.

The next step is to have someone outside of your data link, with a network link close to the same speed as yours, set up a ttcp sending process:

```
# ttcp -ts server.example.com
ttcp-t: buflen=8192, nbuf=2048, align=16384/0, port=5001  tcp
    -> server.example.com
ttcp-t: socket
ttcp-t: connect
```

Let the process run for a few minutes and then press Ctrl+C on the transmitting side to stop the testing. The receiving side then takes a moment to calculate and present the results:

```
# ttcp -rs
ttcp-r: buflen=8192, nbuf=2048, align=16384/0, port=5001  tcp
ttcp-r: socket
ttcp-r: accept from 64.223.17.21
ttcp-r: 2102496 bytes in 70.02 real seconds = 29.32 KB/sec +++
ttcp-r: 1226 I/O calls, msec/call = 58.49, calls/sec = 17.51
ttcp-r: 0.0user 0.0sys 1:10real 0% 0i+0d 0maxrss 0+2pf 0+0csw
```

In this example, the average bandwidth between the two hosts was 29.32 kilobytes per second. On a link suffering from a DDoS, this number would be a mere fraction of the actual bandwidth the data link is rated for.

If the data link is indeed saturated, the next step is to determine where the connections are coming from. A very effective way of doing this is with the netstat command, which is included as part of the base Fedora installation. Type the following to see connection information:

```
# netstat -tupn
```

Table 12-3 describes each of the netstat parameters used here.

**TABLE 12-3**

## netstat Parameters

| Parameter | Description |
| --- | --- |
| **-t, --tcp** | Show TCP socket connections. |
| **-u, --udp** | Show UDP socket connections. |
| **-p, --program** | Show the PID and name of the program to which each socket belongs. |
| **-n, --numeric** | Show numerical address instead of trying to determine symbolic host, port, or usernames. |

The following is an example of what the output might look like:

```
Active Internet connections (w/o servers)
Proto Recv-Q Send-Q Local Address   Foreign Address     State       PID/Program name
tcp    0      0 65.213.7.96:22      13.29.132.19:12545  ESTABLISHED 32376/sshd
tcp    0    224 65.213.7.96:22      13.29.210.13:29250  ESTABLISHED 13858/sshd
tcp    0      0 65.213.7.96:6667    13.29.194.190:33452 ESTABLISHED 1870/ircd
tcp    0      0 65.213.7.96:6667    216.39.144.152:42709 ESTABLISHED 1870/ircd
tcp    0      0 65.213.7.96:42352   67.113.1.99:53      TIME_WAIT   -
tcp    0      0 65.213.7.96:42354   83.152.6.9:113      TIME_WAIT   -
```

```
tcp   0   0 65.213.7.96:42351 83.152.6.9:113       TIME_WAIT  -
tcp   0   0 127.0.0.1:42355    127.0.0.1:783        TIME_WAIT  -
tcp   0   0 127.0.0.1:783      127.0.0.1:42353      TIME_WAIT  -
tcp   0   0 65.213.7.96:850578 19.15.11.1:25        TIME_WAIT  -
```

The output is organized into columns defined as follows:

- **Proto**—Protocol used by the socket.
- **Recv-Q**—The number of bytes not yet copied by the user program attached to this socket.
- **Send-Q**—The number of bytes not acknowledged by the host.
- **Local Address**—Address and port number of the local end of the socket.
- **Foreign Address**—Address and port number of the remote end of the socket.
- **State**—Current state of the socket. Table 12-4 provides a list of socket states.
- **PID/Program name**—Process ID and program name of the process that owns the socket.

**TABLE 12-4**

## Socket States

| State | Description |
| --- | --- |
| ESTABLISHED | Socket has an established connection. |
| SYN_SENT | Socket actively trying to establish a connection. |
| SYN_RECV | Connection request received from the network. |
| FIN_WAIT1 | Socket closed and shutting down. |
| FIN_WAIT2 | Socket is waiting for remote end to shut down. |
| TIME_WAIT | Socket is waiting after closing to handle packets still in the network. |
| CLOSED | Socket is not being used. |
| CLOSE_WAIT | The remote end has shut down, waiting for the socket to close. |
| LAST_ACK | The remote end has shut down, and the socket is closed, waiting for acknowledgement. |
| LISTEN | Socket is waiting for an incoming connection. |
| CLOSING | Both sides of the connection are shut down, but not all of your data has been sent. |
| UNKNOWN | The state of the socket is unknown. |

During a DoS attack, the foreign address is usually the same for each connection. In this case, it is a simple matter of typing the foreign IP address into the search form at ws.arin.net/whois/ so you can alert your ISP.

During a DDoS attack, the foreign address will likely be different for each connection. In this case, tracking down all the offenders is impossible because there will likely be thousands of them. The best way to defend yourself is to contact your ISP and see whether or not it can filter the traffic at its border routers.

# Protecting against intrusion attacks

Crackers have a wide variety of tools and techniques to assist them in breaking into your computer. Intrusion attacks focus on exploiting weaknesses in your security, so the crackers can take more control of your system (and potentially do more damage) than they could from the outside.

Fortunately, many tools and techniques exist for combating intrusion attacks. This section discusses the most common break-in methods and the tools available to protect your system. Although the examples shown are specific to Fedora and other Red Hat Linux systems, the tools and techniques are generally applicable to any Linux or UNIX-like operating system.

## Evaluating access to network services

Linux systems and their UNIX kin provide many network services, and with them many avenues for cracker attacks. You should know these services and how to limit access to them.

What do I mean by a network service? Basically, I am referring to any task that the computer performs that requires it to send and receive information over the network using some predefined set of rules. Routing e-mail is a network service. So is serving Web pages. Your Linux box has the potential to provide thousands of services. Many of them are listed in the /etc/services file. Look at a snippet of that file:

```
# /etc/services:
# service-name   port/protocol   [aliases ...]    [# comment]
chargen          19/tcp               ttytst source
chargen          19/udp               ttytst source
ftp-data         20/tcp
ftp-data         20/udp
# 21 is registered to ftp, but also used by fsp
ftp              21/tcp
ftp              21/udp          fsp fspd
ssh              22/tcp                           # SSH Remote Login Protocol
ssh              22/udp                           # SSH Remote Login Protocol
telnet           23/tcp
telnet           23/udp
# 24 - private mail system
smtp             25/tcp          mail
```

After the comment lines, you will notice three columns of information. The left column contains the name of each service. The middle column defines the port number and protocol type used for that service. The rightmost field contains an optional alias or list of aliases for the service.

As an example, examine the last entry in the file snippet. It describes the SMTP (Simple Mail Transfer Protocol) service, which is the service used for delivering e-mail over the Internet. The middle column contains the text 25/tcp, which tells you that the SMTP protocol uses port 25 and uses the Transmission Control Protocol (TCP) as its protocol type.

What exactly is a *port number*? It is a unique number that has been set aside for a particular network service. It allows network connections to be properly routed to the software that handles that service. For example, when an e-mail message is delivered from some other computer to your Linux box, the remote system must first establish a network connection with your system. Your computer receives the connection request, examines it, sees it labeled for port 25, and thus knows that the connection should be handed to the program that handles e-mail (which happens to be sendmail).

I mentioned that SMTP uses the TCP protocol. Some services use UDP, the User Datagram Protocol. All you really need to know about TCP and UDP (for the purposes of this security discussion) is that they provide different ways of packaging the information sent over a network connection. A TCP connection provides error detection and retransmission of lost data. UDP doesn't check to ensure that the data arrived complete and intact; it is meant as a fast way to send non-critical information.

## Disabling network services

Although hundreds of services (with official port numbers listed in /etc/services) potentially could be available and subject to attack on your Linux system, in reality only a few dozen services are installed and only a handful of those are on by default. In Fedora and RHEL systems, most network services are started by either the xinetd process or by a startup script in the /etc/init.d directory. Other Linux systems use the inetd process instead of xinetd.

xinetd and inetd are daemons that listen on a great number of network port numbers. When a connection is made to a particular port number, xinetd or inetd automatically starts the appropriate program for that service and hands the connection to it.

For xinetd, the configuration file /etc/xinetd.conf is used to provide default settings for the xinetd server. The directory /etc/xinetd.d contains files telling xinetd what ports to listen on and what programs to start (the inetd daemon, alternatively, uses only the /etc/inetd.conf file). Each file in /etc/xinetd.d contains configuration information for a single service, and the file is usually named after the service it configures. For example, to enable the rsync service, edit the rsync file in the /etc/xinetd.d directory and look for a section similar to the following:

```
service rsync
{
    disable = yes
    socket_type        = stream
```

```
wait            = no
user            = root
server          = /usr/bin/rsync
server_args     = --daemon
log_on_failure  += USERID
}
```

Note that the first line of this example identifies the service as rsync. This exactly matches the service name listed in the /etc/services file, causing the service to listen on port 873 for TCP and UDP protocols. You can see that the service is off by default (disable = yes). To enable the rsync services, change the line to read disable = no instead. Thus, the disable line from the preceding example would look like this:

```
disable = no
```

## Tip

The rsync service is a nice one to turn on if your machine is an FTP server. It allows people to use an rsync client (which includes a checksum-search algorithm) to download files from your server. With that feature, users can restart a disrupted download without having to start from the beginning. ∎

Because most services are disabled by default, your computer is only as insecure as you make it. You can double-check that insecure services, such as rlogin and rsh (which are included in the rsh-server package in Fedora and RHEL systems), are also disabled by making sure that disabled = yes is set in the /etc/xinetd.d/rlogin and rsh files.

## Tip

You can make the remote login service active but disable the use of the /etc/host.equiv and .rhosts files, requiring rlogin to always prompt for a password. Rather than disabling the service, locate the server line in the rsh file (server = /usr/sbin/in.rshd) and add a space followed by -L at the end. ∎

You now need to send a signal to the xinetd process to tell it to reload its configuration file. The quickest way to do that in Fedora and RHEL systems is to reload the xinetd service. As the root user, type the following from a shell:

```
# service xinetd reload
Reloading configuration:          [ OK ]
```

You can also tell the xinetd process directly to reread the configuration file by sending it a SIGHUP signal. That works if you are using the inetd daemon instead (on systems such as Debian or Slackware) to reread the /etc/inetd.conf file. For example, type this (as root user) to have the inetd daemon reread the configuration file:

```
# killall -s SIGHUP inetd
```

That's it—you have enabled the rsync service. Provided that you have properly configured your FTP server, clients should now be able to download files from your computer via the rsync protocol.

## Securing servers with SELinux

Security Enhanced Linux (SELinux) is a project developed primarily by the National Security Agency to produce highly secure Linux systems. Although SELinux is available as add-on packages to openSUSE, Debian, Ubuntu, Gentoo, and Yellow Dog, SELinux is installed and turned on by default in Fedora and Red Hat Enterprise Linux systems.

Red Hat, Inc. did a clever thing when it took its first swipe at implementing SELinux in Red Hat systems. Instead of creating policies to control every aspect of your Linux system, it created a "targeted" policy type that focused on securing your system from attacks on those services that are most vulnerable to attacks. The company then set about securing those services in such a way that, if they were compromised, a cracker couldn't compromise the rest of the system as well.

After you have opened a port in your firewall so others can request a service, then started that service to handle requests, SELinux can be used to set up walls around that service. As a result, its daemon process, configuration files, and data can't access resources they are not specifically allowed to access. The rest of your computer, then, is safer.

As Red Hat continues to work out the kinks in SELinux, there has been a tendency for users to see SELinux failures and just disable the entire SELinux service. However, a better course is to find out whether SELinux is really stopping you from doing something that is unsafe. If it turns out to be a bug with SELinux, file a bug report and help make the service better.

If you are enabling FTP, Web (HTTPD), DNS, NFS, NIS, or Samba services on your Fedora or RHEL system, you should consider leaving SELinux enabled and working with the settings from the Security Level Configuration window to configure those services. For information on SELinux that is specific to Fedora, refer to this site:

```
http://fedoraproject.org/wiki/SELinux
```

## Protecting Web servers with certificates and encryption

Previous sections told you how to lock the doors to your Linux system to deny access to crackers. The best deadbolt lock, however, is useless if you are mugged in your own driveway and have your keys stolen. Likewise, the best computer security can be for naught if you are sending passwords and other critical data unprotected across the Internet.

# Exporting Encryption Technology

Before describing how to use the various encryption tools, I need to warn you about an unusual policy of the United States government. For many years, the United States government treated encryption technology like munitions. As a result, anyone wanting to export encryption technology had to get an export license from the Commerce Department. This applied not only to encryption software developed within the United States, but also to software obtained from other countries and then re-exported to another country (or even to the same country you got it from).

Thus, if you installed encryption technology on your Linux system and then transported it out of the country, you were violating federal law! Furthermore, if you e-mailed encryption software to a friend in another country or let him or her download it from your server, you violated the law.

In January 2000, U.S. export laws relating to encryption software were relaxed considerably. However, often the U.S. Commerce Department's Bureau of Export Administration requires a review of encryption products before they can be exported. U.S. companies are also still not allowed to export encryption technology to countries classified as supporting terrorism.

A savvy cracker can use a tool called a *protocol analyzer* or a *network sniffer* to peek at the data flowing across a network and pick out passwords, credit card data, and other juicy bits of information. The cracker does this by breaking into a poorly protected system on the same network and running software, or by gaining physical access to the same network and plugging in his or her own equipment.

You can combat this sort of theft by using encryption. The two main types of encryption in use today are symmetric cryptography and public-key cryptography.

## Symmetric cryptography

*Symmetric cryptography*, also called *private-key* cryptography, uses a single key to both encrypt and decrypt a message. This method is generally inappropriate for securing data that will be used by a third party because of the complexity of secure key exchange. Symmetric cryptography is generally useful for encrypting data for one's own purposes.

A classic use of symmetric cryptography is for a personal password vault. Anyone who has been using the Internet for any amount of time has accumulated a quantity of usernames and passwords for accessing various sites and resources. A personal password vault lets you store this access information in an encrypted form. The end result is that you have to remember only one password to unlock all of your access information.

A few years ago, the United States government was standardized on a symmetric encryption algorithm called DES (Data Encryption Standard) to secure important information. Because there is no direct way to crack DES encrypted data, to decrypt DES encrypted data without a password you would have to use an unimaginable amount of computing power to try to guess the password. This is also known as the *brute force* method of decryption.

As personal computing power has increased nearly exponentially, the DES algorithm has had to be retired. In its place, after a very long and interesting search, the United States government has accepted the Rijndael algorithm as what it calls the AES (Advanced Encryption Standard). Although the AES algorithm is also subject to brute force attacks, it requires significantly more computing power to crack than the DES algorithm does.

For more information on AES, including a command-line implementation of the algorithm, you can visit `http://aescrypt.sourceforge.net/`.

## Asymmetric cryptography

*Public-key cryptography* does not suffer from key distribution problems, and that is why it is the preferred encryption method for secure Internet communication. This method uses two keys, one to encrypt the message and another to decrypt the message. The key used to encrypt the message is called the public key because it is made available for all to see. The key used to decrypt the message is the private key and is kept hidden.

Imagine that you want to send me a secure message using public-key encryption. Here is what we need:

1. I must have a public and private key pair. Depending on the circumstances, I may generate the keys myself (using special software) or obtain the keys from a key authority.

2. You want to send me a message, so you first look up my public key (or more accurately, the software you are using looks it up).

3. You encrypt the message with the public key. At this point, the message can be decrypted only with the private key (the public key cannot be used to decrypt the message).

4. I receive the message and use my private key to decrypt it.

## Secure socket layer

A classic implementation of public-key cryptography is with secure sockets layer (SSL) communication. This is the technology that enables you to securely submit your credit card information to an online merchant. The elements of an SSL encrypted session are as follows:

- SSL-enabled Web browser (Mozilla, Internet Explorer, Opera, Konquerer, and so on)
- SSL-enabled Web server (Apache)
- SSL certificate

To initiate an SSL session, a Web browser first makes contact with a Web server on port 443, also known as the HTTPS port (Hypertext Transport Protocol Secure). After a socket connection has been established between the two machines, the following occurs:

1. The server sends its SSL certificate to the browser.

2. The browser verifies the identity of the server through the SSL certificate.

3. The browser generates a symmetric encryption key.

4. The browser uses the SSL certificate to encrypt the symmetric encryption key.

5. The browser sends the encrypted key to the server.

6. The server decrypts the symmetric key with its private key counterpart of the public SSL certificate.

The browser and server can now encrypt and decrypt traffic based on a common knowledge of the symmetric key. Secure data interchange can now occur.

### Creating SSL certificates

To create your own SSL certificate for secure HTTP data interchange, you must first have an SSL-capable Web server. The Apache Web server, which comes with Fedora and other Linux systems, is SSL-capable. The following procedure for creating SSL certificates is done on a Fedora system that includes Apache from the httpd and mod_ssl packages. This procedure may be different for Apache on other Linux systems.

First install the necessary packages:

```
# yum install httpd mod_ssl openssl
```

Now create SSL certificates:

```
# cd /etc/pki/tls/certs
# make
This makefile allows you to create:
  o public/private key pairs
  o SSL certificate signing requests (CSRs)
  o self-signed SSL test certificates

To create a key pair, run "make SOMETHING.key".
To create a CSR, run "make SOMETHING.csr".
To create a test certificate, run "make SOMETHING.crt".
To create a key and a test certificate in one file, run "make SOMETHING.pem".

To create a key for use with Apache, run "make genkey".
To create a CSR for use with Apache, run "make certreq".
To create a test certificate for use with Apache, run "make testcert".

Examples:
  make server.key
  make server.csr
  make server.crt
  make stunnel.pem
  make genkey
  make certreq
  make testcert
```

The make command utilizes the makefile to create SSL certificates. Without any arguments the make command simply prints the information listed in the preceding example. The following defines each argument you can give to make:

- make server.key—Creates generic public/private key pairs.
- make server.csr—Generates a generic SSL certificate service request.
- make server.crt—Generates a generic SSL test certificate.
- make stunnel.pem—Generates a generic SSL test certificate, but puts the private key in the same file as the SSL test certificate.
- make genkey—Same as make server.key except it places the key in the ssl.key directory.
- make certreq—Same as make server.csr except it places the certificate service request in the ssl.csr directory.
- make testcert—Same as make server.crt except it places the test certificate in the ssl.crt directory.

### Using third-party certificate signers

In the real world, I know who you are because I recognize your face, your voice, and your mannerisms. On the Internet, I cannot see these things and must rely on a trusted third party to vouch for your identity. To ensure that a certificate is immutable, it has to be signed by a trusted third party when the certificate is issued and validated every time an end user taking advantage of your secure site loads it. The following is a list of the trusted third-party certificate signers:

- **GlobalSign**—www.globalsign.com/
- **GeoTrust**—https://www.geotrust.com/
- **VeriSign**—https://www.verisign.com/
- **RapidSSL**— https://www.rapidssl.com/
- **Thawte**—www.thawte.com/
- **EnTrust**—www.entrust.com/
- **ipsCA**—www.ipsca.com/
- **COMODO Group**—www.comodogroup.com/

## Note
**Because of the fluid nature of the certificate business, some of these companies may not be in business when you read this, while others may have come into existence. To get a more current list of certificate authorities, from your Firefox browser select Edit ⇨ Preferences. From the Preferences window that appears, select Advanced ⇨ Encryption, then select the View Certificates button. From the Certificate Manager window that appears, refer to the Authorities tab to see Certificate Authorities from which you have received certificates. ∎**

Each of these certificate authorities has gotten a chunk of cryptographic code embedded into nearly every Web browser in the world. This chunk of cryptographic code allows a Web browser to determine whether or not an SSL certificate is authentic. Without this validation, it would be easy for crackers to generate their own certificates and dupe people into thinking they are giving sensitive information to a reputable source.

Certificates that are not validated are called *self-signed certificates*. If you come across a site that has not had its identity authenticated by a trusted third party, your Web browser will display a message similar to the one shown in Figure 12-5.

A pop-up window alerts you when a site is not authenticated.

 **Secure Connection Failed**

bluestreak uses an invalid security certificate.

The certificate is not trusted because it is self signed.
The certificate is only valid for bluestreak

(Error code: sec_error_untrusted_issuer)

- This could be a problem with the server's configuration, or it could be someone trying to impersonate the server.
- If you have connected to this server successfully in the past, the error may be temporary, and you can try again later.

Or you can add an exception...

This does not necessarily mean that you are encountering anything illegal, immoral, or fattening. Many sites opt to go with *self-signed* certificates, not because they are trying to pull a fast one on you, but because there may not be any reason to validate the true owner of the certificate and they do not want to pay the cost of getting a certificate validated. Some reasons for using a *self-signed* certificate include:

- **The Web site accepts no input**—In this case, you as the end user have nothing to worry about. There is no one trying to steal your information because you aren't giving out any information. Most of the time this is done simply to secure the Web transmission from the server to you. The data in and of itself may not be sensitive, but, being a good netizen, the site has enabled you to secure the transmission to keep third parties from sniffing the traffic.

- **The Web site caters to a small clientele**—If you run a Web site that has a very limited set of customers, such as an Application Service Provider, you can simply inform your users that you have no certificate signer. They can browse the certificate information and validate it with you over the phone or in person.

- **Testing**—Paying for an SSL certificate makes no sense if you are only testing a new Web site or Web-based application. Use a *self-signed* certificate until you are ready to go live.

### Creating a certificate service request

To create a third-party validated SSL certificate from a Fedora Linux system, you must first start with a certificate service request (CSR). To create a CSR, do the following on your Web server:

```
# cd /etc/pki/tls/certs
# make certreq
umask 77 ; \
/usr/bin/openssl req -utf8 -new -key /etc/pki/tls/private/localhost.key
      -out /etc/pki/tls/certs/localhost.csr
    .
    .
    .
```

You will now be asked to enter a password to secure your private key. This password should be at least eight characters long, and should not be a dictionary word or contain numbers or punctuation. The characters you type will not appear on the screen, to prevent someone from shoulder surfing your password.

```
Enter pass phrase:
```

Enter the password again to verify.

```
Verifying - Enter pass phrase:
```

The certificate generation process now begins.

At this point, it is time to start adding some identifying information to the certificate that the third-party source will later validate. Before you can do this, you must unlock the private key you just created. Do so by typing the password you typed for your pass phrase. Then enter information as you are prompted. An example of a session for adding information for your certificate is shown here:

```
Enter pass phrase for /etc/pki/tls/private/localhost.key:  *******
You are about to be asked to enter information that will be incorporated
into your certificate request.
What you are about to enter is what is called
a Distinguished Name or a DN.
There are quite a few fields but you can leave some blank
For some fields there will be a default value,
If you enter '.', the field will be left blank.
-----
Country Name (2 letter code) [GB]:US
State or Province Name (full name) [Berkshire]: Connecticut
Locality Name (eg, city) [Newbury]: Mystic
Organization Name (eg, company) [My Company Ltd]:Acme Marina, Inc.
Organizational Unit Name (eg, section) []:InfoTech
Common Name (eg, your name or your server's hostname) []:www.acmemarina.com
Email Address []: webmaster@acmemarina.com
```

To complete the process, you will be asked whether you want to add any extra attributes to your certificate. Unless you have a reason to provide more information, you should simply press Enter at each of the following prompts to leave them blank.

```
Please enter the following 'extra' attributes
to be sent with your certificate request
A challenge password []:
An optional company name []:
```

### Getting your CSR signed

After your CSR has been created, you need to send it to a signing authority for validation. The first step in this process is to select a signing authority. Each signing authority has different deals, prices, and products. Check out each of the signing authorities listed in the "Using Third-Party Certificate Signers" section earlier in this chapter to determine which works best for you. The following are areas where signing authorities differ:

- Credibility and stability
- Pricing
- Browser recognition
- Warranties
- Support
- Certificate strength

After you have selected your certificate signer, you have to go through some validation steps. Each signer has a different method of validating identity and certificate information. Some require that you fax articles of incorporation, whereas others require a company officer be made available to talk to a validation operator. At some point in the process you will be asked to copy and paste the contents of the CSR you created into the signer's Web form.

```
# cd /etc/pki/tls/certs/
# cat localhost.csr
-----BEGIN CERTIFICATE REQUEST-----
MIIB6jCCAVMCAQAwgakxCzAJBgNVBAYTAlVTMRQwEgYDVQQIEwtDb25uZWN0aWN1
dDEPMA0GA1UEBxMGTXlzdGljMRowGAYDVQQKExFBY211IElhcmluYySwgSW5jLjER
MA8GA1UECxMISW5mb1RlY2gxGzAZBgNVBAMTEnd3dy5hY211bWFyaW5hLmNvbTEn
MCUGCSqGSIb3DQEJARYYd2VibWFzdGVyQGFjbWVtYXJpbmEuY29tMIGfMA0GCSqG
SIb3DQEBAQUAA4GNADCBiQKBgQDcYH4pjMxKM1dyXRmcoz8uBVOvwlNZHyRWw8ZG
u2eCbvgi6w4wXuHwaDuxbuDBmw//Y9DMI2MXg4wDq4xmPi35EsO1Ofw4ytZJn1yW
aU6cJVQro46OnXyaqXZOPiRCxUSnGRU+OnsqKGjf7LPpXv29S3QvMIBTYWzCkNnc
gWBwwwIDAQABoAAwDQYJKoZIhvcNAQEEBQADgYEANv6eJOaJZGzopNR5h2YkR9Wg
18oBl3mgoPH60Sccw3pWsoW4qbOWq7on8dS/++QOCZWZI1gefgaSQMInKZ1II7Fs
YIwYBgpoPTMC4bpOZZtURCyQWrKIDXQBXw7BlU/3A25nvkRY7vgNL9Nq+7681EJ8
W9AJ3PX4vb2+ynttcBI=
-----END CERTIFICATE REQUEST-----
```

You can use your mouse to copy and paste the CSR into the signer's Web form.

After you have completed the information validation, paid for the signing, and answered all the questions, you have completed most of the process. Within 48 to 72 hours you should receive an e-mail with your shiny new SSL certificate in it. The certificate will look similar to the following:

```
-----BEGIN CERTIFICATE-----
MIIEFjCCA3+gAwIBAgIQMI262Zd6njZgN97tJAVFODANBgkqhkiG9w0BAQQFADCB
ujEfMBOGA1UEChMWVmVyaVNpZ24gVHJlc3QgTmV0d29yazEXMBUGA1UECxMOVmVy
aVNpZ24sIEluXy4xMzAxBgNVBAsTKlZlcmlTaWduIEludGVybmF0aW9uYWwgU2Vy
dmVyIENBIC0gZ2xhc3MgMzFJMEcG10rY2g0Dd3LnZlcmlzaWduLmNvbS9DUFMg
SW5jb3JwLmJ51FJlZi4gTElBQklMSVRZIExURC4oYyk5NyBWZXJpU2lnbjAeFw0w
MzAxMTUwMDAwMDBaFw0wNDAxMTUyMzU5NTlaMIGuMQswCQYDVQQGEwJVUzETMBEG
A1UECBMKV2FzaGluZ3RvHiThErE371UEBxQLRmVkZXJhbCBYYXkxGzAZBgNVBAoU
EklETSBTZXJ2aWNlcywgSW5jLjEMMAoGA1UECxQDd3d3MTMwMQYDVQQLFCpUZXJt
cyBvZiB1c2UgYXQgd3d3LnZlcmlzawduLmNvbS9ycGGKGMpMDAxFDASBgNVBAMU
C21kbXNlcnYuY29tMIGfMA0GCSqGSIb3DQEBAQUAA4GNADCBjQKBgQDaHSk+uz0f
7jjDFEnqT8UBa1L3yFILXFjhj3XpMXLGWzLmkDmdJjXsa4x7AhEprlubuVNhJVIO
FnLDopsx4pyr4n+P8FyS4M5grbcQzy2YnkM2jyqVF/7yOW2pD130t4eacYYaz4Qg
q9pTxhUzjEG4twvKCAFWfuhEoGu1CMV2qQ1DAQABo4IBJTCCASEwCQYDVR0TBAIw
ADBEBgNVHSAEPTA7MDkGC2CGSAGG+EUBBxcDMCOwKAYIKwYBBQUHAgEWEHGhOdHBz
Oi8vd3d3LnZlcmlzawduLmNvbS9ycGEwCwYDVRRPBAQDAgWgMCgGA1UdJQQhMB8G
CWCGSAGG+EIEMOOcOwIYBQUHAwEGCCsGAQUFBwmCMDQGCCsGAQUFBwEBBCgwJjAk
BggrBgEFBQcwAYYYaHROcDovL29jc2AudmVyaXNpZ24uY29tMEYGA1UdHwQ/MD0w
O6A5oDeGNWhOdHA6Ly9jcmwudmVyaXNpZ24uY29tL0NsYXNzMOludGVybmF0aW9u
YWxTZXJ2ZXIuY3JsMBkGCmCGSAGG+E+f4Nfc3zYJODA5NzMwMTEyMA0GCSqGSIb3
DQEBBAUAA4GBAJ/PsVttmIDkQai5nLeudLceb1F4isXP17B68wXLkIeRu4Novu13
8lLZXnaR+acHeStRO1b3rQPjgv2ylmwjkPmC1WjoeYfdxH7+Mbg/6fomnK9auWAT
WFOiFW/+a80WRYQJLMA2VQOVhX4znjpGcVNY9AQSHm1UiESJy7vtd1iX
-----END CERTIFICATE-----
```

Copy and paste this certificate into an empty file called `server.crt`, which should reside in the `/etc/pki/tls/certs` directory. Configure the SSLCertificateFile and SSLCertificateKeyFile values in the SSL file (`/etc/httpd/conf.d/ssl.conf`) and restart your Web server:

```
# service httpd restart
```

Assuming your Web site was previously working fine, you can now view it in a secure fashion by placing an "s" after the `http` in the Web address. So if you previously viewed your Web site at `www.acmemarina.com`, you can now view it in a secure fashion by going to `https://www.acmemarina.com`.

### Creating self-signed certificates

Generating and running a self-signed SSL certificate is much easier than having a signed certificate. To generate a self-signed SSL certificate on a Fedora system, do the following:

1. Remove the key and certificate that currently exist:

```
# rm /etc/pki/tls/private/localhost.key
# rm /etc/pki/tls/certs/localhost.crt
```

2. Create your own server key:

```
# cd /etc/pki/tls/certs
# make genkey
```

3. Create the self-signed certificate by typing the following:

```
# make testcert
umask 77 ; \
        /usr/bin/openssl genrsa -des3 1024 >
/etc/pki/tls/private/localhost.key
Generating RSA private key, 1024 bit long modulus
............................++++++
..................................................................++++++
e is 65537 (0x10001)
Enter pass phrase: *******
Verifying - Enter pass phrase: *******
Enter pass phrase for /etc/pki/tls/private/localhost.key: *******
       .
       .
       .
```

At this point, it is time to start adding some identifying information to the certificate. Before you can do this, you must unlock the private key you just created. Do so by typing the password you typed earlier. Then follow this sample procedure:

```
You will be asked to enter information that will be incorporated
into your certificate request.
What you are about to enter is called a Distinguished Name or DN.
There are quite a few fields but you can leave some blank
For some fields there will be a default value,
If you enter '.', the field will be left blank.
-----
Country Name (2 letter code) [GB]: US
State or Province Name (full name) [Berkshire]: Ohio
Locality Name (eg, city) [Newbury]: Cincinnati
Organization Name (eg, company) [My Company Ltd]:Industrial Press, Inc.
Organizational Unit Name (eg, section) []:IT
Common Name (eg, your name or your server's hostname)
[]:www.industrialpressinc.com
Email Address []: webmaster@industrialpressinc.com
```

The generation process in this example creates the file named /etc/pki/tls/certs/local-host.crt. Within the virtual host you created in the /etc/httpd/conf.d/ssl.conf file, identify the certificate file using the following directive:

```
SSLCertificateFile /etc/pki/tls/certs/localhost.crt
```

Then all you need to do is restart your Web server and add `https` instead of `http` in front of your URL. Don't forget that you'll get a certificate validation message from your Web browser, which you can safely ignore.

### Restarting your Web server

By now you've probably noticed that your Web server requires you to enter your certificate password every time it is started. This is to prevent someone from breaking into your server and stealing your private key. Should this happen, you are safe in the knowledge that the private key is a jumbled mess. The cracker will not be able to make use of it. Without such protection, a cracker could get your private key and easily masquerade as you, appearing to be legitimate in all cases.

If you just cannot stand having to enter a password every time your Web server starts, and are willing to accept the increased risk, you can remove the password encryption on your private key. Simply do the following:

```
# cd /etc/pki/tls/private
# /usr/bin/openssl rsa -in localhost.key -out  localhost.key
Enter pass phrase for localhost.key: *******
```

You should now be able to restart the server without entering a pass phrase.

### Troubleshooting your certificates

The following tips should help if you are having problems with your SSL certificate:

- Only one SSL certificate per IP address is allowed. If you want to add more than one SSL-enabled Web site to your server, you must bind another IP address to the network interface.

- Make sure you aren't blocking port 443 on your Web server. All `https` requests come in on port 443. If you are blocking it, you will not be able to get secure pages.

- The certificate lasts for one year only. When that year is up, you have to renew your certificate with your certificate authority. Each certificate authority has a different procedure for doing this; check the authority's Web site for more details.

- Make sure you have the mod_ssl package installed. If it is not installed, you will not be able to serve any SSL-enabled traffic.

# Using Security Tools from Linux Live CDs

If you suspect your computers or networks have been exploited, a wide range of security tools is available for Linux that you can use to scan for viruses, do forensics, or monitor activities of intruders. The best way to learn about and use many of these tools is by using dedicated, bootable Linux distributions built specifically for security.

## Advantages of security live CDs

One great advantage of using live CDs or DVDs to check the security of a system is that it separates the tools you use to check a system from the system itself. In other words, because the tools for finding problems on an installed system may themselves be compromised, a live CD of trusted software can be a good way to ensure that you are testing a potentially infected system with clean tools.

If despite your best efforts (good passwords, firewalls, checking log files, and so on) you believe an intruder may have gained control of your system, you can use a live CD to check it out. Security live CDs such as SystemRescueCd, INSERT, and BackTrack (all included on this book's CD or DVD) are great tools for checking and fixing your system.

### Cross-Reference
**See Chapter 28 for more information on bootable security and rescue CDs.** ■

## Using INSERT to check for rootkits

If an intruder gains access to your Linux system, to try to take over control of that system (and use it for more than just a hit-and-run), the intruder might install what is called a *rootkit*. A rootkit is a set of software that the intruder will use to

- Carry out his intent (such as hosting false Web content from your server)
- Hide his activities from your view

Rootkits can employ different methods for hiding what they do. Often a rootkit will replace common system commands with its own version of those commands. So, for example, replacing `ls` and `ps` could be modified to not list the content added to your machine or not show certain processes running on your system, respectively.

The `chkrootkit` command is a good tool for checking for well-known rootkits, as well as for generally checking system files to see whether they have been infected or not. This tool will check for infections in disk-checking tools (such as `du`, `find`, and `ls`), process table tools (`ps` and `pstree`), login-related commands (`login`, `rlogin`, `slogin`), and many other tools. Here's how to run `chkrootkit` from INSERT:

1. Insert the CD that comes with this book into the CD drive and reboot.
2. From the boot screen, choose Insert. INSERT should boot to a desktop.
3. To be able to check the Linux system installed on your hard disk, you need to mount the partition representing your installed Linux system. Using the mount.app applet (displayed in the lower-right corner of the screen), click the arrows on that applet to click through the available storage media. If Linux was installed on the first partition of the first hard disk, select hda1. Then click the mount button to mount that partition.

4. Open a Terminal window by right-clicking the desktop and selecting Terminal Session ➪ Aterm - super user. A Terminal window opens.

5. Run the chkrootkit command and save the output to a file. For example, run the following command to check the file system mounted on /mnt/hda1 and send the output to a file named chkroot-output.txt:

```
# chkrootkit -r /mnt/hda1 > /tmp/chkroot-output.txt
```

6. When the command completes, page through the output. For example:

```
# less /tmp/chkroot-output.txt
ROOTDIR is '/mnt/hda1/'
Checking 'amd' ... not found
Checking 'basename' ... not infected
   .
   .
   .
```

7. Press the spacebar to page through the output. The output should reveal the following:

- If a rootkit has been planted on your system, some commands will likely come up as infected.

- If any files or directories implanted by commonly known rootkits are detected, those will be noted. The command checks for more than 60 known rootkits.

- If any suspicious-looking files appear, they will be listed so you can check them (although they might not represent the presence of a rootkit).

If the search turns up a rootkit, chances are that someone else has control of your machine. Often the best course of action is to reinstall the system. You may be able to just replace those commands that have been infected, but if you do, you first want to make sure that multiple backdoors have not already been placed on your system.

# Summary

Securing your Linux system is something you need to do from the very beginning and continue as you use your Linux system. By implementing good security practices (such as practices described in the security checklist at the beginning of this chapter), you stand a better chance of keeping out intruders over the long haul.

Going forward, you can help keep your Linux system secure by using encrypted network applications (such as ssh), monitoring log files, and adhering to good password techniques. If your Linux system is being used as a server, you need to take particular care in narrowing the access to the server and protecting data. To that end, you can use such tools as TCP wrappers (to limit who can use your server) and certificates (to ensure that both ends of communications with your Web server are authenticated).

# Part IV

# Setting Up
# Linux Servers

# Running a Linux, Apache, MySQL, and PHP (LAMP) Server

W ith the growing availability of broadband Internet connections and a popular desire to run personal Web sites and Web logs (blogs), an increasing number of people are setting up Web application servers on their home Internet connections. Web applications are also finding more popularity in business environments because Web applications reduce the number of programs that need to be maintained on workstations.

One popular variety of Web application server is known as a *LAMP server* because it brings together Linux, Apache, MySQL, and PHP. LAMP servers combine components from several open source projects to form a fast, reliable, and economical platform for other readily available applications.

This chapter helps you install and configure your own LAMP server. It begins with an introduction to the various components, guides you through the installation and configuration, and finishes with the installation of a sample Web application.

The examples in this chapter are based on a system running Ubuntu but conceptually should work on other distributions, if you take into account that other Linux systems use different ways to install the software and start and stop services. Descriptions of how to set up LAMP configuration files, however, should work across multiple Linux distributions with only slight modifications. You can find more information about Ubuntu in Chapter 17.

## IN THIS CHAPTER

**Components of a LAMP server**

**Setting up your LAMP server**

**Operating your LAMP server**

**Troubleshooting**

**Securing your Web traffic with SSL/TLS**

# Components of a LAMP Server

You're probably familiar with Linux by this point, so this section focuses on the other three components—Apache, MySQL, and PHP—and the functions they serve within a LAMP system. (Sometimes the "P" in LAMP is used to indicate that the Perl or Python scripting language is used for the applications running on a LAMP server.)

## Apache

Within a LAMP server, Apache HTTPD (also known as the Apache HTTP Server) provides the service with which the client Web browsers communicate. The daemon runs in the background on your server and waits for requests from clients. Web browsers connect to the HTTP daemon and send requests, which the daemon interprets, sending back the appropriate data. Apache HTTPD includes an interface that allows modules to tie into the process to handle specific portions of a request. Among other things, modules are available to handle the processing of scripting languages such as Perl or PHP within Web documents and to add encryption to connections between clients and the server.

Apache began as a collection of patches and improvements from the National Center for Supercomputing Applications (NCSA), University of Illinois, Urbana-Champaign, to the HTTP daemon. The NCSA HTTP daemon was the most popular HTTP server at the time, but had started to show its age after its author, Rob McCool, left NCSA in mid-1994.

## Note
**Another project that came from NCSA is Mosaic. Most modern Web browsers can trace their origins to Mosaic.** ■

In early 1995, a group of developers formed the Apache Group and began making extensive modifications to the NCSA HTTPD code base. Apache soon replaced NCSA HTTPD as the most popular Web server, a title it still holds today.

The Apache Group later formed the Apache Software Foundation (ASF) to promote the development of Apache and other free software. With the start of new projects at ASF, the Apache server became known as Apache HTTPD, although the two terms are still used interchangeably. Currently, ASF has more than 60 projects, including Jakarta (open source Java solutions), MyFaces (a Web application framework), and SpamAssassin (an e-mail filtering program).

## MySQL

MySQL is an open source DBMS (database management system) that has become popular among Webmasters because of its speed, stability, and features. MySQL consists of a server that handles storage and access to data, and clients to handle interfacing with and managing the server. Client libraries are also included, and they can be used by third-party programs, such as PHP, to connect to the server.

In a LAMP server, MySQL is used for storing data appropriate to the Web applications that are being used. Common uses include data such as usernames and passwords, entries in a journal, and data files.

## Note

**If you are not sure how a database works, refer to the sidebar "How MySQL Databases Are Structured" later in this chapter. ■**

MySQL was originally developed by Michael (Monty) Widenius of TcX (Sweden). In 1994, TcX needed a backend database for Web applications and decided to use one supporting SQL, a standardized and widely recognized language for interacting with databases.

TcX investigated the free databases that were available at the time, plus some commercial databases, but could not find a system that supported the features it needed and could handle its large databases at the same time. Because it already had experience writing database programs, TcX decided that the best way to get what it wanted was to develop a new system that supported SQL.

In 1995, TcX released the source code for MySQL on the Internet. MySQL was not an open source program at that time (because of some of the restrictions in its license), but it still began to see widespread use. MySQL was later released under the GNU General Public License (GPL) and the company MySQL AB was formed to manage MySQL. In February 2008, Sun Microsystems acquired MySQL AB. After Oracle acquired Sun, it became owner of the MySQL project.

# PHP

PHP is a programming language that was developed specifically for use in Web scripts. It is preferred by many developers because it's designed to be embedded within HTML documents, making it simpler to manage Web content and scripts within a single file.

PHP originated as a set of Perl scripts by Rasmus Lerdorf called *PHP/FI (Personal Home Page/ Forms Interpreter)*. Over time, more features were implemented, and Rasmus rewrote PHP/FI in C.

In late 1997, Andi Gutmans and Zeev Suraski began working on a complete rewrite of PHP/FI. As the language evolved and more features were implemented, Gutmans and Suraski decided that it would be appropriate to rename the project to more accurately reflect these features. The name PHP Hypertext Preprocessor (PHP) was chosen, with Lerdorf's approval, to maintain familiarity for users of PHP/FI.

The core features of PHP are included within the PHP code itself, and additional features are implemented in the form of extensions. The latest stable version of PHP is 5.2.6, but several implementations still include the libapache-mod-php4 (PHP 4) package and PHP 6 is in development. Among the major changes offered in PHP 5 is enhanced security. This release improved the security features that have always been in PHP and fixed some possible holes. This made the language even more stable. Additional information about each release, and what it offers, can be found at `www.php.net/`.

# Setting Up Your LAMP Server

Before proceeding through the examples in this section, be sure that your Linux operating system is installed and configured. The specific instructions in this section were done on an Ubuntu system. However, the same procedure should work on other Debian-based systems with few or no differences. If you try this on a different Linux system, understand that such things as software packaging, the location of startup scripts and configuration files, and other features may be different.

When you install your Linux system, you typically choose whether to install a set of software packages that are appropriate for a workstation or a server. You may choose to set up a server on a system that has been configured using the layout and software packages intended for a workstation. However, that's not recommended unless you are providing services for only a very small number of users whom you know well and trust. In fact, many systems administrators don't even like to have the X Window System and other GUI components installed on a server.

## Note
Another option to using the Apache package that comes with Ubuntu is to use a LAMPP server. LAMPP is an all-in-one LAMP server with PERL support added. The XAMPP project (www.apachefriends.org/en/xampp.html) is one implementation of a LAMPP server (which is available as a Windows server as well). XAMPP is a really good quick and dirty way to get a LAMPP server running. It is also good for testing pages before publishing when you only have one machine. ■

## Installing Apache

The next step toward a functioning LAMP server is to install the Apache HTTP server, which can be found in the apache package. Use APT to retrieve and install the package:

```
$ sudo apt-get install apache2
```

The server should automatically start after the installation is finished, which means that you're now ready to install PHP.

## Installing PHP

Now you're ready to install and test the PHP module in Apache. This is the most common method for installing PHP, but it introduces some security concerns on multiuser systems because all PHP scripts are run as the same user as the Apache daemon. Be sure to read the Security section of the PHP manual at http://php.net/manual/en/security.php before granting other users access to manipulate PHP files on your server.

The PHP Apache module is contained in the php5 package, which is installed using APT. The following lines download and install the Apache php5 module and the MySQL extensions, configure Apache to load the module automatically, and instruct Apache to reload its configuration:

```
$ sudo apt-get install libapache2-mod-php5 php5-mysql php5-gd
$ sudo /etc/init.d/apache2 restart
```

## Note

**Just as the numbering and versions of Apache can sometimes be confusing, similar thoughts can be expressed about PHP. As of this writing, there are active development versions in both 5.*x* and 4.4.*x* (and PHP 6 is under development).** ■

At this point, Apache should be ready to process HTTP requests, complete with processing of PHP files. To test it, create a file named `/var/www/info.php` containing a call to the `phpinfo()` function:

```
$ sudo cat > /var/www/info.php
<?php
    phpinfo();
?>
^D
$ sudo chmod 644 /var/www/info.php
```

The `^D` means that you should press Ctrl+D on your keyboard. This tells the `cat` command that you are at the end of the input. Now try opening the page by going to `http://localhost/info.php`. You should see a page full of information about your Apache and PHP installation, as shown in Figure 13-1.

If, instead of an information page, you are prompted to download the file, check the appropriate PHP installation section (earlier in the chapter) to verify that all the steps were completed successfully.

---

**FIGURE 13-1**

The PHP information page

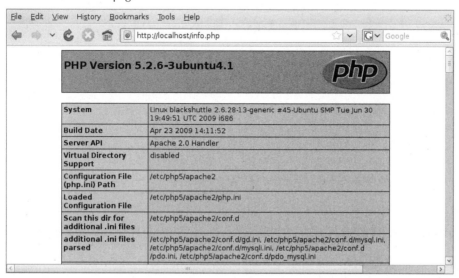

After everything is tested and working, you should remove the info.php file so that it can't be used by potential attackers to gather specifics about your system:

```
$ sudo rm -f /var/www/info.php
```

## Installing MySQL

The MySQL database system is divided into three main packages: the server, clients, and client libraries. The server is contained within the mysql-server package and requires the other two to function. APT is aware of this, which means the packages will be installed automatically when you install mysql-server:

```
$ sudo apt-get install mysql-server
```

### Note

If you are using a Debian system, make sure the host name settings have been configured as described in Chapter 19 before installing the mysql-server package. Failure to do so could result in an error that causes the installation to fail. ■

Access to databases within MySQL is managed based on account information stored within the mysql database. As with UNIX systems, the superuser account is named root. The default installation asks you to set a password on this account. If you don't set it at this point, you can always set it later.

## How MySQL Databases Are Structured

For those who aren't familiar with how a database system is structured, here's a quick introduction:

- *Databases* are the basic organizational block in a database system. Most database systems (including MySQL) are designed to support multiple databases from a single server. This allows separate databases to be created for different users or different functions.

- *Tables* are found within a database. A table is very much like a spreadsheet in that it has *rows* and *columns*. Columns define the different types of data that every entry can or must have, and every entry takes the form of a row. A database can hold multiple tables, allowing you to have many different data sets within a single database.

## Operating Your LAMP Server

With the components of your LAMP server installed and running, you are ready to configure Apache and try it out. For this example, Apache is set up to serve content for your own domain using a feature called *virtual hosting*, after which you'll see how to install the Coppermine Photo Gallery program, which enables you to create an online photo gallery on your LAMP server.

## Editing your apache configuration files

The configuration files for Apache HTTPD are incredibly flexible, meaning that you can configure the server to behave in almost any manner you want. This flexibility comes at the cost of increased complexity in the form of a large number of configuration options (called *directives*), but in practice you'll need to be familiar with only a few directives.

## Note
See `http://httpd.apache.org/docs/` **for a complete list of directives supported by Apache.** ■

In Ubuntu, the Apache configuration is stored in text files read by the Apache server, beginning with `/etc/apache2/apache2.conf`. Configuration is read from start to finish, with most directives being processed in the order in which they are read.

Additional files may also be read based on the `AccessConfig`, `ResourceConfig`, and `Include` directives. On modern installations, the `AccessConfig` and `ResourceConfig` options point to empty files, and the traditional contents of those files have been moved to the main `apache2.conf` file.

The `Include` directive is distinct from `AccessConfig` and `ResourceConfig` in that it can appear more than once and can include more than one file at a time. Files referenced by `Include` directives are processed as if their contents appeared at the location of the relevant `Include` statement. `Include` can point to a single file, to a directory in which all files are read, or to a wildcard that specifies a specific set of files within a directory. For example, virtual host files are included in `apache2.conf` by this line:

```
Include /etc/apache2/sites-enabled/
```

## Note
**Subdirectories are also processed when** `Include` **points to a directory.** ■

The scope of many configuration directives can be altered based on context. In other words, some parameters may be set on a global level and then changed for a specific file, directory, or virtual host. Other directives are always global in nature, such as those specifying which IP addresses the server listens on, and some are valid only when applied to a specific location.

Locations are configured in the form of a start tag containing the location type and a resource location, followed by the configuration options for that location, and finishing with an end tag. This form is often called a *configuration block,* and looks very similar to HTML. A special type of configuration block, known as a *location block,* is used to override settings for specific files or directories. These blocks take the following form:

```
<locationtag specifier>
(options specific to objects matching the specifier go within this block)
</locationtag>
```

Different types of location tags exist and are selected based on the type of resource location that is being specified. The specifier that is included in the start tag is handled based on the type of location tag. The ones you generally use and encounter are Directory, Files, and Location.

## Note

In this chapter, Location **refers specifically to the third type of tag, and** *location* **refers generically to any of the three.** ■

- **Directory** tags are used to specify a path based on the location on the file system. For instance, <Directory /> refers to the root directory on the computer. Directories inherit settings from directories above them, with the most specific Directory block overriding less-specific ones, regardless of the order in which they appear in the configuration files.

- **Files** tags are used to specify files by name. Files tags can be contained within Directory blocks to limit them to files under that directory. Settings within a Files block will override the ones in Directory blocks.

- **Location** tags are used to specify the URI used to access a file or directory. This is different from Directory in that it relates to the address contained within the request and not to the real location of the file on the drive. Location tags are processed last and override the settings in Directory and Files blocks.

Match versions of these tags—DirectoryMatch, FilesMatch, and LocationMatch—have the same function but can contain regular expressions in the resource specification. FilesMatch and LocationMatch blocks are processed at the same time as Files and Location, respectively. DirectoryMatch blocks are processed after Directory blocks.

Apache can also be configured to process configuration options contained within files with the name specified in the AccessFileName directive (which is generally set to .htaccess). Directives in access configuration files are applied to all objects under the directory they contain, including subdirectories and their contents. Access configuration files are processed at the same time as Directory blocks, using a similar "most specific match" order.

## Note

**Access control files are useful for allowing users to change specific settings without having access to the server configuration files. The configuration directives permitted within an access configuration file are determined by the** AllowOverride **setting on the directory in which they are contained. Some directives do not make sense at that level and generally result in a "server internal error" message when trying to access the URI. The** AllowOverride **option is covered in detail at** http://httpd.apache.org/docs/mod/core.html#allowoverride. ■

Three directives commonly found in location blocks and access control files are DirectoryIndex, Options, and ErrorDocument:

- DirectoryIndex tells Apache which file to load when the URI contains a directory but not a filename. This directive doesn't work in Files blocks.

- Options is used to adjust how Apache handles files within a directory. The ExecCGI option tells Apache that files in that directory can be run as CGI scripts, and the Includes option tells Apache that server-side includes (SSI) are permitted. Also commonly used is the Indexes option, which tells Apache to generate a list of files if one of the filenames found in the DirectoryIndex setting is missing. An absolute list of options can be specified, or the list of options can be modified by adding + or - in front of an option name. See http://httpd.apache.org/docs/mod/core. html#options for more information.

- ErrorDocument directives can be used to specify which file to send in the event of an error. The directive must specify an error code and the full URI for the error document. Possible error codes include 403 (access denied), 404 (file not found), and 500 (server internal error). You can find more information about the ErrorDocument directive at http://httpd.apache.org/docs/mod/core.html#errordocument.

Another common use for location blocks and access control files is to limit access to a resource. The Allow directive can be used to permit access to matching hosts, and the Deny directive can be used to forbid it. Both of these options can occur more than once within a block and are handled based on the Order setting. Setting Order to Deny, Allow permits access to any host that is not listed in a Deny directive. A setting of Allow, Deny denies access to any host not allowed in an Allow directive.

As with most other options, the most specific Allow or Deny option for a host is used, meaning that you can Deny access to a range and Allow access to subsets of that range. By adding the Satisfy option and some additional parameters, you can add password authentication. For more information about access control, see http://httpd.apache.org/docs/mod/mod_ access.html.

Location blocks (in the generic sense) can be enclosed within a VirtualHost block. Virtual hosts, which are described in greater detail in the next section, are a convenient (and almost essential) tool for altering server behavior based on the server address or name that a request is directed to. Most global configuration options are applied to virtual hosts but can be overridden by directives within the VirtualHost block.

## Adding a virtual host to Apache

Apache supports the creation of separate Web sites within a single server to keep content separate. Individual sites are configured on the same server in the form of virtual hosts, which also are useful when only a single site will be used. Here's how to configure a virtual host:

Create a file named /etc/apache2/sites-available/example.org.conf using this template:

```
NameVirtualHost *:80
<VirtualHost *:80>
    ServerName      www.example.org
```

```
        ServerAlias      web.example.org
        DocumentRoot     /home/username/public_html/
  DirectoryIndex  index.php index.html index.htm
  </VirtualHost>
```

The NameVirtualHost line tells Apache to determine which virtual host to serve documents from based on the hostname provided by the HTTP client. The *:80 means that requests to port 80 on any IP address will be treated in this manner.

Similarly, the *:80 specification in the VirtualHost block indicates what address and port this virtual host applies to. The port is optional for both the NameVirtualHost and VirtualHost specifications, but should always be used to prevent interference with SSL virtual hosts.

The ServerName and ServerAlias lines tell Apache which names this virtual host should be recognized as, so replace them with names appropriate to your site. You can leave out the ServerAlias line if you do not have any alternate names for the server, and you can specify more than one name per ServerAlias line or have multiple ServerAlias lines if you have several alternate names.

The DocumentRoot specifies where the Web documents for this site are stored. If you plan to have more than one site per user, you will need to modify this layout appropriately. Replace *username* with the name of the account that is administrating the Web site. For this example, each Web site must be administered by a different user account.

Having your virtual host file in the sites-available directory does not enable it. For it to be enabled, you must create a link to that file from the /etc/apache2/sites-enabled directory. In Ubuntu (and other Debian-based systems), you can use the a2ensite command as follows:

```
$ sudo a2ensite example.org.conf
Site example.org.conf installed; run /etc/init.d/apache2 reload to enable
```

With the host enabled, use apache2ctl to check the configuration, and then do a graceful restart:

```
$ sudo apache2ctl configtest
Syntax OK
$ sudo apache2ctl graceful
```

## Note

Unless you have already created it, you will receive a warning about public_html **not existing. Run** mkdir ~/public_html **as the user that owns the Web site in order to create it.** ∎

Additional virtual hosts can be added by repeating the VirtualHost block and repeating the configuration test (configtest) and reload (graceful) steps.

## Note

Keeping individual virtual hosts in separate files is a convenient way to manage virtual hosts. However, you should be careful to keep your primary virtual host in a file that will be read before the others because the first virtual host receives requests for site names that don't match any in your configuration. In a commercial Web-hosting environment, it is common to make a special default virtual host that contains an error message indicating that no site by that name has been configured. ■

## User content and the UserDir setting

In situations in which you do not have the ability to set up a virtual host for every user that you want to provide Web space for, you can easily make use of the mod_userdir module in Apache. With this module enabled (which it is not by default), the public_html directory under every user's home directory is available to the Web at http://*servername*/~*username*/. For example, a user named wtucker on www.example.org stores Web content in /home/wtucker/public_html. That content would be available from http://www.example.org/~wtucker.

To enable the mod_userdir module, as well as other installed modules that are not enabled by default, you need to create links from the appropriate .load and .conf files in the /etc/apache2/mods-available directory to the mods-enabled directory. In Ubuntu, you can do this with the a2enmod command and restart the server as follows:

```
$ a2enmod userdir
Module userdir installed; run /etc/init.d/apache2 force-reload to enable.
$ sudo apache2ctl graceful
```

## Installing a Web application: Coppermine Photo Gallery

After your LAMP server is operational, you can begin installing or creating applications to run on it. One such application is Coppermine Photo Gallery (CPG), the installation of which is demonstrated in this section. CPG is a Web-based photo gallery management system written in PHP. Through its Web interface, you can upload pictures to your own photo galleries, which will be available on the Web through your LAMP server.

You can install CPG under a virtual host or under a user's home directory on your main host. A single server can easily support many CPG installations using either of these methods.

To install CPG on the Ubuntu system described in this chapter, follow these steps:

1. Install the unzip and imagemagick programs. Unzip is used to unpack the CPG program after downloading, and imagemagick is used to resize images and create thumbnails:

```
$ sudo apt-get install unzip imagemagick
```

2. Create a MySQL database for CPG. You can use a database name other than cpg if you want. The database username (the part before the @'localhost' in the GRANT statement) and the database name do not need to match. Be sure to replace *mypassword* with something different:

```
$ sudo mysql -u root -p
Enter password:
Welcome to the MySQL monitor.  Commands end with ; or \g.
Your MySQL connection id is 8
Server version: 5.0.41a-3ubuntu5.1 (Ubuntu)

Type 'help;' or '\h' for help.  Type '\c' to clear the
buffer.

mysql> CREATE DATABASE cpg;
Query OK, 1 row affected (0.00 sec)

mysql> GRANT ALL PRIVILEGES ON cpg.*
TO 'cpg'@'localhost' IDENTIFIED BY 'mypassword';
Query OK, 0 rows affected (0.00 sec)

mysql> \q
Bye
```

3. Log in as the user that will own the CPG installation and download the latest version from the Internet as follows:

```
$ mkdir -p ~/public_html
$ cd ~/public_html
$ wget http://internap.dl.sourceforge.net/sourceforge/coppermine/cpg1.4.18.zip
--19:30:46--  http://internap.dl.sourceforge.net/coppermine/cpg1.4.18.zip
           => `cpg1.4.18.zip'
Resolving internap.dl.sourceforge.net... 64.74.207.41, 66.35.250.221,...
Connecting to internap.dl.sourceforge.net[64.74.207.41]:80... connected.
HTTP request sent, awaiting response...200 OK
Length: 3,824,914 [application/zip]

100%[=======================>] 3,824,914     618.94K/s    ETA 00:00
19:30:53 (611.29 KB/s) - `cpg1.4.18.zip' saved [3824914/3824914]
```

4. Unpack the archive:

```
$ unzip cpg1.4.18.zip
Archive:  cpg1.4.18.zip
  inflating: cpg1418/addfav.php
  inflating: cpg1418/xp_publish.php
[...]
  inflating: cpg1418/zipdownload.php
```

5. Rename the freshly unpacked `cpg` directory, and then set the permissions so that files can be uploaded from PHP:

```
$ mv cpg1418 photos
$ cd photos
$ chmod 777 include
$ find albums -type d | xargs chmod 777
```

6. Go to a Web browser on any machine that can reach your LAMP server over the network and open the `install.php` script under your `coppermine` directory.

   - If you're installing CPG under a user directory under your main host, the URL is `http://servername/~username/photos/install.php`.
   - If you're installing CPG under a virtual host, the URL is `http://virtualhostname/photos/install.php`.

7. Configure CPG to work with your installation by filling in the following fields and selecting Let's Go!:

   - **Username and Password**—The administrative login and password that you will use to administer CPG.
   - **Email Address**—The administrator's (your) e-mail address.
   - **MySQL Host**—The server name that CGP will connect to for the database. In this case, you want to use `localhost`.
   - **MySQL Database Name**—The name of the database that you created in Step 2. (In the example, I used `cpg`.)
   - **MySQL Username and Password**—The username and password that you created in Step 2 for accessing the database. (In the example, I used `cpg` and `mypassword`, respectively.)
   - **MySQL table prefix**—The prefix for the tables that will be used by CPG. The default value (`cpg14x_`) is fine.
   - **ImageMagick path**—The directory containing the imagemagick binary. On Debian systems, this is `/usr/bin`.

8. You're now done installing CPG. At this point you can click Let's Continue to see the default Coppermine Photo Gallery page. You can use this CPG Web interface to create photo galleries and upload photos. Figure 13-2 shows a sample gallery.

**FIGURE 13-2**

A sample Coppermine photo gallery

Although a complete description of the dozens of features of the Coppermine Photo Gallery is beyond the scope of this example, here are a few tips if you want to continue setting up a working photo gallery. To begin, go to the home page of the photo gallery you just created (http:// server/~user/photos) and log in with the administrative user and password you created. Then do the following:

- **Add an Album**—Click the Albums button and then click New. Type a name for the album and select Apply modifications. Then select Continue as instructed.

- **Upload files**—Click the Upload file link at the top of the page. From the Upload file page, add either the full paths to file names (File Uploads) or Web addresses (URI/URL Uploads) of the images you want to install. Then click Continue. If the uploads were successful, click Continue again.

  At this point, you can add information to be associated with each image you just uploaded. Select the Album each will go into, a file title, and a description, and then click Continue. After you have added information for all your uploaded images, click Continue again to return to the main photo gallery. There you can see your images sorted by album, as random files, or by latest additions.

If you installed Coppermine on a public server, you can give the Web address of that server to your friends and family and they can begin viewing your photo albums. You can do a lot to customize your Coppermine Photo Gallery. You can begin by going through the settings on the Configuration page (click the Config link to get there). Click the Users or Groups links to create user or group accounts that give special access to upload or modify the content of your gallery.

# Troubleshooting

In any complex environment, you occasionally run into problems. This section includes tips for isolating and resolving the most common errors that you may encounter.

## Note

This section refers to the Apache HTTPD binary as `apache2`, which is what it is named on Ubuntu and other Debian-based systems. However, in many other distributions, the binary is named `httpd`. On different systems, you may need to substitute *httpd* for *apache* when it appears by itself, although not for commands such as `apache2ctl`. ∎

## Configuration errors

You may occasionally run into configuration errors or script problems that prevent Apache from starting or that prevent specific files from being accessible. Most of these problems can be isolated and resolved using two Apache-provided tools: the `apache2ctl` program and the system error log.

When encountering a problem, first use the `apache2ctl` program with the `configtest` parameter to test the configuration. In fact, it's a good idea to develop the habit of running this every time you make a configuration change:

```
# apache2ctl configtest
Syntax OK
# apache2ctl graceful
/usr/sbin/apache2ctl graceful: httpd gracefully restarted
```

In the event of a syntax error, `apache2ctl` indicates where the error occurs and also does its best to give a hint about the nature of the problem. You can then use the `graceful` restart option (`apache2ctl graceful`) to instruct Apache to reload its configuration without disconnecting any active clients.

## Note

The `graceful` restart option in `apache2ctl` automatically tests the configuration before sending the reload signal to `apache`, but getting in the habit of running the manual configuration test after making any configuration changes is still a good idea. ∎

Some configuration problems pass the syntax tests performed by apache2ctl, but then result in the HTTP daemon exiting immediately after reloading its configuration. If this happens, use the tail command to check Apache's error log for useful information. On Debian systems, the error log is in /var/log/apache2/error.log. On other systems, the location can be found by looking for the ErrorLog directive in your Apache configuration.

An error message that you might encounter looks something like this:

```
[crit] (98)Address already in use: make_sock: could not bind to port 80
```

This error often indicates that something else is bound to port 80 (not very common unless you have attempted to install another Web server), that another Apache process is already running (apache2ctl usually catches this), or that you have told Apache to bind the same IP address and port combination in more than one place.

You can use the netstat command to view the list of programs (including Apache) with TCP ports in the LISTEN state:

```
# netstat -nltp
Active Internet connections (only servers)
Proto   Local Address   Foreign Address   State     PID/Program name
tcp     0.0.0.0:80      0.0.0.0:*         LISTEN    2105/apache2
```

The output from netstat (which was shortened to fit here) indicates that an instance of the apache2 process with a process ID of 2105 is listening (as indicated by the LISTEN state) for connections to any local IP address (indicated by 0.0.0.0) on port 80 (the standard HTTP port). If a different program is listening to port 80, it is shown there. You can use the kill command to terminate the process, but if it is something other than apache2 (or httpd), you should also find out why it is running.

If you don't see any other processes listening on port 80, it could be that you have accidentally told Apache to listen on the same IP address and port combination in more than one place. Three configuration directives can be used for this: BindAddress, Port, and Listen:

- BindAddress—Enables you to specify a single IP address to listen on, or you can specify all IP addresses using the * wildcard. You should never have more than one BindAddress statement in your configuration file.

- Port—Specifies which TCP port to listen on but does not enable you to specify the IP address. Port is generally not used more than once in the configuration.

- Listen—Enables you to specify both an IP address and a port to bind to. The IP address can be in the form of a wildcard, and you can have multiple Listen statements in your configuration file.

Generally, using only one type of these directives is a good idea to avoid confusion. Of the three, Listen is the most flexible, so it is probably the one you want to use the most. A common error when using Listen is to specify a port on all IP addresses (*:80) as well as that same port on a specific IP address (1.2.3.4:80), which results in the error from make_sock.

Configuration errors relating to SSL (discussed later in this chapter) commonly result in Apache failures. Make sure all key and certificate files exist and that they are in the proper format (use openssl to examine them, as shown later in this chapter).

For other error messages, try doing a Web search to see whether somebody else has encountered the problem. In most cases, you can find a solution within the first few matches.

If you aren't getting enough information in the ErrorLog, you can configure it to log more information using the LogLevel directive. The options available for this directive, in increasing order of verbosity, are emerg, alert, crit, error, warn, notice, info, and debug. Select only one of these. Any message that is at least as important as the LogLevel you select will be stored in the ErrorLog. On a typical server, this is set to warn. You should not set it to any lower than crit and should avoid leaving it set to debug because that can slow down the server and result in a very large ErrorLog.

As a last resort, you can also try running apache2 manually to check for crashes or other error messages:

```
# /usr/sbin/apache2 -d /etc/apache2 -F ; echo $?
```

The -d flag tells apache where to look for its configuration file, and the -F flag tells it to run in the foreground. The semicolon separates this command from the echo command, which displays the return code ($?) from Apache after it exits. In the event that apache crashes during this step, you can use tools such as gdb and strace to trace the problem.

## Access forbidden and server internal errors

Two common types of errors that you may encounter when attempting to view specific pages on your server are permission errors and server internal errors. Both types of errors can usually be isolated using the information in the error log. After making any of the changes described in the following list to attempt to solve one of these problems, try the request again and then check the error log to see whether the message has changed (for example, to show that the operation completed successfully).

### Note
**"File not found" errors can be checked in the same way as "access forbidden" and "server internal errors." You may sometimes find that Apache is not looking where you think it is for a specific file. Generally, the entire path to the file shows up in the error log. Make sure you are accessing the correct virtual host, and check for any Alias settings that might be directing your location to a place you don't expect. ■**

- **File permissions**—A "file permissions prevent access" error indicates that the apache process is running as a user that is unable to open the requested file. Make sure that the account has execute permissions on the directory and every directory above it, as well as read permissions on the files themselves. Read permissions on a directory are also necessary if you want Apache to generate an index of files. See the manual page for chmod for more information about how to view and change permissions.

## Note
Read permissions are not necessary for compiled binaries, such as those written in C or C++, but can be safely added unless a need exists to keep the contents of the program secret. ■

- **Access denied**—A "client denied by server configuration" error indicates that Apache was configured to deny access to the object. Check the configuration files for `<Location>` and `<Directory>` sections that might affect the file you are trying to access. Remember that settings applied to a path are also applied to any paths below it. You can override these by changing the permissions only for the more specific path to which you want to allow access.

- **Index not found**—The "Directory index forbidden by rule" error indicates that Apache could not find an index file with a name specified in the `DirectoryIndex` directive and was configured to not create an index containing a list of files in a directory. Make sure your index page, if you have one, has one of the names specified in the relevant `DirectoryIndex` directive, or add an `Options Indexes` line to the appropriate `<Directory>` or `<Location>` section for that object.

- **Script crashed**—"Premature end of script headers" errors can indicate that a script is crashing before it finishes. On occasion, the errors that caused this also show up in the error log. When using `suexec` or `suPHP`, this error may also be caused by a file ownership or permissions error. These errors are indicated in `/var/log/apache2/suexec.log` or `/var/log/apache2/suphp.log`.

# Securing Your Web Traffic with SSL/TLS

You want to add security for your server, including your own certificates. Your data is important, and so is your capability to pass it along your network or the Internet to others. Networks just aren't secure enough by themselves to protect your communications. This section examines ways in which you can help guard your communications.

Electronic commerce applications such as online shopping and banking are generally encrypted using either the Secure Socket Layer (SSL) or Transport Layer Security (TLS) specifications. TLS is based on version 3.0 of the SSL specifications, so they are very similar in nature. Because of this similarity—and because SSL is older—the SSL acronym is often used to refer to either variety. For Web connections, the SSL connection is established first, and then normal HTTP communication is "tunneled" through it.

## Note

**Because SSL negotiation takes place before any HTTP communication, name-based virtual hosting (which occurs at the HTTP layer) does not work easily with SSL. As a consequence, every SSL virtual host you configure should have a unique IP address. You can use some tricks to get name-based virtual hosting to work with apache2, but they are outside the scope of this procedure. (See the Apache site for more information:** `httpd.apache.org/docs/vhosts/name-based.html`.**)** ∎

During connection establishment between an SSL client and an SSL server, asymmetric (public key) cryptography is used to verify identities and establish the session parameters and the session key. A symmetric encryption algorithm such as DES or RC4 is then used with the negotiated key to encrypt the data that are transmitted during the session. The use of asymmetric encryption during the handshaking phase allows safe communication without the use of a preshared key, and the symmetric encryption is faster and more practical for use on the session data.

For the client to verify the identity of the server, the server must have a previously generated private key, as well as a certificate containing the public key and information about the server. This certificate must be verifiable using a public key that is known to the client.

Certificates are generally digitally signed by a third-party certificate authority (CA) that has verified the identity of the requester and the validity of the request to have the certificate signed. In most cases, the CA is a company that has made arrangements with the Web browser vendor to have its own certificate installed and trusted by default client installations. The CA then charges the server operator for its services.

Commercial certificate authorities vary in price, features, and browser support, but remember that price is not always an indication of quality. Some popular CAs include InstantSSL (`www.instantssl.com`), Thawte (`www.thawte.com`), and VeriSign (`www.verisign.com`).

You also have the option of creating self-signed certificates, although these should be used only for testing or when a very small number of people will be accessing your server and you do not plan to have certificates on multiple machines. Directions for generating a self-signed certificate are included in the following section.

The last option is to run your own certificate authority. This is probably practical only if you have a small number of expected users and the means to distribute your CA certificate to them (including assisting them with installing it in their browsers). The process for creating a CA is too elaborate to cover in this book but is a worthwhile alternative to generating self-signed certificates. You can find guides on running your own CA at `http://sial.org/howto/openssl/ca/`.

The following procedure describes how to generate and use SSL keys with the LAMP server (running on an Ubuntu system) configured in this chapter. For a general discussion of SSL keys and procedures specific to Fedora and other Red Hat systems, refer to Chapter 12.

## Generating your keys

To begin setting up SSL, use the `openssl` command, which is part of the OpenSSL package, to generate your public and private key:

1. Use APT to verify that OpenSSL is installed. If it is not present, APT downloads and installs it automatically:

```
$ sudo apt-get install openssl
```

2. Generate a 1024-bit RSA private key and save it to a file:

```
$ sudo su -
# mkdir /etc/apache2/ssl.key/
# cd /etc/apache2/ssl.key/
# openssl genrsa -out server.key 1024
# chmod 600 server.key
```

## Note

You can use a filename other than `server.key` and should do so if you plan to have more than one SSL host on your machine (which requires more than one IP address). Just make sure you specify the correct filename in the Apache configuration later. ■

In higher-security environments, encrypting the key by adding the `-des3` argument after the `genrsa` argument on the `openssl` command line is a good idea:

```
# openssl genrsa -des3 -out server.key 1024
```

3. You are asked for a passphrase, which is needed every time you start Apache.

## Caution

Do not lose this passphrase because it cannot be easily recovered. ■

4. If you plan to have your certificate signed by a CA (including one that you run yourself), generate a public key and a certificate signing request (CSR):

```
# mkdir ../ssl.csr/
# cd ../ssl.csr/
# openssl req -new -key ../ssl.key/server.key -out server.csr

Country Name (2 letter code) [AU]:US
State or Province Name (full name) [Some-State]:Washington
Locality Name (eg, city) []:Bellingham
Organization Name (eg, company) [Internet Widgits Pty
Ltd]:Example Company, LTD.
Organizational Unit Name (eg, section) []:Network
Operations
```

```
Common Name (eg, YOUR name) []:secure.example.org
Email Address []:dom@example.org

Please enter the following 'extra' attributes
to be sent with your certificate request
A challenge password []:
An optional company name []:
```

The Common Name should match the name that clients will use to access your server. Be sure to get the other details right if you plan to have the CSR signed by a third-party CA.

5. When using a third-party CA, submit the CSR to it and then place the certificate it provides you into /etc/apache2/ssl.crt/server.crt (or a different file, as desired).

6. If you don't plan to have your certificate signed, or if you want to test your configuration, generate a self-signed certificate and save it in a file named server.crt:

```
# mkdir ../ssl.crt/
# cd ../ssl.crt/
# openssl req -new -x509 -nodes -sha1 -days 365 -key \
../ssl.key/server.key -out server.crt
Country Name (2 letter code) [AU]: .
State or Province Name (full name) [Some-State]: .
Locality Name (eg, city) []: .
Organization Name (eg, company) [Internet Widgits Pty
Ltd]:TEST USE ONLY
Organizational Unit Name (eg, section) []:TEST USE ONLY
Common Name (eg, YOUR name) []:secure.example.org
Email Address []:dom@example.org
```

## Configuring Apache to support SSL/TLS

After your keys have been generated, you need to enable the mod_ssl Apache module, which adds SSL/TLS support to Apache, and then configure it using the appropriate configuration directives. The mod_ssl module is installed with the basic apache2.2-common package. Here's how to enable it for your virtual hosts:

1. Run the a2enmod command to enable ssl:

```
$ sudo a2enmod ssl
Module ssl installed; run /etc/init.d/apache2 force-reload to enable.
```

2. Add an SSL-enabled virtual host to your Apache configuration files. Using the earlier virtual host as an example, your configuration will look something like this:

```
Listen *:443
<VirtualHost *:443>
```

```
        ServerName       secure.example.org
        ServerAlias      web.example.org
        DocumentRoot     /home/username/public_html/
        DirectoryIndex   index.php index.html index.htm
        SSLEngine        On
        SSLCertificateKeyFile /etc/apache2/ssl.key/server.key
        SSLCertificateFile /etc/apache2/ssl.crt/server.crt
        SSLCACertificateFile /etc/apache2/ssl.crt/ca.crt
</VirtualHost>
```

This example uses a wildcard for the IP address in the VirtualHost declaration, which saves you from having to modify your configuration file in the event that your IP address changes but also prevents you from having multiple SSL virtual hosts. In the event that you do need to support more than one SSL virtual host, replace * with the specific IP address that you assign to that host.

## Note

See the "Troubleshooting" section earlier in the chapter for more information about the Listen **directive.** ∎

A CA generally provides you with a certificate file to place in ca.crt and sometimes also provides you with a separate file that you will need to reference using a SSLCertificateChainFile directive.

3. Test the Apache configuration and then perform a full restart:

```
$ sudo apache2ctl configtest
Syntax OK.
$ sudo apache2ctl stop
$ sudo apache2ctl start
```

4. Browse to https://servername/ and verify the SSL configuration. When using a self-signed certificate, or one signed by a CA, you are asked whether you want to accept the certificate.

# Summary

Combining Linux with an Apache Web server, MySQL database, and PHP scripting content (referred to as a LAMP server) makes it possible for you to configure your own full-featured Web server. The instructions in this chapter showed you how to set up Apache to do virtual hosting, add content to a MySQL database, and allow PHP scripting in the content on your server. For added security, this chapter described how to add your own certificates and troubleshoot problems that might arise with your server.

# Running a Mail Server

E lectronic mail hardly requires an introduction. Communications made through the original forms of e-mail helped shape the Internet. Widespread availability of access to e-mail and enhancements such as MIME (Multipurpose Internet Mail Extensions, which allow for inclusion of attachments and alternate message formats) have helped to make e-mail the most popular application on the Internet.

With a Linux system and a suitable Internet connection, you can easily set up your own mail server for personal or business use. This chapter includes a description of how Internet mail works at the protocol level, and then guides you through the process of setting up a mail server, complete with spam and virus filtering. In the final section, you learn how to secure network communications between clients and your mail server through the use of SSL/TLS (Secure Sockets Layer and Transport Layer Security) protocols.

The examples in this chapter are based on an Ubuntu system. (See Chapter 17 for more information about Ubuntu.) However, much of the knowledge you gain from setting up a mail server in Ubuntu applies to other Linux systems as well.

| IN THIS CHAPTER |
|---|
| **Internet e-mail's inner workings** |
| **About the system and the software used** |
| **Preparing your system** |
| **Installing and configuring the mail server software** |
| **Testing and troubleshooting** |
| **Configuring mail clients** |
| **Securing communications with SSL/TLS** |

## Internet E-Mail's Inner Workings

E-mail messages are generated either by an automated process, such as a form processor on a Web page or an automated notification system, or by an MUA (mail user agent) controlled by an end user. Messages are delivered through one of two methods to the software performing the MTA (mail transfer agent) function on a server:

- **SMTP**—The Simple Mail Transfer Protocol is a network-based protocol that allows for transmission of messages between systems.

- **Local IPC**—Interprocess communications are often used instead of SMTP when transferring a message between programs within a system.

Upon receiving a message, the MTA places it in a queue to be processed by an MDA (mail delivery agent). Mail delivery agents come in two varieties:

- **Local MDAs**—Deliver messages to mailboxes on the local server. Simple versions copy messages directly to a specified mailbox, whereas complex implementations can alter messages or delivery parameters based on user-specified rules.

- **Remote MDAs**—Deliver messages over the network to remote servers. Full remote MDAs use DNS (the Domain Name System) to determine the mail exchanger hosts for recipient addresses and deliver to the best one available for each. Simple remote MDAs (sometimes also called "null clients") forward messages to a central server to continue the delivery process. Most remote MDAs are capable of either method and will act as configured by the administrator who performed the configuration.

## Note

You will often see the term *MTA* used in reference to the software that performs both MTA and MDA functions. This is a carry-over from older designs that did not separate the functions and is still fairly accurate given the fact that most mail server implementations include a minimum of an MTA, remote MDA, and basic local MDA. ■

When a message reaches its destination server, it is written to the user's mailbox by the local MDA. From that point, the message may be viewed by the user using one of three methods:

- **Direct access to the mailbox**—An MUA (mail user agent) with access to the mailbox file, directly or through a network file system, can read messages from the disk and display them for the user. This is generally a console or Web mail application running on the server.

- **Downloaded to a workstation for local viewing**—Most mail users use POP3 (Post Office Protocol, version 3) to download messages to their local computers and view them in applications such as Thunderbird, Evolution, Kmail, or Balsa. By default, messages are removed from the server as they are downloaded by the client.

- **Accessed interactively over the network**—Most clients also support viewing messages while they are still on the server, through IMAP (Internet Message Access Protocol). Unlike POP3, this protocol enables users to access multiple folders on their servers and also allows them to access their messages from anywhere. However, this also creates a heavier burden on the server because it must process (and store) everything that the user decides to keep. Most Web mail applications use IMAP as their backend protocol for accessing mailboxes; this eliminates the need for direct access to the mail files and makes it easier to split functions between server and client systems.

# About the System and the Software Used

The mail server configuration described in this chapter is based on the Exim mail transfer agent. Along with Exim, several other components are added for managing the server and checking e-mail contents for spam and viruses:

- **Exim** (www.exim.org/)—An MTA written and designed by Philip Hazel at the University of Cambridge, with contributions from many people around the world. The version referred to in this chapter includes the Exiscan-ACL patch (http://duncan-thrax.net/exiscan-acl/) from Tom Kistner. This patch allows content scanning from within Exim. Because this patch is integrated with Exim, its features are considered part of Exim for the purposes of this chapter.

- **Maildrop** (www.courier-mta.org/maildrop/)—A local MDA that is part of the Courier MTA package, but is also available as a standalone program. It is used in this configuration to allow the use of advanced features, such as mailbox quotas and server-side message sorting.

- **Courier IMAP** and **POP** (www.courier-mta.org/imap/)—Like Maildrop, these are parts of the Courier MTA that are also available separately. They were chosen for their easy installation, good performance, and compatibility with the Maildir format mail directories.

- **ClamAV** (www.clamav.net)—An open source virus scanner that detects more than 20,000 viruses, worms, and Trojans. It uses a virus pattern database to identify viruses and includes a program named freshclam that handles updating the database automatically. Like SpamAssassin, ClamAV includes a daemon (clamd), a client (clamdscan), and a second command-line tool that does not use the daemon (clamscan).

- **SpamAssassin** (http://spamassassin.apache.org/)—A spam-filtering program written in Perl. It uses a large set of rules to help determine how "spammy" a message looks and assigns a score based on the total of the rule values. For performance reasons, SpamAssassin uses a background daemon called spamd to perform message analysis. Access to this daemon is performed through the spamc client. A spamassassin command that performs the analysis without using spamd is also installed but is not used by either of the example configurations in this chapter.

# Preparing Your System

You will need a few common items for the mail server configuration covered in this chapter, starting with the proper hardware. A personal mail server can easily run on a Pentium-class computer, although you may notice occasional slowdowns while incoming messages are being scanned. Disk space requirements depend mostly on how much mail you want to have room for, so plan on having a few gigabytes for the operating system (which will leave you plenty of extra, just in case), plus the amount of mail you want to store.

The operating system should be installed with only the basic set of packages before you begin these examples. Some general information about the installation is provided in Chapter 17. Although the software described in this chapter works even if you aren't running Ubuntu, the installation methods will not. If you don't have a spare system to act as a dedicated mail server, you can still use it as your workstation, although this is obviously recommended only for personal use.

Your network settings should also be properly configured before you begin installing the mail software. The exact requirements depend on the method by which mail will be delivered to your server:

- **Direct delivery** is the method used by most traditional mail servers. Mail records (MX) on your DNS server tell remote servers that any mail addressed to your domain should be sent to your server via SMTP.

- **Retrieval from a mail host** is also possible using an MRA (mail retrieval agent) such as Fetchmail. This option can be used when you have a mailbox under a shared domain but want to access the mail on your own server. This can also be done in combination with direct delivery if you have both your own domain and mailboxes under shared domains.

## Note
Configuration of Fetchmail is explained in the "Configuring Mail Clients" section of this chapter. ■

## Configuring DNS for direct delivery

For direct delivery to function, the SMTP service (TCP port 25) must be accessible to the outside world through a fixed name in DNS. This name will be in the form of an A (Address) record. "A" records allow DNS resolver processes to determine the IP address associated with a specific name and are used by most of the common protocols on the Internet. A typical DNS A record looks something like this:

```
bigserver.example.org    IN    A    10.0.12.16
```

The first parameter, bigserver.example.org, is the label, and the second parameter is the class (IN for Internet, which is where most DNS records are found). The A indicates the type, and the final parameter is the IP address associated with the label.

After you have your A record, you can direct mail to your server using an MX (Mail eXchanger) record. The A and MX records do not need to be part of the same domain, which allows for much greater flexibility. The following is a sample MX record:

```
widgets.test.    IN    MX    0    bigserver.example.org.
```

This MX record indicates that mail for *any address*@widgets.test should be sent through the server bigserver.example.org. The 0 indicates the numeric priority for this MX record. When more than one MX record exists for a given label, the MX with the lowest priority is tried first. If a temporary error is encountered, the next highest priority mail server is tried, and so on until the list is exhausted. At that point, the sending server will keep trying periodically until the message times out (generally five days). If multiple MX records exist with the same priority, they are tried in a random order.

## Note
**Most mail servers will also fall back on the IP address listed in the A record for a label in the event that no MX records exist. However, it is considered bad practice to rely on this feature.** ∎

In some cases, establishing an A record may be complicated because your IP address frequently changes. Obviously, this is not suitable for commercial purposes, but there is a workaround that is acceptably reliable for personal use. It is achieved through dynamic DNS services that are available (often at no charge) through a number of different companies. A list of these companies is maintained at http://www.dmoz.org/Computers/Internet/Protocols/DNS/ DNS_Providers/Dynamic_DNS/. Two of the most popular are

- **ZoneEdit** (www.zoneedit.com/)—Supported by the ez-ipupdate package
- **No-IP** (www.no-ip.com/)—Supported by the no-ip package

## Note
**The ez-ipupdate package supports both of these, plus a number of others. View the package description** (apt-cache show ez-ipupdate) **for more information.** ∎

Most of these services will provide you with a hostname under a shared domain at no charge and can also provide a similar service for your own domain for a reasonable fee.

## Configuring for retrieval from a mail host

The configuration requirements when retrieving mail from a mail host are pretty limited. Your server should be ready to accept mail addressed to localhost and should generally have a name that is unique to it. In the event that a message sent to one of your mailboxes is rejected, the server will need to have a valid hostname by which to identify itself when sending out the DSN (Delivery Status Notification).

You must be able to access the server from clients, although you may need to do so only from clients within your network. In either case, you should be familiar with the information about DNS and A records in the previous section.

# Installing and Configuring the Mail Server Software

After you have finished with the prerequisites, you are ready to begin the software installation. The software installation and configuration have been divided into two sections. The first section covers the installation of Exim and Courier. The second section covers the installation of ClamAV and SpamAssassin and configuring Exim to use them to filter incoming mail.

## Installing Exim and Courier

Installing and configuring Exim and Courier are very straightforward thanks to the quality of the packages that come with Ubuntu. It is possible that, if you have a new Ubuntu system, it already has a version of Exim installed. However, you'll want to use a specific version of Exim that contains features for content scanning. Here are the installation steps:

1.  Start by installing this Exim package:

    ```
    $ sudo apt-get install exim4-daemon-heavy
    ```

2.  You need to change a few configuration options from the defaults. Run the following command:

    ```
    $ sudo dpkg-reconfigure --priority=medium exim4-config
    ```

    You are asked a number of questions. Here's how to answer them:

    -   **General type:** Select "Mail sent by smarthost; received via SMTP or fetchmail" if you need to send all of your outgoing mail through a server at your Internet service provider. Otherwise, select "Internet site; mail is sent and received directly using SMTP."
    -   **Mail name:** Enter the name of your mail server here.
    -   **IP addresses:** Clear this box (or leave it empty if it is already so) so that Exim will listen on all local IP addresses.
    -   **Destinations to accept mail for:** Enter any domains that your server will be accepting mail for. Be sure to separate them with colons, and not commas or spaces.
    -   **Domains to relay for:** Enter the names of any domains that your machine will relay mail for, meaning that it can receive mail from them but then passes it on. In most cases, you will not want to enter anything here.
    -   **Machines to relay for:** Enter the IP address ranges of any client machines that you want your server to accept mail from. Another (safer) option is to leave this empty and require clients to authenticate using SMTP authentication. SMTP authentication is best performed over an encrypted connection, so this process is described in the security section at the end of this chapter.

- **Rewrite headers:** Select Yes if you want to hide the local mail name in outgoing mail by rewriting the From, Reply-To, Sender, and Return-Path values to a selected system name in outgoing mail. If Yes, you must then set the visible domain name for local users.

- **Split configuration into small files:** Selecting Yes causes Exim to split configuration files into about 50 smaller files (instead of one big one) in the `/etc/exim4/conf.d` directory. Otherwise, the `/etc/exim4/exim4.conf.template` file is used as a single, monolithic file.

3. This configuration uses Maildrop for local mail delivery. Maildrop can deliver messages to the Maildir-style folders that Courier is expecting, and can also handle basic sorting and filtering (as described in the "Configuring Mail Clients" section). This package is not installed by default, so install it as follows:

```
$ sudo apt-get install maildrop
```

4. Create Maildir mail directories for every user already on the system. You must perform this step for every user that is already on the system, and it must be run as the user because running this command as root will result in Maildrop's being unable to write to the folders:

```
$ maildirmake.maildrop $HOME/Maildir
$ maildirmake.maildrop -f Trash $HOME/Maildir
```

5. Create mail directories under `/etc/skel`. The contents of `/etc/skel` will be copied to the home directories of any new accounts that you create after the setup is completed:

```
$ sudo maildirmake.maildrop /etc/skel/Maildir
$ sudo maildirmake.maildrop -f Trash /etc/skel/Maildir
```

6. Configure Maildrop to deliver to the Maildir folders instead of `mbox` files stored in `/var/spool/mail`. Use your favorite text editor to edit `/etc/maildroprc` and uncomment this line at the end of the file:

```
DEFAULT="$HOME/Maildir/"
```

7. Exim needs to be configured to deliver messages using Maildrop. Use your preferred text editor to open `/etc/exim4/update-exim4.conf.conf` and change the `dc_localdelivery` line at the end of the file to read as follows:

```
dc_localdelivery='maildrop_pipe'
```

8. Tell Exim to load the most recent configuration change:

```
$ sudo invoke-rc.d exim4 reload
```

**9.** Install Courier IMAP and Courier POP:

```
$ sudo apt-get install courier-imap courier-pop
```

Select No when asked whether or not the installer should create directories for Web-based administration.

Your system should now be capable of receiving messages. You should also be able to connect to your server using a mail client such as Thunderbird or Evolution. This is a good time to test mail delivery, even if you're planning to follow the directions in the next section to enable virus and spam filters later. More information about configuring a mail client to connect to your server can be found in the "Configuring Mail Clients" section later in this chapter.

## Installing ClamAV and SpamAssassin

Installing and configuring the virus and spam filtering mechanisms is more involved than installing Exim and Courier, but should still go smoothly as long as you follow the steps carefully. Keep in mind, however, that this filtering adds a lot of complexity to the system, so make sure the Exim mail server is working first so that you don't have as many things to check if the system doesn't work as expected.

## Note

The version of ClamAV included with Ubuntu uses an older virus-scanning engine, as does the Debian system on which Ubuntu is based. Because the updated engine is not likely to make it into an update anytime soon because of the Debian upgrade policies, a group of Debian developers has created special sets of the ClamAV packages that are designed for easy installation. For more information about how to use these packages instead of the stock versions, see `http://volatile.debian.net/`. **You may choose to use these packages from the start, or to add the appropriate URIs to your APT configuration later and do an upgrade. In either case, the configuration process detailed in this section is about the same. You can also upgrade the database routinely using** `clamav-freshclam`, `clamav-getfiles` **to generate new** `clamav-data` **packages.** ■

Here's how to install ClamAV and SpamAssassin, and then configure Exim to use them for scanning messages:

**1.** Install the ClamAV and SpamAssassin packages:

```
$ sudo apt-get install clamav-daemon clamav-testfiles \
    spamassassin spamc
```

**2.** Add the clamav user to the Debian-exim group and restart the ClamAV daemon. This step allows the ClamAV daemon access to read the files in Exim's mail queue:

```
$ sudo gpasswd -a clamav Debian-exim
$ sudo invoke-rc.d clamav-daemon restart
```

3.  Replace the report template used by SpamAssassin with one that will fit more easily in a message header. Use a text editor to add these lines to the end of the /etc/spamassassin/local.cf file:

```
clear_report_template
report _YESNO_, score=_SCORE_, required=_REQD_, summary=
report _SUMMARY_
```

4.  Configure the SpamAssassin background daemon to run automatically and change the OPTIONS line to not attempt to create preference files for users. Change the following options in the /etc/default/spamassassin file:

```
ENABLED=1
OPTIONS="--max-children 5"
```

5.  Start the SpamAssassin daemon:

```
$ sudo invoke-rc.d spamassassin start
```

6.  Create the entries that will be included in Exim's ACL (Access Control List) for scanning message data. Use a text editor to create a file named /etc/exim4/acl_check_data_local that contains the following:

```
deny message = $malware_name detected in message
     demime = *
     malware = *

warn message = X-Spam-Score: $spam_score ($spam_bar)
     condition = ${if <{$message_size}{80k}{1}{0}}
     spam = nobody:true/defer_ok

warn message = X-Spam-Status: $spam_report
     condition = ${if <{$message_size}{80k}{1}{0}}
     spam = nobody:true/defer_ok

deny message = Spam score too high ($spam_score)
     condition = ${if <{$message_size}{80k}{1}{0}}
     spam = nobody:true/defer_ok
     condition = ${if >{$spam_score_int}{120}{1}{0}}
```

The first block rejects messages that contain viruses or other malware, and the second and third add headers to messages indicating whether or not SpamAssassin considers them spam. The final block checks $spam_score_int (the spam score multiplied by 10) and rejects the message if it is greater than 120.

The /defer_ok in the last three blocks tells Exim that it is okay to continue processing in the event that the SpamAssassin daemon could not be contacted. You can remove it if you would prefer to have the server return a temporary failure code in such cases. You can also add /defer_ok to the end of the malware = * line if you want processing to continue in the event that a message cannot be scanned by ClamAV.

7. Tell Exim which virus scanner to use and how to connect to SpamAssassin. Use a text editor to create a file named /etc/exim4/conf.d/main/10_exim4-exiscan_acl_ options that contains the following:

```
av_scanner = clamd:/var/run/clamav/clamd.ctl
spamd_address = 127.0.0.1 783

CHECK_DATA_LOCAL_ACL_FILE = CONFDIR/acl_check_data_local
```

8. Tell Exim to load the new configuration:

```
$ sudo invoke-rc.d exim4 reload
```

All messages transmitted through your server should now be checked for viruses using ClamAV. Additionally, messages less than 80 kilobytes will also be checked using SpamAssassin. This is a good time to test the configuration again. You can find fixes for the problems that you are most likely to encounter in the next section.

# Testing and Troubleshooting

This section contains some generic troubleshooting tips, plus specific information about some common errors and how to fix them.

## Checking logs

All logging information for Exim is written to three log files that can be found in /var/log/ exim4: mainlog, rejectlog, and paniclog. The first of these, mainlog, contains log entries for all events, including normal events such as message deliveries. The second, rejectlog, contains entries for rejected messages. The third contains information about configuration or other errors, and is usually empty unless a serious problem has occurred. Every entry in these files generally starts with a timestamp.

Entries in the mainlog often include a string of characters, such as n7MJ123W002743. This is the message identifier for the message that the log entry is related to. Immediately after the message identifier there will generally be a two-character string. Table 14-1 details what those strings mean.

**TABLE 14-1**

## Exim Log File Messages

| Symbol | Description | Explanation |
|--------|-------------|-------------|
| <= | Message arrival | These entries show messages coming into Exim, generally through SMTP or local IPC. |
| => | Message delivery | These entries show message deliveries, whether they are to a local mailbox or to a remote host using SMTP or some other transport. |
| -> | Additional addresses in message delivery | These entries show delivery to additional addresses for messages that have already been delivered to another recipient (and logged with an => entry). |
| ** | Delivery failure | These entries show permanent delivery errors. Errors such as these indicate that the message has been removed from the mail queue and in most cases a DSN (Delivery Status Notification) has been generated and sent to the original message sender. |
| == | Delivery deferral | These entries show temporary delivery problems. The system will continue to retry sending these until delivery succeeds, or a permanent failure occurs as a result of a retry timeout. |

Entries not associated with a message that has not been accepted into the queue will not have the message identifier or two-character flags. Some samples of these types of entries are included in the next section.

Logging information for the Courier IMAP and POP daemons is saved to /var/log/mail.log. Normal entries include LOGIN and LOGOUT messages. DISCONNECTED messages generally indicate that a connection was broken before a normal logout was performed.

## Note

The tail utility is useful for watching for new entries to a log. Use the -f switch to instruct tail to watch for new entries and display them to the screen as they are written to the log. For example: tail -f /var/log/exim4/mainlog. ∎

# Common errors (and how to fix them)

You will encounter two common types of problems with your server: messages being rejected or not delivered by Exim and login failures when connecting to Courier.

### Messages rejected by Exim

The first places to check when messages are rejected by Exim are the `mainlog` and `rejectlog` files. Here are examples of some common errors and tips for fixing them:

- **Relaying Denied**—The following error indicates that the client sending the message is not recognized as a client by Exim and that the recipient domain is not in the list of local or relay domains:

  ```
  H=sample.client [10.0.12.16] F=<sender@example.org> rejected
  RCPT <rcpt@remotesite.example.org>: relay not permitted
  ```

  If the client IP address will not change frequently or is in part of a trusted range of IP addresses, you can add it by running the following:

  ```
  $ sudo dpkg-reconfigure --priority=medium exim4-config
  ```

  The same command can also be used to add the recipient domain as a local or relay domain.

## Caution

**Do not add client IP ranges unless you trust all the users who can connect from those addresses. Likewise, do not add a domain as a relay domain unless you know the owner of the domain and have made arrangements to relay mail for him or her. Doing either of these incorrectly could open up your server as a relay that spammers can use to attack other sites. ■**

  If the client IP address is likely to change frequently and is not part of a trusted range, you should either configure the client to use a mail server that is local to it or configure SMTP authentication in Exim. You can find more information about enabling SMTP authentication on your server in `/usr/share/doc/exim4-base/README.Debian.html` and `/etc/exim4/conf.d/auth/30_exim4-config_examples`.

## Note

**You can enable the Courier authdaemon examples in** `30_exim4-config_examples`, **allowing Exim to use that facility for authentication and negating the need to set up a different mechanism. In order for it to work, however, you need to add the Debian-exim user to the daemon group (sudo** `gpasswd -a Debian-exim daemon`**) and restart Exim. ■**

- ClamAV Misconfiguration—The following error indicates that the ClamAV daemon could not read the temporary message file:

  ```
  1E9PDq-0003Lo-BY malware acl condition: clamd: ClamAV
  returned /var/spool/exim4/scan/1E9PDq-0003Lo-BY:
    Access denied. ERROR
  ```

Make sure you added clamav to the Debian-exim group and restarted ClamAV, as shown in the installation section.

- **ClamAV Unavailable**—This error usually indicates that the ClamAV daemon is not running:

```
1E9PGL-0003MX-38 malware acl condition: clamd: unable to
connect to UNIX socket /var/run/clamav/clamd.ctl
   (No such file or directory)
```

Start the daemon using `invoke-rc.d clamav-daemon start`. You can also use the `clamdscan` program to test the daemon, as follows:

```
$ sudo clamdscan /usr/share/clamav-testfiles/clam.exe
/usr/share/clamav-testfiles/clam.exe: ClamAV-Test-File FOUND
----------- SCAN SUMMARY -----------
Infected files: 1
Time: 0.001 sec (0 m 0 s)
```

## Messages not delivered by Exim

In some cases, messages will be accepted by the server but will not be deliverable. Some of these errors are considered temporary failures and do not generate a bounced message until the retry timer runs out. The error that you are most likely to see looks something like this in the `mainlog` file:

```
1E9PTu-0003jN-QY == user@example.org R=local_user T=maildrop_pipe defer (0):
Child process of maildrop_pipe transport returned 75 (could mean temporary
error) from command: /usr/bin/maildrop
```

This error indicates that Exim attempted to pass the message to Maildrop, but Maildrop returned an error code. The most likely causes are a missing Maildir directory, or a Maildir directory that is owned by the wrong user. The next section shows how to detect and fix these problems.

## Login failures when connecting to Courier

Aside from genuine password errors (which can be remedied by entering the correct password in the mail client), a few other conditions can also result in login failures. Some of these conditions can also result in temporary delivery problems. A normal login failure results in a log entry that looks similar to this:

```
courierpop3login: LOGIN FAILED, ip=[::ffff:1.2.3.4]
```

In this case, a user from IP 1.2.3.4 entered the wrong username or password.

Several of the other errors that may occur will not be logged to the mail log, which means that you may have to test them by connecting manually to the POP3 service (from the mail server, or from a remote machine) and sending a valid username and password. This example shows how to connect to the POP3 service from a shell prompt on the mail server:

```
$ telnet localhost 110
Trying 127.0.0.1...
Connected to localhost.localdomain.
Escape character is '^]'.
+OK Hello there.
USER username
+OK Password required.
PASS password
```

The response you receive from the server should be similar to one of the following:

- **+OK logged in**—This response is normal and should mean that there are no problems with the service.

- **-ERR Maildir: No such file or directory**—This error indicates that the user's account does not have a Maildir directory. Use the maildirmake command to create it, as shown in the "Installing Exim and Courier" section.

- **-ERR Maildir: Permission denied**—This error indicates that the user's Maildir directory cannot be read or belongs to the wrong user. To remedy this, run this command as root:

  ```
  $ sudo chown -R username:groupname ~username/Maildir
  ```

  Be sure to replace *username* and *groupname* with the login name and primary group of the user. In a stock Ubuntu or Debian system, the primary group name will be the same as the username.

- **-ERR Login failed**—If you're certain that you are using the correct username and password, it could be that the Courier authdaemon service is not running. Try to start (or restart) it using this command:

  ```
  # invoke-rc.d courier-authdaemon restart
  ```

# Configuring Mail Clients

Any mail client with support for POP3 or IMAP should be able to access mail from your server. Just use the name of your server in the mail server settings, and follow the troubleshooting steps in the previous section if something doesn't work.

## Cross-Reference

You can find more information about mail clients for Linux in Chapter 6. ■

# Configuring Fetchmail

Fetchmail is an MRA (mail retrieval agent) that you can use to pull mail from a remote account to your new server. It is configured in the `$HOME/.fetchmailrc` file and is very easy to set up. To pull mail to your server, log in as the user to whom the mail should go, and then configure and run it from there.

## Note

Run Fetchmail as the user for whom the mail is being retrieved. You should never run it as root. If you're doing a complex setup in which you retrieve mail from a single mailbox that needs to be sorted out for multiple users, see the Fetchmail man page for information about multidrop mailboxes. ■

A `.fetchmailrc` file can be as simple as this:

```
poll mailserver.yourisp.example protocol pop3 username "foo"
```

If you have more than one mail server, you can add it as an additional line. If the server from which you are pulling mail supports IMAP, you can use `imap` instead of `pop3`. Other options that you can have are `password=your password` and `ssl`. Storing the password in the file enables you to run Fetchmail without entering a password, and the `ssl` option tells Fetchmail to use an SSL/TLS connection to the server.

## Note

Your `.fetchmailrc` file should not be readable by others, and Fetchmail will generally complain if it is. To set the permissions so that only you can read it, run `chmod 0600 $HOME/.fetchmailrc`. ■

Running Fetchmail is as simple as typing

```
$ fetchmail
```

If you want to have Fetchmail run in the background, you can use the `--daemon` (or `-d`) flags with a parameter telling it how often (in seconds) to poll the servers:

```
$ fetchmail --daemon 300
```

To have Fetchmail automatically start when the system boots, add this to your `crontab` file:

```
@reboot    /usr/bin/fetchmail --daemon 300
```

## Note

Fetchmail cannot prompt for passwords when run in this manner, which means that you must store the passwords in `.fetchmailrc` for this to work. ■

If you haven't configured a `crontab` file before, setting it up can be as easy as entering the following three commands:

```
$ cat > mycron
@reboot   /usr/bin/fetchmail --daemon 300
<Ctrl+D>
$ crontab mycron
```

## Configuring web-based mail

If you're running an IMAP server, you can offer Web-based access by installing SquirrelMail (`http://squirrelmail.org/`, also found in the squirrelmail package). Start by configuring your system as a LAMP server (see Chapter 13), and then install and configure the appropriate package.

# Securing Communications with SSL/TLS

Because communication between mail clients and the server often contains sensitive information such as passwords, it is usually desirable to enable SSL/TLS encryption. Here's how to enable SSL/TLS in Exim and Courier:

1. Install the Courier daemons with SSL/TLS support:

   ```
   $ sudo apt-get install courier-imap-ssl courier-pop-ssl
   ```

2. Third-party CA certificates are provided on the ca-certificates package. This will be referenced in the configuration, so install it, too:

   ```
   $ sudo apt-get install ca-certificates
   ```

   Debconf asks you whether you want to trust the CA certificates by default. In most cases, you want to select Yes.

3. If you are going to be using a certificate from a CA that is not already recognized (generally only true if you are running your own CA), place the CA public certificate in its own file in `/etc/ssl/certs/` and update the certificate database:

   ```
   $ sudo update-ca-certificates
   ```

4. Generate the private key and certificate signing request, as described in Chapter 13. The best location for these files is in `/etc/ssl/private/`. Here's an example:

   ```
   $ sudo su -
   # cd /etc/exim4
   ```

```
# openssl genrsa -out mail.key 1024
# chmod 640 mail.key
# openssl req -new -key mail.key -out mail.csr
# chown root:Debian-exim mail.key
```

5. Get your CSR (Certificate Signing Request) signed and place the certificate in /etc/mail/private/mail.crt. Or, to do a self-signed certificate, do the following:

```
# cd /etc/exim4
# openssl req -new -x509 -nodes -sha1 \
  -days 365 -key mail.key -out mail.crt
# chmod 640 mail.crt
# chown root:Debian-exim mail.crt
```

## Caution

Some remote servers will refuse to send messages to your server if your certificate is not signed by a CA that they recognize. Also, make sure the common name (cn) attribute on your certificate matches the name of the server in DNS. ■

6. Concatenate the private key and certificate into a single file for Courier:

```
# cd /etc/courier
# cat /etc/exim4/mail.key /etc/exim4/mail.crt > mail.pem
# chmod 600 mail.pem
```

7. Enable SSL/TLS in the Courier IMAP and POP daemons by editing both /etc/courier/imapd-ssl and /etc/courier/pop3d-ssl and replacing the values for TLS_CERTFILE and TLS_TRUSTCERTS with the following:

```
TLS_CERTFILE=/etc/courier/mail.pem
TLS_TRUSTCERTS=/etc/ssl/certs/ca-certificates.pem
```

8. Tell Exim where it can find the private key and certificate, and enable TLS. Create a file named /etc/exim4/conf.d/main/12_exim4-config_local_tlsoptions containing the following:

```
MAIN_TLS_CERTIFICATE = CONFDIR/mail.crt
MAIN_TLS_PRIVATEKEY = CONFDIR/mail.key
MAIN_TLS_ENABLE = 1
```

9. Restart Exim:

```
$ sudo invoke-rc.d exim4 restart
```

Your server should now support SSL/TLS when communicating with SMTP, POP, and IMAP clients.

# Summary

Using Linux and a good Internet connection, you can set up and maintain your own mail server. Preparing your computer to become a mail server includes configuring your network connection, setting up delivery and retrieval methods, and adding required software packages.

This chapter describes how to install, configure, and troubleshoot the Exim MTA. Exim can be used in tandem with spam filtering software (such as SpamAssassin) and virus scanning software (such as ClamAV). Methods for securing your mail server include configuring support for SSL/ TLS encryption.

# Running a Print Server

Sharing printers is a good way to save money and make your printing more efficient. Very few people need to print all the time, but when they do want to print something, they usually need it quickly. Setting up a print server can save money by eliminating the need for a printer at every workstation. Some of those savings can be used to buy printers that can output more pages per minute or have higher-quality output.

You can attach printers to your Linux system to make them available to users of that system (standalone printing) or to other computers on the network as a shared printer. You can also configure your Linux printer as a remote CUPS or Samba printer. With Samba, you are emulating Windows printing services, which is pretty useful given the abundance of Windows client systems.

This chapter describes configuring and using printers on Linux systems with various desktop environments in use. Some of the details may vary from one distribution to another, but the information included here should work well for the more commonly used distributions. This chapter focuses on Common UNIX Printing Service (CUPS), which is the recommended print service for the majority of Linux installations. Examples in this chapter use the Printer Configuration options in the GNOME and K Desktop environments.

After a local printer is configured, users on your system should easily be able to print Web pages, documents, or images from desktop applications. From the command line, print commands such as lpr are available for carrying out printing. Commands also exist for querying print queues (lpq), manipulating print queues (lpc), and removing print queues (lprm). A local printer can also be shared as a print server for users on other computers on your network.

## IN THIS CHAPTER

**Understanding printing in Linux**

**Setting up printers**

**Using printing commands**

**Managing document printing**

**Sharing printers**

# Common UNIX Printing Service

CUPS has become the standard for printing from Linux and other UNIX-like operating systems. It was designed to meet today's needs for standardized printer definitions and sharing on Internet Protocol-based networks (as most computer networks are today). Nearly every Linux distribution today comes with CUPS as its printing service. Here are some of the service's features:

- **IPP**—CUPS is based on the Internet Printing Protocol (www.pwg.org/ipp), a standard that was created to simplify how printers can be shared over IP networks. In the IPP model, printer servers and clients who want to print can exchange information about the model and features of a printer using HTTP (that is, Web content) protocol. A server can also broadcast the availability of a printer so a printing client can easily find a list of locally available printers.

- **Drivers**—CUPS also standardized how printer drivers are created. The idea was to have a common format that could be used by printer manufacturers so that a driver could work across all different types of UNIX systems. That way, a manufacturer had to create the driver only once to work for Linux, Mac OS X, and a variety of UNIX derivatives.

- **Printer classes**—You can use printer classes to create multiple print server entries that point to the same printer or one print server entry that points to multiple printers. In the first case, multiple entries can each allow different options (such as pointing to a particular paper tray or printing with certain character sizes or margins). In the second case, you can have a pool of printers so that printing is distributed, decreasing the occurrence of congested print queues often caused by a malfunctioning printer or a printer that is dealing with very large documents.

- **Printer browsing**—With printer browsing, client computers can see any CUPS printers on your LAN with browsing enabled. As a result, clients can simply select the printers they want to use from the printer names broadcast on the LAN, without needing to know in advance what the printers are named and where they are connected. You can turn off this feature if you don't want others on the LAN to see your printer.

- **Printer classes**—Printers can be grouped together into *classes*. Clients printing to a particular print class have their print jobs sent to the first available printer, instead of having to wait for a particular printer to become available. CUPS also supports *implicit classes*, which are print classes that are formed by merging identical network printers automatically.

- **UNIX print commands**—To integrate into Linux and other UNIX environments, CUPS offers versions of standard commands for printing and managing printers that have been traditionally offered with UNIX systems.

Many Linux distributions come with simplified methods of configuring CUPS printers. Here are a few examples:

- In Fedora, CentOS, and Red Hat Enterprise Linux systems, the Printer Configuration window (system-config-printer command) enables you to configure printers that use the CUPS facility.

- In Ubuntu, the same Printer Configuration window (select System ➪ Administration ➪ Printing to open it) lets you add, delete, and manage printers.

- In SUSE, the YaST facility includes a printer configuration module. From the YaST Control Center, select Hardware ➪ Printer.

For distributions that don't have their own printer configuration tools, there are several ways to configure CUPS using tools that aren't specific to a Linux distribution. Here are a couple of them:

- **Configuring CUPS from a browser**—CUPS offers a Web-based interface for adding and managing printers. You can access this service by typing **localhost:631** from a Web browser on the computer running the CUPS service. (See the section "Using Web-Based CUPS Administration," later in this chapter.) The KDE desktop comes with a tool for managing CUPS server features. To launch the KDE CUPS Server Configuration window, type **/usr/bin/cupsdconf** from a Terminal window.

- **Configuring CUPS manually**—You also can configure CUPS manually (that is, edit the configuration files and start the cupsd daemon manually). Configuration files for CUPS are contained in the /etc/cups directory. In particular, you might be interested in the cupsd.conf file, which identifies permission, authentication, and other information for the printer daemon, and printers.conf, which identifies addresses and options for configured printers. Use the classes.conf file to define local printer classes.

## Coming from Windows

**You can print to CUPS from non-UNIX systems as well. For example, you can use a PostScript printer driver to print directly from Windows XP to your CUPS server. You can use CUPS without modification by configuring the XP computer with a PostScript driver that uses** http://printservername:631/printers/targetPrinter **as its printing port.** ∎

To use CUPS, you need to have it installed. Most Linux distributions let you choose to add CUPS during the initial system install or will simply add CUPS by default. If CUPS was not added when you first installed your Linux distribution, check your original installation medium (DVD or CD) to see whether it is there for you to install now. Fedora, Slackware, Ubuntu, SUSE, and many other Linux distributions have CUPS on the first CD or DVD of their installation sets.

# Setting Up Printers

Although using the printer administration tools specifically built for your distribution is usually best, many Linux systems simply rely on the tools that come with the CUPS software package. This section explores how to use CUPS Web-based administration tools that come with every Linux distribution and then examines the printer configuration tool system-config-printer, which comes with Ubuntu, Fedora, and Red Hat Enterprise Linux systems to enable you to set up printers.

## Using Web-based CUPS administration

CUPS offers its own Web-based administrative tool for adding, deleting, and modifying printer configurations on your computer. The CUPS print service (using the cupsd daemon) listens on port 631 to provide access to the CUPS Web-based administrative interface.

If CUPS is already running on your computer, you can immediately use CUPS Web-based administration from your Web browser. To see whether CUPS is running and to start setting up your printers, open a Web browser on the local computer and type the following into its location box:

```
http://localhost:631/
```

A prompt for a valid login name and password may appear. If so, type the root login name and the root user's password, and then click OK. If you are using Ubuntu, a screen similar to the one shown in Figure 15-1 appears.

**FIGURE 15-1**

CUPS provides a Web-based administration tool.

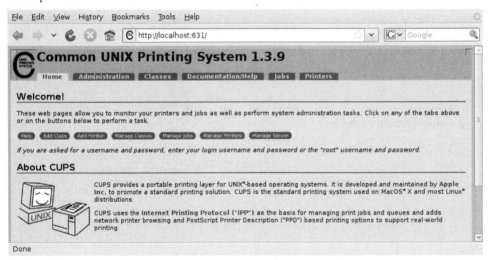

By default, Web-based CUPS administration is available only from the local host. To access Web-based CUPS administration from another computer, you must change the /admin section in the /etc/cups/cupsd.conf file. As recommended in the text of this file, you should limit access to CUPS administration from the Web. The following example includes an Allow line to permit access from a host from IP address 10.0.0.5. You must also add a Listen line, so your CUPS service will listen for requests outside of the local host. In this example, a Listen line is configured to listen on your external interface to your LAN on address 10.0.0.1.

```
Listen localhost:631
Listen 10.0.0.1:631
```

```
<Location /admin>
AuthType Basic
AuthClass System
Order Deny, Allow
Deny from All
Allow From 127.0.0.1
Allow From 10.0.0.5
</Location>
```

From the computer at address 10.0.0.5, you would type

`http://localhost:631/admin`

(substituting the CUPS server's name or IP address for *localhost*), and when prompted, enter the root username and password. For Ubuntu, you can enter your regular user name and password (assuming the user has sudo privileges). You may be asked for that information later in the process of adding a printer.

Now, with the Admin screen displayed, here's how to set up a printer in Ubuntu:

1. Click the Add Printer button. The Add New Printer screen appears.

2. Type a Name, Location, and Description for the printer and click Continue.

3. Select the device to which the printer is connected. The printer can be connected locally to a parallel, SCSI, serial, or USB port directly on the computer. Alternatively, you can select a network connection type for Apple printers (appSocket/HP JetDirect), Internet Printing Protocol (http or ipp), or a Windows printer (using SAMBA or SMB).

4. If prompted for more information, you may need to further describe the connection to the printer. For example, you may need to enter the baud rate and parity for a serial port, or you might be asked for the network address for an IPP or Samba printer.

5. Select the make of the print driver (if you don't see the manufacturer of your printer listed, choose PostScript for a PostScript printer or HP for a PCL printer). For the make you choose, you will be able to select a specific model.

6. If you are asked to set options for your printer, you may do so. Then select Set Printer Options to continue.

7. If the printer is added successfully, the new printer page appears; from it, you can print a test page or modify the printer configuration.

After you are able to print from CUPS, you can return to the CUPS Web-based administration page and do further work with your printers. Here are a few examples of what you can do:

- **List print jobs**—Click Jobs to see what print jobs are currently active from any of the printers configured for this server. Click Show Completed Jobs to see information about jobs that are already printed.

- **Create a printer class**—Click Classes. Then click Add Class and identify a name and location for a printer class. Click Continue. Then, from the list of Printers configured on your server, select the ones to go into this class.

- **Cancel a print job**—If you print a 100-page job by mistake or if the printer is spewing out junk, the cancel feature can be very handy. Click Jobs; then click Show Active Jobs to see what print jobs are currently in the queue for the printer. Select the Cancel Job button next to the print job you want to cancel.

- **View printers**—You can click the Printers link from the top of any of the CUPS Web-based administration pages to view the printers you have configured. For each printer that appears, you can click Stop Printer (to stop the printer from printing but still accept print jobs for the queue), Reject Jobs (to not accept any further print jobs for the moment), or Print Test Page (to print a page). Figure 15-2 shows the Printers page.

**FIGURE 15-2**

Print test pages or temporarily stop printing from the Printers page.

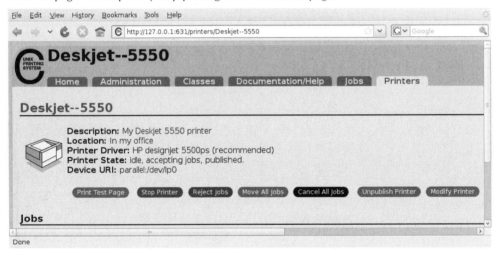

## Using the Printer Configuration window

If you are using Ubuntu, Fedora, RHEL, or other Red Hat–based systems, you can use the Printer Configuration window to set up your printers. In fact, I recommend that you use it instead of CUPS Web administration because the resulting printer configuration files are tailored to work with the way the CUPS service is started on those systems.

To install a printer from your GNOME desktop in Ubuntu or Fedora, start the Printer Configuration window by selecting System ➪ Administration ➪ Printing or as root user by typing **system-config-printer**. This tool lets you add and delete printers and edit printer properties. It also lets you send test pages to those printers to make sure they are working properly.

The key here is that you are configuring printers that are managed by your print daemon (cupsd for the CUPS service). After a printer is configured, users on your local system can use it. You can refer to the "Configuring Print Servers" section to learn how to make the server available to users from other computers on your network.

The printers that you set up can be connected directly to your computer (as on a parallel port) or to another computer on the network (for example, from another UNIX system or Windows system).

### Configuring local printers with the Printer Configuration window

Add a local printer (in other words, a printer connected directly to your computer) with the Printer Configuration window using the following procedure. (See the sidebar "Choosing a Printer" if you don't yet have a printer.)

## Tip

**Connect your printer before starting this procedure. This enables the printer software to autodetect the printer's location and to immediately test the printer when you have finished adding it.** ■

# Choosing a Printer

An excellent list of printers supported in Linux is available from the Linux Foundation site at `www.linux-foundation.org/en/OpenPrinting` (select the OpenPrinting Database link). I strongly recommend that you visit that site before you purchase a printer to work with Linux. In addition to showing supported printers, the site also has a page describing how to choose a printer for use with Linux:

`www.linuxfoundation.org/en/OpenPrinting/Database/DatabaseIntro`

In terms of general guidance when looking for a Linux printer, the PostScript language is the preferred format for Linux and UNIX printing and has been for many years. Every major word-processing product that runs on Fedora, SUSE, Debian, and UNIX systems supports PostScript printing on some level, so a printer that natively supports PostScript printing is sure to work in Linux.

If you get a PostScript printer and it is not explicitly shown in the list of supported printers, simply select the PostScript filter when you install the printer locally. No special drivers are needed. Your next best option is to choose a printer that supports PCL. In either case, make sure that the PostScript or PCL is implemented in the printer hardware and not in the Windows driver.

Avoid printers that are referred to as *Winprinters*. These printers use nonstandard printing interfaces (those other than PostScript or PCL). Support for these low-end printers is hit or miss. For example, some low-end HP DeskJet printers use the pnm2ppa driver to print documents in Printing Performance Architecture (PPA) format. Some Lexmark printers use the pbm217k driver to print. Although drivers are available for many of these Winprinters, many of them are not fully supported.

Ghostscript may also support your printer; if it does, you can use it to do your printing. Ghostscript (found at `www.ghostscript.com`) is a free PostScript-interpreter program. It can convert PostScript content to output that can be interpreted by a variety of printers. Both GNU and Aladdin Ghostscript drivers are available. Although the latest Aladdin drivers are not immediately released under the GPL, you can use older Aladdin drivers that are licensed under the GNU.

### Adding a local printer

To add a local printer from Ubuntu, Fedora, and several other Linux systems, follow these steps:

1. Select System ➪ Administration ➪ Printing from the Desktop menu or type the following as root user from a Terminal window:

   ```
   # system-config-printer &
   ```

   The Printer Configuration window appears.

2. Click New ➪ Printer. A New Printer window appears.

3. If the printer you want to configure is detected, simply select it and click Forward. If it is not detected, choose the device to which the printer is connected (LPT #1 and Serial Port #1 are the first parallel and serial ports, respectively) and click Forward. (Type **/usr/sbin/lpinfo -v | less** in a shell to see all available ports.) You are asked to identify the printer's driver.

4. To use an installed driver for your printer, choose Select Printer From Database, and then choose the manufacturer of your printer. As an alternative, you could select Provide PPD File and supply your own PPD file (for example, if you have a printer that is not supported in Linux and you have a driver that was supplied with the printer). PPD stands for PostScript Printer Description. Select Forward to see a list of printer models from which you can choose.

## Coming from Windows

If you have a printer that works in Windows, but doesn't work in Linux, refer to the disk (probably a CD) that was included with the printer. Choose Provide PPD File, and then look for the PPD file on that disk to test that printer driver with Linux. ■

## Tip

If your printer doesn't appear on the list but supports PCL (HP's Printer Control Language), try selecting one of the HP printers (such as HP LaserJet). If your printer supports PostScript, select PostScript printer from the list. Selecting Raw Print Queue enables you to send documents to the printer that are already formatted for that printer type. ■

5. With your printer model selected, click the Printer, Driver, or PPD buttons at the bottom of the screen. In many cases, you will see useful information from the Linux Printing Database about how your printer is configured and how to tune it further. Click Forward to continue.

6. Add the following information and click Forward:

   - **Printer Name**—Add the name you want to give to identify the printer. The name must begin with a letter, but after the initial letter, it can contain a combination of letters, numbers, dashes (-), and underscores (_). For example, an HP printer on a computer named maple could be named hp-maple.

- **Description**—Add a few words describing the printer, such as its features (an HP LaserJet 2100M with PCL and PS support).

- **Location**—Add some words that describe the printer's location (for example, "In Room 205 under the coffeepot").

7. When the message that you are about to create a new printer appears, click Apply. The new printer entry appears in the Printer Configuration window, as shown in Figure 15-3.

**FIGURE 15-3**

Add printers connected locally or remotely with the Printer Configuration window.

8. If you want the printer to be your default printer, right-click the printer and select Set As Default. As you add other printers, you can change the default printer by selecting the one you want and Set As Default again.

9. Printing should be working at this point. To make sure, open a Terminal window and use the lpr command to print a file (such as `lpr /etc/hosts`). (If you want to share this printer with other computers on your network, refer to the "Configuring Print Servers" section of this chapter.)

### Editing a local printer

After selecting the printer you want to configure, choose from the following menu options to change its configuration:

- **Settings**—The Description, Location, Device URI, and Make and Model information you created earlier are displayed on this dialog. Click Policies to set the following items:

  - **State**—Select check boxes to indicate whether the printer will print jobs that are in the queue (Enabled), accept new jobs for printing (Accepting Jobs), or be available to be shared with other computers that can communicate with your computer (Shared). You also must select Server Settings and click the "Share published printers connected to this system" check box before the printer will accept print jobs from other computers.

  - **Policies**—In case of error, the stop-printer selection causes all printing to that printer to stop. You can also select to have the job discarded (abort-job) or retried (retry-job) in the event of an error condition.

  - **Banner**—Add banner pages at the beginning or end of a job. This is a good practice for a printer that is shared by many people. The banner page helps you sort who gets which print job. The standard banner page shows the ID of the print job, the title of the file, the user who requested the print job, and any billing information associated with it.

- **Access Control**. If your printer is a shared printer, you can select this window to create a list that either allows users access to the printer (with all others denied) or denies users access to the printer (with all others allowed).

- **Printer Options**. Click Printer Options to set defaults for options related to the printer driver. The available options are different for different printers. Many of these options can be overridden when someone prints a document. Here are a few of the options you might (or might not) have available:

  - **Watermark**—Several Watermark settings are available to enable you to add and change watermarks on your printed pages. By default, Watermark and Overlay are off (None). By selecting Watermark (behind the text) or Overlay (over the text), you can set the other Watermark settings to determine how watermarks and overlays are done. Watermarks can go on every page (All) or only the first page (First Only).

    Select Watermark Text to choose what words are used for the watermark or overlay (Draft, Copy, Confidential, Final, and so on). You can then select the font type, size, style, and intensity of the watermark or overlay.

  - **Resolution Enhancement**—You can use the printer's current settings or choose to turn resolution enhancement on or off.

  - **Page Size**—The default is U.S. letter size, but you can also ask the printer to print legal size, envelopes, ISO A4 standard or several other page sizes.

  - **Media Source**—Choose which tray to print from. Select Tray 1 to insert pages manually.

  - **Levels of Gray**—Choose to use the printer's current levels of gray or have enhanced or standard gray levels turned on.

- **Resolution**—Select the default printing resolution (such as 300, 600, or 1,200 dots per inch). Higher resolutions result in better quality but take longer to print.

- **EconoMode**—Either use the printer's current setting or choose a mode where you save toner or one where you have the highest possible quality.

- **Job Options**—Click Job Options to set common default options that will be used for this printer if the application printing the job doesn't already set them. These include Common Options (number of copies, orientation, scale to fit, and pages per side), Image Options (scaling, saturation, hue, and gamma), and Text Options (characters/inch, lines/inch, and margin settings).

- **Ink/Toner Levels**—Click Ink/Toner Levels to see information on how much ink or toner your printer has left. (Not all printers report these values.)

  Click Apply when you are satisfied with the changes you made to the local printer.

## Configuring remote printers

To use a printer that is available on your network, you must identify that printer to your Linux system. Supported remote printer connections include Networked CUPS (IPP) printers, Networked UNIX (LPD) printers, Networked Windows (SAMBA) printers, and JetDirect printers. (Of course, both CUPS and UNIX print servers can be run from Linux systems as well as other UNIX systems.)

In each case, you need a network connection from your Linux system to the servers to which those printers are connected. To use a remote printer requires that someone set up that printer on the remote server computer. See the section "Configuring Print Servers" later in this chapter for information on how to do that on your Linux server.

Use the Printer Configuration window to configure each of the remote printer types. Here is how it is done in Ubuntu:

1. From the Desktop panel, select System ➪ Administration ➪Printing.
2. Click New Printer. The New Printer window appears.
3. Depending on the type of ports you have on your computer, select one of the following:
   - **LPT #1**—For a printer connected to your parallel port.
   - **Serial Port #1**—For a printer connected to your serial port.
   - **AppleSocket/HP JetDirect**—For a JetDirect printer.
   - **Internet Printing Protocol (IPP)**—For a CUPS or other IPP printer.
   - **LPD/LPR Host or Printer**—For a UNIX printer.
   - **Windows Printer via SAMBA**—For a Windows system printer.

Continue with the steps in whichever of the following sections is appropriate.

### Adding a remote CUPS printer

If you chose to add a CUPS (IPP) printer from the Printer Configuration window, you must add the following information to the window that appears:

- **Host**—Hostname of the computer to which the printer is attached (or otherwise accessible). This can be an IP address or TCP/IP hostname for the computer. (The TCP/IP name is accessible from your /etc/hosts file or through a DNS name server.)

- **Queue**—Printer name on the remote CUPS print server. CUPS supports printer instances, which allows each printer to have several sets of options. If the remote CUPS printer is configured this way, you are able to choose a particular path to a printer, such as hp/300dpi or hp/1200dpi. A slash character separates the print queue name from the printer instance.

Complete the rest of the procedure as you would for a local printer (see the "Adding a Local Printer" section earlier in this chapter).

### Adding a remote UNIX printer

If you chose to add a UNIX printer (LPD/LPR) from the Printer Configuration window, you must add the following information to the window that appears:

- **Host**—Hostname of the computer to which the printer is attached (or otherwise accessible). This is the IP address or TCP/IP name for the computer (the TCP/IP name is accessible from your /etc/hosts file or through a DNS name server). Select the Probe button to search for the host.

- **Queue**—Printer name on the remote UNIX computer.

Complete the rest of the procedure as you would for a local printer (see the "Adding a Local Printer" section earlier in this chapter).

## Tip

If the print job you send to test the printer is rejected, the print server computer may not have allowed you access to the printer. Ask the remote computer's administrator to add your hostname to the /etc/lpd. perms file. (Type lpq -P*printer* to see the status of your print job.) ∎

### Adding a Windows (SMB) printer

Enabling your computer to access an SMB printer (the Windows printing service) involves adding an entry for the printer in the Select Connection window.

When you choose to add a Windows printer to the Printer Configuration window (Windows Printer via SAMBA), you are presented with a list of computers on your network that have been detected as offering SMB services (file and/or printing service). At that point, here is how you can configure the printer:

1. Type the URI of the printer, excluding the leading smb://. For example, /host1/ myprinter or /mygroup/host1/myprinter.

2. Select either Prompt user if authentication is required or Set authentication details now.

3. If you chose Set authentication details now, fill in the username and password needed to access the SMB printer. Click Verify to check that you can authenticate to the server.

4. Click Forward to continue.

Alternatively, you can identify a server that does not appear on the list of servers. Type the information needed to create an SMB URI that contains the following information:

- **Workgroup**—The workgroup name assigned to the SMB server. Using the workgroup name isn't necessary in all cases.

- **Server**—NetBIOS name or IP address for the computer, which may or may not be the same as its TCP/IP name. To translate this name into the address needed to reach the SMB host, Samba checks several places where the name may be assigned to an IP address. Samba checks the following (in the order shown) until it finds a match: the local /etc/hosts file, the local /etc/lmhosts file, a WINS server on the network, and responses to broadcasts on each local network interface to resolve the name.

- **Share**—Name under which the printer is shared with the remote computer. It may be different from the name by which local users of the SMB printer know the printer.

- **User**—Username is required by the SMB server system to give you access to the SMB printer. A username is not necessary if you are authenticating the printer based on share-level rather than user-level access control. With share-level access, you can add a password for each shared printer or file system.

- **Password**—Password associated with the SMB username or the shared resource, depending on the kind of access control being used.

## Caution

When you enter a User and Password for SMB, that information is stored unencrypted in the /etc/cups/printers.conf **file. Be sure that the file remains readable only by root.** ■

The following is an example of the SMB URI you could add to the SMB:// box:

```
jjones:my9passswd@FSTREET/NS1/hp
```

The URI shown here identifies the username (jjones), the user's password (my9passswd), the workgroup (FSTREET), the server (NS1), and the printer queue name (hp).

Complete the rest of the procedure as you would for a local printer (see the "Adding a Local Printer" section earlier in this chapter).

If everything is set up properly, you can use the standard lpr command to print the file to the printer. Using this example, employ the following form for printing:

```
$ cat file1.ps | lpr -P NS1-PS
```

**Tip**

If you are receiving failure messages, make sure that the computer to which you are printing is accessible. For the Printer NSI hp example, you can type smbclient -L NS1 -U jjones. Then type the password (`my9passswd`, in this case). The `-L` asks for information about the server; the `-U jjones` says to login the user jjones. If you get a positive name query response after you enter a password, you should see a list of shared printers and files from that server. Check the names and try printing again. ■

# Working with CUPS Printing

Tools such as CUPS Web-based Administration and the Printer Configuration window effectively hide the underlying CUPS facility. There may be times, however, when you want to work directly with the tools and configuration files that come with CUPS. The following sections describe how to use some special CUPS features.

## Configuring the CUPS server (cupsd.conf)

The cupsd daemon process listens for requests to your CUPS print server and responds to those requests based on settings in the `/etc/cups/cupsd.conf` file. The configuration variables in the `cupsd.conf` file are in the same form as those in the Apache configuration file (`httpd.conf` or `apache2.conf`). Type **man cupsd.conf** to see details on any of the settings.

The Printer Configuration window adds access information to the `cupsd.conf` file. For other Linux systems, you may need to configure the `cupsd.conf` file manually. You can step through the `cupsd.conf` file to further tune your CUPS server. Most of the settings are optional or can just be left as the default. Let's take a look at some of the settings in the `cupsd.conf` file.

No classification is set by default. With the classification set to `topsecret`, you can have Top Secret displayed on all pages that go through the print server:

```
Classification topsecret
```

Other classifications you can substitute for `topsecret` include `classified`, `confidential`, `secret`, and `unclassified`.

The `ServerCertificate` and `ServerKey` lines (commented out by default) can be set up to indicate where the certificate and key are stored, respectively:

```
ServerCertificate /etc/cups/ssl/server.crt
ServerKey /etc/cups/ssl/server.key
```

Activate these two lines if you want to do encrypted connections. Then add your certificate and key to the files noted.

The term *browsing* refers to the act of broadcasting information about your printer on your local network and listening for other print servers' information. Browsing is on by default only for the local host (@LOCAL). You can allow CUPS browser information (BrowseAllow) for additional selected addresses. Browsing information is broadcast, by default, on address 255.255.255.255. Here's how these defaults appear in the cupsd.conf file:

```
Browsing On
BrowseProtocols cups
BrowseOrder Deny,Allow
BrowseAllow from @LOCAL
BrowseAddress 255.255.255.255
Listen *:631
```

To enable Web-based CUPS administration, the cupsd daemon can be set to listen on port 631 for all network interfaces to your computer based on this entry: Listen *:631. By default, it only listens on the local interface (Listen localhost:631).

By turning on BrowseRelay (it's off by default), you can allow CUPS browse information to be passed among two or more networks. The source-address and destination-address can be individual IP addresses or can represent network numbers:

```
BrowseRelay source-address destination-address
```

This is a good way to enable users on several connected LANs to discover and use printers on other nearby LANs.

You can allow or deny access to different features of the CUPS server. An access definition for a CUPS printer (created from the Printer Configuration window) might appear as follows:

```
<Location /printers/ns1-hp1>
Order Deny,Allow
Deny From All
Allow From 127.0.0.1
AuthType None
</Location>
```

Here, printing to the ns1-hp1 printer is allowed only for users on the local host (127.0.0.1). No password is needed (AuthType None). To allow access to the administration tool, CUPS must be configured to prompt for a password (AuthType Basic).

## Starting the CUPS server

For Linux systems that use SystemV-style startup scripts (such as Fedora and RHEL), starting and shutting down the CUPS print service is pretty easy. Use the chkconfig command to turn on CUPS so it starts at each reboot. Run the cups startup script to have the CUPS service start immediately. In Fedora and RHEL, type the following as root user:

```
# chkconfig cupsd on
# /etc/init.d/cups start
```

In Ubuntu, type the following:

```
$ sudo /etc/init.d/cups start
```

If the CUPS service was already running, you should use restart instead of start. Using the restart option is also a good way to reread any configuration options you may have changed in the cupsd.conf file.

Other Linux systems vary in how they start up the CUPS service. For example, in Slackware, you can turn on CUPS printing permanently by simply making the rc.cups script executable and then turn it on immediately by executing it (typing the following as root user):

```
# chmod 755 /etc/rc.d/rc.cups
# /etc/rc.d/rc.cups start
```

In Gentoo Linux, you use the add option of the rc-update command to have the CUPS service start at each reboot and run the cupsd run-level script to start it immediately. For example, type the following as root user:

```
# rc-update add cupsd default
# /etc/init.d/cupsd start
```

Most Linux systems have similar ways of starting the CUPS service. You may need to poke around to see how CUPS starts on the distribution you are using.

## Configuring CUPS printer options manually

If your Linux distribution doesn't have a graphical means of configuring CUPS, you can edit configuration files directly. For example, when a new printer is created from the Printer Configuration window, it is defined in the /etc/cups/printers.conf file. Here is what a printer entry looks like:

```
</Printer hp>
<DefaultPrinter printer>
Info HP LaserJet 2100M
Location HP LaserJet 2100M in hall closet
DeviceURI parallel:/dev/lp0
State Idle
Accepting Yes
Shared No
JobSheets none none
QuotaPeriod 0
PageLimit 0
KLimit 0
</Printer>
```

This is an example of a local printer that serves as the default printer for the local system. The Shared No value is set because the printer is currently available only on the local system. The most interesting information relates to `DeviceURI`, which shows that the printer is connected to parallel port `/dev/lp0`. The state is `Idle` (ready to accept printer jobs), and the `Accepting` value is `Yes` (the printer is accepting print jobs by default).

The DeviceURI has several ways to identify the device name of a printer, reflecting where the printer is connected. Here are some examples listed in the `printers.conf` file:

```
DeviceURI parallel:/dev/plp
DeviceURI serial:/dev/ttyd1?baud=38400+size=8+parity=none+flow=soft
DeviceURI scsi:/dev/scsi/sc1d6l0
DeviceURI socket://hostname:port
DeviceURI tftp://hostname/path
DeviceURI ftp://hostname/path
DeviceURI http://hostname[:port]/path
DeviceURI ipp://hostname/path
DeviceURI smb://hostname/printer
```

The first three examples show the form for local printers (parallel, serial, and scsi). The other examples are for remote hosts. In each case, *hostname* can be the host's name or IP address. Port numbers or paths identify the locations of each printer on the host.

## Tip

If you find that you are not able to print because a particular printer driver is not supported in CUPS, you can set up your printer to accept jobs in raw mode. This can work well if you are printing from Windows clients that have the correct printer drivers installed. To enable raw printing in CUPS, uncomment the following line in the `/etc/cups/mime.types` file in Linux:

```
application/octet-stream
```

and uncomment the following line in the `/etc/cups/mime.convs` file:

```
application/octet-stream application/vnd.cups-raw 0 -
```

After that, you can print files as raw data to your printers without using the `-oraw` option to `print` commands. ∎

# Using Printing Commands

To remain backward-compatible with older UNIX and Linux printing facilities, CUPS supports many of the old commands for working with printing. Most command-line printing with CUPS can be performed with the `lpr` command. Word processing applications such as StarOffice, OpenOffice, and AbiWord are set up to use this facility for printing.

You can use the Printer Configuration window to define the filters needed for each printer so that the text can be formatted properly. Options to the `lpr` command can add filters to properly process the text. Other commands for managing printed documents include lpq (for viewing the contents of print queues), lprm (for removing print jobs from the queue), and lpc (for controlling printers).

## Printing with lpr

You can use the lpr command to print documents to both local and remote printers (provided the printers are configured locally). Document files can be either added to the end of the lpr command line or directed to the lpr command using a pipe (|). Here's an example of a simple lpr command:

```
$ lpr doc1.ps
```

When you specify just a document file with lpr, output is directed to the default printer. As an individual user, you can change the default printer by setting the value of the PRINTER variable. Typically, you add the PRINTER variable to one of your startup files, such as $HOME/.bashrc. Adding the following line to your .bashrc file, for example, sets your default printer to lp3:

```
export PRINTER=lp3
```

To override the default printer, specify a particular printer on the lpr command line. The following example uses the -P option to select a different printer:

```
$ lpr -P canyonps doc1.ps
```

The lpr command has a variety of options that enable lpr to interpret and format several different types of documents. These include -# *num*, where *num* is replaced by the number of copies to print (from 1 to 100) and -1 (which causes a document to be sent in raw mode, presuming that the document has already been formatted). To learn more options to lpr, type **man lpr**.

## Listing status with lpc

Use the lpc command to list the status of your printers. Here is an example:

```
$ /usr/sbin/lpc status
hp:
                   printer is on device 'parallel' speed -1
                   queuing is enabled
                   printing is disabled
                   no entries
                   daemon present
deskjet_5550:
                   printer is on device '/dev/null' speed -1
                   queuing is enabled
                   printing is disabled
                   no entries
                   daemon present
```

This output shows two active printers. The first (hp) is connected to your parallel port. The second (deskjet_5550) is a network printer (shown as /dev/null). The hp printer is currently disabled (offline), although the queue is enabled so people can continue to send jobs to the printer.

## Removing print jobs with lprm

Users can remove their own print jobs from the queue with the lprm command. Used alone on the command line, lprm removes all the user's print jobs from the default printer. To remove jobs from a specific printer, use the -P option, as follows:

```
$ lprm -P lp0
```

To remove all print jobs for the current user, type the following:

```
$ lprm -
```

The root user can remove all the print jobs for a specific user by indicating that user on the lprm command line. For example, to remove all print jobs for the user named mike, the root user types the following:

```
$ lprm -U mike
```

To remove an individual print job from the queue, indicate its job number on the lprm command line. To find the job number, type the lpq command. Here's what the output of that command may look like:

```
$ lpq
printer is ready and printing
Rank    Owner            Job Files               Total Size Time
active  root             133 /home/jake/pr1        467
2       root             197 /home/jake/mydoc    23948
```

The output shows two printable jobs waiting in the queue. (The printer is ready and printing the job listed as active.) Under the Job column, you can see the job number associated with each document. To remove the first print job, type the following:

```
# lprm 133
```

# Configuring Print Servers

You've configured a printer so that you and the other users on your computer can print to it. Now you want to share that printer with other people in your home, school, or office. Basically, that means configuring the printer as a print server.

The printers configured on your Linux system can be shared in different ways with other computers on your network. Not only can your computer act as a Linux print server (by configuring

CUPS), but it can also appear as an SMB (Windows) print server to client computers. After a local printer is attached to your Linux system and your computer is connected to your local network, you can use the procedures in this section to share the printer with client computers using a Linux (UNIX) or SMB interface.

## Configuring a shared CUPS printer

Making the local printer added to your Linux computer available to other computers on your network is fairly easy. If a TCP/IP network connection exists between the computers sharing the printer, you simply grant permission to all hosts, individual hosts, or users from remote hosts to access your computer's printing service.

To manually configure a printer entry in the /etc/cups/printers.conf file to accept print jobs from all other computers, make sure the Shared Yes line is set. The following example from a printers.conf entry earlier in this chapter demonstrates what the new entry would look like:

```
</Printer hp>
<DefaultPrinter printer>
Info HP LaserJet 2100M
Location HP LaserJet 2100M in hall closet
DeviceURI parallel:/dev/lp0
State Idle
Accepting Yes
Shared Yes
JobSheets none none
QuotaPeriod 0
PageLimit 0
KLimit 0
</Printer>
```

On Linux systems that use the Printer Configuration window described earlier in this chapter, it's best to set up your printer as a shared printer using that window. Here's how:

1. From the Desktop panel in GNOME, select System ➪ Administration ➪ Printing. The Printer Configuration window appears.

2. Double-click the name of the printer you want to share. (If the printer is not yet configured, refer to the "Setting Up Printers" section earlier in this chapter.)

3. Choose the Policies heading and select Shared so that a checkmark appears in the box.

4. If you want to restrict access to the printer to selected users, select the Access Control heading and choose one of the following options:

   - **Allow Printing for Everyone Except These Users**—With this selected, all users are allowed access to the printer. By typing user names into the Users box and clicking Add, you exclude selected users.

- **Deny Printing for Everyone Except These Users**—With this selected, all users are excluded from using the printer. Type user names into the Users box and click Add to allow access to the printer for only those names you enter.

Now you can configure other computers to use your printer, as described in the "Setting Up Printers" section of this chapter. If you try to print from another computer and it doesn't work, here are a few troubleshooting tips:

- **Open your firewall.** If you have a restrictive firewall, it may not permit printing. You must enable access to port 513 (UDP and TCP) and possibly port 631 to allow access to printing on your computer. See Chapter 27 for information on configuring your firewall.

- **Enable LPD-style printing.** Certain applications may require an older LPD-style printing service to print on your shared printer. To enable LPD-style printing on your CUPS server, you must turn on the cups-lpd service. Most Linux distributions that include CUPS should also have cups-lpd available. In Fedora and RHEL systems, type **yum install cups-lpd** as root user to install it. Then turn on the cups-lpd service and restart the xinetd daemon:

```
# chkconfig cups-lpd on
# service xinetd restart
```

- **Check names and addresses.** Make sure that you entered your computer's name and print queue properly when you configured it on the other computer. Try using the IP address instead of the hostname. (If that works, it indicates a DNS name resolution problem.) Running a tool such as ethereal enables you to see where the transaction fails.

Access changes to your shared printer are made in the `cupsd.conf` and `printers.conf` files in your `/etc/cups` directory.

## Configuring a shared Samba printer

Your Linux printers can be configured as shared SMB printers, so they appear to be available from Windows systems. To share your printer as if it were a Samba (SMB) printer, simply configure basic Samba server settings as described in Chapter 16. All your printers should be shared on your local network by default. The next section shows what the resulting settings look like and how you might want to change them.

### Understanding smb.conf for printing

When you configure Samba, the `/etc/samba/smb.conf` file is constructed to enable all of your configured printers to be shared. Here are a few lines from the `smb.conf` file that relate to printer sharing:

```
[global]
```

```
        .
        .
        .
    load printers = yes
    cups options = raw
;   printcap name = /etc/printcap
;   printing = cups
        .
        .
        .
[printers]
        comment = All Printers
        path = /var/spool/samba
        browseable = yes
        writeable = no
        printable = yes
```

These example settings are the result of configuring Samba from the Samba Server Configuration window in Fedora. You can read the comment lines to learn more about the file's contents. Lines beginning with a semicolon (;) indicate the default setting for the option on a comment line. Remove the semicolon to change the setting.

The selected lines show that printers from /etc/printcap were loaded and that the CUPS service is being used. With cups options set to raw, Samba assumes that print files have already been formatted by the time they reach your print server. This allows the Linux or Windows clients to provide their own print drivers.

The last few lines are the actual printers' definition. By changing the browseable option from no to yes, users can print to all printers (printable = yes).

### Setting up SMB clients

Chances are good that if you are configuring a Samba printer on your Linux computer, you want to share it with Windows clients. If Samba is set up properly on your computer and the client computers can reach you over the network, their finding and using your printer should be fairly straightforward.

The first place a client computer looks for your shared Samba printer is in Network Neighborhood (or My Network Places, for Windows 2000). From the Windows 9x desktop, double-click the Network Neighborhood icon. (From Windows 2000 or XP, double-click the My Network Places icon.) With Windows Vista, you open the Network icon. The name of your host computer (the NetBIOS name, which is probably also your TCP/IP name) appears on the screen or within a workgroup folder on the screen. Open the icon that represents your computer. The window that opens shows your shared printers and folders.

If your computer's icon doesn't appear in Network Neighborhood or My Network Places, try using the Search window. From Windows XP, choose Start ➪ Search ➪ Computer or People ➪ A Computer on the Network. Type your computer's name into the Computer Name box and click

Search. Double-click your computer in the Search window results panel. A window displaying the shared printers and folders from your computer appears.

After your shared printer appears in the window, configure a pointer to that printer by opening (double-clicking) the printer icon. A message tells you that you must set up the printer before you can use it. Click Yes to proceed to configure the printer for local use. The Add Printer Wizard appears. Answer the questions that ask you how you intend to use the printer, and add the appropriate drivers. When you are done, the printer appears in your printer window.

Another way to configure an SMB printer from a Windows XP operating system is to go to Start ➪ Printers and Faxes. In the Printers and Faxes window that appears, click the Add a Printer icon in the upper-left portion of the window, and then select Network Printer from the first window. From there you can browse and/or configure your SMB printer.

# Summary

Providing networked printing services is an essential efficiency on today's business network. With the use of a few network-attached devices, you can focus your printer spending on a few high-quality devices that multiple users can share instead of numerous lower-cost devices. In addition, a centrally located printer can make it easier to maintain the printer, while still enabling everyone to get his or her printing jobs done.

The default printing service in nearly every major Linux distribution today is the Common UNIX Printing Service (CUPS). Any Linux system that includes CUPS offers the CUPS Web-based administrative interface for configuring CUPS printing. It also offers configuration files in the /etc/cups directory for configuring printers and the CUPS service (cupsd daemon).

In Ubuntu, Fedora, and other Linux systems, you can configure your printer with the Printer Configuration windows available in both K Desktop and GNOME environments. A variety of drivers makes it possible to print to different kinds of printers, as well as to printers that are connected to computers on the network.

You can set up your computer as a Linux print server, and you can also have your computer emulate an SMB (Windows) print server. After your network is configured properly and a local printer is installed, sharing that printer over the network as a UNIX or SMB print server is not very complicated.

# Running a File Server

Most networked computers are on the network in the first place so that users can share information. Some users need to collectively edit documents for a project, share access to spreadsheets and forms used in the daily operation of a company, or perform any number of similar file-sharing activities. It also can be efficient for groups of people on a computer network to share common applications and directories of information needed to do their jobs. By far the best way to accomplish the centralized sharing of data is through a file server.

A centralized file server can be backed up, preserving all stored data in one fell swoop. It can focus on the tasks of getting files to end users, rather than running user applications that can use client resources. And a centralized file server can be used to control access to information—security settings can dictate who can access what.

Linux systems include support for each of the most common file server protocols in use today. Among the most common file server types in use today are the Network File System (NFS), which has always been the file-sharing protocol of choice for Linux and other UNIX systems, and Samba (SMB protocol), which is often used by networks with many Windows and OS/2 computers.

## Coming from Windows

Samba allows you to share files with Windows PCs on your network, as well as access Windows file and print servers, making your Linux box fit in better with Windows-centric or mixed organizations. ■

This chapter describes how to set up file servers and clients associated with NFS and Samba.

## Tip

When selecting file services to provide, keep in mind that less is more. If your clients and servers support multiple-file access capabilities (both NFS and SMB, for example), pick the service that lends itself to making the task less complicated for your organization. ■

# Setting Up an NFS File Server

Instead of representing storage devices as drive letters (A, B, C, and so on), as they are in Microsoft operating systems, Linux systems connect file systems from multiple hard disks, floppy disks, CD-ROMs, and other local devices invisibly to form a single Linux file system. The Network File System (NFS) facility enables you to extend your Linux file system in the same way, to connect file systems on other computers to your local directory structure.

An NFS file server provides an easy way to share large amounts of data among the users and computers in an organization. An administrator of a Linux system that is configured to share its file systems using NFS has to perform the following tasks to set up NFS:

1. **Set up the network.** If a LAN or other network link is already connecting the computers on which you want to use NFS, you already have the network you need.

2. **Choose what to share on the server.** Decide which file systems on your Linux NFS server to make available to other computers. You can choose any point in the file system and make all files and directories below that point accessible to other computers.

3. **Set up security on the server.** You can use several different security features to suit the level of security with which you are comfortable. Mount-level security lets you restrict the computers that can mount a resource and, for those allowed to mount it, lets you specify whether it can be mounted read/write or read-only. With user-level security, you map users from the client systems to users on the NFS server so that they can rely on standard Linux read/write/execute permissions, file ownership, and group permissions to access and protect files. Linux systems that support Security Enhanced Linux (SELinux), such as Fedora and Red Hat Enterprise Linux, offer another means of offering or restricting shared NFS files and directories.

4. **Mount the file system on the client.** Each client computer that is allowed access to the server's NFS shared file system can mount it anywhere the client chooses. For example, you may mount a file system from a computer called maple on the /mnt/maple directory in your local file system. After it is mounted, you can view the contents of that directory by typing **ls /mnt/maple**. Then you can use the cd command below the /mnt/maple mount point to see the files and directories it contains.

Figure 16-1 illustrates a Linux file server using NFS to share (export) a file system and a client computer mounting the file system to make it available to its local users.

**FIGURE 16-1**

NFS can make selected file systems available to other computers.

In this example, a computer named oak makes its `/apps/bin` directory available to clients on the network (pine, maple, and spruce) by adding an entry to the `/etc/exports` file. The client computer (pine) sees that the resource is available and mounts the resource on its local file system at the mount point `/oak/apps`, after which any files, directories, or subdirectories from `/apps/bin` on oak are available to users on pine (given proper permissions).

Although it is often used as a file server (or other type of server), Linux is a general-purpose operating system, so any Linux system can share file systems (export) as a server or use another computer's file systems (mount) as a client. Contrast this with dedicated file servers, such as NetWare, which can only share files with client computers (such as Windows workstations) and never act as a client.

## Note

A file system is usually a structure of files and directories that exists on a single device (such as a hard disk partition or CD-ROM). A *Linux file system* refers to the entire directory structure (which may include file systems from several disks or NFS resources), beginning from root (/) on a single computer. A shared directory in NFS may represent all or part of a computer's file system, which can be attached (from the shared directory down the directory tree) to another computer's file system. ■

# Getting NFS

Although nearly every Linux system supports NFS client and server features, NFS is not always installed by default. You'll need different packages for different Linux systems to install NFS. Here are some examples:

- **Fedora and Red Hat Enterprise Linux systems**—You need to install the nfs-utils package to use Fedora as an NFS server. There is also a graphical NFS Configuration tool that requires you to install the system-config-nfs package. NFS client features are in the base operating system. To turn on the nfs service, type the following:

```
# service nfs start
# chkconfig nfs on
```

- **Ubuntu and Debian**—To act as an NFS client, the nfs-common and portmap packages are required; for an NFS server, the nfs-kernel-server package must be added. The following apt-get command line (if you are connected to the Internet) installs them all. Then, after you add an exported file system to the /etc/exports file (as described later), you can start the nfs-common and nfs-kernel-server scripts, as shown here:

```
# apt-get install nfs-common portmap nfs-kernel-server
# /etc/init.d/nfs-kernel-server start
# /etc/init.d/nfs-common start
```

- Gentoo—With Gentoo, NFS file system and NFS server support must be configured into the kernel to use NFS server features. Installing the nfs-utils package (emerge nfs-utils) should get the required packages. To start the service, run rc-update and start the service immediately:

```
# emerge nfs-utils
# rc-update add portmap default
# rc-update add nfs default
# /etc/init.d/nfs start
```

The commands (mount, exportfs, and so on) and files (/etc/exports, /etc/fstab, and so on) for actually configuring NFS are the same on every Linux system I've encountered. So after you have NFS installed and running, just follow the instructions in this chapter to start using NFS.

# Sharing NFS file systems

To share an NFS file system from your Linux system, you need to export it from the server system. Exporting is done in Linux by adding entries into the /etc/exports file. Each entry identifies a directory in your local file system that you want to share with other computers. The entry also identifies the other computers that can share the resource (or opens it to all computers) and includes other options that reflect permissions associated with the directory.

Remember that when you share a directory, you are sharing all files and subdirectories below that directory as well (by default). So, you need to be sure that you want to share everything in that directory structure. There are still ways to restrict access within that directory structure; those are discussed later in this chapter.

## Configuring the /etc/exports file

To make a directory from your Linux system available to other systems, you need to export that directory. Exporting is done on a permanent basis by adding information about an exported directory to the /etc/exports file.

The format of the /etc/exports file is

```
Directory    Host(Options)    # Comments
```

where `Directory` is the name of the directory that you want to share, and `Host` indicates the host computer to which the sharing of this directory is restricted. `Options` can include a variety of options to define the security measures attached to the shared directory for the host. (You can repeat `Host/Option` pairs.) `Comments` are any optional comments you want to add (following the # sign).

As root user, you can use any text editor to configure /etc/exports to modify shared directory entries or add new ones. Here's an example of an /etc/exports file:

```
/cal    *.linuxtoys.net(rw)                # Company events
/pub    (ro,insecure,all_squash)           # Public dir
/home   maple(rw,squash uids=0-99) spruce(rw,squash uids=0-99)
```

The /cal entry represents a directory that contains information about events related to the company. It is made accessible to everyone with accounts to any computers in the company's domain (*.linuxtoys.net). Users can write files to the directory as well as read them (indicated by the rw option). The comment (# Company events) simply serves to remind you of what the directory contains.

The /pub entry represents a public directory. It allows any computer and user to read files from the directory (indicated by the ro option) but not to write files. The insecure option enables any computer, even one that doesn't use a secure NFS port, to access the directory. The all_squash option causes all users (UIDs) and groups (GIDs) to be mapped to the user ID 65534 (which is the nfsnobody user in Fedora and the nobody user in Ubuntu), giving them minimal permission to files and directories.

The /home entry enables a set of users to have the same /home directory on different computers. Say, for example, that you are sharing /home from a computer named oak. The computers named maple and spruce could each mount that directory on their own /home directories. If you gave all users the same username/UIDs on all machines, you could have the same /home/user directory available for each user, regardless of which computer they are logged into. The uids=0-99 is used to exclude any administrative login from another computer from changing any files in the shared directory.

These are just examples; you can share any directories that you choose, including the entire file system (/). Of course, there are security implications of sharing the whole file system or sensitive parts of it (such as /etc). Security options that you can add to your /etc/exports file are described throughout the sections that follow.

### Hostnames in /etc/exports

You can indicate in the /etc/exports file which host computers can have access to your shared directory. If you want to associate multiple hostnames or IP addresses with a particular shared directory, be sure to have a space before each hostname. However, add no spaces between a hostname and its options. For example:

```
/usr/local maple(rw) spruce(ro,root_squash)
```

Notice that there is a space after (rw) but none after maple. You can identify hosts in several ways:

- **Individual host**—Enter one or more TCP/IP hostnames or IP addresses. If the host is in your local domain, you can simply indicate the hostname. Otherwise, use the full host.domain format. These are valid ways to indicate individual host computers:

  ```
  maple
  maple.handsonhistory.com
  10.0.0.11
  ```

- **IP network**—Allow access to all hosts from a particular network address by indicating a network number and its netmask, separated by a slash (/). Here are valid ways to designate network numbers:

  ```
  10.0.0.0/255.0.0.0 172.16.0.0/255.255.0.0
  192.168.18.0/255.255.255.0
  192.168.18.0/24
  ```

- **TCP/IP domain**—Using wildcards, you can include all or some host computers from a particular domain level. Here are some valid uses of the asterisk and question mark wildcards:

  ```
  *.handsonhistory.com
  *craft.handsonhistory.com
  ???.handsonhistory.com
  ```

  The first example matches all hosts in the handsonhistory.com domain. The second example matches woodcraft, basketcraft, or any other hostnames ending in craft in the handsonhistory.com domain. The final example matches any three-letter hostnames in the domain.

## Note

Using an asterisk doesn't match subdomains. For example, `*.handsonhistory.com` would not cause the hostname `mallard.duck.handsonhistory.com` to be included in the access list. ■

- **NIS groups**—You can allow access to hosts contained in an NIS group. To indicate an NIS group, precede the group name with an at (@) sign (for example, `@group`).

### Access options in /etc/exports

You don't have to just give away your files and directories when you export a directory with NFS. In the options part of each entry in `/etc/exports`, you can add options that allow or limit access by setting read/write permission. These options, which are passed to NFS, are as follows:

- `ro`—Client can mount this exported file system read-only. The default is to mount the file system read/write.

- `rw`—Explicitly asks that a shared directory be shared with read/write permissions. (If the client chooses, it can still mount the directory as read-only.)

### User mapping options in /etc/exports

In addition to options that define how permissions are handled generally, you can use options to set the permissions that specific users have to NFS shared file systems.

One method that simplifies this process is to have each user with multiple user accounts have the same username and UID on each machine. This makes it easier to map users so that they have the same permissions on a mounted file system that they do on files stored on their local hard disks. If that method is not convenient, user IDs can be mapped in many other ways. Here are some methods of setting user permissions and the `/etc/exports` option that you use for each method:

- **root user**—The client's root user is generally mapped into the `nfsnobody` username (UID 65534). This prevents a client computer's root user from being able to change all files and directories in the shared file system. If you want the client's root user to have root permission on the server, use the `no_root_squash` option.

## Tip

There may be other administrative users, in addition to root, that you want to squash. I recommend squashing UIDs 0–99 as follows: `squash_uids=0-99`. ■

- **nfsnobody or nobody user/group**—By using the 65534 user ID and group ID, you essentially create a user/group with permissions that do not allow access to files that belong to any real users on the server, unless those users open permission to everyone. However, files created by the 65534 user or group are available to anyone assigned as the 65534 user or group. To set all remote users to the 65534 user/group, use the `all_squash` option.

The 65534 UIDs and GIDs are used to prevent the ID from running into a valid user or group ID. Using anonuid or anongid options, you can change the 65534 user or group, respectively. For example, anonuid=175 sets all anonymous users to UID 175, and anongid=300 sets the GID to 300. (Only the number is displayed when you list file permission unless you add entries with names to /etc/password and /etc/group for the new UIDs and GIDs.)

- **User mapping**—If a user has login accounts for a set of computers (and has the same ID), NFS, by default, maps that ID. This means that if the user named mike (UID 110) on maple has an account on pine (mike, UID 110), he can use his own remotely mounted files on either computer from either computer.

  If a client user who is not set up on the server creates a file on the mounted NFS directory, the file is assigned to the remote client's UID and GID. (An ls -l on the server shows the UID of the owner.) Use the map_static option to identify a file that contains user mappings.

## Exporting the shared file systems

After you have added entries to your /etc/exports file, run the exportfs command to have those directories exported (made available to other computers on the network). Reboot your computer or restart the NFS service, and the exportfs command runs automatically to export your directories. If you want to export them immediately, run exportfs from the command line (as root).

## Tip

Running the exportfs command after you change the exports file is a good idea. If any errors are in the file, exportfs identifies them for you. ∎

Here's an example of the exportfs command:

```
# /usr/sbin/exportfs -a -v
exporting maple:/pub
exporting spruce:/pub
exporting maple:/home
exporting spruce:/home
exporting *:/mnt/win
```

The -a option indicates that all directories listed in /etc/exports should be exported. The -v option says to print verbose output. In this example, the /pub and /home directories from the local server are immediately available for mounting by those client computers that are named (maple and spruce). The /mnt/win directory is available to all client computers.

Running the exportfs command temporarily makes your exported NFS directories available. To have your NFS directories available on an ongoing basis (that is, every time your system reboots), you need to set your nfs startup scripts to run at boot time. This is described in the next section.

### Starting the nfs daemons

If NFS has been disabled on your system (or is not active by default), you need to start the service. Different Linux distributions have different ways of turning on the NFS service, as you saw in the "Getting NFS" section earlier in the chapter. This section explores how the service is turned on in Fedora and Red Hat Enterprise Linux systems.

In Fedora, you can use the `chkconfig` command to turn on the NFS service so that your files are exported and the nfsd daemons are running when your system boots. There are two startup scripts you want to turn on for the service to work properly. The NFS service exports file systems (from `/etc/exports`) and starts the nfsd daemon that listens for service requests. The nfslock service starts the lockd daemon, which helps allow file locking to prevent multiple simultaneous use of critical files over the network.

To turn on the NFS service, type the following as root user:

```
# chkconfig nfs on
# chkconfig nfslock on
```

The next time you start your computer, the NFS service will start automatically, and your exported directories will be available. If you want to start the service immediately, without waiting for a reboot, type the following:

```
# /etc/init.d/nfs start
# /etc/init.d/nfslock start
```

The NFS service should now be running and ready to share directories with other computers on your network.

## Using NFS file systems

After a server exports a directory over the network using NFS, a client computer connects that directory to its own file system using the `mount` command. That's the same command used to mount file systems from local hard disks, CDs, and floppies, but with slightly different options.

`mount` can automatically mount NFS directories added to the `/etc/fstab` file, just as it does with local disks. NFS directories can also be added to the `/etc/fstab` file in such a way that they are not automatically mounted (so you can mount them manually when you choose). With a `noauto` option, an NFS directory listed in `/etc/fstab` is inactive until the `mount` command is used, after the system is up and running, to mount the file system.

### Manually mounting an NFS file system

If you know that the directory from a computer on your network has been exported (that is, made available for mounting), you can mount that directory manually using the `mount` command. This is a good way to make sure that it is available and working before you set it up to mount permanently. Here is an example of mounting the /tmp directory from a computer named maple on your local computer:

```
# mkdir /mnt/maple
# mount maple:/tmp /mnt/maple
```

The first command (mkdir) creates the mount point directory (/mnt is a common place to put temporarily mounted disks and NFS file systems). The mount command identifies the remote computer and shared file system separated by a colon (maple:/tmp), and the local mount point directory (/mnt/maple) follows.

## Note

**If the mount fails, make sure the NFS service is running on the server and that the server's firewall rules don't deny access to the service. From the server, type ps ax | grep nfsd to see a list of nfsd server processes. If you don't see the list, try to start your NFS daemons as described in the previous section. To view your firewall rules, type iptables -L (see Chapter 27 for a description of firewalls). By default, the nfsd daemon listens for NFS requests on port number 2049. Your firewall must accept udp requests on ports 2049 (nfs) and 111 (rpc). In some Linux systems, such as Fedora, you may need to set static ports for related services, then open ports for those services. To accomplish this, you can open the /etc/sysconfig/nfs file and set static port numbers for RQUOTAD_PORT, LOCKD_TCPPORT, LOCKD_UDPPORT, MOUNTD_PORT, STATD_PORT, and STATD_OUTGOING_PORT. ∎**

To ensure that the mount occurred, type **mount**. This command lists all mounted disks and NFS file systems. Here is an example of the mount command and its output (with file systems not pertinent to this discussion edited out):

```
# mount
/dev/sda3 on / type ext3 (rw)
...
...
...
maple:/tmp on /mnt/maple type nfs (rw,addr=10.0.0.11)
```

The output from the mount command shows the mounted disk partitions, special file systems, and NFS file systems. The first output line shows the hard disk (/dev/sda3), mounted on the root file system (/), with read/write permission (rw), with a file system type of ext3 (the standard Linux file system type). The just-mounted NFS file system is the /tmp directory from maple (maple:/tmp). It is mounted on /mnt/maple and its mount type is nfs. The file system was mounted read/write (rw), and the IP address of maple is 10.0.0.11 (addr=10.0.0.11).

This is a simple example of using mount with NFS. The mount is temporary and is not remounted when you reboot your computer. You can also add options for NFS mounts:

- -a—Mount all file systems in /etc/fstab (except those indicated as noauto).
- -f—This goes through the motions of (fakes) mounting the file systems on the command line (or in /etc/fstab). Used with the -v option, -f is useful for seeing what mount would do before it actually does it.

- -F—When used with -a, you tell mount to fork off a new incarnation of mount for each file system listed to be mounted in the /etc/fstab file. An advantage of using this option, as it relates to NFS shared directories, is that other file systems can be mounted if an NFS file system isn't immediately available. This option should not be used, however, if the order of mounting is important (for example, if you needed to mount /mnt/pcs and then /mnt/pcs/arctic).
- -r—Mounts the file system as read-only.
- -w—Mounts the file system as read/write. (For this to work, the shared file system must have been exported with read/write permission.)

The next section describes how to make the mount more permanent (using the /etc/fstab file) and how to select various options for NFS mounts.

## Automatically mounting an NFS file system

To set up an NFS file system to mount automatically each time you start your Linux system, you need to add an entry for that NFS file system to the /etc/fstab file. That file contains information about all different kinds of mounted (and available to be mounted) file systems for your system.

Here's the format for adding an NFS file system to your local system:

```
host:directory    mountpoint    nfs    options    0    0
```

The first item (host:directory) identifies the NFS server computer and shared directory. mountpoint is the local mount point on which the NFS directory is mounted. It's followed by the file system type (nfs). Any options related to the mount appear next in a comma-separated list. (The last two zeros configure the system to not dump the contents of the file system and not to run fsck on the file system.)

The following are examples of NFS entries in /etc/fstab:

```
maple:/tmp    /mnt/maple nfs    rsize=8192,wsize=8192  0 0
oak:/apps     /oak/apps  nfs    noauto,ro             0 0
```

In the first example, the remote directory /tmp from the computer named maple (maple:/tmp) is mounted on the local directory /mnt/maple (the local directory must already exist). The file system type is nfs, and read (rsize) and write (wsize) buffer sizes (discussed in the "Using mount options" section later in this chapter) are set at 8192 to speed data transfer associated with this connection. In the second example, the remote directory is /apps on the computer named oak. It is set up as an NFS file system (nfs) that can be mounted on the /oak/apps directory locally. This file system is not mounted automatically (noauto), however, and can be mounted only as read-only (ro) using the mount command after the system is already running.

## Tip

The default is to mount an NFS file system as read/write. However, the default for exporting a file system is read-only. If you are unable to write to an NFS file system, check that it was exported as read/write from the server. ■

### Mounting noauto file systems

Your /etc/fstab file may also contain devices for other file systems that are not mounted automatically. For example, you might have multiple disk partitions on your hard disk or an NFS shared file system that you might want to mount only occasionally. A noauto file system can be mounted manually. The advantage is that when you type the mount command, you can type less information and have the rest filled in by the contents of the /etc/fstab file. So, for example, you could type:

```
# mount /oak/apps
```

With this command, mount knows to check the /etc/fstab file to get the file system to mount (oak:/apps), the file system type (nfs), and the options to use with the mount (in this case ro for read-only). Instead of typing the local mount point (/oak/apps), you could have typed the remote file system name (oak:/apps) and had other information filled in.

## Tip

When naming mount points, including the name of the remote NFS server in that name can help you remember where the files are actually being stored. This may not be possible if you are sharing home directories (/ home) or mail directories (/var/spool/mail). For example, you might mount a file system from a machine called duck on the directory /mnt/duck. ■

### Using mount options

You can add several mount options to the /etc/fstab file (or to a mount command line itself) to influence how the file system is mounted. When you add options to /etc/fstab, they must be separated by commas. For example, here, the noauto, ro, and hard options are used when oak:/apps is mounted:

```
oak:/apps    /oak/apps   nfs   noauto,ro,hard    0 0
```

The following are some options that are valuable for mounting NFS file systems:

- hard—If this option is used and the NFS server disconnects or goes down while a process is waiting to access it, the process will hang until the server comes back up. This is helpful if it is critical that the data you are working with not get out of sync with the programs that are accessing it. (This is the default behavior.)
- soft—If the NFS server disconnects or goes down, a process trying to access data from the server will time out after a set period of time when this option is on. An input/output error is delivered to the process trying to access the NFS server.

- rsize—The number of bytes of data read at a time from an NFS server. The default is 1024. Using a larger number (such as 8192) will get you better performance on a network that is fast (such as a LAN) and is relatively error-free (that is, one that doesn't have a lot of noise or collisions).

- wsize—The number of bytes of data written at a time to an NFS server. The default is 1,024. Performance issues are the same as with the rsize option.

- timeo=#—Sets the time after an RPC timeout occurs that a second transmission is made, where # represents a number in tenths of a second. The default value is seven-tenths of a second. Each successive timeout causes the timeout value to be doubled (up to 60 seconds maximum). Increase this value if you believe that timeouts are occurring because of slow response from the server or a slow network.

- retrans=#—Sets the number of minor timeouts and retransmissions that need to happen before a major timeout occurs.

- retry=#—Sets how many minutes to continue to retry failed mount requests, where # is replaced by the number of minutes to retry. The default is 10,000 minutes (which is about one week).

- bg—If the first mount attempt times out, try all subsequent mounts in the background. This option is very valuable if you are mounting a slow or sporadically available NFS file system. By placing mount requests in the background, your system can continue to mount other file systems instead of waiting for the current one to complete.

## Note

If a nested mount point is missing, a timeout to allow for the needed mount point to be added occurs. For example, if you mount /usr/trip and /usr/trip/extra as NFS file systems and /usr/trip is not yet mounted when /usr/trip/extra tries to mount, /usr/trip/extra will time out. If you're lucky, /usr/trip comes up and /usr/trip/extra mounts on the next retry. ∎

- fg—If the first mount attempt times out, try subsequent mounts in the foreground. This is the default behavior. Use this option if it is imperative that the mount be successful before continuing (for example, if you were mounting /usr).

Any of the options that don't require a value can have no appended to them to have the opposite effect. For example, nobg indicates that the mount should not be done in the background.

### Using autofs to mount NFS file systems on demand

Recent improvements to auto-detecting and mounting removable devices have meant that you can simply insert or plug in those devices to have them detected, mounted, and displayed. However, to make the process of detecting and mounting remote NFS file systems more automatic, you still need to use a facility such as autofs (short for automatically mounted file systems).

The autofs facility will mount network file systems on demand when someone tries to use the file systems. With the autofs facility configured and turned on, you can cause any NFS shared directories to mount on demand. To use the autofs facility, you need to have the autofs package installed. (For Fedora and RHEL, you can type `yum install autofs` or for Ubuntu or Debian `apt-get install autofs` to install the package from the network.)

With autofs enabled, if you know the hostname and directory being shared by another host computer, simply change (`cd`) to the autofs mount directory (`/net` or `/var/autofs` by default). This causes the shared resource to be automatically mounted and made accessible to you.

The following steps explain how to turn on the autofs facility in Fedora:

1. In Fedora, as root user from a Terminal window, open the `/etc/auto.master` file and look for the following line:

   ```
   /net    -hosts
   ```

   This causes the `/net` directory to act as the mount point for the NFS shared directories you want to access on the network. (If there is a comment character at the beginning of that line, remove it.)

2. Start the autofs service by typing the following as root user:

   ```
   # /etc/init.d/autofs start
   ```

3. On a Fedora system, set up the autofs service to restart every time you boot your system:

   ```
   # chkconfig autofs on
   ```

Believe it or not, that's all you have to do. If you have a network connection to the NFS servers from which you want to share directories, try to access a shared NFS directory. For example, if you know that the `/usr/local/share` directory is being shared from the computer on your network named shuttle, you can do the following:

```
$ cd /net/shuttle
```

If that computer has any shared directories that are available to you, you can successfully change to that directory.

You also can type the following:

```
$ ls
usr
```

You should be able to see that the `usr` directory is part of the path to a shared directory. If there were shared directories from other top-level directories (such as `/var` or `/tmp`), you would see those as well. Of course, seeing any of those directories depends on how security is set up on the server.

Try going straight to the shared directory as well. For example:

```
$ cd /net/shuttle/usr/local/share
$ ls
info man music television
```

At this point, the `ls` should reveal the contents of the `/usr/local/share` directory on the computer named shuttle. What you can do with that content depends on how it was configured for sharing by the server.

This can be a bit disconcerting because you won't see any files or directories until you actually try to use them, such as changing to a network-mounted directory. The `ls` command, for example, won't show anything under a network-mounted directory until the directory is mounted, which may lead to a sometimes-it's-there-and-sometimes-it's-not impression. Just change to a network-mounted directory, or access a file on such a directory, and autofs will take care of the rest.

## Unmounting NFS file systems

After an NFS file system is mounted, unmounting it is simple. You use the `umount` command with either the local mount point or the remote file system name. For example, here are two ways you could unmount `maple:/tmp` from the local directory `/mnt/maple`.

```
# umount maple:/tmp
```

```
# umount /mnt/maple
```

Either form works. If `maple:/tmp` is mounted automatically (from a listing in `/etc/fstab`), the directory will be remounted the next time you boot Linux. If it was a temporary mount (or listed as `noauto` in `/etc/fstab`), it won't be remounted at boot time.

### Tip
**The command is** `umount`**, not unmount. This is easy to get wrong.** ∎

If you get the message `device is busy` when you try to unmount a file system, it means the unmount failed because the file system is being accessed. Most likely, one of the directories in the NFS file system is the current directory for your shell (or the shell of someone else on your system). The other possibility is that a command is holding a file open in the NFS file system (such as a text editor). Check your Terminal windows and other shells, and `cd` out of the directory if you are in it, or just close the Terminal windows.

If an NFS file system won't unmount, you can force it (`umount -f /mnt/maple`) or unmount and clean up later (`umount -l /mnt/maple`). The `-l` option is usually the better choice because a forced unmount can disrupt a file modification that is in progress.

## Other cool things to do with NFS

You can share some directories to make it convenient for a user to work from any of several different Linux computers on your network. Some examples of useful directories to share are:

- /var/spool/mail—By sharing this directory from your mail server and mounting it on the same directory on other computers on your network, users can access their mail from any of those other computers. This saves users from having to download messages to their current computers or from having to log in to the server just to get mail. There is only one mailbox for each user, no matter from where it is accessed.

- /home—This is a similar concept to sharing mail, except that all users have access to their home directories from any of the NFS clients. Again, you would mount /home on the same mount point on each client computer. When the user logs in, she has access to all of the startup files and data files contained in her /home/user directory.

## Tip

If your users rely on a shared /home directory, you should make sure that the NFS server that exports the directory is fairly reliable. If /home isn't available, the user may not have the startup files to log in correctly, or any of the data files needed to get work done. One workaround is to have a minimal set of startup files (.bashrc, .Xdefaults, and so on) available in the user's home directory when the NFS directory is not mounted. This enables the user to log in properly at those times. ∎

- /project—Although you don't have to use this name, a common practice among users on a project is to share a directory structure containing files that people on the project need to share so that everyone can work on original files and keep copies of the latest versions in one place. (Of course, a better way to manage a project is with CVS or some other version control–type software, but this is a poor person's way to do it.)

- /var/log—An administrator can keep track of log files from several different computers by mounting the /var/log file on the administrator's computer. (Each server may need to export the directory to enable root to be mapped between the computers for this to work.) If there are problems with a computer, the administrator can then easily view the shared log files live.

If you are working exclusively with Linux and other UNIX systems, NFS is probably your best choice for sharing file systems. You can mount NFS shares on a Windows client, but only if you have NFS client software for Windows, which does not come with Windows by default. If your network consists primarily of Microsoft Windows computers or a combination of systems, you may want to look into using Samba for file sharing.

# Setting Up a Samba File Server

Samba is a software package that comes with Ubuntu, Fedora, and Red Hat Enterprise Linux systems and many other Linux systems. (You can obtain the Samba software package from www.samba.org if it is not included with your distribution.) Samba enables you to share file systems and printers on a network with computers that use the Server Message Block (SMB) or Common Internet File System (CIFS) protocols. SMB is the Microsoft protocol that is delivered with Windows operating systems for sharing files and printers. CIFS is an open, cross-platform protocol that is based on SMB. Samba contains free implementations of SMB and CIFS.

## Note

In Windows file and printer sharing, SMB is sometimes referred to as CIFS (Common Internet File System), which is an Internet standard network file system definition based on SMB, or NetBIOS, which was the original SMB communication protocol. ■

The Samba software package contains a variety of daemon processes, administrative tools, user tools, and configuration files. To do basic Samba configuration, start with the Samba Server Configuration window, which provides a graphical interface for configuring the server and setting directories to share.

Most of the Samba configuration you do ends up in the /etc/samba/smb.conf file. If you need to access features that are not available through the Samba Server Configuration window, you can edit /etc/samba/smb.conf by hand or use SWAT, a Web-based interface, to configure Samba.

Daemon processes consist of smbd (the SMB daemon) and nmbd (the NetBIOS name server). The smbd daemon makes the file-sharing and printing services you add to your Linux system available to Windows client computers. The Samba package supports the following client computers:

- Windows 9x
- Windows NT
- Windows ME
- Windows 2000
- Windows 2007
- Windows XP
- Windows Vista
- Windows for workgroups
- MS Client 3.0 for DOS
- OS/2
- Dave for Macintosh computers
- Mac OS X
- Samba for Linux

## Note

Mac OS X Server ships with Samba, so you can use a Macintosh system as a server. This chapter, however, discusses using a Linux system as a server. You can then have Macintosh, Windows, or Linux client computers. In addition, Mac OS X ships with both client and server software for Samba. ■

As for administrative tools for Samba, you have several shell commands at your disposal: `testparm` and `testprns`, with which you can check your configuration files; `smbstatus`, which tells you what computers are currently connected to your shared resources; and the `nmblookup` command, with which you can query computers.

Samba uses the NetBIOS service to share resources with SMB clients, but the underlying network must be configured for TCP/IP. Although other SMB hosts can use TCP/IP, NetBEUI, and IPX/SPX to transport data, Samba for Linux supports only TCP/IP. Messages are carried between host computers with TCP/IP and are then handled by NetBIOS.

## Getting and installing Samba

You can get Samba software in different ways, depending on your Linux distribution. Here are a few examples:

- **Ubuntu and Debian**—To use Samba in Ubuntu or Debian, you must install the samba and smbclient packages using `apt-get`. Then start the Samba service by running the appropriate scripts from the `/etc/init.d` directory, as follows:

  ```
  # apt-get install samba samba-common smbclient swat
  # /etc/init.d/samba start
  ```

- **Gentoo**—With Gentoo, you need to have configured net-fs support into the kernel to use Samba server features. Installing the net-fs package (`emerge net-fs`) should get the required packages. To start the service, run `rc-update` and start the service immediately:

  ```
  # emerge samba
  # rc-update add samba default
  # /etc/init.d/samba start
  ```

- **Fedora and other Red Hat Linux systems**—You need to install the samba, samba-client, samba-common, and optionally, the system-config-samba and samba-swat packages to use Samba in Fedora. You can then start Samba using the `service` and `chkconfig` commands as follows:

  ```
  # service smb start
  # chkconfig smb on
  ```

The commands and configuration files are the same on most Linux systems using Samba. The Samba project itself comes with a Web-based interface for administering Samba called Samba Web Administration Tool (SWAT). For someone setting up Samba for the first time, SWAT is a good way to get it up and running.

## Note

If your Linux installation does not have help documents for Samba available, consult the documentation on the Samba project home page (www.samba.org). Also, check the extensive help information that comes with SWAT. ∎

# Configuring Samba with SWAT

In addition to offering an extensive interface to Samba options, SWAT also comes with an excellent help facility. And if you need to administer Samba from another computer, SWAT can be configured to be remotely accessible and secured by requiring an administrative login and password.

## Turning on the SWAT service

Before you can use SWAT, you must do some configuration. The first thing you must do is turn on the SWAT service, which is done differently in different Linux distributions.

Here's how to set up SWAT in Fedora and Red Hat Enterprise Linux systems:

1. Turn on the SWAT service by typing the following, as root user, from a Terminal window:

   ```
   # chkconfig swat on
   ```

2. Pick up the change to the service by restarting the xinetd startup script as follows:

   ```
   # service xinetd restart
   ```

Linux distributions such as Debian, Slackware, and Gentoo turn on the SWAT service from the inetd superserver daemon. After SWAT is installed, you simply remove the comment character from in front of the swat line in the /etc/inetd.conf file (as root user, using any text editor) and restart the daemon. Here's an example of what the swat line looks like in Ubuntu and Debian:

```
swat    stream    tcp    nowait.400    root    /usr/sbin/tcpd    /usr/sbin/swat
```

With the SWAT service ready to be activated, restart the inetd daemon so it rereads the inetd.conf file. To do that in Debian, type the following as root user:

```
# /etc/init.d/inetd restart
```

The init.d script and xinetd services are the two ways that SWAT services are generally started in Linux. So if you are using a Linux distribution other than Fedora or Debian, look in the /etc/inetd.conf file or /etc/xinetd.d directory (which is used automatically in Fedora) for the location of your SWAT service.

When you have finished this procedure, a daemon process will be listening on your network interfaces for requests to connect to your SWAT service. You can now use the SWAT program, described in the next section, to configure Samba.

### Starting with SWAT

You can run the SWAT program by typing the following URL in your local browser:

```
http://localhost:901/
```

Enter the root username and password when the browser prompts you. The SWAT window (see Figure 16-2) appears.

## Tip

Instead of running SWAT from your local browser, you can run it from another computer on the network by substituting the server computer's name for localhost. (To allow computers besides localhost to access the swat service on Fedora systems, you must change or remove the `only_from = 127.0.0.1` line from the `/etc/xinetd.d/swat` file and restart the xinetd service.) This is not necessary with Ubuntu systems. ■

### FIGURE 16-2

Use SWAT from your browser to manage your Samba configuration.

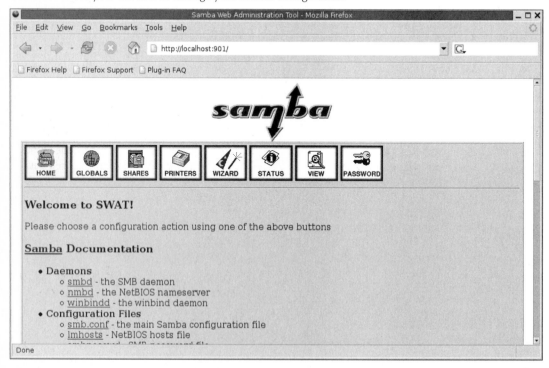

The following sections explain how to use SWAT to create your configuration entries (in /etc/samba/smb.conf) and to work with that configuration.

## Caution

Any time you use a GUI to change a plain-text configuration file (as you do with SWAT), you may lose some of the information that you put in by hand. In this case, SWAT deletes comment lines and rearranges other entries. To protect changes you have made manually, make a backup copy of your /etc/samba/smb.conf file before you edit it with SWAT. ■

### Creating global Samba settings in SWAT

A group of global settings affects how file and print sharing are generally accomplished on a Samba server. These settings appear under the [global] heading in the /etc/samba/smb.conf file. To view and edit global variables, click the GLOBALS button on the SWAT window.

Several types of options are available: base, security, logging, protocol, tuning, printing, browse, WINs, eventlog, and miscellaneous.

## Note

Each option relates to the exact parameters used in the /etc/samba/smb.conf file. You can refer to the smb.conf man page (type **man smb.conf**) to get more information on these parameters. ■

### Base options

The following options relate to basic information associated with your Samba server:

- **Workgroup**—The name of the workgroup associated with the group of SMB hosts. By default, the value for this field is WORKGROUP.

- **Realm**—If you are using kerberos authentication, this value indicates the kerberos realm to use. Typically, that is reflected by the hostname of the server providing the service.

- **NetBIOS name**—The name assigned to this Samba server. You can use the same name as your DNS hostname or make it blank, in which case the DNS hostname is used automatically. Your DNS hostname is filled in for you by default.

- **NetBIOS alias**—Enables you to set a way of referring to a host computer (an alias) that is different from the host's TCP/IP DNS name.

- **Server string**—A string of text identifying the server. This name appears in places such as the printer comment box. By default, it says Samba and the version number.

- **Interfaces**—Enables you to set up more than one network interface and let Samba browse several different subnetworks. The form of this field can be IP Address/Subnetwork Mask. Or, you could identify a network interface (such as eth0 for the first Ethernet card on your computer). For example, a Class C network address may appear as

192.168.24.11/255.255.255.0

### Security options

Of the security options settings, the first (security) is the most important one to get right. It defines the type of security used to give access to the shared file systems and printers to the client computers. (To see some of the fields described here, you need to click the Advanced view.)

- **Security**—Sets how password and user information is transferred to the Samba server from the client computer. As noted earlier, it's important to get this value right. Samba 2.0 and later has a different default value for security (security=user) than the earlier versions of Samba do (security=share). If you are coming from an earlier version of Samba and clients are failing to access your server, this setting is a good place to start. Here are your options:

  - **user**—The most common type of security used to share files and printers to Windows 95/98/2000/NT/XP clients. It is the default set with Samba in the current release. This setting is appropriate if users are doing a lot of file sharing (as opposed to a Samba server used mostly as a print server). It requires that a user provide a username/password before using the server. The easiest way to get this method working is to give a Linux user account to every client user who will use the Samba server, therefore providing basically the same file permissions to a user account through Samba as the same user would get if he or she were logged in directly to Linux.

  - **share**—The share value for security works best for just print sharing or for providing file access that is more public (guest sharing). A client doesn't need to provide a valid username and password to access the server. However, the user typically has a guest level of permission to access and change files. See the "Assigning Guest Accounts" sidebar in this chapter for further information.

  - **server**—From the client's point of view, this is the same as user security in that the client still has to provide a valid username/password combination to use the Samba server at all. The difference is on the server side. With server security, the username/password is sent to another SMB server for validation. If that fails, Samba tries to validate the client using user security.

  - **domain**—From the client's point of view, this also looks the same as user security. This setting is used only if the Samba server has been added to a Windows NT domain (using the smbpasswd command). When a client tries to connect to the Samba server in this mode, its username and password are sent to a Windows NT Primary or Backup Domain controller. This is accomplished the same way that a Windows NT server would perform validation. Valid Linux user accounts must still be set up.

  - **ads**—This security option causes Samba to act as a domain member in an ADS realm. Kerberos must be installed on the Samba machine to use this option. Samba must also join the ADS realm (see the net utility).

- **auth methods**—Sets the authentication method used by the Samba server (smbd). Leave the default in most cases. Authentication methods you can choose include anonymous access (guest), relay authentication through winbind (winbind), pre-winbind

NT authentication (ntdomain), local lookups based on netbios or domain name (sam), or remote DC authentication of trusted users (trustdomain).

- **Encrypt passwords**—Controls whether encrypted passwords can be negotiated with the client. This is on (Yes) by default. For domain security, this value must be Yes. Later versions of Windows NT (4.0 SP3 or later) and Windows 98 and Windows 2000 expect encrypted passwords to be on.

- **client schannel**—Choose if the client is to require the use of netlogin schannel (yes), offer schannel but doesn't enforce it (auto), or not even offer schannel (no).

- **server schannel**—Choose if the server requires clients to use netlogin schannel (yes), offers schannel but doesn't enforce it (auto), or doesn't even offer schannel (no). If you set this to no, you must apply the Windows XP WinXP_SignOrSeal.reg patch available from the Samba project.

- **map to guest**—Lets you select to map clients into your guest account (minimal permissions) in selected situations. For example, you can map user names that are not valid (Bad User), users that provide the wrong password (Bad Password), or users with an invalid user ID (Bad Uid). Or you can select Never to never map those users to guest.

- **Obey PAM restrictions**—Turn this on (Yes) if you want to use PAM for account and session management. Even if activated, PAM is not used if the encrypted passwords feature is turned on (encrypt passwords = yes). (PAM stands for *Pluggable Authentication Modules* and is used for authenticating host computers and users.)

- **PAM password change**—Indicates to use the PAM password change control flag for Samba. If this is on (Yes), SMB clients will use PAM instead of the program listed in the Password Program value for changing SMB passwords.

- **Passwd program**—Indicates which password program to use to change Linux user passwords. By default, /usr/bin/passwd is used, with the current username (%u) inserted.

- **Passwd chat**—Sets the chat that goes on between the Samba daemon (smbd) and the Linux password program (/usr/bin/passwd by default) when smbd tries to synchronize SMB passwords with Linux user passwords.

- **UNIX password sync**—With this on (Yes), Samba tries to update a user's Linux user password with his or her SMB password when the SMB password is changed. To do this, SMB runs the passwd command as the root user. This is on by default.

- **Guest account**—Specifies the username for the guest account. When a service is specified as Guest OK, the name entered here is used to access that service. The account is usually the nobody username.

## Tip

**Make sure that the guest account is a valid user. (The default of nobody should already be set up to work.) With an invalid user as the guest account, the IPC$ connection that lists the shared resources fails.** ∎

- **Hosts allow**—Contains a list of one or more hosts that are allowed to use your computer's Samba services. By default, users from any computer can connect to the Samba server (of course, they still have to provide valid usernames and passwords). Generally, you use this option to allow connections from specific computers (such as 10.0.0.1) or computer networks (such as 10.0.0.) that are excluded by the hosts deny option.

- **Hosts deny**—Contains a list of one or more hosts from which users are not allowed to use your computer's Samba services. You can make this option fairly restrictive, and then add the specific hosts and networks you want to use the Samba server. By default, no hosts are denied.

- **Preload modules**—You can add services that you want to add to the browse list to the preload option.

### Logging options

The following options help define how logging is done on your Samba server:

- **Log file**—Defines the location of the Samba smb log file. By default, Samba log files are contained in /var/log/samba (with filenames log.nmbd, log.smbd, and smb.log). In this option, the %m is replaced by smb to set the smb log file as /var/log/samba/smb.log.

- **Max log size**—Sets the maximum amount of space, in kilobytes, that the log files can consume. By default, the value is set to 0 (no limit).

## Assigning Guest Accounts

Samba always assigns the permissions level of a valid user on the Linux system to clients who use the server. In the case of share security, the user is assigned a guest account (the nobody user account by default).

If the guest account value isn't set, Samba goes through a fairly complex set of rules to determine which user account to use. The result is that ensuring which user permissions will be assigned in each case can be hard. That's why user security is recommended if you want to provide more specific user access to your Samba server.

### Protocol options

Use the **svcctl list** option if you want to set a list of initialization scripts that the smbd daemon will use for starting and stopping Unix services by way of the Win32 ServiceControl API. Using this feature, Windows administrators can use the Microsoft Management Console plug-ins to manage a Unix server running Samba.

### Tuning options

Use the **cluster addresses** option to add additional addresses for nmbd to register with a WINS server.

### Printing options

The printing options are used to define how printer status information is presented. For the overwhelming majority of Linux systems, the `printing` value is set to `cups`. You can use printing styles from other types of operating systems, such as UNIX System V (`sysv`), AIX (`aix`), HP UNIX (`hpux`), and Berkeley UNIX (`bsd`), to name a few. LPRng (`lprng`), offered by many UNIX systems, is also included. Other printing options enable you to redefine the location of basic printing commands (`lpq`, `lprm`, and so on) and printing files (such as the name of the printcap file).

### Browse options

A browse list is a list of computers that are available on the network to SMB services. Clients use this list to find computers that are on their own LAN and also computers in their workgroups that may be on other reachable networks.

In Samba, browsing is configured by options described later in this section and implemented by the nmbd daemon. If you are using Samba for a workgroup within a single LAN, you probably don't need to concern yourself with the browsing options. However, if you are using Samba to provide services across several physical subnetworks, you might want to consider configuring Samba as a domain master browser. Here are some points to think about:

- Samba can be configured as a master browser, which allows it to gather lists of computers from local browse masters to form a wide-area server list. (Browse masters keep track of available shared directories and printers on the network of Samba systems and broadcast information about those resources as necessary.)

- If Samba is acting as a domain master browser, Samba should use a WINS server to help browse clients resolve the names from this list.

- Samba can be used as a WINS server, although it can also rely on other types of operating systems to provide that service.

- There should be only one domain master browser for each workgroup. Don't use Samba as a domain master for a workgroup with the same name as an NT domain.

If you are working in an environment that has a mix of Samba and Windows NT servers, use an NT server as your WINS server. If Samba is your only file server, choose a single Samba server (nmbd daemon) to supply the WINS services.

## Note

A WINS server is basically a name server for NetBIOS names. It provides the same service that a DNS server does with TCP/IP domain names: It can translate names into addresses. A WINS server is particularly useful for allowing computers to communicate with SMB across multiple subnetworks where information is not being broadcast across the subnetworks' boundaries. ■

To configure the browsing feature in Samba, you must have the workgroup named properly (described earlier in this section). Here are the global options related to SMB browsing:

- **OS level**—Set a value to control whether your Samba server (nmbd daemon) may become the local master browser for your workgroup. Raising this setting increases the Samba server's chance to control the browser list for the workgroup in the local broadcast area.

  If the value is 0, a Windows machine will probably be selected. A value of 60 ensures that the Samba server is chosen over an NT server. The default is 20.

- **Preferred master**—Set this to Yes if you want to force selection of a master browser and give the Samba server a better chance of being selected. (Setting Domain Master to Yes along with this option ensures that the Samba server will be selected.) This is set to Auto by default, which causes Samba to try to detect the current master browser before taking that responsibility.

- **Local master**—Set this to Yes if you want the Samba server to become the local browser master. (This is not a guarantee, but gives it a chance.) Set the value to No if you do not want your Samba server selected as the local master. Local Master is Auto by default.

- **Domain master**—Set this to Yes if you want the Samba server (nmbd daemon) to identify itself as the domain master browser for its workgroup. This list will then allow client computers assigned to the workgroup to use SMB-shared files and printers from subnetworks that are outside their own subnetwork. This is set to No by default.

# Note

If browsing isn't working, check the nmbd log file (/var/log/samba/log.nmbd). To get more detail, increase the debug information level to 2 or 3 (described earlier in this section) and restart Samba. The log can tell you whether your Samba server is the master browser and, if so, which computers are on its list. ■

### WINS options

Use the WINS options if you want to have a particular WINS server provide the name-to-address translation of NetBIOS names used by SMB clients:

- **WINS server**—If there is a WINS server on your network that you want to use to resolve the NetBIOS names for your workgroup, enter that server's IP address here. Again, you probably want to use a WINS server if your workgroup extends outside the local subnetwork.

- **WINS support**—Set this value to Yes if you want your Samba server to act as a WINS server. (It's No by default.) Again, this is not needed if all the computers in your workgroup are on the same subnetwork. Only one computer on your network should be assigned as the WINS server.

In addition to the values described here, you can access dozens more options by clicking the Advanced View button. When you have filled in all the fields you need, click Commit Changes on the screen to have the changes written to the /etc/samba/smb.conf file.

### EventLog options

You can use the **eventlog list** option to create a list of log names for Samba to report to the Microsoft EventViewer utility.

### Miscellaneous options

Two options in this category, **usershare prefix allow** and **usershare prefix deny**, let the administrator restrict which directories can be shared in user-defined shares. The deny list is defined first to allow the most restrictive interpretation of the list.

## Configuring shared directories with SWAT

To make your shared directory available to others, add an entry to the SWAT window. To use SWAT to set up Samba to share directories, do the following:

# Note

You may see one or more security warnings during the course of this procedure. These messages warn you that someone can potentially view the data you are sending to SWAT. If you are working on your local host or on a private LAN, the risk is minimal. ■

**1.** From the main SWAT window, click the SHARES button.

**2.** Type the name of the directory that you want to share in the Create Share box, and then click Create Share.

**3.** Add any of these options:

- **Comment**—A few words to describe the shared directory (optional).

- **Path**—The path name of the directory you are sharing.

- **Invalid users**—Lets you add a list of users who are not allowed to log in to the Samba service. Besides identifying usernames directly (from your /etc/passwd file), invalid users can be identified by Linux group or NIS netgroup, by adding a + or & in front of the name, respectively. Precede the name with @ to have Samba first check your NIS netgroup, then the Linux group for the name.

- **Valid users**—Add names here to identify which Linux user accounts can access the Samba service. As with invalid users, names can be preceded with +, &, or @ characters.

- **Admin users**—Lets you identify users who have administrative privilege on a particular share. This is available with security = share type of security only.

- **Read list**—Add users to this list if you want to grant read access to shares only (even if a share is available with read-write access). This is available with security = share type of security only.

- **Write list**—Add users to this list to grant write access by those users to shares, even if the share is available to all others with read-only access. This is available with security = share type of security only.

- **Guest account**—If Guest OK is selected, the username that is defined here is assigned to users accessing the file system. No password will be required to access the share. The `nobody` user account (used only by users who access your computer remotely) is the default name used as the guest account. (The FTP user is also a recommended value.)

- **Read only**—If Yes, files can only be read from this file system, but no remote user can save or modify files on the file system. Select No if you want users to be allowed to save files to this directory over the network.

- **Hosts allow**—Add the names of the computers that will be allowed to access this file system. Separate hostnames by commas, spaces, or tabs. Here are some valid ways of entering hostnames:

  - **localhost**—Allows access to the local host.

  - **192.168.12.125**—IP address. Enter an individual IP address.

  - **192.168.12.**—Enter a network address to include all hosts on a network. (Be sure to put a dot at the end of the network number or it won't work!)

  - **pcren, pcstimpy**—Enables access to individual hosts by name.

  - **EXCEPT** *host*—If you are allowing access to a group of hosts (such as by entering a network address), use EXCEPT to specifically deny access from one host from that group.

- **Hosts deny**—Denies access to specific computers by placing their names here. By default, no particular computers are excluded. Enter hostnames in the same forms you used for Hosts Allow.

- **Browseable**—Indicates whether you can view this directory on the list of shared directories. This is on (Yes) by default.

- **Available**—Enables you to leave this entry intact but turns off the service. This is useful if you want to close access to a directory temporarily. This is on (Yes) by default. Select No to turn it off.

4. Select Commit Changes.

At this point, the shared file systems should be available to the Samba client computers (Windows 9x, Windows NT, Windows 2000, OS/2, Linux, and so on) that have access to your Linux Samba server. Before you try that, however, you can check your Samba configuration.

## Checking your Samba setup with SWAT

From the SWAT window, select the STATUS button.

From this window, you can restart your smbd and nmbd processes. Likewise, you can see lists of active connections, active shares, and open files. (The preferred way to start the smbd and nmbd daemons is to set up the smb service to start automatically. Type **chkconfig smb on** to set the service to start at boot time.)

# Working with Samba files and commands

Although you can set up Samba through the Samba Server Configuration window or SWAT, many administrators prefer to edit the /etc/samba/smb.conf directly. As root user, you can view the contents of this file and make needed changes. If you selected User security (as recommended), you will also be interested in the smbusers and smbpasswd files (in the /etc/samba directory). These files, as well as commands such as testparm and smbstatus, are described in the following sections.

## Editing the smb.conf file

Changes you make using the Samba Server Configuration window or SWAT Web interface are reflected in your /etc/samba/smb.conf file. Here's an example of a smb.conf file (with comments removed):

```
[global]
workgroup = ESTREET
server string = Samba Server on Maple
hosts allow = 192.168.0.
printcap name = /etc/printcap
load printers = yes
printing = cups
log file = /var/log/samba/%m.log
max log size = 0
smb passwd file = /etc/samba/smbpasswd
security = user
encrypt passwords = Yes
unix password sync = Yes
passwd program = /usr/bin/passwd %u
passwd chat = *New*password* %n\n *Retype*new*password* %n\n *passwd:
            *all*authentication*tokens*updated*successfully*
pam password change = yes
obey pam restrictions = yes
socket options = TCP_NODELAY SO_RCVBUF=8192 SO_SNDBUF=8192
username map = /etc/samba/smbusers
dns proxy = no

[homes]
comment = Home Directories
browseable = no
writable = yes
valid users = %S
create mode = 0664
directory mode = 0775

[printers]
comment = All Printers
path = /var/spool/samba
browseable = no
```

```
guest ok = no
writable = no
printable = yes
```

I won't go through every line of this example, but here are some observations. In the [global] section, the workgroup is set to ESTREET, the server is identified as the Samba Server on Maple, and only computers that are on the local network (192.168.0.) are allowed access to the Samba service. You must change the local network to match your network.

Definitions for the local printers that will be shared are taken from the /etc/printcap file, the printers are loaded (yes), and the CUPS printing service is used.

Separate log files for each host trying to use the service are created in /var/log/samba/%m.log (with %m automatically replaced with each hostname). There is no limit to log file size (0).

This example uses the user-level security (security = user), which allows a user to log in once and then easily access the printers and the user's home directory on the Linux system. Password encryption is on (encrypt passwords = yes) because most Windows systems have password encryption on by default. Passwords are stored in the /etc/samba/smbpasswd file on your Linux system.

The dns proxy = no option prevents Linux from looking up system names on the DNS server (used for TCP/IP lookups).

The [homes] section enables each user to access his or her Linux home directory from a Windows system on the LAN. The user will be able to write to the home directory. However, other users will not be able see or share this directory. The [printers] section enables all users to print to any printer configured on the local Linux system.

### Adding Samba users

Performing user-style Samba security means assigning a Linux user account to each person using the Linux file systems and printers from his or her Windows workstation. (You could assign users to a guest account instead, but in this example, all users have their own accounts.) Then you need to add SMB passwords for each user. For example, here is how you would add a user whose Windows workstation login is chuckp:

1. Type the following as root user from a Terminal window to add a Linux user account:

   ```
   # useradd -m chuckp
   ```

2. Add a Linux password for the new user as follows:

   ```
   # passwd chuckp
   Changing password for user chuckp
   New UNIX password: ********
   Retype new UNIX password: ********
   ```

3. Repeat the previous steps to add user accounts for all users from Windows workstations on your LAN that you want to give access to your Linux system.

4. Type the following command to create the Samba password file (`smbpasswd`) on Fedora Linux systems:

```
# cat /etc/passwd | /usr/bin/mksmbpasswd.sh > /etc/samba/smbpasswd
```

In Ubuntu and Debian systems, use the `/usr/sbin/mksmbpasswd` command instead of `mksmbpasswd.sh`.

5. Add an SMB password for the user as follows:

```
# smbpasswd chuckp
New SMB password: **********
Retype new SMB password: **********
```

6. Repeat this step for each user. Later, each user can log in to Linux and rerun the `passwd` and `smbpasswd` commands to set private passwords.

## Note

In the most recent version of Samba, options are available in the `smb.conf` file that cause SMB and Linux passwords to be synchronized automatically. See descriptions of the passwd program, passwd chat, and UNIX password sync options in the SWAT section of this chapter. ∎

### Starting the Samba service

When you have your Samba configuration the way you want it, restart the Samba server as described earlier in the "Getting and installing Samba" section. You can now check SMB clients on the network to see whether they can access your Samba server.

### Testing your Samba permissions

You can run several commands from a shell to work with Samba. One is the `testparm` command, which you can use to check the access permissions you have set up. It lists global parameters that are set, along with any shared directories or printers.

### Checking the status of shared directories

The `smbstatus` command can view who is currently using Samba shared resources offered from your Linux system. The following is an example of the output from `smbstatus`:

```
# smbstatus

Samba version 3.2.0-17.fc9
PID     Username      Group         Machine
-------------------------------------------------------------------
25770   chris         chris         booker      (10.0.0.50)
```

```
25833    chris        chris        10.0.0.50    (10.0.0.50)

Service    pid    machine      Connected at
----------------------------------------------------------
IPC$       25729  booker       Tue Aug 25 12:06:29 2009
mytmp      25770  booker       Tue Aug 25 12:16:03 2009
mytmp      25833  10.0.0.50    Tue Aug 25 12:25:52 2009
IPC$       25730  booker       Tue Aug 25 12:06:29 2009

Locked files:
Pid   Uid DenyMode  Access   R/W  Oplock SharePath   Name    Time
----------------------------------------------------------------------
25833 501 DENY_NONE 0x12019f RDWR NONE   /tmp .b.txt.swp Tue Aug 25 12:26:18 2009
```

This output shows that from your Linux Samba server, the `mytmp` service (which is a share of the `/tmp` directory) is currently open by the computer named booker. PID 25833 is the process number of the smbd daemon on the Linux server that is handling the service. The file that is open is the `/tmp/.b.txt.swap` file, which happened to be opened by a `vi` command. It has read/write access.

## Using Samba shared directories

After you have configured your Samba server, you can try using the shared directories from a client computer on your network. The following sections describe how to use your Samba server from another Linux system or from various Windows systems.

### Using Samba from Nautilus

To connect to a Samba share from a Nautilus file manager, use the Open Location box by clicking File ⇨ Open Location. Then type **smb:** into your Nautilus file manager Location box.

A list of SMB workgroups on your network appears in the window. You can select a workgroup, choose a server, and then select a resource to use. This should work for shares requiring no password.

The Nautilus interface seems to be a bit buggy when you need to enter passwords. It also requires you to either send clear-text passwords or type the username and password into your location box. For example, to get to my home directory (`/home/chris`) through Nautilus, I can type my username, password, server name, and share name as follows:

    smb://chris:my72mgb@arc/chris

### Mounting Samba directories in Linux

Linux can view your Samba shared directories as it does any other medium (hard disk, NFS shares, CD-ROM, and so on). Use `mount` to mount a Samba shared file system so that it is permanently connected to your Linux file system.

Here's an example of the `mount` command in which a home directory (`/home/chris`) from a computer named `toys` on a local directory (`/mnt/toys`) is mounted. The command is typed, as root user, from a Terminal window:

```
# mkdir /mnt/toys
# mount -t smbfs -o username=chris,password=a72mg //toys/chris /mnt/toys
```

The file system type for a Samba share is smbfs (`-t smbfs`). The username (`chris`) and password (`a72mg`) are passed as options (`-o`). The remote share of the home directory on `toys` is `//toys/chris`. The local mount point is `/mnt/toys`. At this point, you can access the contents of `/home/chris` on `toys` as you would any file or directory locally. You will have the same permission to access and change the contents of that directory (and its subdirectories) as you would if you were the user `chris` using those contents directly from `toys`.

To mount the Samba shared directory permanently, add an entry to your `/etc/fstab` file. For the example just described, you would add the following line (as root user):

```
//toys/chris    /mnt/toys    smbfs    username=chris,password=a72mg
```

## Troubleshooting your Samba server

A lot can go wrong with a Samba server. If your Samba server isn't working properly, the descriptions in this section should help you pinpoint the problem.

### Basic networking in place?

You can't share anything with other computers without a network. Before computers can share directories and printers from Samba, they must be able to communicate on your LAN.

Your Samba server can use the TCP/IP name as the NetBIOS name (used by Window networks for file and printer sharing), or a separate NetBIOS name can be set in the `smb.conf` file. It is critical, however, that the broadcast address be the same as the broadcast address for all clients communicating with your Samba server. To see your broadcast address, type the following (as root user):

```
# ifconfig -a
eth0      Link encap:Ethernet  HWadd 00:D1:B3:75:A5:1B
          inet addr:10.0.0.1  Bcast:10.0.0.255  Mask:255.255.255.0
```

The important information is the broadcast address (`Bcast: 10.0.0.255`), which is determined by the netmask (`Mask:255.255.255.0`). If the broadcast address isn't the same for the Samba server and the clients on the LAN, the clients cannot see that the Samba server has directories or printers to share.

### Samba service running?

A basic troubleshooting check is to see whether the service is running. Try the `smbclient` command from your Linux system to see that everything is running and being shared as you expect it to be. The `smbclient` command is a great tool for getting information about a Samba server and even accessing shared directories from both Linux and Windows computers. While logged in as root or any user who has access to your Samba server, type the following:

```
$ smbclient -L localhost
Password: **********
Domain=[ESTREET] OS=[Unix] Server=[Samba 3.0.3-4]

        Sharename       Type        Comment
        ---------       ----        -------
        homes           Disk        Home Directories
        IPC$            IPC         IPC Service (Samba Server)
        ADMIN$          Disk        IPC Service (Samba Server)
        hp-ns1          Printer
Domain=[ESTREET] OS=[Unix] Server=[Samba 3.0.8-4]

        Server                  Comment
        ---------               -------
        PINE                    Samba Server
        MAPLE                   Windows XP
        NS1                     Samba Server

        Workgroup               Master
        ---------               -------
        ESTREET                 PINE
```

The Samba server is running on the local computer in this example. Shared directories and printers, as well as servers in the workgroup, appear here. If the Samba server is not running, you see `Connection refused` messages, and you need to start the Samba service as described earlier in this chapter.

### Firewall open?

If the Samba server is running, it should begin broadcasting its availability on your LAN. If you try to access the server from a Windows or Linux client on your LAN but get a `Connection refused` error, the problem may be that the firewall on your Linux Samba server is denying access to the NetBIOS service.

## Cross-Reference
Chapter 27 covers firewalls. ■

If you have a secure LAN, you can type the following (as root user) to flush your firewall filtering rules temporarily:

```
# iptables -F
```

Try to connect to the Samba server from a Windows or Linux client. If you find that you can connect to the server, turn the firewall back on:

```
# /etc/init.d/iptables restart
```

You then need to open access to ports 137, 138, and 139 in your firewall so that the Samba server can accept connections for services. Keep in mind, however, that opening those ports can cause a host of security problems for Windows systems. (See Chapter 27 for information about modifying your firewalls.)

### User passwords working?

Try accessing a shared Samba directory as a particular user (from the local host or other Linux system on your LAN). You can use the smbclient command to do this. Here is an example:

```
# smbclient //localhost/tmp -U chris
added interface ip=10.0.0.1 bcast=10.0.0.255 nmask=255.255.255.0
Password: *******
Domain=[ESTREET] OS=[Unix] Server=[Samba 2.2.7a]
smb: \>
```

In this example, smbclient connects to the directory share named tmp as the Samba user named chris. If the password is accepted, you should see information about the server and an smb: \> prompt. If you cannot access the same shared directory from a Windows client, it's quite possible that the client is passing an improper username and password. Part of the problem may be that the Windows client is not providing encrypted passwords.

For certain Windows clients, using encrypted passwords requires that you change a Windows registry for the machine. One way to change the registry is with the Windows regedit command. Registry changes required for different Windows systems are contained within the /usr/share/doc/samba-*/docs/Registry directory.

## Tip

The smbclient **command, used here to list server information and test passwords, can also be used to browse the shared directory and copy files after you are connected. After you see the** smb: \> **prompt, type help to see the available commands. The interface is similar to any ftp client, such as sftp. ■**

If your particular problem has not been addressed in this troubleshooting section, please refer to the user documentation that accompanies the Samba project. On Fedora systems, look in the /usr/share/doc/samba-*/htmldocs directory for some excellent documentation you can read from your Web browser. In particular, refer to the Samba-HOWTO-Collection/diagnosis.html file for help with troubleshooting.

# Summary

By providing centralized file servers, an organization can efficiently share information and applications with people within the organization, with customers, or with anyone around the world. Several different technologies are available for making your Linux computer into a file-serving powerhouse.

The Network File System (NFS) protocol was one of the first file server technologies available. It is particularly well suited for sharing file systems among Linux and other UNIX systems. NFS uses standard `mount` and `umount` commands to connect file systems to the directory structures of client computers.

The Samba software package that comes with many Linux distributions (or can be easily installed if it doesn't) contains protocols and utilities for sharing files and printers among Windows and OS/2 operating systems. It uses SMB protocols that are included with all Microsoft Windows systems and therefore provides a convenient method of sharing resources on LANs containing many Windows systems.

# Part V

# Choosing and Installing Different Linux Distributions

# Running Ubuntu Linux

Ubuntu Linux (www.ubuntu.com) has experienced a meteoric rise in popularity since its first release at the end of 2004. Relying on a constantly expanding number of core developers and contributions from its growing legion of advocates and users, Ubuntu has become one of the most popular distributions around the world for Linux enthusiasts.

"Ubuntu" is an African word that means "humanity to others." The project pursues the meaning of its name by

- Making the distribution freely available; in fact, the project will even mail you pressed CDs without charge, although it can take up to 10 weeks to receive them (https://shipit.ubuntu.com)

- Providing support for many languages

- Offering features to make it usable by people with disabilities

Ubuntu is based on Debian GNU/Linux but offers more focused goals than Debian. The original goals of Ubuntu were to provide a tested, easy-to-use Linux distribution with a regular release schedule (every six months), to provide support and updates for those releases for an extended period of time, and to fit this easy-to-use desktop Linux on one installation CD. Ubuntu now offers Desktop and Server install CDs, as well as an Alternate install CD to help with automated deployments, partitioning, and low-resource system installs.

Ubuntu provides its own repositories of freely available software on the Internet, providing a huge assortment of software organized in the traditional licensing-oriented Debian fashion. These packages can be installed using the familiar apt-get, aptitude, and synaptic software management tools.

This chapter describes some of the major features of Ubuntu. It also describes how to install Ubuntu on your computer or run the live CD version of Ubuntu.

# Overview of Ubuntu

Although Ubuntu is primarily a Debian distribution on the inside, Ubuntu's focus on internationalization and general usability, its regular release schedule, and its simplified installation process are what make it different from Debian.

South African businessman, Internet entrepreneur, and long-time Debian advocate, Mark Shuttleworth sponsors Ubuntu Linux through his organization Canonical Limited (`www.canonical.com`). Some of the best and brightest open source developers (many originally from the Debian project) are on Canonical's team for producing Ubuntu. The organization's commitment to free distribution and rapid development has attracted a large and active user and development community for Ubuntu.

## Ubuntu releases

Coming into 2009, the Ubuntu project has produced eleven releases, which recently have followed Ubuntu's promised every-six-month release cycle. Each release carries a version number derived from the year and month in which it was released, and is named after a woodland creature:

- **Warty Warthog**—Released in October 2004 under Ubuntu version number 4.10
- **Hoary Hedgehog**—Released in April 2005 under Ubuntu version number 5.04
- **Breezy Badger**—Released in October 2005 under Ubuntu version number 5.10
- **Dapper Drake**—Released in June 2006 under Ubuntu version number 6.06
- **Edgy Eft**—Released in October 2006 under Ubuntu version number 6.10
- **Feisty Fawn**—Released in April 2007 under Ubuntu version number 7.04
- **Gutsy Gibbon**—Released in October 2007 under Ubuntu version number 7.10
- **Hardy Heron**—Released in April 2008 under Ubuntu version number 8.04
- **Intrepid Ibex**—Released in October 2008 under Ubuntu version number 8.10
- **Jaunty Jackalope**—Released April 2009 under Ubuntu version number 9.04
- **Karmic Koala**—Released October 2009 under Ubuntu version number 9.10

## Note

In addition to the regular releases, Ubuntu also releases an LTS version for Long Term Support for those who want reliability above features. The LTS version offers support for three years on desktop versions and five years on server versions. Ubuntu 8.04 is the most recent version offering LTS. ∎

If you are new to Linux, Ubuntu is designed with you in mind. The standard Ubuntu desktop installer provides a great set of defaults for most installation options. Ubuntu, however, also provides other installers that include many more choices for customization when you install it. If you are transitioning from Debian (or another Debian derivative, such as KNOPPIX), you will find it easy to work with Ubuntu. You install and remove packages and manage services with Ubuntu using the same methods as with Debian.

Beginning with the Dapper Drake release, the Ubuntu project offers each release as three different CDs or a single DVD. The CDs are as follows:

- **Desktop Install CD**—This boots directly to Ubuntu, where you can either experiment with Ubuntu (without changing anything on your existing system) or install Ubuntu to a hard drive. This is the equivalent of the live CD provided by many distributions, except that it also provides an easy way to install Ubuntu Linux permanently if you decide to do so. (This CD is included on the DVD that comes with this book.)

- **Server Install CD**—Lets you install various server configurations, ranging from a basic server to a standard LAMP (Linux/Apache/MySQL/Perl) Web server.

- **Alternate Desktop CD**—Enables you to install an Ubuntu desktop system from the command line in a more complex fashion than that provided by the Desktop CD's graphical installer (such as using Logical Volume Management). It also supports OEM firms that want to customize and ship Ubuntu-based systems, and provides a custom server installation mechanism. It does not include the Live CD.

Getting started with Ubuntu is easy because the Desktop Install CD boots to a fully functioning desktop system. The Ubuntu Desktop Install CD does a great job at detecting hardware, setting up your video card environment (mouse, keyboard, and video card), and booting right to a GNOME desktop without changing anything on your existing system. It includes an icon on the desktop that enables you to install Ubuntu to your computer's hard disk after walking through just a few simple configuration screens (discussed later in this chapter).

The following sections describe the desktop and server features in Ubuntu 9.10 (Karmic Koala).

## Ubuntu installer

The Ubuntu installer has helped make Ubuntu a tremendously popular distribution, showing Ubuntu's commitment to usability right out of the gate. The desktop Ubuntu install process does an excellent job of detecting hardware and system configuration information. Ubuntu's Desktop Install CD "test-drive" needs only a few additional bits of information in order to install its whole set of software packages to your hard drive.

The other Ubuntu CDs feature a more traditional, text-based installer that should be familiar to users of any Debian-like system and are designed to work on almost any system with VGA graphics and 128MB or so of memory. This chapter focuses on the graphical Ubuntu installer, but the text-based installer on the Server and Alternate Install CDs is also quite easy to use.

Many ease-of-use features are built into the Ubuntu installer. For example, if you are not sure which type of keyboard you have, you have the option to type a few keys (as prompted by the installer) and have it try to figure out the type of keyboard you have. You also have the option to resize existing partitions on your disk during installation (a very handy feature if you have a hard disk with only one big Windows partition that you don't want to completely delete).

## Ubuntu as a desktop

As promised, Ubuntu 9.10 contains the latest desktop features available at the time it was released. Along with the latest desktop components you would expect (GNOME, OpenOffice.org, and so on), Ubuntu 9.10 also includes improved features for installing applications and customizing the desktop experience. Here are some of the features in Ubuntu 9.10:

- **GNOME Desktop**—GNOME 2.26 provides the desktop environment for this release of Ubuntu. Ubuntu's default desktop theme, Human, is a calm, brown theme in keeping with the standard Ubuntu color scheme.

- **Flash experience**—Improved handling of Flash content. This includes improved ways of using the plug-in finder wizard, better experiences with Web sites that use the Flash detection kit, and more help to users who want to select alternatives.

- **Firefox 3**—This major Firefox release provides improved security, ease-of-use, and performance. (See Chapter 6 for details.)

- **Print driver downloads**—When you use the Printer Setup tool in Ubuntu and your system doesn't have the driver needed for your printer, the new tool will automatically grab the print driver needed from the OpenPrinting database.

Beyond these features, Ubuntu contains a broad range of open source applications suitable for the desktop. Leading the list are the latest versions of OpenOffice.org (popular office productivity suite), The GIMP (image manipulation software), and Firefox (Web browser).

Many of the tools for configuring and setting preferences for the desktop that come with the GNOME project also fit well into the Ubuntu goals of accessibility and ease-of-use. GNOME's Removable Drives and Media Preferences window is set to immediately launch appropriate applications when you insert a CD or DVD, attach an external hard disk, or plug in a camera, printer, or scanner. The Assistive Technology Preferences window enables someone who is visually or physically impaired to use magnifiers and onscreen keyboards.

Figure 17-1 shows examples of some of these GNOME tools and applications.

## Ubuntu as a server

Many features that are not useful for a desktop Linux system but are important to servers have been built into the Ubuntu default server installer, available on the Ubuntu Server Install CD (or the complete Ubuntu Install DVD).

FIGURE 17-1

Assistive technology and easier device management with Ubuntu

As a central computing resource, servers tend to need to grow, and features such as the Ubuntu server installer's ability to create LVM partitions during installation make it easier for you to add disk space to your server on-the-fly in the places it is needed. Unlike the graphical Ubuntu Desktop installer described later in this chapter, the Ubuntu server installer is a non-graphical, terminal-oriented installer that is fast and easy to use regardless of the graphical capabilities of your server.

The default server installation supports up to 4GB of RAM on 32-bit PCs, and also provides kernel support for the GFS and OCFS2 cluster file systems. Although GFS and OCFS2 are still relatively new file systems, and therefore may not be ready for use on your productions systems, they are available for you to try out in Ubuntu.

To use Ubuntu as a thin-client server, Linux Terminal Server Project software is included in the Ubuntu server. You can read about how to use LTSP on the Ubuntu Thin Client HOWTO (https://help.ubuntu.com/community/ThinClientHowto).

The default server install takes up only about 400MB of disk space, although it is a very bare-bones system. Besides base system packages and core utilities, you get software for managing your network connections and file systems, but not much else. Luckily, however, you do get application management utilities (such as apt-get), so any open source software you want to add to your server is just an `apt-get` away with an Internet connection.

The most common type of server that many people install is a LAMP server system, which uses Linux to support an Apache Web server and provides the MySQL database. It also supports the Perl programming language, in which many Web applications are written. The Ubuntu Server Install CD provides a separate installer for this type of server system, highlighting Ubuntu's awareness of (and sensitivity) to the needs of its users, regardless of whether they are sitting in front of their desktop computer system or are cloistered in a machine room somewhere.

## Ubuntu spin-offs

Because no single CD set of software is going to please everyone, some spin-off projects have already been created from Ubuntu. The following are three partner projects associated with Ubuntu Linux:

- **Kubuntu** (www.kubuntu.org)—This project combines the latest version of the KDE desktop with each desktop Ubuntu release. KDE replaces the GNOME desktop, which is used by default with Ubuntu.

- **Xubuntu** (www.xubuntu.org)—This project blends the power and usability of Ubuntu with the lightweight Xfce desktop system, delivering a full-featured Ubuntu system that is less demanding of system and graphics resources. Xubuntu runs well on older or less-powerful systems, and is ideal for laptops.

- **Edubuntu** (www.edubuntu.org)—This project focuses on producing a version of Ubuntu that is suitable for use in classrooms. Edubuntu combines Ubuntu with software geared toward education (such as KDE Edutainment software) and software used for creating inexpensive computer clusters (such as the Linux Terminal Server Project). As a result, Edubuntu can be used to fill a school's whole computer lab with working, educational workstations at very little cost.

Other Ubuntu spin-offs that have different levels of association with the main Ubuntu project include Mythbuntu (multimedia player spin centering on MythTV), Ubuntu Studio (multimedia-creator spin), Ubuntu JeOS (virtual appliance spin), Ubuntu Mobile (spin designed for Intel Mobile Internet devices), and Ubuntu Netbook Remix (like Ubuntu Mobile, but for subnotebooks). The Gobuntu spin (Ubuntu with no non-free software) has been abandoned to focus on installation tools that let you choose to only have free software during an install. Linux Mint is a user-friendly version of Ubuntu that includes many popular multimedia codecs.

Because of Ubuntu's commitment to help people of different cultures, with support for many different languages and keyboard types, there are Ubuntu communities to support users from all over the world. There's Ubuntu China (`www.ubuntu.org.cn`), Ubuntu Germany (`www.ubuntu-forum.de`), Ubuntu Sweden (`www.ubuntulinux.se`), Ubuntu Indonesia (`www.ubuntulinux.or.id`), Ubuntu Portugal (`www.ubuntu-pt.org`), and many other international Ubuntu sites.

## Challenges facing Ubuntu

Despite its rise to stardom, Ubuntu is bound to suffer some growing pains. Some possible challenges Ubuntu faces include

- **Peaceful coexistence with Debian**—As a Debian-inspired distribution, Ubuntu was originally quite dependent on Debian and continued many of the licensing, usability, and stability issues that are heavily emphasized in Debian Linux. Some members of the Debian community initially saw Ubuntu as hijacking the hard work of the Debian project. The success of Ubuntu, however, speaks for both itself and the technical excellence and commitment of the Debian community. Ubuntu pushes its fixes and enhancements back to the Debian community, as well as to the developers who support individual open source packages. The two distributions need to continue to work together to improve both distributions and GNU/Linux in general.

- **Fast release cycles**—Ubuntu has set itself a pace of six-month release cycles. In terms of major free Linux distributions, only Fedora has stayed close to a six-month release cycle. Debian has certainly not been known to rush to release new versions—the slowness of Debian releases was one of the initial inspirations for Ubuntu.

- **Business model**—Although the Ubuntu project does offer shirts, hats, teddy bears, and other products you can purchase that carry the Ubuntu logo (`https://shop.canonical.com/`), proceeds from that and donations are clearly not going to be enough to support a long-term development effort. The project has made it clear that it intends to be committed to software that is "100% free of charge" going forward. Canonical, Ltd, and many other vendors around the world, provide paid commercial support for Ubuntu releases, but "paid support" business models for Linux have rarely been successful. Only time (and a growing number of home, small, and medium business, and enterprise Ubuntu users) will tell whether Ubuntu can manage to succeed without adopting a free/paid community model such as those of Fedora/Red Hat and openSUSE/SUSE.

- **Commitment to open source**—Desktop computer users expect that their wireless cards will just work and their multimedia content will just play. Some of the software needed to do those things, however, are either encumbered by patent claims or not available in open source. To compete, Ubuntu has made some of this non-free software available to its users—sometimes from Ubuntu repositories and sometimes through for-pay software (offered through services such as `www.cnr.com`). Whether this non-purist approach to the free software world will have long-term negative effects (some have already begun complaining about it) remains to be seen.

- **Freedom and responsibility**—Endeavors with goals such as freedom and equality as guiding lights can sometimes suffer from a lack of control. As philosophically inspired distributions become more popular, technical discussions can sometimes spin out of control to become almost religious discussions. Ubuntu seems to resist the response that some profit-oriented Linux projects ultimately resort to: "Because we say so," but the line between openness and determinism is a tough one to walk.

Ubuntu's leadership has done a good job setting up a structure to make hard decisions in a free environment. For example, Ubuntu now has a Community Council (to create teams and projects, as well as leaders for each team) and a Technical Board (to guide the technical direction of Ubuntu). There is also now a Code of Conduct (`www.ubuntu.com/community/conduct`) presented to keep everyone participating in the project on the same path.

Ubuntu has prospered and increased in popularity far beyond the initial excitement inspired by being the new kid on the block. Ubuntu is holding up well under the pressure and continues to grow both in the size of its development and support communities and its popularity.

# Installing Ubuntu

Installing Ubuntu to hard disk requires a computer with at least 64MB of RAM for an Ubuntu Server, and 256MB of RAM for an Ubuntu Desktop installation. However, to use the live CD–based installer, you need at least 384MB of RAM.

As for hard disk space, you will need at least 4GB of space to install a desktop system or 500MB of disk space for a minimal server system. For the minimal server, you need to be able to work from the command line (no GUI is installed).

## On the DVD
**The Ubuntu 9.10 Desktop Install CD image is included on the DVD that comes with this book. If you are using that DVD instead of an Ubuntu CD image, select Ubuntu after booting the DVD and skip ahead to Step 4. ■**

If you are setting up Ubuntu to dual-boot on a desktop computer with a Windows system currently installed, you can resize your Windows partition during the installation process. It is easier, however, to first make sure that the free disk space exists outside of the Windows partition. See Chapter 8 for information on resizing hard disk partitions to make space for a Linux installation. Of course, you should also back up any important data files at this point.

The following procedure describes how to boot and install Ubuntu:

1. Insert the Ubuntu Desktop Install CD and reboot your computer. You should see the Ubuntu CD's boot screen, as shown in Figure 17-2. (If your system doesn't boot from the CD or you don't see the Ubuntu splash screen, make sure your computer is capable of booting from a CD, as described in Chapter 8.)

**FIGURE 17-2**

The Ubuntu Desktop Install CD Boot screen

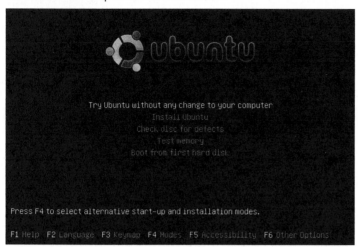

Try Ubuntu without any change to your computer
Install Ubuntu
Check disc for defects
Test memory
Boot from first hard disk

Press F4 to select alternative start-up and installation modes.

F1 Help  F2 Language  F3 Keymap  F4 Modes  F5 Accessibility  F6 Other Options

2. The boot screen for the Ubuntu Desktop Install CD provides a number of different options for booting your system, testing the installation CD or your system's memory, and so on. It also provides a number of special menus and screens that you can view to activate capabilities that might help you if you have special requirements during the install. The following is a list of the function keys that you can press and descriptions of each resulting menu or screen:

- **Help (F1)**—Lists what is available on the boot screens.

- **Language (F2)**—Enables you to set the language used by Ubuntu and the Ubuntu installer.

- **Keymap (F3)**—Enables you to specify the type of keyboard used by Ubuntu and the Ubuntu installer.

- **Modes (F4)**—Enables you to specify the graphics capabilities, add extra drivers from an update CD, and do a special OEM install of the system on which you are booting or installing Ubuntu.

- **Accessibility (F5)**—Enables you to activate various accessibility-related options in the Ubuntu installer, including a screen magnifier, onscreen keyboard, audio reading of various prompts, and so on.

- **Other Options (F6)**—Enables you to modify the kernel command line used to boot Ubuntu, which lets you deactivate certain hardware systems (such as power control), turn on more verbose debugging, and so on.

3. To proceed without modifying any of these options, simply press Enter to select "Try Ubuntu without any change to your computer." That boots Ubuntu and starts a default

desktop. The icon for installing Ubuntu to your hard disk appears in the upper-left corner of the screen, as shown in Figure 17-3.

The Ubuntu Desktop and the icon for the Graphical Installer

4. After the Ubuntu desktop displays, you can experiment with Ubuntu Linux on your current system without making any changes to your hard drive, or install Ubuntu to your system. To install Ubuntu on your computer system, double-click the Install icon to begin the installation process.

5. Select the language you want to use for Ubuntu. (The default is English.) To accept the selected value and proceed to the next screen, click Forward. You are asked to enter your location.

6. Choose your location. Your location will refine the language used (in other words, US English might be different from Canadian English), and will also be used to set the current time. If the time shown is incorrect for your location, you can click the Set Time button to display a dialog that enables you to correctly specify the local time. To accept the selected values and proceed to the next screen, click Forward. You are asked to enter your keyboard layout.

7. Select your keyboard type. To accept the selected value and proceed to the next screen, click Forward.

## Caution

**Changing or removing existing disk partitions can result in data being lost. Consider your options carefully before selecting a partitioning method. ■**

8. Choose your network connection. If you have a wired network interface card you can choose to automatically configure it with DHCP or enter a static IP address. In either case, you are asked to also enter a hostname.

9. Configure your clock by entering your time and timezone.

10. You are asked to begin partitioning your hard disk. Select one of the following choices for partitioning your hard disk. Selections for configuring LVM partitions may only

appear if you are using the alternate Ubuntu CD. (See Chapter 8 for further information on disk partitioning.)

- **Guided - resize**—Select this choice if you want to take disk space from an existing partition to use for your Ubuntu installation. Move the slider bar to take disk space from the selected partition. (You can use this if the entire hard disk is devoted to Windows and you want to be able to dual boot with Ubuntu.)

- **Guided - use entire disk**—This erases your entire hard disk, and then repartitions it automatically. If you have more than one hard disk, it lets you choose which one to use. Choose this method if you are prepared to remove all the data on your hard disk. Ubuntu installer will repartition using common Linux file system types.

- **Guided - use entire disk and set up LVM**—This allows you to install Ubuntu with hard disk partitions that use Logical Volume Manager (LVM). LVM is useful if you suspect that you will ever need to resize your disk partitions.

- **Guided - use entire disk and set up encrypted LVM**—This allows you to add encrypted logical volumes when you install Ubuntu, so your data can be secured and password protected.

- **Guided - use the largest continuous free space**—This allows you to install Ubuntu on a system on which another operating system is already installed, as long as you have sufficient, unallocated space available on your system's disk(s). Chapter 8 explains how to repartition an existing system in order to free up space for this option.

- **Manual**—This lets you manually create your own hard disk partitions. This is the best choice if you want to keep existing partitions from being erased. This is also the best choice if you have special needs, such as creating separate partitions to hold user data (/home) or server data (/var), or using a particular file system type for an area of your hard disk. Manual partitioning is considered to be a more advanced skill.

If you selected to manually edit the partition table, proceed to the next step. Otherwise, skip ahead past the partitioning steps.

11. During the manual partitioning phase, you can specify information about how you want to use partitions on the system where you are installing Ubuntu. You must define at least two partitions. One partition is used as swap space, which is a special partition format that Linux systems use for managing virtual memory. A second partition is used to hold the top-level directory of your Ubuntu Linux installation, known as the root directory and mounted as "/" on your Ubuntu system.

In the initial partitioning dialog, you select the free disk space in which you want to create a partition and click New Partition, which enables you to specify the type of file system that you want to use on the partition and whether it is a primary or extended partition. You can have only four primary partitions on a single disk drive—to create more than four partitions on a single disk drive, at least one of the four primary partitions must be defined as an extended partition, in which other (logical) partitions can then be defined.

12. After you agree to the partitioning scheme, your disk is partitioned, the base system is installed, and you need to provide information about a user account that you want to create on this system. This account will have administrative privileges, so you should create your own account at this point. Enter your full name (for example, John Smith), a username (for example, jsmith) that you will use to log in as this user, a password (twice) for the new user, and a name for this computer (which can be anything).

    To accept the selected values and proceed to the next screen, click Forward. At this point you may be asked whether you want to encrypt your home directory. Doing so can add a level of security to your system, in case it is stolen.

13. If the installer finds user accounts from any partitions on your hard disk, it asks whether you want to import settings (such as from Firefox or Evolution) to your new Ubuntu installation. Select any accounts for which you want to import information and click Forward.

14. You are asked whether you need a proxy server. If you need to indicate a proxy server to access the Internet, enter the location of that proxy server.

15. A confirmation screen summarizes the installation options that you have selected. To begin the installation, click Install. You can click Back to return to previous screens and change the values that you selected, or click Cancel to abort the installation process without changing anything on your system. If you select Forward, the Ubuntu installer begins the installation process. When the process is complete, the installer ejects the CD, reminds you to remove it from your system's CD drive, and asks you to press Return to reboot your system.

16. When installation is complete, the Desktop CD installer displays an Installation Complete dialog that confirms a successful installation. When you see this dialog, you can either click Continue Using the live CD to continue experimenting with Ubuntu from the CD, or click Restart Now to reboot your system and begin running Ubuntu directly from your system's hard drive(s).

    When you boot your system, Ubuntu displays a splash screen and progress dialog as it boots, followed by a graphical login screen. Congratulations—you're running Ubuntu Linux!

Ubuntu systems automatically run a graphical application called the Update Manager to notify you when system updates are available and to simplify retrieving and installing those updates. If updates to your system are available, the Update Manager displays a message to this effect and provides an icon at the right of the top panel that you can select to install those updates and keep your system current. You will need to provide your password in order to perform this (or any other) administrative operation. You can also check for updates manually at any time by selecting the System ⇨ Administration ⇨ Update Manager menu item.

To add other software packages, you can open the Synaptic Package Manager Window (select System ⇨ Administration ⇨ Synaptic Package Manager) or Add/Remove Applications window (select Applications ⇨ Add/Remove Programs). Using Synaptic, you can add the software you want individually. Software not available on the CD will be downloaded from the Internet (provided you have an active Internet connection).

# Getting Started with Ubuntu

On the surface, Ubuntu is not very different in appearance from other Linux desktop systems using GNOME. Underneath, the tools for managing your software packages are the same as you would expect with Debian systems. Many of the differences are subtle and do a lot to make using Linux easier for the end user.

Log in using the username and password you entered during installation. Figure 17-4 shows an example of an Ubuntu desktop with several applications started.

**FIGURE 17-4**

The Ubuntu desktop incorporates GNOME with ease-of-use additions.

# Trying out the desktop

With the latest GNOME interface, menus are available on the top panel. You won't have all the applications you would expect from a full-featured desktop system. However, you can easily add lots of other applications from the Internet (as described later). A good way to familiarize yourself with the Ubuntu GNOME desktop is to check out some of the menus.

- On the upper-left panel, the following categories of software are available from the **Applications** menu (I've added some notes about additional applications that you can grab from other locations):

  - **Accessories**—From this menu, select some basic desktop utilities that are part of the GNOME project. Text Editor starts the gedit graphical text editor (so you don't have to use the unintuitive vi editor to edit plain text documents). To go to a shell, you can launch the Terminal application from this menu. Other Accessories include a Calculator and a Character Map.

  - **Games**—Under the Games menu, you have a selection of about 17 GNOME games. Some are similar to ones you would find on a Windows desktop (for example, Mines, AisleRiot Solitaire, and FreeCell Solitaire). There are also Tetris-like games (Gnometris) and board games (Mahjongg). You don't get any of the more demanding open source games (such as Tux Racer) or networked games (such as the BZFlag networked tank battle game), but these can easily be installed using the Synaptic Package Manager.

  - **Graphics**—The Ubuntu desktop install includes the GIMP open source graphic manipulation application. It also includes the F-Spot Photo Manager for managing collections of digital photographs, and the gThumb Image Viewer. To import images from a scanner, Ubuntu includes the XSane image scanning application. No document viewers are included here, but Evince (which can be used to view PostScript and PDF files) and the more traditional Adobe Acrobat viewer can be installed using Synaptic.

  - **Internet**—Popular, standard open source Internet clients can be launched from this menu. The Ekiga Softphone application enables you to make voice-over-IP phone calls directly from your Ubuntu system. Evolution (a resource-intensive but full-featured mail client and personal information manager) can be used for reading and managing your e-mail. Firefox is the default Ubuntu Web browser and Pidgin (formerly known as GAIM) is used for instant messaging. This menu also includes a Terminal Server Client if you need to connect to Microsoft Windows Terminal servers (in the rare event that you still need access to a Microsoft Windows system).

  - **Office**—A full set of OpenOffice.org office productivity applications is available for Ubuntu, although it is not included with the initial live CD install. Available selections include OpenOffice.org Calc (spreadsheet), Draw (drawing and flowcharts), Impress (presentations), Math (formulas and equations), and Writer (word processing). OpenOffice.org Database lets you create and access a database.

- **Sound & Video**—Ubuntu provides a movie player, the Rhythmbox Music Player for online audio, the Serpentine CD creator, and the Sound Recorder audio recording application. Like other commercial Linux distributions, Ubuntu doesn't include the software needed to play MP3 music out of the box. However, if you try to play MP3 music from Rhythmbox or some other music players, you are asked whether you want to add these capabilities from the Ubuntu repositories.

  The movie player included with Ubuntu (and other GNOME desktops) is the Totem Movie Player (identified simply as Movie Player). Additional non–open source codecs are needed to enable that video player to play commercial DVD movies. Movie players such as xine and MPlayer, whose use requires codecs that cannot be freely distributed, are not included with Ubuntu by default, but can also be added through the Ubuntu repositories.

- The **Places menu** keeps track of places you want to go, lets you connect to remote servers, and lets you see (and, if you like, connect) to recently opened documents. There is also an option available to search your system for files.

- The **System menu** provides selections for changing desktop preferences and doing system administration tasks.

## Adding more software

Although Ubuntu manages to install around 2GB of applications from a single Ubuntu CD, it's still only 2GB. By contrast, other implementations with multiple CDs in a set can install about 7GB of applications or more. To add more software to Ubuntu, you can use the common Debian packaging tools (apt-get, aptitude, and even dpkg). You can also use the Synaptic Package Manager for adding and removing software packages, which provides a friendly graphical interface, a handy Search function to help you find packages, and many other usability improvements over the command-line tools.

To open the Synaptic Package Manager window, select System ➪ Administration ➪ Synaptic Package Manager. Figure 17-5 shows the Synaptic Package Manager window.

Using Synaptic Package Manager, you can install more software by selecting the Not Installed entry in the next column, and then selecting the package you want to install to the left. With one or more packages selected, select Apply and the software packages you selected will be downloaded from an Internet repository and installed.

As Ubuntu is delivered, it will check only official Ubuntu software repositories to find and download the software you add to Ubuntu. There are times, however, when you want to add community-built software that is outside the official distribution, in areas referred to as Universe and Multiverse:

- **Universe**—Packages stored in Ubuntu Universe repositories include software that is not yet stable enough to be officially included in the project. Although the software has been built against Ubuntu libraries by the Ubuntu community, and will work well in most cases, it comes without guarantee of support or security fixes.

- **Multiverse**—Packages in Multiverse repositories contain software that is not free. This means that the software licensing might not meet Ubuntu requirements, the software may be encumbered by patent issues, or that only binary versions are available. Users are encouraged to research licensing and other legal issues themselves before using software from these repositories.

**FIGURE 17-5**

Synaptic Package Manager displays and installs Ubuntu software.

Follow these steps to add the Universe and Multiverse repositories to Synaptic Package Manager so that you can use them to get additional Ubuntu software that simply might not be stable enough to be part of the Ubuntu release:

1. From the Synaptic Package Manager main window, select Settings ➪ Repositories. The Software Sources window appears, displaying the software repositories that are active for your system, as shown in Figure 17-6.

**FIGURE 17-6**

Add repositories to get software from Universe or outside the official distribution.

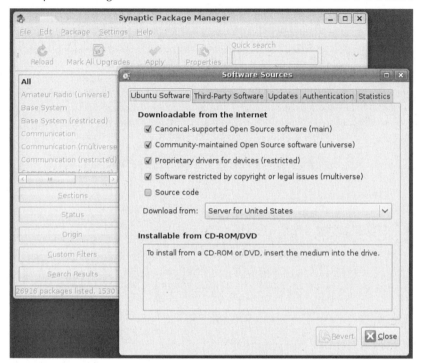

2. Select the Community-maintained Open Source software (Universe) or Software restricted by copyright or legal issues (Multiverse) repositories to enable you to explore or install software from them. (These repositories might already be enabled.)

3. Click Close to close this dialog and return to Synaptic. You will see a confirmation dialog, alerting you to update Synaptic's package list. Click OK.

4. Select Reload from the main Synaptic window. Software from the added repositories now appears in the list of software you can install in your system.

At this point, you can install any of the software that was added to your software list. Keep in mind, however, that because software in the Universe and Multiverse repositories is not supported by Ubuntu, it will not receive official patches or security updates from the Ubuntu development team. In other words, you are on your own (aside from asking for help on the Ubuntu forums or from the open source community in general).

If you want to stray further from the officially supported Ubuntu software, you can add custom repositories to your Ubuntu repository list. This is where you need to be particularly careful, so be sure to read the caution before proceeding.

## Caution

As with any Linux distribution, any time you use a repository other than the official repositories supported by that distribution, you should carefully scrutinize that repository. Unofficial repositories can break software compatibility, can contain software that you cannot use legally, and might even contain malicious software. Although it is still no guarantee of safety, check Ubuntu forums and mailing lists to find outside repositories that others have found to be reliable before using them yourself. Also, look for repositories that are specific to your version of Ubuntu because software from earlier Ubuntu releases or Debian-specific releases may not work. ■

To add a custom repository to Ubuntu, do the following from the Synaptic Package Manager window:

1. Select Settings ➪ Repositories. The Software Sources window appears.

2. Select the Third-Party Software tab.

3. Click Add. You are asked to add a complete line identifying the repository.

4. Type the line identifying the repository that contains the outside software you want to install. (The following is an example of a line identifying a fictitious repository.)

   ```
   deb http://ubuntu.example.com/ubuntu eft main
   ```

5. Click Add Source to have the line you just created added to your list of Ubuntu software repositories.

6. Click Close in the Software Sources dialog. You are warned that your repository information changed and that you can now reload your package list.

7. Click Close.

At this point, you can install any packages that appear in your new package list. (Click Not Installed in the left column to see any packages that have not yet been installed from any of the repositories identified in your repository list.)

# Getting More Information about Ubuntu

Ubuntu's popularity has led to many online resources for supporting it. One of the best places to start learning more about Ubuntu or finding answers to specific questions is the Ubuntu Forums site (www.ubuntuforums.org). To begin participating in that site, I suggest you read the usage guidelines and policies in the Ubuntu Forums FAQ at http://ubuntuforums.org/faq.php?faq=policy.

This FAQ describes conduct rules and suggests the best ways of having your technical support questions answered. As with most forums, browsing through topics of interest and doing keyword searches are good ways to find the information you need.

A few resources from the Ubuntu forums are particularly useful for someone starting out with Ubuntu. I recommend the following:

- **FAQs, HowTo, Tips, & Tricks** (`http://ubuntuforums.org/forumdisplay.php?f=100`)—This forum lists common steps that many people do after installing Ubuntu, such as adding support for certain video cards or multimedia software.

- **Absolute Beginner Talk** (`http://ubuntuforums.org/forumdisplay.php?f=73`)—Posts in this forum can help you understand what Linux is all about and whether or not Ubuntu will suit your needs. You can ask very basic questions here as well.

- **Ubuntu Cafe** (`http://ubuntuforums.org/forumdisplay.php?f=11`)—To catch the spirit of the Ubuntu community, you can check out the Ubuntu Cafe forum and get a taste of what's on people's minds.

The Ubuntu community also has a wiki (`https://wiki.ubuntu.com`) that continues to gain useful content for people using Ubuntu. Currently, the wiki includes areas for Ubuntu documentation, community information, support for different languages, events, and much more. There are also specific areas devoted to each Ubuntu release.

# Summary

Ubuntu is certainly the rising star of Linux distributions. Ubuntu started with Debian (one of the most respected but challenging distributions for beginners), simplifying the packaging and installation. It has demonstrated a commitment to frequent, well-designed, and supported releases. Today, Ubuntu is far more than a Debian spin-off, with its own community, advocates, and well-established development and maintenance groups.

Using a single installation CD, a user can install a set of useful desktop software or a streamlined server system. Ubuntu's graphical installer greatly simplifies the installation process by combining a graphical installer with a live distribution that you can run directly from the CD, which has made it easier than ever to test-drive and install Linux.

Along with the growth in popularity of Ubuntu has come an active community of developers and users. To become involved with Ubuntu, a good place to start is with community forums and the Ubuntu wiki.

# Running Fedora and Red Hat Enterprise Linux

I n September 2003, the world's leading Linux distribution, Red Hat Linux, disappeared. Red Hat, Inc., the company that created Red Hat Linux, divided its development efforts in two directions: the Fedora Project, which produces the Fedora operating system (originally called Fedora Core), and Red Hat Enterprise Linux. The split came from trying to better serve two diverse groups with one operating system. Fedora focused on encouraging the open source development community interested in helping develop and test software that would one day go into Red Hat products. Red Hat Enterprise Linux focused on the needs of paying customers who needed enterprise computing solutions.

## On the DVD

The Fedora 11 GNOME live/install CD is included on the DVD that comes with this book. You can try out the live version and then install a working Fedora desktop system from this DVD, using descriptions in Appendix A and the "Installing Fedora" section later in this chapter. If you don't have a DVD drive, you can get the software on CDs by downloading them from the Internet (http://fedoraproject.org/get-fedora) and burning them to CD, as described in Appendix A. ■

Fedora and Red Hat Enterprise Linux both come from a base of code that stems from the Red Hat Linux legacy. The two distributions have different goals and audiences and may drift farther apart over time. For the time being, however, Fedora is a community-driven distribution that is intended to include the latest Linux technology. Fedora is used as the basis for Red Hat Enterprise Linux releases.

Although Fedora is primarily sponsored by Red Hat, Inc. and staffed by Red Hat employees, the Fedora Project encourages community leadership and involvement. The latest Fedora includes many more features than Red

Hat Enterprise Linux, but those features have less guarantee of stability and no guarantee of support. However, important decisions about the direction of Fedora are still very much under the control of Red Hat, Inc. Likewise, Red Hat owns Fedora trademarks and makes legal decisions for Fedora based on its own legal counsel. Nearly all financial support for Fedora comes from Red Hat.

## Note

**Fedora follows the legacy of Red Hat Linux. The final version of Red Hat Linux was version 9. Fedora Core 1 and Red Hat Enterprise Linux 3 followed Red Hat Linux 9. At the time of this writing, Fedora 11 (the "Core" having been dropped) and Red Hat Enterprise Linux 5.3 are the latest versions of those two operating systems. ∎**

Red Hat Enterprise Linux (RHEL), which is actually represented by multiple products for desktop and server computer systems, is licensed commercially. Red Hat puts all its documentation, training, and support effort behind RHEL, which it sells to customers in the form of subscriptions. The intent is to have RHEL be a rock-solid Linux system that can be deployed across entire enterprises.

Despite the confusion it unleashed by dumping its flagship Red Hat Linux line and fears by some that Red Hat might become another Microsoft, Red Hat is still the dominant player when it comes to commercial Linux products. Many people have been happy to upgrade their critical Linux systems to Red Hat Enterprise Linux products.

In fact, when Microsoft announced its patent agreement with Novell, Red Hat was reported to have turned down a similar offer of cooperation with Microsoft, calling such an arrangement an "innovation tax." So, Red Hat, which was once viewed by some in the free software community as a threat to the free software movement, is now being viewed more often as a great defender of free and open source software rights. In fact, Fedora has a reputation for its extraordinary commitment to remain freely redistributable and as free as possible from patent-encumbered software.

## Note

**One reflection of the quality of the source code that Red Hat releases into the world is the success of the CentOS project. With no affiliation to Red Hat, members of the CentOS project build their own binary distribution of the RHEL source code with an aim at 100% binary compatibility with RHEL. Today, many people who don't have the need for the support, certification, and other assurances that come with RHEL are using CentOS in their organizations. ∎**

To its credit, Red Hat has managed to become a profitable venture while making some remarkable contributions to the open source effort. Releasing its installer (anaconda) and software packaging tools (RPM Package Management) under the GNU Public License (GPL) has enabled other Linux distributions to use and enhance those features. Within Red Hat Linux and now Fedora, Red Hat, Inc. has worked hard to include only software that could be freely distributed (removing most software with patent and copyright issues).

Despite continued emphasis from Red Hat, Inc. that Fedora comes with no guarantees, Fedora is an excellent Linux distribution. I know of universities that have deployed hundreds of Fedora desktop systems in their computer labs and small companies that run their businesses exclusively with Fedora. Those organizations have simply accepted responsibility for maintaining those systems themselves and upgrading their systems more often.

Even if you prefer to bet your business on Red Hat Enterprise Linux, Fedora is a great way to evaluate and use technology that is in all Linux distributions from Red Hat. Features in the current Fedora system are those that are being prepared for a later release of RHEL. Both Fedora and RHEL are discussed in this chapter, so you can determine which distribution is right for you.

# Digging into Features

There are many opinions on why Red Hat Linux and other distributions from the Red Hat Linux legacy have been so popular. The following sections describe some features of Red Hat Linux distributions commonly believed to have led to its success and that now add to the popularity of Fedora and Red Hat Enterprise Linux distributions.

## Red Hat installer (anaconda)

When many Linux distributions still had you struggling from the command line to get the distribution installed, Red Hat created its own installer called anaconda. anaconda includes both graphical and text-based procedures for installing Linux, and is one of the oldest graphical installers continuously shipping. When you're done installing Fedora or Red Hat Enterprise Linux, you have the following:

- A set of software packages installed that suits how you want to use your computer (as a desktop, workstation, server, or some custom configuration).

- Configured online software repositories. By identifying Fedora and third-party repositories, you can choose from thousands of software packages to easily download and install.

- Standard information, such as date, time, time zone, and language set.

- A configured mouse, keyboard, video card, and monitor.

- An appropriately partitioned hard disk.

- A configured network card and firewall, to immediately connect to a LAN.

- A configured boot loader, to define how Linux starts up.

In addition to being easy to use, anaconda is loaded with features to make it easy to manage the installation of multiple RHEL or Fedora systems. For example, these power features are built into the anaconda installer:

- **Network installs**—After booting the install process, the actual Fedora or RHEL distribution can be on a network server that is accessible via a Web server (HTTP), FTP server (FTP), or UNIX file server (NFS).

- **Kickstart installs**—It's not so bad to sit there and click through the answers to run the installation of one Fedora system, but if you're doing dozens or hundreds of installs (especially on similar computers), automating that task can be a major time-saver. anaconda supports kickstart installs, for which you use a preconfigured kickstart file to answer the questions that come up during a Fedora or RHEL installation. If you answer all the questions in the file, you can launch the installation and have it run from start to finish without you in attendance.

- **Upgrades**—With an existing Fedora system installed, anaconda enables you to easily upgrade to a newer Fedora system. A lot of nice features for saving backups of configuration files and logging the upgrade activities are built into that process. During an upgrade, anaconda takes into consideration any dependency issues, so the upgraded software packages will have all the libraries and commands that the features in those packages need.

Major enhancements to anaconda have come with recent releases of Fedora. In particular, anaconda now incorporates the yum facility for gathering, downloading, and installing packages. During initial installation, you can add multiple yum-enabled Fedora software repositories to install software from those repositories.

You'll find a detailed description of installing Fedora using the anaconda installer at the end of this chapter.

## Custom spins, install sets, and live CDs

By extending anaconda installer features to tools such as `livecd-creator` and `pungi`, you can create your own software repositories, live CDs, and custom software install CDs/DVDs. So if you want to create your own software (or grab software from outside the Fedora repositories) and package it up with Fedora, the Fedora Project has easy-to-use tools to help you do that. The resulting CD or DVD ISO images are referred to as *custom spins*.

Using `livecd-creator`, you can select which software packages you want to use in your own live CD and which settings you want with it (user accounts, desktop settings, network configuration, and so on). With `pungi`, you create custom installation media, so your customers or friends can install exactly the system you offer them.

Both `livecd-creator` and `pungi` can run from the same type of kickstart file used with anaconda, allowing you to save the packages and settings you choose. So it becomes easy to update your custom spin by rerunning the build command with the kickstart file as updated packages become available.

Custom spins created directly from the Fedora Project itself or from members of the community are already available. For example, there are Fedora live CDs featuring gaming, electronics tools, KDE desktops, and Creative Commons live content.

# RPM Package Management

All Red Hat and Fedora distributions use the RPM Package Management (RPM) software packaging format to store and maintain software. Fedora and RHEL contain a set of tools for installing, upgrading, maintaining, and querying software packages in RPM format. Essentially, the RPM software packages that are installed are maintained in a local database, so you can list the contents of packages, view descriptions, and even check for tampering of the files in those packages you have installed.

Using RPM, add-on software can also be easily included in and maintained for Fedora systems. So users who once had to know how to deal with tarballs and makefiles to compile their own software can now simply install an RPM package to get the features they want. With other Linux distributions (such as SUSE and Mandrake) also using RPM packaging, your RPM tool skills can help you manage software on those distributions as well.

You can check out ongoing development of the RPM from the RPM project (`http://rpm.org`) site. Fedora 11 includes RPM 4.7. Improvements in RPM 4.7 include features to provide support for larger files, better compression, improved architecture dependency, and better cleanup of stale lock files. For end users, these improvements should result in better reliability, security, and performance.

Because of the popularity of Red Hat Linux systems, lots of software repositories and third-party software management tools have been created to further automate and simplify handling software in Red Hat systems. Tools such as yum (`http://yum.baseurl.org`) and apt4rpm (`http://apt4rpm.sourceforge.net`) are available for updating selected software.

As noted earlier, the yum facility forms the foundation for installing RPM packages in Fedora and RHEL. For several reasons, yum is usually preferred over the `rpm` command. First, it can be used to install from network repositories. Second, it can find and install dependent packages needed by the packages you request. And last, it is preferred because there are related tools for searching and managing repositories. Yum can also be used to install software from local media and, unlike rpm, resolve dependencies automatically.

# Latest desktop technology

By keeping up with the latest technologies, the Fedora Project helps users discover the latest innovations in desktop technology. In the past year, Fedora releases have featured major new desktop technology such as KDE 4.2 and the new Lightweight X11 Desktop Environment (described in Chapter 3).

Fedora was the first major distribution to include KDE 4 as its default KDE environment. The most obvious new features include the ability of the new Plasma desktop to place widgets directly on the desktop. This allows mini-applications such as photo viewers, system monitors, and stock tickers to sit directly on the desktop. The Photon multimedia feature provides a single framework for KDE music and video applications. New Oxygen Artwork provides a whole new look to the KDE desktop. A lightweight file manager named Dolphin is now used as the default file manager.

The Lightweight X11 Desktop Environment (www.lxde.org) has been added recently to Fedora. LXDE was designed to perform well on low-RAM computers such as handhelds or on live CDs. (To use LXDE in Fedora, type **yum groupinstall LXDE** as root user. Then select LXDE as your desktop session when you log in.) Figure 18-1 shows an example of the LXDE desktop.

LXDE has its own set of efficient desktop applications. It uses PCMan as its file manager and GPicView to view images, as shown in Figure 18-1.

**FIGURE 18-1**

Fedora includes the new Lightweight X11 Desktop Environment (LXDE).

## System configuration tools

Red Hat created a set of simplified, graphical tools for configuring and administering many basic administrative features in Red Hat systems. Using these tools, you can add printers, configure your network, add users, set up your sound card, and tune up your video card, to name a few of the features they cover.

Red Hat's graphical configuration tools (described in Chapter 10) can be launched from the Administration menu or from the command line.

### Note

**Several releases ago, the beginnings of these configuration tools' command names changed from** `redhat-config` **to** `system-config`**. For example, the tool to configure your network in Fedora is now called** `system-config-network` **(instead of** `redhat-config-network`**).** ∎

# Going Forward with Fedora

Fedora has done a particularly good job in serving the open source software development community and those who want to repackage Linux for different purposes. Fedora is particularly good if you want to use it in the following ways:

- **Personal desktop**—If you are on the technical side and want to have the latest Linux technology, Fedora can be a great choice. You may have to deal with more software updates and deal with some less-complete features than with Red Hat Enterprise Linux. However, those negatives can be a small price for those who are always looking to try out the latest desktop features available.

- **Personal server**—Many people use Fedora for a personal file, print, or Web server with great results. Incorporating SELinux security can help make a Fedora server among the most secure server platforms available today, while still providing cutting edge server features.

- **Build your own Linux system**—By building your own live CD or install CD, you can repackage Fedora to have exactly the software you want. You can even build in your own software packages and repositories with Fedora tools. Because Fedora is made so that people can redistribute it, you have fewer concerns about potential copyright or patent infringements.

- **Develop software**—Many people use Fedora for developing their open source software projects. Using Fedora, software developers can test their own software on the latest systems. For enterprise software products, developers can test out features that will eventually make their way into Red Hat Enterprise Linux. Linus Torvalds himself uses Fedora to develop the latest Linux kernel technology, primarily because of its excellent support for PowerPC hardware.

The Fedora Project remains committed to the principle that everything in Fedora be freely redistributable and that almost everything be open source (with the exception of some firmware drivers, such as wireless LAN card drivers). Although not offering some non-free software (particularly multimedia codecs) makes Fedora less attractive to some casual users, true open source enthusiasts have found Fedora to be a trustworthy distribution.

Beyond its value to the development community, many non-technical people use Fedora. Statistics gathered by the Fedora Project (`http://fedoraproject.org/wiki/Statistics`) show that Fedora system updates were downloaded from nearly 1 million unique IP addresses during the first 12 weeks that Fedora 11 was released. Because many Fedora systems are behind NAT firewalls, with multiple systems behind a single IP address, the number of installed Fedora 11 systems is probably much higher than that.

If Fedora sounds interesting to you, the following sections describe some ways you can get involved. To become an official member of the Fedora community, you can go to the Join Fedora page (`http://fedoraproject.org/join-fedora`), which will lead you through opportunities with the Fedora Project and help you sign up.

## Growing community support for Fedora

In the past few years, new initiatives and Web sites have popped up to support Fedora. Two of the best official assets of the Fedora Project are FedoraProject.org (the official Fedora Project site) and FedoraForum.org (which has been recognized as the official end-user forum of choice).

FedoraProject.org is the site for official information about schedules, goals, and initiatives that make up the Fedora Project. If you want to become involved in Fedora-related projects, such as Ambassadors, Marketing, Live CD, or Documentation, FedoraProject.org is the focal point for pursuing those initiatives.

FedoraForum.org features news, galleries, and (as you might guess) forums for sharing questions and information about Fedora. As of this writing, FedoraForum.org had more than 100,000 members.

The Unofficial Fedora FAQ (`www.fedorafaq.org`) has become an excellent resource for getting answers to the most constant, nagging questions about Fedora. This FAQ is a good place to start for learning how to get all those things you need (MP3 players, viewing DVD movies, instant messaging, video players, access to your Windows XP NTFS file system, and so on).

On the whole, the total amount of software available and greater stability among software repositories has meant that it's possible to get a much better total experience with Fedora than was possible even with Red Hat Linux.

## Joining Fedora special interest groups

People in the Fedora community join together into special interest groups (SIGs) to pursue common goals with Fedora. Some of the groups stay in touch using mailing lists, regular meetings on

IRC chat channels, and Fedoraproject.org wiki pages. Here are a few Fedora SIGs you might find interesting:

- **One Laptop Per Child SIG** (http://fedoraproject.org/wiki/OLPC)—You may have heard of the OLPC project's (www.laptop.org) goal of bringing low-cost laptops to children around the world. But you may not know that the operating system inside those laptops is Fedora. The Fedora OLPC SIG explores ways for the Fedora Project to provide software and infrastructure support to OLPC.

- **Games SIG** (http://fedoraproject.org/wiki/SIGs/Games)—The Fedora Games SIG has done a great job packaging open source and liberated commercial games to run on Fedora. To participate, you can join the fedora-games-list mailing list, chat on the #fedora-games channel on irc.freenode.net, or just check out the Games SIG wiki page.

- **Artwork Team** (http://fedoraproject.org/wiki/Artwork)—The Fedora Artwork team provides an avenue for creative people to contribute to Fedora. While encouraging the use of open source tools, the Artwork team has created logos, backgrounds, promo banners, posters, and other art to support Fedora.

- **Education SIG** (http://fedoraproject.org/wiki/SIGs/Education)—The Fedora Education SIG is working to get more educational applications into Fedora, and then produce a Fedora Education Spin to efficiently distribute that software.

- **Spins SIG** (http://fedoraproject.org/wiki/SIGs/Spins)—The Spins SIG was created to help people create their own custom spins of Fedora software. Anyone can create a spin and submit it for approval from the Spins SIG. If it meets Fedora Project requirements, the spin could be hosted by Fedora or simply have the instructions for producing the spin (typically a kickstart file) stored by Fedora for others to use.

Other interesting SIGs include the Fedora Robotics SIG, the Astronomy SIG, Embedded Systems SIG, and Store SIG. There are also efforts you can join to improve documentation, the wiki, translations, marketing, and other areas.

## Forums and mailing lists

If you want to get into the flow of the Fedora community, I recommend starting with the Fedora Project's own mailing lists. You can choose the Fedora mailing list that interests you from the Red Hat Mailing Lists page (http://redhat.com/mailman/listinfo). Start with the Fedora-list or Fedora-announce-list mailing list.

# Fedora Comes of Age

Most people who follow Linux would agree that Fedora has become a strong, viable Linux system in its own right, and not just a test release for Red Hat Enterprise Linux. The project has continued to grow and flourish and the current Fedora release is the latest incarnation in a great line. Figure 18-2 shows a standard desktop.

**FIGURE 18-2**

Fedora includes the GNOME desktop, with many productivity tools and games available.

While still laying the foundation for Red Hat Enterprise Linux, Fedora has also added some fun and powerful features to distinguish itself from other Linux systems. Here are some examples:

- **Package Kit**—In the past year, Fedora has dropped its graphical tools for installing and updating software (pup and pirut) in favor of the PackageKit facility. While Fedora is still shaking some bugs out of PackageKit, PackageKit offers simplified tools for getting new packages and software updates. A PackageKit applet in the panel alerts you when updates are available and lets you select to get and install them.

- **NetworkManager**—The NetworkManager facility has recently been added as the default tool for starting and stopping your network connections. By starting the NetworkManager service and selecting the NetworkManager applet in the panel, you can see the wireless access points that have been detected and select which one you want to connect to. You can also start and stop any wired network interfaces.

- **KVM and Xen Virtualization**—The ability to run multiple operating systems instances on one computer is just the beginning of the promise that virtualization brings to Linux. In today's server computing model, often an entire server is devoted to running a particular application that may be tied to a particular operating system. As a result, the entire computer may be underutilized if it is not a high-demand application.

  With virtualization, you have the opportunity to run multiple instances, including an entire operating system, an application, and a data combination. Those instances (called *guests*) can be Linux, Windows, or any other operating system that runs on the computer hardware. Guests operate separately from each other, and so remain secure from each other. As demand slows or increases for a guest, it can be moved to different machines to make the best use of available hardware.

  Red Hat, Inc. has thrown some strong development support into the KVM virtualization software that is built into the Linux kernel. It also continues to support Xen virtualization in RHEL (Xen is now part of Citrix Systems). Tools for starting, stopping, and otherwise managing multiple guest operating systems are all included in the KVM and Xen versions that come with Fedora 11.

- **AIGLX desktop eye candy**—The Accelerated Indirect GLX (AIGLX) project is a cooperative effort between the Fedora community and the X.Org X Window server project. With a video card that supports DRI and GLX (see `http://fedoraproject.org/wiki/RenderingProject/aiglx` for information on supported cards), you can see some eye-popping desktop effects.

If Fedora is such a great product, you may wonder why someone would want to pay for Red Hat Enterprise Linux. The major reason for using RHEL over Fedora is the promise of support behind your critical systems. You may also need a longer period of promised support for critical fixes and security patches than is available with Fedora. With Red Hat Enterprise Linux you can also get

- **Training**—Red Hat, Inc. offers training courses in system administration, software development, and other areas. (See `www.redhat.com/courses`.)

- **Certification**—Red Hat offers certifications for Red Hat Certified Technician and Engineer (RHCT and RHCE), Datacenter Specialist (RHCDS), Security Specialist (RHCSS), and Architect (RHCA). (See `www.redhat.com/certification`.)

- **Third-party hardware and software**—Through a variety of alliances with hardware vendors, software vendors, and resellers, you can be assured of finding certified hardware, certified software, and services to back up your Red Hat Enterprise Linux installations.

Many people I know, especially those who like to have the latest cool bits available, use Fedora for their personal desktop and server systems and use Red Hat Enterprise Linux at work. They don't mind upgrading their home desktop system every six months or so and can accept a certain level of instability. If you have a similar aesthetic, Fedora could be an excellent Linux distribution for you.

# Installing Fedora

The Linux operating system Fedora, sponsored by Red Hat, is included on this book's DVD. The rest of this chapter leads you through its installation.

Before you install Fedora on your computer, ensure that your computer hardware supports it. You should also choose a method of installing Fedora. Those topics are discussed in the following sections.

## Choosing computer hardware

This book comes with a standard PC (x86) version of Fedora. For different hardware (such as PowerPC or a 64-bit machine), see the Get Fedora Web page (`http://fedoraproject.org/get-fedora`) for information on downloading the Fedora medium for your architecture. To install the Fedora system from the DVD that comes with this book, the computer must have the following:

- **Processor**—The Pentium-class PC needs to be at least 200 MHz for text mode and 400 MHz Pentium II for GUI.

- **RAM**—You need at least 64MB of RAM to install Fedora. If you are running in graphical mode, you need at least 192MB. The recommended RAM for graphical mode is 512MB.

- **DVD or CD drive**—You need to be able to boot up the installation process from a DVD or CD (the latter requires you get Fedora installation CDs as described at `http://fedoraproject.org/get-fedora`). If you can't boot from a DVD or CD, there are ways to start the installation from a hard disk or using a PXE install, as the following section, "Choosing an installation method," explains.

- **Hard disk**—With no preset install types in Fedora 11, essentially every installation is a custom installation. Therefore, depending on which packages you choose to install, the disk space you need can range from about 600MB (for a minimal server with no GUI installed) to 7GB (to install all packages from an official Fedora install DVD).

  For installing from a Fedora desktop live CD, I recommend at least 2GB to 3GB of disk space. (The Fedora Project recommends at least five percent of additional free space, plus any disk space you require for user data.)

- **Keyboard and monitor**—You need a keyboard and monitor at least during installation. (You can operate Fedora quite well over a LAN using either a shell interface from a network login or an X terminal.)

As mentioned earlier, although not included with this book, Fedora versions are available for the PowerPC and 64-bit architectures. Red Hat Enterprise Linux versions (which you have to purchase from Red Hat, Inc.) are available for other hardware, such as Intel Itanium, IBM PowerPC, and IBM mainframe.

Most of the software described in this book will work the same in any of those hardware environments. (Check out Fedoraproject.org for sites that offer Fedora for different computer hardware architectures.)

To begin installing Fedora, you also need to have installation media, such as the *Linux Bible 2010 Edition* DVD that comes with this book (or a set of official Fedora installation CDs or DVD that you obtain yourself). Also you must either be dedicating your entire hard disk (or an added hard disk) to Linux, have a preconfigured Linux partition, or have sufficient free space on your hard disk outside any existing Windows partition.

## Note

**If you are not dedicating your whole hard disk to Fedora and you don't understand partitioning, refer to Chapter 8, which describes how to set up partitioning to allow multiple computer operating systems to coexist on the same hard drive. Always be sure to back up everything before installing a new operating system or making a significant change. ∎**

## Choosing an installation method

You can also install Fedora from any of several different types of media. You can still start the install process by booting a Fedora install from one of the following media:

- **Fedora installation CD or DVD**—These media contain both the installer and the actual software packages needed to install Fedora.

- **Fedora boot CD**—A CD that has only the Fedora installer (not the actual software packages) can be used to start the install process. You can make your own boot CD by burning the `boot.iso` file that comes on official Fedora install media (look in the `images` directory) to a blank CD. You must then continue the installation from one of the install methods listed later in this section.

- **Network Interface Card (PXE)**—If your computer's network interface card (NIC) can support PXE booting, and there is a computer offering a Fedora install server over PXE on your LAN, you can simply boot from that NIC to start a Fedora installation. No other boot media is required.

After booting the install process you can continue to install from the local medium (provided that the software packages are on that medium). Or, type `linux askmethod` at the boot prompt, which offers you the choice of installing Fedora from the following locations:

- **Local DVD or CD-ROM**—This is the most common method of installing Fedora and the one you get by pressing Enter from the Fedora installation boot prompt. Use this section for both DVD and CD installs. (You may need to change the BIOS if the DVD or CD doesn't boot.) To boot and install the Fedora live CD that is included on the DVD that comes with this book, select **fedora** from the startup menu. The official Fedora install DVD or set of Fedora install CDs can be used to install without first booting live.

- **HTTP**—Lets you install from a Web address (http://) that contains a Fedora installation directory.

- **FTP**—Lets you install from an FTP site (ftp://) that contains a Fedora installation directory.

- **NFS image**—Allows you to install from any shared directory on another computer on your network that contains Fedora installation images using the Network File System (NFS) facility.

- **Hard drive**—If you can place a copy of the Fedora distribution on your hard drive, you can install it from there. (The ISO images of the Fedora installation media should be on a hard drive partition to which you are *not* installing.)

### Installing on multiple computers

If you're installing Fedora on many computers with similar configurations, you can save yourself some time by using the Kickstart installation, which enables you to create a set of answers to the questions Fedora asks you during installation. After you install your Fedora system, a kick-start.ks file is copied to your /root directory. You can use that kickstart file as the basis for future Fedora installations, so you can make the same selections for subsequent installs.

### Installation guides

Fedora installation guides are available in several different languages. To download a tarball of an installation guide or simply read it online, refer to this site:

    http://docs.fedoraproject.org/install-guide/

## Choosing to install or upgrade

Are you doing a new install or an upgrade? If you are upgrading a Fedora system to the latest version, the installation process will try to leave your data files and configuration files intact as much as possible. This type of installation takes longer than a new install. A new install simply erases all data on the Linux partitions (or whole hard disk) that you choose.

If you are upgrading an existing Fedora system to this release, you should consider first removing any unwanted packages from your old Fedora system. The fewer packages to be checked during an upgrade, the faster the upgrade installation (and the less space used).

## Note

**You can upgrade to Fedora 11 from previous Fedora systems. The further you are from the current release, however, the greater the chance of something going wrong. You cannot upgrade to Fedora from a Red Hat Enterprise Linux or CentOS system or vice versa.** ∎

To upgrade, you must have at least a Linux 2.0 kernel installed. With an upgrade, your configuration files that are replaced are saved as *filename*.rpmsave (for example, the hosts file is saved as /etc/hosts.rpmsave). More often, however, your old configuration files will remain in place, while the system copies new configuration files to `filename.rpmnew`. The locations of those files, as well as other upgrade information, is written to `/tmp/upgrade.log`. The upgrade installs the new kernel, any changed software packages, and any packages that the installed packages depend on being there. Your data files and configuration information should remain intact. By clicking the Customize box, you can choose which packages to upgrade.

A recent feature that is available when you are upgrading to Fedora 11 is the preupgrade package. By installing preupgrade on a Fedora 10 system (`yum install preupgrade`), if you have an Internet connection you can prepare your system to upgrade to Fedora 11 by launching a single application to

- Determine which packages need to be downloaded to upgrade to Fedora 11
- Download the packages needed to complete the upgrade (while Fedora 10 is still running)
- Download the boot images needed for the upgrade

The advantage to using preupgrade is that you can continue using your system while you do most of the time-consuming work (such as downloading packages) that needs to be done to complete an upgrade. Also, before you get into running the installer, you will be able to see whether there are any package dependencies you should deal with (before committing to the actual upgrade).

With the preupgrade package installed, you can start the GUI version of preupgrade by typing **preupgrade** from a Terminal window as root user. Files needed for the upgrade are copied to the `/var/cache/yum/anaconda-upgrade` directory (so make sure there is plenty of disk space there before you start). When preupgrade is complete, you can reboot and the Fedora upgrade will begin from the GRUB bootloader.

## Coming from Windows

If you are installing a dual-boot system that includes a Windows operating system, install the Windows system first and the Fedora system afterward. Some Windows systems blow away the Master Boot Record (MBR), making the Fedora partition inaccessible.

If, when installing Windows or Fedora, you find that the other operating system is no longer available on your boot screen, don't panic and don't immediately reinstall. You can usually recover from the problem by booting with the Fedora emergency boot disk and then using either the grub-install or lilo command to reinsert the proper MBR. If you are uncomfortable working in emergency mode, seek out an expert to help you.

Red Hat provides a description of how to configure a dual-boot system at `www.redhat.com/docs/manuals/linux/RHL-9-Manual/install-guide/ch-x86-dualboot.html`. ■

## Beginning the installation

After you have selected the right type of installation for your needs, you can begin the installation procedure. Throughout most of the procedure, you can click Back to make changes to earlier screens. However, after you are warned that packages are about to be written to hard disk, there's no turning back. Most items that you configure can be changed after Fedora is installed.

## Coming from Windows

It is quite possible that your entire hard disk is devoted to a Windows 95, 98, 2000, ME, NT, XP, Windows 7 or Vista operating system, and you may want to keep much of that information after Fedora is installed. Although there are installation choices that let you retain existing partitions, they don't let you take space from existing DOS or NTFS partitions without destroying them. If you like, you can try resizing your Windows partition using the qtparted utility. You can run qtparted by booting the KNOPPIX distribution that comes on the DVD included with this book. Just be aware that, if used improperly, qtparted (or any disk partitioning tool) can damage or erase important data from your hard disk. ■

Ready to install? (Have you backed up any data you want to keep safe?) Okay, then here's what to do:

1. **Insert the DVD into the DVD drive.** If you are not able to boot from the DVD, obtain an official Fedora installation CD set as described earlier in this chapter and continue with this procedure by inserting the first CD into the drive.

2. **Reboot your computer.** If you see the Linux Bible boot screen or the Fedora installation screen, continue to the next step.

## Tip

If you don't see the installation screen, your DVD or CD-ROM drive may not be bootable. You may be able to make the drive bootable, however. Here's how: Restart the computer. Immediately, you should see a message telling you how to select the boot device, such as by pressing the F12 or Del key. From the list that appears, select the CD/DVD drive and press Enter. ■

3. **Boot the install medium.** What you do next depends on whether you are booting the Fedora live CD (as comes on the DVD with this book) or Fedora install DVD. From the boot screen do one of the following:

   - **Linux Bible DVD or Fedora live CD**—From the Linux Bible DVD boot screen, type **fedora**. From a Fedora live CD, either wait for the boot screen to time out or with Boot highlighted on the boot menu, press Enter to start the live CD. When the CD or DVD boots up to a desktop system, double-click the Install to Hard Drive icon to begin the installation.

   - **Fedora Install DVD**—As noted earlier, you need to obtain a Fedora install DVD on your own (as one doesn't come with the book). With "Install or upgrade" highlighted on the boot menu, press Enter to begin the installation.

## Note

Although many of the steps are the same, the live CD and install DVD installs are different in a few key ways. In particular, the DVD install lets you select which packages to install. The CD install simply copies what is essentially an installed system from the live CD to your hard disk. So some of the steps that follow won't apply to the live CD install. ■

If your computer won't let you install in graphical mode (16-bit color, 800 × 600 resolution, framebuffer), refer to the "Choosing Different Install Modes" sidebar. The boot screen is menu-driven. So if you want to change any of the boot options for a menu selection, highlight that selection and press the Tab key. You can then remove or add options before pressing Enter to continue. For example, to install from a different medium (such as over the network), add the askmethod boot option. See the sidebar "Choosing Different Install Modes" for more boot options.

4. **Media check.** If you're asked to check your installation media, press Enter. If the CD or DVD is damaged, this step saves you the trouble of getting deep into the install and then failing. After the DVD is checked, select Skip to continue.

5. **Continue.** When the welcome screen appears, click Next to continue.

6. **Choose an installation language.** If you are asked to choose an installation language, move the arrow keys to the language you want and then select Next. (Later, you will be able to add additional languages.)

7. **Choose install type.** If there is an existing version of Fedora on your hard disk, from the install medium (as opposed to the live CD), you are asked to select one of the following: Install Fedora for a new install or Upgrade an Existing Installation to upgrade an existing version of Fedora.

## Choosing Different Install Modes

Although most computers enable you to install Fedora in the default mode (graphical), there may be times when your video card does not support that mode. Also, although the install process detects most computer hardware, there may be times when your hard disk, Ethernet card, or other critical piece of hardware cannot be detected and will require you to enter special information at boot time.

The following is a list of commands that you can type at the installation boot prompt to change installation modes to start the Fedora install process. You typically try these modes only if the default mode fails (that is, if the screen is garbled or installation fails at some point). For a list of other supported modes, refer to the /usr/share/doc/anaconda*/command-line.txt file or press F2 to see short descriptions of some of these types.

| Command | Description |
| --- | --- |
| text | Runs installation in a text-based mode. Do this if installation doesn't seem to recognize your graphics card. |
| ks | Type **ks** to run a Fedora installation using a kickstart file. A kickstart file provides some or all of the installation options you would otherwise have to select manually. |
| lowres | Runs installation in 640 × 480 screen resolution for graphics cards that can't support the higher resolution. To choose a particular resolution, use the resolution option. For example: resolution=1024x768. |
| nofb | Turns off frame buffer. (With frame buffer on, the video display is driven from a memory buffer holding a complete data frame.) |

*continued*

*continued*

| Command | Description |
|---|---|
| noprobe | Installation won't probe to determine your hardware; you must load any special drivers that might be needed to install it. Typically, installation auto-probes to determine what hardware you have on your computer. |
| mediacheck | Check your DVD or CDs before installing. Because media checking can be done in the normal installation process, do this only to test the media on a computer you are not installing on. |
| rescue | Boots from CD, mounts your hard disk, and lets you access useful utilities to correct problems that are preventing your Linux system from operating properly. (Not really an installation mode.) |
| vnc | Type **vnc vncconnect=***hostname* **vncpassword=****** to run the install in VNC mode. In this mode, you step through the installation process from another system (a VNC client represented by *hostname*). The other system must be running a VNC server to do this type of install. |
| dd | Type **dd** if you have a driver disk you want to use to install. |
| expert | Bypasses probing so you can choose your mouse, video memory, and other values that would otherwise be chosen for you. Use if you believe that the installation process is not properly auto-probing your hardware. |
| askmethod | Has the installation process ask where to install from (local CD, NFS image, FTP, HTTP, or hard disk). |
| nocddma | Type **nocddma** to turn off DMA. Errors with some CD drives can be overcome by turning off the DMA feature. This is a good option to try if an install CD or DVD you know to be good fails media check. You could also try ide=nodma to turn off DMA for all IDE devices. |
| updates | To install from an update disk. |

You can add other options to the linux boot command to identify particular hardware that is not being detected properly. For example, to specify the number of cylinders, heads, and sectors for your hard disk (if you believe the boot process is not detecting these values properly), you can pass the information to the kernel as follows: linux hd=720,32,64. In this example, the kernel is told that the hard disk has 720 cylinders, 32 heads, and 64 sectors. You can find this information in the documentation that comes with your hard disk (or stamped on the hard disk itself on a sticker near the serial number).

There are also other boot options you can add to the installation prompt to instruct the installation boot prompt how to start the installation. Many of these options are described in Chapter 21.

8. **Enter hostname.** Identify the network name used by this computer. You may enter a fully qualified domain name (such as `host.example.com`).

9. **Choose a time zone.** Select the time zone. Either click a spot on the map or choose from the drop-down box. Before you click your exact location on the map, click on the area of the map that includes your continent or move the slider to zoom in. Then select the specific city. You can click "System clock uses UTC" to have your computer use Coordinated Universal Time (also known as Greenwich Mean Time). With multiple operating systems installed, you might want to uncheck this box, because some operating systems expect the BIOS to be set to local time.

10. **Set root password.** You must choose a password for your root user at this point. The root password provides complete control of your Fedora system. Without it, and before you add other users, you will have no access to your own system. Enter the root password, and then type it again in the Confirm box. (Remember the root user's password and keep it confidential! Don't lose it!) Click Next to continue.

## Tip

Use the `passwd` command to change your password later. See Chapter 12 for suggestions on how to choose a good password. See Chapter 11 for information on setting up user accounts. ■

11. **Choose your partitioning strategy.** You have the following choices related to how your disk is partitioned for a Fedora installation:

## Note

Instead of installing to a local hard disk, you can identify an ISCSI initiator as the storage device by selecting the Advanced Storage Configuration button and entering the IP address and ISCSI Initiator Name of the SCSI device. After that is identified, you can use that device for installing Fedora. ■

- **Use entire drive**—This erases the entire contents of the hard disks you select.

- **Replace existing Linux system**—This erases all Linux partitions, but leaves Windows partitions intact.

- **Shrink current system**—This allows you to resize the disk partitions for the currently installed Linux or Microsoft Windows system so you can then use the remaining space to install Linux.

- **Use free space**—This works only if you have enough free space on your hard disk that is not currently assigned to any partition. (You can choose this option if you resized your Windows partition to make space for Linux.)

- **Create custom layout**—Select this if you want to create your own custom partitioning.

## Note

If you selected to create a custom layout, refer to the section on partitioning your hard disk later in this chapter for details on using those tools. ■

If you have multiple hard disks, you can select which of those disks should be used for your Fedora installation. Check the Encrypt system box if you want to have an encrypted file system. Check the Review and Modify Partitioning Layout check box to see how Linux is choosing to partition your hard disk. Click Next to continue.

12. **Review and modify partitioning layout.** If you chose to review or customize your partitioning, you will see the Disk Setup tool with your current partitioning layout displayed. You can change any of the partitions you choose, provided that you have at least one root (/) partition that can hold the entire installation and one swap partition. A small /boot partition (about 100MB) is also recommended. Note that LVM partitions are assigned by default to your root partition and swap space. This will enable you to easily resize those partitions in the future.

## Caution

**Partitioning your disk improperly can cause you to lose your data. Refer to the "Partitioning Hard Drives" section in Chapter 8 for further information on disk partitioning.** ■

The swap partition is often set to twice the size of the amount of RAM on your computer (for example, for 512MB RAM you could use 1024MB of swap). Linux uses swap space when active processes have filled up your system's RAM. At that point, an inactive process is moved to swap space. You get a performance hit when the inactive process is moved to swap and another hit when that process restarts (moves back to RAM). For example, you might notice a delay on a busy system when you reopen a window that has been minimized for a long time.

The reason you need to have enough swap space is that when RAM and swap fill up, no other processes can start until something closes. Bottom line: Add RAM to get better performance; add swap space if processes are failing to start. The Fedora Project suggests a minimum of 32MB and maximum of 4GB of swap space.

Click the Next button (review partitions that are being reformatted and select Format if the changes are acceptable) to continue.

13. **Configure boot loader.** All bootable partitions and default boot loader options that are detected are displayed. By default, the install process will use the GRUB boot loader, install the boot loader in the master boot record of the computer, and choose Fedora as your default operating system to boot.

## Note

**If you keep the GRUB boot loader, you have the option of adding a GRUB password. The password protects your system from having potentially dangerous kernel options sent to the kernel by someone without that password. This password can and should be different from the root password you are asked to enter later.** ■

The names shown for each bootable partition will appear on the boot loader screen when the system starts. Change a bootable partition name by clicking it and selecting Edit.

## Caution

Before proceeding to the next step, you need to know that for the live CD install, the live CD image is simply copied to your hard disk when you continue. You won't get a chance to back out after this, so make sure you mean it. ■

Here is where the procedures for the Fedora live CD install (such as the one that comes on the *Linux Bible* DVD) and the Fedora install DVD diverge. Follow Step 14 for the live CD install (which is on the Linux Bible DVD); skip to Step 15 for an official Fedora Installation DVD install.

14. **Fedora Live CD install.** For the live CD install, the software from the live CD is simply copied to your hard disk. When the install is complete, click the Close button. Then select System ➪ Shut Down and choose Restart. Remove the live CD/DVD to reboot your installed system.

15. **Fedora Installation DVD install.** For a new install, the installer automatically selects a set of basic software to install. In addition to that set, you can choose one or more of the following groups of software, referred to as tasks. For each of these installation tasks, you have the opportunity to install a set of preset packages or customize that set.

    ● **Office and Productivity**—Installs software appropriate for a home or office personal computer or laptop computer. This includes the GNOME desktop (no KDE) and various desktop-related tools (word processors, Internet tools, and so on). Server tools, software development tools, and many system administration tools are not installed.

    ● **Software Development**—Similar to an Office and Productivity installation but adds tools for system administration and software development. (Server software is not installed.)

    ● **Web Server**—Installs the software packages that you would typically need for a Linux Web server (in particular, Apache Web server and print server). It does not include many other server types by default (FTP, DHCP, mail, DNS, FTP, SQL, or news servers). The default server install also includes a GUI (GNOME only).

    A recent feature in Fedora lets you select software repositories outside of Fedora, from which you can select packages to install during the initial Fedora installation. Use the check box to be able to install from other software repositories. Select Add additional software repositories to add other repositories (such as RPMfusion.org or ATRpms repositories). Then, select the Customize Now button if you want to further specifically select which packages in the selected tasks are installed:

16. **Customize Now**—Select the Customize Now button after selecting the task (or tasks) you want to install. This lets you see which categories from each task and which packages within those categories are selected to be installed. It also lets you add or remove package selections. Note that packages from multiple repositories can appear in the same category (for example, you would see games from both Fedora and RPM Fusion packages appearing in the Games category if the RPM Fusion repository were enabled).

Unlike previous versions, this version of Fedora does not offer an Everything install type or a Minimal install type. Select install classes you want, and then choose Customize Now to see the packages to be installed (based on install categories and package groups). Unselecting the major categories can get you a pretty good minimal install, if you like to build from a barebones install. In the following step, the procedure will continue as if you had chosen Customize Now.

17. **Customize categories**—If you selected Customize Now, you are presented with categories of software on the left side of the screen and package groups on the right side.

    Select a category to see which groups it contains. Select a group and click the Optional packages to see which optional packages are available in that group and which are selected to be installed. Categories include

    - **Desktop Environments**—The GNOME desktop environment is selected by default. KDE and Xfce are the other available desktop environments, depending on which install medium you are using. (Desktop environments are described in Chapter 3.)

    - **Applications**—This category includes packages of office applications, games, sound and video players, Internet tools, and other applications. (Many of these applications are described in Chapters 4 through 7.)

    - **Development**—General and specialized software development tools are included in packages in this category.

    - **Servers**—Packages in this category are for Web, mail, FTP, database, and a variety of other network server types.

    - **Base System**—Contains basic system administration tools, many common utilities, and support for basic system features (such as X Window System, Java, and Legacy software support).

    - **Languages**—Packages containing support for multiple languages are contained in this category.

    After you have chosen the packages you want to install, select Next to continue. The installer will take some time to check for dependencies among the packages you selected.

    A screen tells you that you are about to begin writing to hard disk. You can still back out, and your hard disk will not have changed. Click Next to proceed. (To quit without changes, eject the DVD or CD and restart the computer.) Now the file systems are created and the packages are installed. This typically takes from 20 to 60 minutes to complete, although it can take much longer on older computers.

18. **Finish installing.** When you see the Congratulations screen, you are done. Eject the DVD or CD and click Reboot.

19. **Your computer restarts.** If you installed GRUB, you will see a graphical boot screen that displays the bootable partitions. Press the up or down arrow key to choose the

partition you want to boot, and press Enter. If Fedora is the default partition, you can simply wait a few moments and it boots automatically.

The first time your system boots after installation, the Fedora Setup Agent (Firstboot) runs to do some initial configuration of your system. The next section explains how Fedora Setup Agent works.

## Running the Fedora Firstboot

The first time you boot Fedora after it is installed, the Fedora Firstboot runs to configure some initial settings for your computer.

The Welcome screen displays. From it, step through screens to read (and agree to) the license, create a regular user, set time and date, and view your hardware profile. Click the Finish button and you are ready to log in to Fedora.

## Note

The Fedora Firstboot runs automatically only if you have configured Fedora to boot to a graphical login prompt. To start it from a text login, log in as root and switch to init state 5 temporarily (type init 5). Log in to the graphical prompt. From a Terminal window, as root user, type

```
# rm /etc/sysconfig/firstboot
# /usr/sbin/firstboot ■
```

## Adding cool stuff to your Fedora desktop

If you are used to Windows or a Mac desktop, you will notice that some features are missing from the Fedora desktop that you expect to have. Mostly because of patent and licensing issues, Fedora cannot freely distribute software for playing MP3s, commercial DVD movies, and other multimedia content (see Chapter 4 for discussions of multimedia patent issues).

Some of this software can be used legally, but cannot be redistributed. So you just need to know where to look. To find out about how to get and install software for NVIDIA video drivers, Adobe Flash content, MP3 music, DVD movies, and other stuff, refer to the Personal Fedora 11 Installation Guide at www.mjmwired.net/resources/mjm-fedora-f11.html.

# Summary

Since leaving its well-known Red Hat Linux name behind, Red Hat, Inc. focused its development efforts into the free Fedora Project and commercial Red Hat Enterprise Linux. In the past few releases, Fedora has emerged as an exceptional distribution in its own right, with new features such as PackageKit, NetworkManager, KVM, and Xen virtualization, and powerful extensions to its anaconda installer.

Fedora and Red Hat Enterprise Linux distributions distinguish themselves from other Linux distributions with their simplified installer (anaconda), graphical configuration tools, RPM Package Management tools, and a tenacious commitment to supporting open source software. Fedora is freely available, whereas Red Hat Enterprise Linux is available on a paid subscription basis.

A live/install CD version of Fedora is included on the DVD that comes with this book. You can install the Fedora distribution by following the detailed instructions included in this chapter.

# Running Debian GNU/Linux

**D**ebian GNU/Linux is a creation of the Debian Project. Founded in 1993 by Ian Murdock, the Debian Project is an association of individuals who have made a common cause to create a free, coherent, and complete operating system.

## Note

Ian Murdock later became associated with Sun (now owned by Oracle), and continues to be an outspoken visionary on Debian, Linux, and operating systems in general. He regularly contributes to a blog that is worth reading and can be found at http://ianmurdock.com/. The name Debian is a combination of Ian's wife's name (Deb) and his own. ■

The principles of the Debian Project are defined in the Debian Social Contract. This contract is a commitment to the free software community that basically states the following:

- All software within the Debian system will remain free, as defined in the Debian Free Software Guidelines (DFSG).

- The Debian Project will contribute to the free software community by licensing any software developed for the Debian system in accordance with the DFSG, developing the best system it can, and by sharing improvements and fixes with the original developers of any programs incorporated into Debian GNU/Linux.

- Problems will not be hidden from users, and any bug reports filed against Debian components will be made promptly available to the public through the Debian Bug Tracking System (BTS).

- The Debian Project will focus on the needs of its users and on the principles of free software.

- Provisions will be made for the support of programs that do not meet the standards in the DFSG because some users may depend on these programs to make effective use of the system. The bug tracking and support systems will always include mechanisms for handling these programs when they are provided with the Debian system.

Debian's commitment to free software distribution and openness has earned it a huge following in the technical community. More than any other Linux system, Debian has been used as the basis for other Linux distributions, including KNOPPIX, Ubuntu, Damn Small Linux, and many others.

The success of Debian has come despite the lack of large corporate sponsors, formal enterprise initiatives, or official certification and training programs. Debian enthusiasts will tell you that it is the most stable and reliable Linux system. It is thoroughly tested, and new versions aren't released until the Debian leadership believes that the software is extraordinarily stable.

## On the CD

**A single Debian GNU/Linux network install CD image is contained on the CD that comes with this book. You can install Debian directly from that CD as described in this chapter. This installation provides a suitable base system for setting up a Web server (LAMP server), a mail server, or a desktop system. An Internet connection is needed to get those additional components.** ∎

# Inside Debian GNU/Linux

As with most modern operating systems, software programs in Debian GNU/Linux are bundled into packages for easy distribution and management. The package format and management tools used in Debian GNU/Linux were created by the Debian Project and are arguably the most sophisticated of their type. Additionally, careful adherence to packaging policies and quality-control measures ensure compatibility and help make upgrades go smoothly. Debian is one of the operating system distributions in which all components (except the kernel) can be upgraded without rebooting the system.

## Debian packages

Debian packages come in two forms: binary and source. Binary packages contain files that can be extracted directly onto the system by the package management tools. Source packages contain source code and build instructions that the Debian build tools use to create binary packages.

In addition to programs and their associated data files, Debian packages contain control data that enable the package management tools to support advanced features:

- A main control file contains version and package interrelationship data. The version can be compared to an installed version of the same package to determine whether an upgrade is needed. The interrelationship data tell the package management tools which packages must or cannot be installed at the same time as the package.

## Note

**Package interrelationship fields include Depends, Conflicts, Replaces, Provides, Recommends, Suggests, and Enhances. For a complete list of control file fields, see** `www.debian.org/doc/debian-policy/ch-controlfields.html.` ■

- Optional `preinst`, `postinst`, `prerm`, and `postrm` files can instruct the package management tools to perform functions before or after package installation or removal. For example, most packages containing daemons (such as Apache HTTPD) include a `postinst` script that starts the daemon automatically after installation.
- A `conffiles` file can designate specific files in the package as configuration files, which are not automatically overwritten during upgrades. By default, all files under the `/etc/` directory are configuration files.

Two special package types, meta and virtual, also exist. Meta packages are standard binary packages that do not contain any files, but depend on a number of other packages. Installation of a meta package results in the automatic installation of all packages that they depend on. These can be used as a convenient method for installing a set of related packages.

Virtual packages do not actually exist as files but can be referenced in the package interrelationship fields. They are most commonly used in cases where more than one package fulfills a specific requirement. Packages with this requirement can reference the virtual package in their `Depends` field, and packages that satisfy this dependency reference it in their `Provides` field.

Because most programs providing a virtual package are mutually exclusive, they also include the virtual package in their `Conflicts` field to prevent the installation of conflicting packages. An example of this is the mail-transport-agent virtual package, which is required by most system programs in order to send mail.

## Note

**An easy way to browse the list of available packages is through the Debian Web site at** `www.debian.org/distrib/packages.` **The current release comes with more than 29,400 packages.** ■

# Debian package management tools

Perhaps the most interesting and well-known part of the Debian package management system is APT, the Advanced Package Tool. APT, through the `apt-get` utility, maintains a database of packages available in the repositories that it is configured to check and can handle automatically downloading new or upgraded packages. A program named `aptitude` has been added to simplify package management. `aptitude` acts as an interface for the command-line operations of `apt-get`.

When installing or upgrading packages, APT downloads the necessary files to a local cache directory and then instructs the `dpkg` tool to take the appropriate actions. Among other things, this allows the user to select programs for addition or removal without having to manually instruct the system to handle any package dependencies.

Most basic package management functions are performed by dpkg, although not always at the direct request of the user. This tool handles medium-level package installation and removal and also manages the package status database. That database contains information about every package known to dpkg, including the package meta information and two other important fields: the package state and selection state.

## Note

**You can find more information about how to determine the state of a package in the "Querying the package database" section of this chapter. ■**

As its name suggests, the package state indicates the present state of the package, which is one of the following:

- **not-installed**—The package is known but is not installed on the system.
- **half-installed**—An attempt was made to install the package, but an error prevented it from finishing.
- **unpacked**—The files have been extracted from the package, but any post-extract configuration steps have not yet been performed.
- **half-configured**—The post-extract configuration was started, but an error prevented it from finishing.
- **installed**—The package is fully installed and configured.
- **config-files**—The package was removed, but the configuration files still exist on the system.

## Note

**If you have manually removed a configuration file and want to get it back by reinstalling the package, you can do so by passing the --force-confmiss option to dpkg. Doing so will not overwrite the other configuration files for that package. If you want to start over with all the original configuration files, you can also pass the --force-confnew option. ■**

The package selection state indicates what state you want the package to be in. Changes to package status through dpkg happen immediately when using the --install, --remove, and --purge options on a package, but other uses and tools will instead set this flag and then process any pending changes in a batch. The package selection state is one of the following:

- **install**—The package should be installed.
- **deinstall**—The package files should be removed, with the exception of configuration files.
- **purge**—All package files and configuration files should be removed.
- **hold**—dpkg should not do anything with the package unless explicitly told to do so with the --force-hold argument.

Some packages are designed to enable you to select configuration options as they are being installed. This configuration is managed through the debconf utility. The debconf utility supports a number of different interfaces, including a command prompt and a menu-based interface. A database of configuration options is also maintained by debconf, allowing it to automatically answer repeated questions, such as those you might encounter while upgrading or reinstalling a package.

Examples of how to use these utilities are included in the section "Managing Your Debian System" later in this chapter.

## Debian releases

In Debian terms, a distribution is a collection of specific package versions. From time to time, a distribution is declared ready for release and becomes a release. In practice, these two terms are often used interchangeably when referring to Debian distributions that have reached the "stable" milestone.

Debian distributions are given code names (recent ones include potato, woody, sarge, etch, lenny, and squeeze, named for characters in the movie *Toy Story*) to identify their archive directory on the Debian servers. While a particular distribution release is active, it will be referenced by one of three release tags, each one pointing to one of the three active releases. The tags—unstable, testing, and stable—identify the state of the release within the release cycle. At the time of this writing, the current stable release is lenny, and the testing release is squeeze. The unstable release is special in that it is always named sid (after the kid who broke all the toys).

New packages, and new versions of packages, are uploaded to the Debian archive and are imported into the unstable distribution. This distribution always contains the newest version of every package, which means that changes have not yet been thoroughly tested to verify that installing them will not cause unexpected behavior.

After a package has been assigned to the unstable area for a few days and testing shows that it has not had any significant bugs filed against it, it is imported into the testing distribution. The testing distribution remains open to changes (just as the unstable area was) until it is frozen in preparation for release as the next stable distribution. When testing is in the frozen state, only changes necessary to fix significant bugs are imported.

After all release-critical bugs have been fixed in the frozen testing distribution, the release manager declares the release ready and it replaces the stable distribution. When the previous stable version becomes obsolete (but remains on the Debian archive for a reasonable period of time), a new testing distribution is created from the changes that went into packages in the unstable area while testing was frozen, and the process begins again.

# Getting Help with Debian

The Debian project has a mature set of resources to support those who use, administer, and develop software for Debian systems. A place to begin learning more about Debian is the Debian

Support page (www.debian.org/support). Here are some of the resources you can connect to from that page:

- **Documentation** (www.debian.org/doc/)—From this page, you can find links to both Debian-specific and general Linux documentation. For specific Debian information, refer to the Release Notes, Installation Guide, Debian GNU/Linux FAQ, and various user, administrator, and programming manuals. General Linux information includes manuals, HOWTOs, and FAQs.

- **Mailing lists** (www.debian.org/MailingLists)—Ways of accessing (and behaving on) a Debian mailing list are described on this page. A complete listing of the more than 200 Debian mailing lists is available from http://lists.debian.org/completein-dex.html.

- **Bug tracking** (www.debian.org/Bugs)—If you are interested in following the bug tracking system for Debian, links from the support page can take you to the Bug Tracking System site. If you are having problems with any Debian software, you can search this site for bug reports and file a bug report, if your bug was not yet reported.

- **Help** (www.debianhelp.org)—This site offers connections to a range of information about Debian. In particular, you can find Debian forums from this site, containing literally thousands of posts. The Debian User Forums site (http://forums.debian.net) is another place you can go to post questions about Debian.

If you are interested in becoming a Debian developer, start at the Debian Developers' Corner (www.debian.org/devel). That site acts as a guide to ways in which you can enter the Debian development community. There are Debian developers all over the world. The largest concentrations of Debian developers are in Europe and the United States, as you can see from the Debian Developer Location map (www.debian.org/devel/developers.loc).

# Installing Debian GNU/Linux

The Debian CD image included with this book contains the most commonly used packages in the Debian system. Additional packages can be downloaded and installed from the Internet after the base system has been installed and an Internet connection established. For information about how to obtain additional Debian packages on CD or DVD, see www.debian.org/distrib/.

## Hardware requirements and installation planning

To run Debian, you need at least a 486 processor and 32MB of RAM. For a server or a graphical workstation (running the X Window System), you should plan on having at least 128MB of memory and a Pentium-class processor.

A minimal set of packages requires 250MB of disk space, and a normal installation of desktop applications can require at least 2–4 gigabytes. Additional space will be needed to store any data files that you want to keep on the system.

Most ISA and PCI network cards are supported under Linux, although ISA models are not usually detected automatically by the installer. Inexpensive cards based on RealTek 8139 chipsets can be found at most PC dealers and will work fine for low-demand applications. Intel PRO/100 and PRO/1000 adapters are supported in Linux and will work well in high-demand applications, as will cards based on the "tulip" chipsets and most 3com network cards.

Many newer systems include software-based modems that are not supported by the manufacturer under Linux. If you require a dial-up connection for Internet access, see Chapter 11 and check out http://tldp.org/HOWTO/Modem-HOWTO-2.html before you start the installation process.

Many other devices, such as sound and video capture cards, can also be used under Linux. For more information about hardware compatibility, see the Hardware Compatibility HOWTO at http://tldp.org/HOWTO/Hardware-HOWTO/.

### Workstations

In most cases, workstation users will want to run the X Window System (X11). The ability to run X11 depends on compatibility with the video chipset on your video card or mainboard.

### Servers

A Linux server installation generally consists of only the minimum set of packages required to provide the service for which it was designed. In particular, this means that servers do not usually have a graphical interface installed.

Server hardware is generally more expensive than workstation hardware, although you can still run smaller servers on less-expensive desktop hardware. If you are planning to store important data on your server, look into a RAID array for storage. A number of inexpensive ATA RAID controllers work well under Linux.

## Note

**More information about ATA RAID compatibility is available at the following sites:** http://linuxmafia .com/faq/Hardware/sata.html **and** http://ibiblio.org/pub/Linux/docs/HOWTO/other-for-mats/html_single/Hardware-HOWTO.html#IDERAID. ∎

Higher-end servers will, of course, require more expensive hardware. In applications such as mail servers where you will have a lot of disk activity, plan on splitting the disk-intensive tasks across multiple arrays. When it comes to CPU and RAM, more of both is good, but most applications benefit more from extra RAM than they do from multiple CPUs.

# Running the installer

The latest Debian installation process is done in one stage, where it used to require two stages (with a reboot in the middle of the process). During this procedure, you create the settings needed for your computer (time zone, language, keyboard, user accounts, and so on), partition your disk as needed, install a base system to disk, and download additional software as needed.

## Caution

Before you begin installing Debian to your hard disk, be sure to back up any data that is important to you. A simple mistake during partitioning can result in losing some or all of your data. Refer to Chapter 8 for information on disk partitioning. It can help you decide how to divide up your hard disk or even resize existing disk partitions to make room for the new Debian installation. ■

Here's the Debian installation procedure from the CD image included on the CD that comes with this book:

## Note

Because the Debian CD image included with this book is the network install image, the CD itself will provide software for installing only a minimal Debian system. You will need a network connection or other Debian software CDs to install, for example, a full desktop system or the LAMP and mail servers (similar to those described for Ubuntu in Chapters 13 and 14). ■

1. **Boot CD**—Boot the CD that comes with this book and type **debian** from the boot prompt to begin the Debian installer. (If you download your own copy of the CD, type **linux** instead.)

## Note

Some systems may require special parameters in order to boot. Other options are also available, such as the option to use a Linux kernel from the 2.6 series. Press F1 at the boot: prompt for more information. ■

2. **Language, Region, Keyboard**—After the installer has finished booting, you are presented with the series of menus that make up the installation process. Use the arrow keys to navigate through the menus and select your language, region, and keyboard mapping.

3. **Network**—Configure the network connection. This step is skipped automatically if no network card is detected in your system.

   If a network card is detected in your system, the installer will attempt to automatically detect the network using the DHCP protocol. This involves the computer sending out requests on the network for configuration details from a DHCP server. Most networks and broadband routers support this service.

   If the DHCP configuration fails, you are presented with four options:

   - **retry**—Select this option if you suspect that a temporary problem prevented your computer from communicating with the DHCP server.

   - **retry with hostname**—Select this option if your network provider requires you to enter a DHCP hostname. This used to be common on cable modem networks, but is rarely seen anymore.

- **manual configuration**—Select this option if you have static IP address information that must be entered for your Internet connection.

- **do not configure at this time**—Select this option if you do not have an Internet connection, are using a dial-up connection, or have a broadband connection that requires the use of PPPoE. In the latter two cases, you'll want to establish the connection at the point that it is noted during stage 2 of the installation.

## Cross-Reference

See Chapter 11 for information about IP addresses, network masks, and other material related to setting up a network card connection. ■

4. **Time zone**—Select your time zone and select Continue.

5. **Hostname**—Provide a hostname (a single-word name that you give to your system, such as debian, littlebeigebox, or yoda) and a domain name. If you do not have your own domain name, you can make one up, such as myhouse.local.

6. **Partitions**—Next, you will be asked to configure your disk partitions for Debian. If you haven't already done so, read Chapter 8 for more information about partitioning.

   If you already have partitions on your drive and have room for more, you are given the option to use this space for your Debian system. Another option is to erase the entire disk and use the whole thing for Debian. Either of these two options takes you through the guided partitioning, which is covered in this section.

   A third option, manually editing the partition, enables you to be more exacting about your partition setup, but you should not try this without help or at least without reading Chapter 8.

   The guided partitioning section presents three partitioning schemes. Each of the options includes a suitable amount of swap space but has different benefits based on your situation. You must select one from the list before you proceed. See the sidebar "Selecting a Partition Scheme" for more information.

## Note

When installing to small disk drives (those under a few gigabytes in size), you should use ext2 file systems instead of ext3. The journaling feature in ext3 requires that a portion of the disk be set aside for the journal, but the feature is of limited usefulness on small file systems. You can change file system types by going into the partition properties. To do this, highlight the partition using the arrow keys and press Enter. ■

## Selecting a Partition Scheme

The guided partitioning feature allows you to select one of three templates to use to create your partitions. Use these guidelines to select the template that is correct for you.

- **All files in one partition**—Makes a single Linux partition for files. This is the easiest option to manage because you don't have to worry about balancing the sizes of your partitions. This can also be dangerous because users have the capability to fill up the entire disk, which can cause problems for the operating system. Do not use this option unless you are prepared to monitor disk space carefully.

- **Separate /home partition**—This option is recommended for a desktop system. It gives the operating system its own space and gives home directories their own space. This option is a good trade-off between the convenience of a single partition and the increased safety of the multiuser scheme. However, the /tmp/ directory is still part of the operating system partition, meaning that it is still fairly easy for people who habitually use that directory to fill up the operating system partition.

- **Separate /home, /usr, /var, and /tmp partitions**—Creates separate partitions for the root file system, /usr, /var, /tmp, and /home. You can choose this option when you are using this system as a server. It may also be a good choice for systems that will be used by more than just you, your relatives, and your close friends. The trade-off is that you may run out of room on a given partition even though the others have plenty of space, which means that you will need to plan carefully.

In some situations, you may need to adjust the partition sizes selected by the multiuser partitioning scheme to put more room where you are likely to need it:

- If you are planning to compile a lot of large software packages, you'll need to have plenty of space in the /usr/ partition.

- Active servers (especially Web and mail servers) may need extra room in /var/ for log files. Mail servers also use this space for the mail queue, and the default mail system also stores incoming mail here (you may also want to consider making /var/mail/ a separate partition in these cases).

- Web browsers such as Mozilla use /tmp/ for storing files while they are downloaded. This file system must be big enough to hold any large files that you want to download through there, plus any other files that may be there at the same time.

Note that with the server-style partitioning scheme, the /home/ partition generally ends up receiving most of the space on larger disks. This usually makes it a good place to "borrow" space from when you want to make other partitions larger. However, because partman (the partitioning tool used by the Debian installer) has already mapped out the partitions, you actually need to delete /home/ and then re-add it after you increase the size of the other partition. If other partitions are between /home/ and the one that you are increasing in size, you also need to delete them, and then add them back in an appropriate order.

## Caution

**The next step modifies the contents of your hard disk. Check your partition settings carefully. You receive an additional confirmation before proceeding.** ■

7. **Write Changes**—With your partition configuration chosen, select Finish Partitioning and Write Changes to Disk. This is your last chance to cancel changes that could cause damage to any other operating systems you may have on the disk, so check the screen carefully before proceeding!

   The installer writes the partitions to disk and creates the necessary file systems. After they have been prepared and mounted, the Debian base system is extracted from the CD and installed to the target partitions.

8. **Root password**—The base system includes an empty password for the root (superuser) account, which means that you want to set one here. Select a password that you can remember but that others will not be able to guess easily.

9. **User account**—Add a non-administrative account that you can use for your day-to-day tasks on the server. Enter a username (this should not contain any spaces or punctuation other than dashes, must not start with a number, and is generally all in lowercase), and a password for this account. If you have more users to add, you can do so later, as described in Chapter 10.

10. **Install from mirror**—You are asked to select your country so that Debian can locate a network mirror from which to get software over the Internet (using only the install CD that comes with this book, you will only get a minimal system).

11. **Choose mirror**—Select a mirror site that is close to your region and press Enter.

12. **Proxy**—If you need to use an HTTP proxy to reach the Internet, type the name or IP address of that system. Otherwise, just leave the field blank and press Enter.

13. **Survey**—You are asked to participate in a survey of the most popular packages in Debian. Select Yes if you don't mind submitting anonymous information about the packages you install and use, with information updated about every week. (You can see the results of this survey at `http://popcon.debian.org`.)

14. **Software selection**—Select the software categories you want to install. To start with a basic desktop system, you can use the Desktop Environment and Standard System categories that are selected by default. Highlight a category and press the spacebar to select or unselect a category. Press Enter to begin downloading and installing software.

15. **Package settings**—If any of the packages you just installed require extra settings, you are asked to enter them now. For example, if you installed file sharing, you are asked to enter the workgroup/domain name for your Samba Server.

16. **Install boot loader**—The final step is to install GRUB, the boot loader. The default setting is to install to the master boot record (MBR), which is generally the best option. Accept the defaults and continue. The installer ejects the CD and prompts you to remove the CD. Remove the CD and press Enter to continue. Your computer should restart from the Debian system installed on your hard disk.

You now have a functional Debian GNU/Linux system. If you left the default selection to install a desktop interface you will have a good, basic GNOME desktop to start with. The system is also ready to be used for the LAMP and mail server examples in this book (examples for how to install those servers in Ubuntu, which is very similar to Debian, are available in Chapters 13 and 14, respectively). Take some time, as needed, to browse through Chapter 9 and familiarize yourself with the command line before continuing with the next section.

# Managing Your Debian System

Some of the basic tasks that you may encounter while running Debian GNU/Linux include package installation, configuration, and removal, as well as handling some special situations that you may come across.

All these steps require that you be logged in as the superuser (root). If you have just finished installing the system, you can log in as root from the login prompt.

## Configuring network connections

Debian includes a set of tools for managing most types of network interfaces, including Ethernet, PPP, wireless, and even ATM. You may find that you need to add or change network settings after the system has been installed.

### IP networks: Ethernet and wireless

On Debian systems, standard network connections are configured in the `/etc/network/interfaces` file. If you have a network card configured to obtain an IP address automatically, this file will look like this:

```
# This file describes the network interfaces available on
# your system and how to activate them. For more information,
# see interfaces(5).

# The loopback network interface
auto lo
iface lo inet loopback

# The primary network interface
auto eth0
iface eth0 inet dhcp
```

## Caution
Do not modify the `loopback` entry unless you are absolutely certain that you know what you are doing. ∎

In some cases, such as when the system will be acting as a server, you want to configure your network interface with a fixed IP address. To do so, edit `/etc/network/interfaces` and replace the `iface eth0 inet dhcp` line. Use the following block as a template, replacing the parameters with the correct settings for your network:

```
iface eth0 inet static
       address 192.168.1.220
       netmask 255.255.255.0
       gateway 192.168.1.1
```

## Note

**You can obtain IP network settings from your ISP or network administrator. ■**

Wireless interfaces can also be configured using the interfaces file but require that the wireless-tools package be installed. Use `dpkg` or `apt-get` to install the wireless-tools package. Then add the necessary parameters to the entry for your wireless network interface. This example shows the settings for a wireless network with an access point (managed mode) set to the ESSID Home, and operating on channel 11:

```
iface eth0 inet dhcp
       wireless_essid Home
       wireless_mode Managed
       wireless_channel 11
```

## Note

**If your wireless network is using encryption, you need to specify a `wireless_key` parameter. You can find a complete list of wireless options in the `iwconfig` man page and `/usr/share/doc/wireless-tools/README.Debian`. ■**

### Dial-up PPP connections

Dial-up connections can be managed using the pppconfig utility. After installing the pppconfig package, run `pppconfig`. You are provided with a menu from which you can create, modify, and delete dial-up connections. If you have not created a connection yet, you want to select that option from the menu. Otherwise, you can edit your existing connections instead.

The pppconfig utility asks a number of questions during the connection creation process. Start by selecting "Create a connection," and then enter the following information as prompted:

1. **Provider name**—Enter any name you like to identify this connection. For the dial-up entry to your primary ISP, you can simply leave the name `provider` as the Provider name.

2. **DNS server configuration method**—Here you can configure the connection to static DNS servers if needed. This is probably not necessary unless your service provider included the DNS server information in the information that it provided about the connection. If you aren't certain, select Dynamic DNS and change it later if needed.

3. **Authentication method**—This is the method that your computer will use to identify itself to the dial-up server. PAP is the most commonly used protocol, and some systems also support CHAP. The CHAP option should be used if the dial-up servers use text prompts to ask for the username and password. If in doubt, select PAP.

4. **User name and password**—Enter the username and password that will be recognized by the dial-up server.

5. **Speed**—This is the speed that your computer and your modem will communicate with one another. In most cases, this should be set to 115200.

6. **Dialing method**—If your telephone system requires pulse dialing, you can configure that here.

7. **Phone number**—Enter the number that you need to dial in order to reach the dial-up server, including any area codes and other codes that may be needed. For example, if you have to dial 9 in order to reach an outside line, use 9,<number to dial>. The comma tells your modem to pause before continuing the dialing process. You may also enter the appropriate numbers for disabling features such as call waiting through your telephone service.

8. **Modem configuration method**—Here, you can have pppconfig attempt to automatically find the port that your modem is on. If a modem is not found, you are then given the chance to enter the path to the modem device. You can find more information about what to enter here in the "Identifying and Configuring Your Modem" sidebar later in this chapter.

Save your settings by selecting Finished from the menu, and then exit the pppconfig utility.

# Identifying and Configuring Your Modem

If your modem is not automatically on COM1, 2, 3, or 4, you may need to perform some additional configuration steps before it can be used for PPP connections. Plug-and-play and PCI modems are often found on higher ports such as ttyS4 ("COM5"). This information is often found in the output from the dmesg utility. If you reached this point from stage 2 of the install, you can get to a prompt by pressing Alt+F2 and logging in as root.

```
# dmesg | grep tty
ttyS00 at 0x03f8 (irq = 4) is a 16550A
ttyS04 at port 0xa800 (irq = 5) is a 16550A
```

In this case, ttyS00 is the on-board serial port (most PC motherboards have at least one of these) and ttyS04 is probably the modem. If you have several serial ports showing up, you can create devices for all of them (as shown following) and try them until you find your modem.

The system includes only ttyS0 through ttyS3 by default, so this device will need to be created using the MAKEDEV command. When running MAKEDEV, you need to leave out any leading zeros in the device number. In this example, ttyS04 becomes ttyS4:

```
# (cd /dev && sh MAKEDEV ttyS4)
```

If you reached this point while performing stage 2 of the install, you can get back to the install menu by pressing Alt+F1.

See Chapter 11 for more information on using modems to get on the Internet.

Dial a connection by using the pon command, replacing peer with the name you assigned to your connection, or by leaving it out if your connection is named provider:

```
# pon peer
```

You can disconnect using the poff command and can view logs (for diagnosing problems or determining status) using the plog command. The user that was created during the base system configuration will automatically have access to run these commands. You will need to add any other users who need to run them to the dialout group through the use of the gpasswd utility:

```
# gpasswd -a <username> dialout
```

### PPPoE connections

Some DSL and cable modem providers require that you use PPPoE (PPP over Ethernet) to connect to their systems. PPPoE connections are managed using the pppoeconf program. (You may need to install pppoeconf since it is not installed by default.) As long as your computer is connected to a broadband connection, it should be able to detect most of the settings automatically.

## Package management using APT

For most users, APT will be the primary tool for installing, removing, and upgrading packages. This section shows how to use the apt-get and apt-cache utilities. From the console, you can also use the aptitude utility, which acts as an interface to apt-get.

When you run aptitude with no options, you can manage packages in interactive mode. From the aptitude screen, you can get security updates or view new packages. You can work with installed packages or those that are not yet installed (or virtual packages that only exist to provide functions needed by other packages). Installing tasks, however, is one of the most useful features.

The Add/Remove Applications window is another popular application to install software from a GNOME desktop in Debian. Select this application from the System Administration menu. Figure 19-1 shows an example of the Add/Remove Applications window.

Select the Search box to type a term related to the package you want to install. Alternatively, you can select a category and scroll through available packages in that category. Select the check boxes of the applications and click Apply Changes. The packages, and any dependent packages needed by those packages, are downloaded and installed on your system.

---

**FIGURE 19-1**

Use Add/Remove Applications interactively to view and install packages.

## Managing the list of package repositories

The configuration file /etc/apt/sources.list contains a list of Debian package repositories that APT will use. As with most configuration files on a Linux system, you can view this plain-text file using any text editor or pager. To view its contents, run the following:

```
# pager /etc/apt/sources.list
#deb cdrom:[Debian GNU/Linux 5.0.1 _Lenny_ Official i386 NETINST]/ lenny main

deb http://ftp.us.debian.org/debian/ lenny main
deb-src http://ftp.us.debian.org/debian/ lenny main

deb http://security.debian.org/ lenny/updates main contrib
deb-src http://security.debian.org/ lenny/updates main contrib
```

## Note

**Depending on which pager is configured as your default, you may need to press the Q key in order to return to a prompt. ■**

Your output will differ from this example's, of course, but the kind of information remains the same. The first part of each line indicates whether the repository is to be used for binary packages (indicated by the deb prefix) or source packages (deb-src). The rest of the line defines the method (in this case, cdrom or http), the location, the distribution (etch), and the sections (main). The contrib section is also added. If you want to use software from the non-free section, you can use a text editor to add them after main and contrib.

## Note

Run man sources.list **on any Debian system for more information.** ∎

If you aren't going to have your Debian CD available all the time, you may want to remove the cdrom: entry from the file (or comment out the line, as shown earlier). Use a text editor (as root user) to edit the file:

```
# editor /etc/apt/sources.list
```

Make any changes you need to the file, exit the editor, and then update the package database as described in the following section.

## Note

**Astute readers may notice that the** pager **and** editor **commands used in this section are not common UNIX commands. Both are pointers to programs and are managed using Debian's alternatives system, which is discussed later in this chapter.** ∎

### Updating the APT package database

Because the lists of packages available in the Debian package repositories may change from time to time, you need to instruct APT to download these lists and update its database occasionally. To perform this process, run the following command:

```
# apt-get update
```

You generally want to run this command before installing new packages so that you do not download an older version. Run it before checking for upgrades as well.

### Finding and installing packages

When looking for new packages to install, you may not always know what package you want. The package database maintained by APT includes package descriptions and other fields that can be searched using the apt-cache utility:

```
# apt-cache search tetris
bsdgames--a collection of classic textual unix games
pytris--two-player networked console tetris clone
stax--collection of puzzle games similar to Tetris Attack.
...
```

## Tip

**Specifying multiple keywords in a search prevents** apt-cache **from listing packages that do not contain all the keywords you specify. This enables you to do very specific searches, such as** word processor. ∎

You can also use this utility to find out more information about a specific package in the repositories:

```
# apt-cache show pytris
Package: pytris
Priority: optional
Section: games
Installed-Size: 96
Maintainer: Radovan Garabik <garabik@kassiopeia.juls.savba.sh>
Architecture: i386
Version: 0.98
Depends: python (>=2.1), libc6 (>= 2.3.5-1)
Filename: pool/main/p/pytris/pytris_0.98_i386.deb
Size: 16258
MD5sum: d08e8ed6cce5e7b78e2c799eb83d463b
SHA1: 8cca87b2689ab69b5d3a07fda7ef4a47f06d2042
SHA256:
   9353512ee65466fc72105d535453a55cdf3ba8f1b07aa8fd09818e5c65ffe095
Description: two-player networked console tetris clone
 two-player networked console based tetris clone, written
 in python, similar to xtet42.
Tag: game::tetris, implemented-in::python, interface::x11,
   role::program, use::gameplaying, x11::application
```

## Note

To view information about a specific package that is already installed on your system, use dpkg, as discussed later in this chapter. ∎

After you know the name of the package you want to install, use the install method to download it and any packages on which it depends. For example, the ssh package is very useful for remotely accessing systems and is probably one of the first programs that you will want to install:

```
# apt-get install ssh
```

On this command, APT retrieves and installs the ssh package. If additional packages are required, a list of those packages is displayed by APT. If you choose to continue, APT will download and install those packages along with the package you requested.

## Note

When installing packages that support automatic configuration through debconf, you're prompted to answer the appropriate configuration questions. Although the Debian package developers have gone to great lengths to ensure that the default options for these questions will work in most situations, it's best to read the questions thoroughly to be sure that the defaults work for you. ∎

### Removing packages

You can also use APT to remove packages from your system. Unlike dpkg, which removes only the package you tell it to remove, apt-get also removes any packages that depend on the package you are removing. This is best used in conjunction with the -s option to simulate what would happen if the removal were actually performed:

```
# apt-get -s remove python2.3
Reading Package Lists... Done
Building Dependency Tree... Done
The following packages will be REMOVED:
  bittornado python python2.3 python2.3-dev
0 upgraded, 0 newly installed, 4 to remove and 0 not upgraded.
Remv pytris (0.96 Debian:testing)
Remv python (2.3.4-1 Debian:testing)
Remv python2.3-dev (2.3.4-5 Debian:testing)
Remv python2.3 (2.3.4-5 Debian:testing)
```

In this example, several other packages depend on the python2.3 package and also need to be removed. To proceed with removing python2.3 and all packages that depend on it, run the command again without the -s flag.

### Upgrading your system

As new versions of packages become available, you can instruct APT to download and install them, automatically replacing the older versions. This is as simple as updating your package list, followed by a simple command:

```
# apt-get upgrade
```

APT begins by downloading the necessary packages, and then moves on to installing and configuring them. If necessary, you can abort the upgrade during the download process by pressing Control+C. APT may also be able to recover if you have to abort during the installation or configuration steps, but it is still best to let the process run without interruption after it has begun installing packages.

## Note

When upgrading to a newer distribution, use dist-upgrade instead of upgrade. This changes the rules that APT uses when deciding which actions to take, making it expect major changes in dependencies and handle them appropriately. ■

# Package management using dpkg

As mentioned earlier, the dpkg utility is the core package management tool in Debian. Most other package management tools within the system, including APT, use dpkg to perform the midlevel work, and dpkg in turn uses dpkg-deb and dpkg-query to handle a number of the low-level functions. In most cases, you will want to use APT or Aptitude for package management, and use dpkg in only a few situations.

Far too many commands associated with dpkg exist to list in this chapter, but the most common ones are explained in the following sections. In most cases, there are both short and long commands to perform the same function. Use whichever is easier for you to remember.

### Installing and removing packages

You can install packages with dpkg using the -i or --install flags and the path to the .deb file containing the package. The path must be accessible as a file system path (HTTP, FTP, and other methods are not supported), and you can specify more than one package:

```
# dpkg --install /home/wayne/lsof_4.77.dfsg.1-3_i386.deb
```

Package removal through dpkg is also straightforward and is done with the -r or --remove commands. When configuration files are to be removed, you can use the -P or --purge command instead. Both commands can also be used to specify multiple packages to remove:

```
# dpkg --remove lsof
```

or . . .

```
# dpkg --purge lsof
```

### Querying the package database

You often need to obtain more information about packages that are already installed on your system. Because these operations do not modify the package database, you can do them as a non-root user.

To list all packages known to dpkg, use the -l or --list commands:

```
$ dpkg --list
```

You can restrict the list by specifying a glob pattern:

```
$ dpkg --list "*lsof*"
```

## Note

**The quotes are used to prevent the shell from replacing the wildcard with a list of matching files in the current directory. For more information about wildcards, see Chapter 9 or type** man 7 glob **to see a list of wildcards. ∎**

To view detailed information about a specific package, use the -s or --status command:

```
$ dpkg --status lsof
Package: lsof
Status: install ok installed
Priority: standard
Section: utils
...
```

To determine the origin package for a file use the -S or --search command:

```
$ dpkg --search /bin/ls
coreutils: /bin/ls
```

To view the list of files in an installed package use the `-L` or `--listfiles` command:

```
$ dpkg --listfiles lsof
/.
/usr
/usr/sbin
/usr/bin
/usr/bin/lsof
...
```

## Examining a package file

You can examine package files before installing them using either the `--info` (`-I`) or the `--contents` (`-c`) command. You can use these options on packages in a local directory, as opposed to using them to examine packages on a remote server.

The following `--info` option shows the lsof package name, version information, and sizes of different parts of the package. Beyond that (although shortened here for space considerations) you would be able to see a list of packages `lsof` depends on and descriptive information about the package.

```
$ dpkg --info lsof_4.77.dfsg.1-3_i386.deb
new debian package, version 2.0.
size 205312 bytes: control archive= 1207 bytes.
    517 bytes,     15 lines        control
   1615 bytes,     22 lines        md5sums
Package: lsof
Version: 4.77.dfsg.1-3
...
Description: List open files
 Lsof is a Unix-specific diagnostic tool.  Its name stands
 for LiSt Open Files, and it does just that.  It lists
 information about any files that are open, by processes
 currently running on the system.
```

The following `--contents` option lets you see the full contents of the package you choose as if you were listing the contents with an `ls -l` command. You can see the name and path to each file, its permission settings, and file/group ownership:

```
$ dpkg --contents lsof_4.77.dfsg.1-3_i386.deb
drwxr-xr-x root/root         0 2006-05-15 18:09 ./
drwxr-xr-x root/root         0 2006-05-15 18:09 ./usr/
drwxr-xr-x root/root         0 2006-05-15 18:09 ./usr/bin/
...
```

# Installing package sets (tasks) with tasksel

Some package sets are too large to be managed practically through meta packages, so tasks have been created as an alternative. You install and remove tasks with the `tasksel` utility. When run without any arguments, `tasksel` presents a menu from which you can select tasks to install or remove.

## Caution

Do not install any tasks if you plan to use this system in conjunction with the server examples in Chapters 13 and 14. Packages installed by the tasks might conflict with the packages installed in those chapters. ■

Additional options are available from the command line:

- To see a list of known tasks, run `tasksel --list-tasks`.
- To list the packages that are installed by a task, run `tasksel --task-packages <task name>`.

Refer to the `/usr/share/tasksel/debian-tasks.desc` file for a list of tasks that APT knows about, along with descriptions of those tasks.

## Caution

When a task is removed, all programs associated with that task, whether installed manually or as part of that task, are removed! ■

If you want to try a desktop other than the GNOME desktop installed by default, you can use `tasksel` to install a KDE or Xfce desktop. Use the `kde-desktop` task to install KDE or `xfce-desktop` to install the Xfce desktop. Note that the `kde-desktop` task takes a long time to download and install and requires several hundred megabytes of disk space to complete. To start the `kde-desktop` task, run the following:

```
# tasksel install kde-desktop
```

# Alternatives, diversions, and stat overrides

In cases where more than one installed program provides a specific function, package maintainers have the option of utilizing Debian's alternatives system. The alternatives system manages which program is executed when you run a specific command. For example, the ed, nano, and nvi packages each provide a text editor. An alternative maintained in the system guarantees that a text editor is accessible through the generic `editor` command, regardless of which combination of these packages is installed.

The system administrator can designate which program is referenced in the alternatives database through the use of the `update-alternatives` command:

```
# update-alternatives --config editor

These are alternatives that provide 'editor'.
  Selection    Alternative
------------------------------------------------
      1        /bin/ed
*+    2        /bin/nano
      3        /usr/bin/nvi
```

```
Press enter to keep the default[*],
or type selection number: 2
```

You can also use the `--all` command with `update-alternatives` to configure every entry in the alternatives database, one at a time. You can find more details by typing the following: **man update-alternatives**.

## Note

**By default, all alternatives are in automatic mode, meaning that the system automatically selects a suitable program from the available candidates. Installing a new candidate program generally results in the automatic updating of the appropriate alternatives. Manually configuring an alternative disables automatic mode, preventing the system from changing these settings without prior knowledge of the system administrator. ■**

The Debian package management tools also provide a mechanism for renaming specific files in a package and for overriding the ownership and permission settings on files. Unlike when these changes are made manually, using `mv`, `chmod`, or `chown`, changes made through the Debian tools remain in place across package upgrades and reinstallations.

For example, if you want to replace `/usr/bin/users` without modifying the coreutils package, you can divert it to `/usr/bin/users.distrib`:

```
# dpkg-divert --local --rename --add /usr/bin/users
Adding 'local diversion of /usr/bin/users to /usr/bin/users.distrib'
```

Removing the diversion returns the original filename:

```
# dpkg-divert --remove /usr/bin/users
Removing 'local diversion of /usr/bin/users to /usr/bin/users.distrib'
```

Stat overrides are useful when you want to disable access to a program, or when you want to make it set-UID. For example, to disable access to the `wall` program, type the following:

```
# dpkg-statoverride --update --add root root 0000 /usr/bin/wall
```

This sets the owner and group of `/usr/bin/wall` to root and disables all permissions on the file.

## Note

**You can find more information about file permissions in the section "Understanding file permissions" in Chapter 9. ■**

Unlike `dpkg-divert`, `dpkg-statoverride` does not keep track of the original file permissions. As a result, removing an override does not restore the old permissions. After removing the override, you need to either set the permissions manually or reinstall the package that contained the file:

```
# dpkg-statoverride --remove /usr/bin/wall
# apt-get --reinstall install bsdutils
Reading package lists... Done
```

```
Building dependency tree... Done
0 upgraded, 0 newly installed, 1 reinstalled, 0 to remove and 1 not upgraded.
Need to get 0B/68.5kB of archives.
After unpacking 0B of additional disk space will be used.
Do you want to continue? [Y/n]Y
(Reading database ... 16542 files and directories currently installed.)
Preparing to replace bsdutils 1:2.12r-19etch1 (using .../bsdutils_1%3a2.12r-
19etch1_i386.deb) ...
Unpacking replacement bsdutils ...
Setting up bsdutils (2.12r-19etch1) ...
```

## Managing package configuration with debconf

All packages that include support for configuration management through debconf are configured as they are being installed. If you want to change a configuration option later, you can do
so using the dpkg-reconfigure command. For example, you can change the configuration
options for ssh using the following command:

```
# dpkg-reconfigure ssh
```

Every configuration parameter is assigned a priority by the package maintainer. This allows
debconf to select the default values for settings below a specific priority. By default, you will be
prompted to answer questions of only medium, high, or critical priority; low-priority questions
are answered automatically. You can change this by reconfiguring the debconf package:

```
# dpkg-reconfigure debconf
```

## Note

**Advanced users maintaining multiple systems may want to create a database of configuration settings that can
be distributed to every computer (or to sets of computers) to reduce the number of repeated steps. This process is documented in the** debconf **and** debconf.conf **man pages.** ∎

# Summary

The reliability of Debian GNU/Linux, combined with the large number of high-quality packages available for it, make Debian a great choice for both workstations and servers. The carefully
executed releases and the capability to upgrade most software without rebooting serve to further
increase its suitability as a server operating system.

APT is a primary tool for installing, removing, and upgrading packages. This chapter explored
how to use the aptitude, apt-get, and apt-cache utilities for package management. The
chapter also covered the installation of package sets (tasks) using the tasksel utility and managing package configuration with the dpkg-reconfigure utility.

# Running SUSE and openSUSE Linux

F or the past few years, SUSE Linux distributions have been the most popular Linux distribution in Europe. Since the U.S. networking company Novell, Inc. purchased SUSE in November 2003, SUSE Linux Enterprise (SLE) products have been positioned to challenge Red Hat to become the dominant Linux distribution for large enterprise computing environments worldwide.

Like Fedora and Red Hat Enterprise Linux, openSUSE and SUSE Linux Enterprise are excellent for people who are looking for a career with Linux systems. Because Novell's Linux product line is geared toward enterprise computing, the skills you gain using SUSE on your home Linux system will be useful in a business environment as well.

SUSE systems have a slick graphical installer that leads you through installation and intuitive administrative tools, consolidated under a facility called YaST. SUSE and its parent company, Novell, offer a range of Linux products and support plans that scale from free versions of openSUSE with community support, to supported SUSE distributions for enterprise desktop (SUSE Linux Enterprise Desktop, or SLED), all the way up to SUSE's Linux Enterprise Server (SLES) product.

In 2005, Novell refocused its development efforts to do as Red Hat does with its Red Hat Enterprise Linux product and Fedora project: Novell formed the openSUSE project, which, like the Fedora project, produces a free community-driven Linux system with relatively frequent releases that feed into Novell's for-profit Linux systems. Unlike Fedora, however, openSUSE can also be purchased in a boxed set. With the openSUSE box set, Novell offers only 90-day installation support, whereas it offers multiple support options with SUSE Linux Enterprise. See the Comparative

## IN THIS CHAPTER

**Understanding SUSE**

**What's in SUSE**

**Getting support for SUSE**

**Installing openSUSE**

Features and Benefits page at `www.novell.com/products/opensuse/comparative.html` for more differences.

## On the DVD

**The DVD that comes with this book contains the openSUSE 11.1 KDE live/install CD. ■**

This chapter describes the features and approach to Linux that sets SUSE Linux Enterprise apart from other Linux distributions. It also explains how to install the openSUSE Linux 11 distribution that is included with this book.

The current version of openSUSE features the YaST installer, and the current versions of KDE 4 desktop environment, GNOME 2.22, Firefox 3.0, GIMP 2.4.5, Apache 2.2.8, MySQL 5.0.51a, and OpenOffice.org 2.4.0. To see all the packages available with openSUSE, visit one of the openSUSE mirror sites (`http://en.opensuse.org/Mirrors_Released_Version`).

## Note

**With the split between SUSE Linux Enterprise and openSUSE, Linux product names from Novell have changed significantly in the past few years. Most significantly, what was previously called SUSE Professional Linux is now called SUSE Linux Enterprise. ■**

# Running with the Enemy: The SUSE/Microsoft Deal

In November, 2006, Novell announced that it had struck a deal with Microsoft to further collaboration and interoperability with Microsoft products. This deal includes indemnification against patent-related lawsuits, and has raised a fair amount of concern and controversy in the open source community. In reality, Novell hasn't admitted and doesn't see any evidence of the use of Microsoft's intellectual property (IP) in Linux, but indemnification against patent liabilities has become an important part of the Linux scene ever since SCO launched its series of questionable IP lawsuits against Linux. Red Hat and Oracle already offer indemnification against this sort of thing.

Paranoia aside, this deal is important if for no other reason than that it is a statement by Microsoft that Linux is important to its customers and a viable enterprise operating system. As always, the long-term effects of this deal remain to be seen.

Many members of the open source community are concerned that Microsoft will sneak its IP into the GNU/Linux code base, setting the stage for future lawsuits against non-partners. The agreement with Novell is of primary concern, but Microsoft's agreement with Xandros (a leading commercial Linux desktop producer) is also seen as a major threat. (See Chapter 25 for descriptions of Xandros and its purchase of the other leading Linux commercial desktop producer, Linspire.)

# Understanding SUSE Linux Enterprise and openSUSE

If you are looking for a Linux system with the stability and support on which you can bet your business, SUSE offers impressive, stable Linux products backed by a company (Novell, Inc.) that has been selling enterprise solutions for a long time. SUSE Linux Enterprise products range from desktop systems to enterprise-quality servers.

SUSE (originally written as SuSE) began as a German version of Slackware in 1992, on 40 floppy disks, and was first officially released on CD (SUSE Linux 1.0) in 1994. Founded by Hubert Mantel, Burchard Steinbild, Roland Dyroff, and Thomas Fehr, SUSE set out as a separate distribution from Slackware to enhance the software in the areas of installation and administration.

Although SUSE had success and respect with its Linux distribution, it was not profitable, and Novell's $210 million offer for SUSE was seen as a good thing both for SUSE and for Linux in general. SUSE was running short on cash, and Novell was looking for a way to regain its stature as a growth company in the enterprise and network-computing arena.

In the 1980s and early 1990s, Novell was the world's number-one computer networking company. Before the Internet took hold, Novell's NetWare servers and IPX/SPX protocols were the most popular ways to connect PCs together on LANs. International training, support, and sales teams brought Novell products to businesses and organizations around the world.

Despite Novell's huge lead in the network computing market, file- and printer-sharing features in Microsoft Windows and late entry into the TCP/IP (Internet) arena caused Novell to lose its market dominance in the 1990s. Although its NetWare products contained excellent features for directory services and managing network resources, Novell didn't have end-to-end computing solutions and relied on Windows for client computers.

Novell's association with the UNIX operating system in the early 1990s makes an interesting footnote in the history of Linux. Novell purchased UNIX System V source code from AT&T and set out to make its resulting UnixWare product (a UNIX desktop product for x86 processors) a competitor to Microsoft's growing dominance on the desktop. The effort was half-hearted, and in the mid-1990s Novell gave the UNIX trademark to the Open Group and sold the UNIX source code to SCO.

Novell's purchase of SUSE marked its second major attempt to fill in its product line with a UNIX-like desktop and server product. In its first few years of supporting Linux, Novell is already doing a better job with Linux than it did with UNIX.

# What's in SUSE Distributions?

Unlike distributions geared toward more technical users, such as Gentoo and Slackware, you can configure and launch most major features of SUSE Linux by selecting menus on the desktop. New Linux users should find SUSE to be very comfortable for daily use and basic administration.

Like Red Hat Enterprise Linux, SUSE is made to have a more cohesive look-and-feel than most Linux distributions that are geared toward Linux enthusiasts. In other words, you aren't required to put together a lot of SUSE by hand just to get it working. Although SUSE is ultimately aimed more toward enterprise computing, it also works well as a home desktop system.

The following sections explore what openSUSE and SUSE Linux Enterprise offer you.

## Installation and configuration with YaST

A set of modules that you can use to configure your SUSE system is gathered together under the YaST facility. Because many of the features needed in a Linux installer are also needed to configure a running system (network, security, software, and other setup features), YaST does double duty as an installer and an administrative tool.

YaST (which stands for Yet Another Setup Tool) was originally proprietary code that was not available as open source. However, to gain wider acceptance for YaST among major computing clients as a framework for managing a range of computing services, Novell released YaST under the GNU Public License in March 2004.

YaST makes obvious what you need to do to install Linux. Hardware detection is done before your eyes. You can set up your disk partitions graphically (no need to remember options to the fdisk command). Setting up the GRUB boot loader is done for you, with the option to modify it yourself.

One of the nice features of YaST installation is that you can scan the configuration process without stepping through every feature. If you scan through the mouse, keyboard, installation mode, partitioning, and other information and they look okay, you can click Accept and just keep going. Or you can change any of those settings you choose. (The "Installing openSUSE" section later in this chapter details the installation process with YaST.)

Because YaST offers both graphical (QT) and text-based (ncurses) interfaces, you can use YaST as a configuration tool from the desktop or the shell. To start YaST from the KDE desktop, click the Computer button on the desktop panel and select YaST from the System menu. Figure 20-1 shows the graphical version of the YaST utility.

Launching the YaST utility actually involves running the /sbin/yast2 command. When you run /sbin/yast2, YaST starts in graphical mode by default. (An alternative is to run /sbin/yast as root user from a Terminal window, which starts YaST in text mode.) Figure 20-2 shows what YaST looks like when started in text mode from a Terminal window.

**FIGURE 20-1**

Configure common Linux features using the YaST utility.

**FIGURE 20-2**

Use the arrow and Tab keys to navigate YaST in text mode.

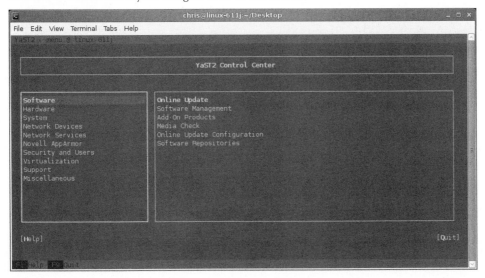

YaST offers you some intuitive tools for configuring your system and comes preconfigured so you start with a nice set of defaults. YaST also does a good job detecting your hardware, finding partitions, and the like, so a new user can often just accept the settings YaST chooses. Here are some examples of what YaST does for you:

- **Detects hardware**—You don't have to check through /etc configuration files or run lsmod, lspci, or hwinfo to see the drivers for your hardware or how your hardware has been configured in SUSE. From the Hardware section, you can select icons representing your graphics cards, printers, joysticks, scanners, sound cards, and mice. Click the Hardware information icon to see your full list of detected hardware.

- **Manages system configuration**—Like Red Hat Enterprise Linux, SUSE stores much of the information it uses to configure services at boot time in files in the /etc/sysconfig directory. The information in those files is in the form VARIABLE="VALUE".

  Under the YaST System heading (in the left-hand pane), you can select the sysconfig Editor, which lets you select each file and then view and possibly change each variable so that you don't have to guess what variables are available for each configuration. For more advanced system administrators, this is a great way to fine-tune the startup services for your system.

  SUSE also includes a Profile Manager applet, which lets you store and manage a collection of system settings so it can be used again later.

- **Configures network devices**—YaST detects your dial-up modem, Ethernet card, DSL modem, or ISDN hardware, and gives you the opportunity to configure each piece of hardware. SUSE also does a much better job than most distributions at getting Winmodems working in Linux, which is particularly useful for using dial-up features on laptops that have cheap, built-in modems.

- **Defines network services**—With a connection to your LAN or WAN, YaST provides some helpful graphical tools for configuring some services that can be unintuitive to configure from the command line. NetworkManager (which is enabled by default in openSUSE) tries to detect and configure your network interfaces automatically. However, to scan available network interfaces and manually override those settings from YaST, select Network Settings from the Network Devices category.

- **Changes security settings**—Security settings in Linux are often among the most unintuitive features to configure, while at the same time being among the most important. Although features such as iptables work great for most Linux gurus for setting up a firewall, people who are accustomed to graphical interfaces may find them challenging.

  From the YaST Security and Users selection, the Firewall icon enables you to step through your network interfaces and add access to those services you want by name (such as Web Server, Mail Server, and Other Services) or by port number. It even enables you to do initial setup of more complex firewall features, such as packet forwarding, IP Masquerading, and logging.

To make your way around the graphical YaST interface, you need only to click the mouse and use the Tab key to move between fields. For the text-based YaST interface, you can use the Tab and arrow keys to move among the selections and the Enter key to select the currently highlighted item.

## RPM package management

Like Red Hat Enterprise Linux and Fedora, SUSE packages its software using the RPM package management file format and related tools. RPM contains a lot of features for adding, removing, and managing software in SUSE. Although software packages in the Red Hat and SUSE distributions are different, the tools you use for managing packages in those two distributions from the command line are very much the same.

In most cases, you will use the YaST Software Manager to find, install, and uninstall software packages in SUSE distributions. However, you also can run the rpm utility to work with RPM software packages from the command line. Here's a list of some of its features:

- **Installing local or remote packages**—You can use the rpm command to add a software package to SUSE, and rpm doesn't care if the package is in the local directory, CD, or remote computer (providing you have network access to that computer). A remote package can be available on a Web server (http://) or FTP server (ftp://). Here's an example of using an rpm command to install a software package from an FTP server:

```
# rpm -iv ftp://ftp.linuxtoys.net/pub/suse/11/abc.i586.rpm
```

In this example, the -i option says to install the package, and the -v option says to give verbose output as the package is installed. The fictitious package (abc.i586.rpm) is installed from an FTP repository. If there are dependency or access issues, rpm informs you and fails. Otherwise, the package is installed. (The -U option is often used instead of the -i option to install RPMs because -U succeeds even if the package is already installed. The -U says to upgrade the package.)

- **Querying the RPM database**—One of the best features of the RPM facility is that you can find out a lot of information about the software packages that are installed. The query option (-q) lets you list package names, descriptions, and contents in various ways. Here are a few examples:

```
# rpm -qa coreutils
# rpm -ql coreutils| less
# rpm -qi coreutils| less
```

The first example (-qa) searches for the coreutils package and reports the current version of the package that is installed. In the second, -ql lists all files in the coreutils package and then pipes that output to the less command to page through it. And finally, -qi displays a description and other information about the coreutils package.

● **Verifying installed packages**—Use rpm to verify the contents of an RPM package. The -V option enables you to check whether any of the files in a package have been tampered with. Here is an example:

```
# rpm -V aaa_base
..5....T c /etc/inittab
S.5....T   /etc/profile.d/alias.ash
```

The -V checks whether any of the contents of the aaa_base package (which contains some basic system configuration files) have been modified. The output shows that the inittab and alias.ash files have been modified from the originals. The 5 indicates that the md5sums of the files differ, while the T indicates that the time stamp on the file differs. On the alias.ash file, the S shows that the size of the file is different.

The rpm command has many other options as well. To find out more about them, type man rpm or rpm --help from any shell.

## Automated software updates

SUSE Linux includes an automatic update agent, referred to as the YaST Online Update (YOU) utility. This utility is built right into the YaST facility and offers an easy way to get updates, security patches, and bug fixes for SUSE Linux Enterprise or openSUSE by downloading and installing them from software repositories over the network. You can also execute YOU from the command line as root user, using the you command.

From within YaST, select Software ⇨ Online Update. YaST uses software installation sources that have been defined in YaST's Installation Source module to enable you to begin retrieving software updates with a single click. It presents you with a list of patches from which you can choose. Security patches are in red, all recommended patches are selected, and optional patches are shown (unselected). It's easy to see all available patches and read their descriptions to determine whether you want them.

After you have selected the updates you want and clicked OK, you can watch the progress as each patch and updated package is downloaded and installed. Having security-related patches and other fixes separated and having the ability to read all about each software update and patch right on the YaST window before you start downloading are features that make YaST Online Update a powerful and easy-to-use software update mechanism.

## Managing software with zypper

Although the rpm command is good for managing single applications, SUSE needed a tool that could work well with online repositories and deal with issues of dependent packages and updates. The recently added zypper utility is just such a tool.

The zypper utility is similar to the yum utility that is used with Fedora and other Red Hat systems. With zypper, not only can you install packages, but you can also search, download, and query packages from online SUSE repositories. The zypper utility is also designed to support several different software backends, including Novell Rug (Red Carpet updater), ZENworks software manager, and yum repositories.

# Getting Support for SUSE Linux Enterprise and openSUSE

There is no support offered for openSUSE if you download it yourself or get it with a book (as you do here). However, if you purchase the boxed set of openSUSE from Novell, you get 90 days of installation support. Besides that, anyone can get free support from the openSUSE community.

The Discover It page (http://en.opensuse.org/Welcome_to_openSUSE.org) is the place to search for answers about using openSUSE. From this page you can immediately find links to download openSUSE, participate in projects, report bugs, or learn more about openSUSE.

Select the Support link to find several ways to get more information about the openSUSE project or any problems you may have using openSUSE. You can use online forums, IRC chats, mailing lists, news portals, and other features of the site to learn more about openSUSE.

With the split of openSUSE and SUSE Linux Enterprise, many of SUSE's online resources have been divided as well. For example, many general SUSE resources are directed to either Novell. com or openSUSE.org sites. If you are learning or trying out openSUSE as your entry into SUSE Linux Enterprise products, you should start at the openSUSE.org site for information.

# Installing openSUSE

The DVD that comes with this book includes the openSUSE 11.1 KDE live/install CD, remastered to coexist with other Linux systems on the DVD. If you like openSUSE and want a boxed set, you can purchase one from the openSUSE project. The boxed set of SUSE Linux includes installation support and hardcopy documentation.

## Note
The installation description in this chapter covers installs on Intel x86 PCs. If you have an AMD 64-bit or Intel Extended Memory 64 Technology system (x86_64) or PowerPC (ppc), you can download those versions of openSUSE from an openSUSE mirror site (see http://software.opensuse.org). Live CDs, as well DVD and install media, are available to download and burn. You can purchase boxed sets from that site as well. ■

# Before you begin

There is a variety of ways to install openSUSE from either local media (CD, DVD, and so on) or from network software repositories. The install itself can be launched from a live CD, an install CD/DVD, or a PXE boot from your network card. In this openSUSE install procedure, I focus on the following media types:

- **Live media**—The openSUSE project produces live CDs containing KDE and GNOME desktops. The openSUSE KDE live CD is included with the DVD that comes with this book. You can boot these media live to try out openSUSE, and then install the contents of those media to your hard disk from an icon on the desktop. With this type of install, you get fewer install choices, but the procedure is a bit easier.

- **Install media**—The openSUSE project also produces CD and DVD media that boot directly to an openSUSE installer. You can download the openSUSE install DVD. Or you can do a network install from the CD included with this book.

For further information on different ways of installing openSUSE, refer to the openSUSE Installation page at `http://en.opensuse.org/installation`.

To use the openSUSE live CD that comes with this book, you should have at least 512MB of main memory. To install minimal systems from other openSUSE installation media, you need at least 96MB of main memory (text-only interface), although more is always better, and future releases may require greater amounts of memory for installation and usability. For a desktop install, however, I recommend at least 256MB of main memory.

The default installation of openSUSE 11.1 from the KDE live CD included on the DVD with this book requires at least 2.5GB of disk space. The default installation from an official openSUSE 11.1 DVD requires 3.25GB of disk space. You can get by with less by deselecting packages during installation from install media. From the live CD, it simply installs the entire contents of the CD. Installation should work on any Pentium-class x86 PC.

The descriptions here explain how to install by booting the openSUSE live CD on the DVD that comes with this book. Other than the boot screen, the procedure is the same as if you had downloaded the openSUSE live CD yourself. The network install CD requires that your computer have an Ethernet connection to the Internet. (Refer to `http://en.opensuse.org/INSTALL_Internet`, the openSUSE Internet installation procedure, for details on installing from a network install CD.)

## Note

When the openSUSE live CD first boots, there is no root password assigned. If you need to run any system administration commands, the `sudo` facility is configured to allow the live CD user to run administrative commands. During installation, you have a chance to assign a root password for your installed system. ∎

# Starting installation

The following are the steps for installing openSUSE Linux on your hard disk from the openSUSE live CD included on the DVD accompanying this book. This procedure has fewer steps than installing from install media. In particular, instead of letting you choose which software packages to install, the live CD media simply copies the exact live CD software to your hard disk.

1. **Insert the DVD that comes with this book in your drive.** Reboot the computer. The boot screen appears.

2. **Select suse from the boot screen.** (If you are using media obtained directly from the openSUSE project, select Installation and press Enter.) A live version of openSUSE boots up to a live openSUSE desktop.

3. **Start installing.** Open the Live Installer icon from the desktop. A Welcome screen appears. (You may get a warning that you need at least 1GB of RAM to do a full install.)

4. **License, Language and Keyboard.** You can change the default language and keyboard from English (US) if you need to on this screen. Then read the Novell Software License Agreement. If you agree, select the check box and click Next. (Selecting No ends the install process.) If an earlier version of openSUSE is detected, you are prompted to select an install mode. The system is probed to make sure minimum hardware requirements are met. If additional drivers are needed than are available on the installation medium, they will be downloaded from the Internet.

## Note

Sometimes installation can fail because the computer hardware doesn't support certain features, such as power management (ACPI or APM) or DMA on hard drives or removable media. For those cases, you can try starting installation by selecting ACPI Disabled (which turns off ACPI) or Safe Settings (which turns off ACPI and APM as well as turning off DMA for any IDE CD, DVD, or hard drives). ■

5. **Clock and time zone.** Select the geographic region and time zone in which you're located. If the time is wrong, click Change, and type your new date and/or time and click Accept. Note that other operating systems may not expect the Hardware Clock (in the BIOS) to be set to UTC (Coordinated Universal Time). If you dual-boot, you may want to consider setting this to Local time so it does not conflict with other operating systems. Linux works with either mode. Select Next to continue.

6. **Partitioning.** Partitioning is very important, especially if you want to protect any data currently on your hard disk. The openSUSE install screen recommends a partitioning scheme. (If your disk is already partitioned, openSUSE tries to use that scheme.) You can simply accept that scheme (just click Next) or select the Edit Partition Setup button.

   The Edit Partition Setup selection enables you to use a partitioning interface that is very similar to the partition screen used when installing Fedora. See the description of partitioning in Chapter 8 for information on partitioning your hard disk. If you ever plan to move your partitions around with a tool such as Partition Magic, you should assign your Linux partition to the ext3 file system type. (If you are an expert and want to use the `fdisk` command you can open a shell as root user and do that.)

7. **Create New User.** You will want to add at least one user account, as prompted, for your computer. Right now, you have only the root user account set up for use on a standalone machine. Using that account for e-mail, Web browsing, or other common tasks is considered bad security practice. So be sure to add at least one user account for non-administrative use of your computer. Add your full name, a short, one-word login name, and a password to protect that account.

   You can choose to have the same password for your regular user be used as the password for the root user. If you want to have this user automatically logged in on the system whenever you restart, leave the Automatic Login check box selected. Otherwise, deselect it to see a standard login prompt whenever you boot your system. You can also check the Receive System Mail check box to ensure that the user account that you have just created automatically receives a copy of any mail sent to the root user on your system, which is often sent by administrative applications. To proceed, click Next.

8. **Installation Settings.** Installation headings are displayed for System, Partitioning, Booting, Keyboard Layout, Time Zone, and Default runlevel. Review those settings and click on the heading representing any settings you want to change. Here are descriptions of those headings:

   - **System**—Select System to probe your computer hardware. The result is details about the type and model of each hardware item on your computer. You can save this information to your hard disk (if there is an available partition) or to a floppy disk. Click Details to see further information about any selected item. You might find this information useful if, for some reason, the hardware is not properly configured after the install is complete. It gives you information you need to search the Web or ask a question on a Linux forum about your hardware problem.

   - **Partitioning**—Select Partitioning to review and optionally change the partitioning as described earlier.

   - **Booting**—Select Booting to see the information that is added to your boot loader (GRUB, by default, but you can use the LILO boot loader as well). The boot loader includes the information needed to boot Linux: the location of the boot loader, default operating system to boot, and other information.

   - **Keyboard Layout**—Select this option to set the keyboard to be used by the system.

   - **Time Zone**—Select Time Zone to change the time zone and related clock setting on your computer system.

   - **Default runlevel**—Normally you use the default (5) to boot to a full multiuser, networked desktop system with a graphical login screen. The other common default is 3, which provides a text-based login screen but is otherwise the same. (If you choose 3, you can start the GUI after login by typing the `startx` command.)

9. **Start the install.** If the Installation settings all look okay, click Install to begin the install process. Remember that this is your last chance to back out! When the confirmation dialog box appears, click Back to return to the installer so that you can modify or abort the install process, or click Install to start the installation.

If you select Install, openSUSE formats your hard disk and installs the entire contents of the openSUSE live CD. After installation finishes, a message tells you to reboot.

10. **Reboot your computer.** Reboot the computer (select Shutdown and Restart from the Computer menu). Remove the CD or DVD before the computer boots up again. After your system starts up (this time from hard disk), openSUSE probes for information about your video card, printers, and network. It then tries to automatically configure those devices.

At this point you should have a working openSUSE system. You can go ahead and start using openSUSE as described in the next section.

# Starting with openSUSE

If you created a user account during the preceding installation and left Automatic Login selected when you created that account, openSUSE should automatically log you in as that user and present you with the KDE desktop. (If you are presented with a graphical login screen instead, log in as that user now.) Here are a few things to help you get started using openSUSE:

- **Desktop applications**—The default openSUSE install is configured as a desktop system that includes a set of easily accessible desktop applications. Select the Application Launcher to see icons for starting popular desktop applications: Firefox (Web browser), Banshee Media Player, F-Spot (photo browser), Evolution (mail and calendar), OpenOffice.org Writer (word processor), and Nautilus (file browser).

- **Home folder**—The Home folder on the desktop gives you access to your Desktop, Documents, and `public_html` folders in a file manager window.

- **Reconfigure your computer**—Get to the YaST administration tool by selecting Computer ⇨ YaST from the openSUSE menu. Reconfigure your system hardware and software from the YaST Control Center that appears.

If you want to configure your desktop (change backgrounds, screen savers, or themes), just right-click the desktop and select Desktop Settings. A KDE Control Center is also available from the openSUSE menu, to further configure your system.

# Summary

SUSE Linux Enterprise is generally considered to be the next best choice for enterprise-quality Linux systems in the United States, after Red Hat Enterprise Linux. However, SUSE Linux Enterprise is very popular in Europe. The openSUSE distribution on which SUSE Linux Enterprise is based is recommended for home users and enthusiasts. Both distributions offer graphical installation and administrative tools (implemented in a facility called YaST) that help set them apart from other Linux distributions geared more toward technical users.

Since SUSE was acquired by Novell in 2003, SUSE Linux Enterprise has become part of a larger, enterprise-ready product line. Boxed sets of openSUSE Linux are also available from Novell. Support offerings are available at many different levels. With Novell's worldwide sales and training organization, SUSE Linux has the backing it needs to compete to become the world's most popular commercial Linux system. The release of SUSE to the open source community as the openSUSE project ensures that the latest and greatest features are available or are in the SUSE development pipeline.

Because so much work has gone into the YaST installer and administrative interface, even an inexperienced user can be up and running on a newly installed SUSE Linux Enterprise or openSUSE system within an hour. It's then easy to begin using a variety of desktop and personal productivity applications from the SUSE desktop.

# Running KNOPPIX

A computer's operating system usually resides on the hard disk—but it doesn't have to. When a computer boots up, it typically checks first whether a CD, floppy disk, or DVD is in a drive and tries to boot from there (depending on BIOS settings). So, with up to 700MB (CD) or 8.4GB (dual-layer DVD) of space on those media, why not use them to boot whole operating systems?

Well, that's exactly what bootable Linux distributions (also called *live CDs*) such as KNOPPIX do. In the case of KNOPPIX, one CD holds up to 2GB of compressed software for you to run that uncompresses on-the-fly. Start it up and you can try out all the features of a well-stocked Linux system, without touching the contents of your hard disk.

## On the DVD

KNOPPIX is included on the DVD that comes with this book. In fact, it is the default option. Insert the DVD into your PC's DVD drive, and when you see the boot screen, press Enter. KNOPPIX should just start up, and you can begin using it as described in this chapter. ■

If you have never used Linux before, KNOPPIX gives you the chance to do so in a very safe way. If you are experienced with Linux, KNOPPIX can be used as a tool to take Linux with you everywhere, troubleshoot a computer, or check whether a computer will run Linux. In any case, you can use this chapter to take a little tour of some great Linux features that you can try out with KNOPPIX.

# KNOPPIX Features

KNOPPIX has so many features it's hard to find a place to start. The latest official version of KNOPPIX at the time of this writing (KNOPPIX 6.0.1), features X.Org 7.3, OpenOffice.org 3.0.1, LXDE 0.3.2, GIMP 2.4.7, Linux kernel 2.6.28, as well as many accessories. The KNOPPIX CD version is included on this book's DVD (a KNOPPIX DVD version is available for download). More information on downloads and other topics can be found on the KNOPPIX home page (www.knoppix.com).

One of the most useful features of KNOPPIX is the ease with which you can create your own, personalized KNOPPIX disk. The available options are so vast that there is not enough room to cover them in this book. For more information on how to create your own version of KNOPPIX, see www.knoppix.net/wiki/Knoppix_Remastering_Howto.

## Coming from Windows

**KNOPPIX includes support for NTFS file systems, so you can use KNOPPIX on a computer with Windows XP installed and access your files from your hard disk. This is a good way to try out your documents, music, movies, or other content from Windows using Linux applications (before you switch permanently). NTFS transparent write access, which is not available in every Linux distribution, makes writing to NTFS partitions safer than it was in previous versions.** ■

# Understanding KNOPPIX

If you are impatient to get started, you don't have to read any further. In most cases, you can just insert your DVD into your PC, reboot the computer, and start using KNOPPIX. If you have the time, however, read on a bit more.

KNOPPIX is a bootable Linux that includes a nice selection of open source software. Originally, there was a CD version of KNOPPIX (about a 700MB image). Now, there is also a DVD version (about a 4GB image). It is the KNOPPIX CD image that is included on the DVD that comes with this book.

KNOPPIX was the trailblazer of Linux live CDs. In fact, for a long time KNOPPIX was used as the basis for creating many specialized Linux live CDs, including Gnoppix (featuring GNOME instead of LXDE), KNOPPIX STD (security), KnoppMyth (MythTV media player), Damn Small Linux (mini desktop), and KnoppiXMAME (console game player), to name a few. To try out the latest features, however, you should start with the most recent version of KNOPPIX, as described in the rest of this chapter.

## Looking inside KNOPPIX

After automatically detecting and configuring your computer hardware, KNOPPIX boots right up to a fast, lightweight desktop system with a handful of ready-to-use desktop applications (no login required). It includes some powerful server and power user features.

The latest KNOPPIX release (6.0.1) marks a departure from earlier KNOPPIX releases (such as 5.1.1). Instead of including a boatload of applications, it includes a good set of standard applications and seems to otherwise focus on making the desktop rock solid and blazing fast.

If you have used earlier versions of KNOPPIX the first thing you'll notice is how quickly it boots up to a desktop. Then you'll notice that the KDE desktop is gone and is replaced by the Lightweight X11 Desktop Environment (www.lxde.org). So you lose a few dozen KDE utilities (including applications like Konqueror) but you gain tremendous efficiency, even with desktop effects enabled by default (Compiz is the default window manager)!

Take a look at the following list of some of KNOPPIX's major components:

- **LXDE**—A lightweight, efficient desktop environment that runs well, even with cool desktop effects (screen wobble, deleted windows bursting into flames, and so on).

- **OpenOffice.org**—The OpenOffice.org suite of office productivity tools so that you can create documents, graphics, presentations, spreadsheets, and most anything you expect to be able to do with office applications. With KNOPPIX, you can give a presentation created in OpenOffice.org software anywhere that you have access to a PC. (See Chapter 5 for descriptions of OpenOffice.org productivity applications.)

- **Internet tools**—Web browser (Iceweasel, which is a streamlined version of Firefox), e-mail clients (Icedove and mutt), an instant messaging client (Pidgin), Linphone webphone, and several other applications for using the Internet. (See Chapter 6 for descriptions of popular Web browsers and mail clients.)

- **Multimedia software**—Applications for playing music and video (Mplayer), working with graphics (GIMP), and displaying images (GPicView). (Chapter 4 covers music and video players.)

- **Administrative tools**—Under the System Tools menu you can find tools for installing KNOPPIX to hard disk or USB flash disk, setting up special network connections and editing your desktop configuration. Select the Synaptic Package Manager, select to update your packages list, and, provided you have an Internet connection, you can download and install from thousands of packages available from the Debian software repository.

- **Servers**—Only a few server packages have been retained in the latest version of KNOPPIX. However, you can still configure KNOPPIX as an NFS or a DHCP server.

## Coming from Windows

**Using KNOPPIX (or any of the other bootable server Linux systems described in Chapter 28) as a server opens some amazing possibilities for serving the data from a Windows or other operating system to a network, while completely bypassing that operating system on the computer's hard disk. ∎**

KNOPPIX is based on Debian GNU/Linux, so a Debian user will be particularly comfortable with the selection and organization of features. KNOPPIX software packages are also done in deb package format, so you can use apt, dpkg, and related tools to list and otherwise manage the packages. A graphical tool for working with software packages that comes with KNOPPIX is the Synaptic Package Manager.

## Note

**Refer to Chapter 19 for information on using apt and dpkg tools for managing software in Debian. Even if you don't install any new software, those tools provide an excellent way to search, list, or even upgrade software packages that are running in KNOPPIX. ■**

## What's cool about KNOPPIX

The features just described are ones that come with many different Linux distributions. What makes them special with KNOPPIX is that you can often be up and using those features within a few minutes—without having to repartition your disk, install software, or do any configuration. For just trying out Linux or using it for some special, quick task such as playing or displaying music, documents, or spreadsheets from a computer's hard disk, KNOPPIX is quite awesome.

Some features, however, are specific to KNOPPIX and other live CDs (as compared to a Linux system you would run from a hard disk). Many of those special features are there to help you through issues related to the fact that you're working in a setup that's not permanent. In particular, KNOPPIX includes the following:

- **Extraordinary hardware detection**—The capability to properly detect and configure hardware is one of the best features. During the boot-up procedure, KNOPPIX finds most common PC hardware components and loads the proper modules so it can use them. Its hwsetup tool relies on the Red Hat libkudzu facility to identify hardware, load appropriate modules, and create necessary device files.

  For hardware that can't be detected, there are many boot options you can add to properly identify (or skip over) selected hardware devices. Some of them deal with particularly sticky issues related to video cards and running on laptop computers. (See Tables 21-1 through 21-3.)

- **Automatic desktop startup**—Instead of just dropping you to a command line, KNOPPIX does its best to start up a complete LXDE desktop environment. Try some of the great desktop 3D effects: Use your mouse's wheel to rotate between your desktop workspaces or press Ctrl+Alt and hold the left mouse button to spin the whole desktop on a cube. (Your keyboard may require a key other than the Alt key.)

- **Save setup**—You don't have to lose the configuration you have done for KNOPPIX every time you reboot. Click the System Tools menu and make the appropriate selection to save your complete KNOPPIX desktop software and data to either hard disk or USB flash drive.

- **Work with Windows files**—KNOPPIX includes drivers for using Microsoft Windows NTFS file systems. The drivers enable you to read and write files from your hard disk if you are booting KNOPPIX from a PC with Windows installed. (Writing to NTFS partitions from KNOPPIX is still considered experimental, so consider using an NTFS partition in read-only mode if the partition contains critical data.)

For example, say that you have your entire music collection, images downloaded from your digital camera, and personal Web pages on your hard disk on a computer that was set up to be booted by Microsoft Windows XP. You boot KNOPPIX instead (notice that Microsoft Windows is not running at all). Suddenly your hard disk is just a place that holds a lot of files. You can now use applications that come with KNOPPIX to open the files on your hard disk to play the music, view or manipulate images, and display or change Web pages.

To see and access your available hard disk or USB flash drive partitions, open the PCMan File Manager icon on the desktop. Then select the folder representing the partition you want to open (including any Linux, Windows, or other partitions on your computer's storage devices).

A testament to how well KNOPPIX is respected is how many other bootable Linux distributions are based on it. The KNOPPIX project even provides a KNOPPIX-customize package that lets anyone make his own customized KNOPPIX. Specialized KNOPPIX derivatives can be used to rescue a broken computer, play a range of multimedia content, or run a specific application.

## Cross-Reference

See Chapter 27 for information on using a bootable Linux distribution as a firewall/router and Chapter 28 for descriptions of many other bootable Linux distributions. ■

# Examining challenges with KNOPPIX

For most people, KNOPPIX is a special-use Linux system. It's a great way to try Linux or to access a computer that isn't set up the way you like. However, there are a few challenges with using KNOPPIX that you should keep in mind:

- **Reboot clears out KNOPPIX**—Unless you save your data to some other media (which you can do, as I describe later in this chapter), the entire KNOPPIX system goes away when you reboot. That means files on the desktop, installed software, system configuration, and anything else you do during your KNOPPIX session will be gone unless you explicitly save that information to a hard disk or some removable medium (floppy, CD, and so on).

- **Memory limitations**—KNOPPIX is made to be able to run without touching your hard disk, so when you save files to KNOPPIX, they are (by default) stored in your computer's memory (RAM). As a result, precious memory is devoted to holding files that might otherwise be used for running demanding applications.

- **Performance hits**—By moving to the LXDE desktop, KNOPPIX has vastly improved some of the performance problems that plague live CDs in general. The latest KNOPPIX live CD runs quite well with only about 512MB of RAM, where earlier versions of KNOPPIX and other full-featured live CDs would run slowly.

- **Uses your CD/DVD drive**—Because KNOPPIX relies so heavily on data from the CD or DVD, you can't remove it while you are using the system. So, if you have only one drive for removable media, you can't use it to access a music CD, install from another software disk, or burn data while you are using KNOPPIX.

## Note

If you have more than 1GB of RAM on your computer, you can use the `toram` boot option to run KNOPPIX. This will not only allow you to remove the KNOPPIX disk, because everything is running from RAM, but will also cause KNOPPIX to run faster than a Linux system installed on a hard disk. ∎

I must admit that the challenges described here are more of an explanation of how KNOPPIX works than they are problems with KNOPPIX itself. The idea that you can run a full-blown desktop and server operating system from a single CD (with nearly 2GB of available applications) is an awesome concept for someone who still remembers DOS and character terminals.

## Seeing where KNOPPIX comes from

KNOPPIX was created by Klaus Knopper in Germany. Knopper follows in the great tradition of naming a distribution using a part of the creator's own name with "ix" or "ux" stuck on the end.

Although a groundswell of interest and support has appeared for KNOPPIX in the past few years, Knopper himself admits that KNOPPIX started out more as a collection of tools he needed than as a full Linux distribution. Knopper works to provide only software that can be distributed freely, for both noncommercial and commercial use. He doesn't even include some free software (such as browser plug-ins) that might restrict free redistribution, although he doesn't object to including non–open source software that can still be freely distributed.

There is no big company behind KNOPPIX, and development efforts continue to be headed up by Knopper himself. However, many people contribute bug reports and enhancement requests (see `www.knoppix.net/wiki/bugs`), and other developers have helped create software specifically for KNOPPIX (in particular, Fabian Franz who, among other things, has contributed significant work to KNOPPIX installer-related features).

The official KNOPPIX Web site is Knopper's own personal site: `www.knopper.net/knoppix/index-en.html`. If you are looking for a way to get information and become involved with others who use and develop the system, the `Knoppix.net` site offers a very active forum and links to information about other KNOPPIX resources. It's a great place not only to get your questions answered, but also to find a wealth of links to FAQs, HOWTOs, and related projects. There is also an IRC channel (#knoppix on `irc.freenode.net`) and a wiki used primarily to gather documentation (`www.knoppix.net/wiki/Main_Page`).

# Exploring uses for KNOPPIX

Because you can do so much with KNOPPIX, choosing just a few uses to highlight is hard. Consider the following possibilities:

- **Your own portable operating system**—You don't have to carry around a laptop or whole PC to make sure you have the software you need. Instead, you can use any PC that is available (with the exception of some unsupported hardware) and boot your whole computing environment with a single CD. By customizing your own KNOPPIX, you can add your own data and pick and choose applications as well.

- **A tool for managing data on any PC**—You can bypass the operating system and other software on any computer and use the applications on your KNOPPIX disk to manage the data on that computer.

Of course, these concepts are not exclusive to KNOPPIX because you could conceptually do the same thing with any boot floppy since the days of DOS (as well as any other bootable Linux). The difference is that KNOPPIX does those things so well. It lets you take over a computer, not just with a tiny rescue disk capable of running a few obtuse commands, but with a full-scale desktop, server, and administrative toolkit operating system. With that in mind, here are some ways people are using KNOPPIX:

- **Showing off Linux**—A demo can lack some punch when you have to spend an hour installing before you can make your point. With KNOPPIX, it can take about 5 minutes from the time you tell your friend about Linux to the time you have a complete desktop system running on his PC. And in the process, you don't have to worry about harming anything on his computer because you don't even need to touch his hard disk.

- **Testing a computer for Linux**—Instead of getting halfway through an install to see whether your PC is capable of running Linux, you can boot KNOPPIX. If it works, you can check to see what drivers were loaded to deal with your hardware (type **lsmod** from a shell) and then go ahead and install any Linux you like to the hard disk.

- **Rescuing a computer or network**—Many tools for tracking down and fixing problems on both Linux and Windows systems are included in KNOPPIX. The Knoppix-STD edition also includes dozens more tools for rescuing broken systems and tracing network problems (see www.knoppix-std.org).

- **Taking over a broken server**—If a Web server, file server, or firewall has been cracked or otherwise broken, you might be able to use KNOPPIX to safely serve the data from a KNOPPIX boot disk while you fix the problem. If the exact software is not on KNOPPIX, you can simply use the Synaptic Package Manager to download and install it (provided you have an Internet connection).

- **Doing anything you want**—For those of us who have gotten used to using Linux, going somewhere and having to do work or make a presentation on a computer that doesn't have the tools you need is a pain. By bringing the whole operating system, all your software tools and sometimes even your data (with a customized CD, separate floppy, pen drive, or downloaded files), your computing environment can be the same wherever you go.

Now that you have some idea of what to do with KNOPPIX, let's get started.

# Starting KNOPPIX

In most cases, starting KNOPPIX is very easy. With KNOPPIX in hand, all you really need is a PC that meets the minimum specifications.

## Getting a computer

If you are ready to start KNOPPIX, I recommend the following:

- **A PC**—You need a PC that meets the minimal processor and memory requirements described a bit later. There are no hard disk space requirements because you don't need to touch the hard disk. To get better performance on low-RAM systems, however, you might want to create a swap partition, or swap file, on hard disk to enable you to run more processes (as described later).

- **Permission to reboot**—KNOPPIX is going to take over operation of the PC, so you need to be sure that it's okay to reboot it. Make sure that nobody else is currently using the computer or relying on it to be accessible over a network. (It is possible to run KNOPPIX on a running Windows or Linux system, using virtualization tools such as Qemu or VMWare. To run KNOPPIX, however, you need a computer that has extra available RAM. Otherwise, you will get poor performance.)

- **Internet connection (optional)**—It isn't necessary, but if your computer has an Ethernet card and a connection to the Internet, you can immediately start using KNOPPIX to browse the Web and otherwise take advantage of its communications tools. KNOPPIX will try to detect a DHCP server (to get an IP address and other information) and automatically configure itself to use the Internet or other network that is available.

The system requirements for running KNOPPIX are much lower than you need for most of the latest Linux systems. According to Klaus Knopper, you need

- **CPU**—Intel-compatible i486 or better.

- **RAM**—20MB (for text mode), 82MB (for graphics mode), or 128MB (to also run most office applications). (These are the most recent memory requirements I could find. It's possible that these numbers are higher now.)

- **Bootable drive (DVD drive to use the DVD or CD to use a CD)**—KNOPPIX is able to boot from drives that are IDE/ATAPI, FireWire, USB, or SCSI (provided that your computer can boot from those devices). If you have a DVD drive, you can boot KNOPPIX directly from the DVD that comes with this book.

- **Graphics card**—Must be SVGA-compatible.
- **Mouse**—Supports any standard serial mouse, PS/2 mouse, or IMPS/2-compatible USB mouse.

## Booting KNOPPIX

If you have a PC in front of you that meets the requirements, you can get started by following these steps:

1. Insert your KNOPPIX DVD or CD into the appropriate drive.
2. Reboot the computer. After a few moments, the boot screen appears.

### Note

**Although the boot screens look different for the *Linux Bible 2010 Edition* DVD and a regular KNOPPIX CD, you can proceed with the boot process the same way. ■**

3. Press Enter. If all goes well, you should see the KNOPPIX desktop, and you can proceed to the "Using KNOPPIX" section. If KNOPPIX doesn't boot up properly or if you want to tune it further before it boots, continue on to the next section. In particular, you might want to use some of the boot options shown in Table 21-1.

## Correcting boot problems

By understanding a bit about the boot process you can, in most cases, overcome any problems you might have installing KNOPPIX. Here are some things you should know:

- **Check boot order**—Your computer's BIOS has a particular order in which it looks for bootable operating systems. A typical order would be floppy, CD or DVD, and hard disk. If your computer skips over the KNOPPIX boot disk and boots right from hard disk, make sure that the boot order in the BIOS is set to boot from CD or DVD. To change the BIOS, restart the computer and as it first boots the hardware enter Setup (quickly) as instructed (usually by pressing F1, F2, or DEL). Look for a selection to change the boot order so that your CD or DVD boots before the hard disk.
- **Add boot options**—Instead of just letting the boot process autodetect and configure everything about your hardware, you can add options to the boot prompt that will override what KNOPPIX autoconfiguration might do. Press F2 from the boot prompt to see additional boot options.

Some boot options are available with which you can try to overcome different issues at boot time. KNOPPIX refers to these options as *cheat codes*. For a more complete list, refer to the file knoppix-cheatcodes.txt, which you'll find in the KNOPPIX directory when you mount the CD or the DVD that comes with this book on any operating system.

## Note

**Many boot options can be used with different Linux systems. So if you are having trouble installing or booting a different Linux distribution, you can try any of these options to see if they work. Instead of the word "knoppix," you will probably use a different word to launch the install or boot process for other distributions (such as "linux" for Fedora systems or "morphix" for Morphix Live-CD, depending on the distribution). See Appendix A for information on how to start each Linux distribution. ■**

When KNOPPIX first begins the boot process, you see the boot screen, with the boot: prompt at the bottom. The following tables provide boot prompt options that can help you get KNOPPIX running the way you like. Table 21-1 shows options to use when you want specific features turned on that may not be turned on by default when you boot.

**TABLE 21-1**

## Boot Options to Select Features

| Option | Feature |
|---|---|
| knoppix lang=?? | Choose a specific language/keyboard. Replace *??* with one of the following: cn, de, da, es, fr, it, nl, pl, ru, sk, tr, tw, uk, or us. |
| knoppix blind | Start BrailleTerminal (running without X). (Note that there is a special version of KNOPPIX called Adriane KNOPPIX that contains special accessibility features.) |
| knoppix brltty= type,port,table | Add parameters to use for the Braille device. |
| knoppix wheelmouse | For a wheel mouse, enable IMPS/2 protocol. |
| knoppix nowheelmouse | For a regular PS/2 mouse, force PS/2 protocol. |
| knoppix keyboard=us xkeyboard=us | Assign different keyboard drivers to use with text (shell) and graphical (X). |
| knoppix dma | Turn on DMA acceleration for all IDE drives. |
| knoppix gmt | Use time that is based on Greenwich Mean Time. You can use utc instead of gmt to get the same result. |
| knoppix tz= *country/city* | Specify a particular time zone, based on country and city. |
| knoppix noeject | Don't eject the CD after KNOPPIX has stopped. |
| knoppix noprompt | Don't prompt to remove CD after KNOPPIX stops. |

If hardware is being improperly detected or configured, you can have KNOPPIX skip over that hardware. Table 21-2 contains options for skipping or turning off various hardware features.

**TABLE 21-2**

## Boot Options to Turn Off or Debug Hardware

| Option | Result |
| --- | --- |
| knoppix debug | Run KNOPPIX with verbose kernel messages. |
| knoppix atapicd | No SCSI-Emulation for IDE CD-ROMs. |
| knoppix noagp | No detection of AGP graphics card. |
| knoppix noapic | Disable Advanced Programmable Interrupt Controller (can overcome some problems on SMP computers). |
| knoppix acpi=off | Disable Advanced Configuration and Power Interface (ACPI). |
| knoppix noapm | No Advanced Power Management support. (With a working acpi, apm will be off by default. Only one can be active at a time.) |
| knoppix noaudio | No sound support. |
| knoppix nodhcp | Don't try to start your network connection automatically via DHCP. |
| knoppix fstab | Don't read the fstab file to find file systems to mount or check. |
| knoppix nofirewire | No detection of Firewire devices. |
| knoppix nopcmcia | No detection of PCMCIA card slots. |
| knoppix noscsi | No detection of SCSI devices. |
| knoppix noswap | No detection of swap partitions. |
| knoppix nousb | No detection of USB devices. |
| knoppix nousb2 | Disable extensions for USB 2.0. |
| knoppix pnpbios=off | Don't initialize plug-and-play (PnP) in the BIOS. |
| knoppix failsafe | Do almost no hardware detection. |

Table 21-3 lists options that may help if you are having trouble with your video card. Several of these options are particularly useful if you are having trouble with X on a laptop.

**TABLE 21-3**

## Boot Options to Fix Video Problems

| Option | Result |
|---|---|
| knoppix screen=?? | Pick X screen resolution. Replace ?? with 640 × 480, 800 × 600, 1024 × 768, 1280 × 1024, or any other resolution supported by your video card. |
| knoppix xvrefresh=60 | Set vertical refresh rate to 60 Hz for X (or other value as specified by monitor's manual). |
| knoppix xhrefresh=80 | Set horizontal refresh rate to 80 Hz for X (or other value as specified by monitor's manual). |
| knoppix xserver=?? | Replace ?? with XFree86 or XF86_SVGA. |
| knoppix xmodule=?? | Select the specific driver to use for your video card. Replace ?? with one of the following: ati, fbdev, i810, mga, nv, radeon, savage, s3radeon, svga, or i810. |
| knoppix 2 | Runlevel 2, Text mode only. |
| knoppix vga=normal | No-framebuffer mode, but X. |
| knoppix fb1280x1024 | Use fixed framebuffer graphics (1). |
| knoppix fb1024x768 | Use fixed framebuffer graphics (2). |
| knoppix fb800x600 | Use fixed framebuffer graphics (3). |

### Customizing KNOPPIX

Several boot options exist that tell KNOPPIX to run in special ways. For example, you can tell KNOPPIX to run entirely from RAM or tell it to install KNOPPIX to hard disk instead of running live. Table 21-4 describes some of these special boot options.

**TABLE 21-4**

## Special Boot Options

| Option | Result |
|---|---|
| knoppix mem=???M | Make the specified amount of memory available to KNOPPIX (for example, 128M). |
| knoppix toram | Copy the contents of the CD to RAM and run it from there. (For a live CD, you should have at least 1GB of RAM available to use toram.) |

| Option | Result |
| --- | --- |
| knoppix tohd=/dev/???? | Copy the contents of the CD to a hard disk partition and run it from there. Replace ???? with the device name, such as hda1 or sda1. The partition must be ext2 or VFAT to use this feature. |
| knoppix fromhd | Look for KNOPPIX to run on hard disk, instead of the CD. |
| knoppix fromhd=/dev/???? | Look for KNOPPIX to run from a particular partition on hard disk, instead of the CD. Replace ???? with the device name, such as hda1 or sda1. |
| knoppix bootfrom=/dev/???? | If the KNOPPIX image is on an NTFS or ReiserFS file system, use this option to boot the image from there. |
| knoppix bootfrom=/dev/????/KNX.iso | Select a particular image name to boot from, when the image exists on an NTFS or ReiserFS file system on the selected hard disk. The kernel versions on the CD and hard disk image must match. |

## Special features and workarounds

Other boot options are described in the knoppix-cheatcodes.txt file that comes on the KNOPPIX CD (open the KNOPPIX folder from the KNOPPIX icon on the desktop to find the file). Things you can do with boot options include changing the splash screen when KNOPPIX boots, running in expert mode so you can load your own drivers, testing your computer's RAM, and trying to overcome special problems with laptop computers.

- **Testing the CD**—If you suspect that you have a bad KNOPPIX CD, I recommend running this from the boot prompt:

```
knoppix testcd
```

  If you are still not able to boot KNOPPIX at this point, it might be that your hardware is either not supported or is broken in some way. To further pursue the problem, check out an appropriate forum at www.knoppix.net.

- **Running KNOPPIX from RAM**—To improve performance, KNOPPIX offers a way to run the entire KNOPPIX distribution from RAM (provided you have enough available) or install it on hard disk and run it from there. Provided that you have more than 1GB of RAM, you can run KNOPPIX entirely from RAM (so you can remove the KNOPPIX DVD or CD and use that drive while you run KNOPPIX) by typing the following from the boot prompt:

```
knoppix toram
```

- **Installing KNOPPIX to hard disk**—You can run KNOPPIX entirely from hard disk if your hard disk is either a FAT or EXT2 file system type and contains at least 800MB of space. To do this, you must know the name of the hard disk partition you are installing on. For example, to use the first partition on the first IDE drive you would use /dev/hda1. In that case, to copy KNOPPIX to that disk partition, you would type this at the boot prompt:

```
knoppix tohd=/dev/hda1
```

You can watch as KNOPPIX is copied to your hard disk partition and then boots automatically from there. The next time you want to boot KNOPPIX, you can boot it from hard disk again by inserting the KNOPPIX medium and typing the following:

```
knoppix fromhd=/dev/hda1
```

With KNOPPIX running from your hard disk, you can safely eject your CD or DVD and use the drive for other things (type **eject /dev/cdrom**). Refer to the knoppix-cheatcodes.txt file for information on other things you can do from the KNOPPIX boot prompt.

# Using KNOPPIX

LXDE is the default desktop environment that comes with KNOPPIX. You can get an earlier version of KNOPPIX if you prefer KDE or get a Gnoppix disk instead to use the GNOME environments.

Although KNOPPIX contains many of the standard applications described in other parts of the book (OpenOffice.org office suite, Web browser, e-mail, and instant messaging applications), the most fun features to try out with KNOPPIX are the 3D desktop effects. Here are some desktop tricks you can try with the latest version of KNOPPIX:

- **Wobbling windows**—Open any desktop application. Grab the title bar of the application's window and drag it across the desktop. Instead of just moving in a fixed rectangle, it turns transparent and wobbles as it moves.

- **Drag windows to other workspaces**—Continue to drag a window all the way to the left or right. As if on a cube the next available workspace will rotate into place.

- **Go to next workspace**—Hold Ctrl+Alt keys and press the right- and left-arrow keys. Your workspaces rotate to the right and left.

- **Rotate workspaces on a cube**—Hold Ctrl+Alt keys and click and hold the left mouse button. While holding down the keys and button, move the mouse around. Your workspaces move around as if on a cube in all directions. Figure 21-1 shows an example of the KNOPPIX desktop workspaces rotating on a cube.

**FIGURE 21-1**

KNOPPIX lets you spin your workspaces on a cube.

- **Exploding windows**—When you close an application's primary window, it appears to explode into dozens of little blocks. When you close a pop-up window, it explodes in flames. Figure 21-2 shows an exploding primary window.

- **Show all desktops**—Move your mouse so that the cursor is all the way to the upper-left corner of the screen. All workspaces then appear as if they were propped up on a reflecting mirror, as shown in Figure 21-3. Double-click the workspace you want to work on for it to fill the screen or move the mouse cursor to the upper-left corner again to return to your previous workspace.

**FIGURE 21-2**

Windows explode into blocks when they are closed.

- **Show all desktop applications**—If you want to return to a running desktop application, but can't remember exactly which workspace it is on, move your mouse cursor to the upper-right corner of the screen. All running desktop applications are shrunk down and displayed on a single screen. Select the one you want to go directly to that application or move the mouse cursor to the upper-right corner again to return to the current workspace. Figure 21-4 shows an example.

**FIGURE 21-3**

See all workspaces on a reflecting base.

**FIGURE 21-4**

Show all open desktop applications on one screen.

To find out more about Compiz desktop effects you can use in KNOPPIX, refer to the description of 3D effects in Chapter 3. To change Compiz effects in KNOPPIX, from the main menu in the bottom panel, select Settings ➪ CompizConfig Settings Manager. Figure 21-5 shows an example of that window:

**FIGURE 21-5**

Change desktop effects from the CompizConfig Settings Manager window.

Besides allowing you to configure desktop effects, the CompizConfig Settings Manager window also enables you to turn on accessibility features with KNOPPIX.

## Getting on the network

If you have an Ethernet card and a connection to a network that has a DHCP server, your KNOPPIX system should just start up and offer immediate access to that network (and possibly the Internet if it offers such a connection). If not, KNOPPIX lets you configure your network interfaces manually using the NetworkManager facility.

To configure NetworkManager, right-click the NetworkManager icon (it looks like two small computer displays) in the lower-right panel. Select Edit Connections. From the window that pops up you can manually configure a wired or wireless Ethernet connection, as well as other networking features. (See Chapter 11 for further information on NetworkManager.)

# Installing software in KNOPPIX

Despite the fact that KNOPPIX includes a wide range of software applications, there may be some software package you want to use with it that isn't included. To install software while you are running KNOPPIX from the DVD, you can use Synaptic.

To start Synaptic, from the main KNOPPIX menu, select System Tools ➪ Synaptic Package Manager. The Synaptic Package Manager window opens, displaying lists of installed packages. Here's what you do to install a package:

1. **Reload package list.** To see which packages are available for you to install, select the Reload button. Synaptic searches online repositories configured for KNOPPIX for available packages and loads them into the Synaptic window. New package categories and packages appear.

2. **Select package.** Choose a category on the left and any package you want from that category on the right. A description of the package appears in the lower pane. Figure 21-6 shows an example of Synaptic with the bzflag package selected.

**FIGURE 21-6**

Choose packages to install in KNOPPIX using Synaptic Package Manager.

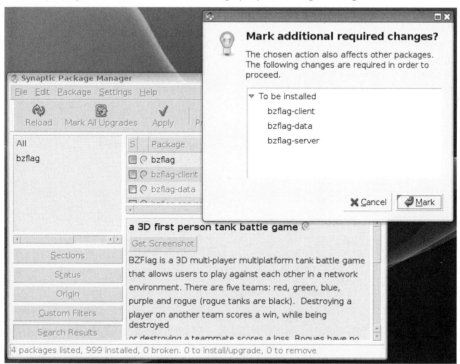

3. **Mark for install.** With the package that you want to install highlighted, select Package ⇨ Mark for Installation. If any changes to existing packages or additional packages are needed, a pop-up window alerts you. Click Mark to continue.

4. **Apply changes.** After you have selected all the new packages you want, select Apply. If the changes noted in a pop-up window are okay, select Apply again. Synaptic begins downloading and installing the selected packages.

Remember that the software is being installed in the version of KNOPPIX that is running in RAM. So, the software will disappear the next time you reboot, unless you do something to preserve your data.

# Summary

KNOPPIX offers what many feel is the best bootable Linux today. It gives you a lightweight, yet powerful Linux desktop system available virtually anywhere you can find a bootable PC.

By moving from a KDE to an LXDE desktop environment in its latest release, KNOPPIX lets you use many state-of-the-art 3D desktop effects, such as spinning workspaces on a cube. In addition to desktop features, KNOPPIX contains software for many server and troubleshooting features of Linux as well.

KNOPPIX is particularly valuable as a tool for accessing a damaged computer so that you can troubleshoot it. With a KNOPPIX disk booted on a computer that was installed to use Microsoft Windows or another operating system, you can use KNOPPIX to access and work with data on that computer's hard disk.

# Running Yellow Dog Linux

Yellow Dog Linux is a Linux distribution for Cell (Cell/BE) and PowerPC (PPC) platforms. Offered by Fixstars Corporation (www .fixstars.com/en/products/ydel), Yellow Dog Linux runs on older Mac machines (G4/G5) as well as cool gaming systems and machines with PowerPC architectures (such as PlayStation 3 and IBM QS2x systems).

Unlike other Linux distributions that aim primarily for the Intel/AMD (x86) platform, Yellow Dog Linux focuses on the world of PowerPCs. Although it's not the only Linux distribution that provides PowerPC versions of their releases (Fedora and Ubuntu have dedicated PowerPC developers, as well), Yellow Dog has always been a leader in that area.

Terra Soft Solutions originally produced Yellow Dog as a port of Red Hat Linux for Mac PowerPC users, and Yellow Dog's new owner (Fixstars Corporation, headquartered in Tokyo, Japan) has expanded its offerings into the Enterprise. Yellow Dog Enterprise Linux runs on IBM ZS2x Cell blades and Sony ZEGO BCU-100 systems. Fixstars Corporation has also moved Yellow Dog's porting base to the CentOS Linux system, so it can rely on source code that was first built by Red Hat, Inc. for enterprise applications.

This chapter introduces you to Yellow Dog Linux and explains how it is moving forward to cater not only to those who love Apple's older PowerPC hardware and are drawn to Linux, but also to those wanting an enterprise-quality PowerPC-based Linux operating system.

Yellow Dog Linux is not included on the CD or DVD that come with this book. You can purchase Yellow Dog Linux from Fixstars Corporation or download the current installation DVD or set of CDs from a Yellow Dog Linux mirror site:

```
http://us.fixstars.com/support/downloads
```

Check the OVERVIEW file from a mirror directory to help you choose which ISO images to download. See Appendix A for information on burning DVD and CD ISO images.

# Understanding Yellow Dog Linux

Terra Soft Solutions, which originally created Yellow Dog Linux, focused its efforts on making Yellow Dog Linux work for a wide range of Apple products. This focus resulted in less chance of hardware incompatibilities, which became one of the distribution's strengths. As an Apple Authorized OEM Value Added Reseller, Terra Soft Solutions had permission from Apple to install Linux on Apple hardware, retaining any hardware warranties provided by Apple.

## Note

**The latest Apple hardware uses x86 chips in the form of Intel's Core Duo processors. Although not its original mission, Yellow Dog Linux is also now available for x86 platforms as well. See the section "Going Forward with Yellow Dog" for more information. ■**

In 2008, Fixstars purchased Terra Soft Solutions. Terra Soft's CEO, Kai Staats, became COO of the Fixstars subsidiary Fixstars Solutions, where he continues to work on Yellow Dog Linux. With the popularity of PowerPC architecture computers in enterprise computing, Fixstars has gone forward on the natural move toward development on those architectures with the Yellow Dog Enterprise Linux distribution.

A few different versions of Yellow Dog Linux are currently available:

- **Yellow Dog Linux 6.2**—Released in June, 2009, this version of Yellow Dog Linux supports Apple PowerPC (G4/G5), Sony Playstation 3, and YDL PowerStation hardware. Yellow Dog Linux kernels run on PPC64 (2.6.29 kernel) and PPC32 (2.6.27) platforms. On the desktop, Yellow Dog added the Xfce 4 Desktop Environment (GNOME, KDE, and Enlightenment are already available) and many applications, such as the OpenOffice.org 3.0 office suite and Firefox 3.0.6 browser. With YDL.net, you get access to private software repositories, support features, a secure webmail account, and a personal calendar and blog.

- **Yellow Dog Enterprise Linux**—Based on CentOS Linux, Yellow Dog Enterprise Linux (YDEL) aims at enterprise customers. YDEL can be installed on IBM QS2x Cell blade and Sony ZEGO BCU-100 computers. It is designed to install quickly on entire blade centers, with low-cost yearly support contracts.

- **Yellow Dog Linux 6.1**—Besides providing support for PlayStation 3, Apple G4 and G5, IBM 510, 520, and 540, and JS20 and 21 computers, this product offers access to the YDL.net site. This and earlier versions of Yellow Dog Linux are not officially supported by Fixstars. However, you can still download ISO images of that software from Fixstars.

- **Yellow Dog Linux 6.0 DVD for Sony PlayStation 3**—This version of Yellow Dog Linux came with a printed guide for the Sony PS3, a Yellow Dog Linux sticker, and optional six months of installation support. Today it is still available for download.

●   **Yellow Dog Linux 6.0 DVD for Apple PowerPC and IBM System p**—An install DVD and source DVD comes with this Yellow Dog Linux package. The printed guide describes how to install Yellow Dog on Apple PowerPC (G4 and G5) and IBM System p. Online guides cover how to install on OpenPower, 510/520/540 systems, and JS20/21 systems. Optional six-month support contracts are available.

# Going Forward with Yellow Dog

Despite the fact that Apple has moved its product line from the PowerPC to the x86 (standard PC) architecture, Fixstars continues developing Yellow Dog Linux for the Power architecture. Although its new subsidiary Fixstars Solutions remains a top-tier value-added partner of Apple's, it also sells pre-installed Linux systems on hardware from other manufacturers.

Simply put, Yellow Dog's mission is to support the latest Power architecture systems, such as the Sony PlayStation 3, Cell-based and high-end PowerPC systems from vendors such as IBM and Mercury Computer, and to continue to deliver PowerPC-focused Linux for the 10 or 20 million people like myself who have PowerPC-based Macs but want to take advantage of the power of Linux on those systems.

For high-end server systems, Fixstars offers its operating systems on IBM 970 BladeCenter 42U rack servers and Mercury Computer XR9 64-bit extended ATX 1U and 4U rack servers. A cluster management software suite is also available, so you can centrally manage multiple Power-based Y-HPC servers.

On the workstation end, for many people Yellow Dog Linux is still the preferred Linux distribution for the Sony PlayStation 3. After having worked closely with Sony to ensure complete support and interoperability, Terra Soft delivered Yellow Dog Linux 5.0 for the PS3 at the end of November 2006, and now offers version 6.2 through Fixstars.

The bottom line here is that you can expect Yellow Dog Linux to continue with its support for Power architecture both on server and desktop systems. So, Apple users who love their PowerPCs can find a way to continue using that hardware by moving over to a Yellow Dog Linux system. Also, because of the Power architecture's support for multimedia hardware and Yellow Dog's inclusion of software for playing a variety of audio and video content, the combination adds a bit of sparkle to the standard Linux desktop systems that are around today.

With Yellow Dog Linux being acquired by Fixstars, which has a large, dedicated team of Cell processor developers, you can expect Yellow Dog Linux development to continue to move toward features that support enterprise customers.

# Digging into Yellow Dog

Yellow Dog Linux offers a CentOS, RPM-based distribution that is compatible with most available open source software. By basing the Yellow Dog distribution on a widely deployed and used x86 distribution such as CentOS (which is based on Red Hat Enterprise Linux), YDL developers have been able to quickly deploy a very uniform, user-friendly experience for its user base. This section takes a look at some of the highlights of the Yellow Dog distribution.

## Note

This chapter focuses on Yellow Dog 6.2, which was released in June, 2009 on DVD. Besides being a commercial product, it is also freely available for download. Earlier versions of Yellow Dog Linux are available on a four-CD set. So if you have a pre-Intel Mac, you can use those CDs to install older versions of Yellow Dog. ∎

Yellow Dog Linux 6.2 offers software on DVD with the following applications and components:

- 2.6.29 Linux kernel

- X Window System server (X.Org 1.4)

- KDE 3.5.4 desktop (unified with GNOME to provide easy access to programs from either desktop environment)

- GNOME 2.16 desktop (again, unified with KDE to provide easy access to programs from either desktop environment)

- Xfce 4.4 desktop (a lightweight desktop environment that runs well on low-CPU, low-RAM computers)

- OpenOffice 3.0 (suite of productivity tools including a spreadsheet program, drawing program, presentation software, and a full-featured, Microsoft Word–compatible word processor)

- More than 1,300 other application packages from programming tools to Web browsers

The wide range of applications included on the Yellow Dog DVD is enough to keep even the most computer-savvy person happy, but many more choices are available on the Internet, so you should be able to find an application that fits your needs.

As a derivative of CentOS, Yellow Dog Linux can offer the advantages of the features of the aforementioned Linux systems on a PowerPC platform, including:

- **Red Hat Package Manager (RPM) software**—Starting with software packages from the Fedora project helps Yellow Dog Linux avoid compatibility problems suffered by some Linux distributions. Users can also rely on well-known RPM packaging tools for adding, removing, and managing software.

- **Extended Packages for Enterprise (EPEL) repositories**—Many software packages in Fedora that are not produced directly for Red Hat Enterprise Linux (RHEL) are built and made available for RHEL distributions. As a derivative of RHEL systems, Yellow Dog Linux can also be configured to include EPEL repositories to use the yum facility to grab packages.

- **anaconda installer**—Yellow Dog takes advantage of the well-tested anaconda installer for easy installation.

- **HAL hardware daemon**—The Hardware Abstraction Layer (HAL) daemon collects and maintains information about your computer hardware, which allows such features as plugging in a USB printer, Webcam, or flash memory stick and having HAL pass information about that device to the operating system so an application can be launched to handle the device (such as a video application or a file manager window).

## Cross-Reference

Refer to Chapter 18 for more information on Fedora and some of the specifics regarding its implementation. ∎

# Installing Yellow Dog Linux

The first and most recommended avenue for acquiring Yellow Dog Linux is to purchase it from the vendor. You benefit because you both acquire the distribution from the source as well as support the company that creates Yellow Dog Linux so it can continue development for the PowerPC platform. Alternatively, you can get a copy from a Yellow Dog Linux mirror site.

## Note

Yellow Dog Linux makes its distribution freely available and downloadable from its mirror sites. At the time of this writing, version 6.2 is both commercially available and freely available as ISO images you can download and burn. Check the Fixstars downloads page for a mirror site (`http://us.fixstars.com/support/downloads`). ∎

To purchase Yellow Dog Linux from Fixstars, visit the Fixstars Web store at `http://us.fixstars.com/store/`. When purchasing Yellow Dog Linux, you receive the following in a box set:

- Install and source DVDs.

- *Getting Started with Yellow Dog Linux,* a book that covers all the information a beginning Linux user would need to know to get a fully operational Yellow Dog Linux system running.

- Optional 60 days of installation support (you can purchase the box set with or without support, depending on your needs and skill level with Linux).

- Other goodies (sticker, flexible flier cloth flying disc, depending on package purchased).

- The knowledge that you are supporting the company that created the product, allowing further development.

Alternatives to purchasing the Yellow Dog Linux box set include:

- **Purchasing a subscription to YDL.net**—This is an online resource for Yellow Dog Linux users. You can get e-mail accounts and Web space as well as prerelease access to the latest version of Yellow Dog Linux before it is available for general release. The costs vary depending on which version you choose. More information is available at www.ydl.net.

- **Downloading and creating your own ISO**—Refer to this page for instructions on downloading and burning your own Yellow Dog Linux ISO image: http://us.fixstars.com/support/downloads.

- **Run from USB drive**—Yellow Dog Linux can be installed and run from a USB thumb drive. With Yellow Dog Linux on a USB drive, you can safely boot and run Yellow Dog without disturbing the contents of your PlayStation 3 gaming system or other hardware.

- **Purchasing online**—If you have a slow Internet connection and want to try Yellow Dog, you can purchase burned CDs or DVDs (depending on the release of Yellow Dog that you want to run) from various Linux stores on the Internet. Use your favorite search engine to locate one near you.

Links to guides for installing different Yellow Dog Linux versions are available from the Download page (http://us.fixstars.com/support/downloads).

## Hardware support

Hardware support with the Linux operating system was a major issue in the past, but as Linux's popularity has grown, many device makers have provided access to their hardware drivers or in some cases have created hardware drivers for Linux.

Although hardware support is still an issue with hardware that is brand new in the x86 community, the effects are lessened with the PowerPC platform because all hardware is generally created to Apple's exacting standards. Fixstars Solutions' focus on Apple hardware and generally fewer variations in hardware add up to support being much faster for the PowerPC platform.

One of the great things about Yellow Dog Linux is that as you dig into it, you discover that some of the hardware compatibility issues faced by the x86 Linux crowd (such as with Winmodems, the plethora of hardware configuration options, and so forth) are minimized or eliminated. With Fixstars Solutions, a fully authorized Apple Value Added Reseller, you are assured that the hardware you are using will be supported.

In addition to being able to install Yellow Dog Linux on your own PowerPC hardware, you can purchase PowerPC hardware from Fixstars Solutions with Yellow Dog Linux preinstalled.

Fixstars Solutions has a list of supported hardware for Yellow Dog Linux (http://us.fixstars.com/support/hardware). With Yellow Dog Linux 6.2, official support for many older hardware configurations has been dropped. Officially supported hardware includes:

- Fixstars' GigaAccel 180 IBM PXCAB (Requires Yellow Dog Enterprise Linux BSP)
- Fixstars' YDL PowerStation
- Sony PlayStation 3

- Sony ZEGO BCU-100 (Cell and RSX are fully supported)
- IBM JS2x, IBM QSx, IBM Power
- Mercury Cell
- Apple Power Mac G4 (Power Mac G4 PCI 350–400 MHz G4 and above)
- Apple Power Mac G5 (1.6 GHz G5 and above)
- Apple Xserve (G4 and G5)
- Apple iMac (Rev A,B 233 MHz G3), eMac G4, and iMac G5
- Apple iBook (800 MHz 1.2 GHz G4)

## Note

You can use earlier versions of Yellow Dog for older computers. For older computers, Yellow Dog 5.0.2 should run on any PPC-based Mac system released before January, 2006, with the exception of Old World ROM or beige G3 and earlier hardware such as 8500s, 7200s, and Performa PowerPCs. YDL 3.0.1 supports this older hardware and much of the hardware currently supported by Yellow Dog Linux 4.1 (certainly anything that was manufactured by Apple before September, 2003, which is when 3.0.1 was released). The hardware supported and tested for Yellow Dog Linux 3.0.1 includes Power Mac 4400–9600, Power Mac beige G3 models and blue-and-white G3 models, and most hardware supported by Yellow Dog Linux 4.0 and 4.0.1.

If you have older PPC hardware that isn't officially supported, you should still be able to use Yellow Dog Linux 4.1, but you'll be running in an unsupported configuration, so *caveat emptor*. Fixstars Solutions dropped support for many older hardware configurations so that it could focus on the most likely configurations. Also, trying to support outdated computer architectures, which on the Old World ROM systems were particularly troublesome, doesn't offer much return for a commercial Linux venture. ■

Descriptions in the rest of this section focus on Yellow Dog Linux installation on the Fixstars YDL PowerStation:

```
http://us.fixstars.com/support/hardware/powerstation.shtml
```

## Installing Yellow Dog Linux on a PowerStation

To boot the PowerStation, Yellow Dog Linux installs the Yet Another Bootloader (yaboot) boot loader. To begin, you must get the latest Yellow Dog Linux installation DVD, as described earlier in this chapter. With that in hand, and your PowerStation in front of you, here's how to proceed:

1. **Insert the Yellow Dog Linux DVD into your computer.**
2. **Reboot.**
3. **Press s as instructed to enter Open Firmware.**
4. **At the firmware prompt, type**

   ```
   boot cdrom
   ```

   The yaboot prompt appears.

5. **Boot the install process.** Type the following to begin the install process:

```
install-ppc64
```

6. **Select your Language and keyboard, as prompted.** The Partition screen appears, as shown in Figure 22-1.

---

**FIGURE 22-1**

Partition your disk during Yellow Dog installation.

The partition screen is derived from the same screen used in CentOS, Fedora, and Red Hat Enterprise Linux systems to partition disks, so you can use the descriptions in the Fedora chapter (Chapter 18) or installation chapter (Chapter 8) if you have questions about partitioning your disks.

You are asked to configure networking.

7. **Set up Networking.** Configure your Ethernet port (eth0 or eth1) to connect to your LAN or Internet hardware. The first port (eth0) is labeled Port 2 on the PowerStation and will be enabled automatically to detect and start up from a DHCP server, if one is available. Port 1 (eth1) is not enabled by default.

8. **Set root password.** Enter the password for your root user (at least eight characters).

## Caution
**It is critical that you remember this password and don't share it with anyone you don't trust to have full access to your computer.** ■

9. **Select packages.** Choose to install the pre-set groups of packages or select to customize the packages installed on your computer. Fixstars has a list of packages at its Web site: `http://us.fixstars.com/products/ydl/apps.shtml`. When you have selected packages you want, the installer takes several minutes to check for dependencies.

10. **Begin installing.** Click Next to begin installing packages to the hard disk. This process should take a half hour or more to complete, depending on how many packages you selected and the speed of your hardware.

11. **Reboot.** When installation is complete, eject the DVD and reboot the computer.

As with Fedora, Red Hat Enterprise Linux, and related Linux distributions, the first time you boot your Yellow Dog Linux system, the Firstboot screen appears. Firstboot, which runs only this one time after installation, lets you agree to the licensing, set date and time, configure your display, create a regular user account, and set up your sound card.

After you complete Firstboot, the graphical login screen appears, ready for you to log in and start using Yellow Dog Linux.

# Updating Yellow Dog Linux

The Yellow Dog Updated, Modified tool (yum) is included with Yellow Dog and ships with Fedora, Mandriva, and other Linux distributions as well. It's a utility that enables you to update your system packages to the latest available version. Because new security vulnerabilities are released on all operating systems frequently, updating your system packages regularly is essential.

Updating your packages also gives you the newest features available for the applications you are using. Table 22-1 shows some of the most widely used options available with yum (replace *package* with the name of your package).

**TABLE 22-1**

## Using yum to Work with Software Packages

| Option | Description |
|---|---|
| yum list | Shows all the packages available to be installed (but not installed). |
| yum list installed | Shows installed packages. |
| yum list updates | Shows all installed packages that have updates (patches) available. |
| yum install *package* | Installs the package you identify in *package*. |
| yum update *package* | Updates the package you identify in *package*. The great thing about this option is it installs all package dependencies, which used to be a major headache when administering patches. |
| yum update | Updates all packages on the system. (Same as preceding option but does not specify package name.) |
| yum remove *package* | Removes the package identified in *package*. |
| yum info *package* | Provides detailed information on the package identified in *package*. |

Using this information, assume that you want to run gimp—GNU Image Manipulation Project (GIMP) is a very popular graphics editing program—and you haven't installed it previously. If you want to get more information on it, run the following:

```
# yum info gimp
```

If you decide you want to install it, run the following:

```
# yum install gimp
```

If an update becomes available a week later and you want to patch it, run the following:

```
# yum update gimp
```

If it has been a month and you decide you no longer need gimp, you can remove it with the following:

```
# yum remove gimp
```

yum makes updating packages very easy and you should use it regularly to keep your system updated with the latest patches (you can even run it from a cron job for true automation).

# Support Options

If you run into problems using or installing Yellow Dog Linux, you can obtain support in many ways. The Linux community is very supportive, proffering numerous Web pages available to assist the newcomer. If you encounter problems with hardware, try one of the following options:

- **Yellow Dog Community Board**—Another free support option that is run by Yellow Dog Linux enthusiasts. It is available at `http://yellowdog-board.com/`.

- **Yellow Dog Mail Lists**—If your questions don't get answered through the preceding sites, you can subscribe to some of the numerous Yellow Dog mailing lists where you can ask your questions. Directions for use are at `http://lists.fixstars.com/mailman/listinfo`.

- **Yellow Dog Linux User Channel**—If you are comfortable with IRC (Internet Relay Chat), you can use `irc.freenode.net` and join #yellowdog for community-driven interactive support.

- **Yellow Dog Official Support**—Information on installation support for Yellow Dog Linux is available from Fixstars: `http://us.fixstars.com/support/installation`. Fixstars also has paid support options you can refer to at `http://us.fixstars.com/services/quote-request.shtml`.

# Summary

Yellow Dog Linux is a stable, fully functioning distribution, based on CentOS that is available on the PowerPC and Cell/BE platforms. It has the capability to extend the life of your PowerPC Mac hardware and to run on enterprise-quality IBM QS2x BladeCenter products.

Linux is not just tied to x86 computers. Yellow Dog Linux enables PowerPC users to use Linux through multi-booting, while still enjoying their Mac OS or Mac OS X environment when needed.

Apple's move from the PowerPC to the x86 architecture has made Linux an even more attractive proposition for existing PowerPC systems. Although Mac OS X itself is based on a free version of Linux (a FreeBSD derivative called Darwin), running Linux on your PPC Mac software is the easiest way to guarantee that you'll always be able to run the latest and greatest open source software on your PowerPC Macintosh hardware.

Besides offering Yellow Dog Linux for older Mac (G4/G5) systems, Fixstars Solutions (formerly Terra Soft Solutions) also delivers Linux on newer Power Architecture systems (most notably the Sony PlayStation 3) and systems using Cell processors. Fixstars also provides Linux for various high-performance rack-mounted computers and continues to support Linux for Macintosh systems and other PPC workstations (such as the YDL PowerStation) with a focus on strong multimedia support and high-quality graphics.

# Running Gentoo Linux

Several years ago, Gentoo (www.gentoo.org) was the rising star of Linux distributions among Linux enthusiasts. Of all the popular Linux distributions, this is the first one I would recommend to a technically oriented friend who wanted to tune his own Linux system to the $n$th degree, and the last one I'd recommend to my wife ("Just show me what button to click for my e-mail."). That's because to install and maintain Gentoo effectively, you have to care (to an almost unnatural extent) about what is going on with your computer.

Gentoo is named after the gentoo penguin, believed to be the fastest under-water swimmers of all penguin species. So Gentoo Linux gives a nod both to the Linux mascot (a penguin named Tux) and to the distribution's own goals to provide tools to create a fast and efficient operating system. (To pronounce Gentoo, use the $G$ sound as you would in the word *gentle*.)

This chapter describes why you might want to use Gentoo, what the Gentoo community is like, and how to get and install Gentoo Linux.

## On the DVD

The Gentoo live/install CD is included on the DVD that comes with this book. You can use this Gentoo CD as described in Appendix A. The Gentoo live/install CD image lets you run, and then install, a solid, basic desktop system. You will need an Internet con-nection or some medium containing the needed Gentoo packages (CD, DVD, or hard disk) to get additional packages for your Gentoo installation. ■

# Understanding Gentoo

Performance and efficiency were the critical goals that led to the creation of the Gentoo Linux distribution. A dedication to the spirit of open source software (and to those drawn to it) was vital to Gentoo's early rapid and incredible growth.

In the few years it has been in existence, Gentoo has grown from having one maintainer—its creator, Daniel Robbins—to having about 250 active developers. Although Robbins has moved on to other endeavors, Gentoo still boasts one of the strongest user communities among all Linux distributions. Gentoo users seem willing to contribute so freely because they feel that they get back what they give to Gentoo.

The Portage software distribution management system is the key technology that separates Gentoo from other Linux distributions. Based on the BSD Ports system, Portage can be used to build almost the entire Gentoo distribution from source code, and manage and upgrade that software as well.

## Gentoo's open source spirit

Although Gentoo could some day produce a commercial Linux distribution, the Gentoo project is committed to the goals of open source software, while still allowing those who use the software to make money. Ways that those goals are reflected in Gentoo—and not in some other distributions—include

- **Passing bug fixes upstream**—Software bugs in open source projects are often shaken out when actual Linux distributions are put together. When a distribution finds a bug, it is considered good practice to pass the fix to that bug upstream, to the project maintaining the original software.

  Not passing bug fixes upstream could potentially give a commercial Linux distribution an advantage over other distributions that don't have the fix. There have been many cases where fixes in some distributions have not made it to the upstream projects. Gentoo, on the other hand, has a reputation for sharing bug fixes with the open source community.

- **Transparent development process**—Not only is the open source software made available to everyone, but the tools for building that software are also freely distributed. Gentoo users can see exactly what their software contains, along with all the decisions made to build that software. It is also a fairly simple procedure for users in the process of building their own Gentoo software to change any of those build decisions.

- **Choices for creating Gentoo**—You can build your own Gentoo Linux from the source code pages or start from prebuilt binary packages provided by the Gentoo project. Freedom, in the Gentoo philosophy, means letting users create the kind of Linux system they want. So, if users don't want to make decisions about how their packages are built, they can simply take ready-made packages from the Gentoo project.

- **Thousands of packages**—The Gentoo software repository contains more than 10,000 packages. The upside to this is that you have an incredibly diverse set of software to choose from in every major software category. The downside is that not every package gets the same care that you might expect from a distribution that offers a smaller number of packages. Those who build their own Gentoo systems are expected to have some expertise fixing software build problems themselves.

- **Not-for-profit organization**—When the Linux distribution is dedicated to the community and not beholden to stockholders, open source enthusiasts often feel better about freely contributing to improving that distribution. Gentoo is a not-for-profit organization.

This open source spirit has also helped Gentoo gain a community that is extraordinarily active and helpful to one another.

## The Gentoo community

The open source spirit of Gentoo pervades its community. The size and activity of that community is best reflected in its forums (http://forums.gentoo.org), in which there are literally hundreds (and sometimes thousands) of new posts per day. If there's something about Gentoo you can't find using Google, try searching the Gentoo forums.

To get a sense of the activity levels on the forums, check out the board statistics (http://forums.gentoo.org/statistics.php). You can see how many posts, topics, and users there are in the forums per day. You can also see, and visit, the most active topics in the forums.

Many Gentoo enthusiasts seem to live on the forums. Although most of the posts stick closely to Linux, nobody seems to blink an eye when someone posts questions about the existence of God or what to do when a guy's wife has left him. At times, the forums have the distinct feel of a coffeehouse.

It never hurts to start with the Frequently Asked Questions (FAQ) forums. However, I think most will want to start with the Installing Gentoo forum (because it's quite possible to get hung up on installation when you first try installing it). If you are interested in live communications about Gentoo, try the Gentoo IRC #gentoo channel at irc.freenode.net (you can use xchat in most Linux systems to access IRC channels). Another good starting forum is the Documentation, Tips, & Tricks forum, where you can find cool little tricks to tweak your system.

## Building, tuning, and tweaking Linux

Gentoo is sometimes referred to as the build-from-source Linux system. Most other Linux distributions give you a set of prebuilt packages to install and never expect you to build the whole system yourself. Although you can get Gentoo with packages prebuilt for you, the distribution was made for you to be able to build the Linux kernel and all packages right on the machine where you will install it.

When you install from prebuilt binary software packages, which is expected with Gentoo and most other Linux distributions, many decisions have already been made for you about what each package includes and what it is tuned for. For a first-time user, the Gentoo project has made a first installation easy by including an installer that you can launch right from the desktop of the Gentoo live CD (which is included on the DVD that comes with this book).

By building a Gentoo distribution from source code, however, you can create a distribution that specifically takes into account the following about your situation:

- **What processor you are running**—Most distributions choose a particular architecture (such as x86, PowerPC, or Sparc) and a generic selection of settings for using the processor. With Gentoo, however, you can choose the exact type of processor you're using and compile all software to take advantage of features from that processor (while not including features specific to other processors).

- **What hardware you might have**—Most distributions install tons of modules to support hardware that you might some day add (it loads them as you need them into the kernel). It also builds a kernel for you that includes support for features that it believes you do need (for example, some distributions include ext3 file system support, expecting that to be your basic file system type, but may not have reiserfs file system support built into the kernel). With Gentoo, you can choose exactly which features are in the kernel to support only the hardware you know you have. Likewise, you can get and install drivers for hardware not connected to your computer if you expect to install that hardware later.

- **What services you want**—Some Linux distributions suffer performance problems because they have processes taking up memory for services that you don't necessarily want (such as daemons for Web, file, print, and other server types). With Gentoo, you can be selective down to the most minute detail about the services that are installed and running on Gentoo (including the order in which they are started).

- **What software is available**—Linux distributions such as Red Hat Enterprise Linux offer a preset selection of software packages that are well-tested and integrated into a set of CDs or DVDs. Gentoo has a massive repository of software packages from which you can choose the exact packages you need. Each package carries its own set of dependencies with it as well, so you don't have to add every library or utility to your system to support software you might want some day. With an Internet connection and Gentoo's emerge tool, you can always add software you need, when you need it.

- **What features are available**—Because in Gentoo you are making decisions about what software you use at compile time, you can select to turn on or off optional features within each software component. For example, if you are building an e-mail client, you can choose whether the package you build will include support for LDAP address books. In theory, removing support for unneeded features makes the software you end up with run faster and use less memory. However, if you need the support at a later date, you will need to recompile the application (and possibly others that depend on it).

The features just described help characterize the type of person who is attracted to Gentoo. Gentoo enthusiasts like to configure, tune, tweak, and update their Linux systems continuously, and Gentoo users generally end up with systems that run faster, take up less disk space, and run in less memory than would be the case with any other Linux that you get off the shelf.

## Where Gentoo is used

As you may have guessed by now, Gentoo is most popular with Linux enthusiasts as their personal Linux systems. Among Gentoo users you find those who like to tinker with desktops and run servers where performance is critical (such as game servers). Because Gentoo can be so easily configured and tuned, users can make very efficient Linux desktop and server systems that include only the software needed for the particular job.

Given its slant toward personal use, there is a lot of interest in Gentoo forums for configuring desktops, configuring multimedia applications, and getting popular games running. There are also significant discussions on securing Gentoo because most of its security tools don't come with friendly, graphical interfaces and require a lot of manual setup.

Despite the fact that you can use Gentoo to create an extraordinarily efficient, finely tuned Linux desktop or server, the distribution is not yet widely accepted in business or educational institutions. There are probably several reasons for that:

- **Stability**—To stay on the bleeding edge of the latest Linux software, Gentoo sacrifices the level of stability demanded by most businesses.
- **Support**—No official support packages are offered with Gentoo, so if something goes wrong, no official help is available (although the forums can be quite helpful).
- **Training**—If you are setting up many machines, the people who use those machines will need training. Unlike Red Hat Enterprise Linux or SUSE Linux Enterprise, you can't get official training from Gentoo's developers.

## Note
People I know who use Gentoo on their personal computers tend to use Ubuntu, Debian, or Fedora for small Web, file, or print servers when they do consulting work, and Red Hat Enterprise Linux or SUSE Linux Enterprise for larger enterprise installations. ■

So far, the factors just mentioned have kept Gentoo from making any significant inroads into enterprise computing. However, as a learning tool and a personal Linux distribution, Gentoo is hard to beat.

# What's in Gentoo

No two Gentoo systems are alike because you can select and build only the pieces of Linux you want to use. In late 2009, more than 10,000 software packages were available for the project, and the list was growing.

Unlike distributions such as Red Hat Enterprise Linux and SUSE Enterprise Linux, Gentoo tends to not force its own look-and-feel on the projects it includes. Each software package ported to a Gentoo system gives the user a view of the included open source software packages as they were intended from the individual projects. For example, a KDE desktop will look like a KDE desktop as it was delivered from the KDE project itself; there are no "Gentoo-ized" menus and icons or graphical administration tools to alter it.

Gentoo's focus on tools for managing and building source code has helped make Gentoo extraordinarily portable. Besides the common Intel x86 (PC) version of Gentoo, packaged versions of Gentoo ports exist for HP Alpha, AMD64, HPPA, iA64, PowerPC, PowerPC64, and Sparc 64 computer architectures. Available, but unsupported architectures include ARM, MIPS, and s390. Optimized Linux kernels are also available with Gentoo for different specific processors within each architecture. Still, some of the ports are works in progress, so for the time being you will probably get the best experience using an x86 platform to run Gentoo.

To explore Gentoo, starting with the tools for getting what you want is more appropriate than talking about what you end up with. If you build Gentoo tuned to your hardware and include just the software that you need, your system isn't going to look like any other Gentoo system.

## Managing software with Portage

At the heart of Gentoo is the Portage software management system. Based on the FreeBSD Ports system, Portage enables you to find, download, configure, build, and install the exact software you choose.

Using the Portage system can give you some excellent insights into how Linux is created. As Daniel Robbins said, " ...we are documenting how to build a Linux system at the same time we are moving Gentoo Linux development forward."

Those developing software are encouraged not only to contribute their software to the Gentoo project but also to contribute the scripts they use to build that software. Portage tools and build scripts open up Linux technology beginning at the source-code level.

Key components of the Portage package management system include the `emerge` command and the package build scripts (contained in the `/usr/portage` directory). You can use these tools to build the entire Gentoo distribution from scratch, or rely on some prebuilt binaries to save some compile time. In most cases, you won't have to modify any configuration files to get a solid Gentoo installation.

For examples of how to use the `emerge` command with Gentoo, refer to the section "Getting Software with emerge" later in this chapter.

## Finding software packages

Part of the Gentoo installation process includes installing the Portage directory tree in the `/usr/portage` directory. You can step around that directory to see the packages that are available. As I mentioned earlier, several thousand are available.

Most software packages fall into the following major categories:

- **app**—Applications software package subcategories, such as editors, antivirus software, administrative tools, accessibility tools, CD writing applications, and many other subcategories have packages under the app category.
- **dev**—A wide variety of development tools.
- **games**—Dozens of board, arcade, first-person-shooter, puzzle, and strategy games, and games servers fall into subcategories of games.
- **gnome**—Packages for the GNOME desktop environment are contained in base and extra subcategories.
- **kde**—Packages for the KDE desktop environment are contained in base and misc subcategories.
- **mail**—Mail servers, clients, and filters software packages.
- **media**—A variety of audio, video, and other multimedia tools.
- **net**—Communications, server, firewall, and other network tools.
- **sci**—Astronomy, biology, chemistry, electronics, physics, and other scientific tools.
- **sys**—System configuration tools.
- **www**—Web communications servers and related software packages.
- **x11**—Miscellaneous tools for the X Window System graphical interface, along with related themes and window managers.
- **xfce**—Packages for the XFCE desktop environment are in base and extra subcategories.

Simply step through the /usr/portage directory structure to see the software packages you can install, information about how each is built, and patches that are available.

## Gentoo features

To showcase Gentoo, the official live CD from the Gentoo project features an Xfce desktop, instead of KDE or GNOME. Using the lightweight Xfce desktop allowed more space for applications than you would get by adding KDE and GNOME software to a live CD.

An icon on the Gentoo Xfce live CD's desktop lets you install the contents of the live CD to hard disk without needing access to the Internet. After the Xfce desktop system is installed, you can add a GNOME desktop, KDE desktop, or other software using ebuild tree on the live CD.

Improvements to the Gentoo installer represent another major area of change in the latest version of Gentoo. No network connection is required to do your initial install because all the software you need to get started with a basic desktop is on the live CD. However, with a network install CD, you won't get more than a minimal system without a network connection. Partitioning has been simplified and a Quickstart install has been added to do automated installations.

Many drivers were added to Gentoo in recent releases. Many of those come with the kernel update to release 2.6.24. The C language compiler (gcc) and associated libraries (glibc) have been updated to 4.12 and 2.6.1, respectively. The release of Portage is 2.1.4.4. Then, of course, there is the continuing development of the 10,000 software packages in the Gentoo Portage tree that is reflected in the latest release of Gentoo.

# Installing Gentoo

A traditional Gentoo installation is more like building your own Linux than it is like typical Linux installs. However, improvements to the Gentoo installer, including the ability to install directly from the Gentoo live CD, makes installing Gentoo a much easier proposition for the first-time Gentoo user.

Two different Gentoo installation procedures are included in this chapter:

- **Live CD Install**—Using the Gentoo live CD included on the DVD that comes with this book, you can boot to a live Gentoo system. Then, by opening an icon on the desktop, you can begin the process of installing Gentoo on your hard disk with a basic, pre-set desktop system. If you are new to Gentoo, you should use this install type.

- **Minimal CD Install**—If you prefer a more tuned and selective Gentoo install, download and burn a Gentoo minimal install CD from the Gentoo site (`www.gentoo.org/main/en/where.xml`). To get a useful system from this procedure, you need an Internet connection to your computer. The minimal CD install is really only for those who are comfortable working from the command line and have a lot of time and a fast Internet connection.

## Getting Gentoo

The Gentoo Linux distribution is available in several different forms. The live CD install is the easiest to do and is the one that is included with this book. However, you might want to look into more customizable install types as well. Regardless of your initial install, however, you still have the opportunity to add and remove software as you please.

If you are new to Gentoo, I recommend you try the live CD install procedure described next. If you are more experienced with Linux or you want to learn more about the detailed features that go into an installation, use the Minimal/Universal install described later.

### Live CD install

You can use the Gentoo live CD, included on this book's DVD, to install a basic desktop system. This CD is for x86 computer architectures. If you are installing for a different architecture, you can find other live/install CDs from the "Where to Get Gentoo Linux" page (`www.gentoo.org/main/en/where.xml`). Then follow the procedures in the "Starting Gentoo installation from a live CD" section later in this chapter.

### Minimal/Universal install CD

To provide the full feel of installing Gentoo, you could begin with as little as a minimal disk image. From a minimal install disk, you can download and compile most of the software you need (including the kernel itself). To do this procedure, you need a broadband Internet connection (no dial-up). For architectures other than i686 and AMD64, there are also Universal and Package Gentoo CDs that you can use without having a live Internet connection.

For the minimal install, begin with the following CD image: `install-x86-minimal-YYYYM-MDD.iso`, where YYYYMMDD are replaced by the year, month and day of the current build. This bootable minimal install CD image (80MB) includes just enough software to begin the install procedure. You can find this image in any Gentoo mirror site (in the `releases/x86/auto-builds/current-iso` directory).

If you have computers that have non-x86 or AMD64 architectures, I recommend that you get the Universal CD for your particular architecture. The Universal Install CD (`install-*-universal-*.iso`) is a bootable install CD image, containing enough software to enable you to have a working Gentoo system without going on the Internet. Look for the Universal Install CD link on the "Where to Get Gentoo Linux" page for your architecture (`www.gentoo.org/main/en/where.xml`).

The Universal CD enables you to do a complete Gentoo install without requiring that you access the Internet. You can download the disk images from Gentoo mirror sites (refer to `www.gentoo.org/main/en/mirrors.xml` for the locations of these sites).

For a more detailed description of the Gentoo install process, refer to the *Gentoo Linux x86 Quick Install Guide* and the larger, more general *Gentoo Linux Handbook*. Look for these documents from links on the Gentoo Documentation Resources page (`www.gentoo.org/doc/en/index.xml`). Select Installation Related Resources for guides directly related to installation.

## Starting Gentoo installation from a live CD

Here are the minimum computer requirements for a Gentoo installation using the live CD procedure described in this section:

- 1.5GB of hard disk space
- 256MB of RAM
- A 686 processor (or better) is recommended
- 256MB of swap space

Boot the Gentoo live CD from the DVD that accompanies this book:

1. **Insert the DVD.** Insert the DVD that comes with this book. Then, restart the computer and select to boot the Gentoo live CD image contained on that DVD. (You can get a list of available kernels by pressing F1 from the boot prompt. Press F2 through F7 function keys for other boot information.)

2. **Start the graphical installer.** The live CD boots to a graphical Xfce desktop system. From icons on the desktop, you have a choice of starting a graphical or text-based install. Then select either a standard or networkless install. If possible, I recommend starting the graphical (GTK) install. Figure 23-1 shows the graphical and text-based installer icons and the first screen of the graphical Gentoo installer (Partitioning).

**FIGURE 23-1**

Start the installer (GTK or command line) from the Gentoo desktop.

## Caution

**Although some Linux installations save your selections and don't change or delete your disk partitions or write to disk until all your selections are done, Gentoo tends to make changes as you go along. So, for example, when you delete a partition, it will be gone immediately (with no going back). If you have a problem on any of the screens, select View Log to see error messages that have occurred. ■**

3. **Partition your hard disk.** Choose which drive to install Gentoo on from the drop-down box. Partitions for that drive are displayed. Click on each partition in the bar to see the device name (such as /dev/sda1), type of partition (primary or extended), file system type (such as Windows fat32 or Linux ext3), and the size of the partition. At this point, you can

   ● **Clear partitions**—Select this button if you want to delete everything from the entire hard disk. (Be sure the disk doesn't have any data you still need before you do this.)

   ● **Recommended layout**—Select this button if you want Gentoo to recommend how to partition your disk.

   ● **Delete a partition**—With a partition selected, click the Delete button to delete it. (Be sure the partition doesn't have any data you still need before you do this.)

   ● **Create a new partition**—If free space is available on the disk, select the free space bar and select to create a new partition.

When you are done, you should have at least a 1GB swap partition and probably at least a 3GB or 4GB partition to use as root (/), typically an ext3 file system (although some use reiserfs). A 100MB /boot partition is also recommended. If you have extra space, assign it to the root partition. You can delete partitions if you need more space, but first make sure to back up any data you need. Click Next to continue.

4. **Assign mount points.** With your partitions created, you need to indicate where each partition should be mounted. You need at least a root (/) partition (as noted earlier) to be mounted. If you are dual-booting, you could mount your Windows partition on /mnt/windows (for example). If you have a spare partition, consider creating a separate /home partition, so you can keep the operating system separate from your data.

   The installer begins downloading (if needed) and unpacking the stage tarballs. Then the installer prompts you for a root password.

5. **Enter root password.** Type in your root password and repeat. Click Next to continue.

6. **Time zone selection.** Choose your time zone from the map or list shown on the screen. Then click Next to go to the Networking screen.

7. **Configure networking.** Choose your network interface (usually eth0) from the Interface box. Then either select DHCP or select Static (and add your IP address and other information by hand) and a hostname. For a wireless interface, select the Wireless box and type your ESSID and Key. If you need to connect to the Internet via a proxy server, you can enter the location of the proxy server on this screen as well. Click the Save button to save the interface settings. Click Next to see the Daemons page.

8. **Add a user.** Add a user account for everyday computer use. Type your username, password (six characters at least), group (can be the same as the username), shell (such as /bin/bash), home directory (such as /home/chris), user ID (can be blank to have one selected for you), and comment (usually your full name). Click Accept Changes. Then click Next to continue.

9. Choose **extra packages.** Here you have the choice to decide which packages from the live CD you want to install. You can select them all to install all the saved software that is on the live CD. Click Next to continue.

10. **Choose services.** Turn on the services that will start up at boot time. Services you should consider turning on include sound (alsasound), printing (cupsd), text-based mouse support (gpm), firewall (iptables), remote login (sshd), and others. Click Next to go to the Other Settings screen.

11. **Select settings.** Choose settings associated with the display manager, keymaps, and other features that interest you. You also have the choice of setting the BIOS clock to UTC time. Click Next to continue.

12. **Finish installing.** Click Exit to close the installer after you see the "Your install is complete!" message.

13. **Exit and reboot.** Select to log out, and then choose to reboot the computer. After the system shuts down, remove the live CD and reboot the newly installed Gentoo system.

At this point, you can use the emerge command to add additional software packages to your installed Gentoo system. See the "Getting Software with emerge" section later in this chapter.

## Starting Gentoo installation from a minimal CD

The Gentoo minimal install procedure described here is for people who are comfortable working from a Linux command line shell. If you are not, you should consider installing from a Gentoo live CD or using a different Linux distribution.

There are many opportunities for error in this procedure and completing it can take a very long time, with all the downloading and compiling that must be done. However, if it works, the result can be a fully-tuned, custom Gentoo install that can run very well on your particular computer.

Here are the minimum computer requirements for a Gentoo installation using the minimal install procedure described in this chapter:

- 1.5GB of hard disk space
- 256MB of RAM
- A 686 processor (or better)
- 256MB of swap space

If you have a slow processor, consider getting precompiled packages because the full compilation process can take a long time.

For this installation, you will need to download the disk image as described earlier in the "Minimal/Universal install CD" section and burn that image to a CD as described in Appendix A. With this CD in hand, here's how to install Gentoo on your computer:

1. **Insert CD.** Insert the CD into your computer's CD or DVD drive.
2. **Reboot.** Reboot your computer.
3. **Boot CD.** Type **gentoo** at the boot: prompt to start the Gentoo minimal install CD, or press the designated Gentoo function key to see other options for running Gentoo.

    Gentoo should detect your computer hardware, start the install process, and display a boot prompt.

4. **Set date.** Type the date command to make sure the date and time are set correctly. If they need to be changed, use the date command (with options) to change them. For example, to set the date to 8:15 a.m., June 15, 2010, type

    ```
    # date 061508152010
    ```

5. **Load modules.** If some piece of hardware was not auto-detected, you may have to load the module you need to access that hardware. Use the modprobe command with the

name of the module you want to load. For example, to load the module for an Orinoco wireless LAN card, you can type

```
# modprobe orinoco
```

## Tip

**Do a Web search for "Linux" and the name of the hardware not being detected to find out what module to load.** ∎

6.  **Configure network.** Type ifconfig eth0 to see if the Internet connection to your first Ethernet card is up and running. Then try to ping a computer on the Internet to make sure you can get out (for example, ping www.gentoo.org). If you are not able to pick up a DHCP server to automatically connect to the Internet, you can set up your Internet connection manually, by typing

```
# net-setup eth0
```

Refer to the network configuration information in the installation procedure in Chapter 8 to help you answer questions about setting up your Internet connection manually.

7.  **Partition hard disk.** Partition your hard disk to prepare it to receive your Gentoo installation. You can use the fdisk utility to do this. Gentoo recommends a 64MB boot volume (ext2 file system), a swap partition that's double the size of your RAM, and a large root (/) partition (reiserfs file system). Start fdisk by following the command with the name of your first hard disk (such as /dev/hda or /dev/sda for your first IDE or SCSI hard disk, respectively). Then type **h** to display a list of commands. (See Chapter 8 for information on using fdisk to partition your hard disk.)

## Caution

**Repartitioning your disk destroys existing data on your hard disk. Back up any data you value before starting this procedure. Be sure not to delete or change any partitions that have data on them that you want to keep.** ∎

```
# fdisk /dev/hda
```

8.  **Make file systems.** To create the appropriate file systems on your disk partitions, use the mk2fs and mkswap commands. For example, with an IDE hard drive that has the first partition as the boot partition (/dev/hda1), the second as swap (/dev/hda2), and the third as the root (/) partition (/dev/hda3), you can type the following:

```
# mke2fs /dev/hda1
# mkswap /dev/hda2
# mkreiserfs /dev/hda3
```

9.  **Turn on swap.** Use the swapon command to turn on your swap partition. For our example (with hda2 being the swap partition), type

```
# swapon /dev/hda2
```

10. **Mount root (/) partition.** You need to mount the root (/) partition temporarily to begin installing Gentoo to it. In this example (with the root file system on /dev/hda3), type

```
# mount /dev/hda3 /mnt/gentoo
```

11. **Mount the /boot partition.** Mount the boot partition so you can install boot files to that partition:

```
# mkdir /mnt/gentoo/boot
# mount /dev/hda1 /mnt/gentoo/boot
```

12. **Get the stage1 tarball.** Assuming that you have the minimal Gentoo installation CD, you need to download the stage1 tarball. Find a mirror site near you (as described earlier). Then make a directory on your hard disk to copy it to and download the tarball using a tool such as wget. Here is an example:

## Note

If you are using the Universal CD, the stage1 tarball is available there. Instead of downloading it, jump to the next step and extract the tarball from /mnt/cdrom/stages/stage1*.tar.bz2. If you are using a later version of Gentoo, the link you use will be different. ■

```
# mkdir /mnt/gentoo/tmp2
# cd /mnt/gentoo/tmp2
# wget -c http://gentoo.osuosl.org/releases/x86/2008.0/
  stages/stage1-x86-2008.0.tar.bz2
```

## Note

The wget command, which appears on multiple lines here, should all be typed on one line. (There's no space between the slash at the end of the first line and the word "stages" at the beginning of the next.) If the download should stop in the middle, you can restart it by running the same command again in the same directory. ■

13. **Extract the stage 1 tarball.** Use the following commands:

```
# cd /mnt/gentoo
# tar -xvjpf /mnt/gentoo/tmp2/stage1-*.tar.bz2
```

You can remove the stage1 tarball after you have untarred it.

14. **Select mirror site.** Use the mirrorselect command to search for a Gentoo mirror site from which you can efficiently download the files you need to do the install. Run the following command to select an efficient mirror and add it to your make.conf file (it will take a while to test download speed from more than 150 servers):

```
# mirrorselect -s4 -o |grep GENTOO_MIRRORS >> /mnt/gentoo/etc/make.conf
```

## Note

If, when you run emerge commands later in this procedure, you see messages that files are not found from any of the download sites, you might need to add other mirror sites to the make.conf file. ■

15. **Mount file systems.** Mount the /proc file system as follows:

    ```
    # mount -t proc proc /mnt/gentoo/proc
    ```

16. **Change root directory.** Use the chroot command to change /mnt/gentoo to be your root directory, but first copy the resolve.conf file so it can be used from there:

    ```
    # cp /etc/resolv.conf /mnt/gentoo/etc/resolv.conf
    # chroot /mnt/gentoo /bin/bash
    ```

17. **Update Portage tree.** Type the following command to have the latest package information installed to your /usr/portage directory:

    ```
    # emerge --sync
    ```

18. **Update environment.** Read in environment variables as follows:

    ```
    # env-update; source /etc/profile
    ```

19. **Modify make.conf.** Use the nano text editor to change the make.conf file that is used to build your Gentoo system because that is the text editor available at this point. Here's how:

    ```
    # nano -w /etc/make.conf
    ```

    (Use the -w option of nano so that configuration lines aren't wrapped around. For more nano options, type nano --help.)

    If you don't know what to change, refer to the /etc/make.conf.example file for information on the settings you may want to change before continuing. If you don't know what processor your computer has, type cat /proc/cpuinfo.

20. **Bootstrap Gentoo.** This step will take a fairly long time. Run bootstrap.sh to bootstrap Gentoo as follows:

    ```
    # cd /usr/portage/ ; scripts/bootstrap.sh
    ```

21. **Install Gentoo.** Before running the next command, understand that it could take a *very* long time to complete. With an old computer and slow Internet connection, it could take anywhere from hours to days to complete. If you are okay with that, run the following emerge command to install:

    ```
    # emerge -e system
    ```

# Note

As noted earlier, it takes a long time for the emerge -e system command to complete. If it fails before it is finished, check that the settings in your make.conf file are correct. ∎

22. **Set the time zone.** Use the following command:

    ```
    # ln -sf /usr/share/zoneinfo/path /etc/localtime
    ```

    You need to replace *path* with the path to the file that represents the time zone your computer is in. For example, the entire path for Central time in the United States is /usr/share/zoneinfo/US/Central. (If your date and time are set incorrectly, you can run the hwclock -s command to set the system date and time from the BIOS.)

23. **Create file system table.** Add the file systems you want to mount automatically at boot time to your /etc/fstab file. Here's an example:

    ```
    # nano -w /etc/fstab
    ```

    Here's what /etc/fstab might look like (given the partitions created earlier in this example procedure):

    ```
    # <fs>                  <mountpoint> <type>   <opts>            <dump/pass>
    /dev/hda1               /boot        ext2     noauto,noatime    1 2
    /dev/hda2               none         swap     sw                0 0
    /dev/hda3               /            reiserfs noatime           0 1
    /dev/cdroms/cdrom0      /mnt/cdrom   auto     noauto,user       0 0
    none                    /proc        proc     defaults          0 0
    none                    /dev/shm     tmpfs    defaults          0 0
    ```

24. **Build kernel.** Either install a prebuilt kernel or build one yourself. To build one, you need a kernel sources package (gentoo-sources is recommended). Type the emerge command as follows to get the gentoo-sources package:

    ```
    # emerge gentoo-sources
    ```

    Next, use the following command to get the genkernel package and configure a kernel using menuconfig:

    ```
    # emerge genkernel
    # genkernel --menuconfig all
    ```

    After you have made any changes you want to your kernel configuration, select Exit, and then choose Yes to save it. At this point, genkernel makes your new kernel. This takes a while.

    After genkernel is complete, note the names of the kernel and boot loader. (Type **ls /boot** to see the names.)

25. **Configure system services.** Install your system services—system logger, cron service, hotplug, and reiserfs service—and set the domain name. Then turn on each of those services, as follows:

```
# emerge syslog-ng
# rc-update add syslog-ng default
# emerge vixie-cron
# rc-update add vixie-cron default
# emerge hotplug
# rc-update add hotplug default
# emerge reiserfsprogs
```

26. **Add special driver support.** There may be particular kernel modules required by your computer at this point. For example, if you have a special Ethernet adapter or a special type of video card, use the emerge command to install kernel modules now. You may not need any of them. Here are a few examples:

```
# emerge nvidia-kernel
# emerge nforce-audio
# emerge e1000
# emerge ati-drivers
```

These emerge command lines are used only if you have special hardware associated with the kernel drivers. Respectively, those commands load drivers for accelerated NVIDIA video cards, audio for NVIDIA NForce motherboards, Intel e1000 Gigabit Ethernet cards, and ATI Radeon+/FireGL graphics acceleration video cards.

27. **Add user and machine information.** Add a password for the root user, a regular user account name of your choosing (chris in this example), a machine name, and a domain name. If you like, you can also edit the /etc/hosts and /etc/rc.conf files to add IP addresses and hostname or change the basic system startup script.

```
# passwd
# useradd chris -m -G users,wheel,audio -s /bin/bash
# passwd chris
# echo mymachine > /etc/hostname
# echo mydomain.com > /etc/dnsdomainname
# nano -w /etc/hosts
# nano -w /etc/rc.conf
```

28. **Set up networking.** Edit the net file, and then run rc-update to add the eth0 interface as the default. (You can skip editing the net file if you just want to use DHCP to start up automatically on your eth0 interface.)

```
# nano -w /etc/conf.d/net
# rc-update add net.eth0 default
```

29. **Add kernel modules.** Add any extra kernel modules that you need to add at boot time. You usually need to do this only if some piece of hardware isn't detected and the module needed to use it isn't automatically loaded. Edit either the kernel-2.4 or kernel-2.6 file, depending on which kernel you are using.

```
# nano -w /etc/modules.autoload.d/kernel-`uname -r`
```

You can type **uname** -a to see what your current kernel version is.

30. **Configure the boot loader.** You need to install a boot loader (grub in this example) and configure it. The example makes the following assumptions about your setup. You need to replace any of the following information with the settings for your particular setup:

   - Gentoo is installed on your first IDE hard disk (/dev/hda).
   - You have a separate /boot partition on /dev/hda1.
   - Your initrd file in the /boot directory is initramfs-genkernel-x86-2.6.25-gentoo-r6.
   - Your kernel file in the /boot directory is kernel-genkernel-x86-2.6.25-gentoo-r6.

   If any of that information is different for your setup, you need to adapt the following step appropriately. To configure grub, install it with emerge, run the grub command, and then create the grub.conf file as follows:

```
# emerge grub
# grub
grub> root (hd0,0)
grub> setup (hd0)
grub> quit
```

   When you create the grub.conf file, you need to do the following:

```
# cd /boot/grub
# nano -w /boot/grub/grub.conf
default 0
timeout 15
splashimage=(hd0,0)/grub/splash.xpm.gz

title=Gentoo Linux
  root (hd0,0)
  kernel /kernel-genkernel-x86-2.6.25-gentoo-r6 root=/dev/hda0
  initrd /initrd-genkernel-x86-2.6.25-gentoo-r6
```

**31.** **Reboot.** Exit from your chroot partition by running `umount` to unmount all partitions and then rebooting as follows:

```
# exit
# cd /
# umount /mnt/gentoo/proc /mnt/gentoo
# reboot
```

Remove the installation disk and allow the computer to boot from hard disk. After a few moments, you should see the GRUB boot screen. Select Gentoo Linux (press Enter).

## Note

From here on you will be booting from the hard disk and working directly from the operating system you installed. If you see error messages, such as missing kernel drivers, I recommend that you go to `http://forums.gentoo.org` and search for the driver that's causing problems. Chances are that someone else has had the same problem and can offer you a solution. ■

**32.** **Install a desktop.** For most of us, it's not much fun just working from the command line. The following command installs a basic set of desktop packages, including the X Window System (xfree), KDE desktop (kde), Mozilla browser (mozilla), and Openoffice.org office suite (openoffice-bin). (This takes a long time to install over the network!)

```
# emerge xorg-x11
```

At this point you can add a simple window manager, such as enlightenment. You could add the entire KDE desktop (`emerge kde`) or GNOME desktop, but I warn you that it will take a very, very long time to complete over the network. The Gentoo quick install guide shows an example GNOME install (`emerge -vp gnome`) as taking nearly nine hours to complete and a complete KDE install (`emerge -vp kde-meta`) taking more than 19 hours to complete.

Here is an example of installing the enlightenment window manager:

```
# emerge enlightenment
```

After that, you should choose some desktop applications to install. For example, here's how to install the Firefox Web browser and Abiword word processor:

```
# emerge mozilla-firefox abiword
```

**33.** **Configure the X server.** Now that your desktop software is installed, you need to configure the X Window System to work properly with your video card and monitor. Type the following to configure your video card and monitor:

```
# Xorg -configure
```

The previous command creates a sample configuration file: `/root/xorg.conf.new`.
Type the following command to test that configuration file:

```
# X -config /root/xorg.conf.new
```

If you see a gray screen with your mouse cursor represented by an X and able to move,
the configuration file is basically working. To exit from X, press Ctrl+Backspace. Copy
the file to its permanent location:

```
# cp /root/xorg.conf.new /etc/X11/xorg.conf
```

Now, you should be able to start your desktop interface.

```
# startx
```

If no window manager is found, or if you get a window manager you don't want such as
twm, create a `$HOME/.xinitrc` file and indicate the file manager to use. For example,
to use fluxbox as your window manager, add the following line to your .xinitrc file:

```
XSESSION=enlightenment
```

You can run `startx` again to start your desktop with the new window manager.

At this point you should have a working desktop. If you need help getting it working, refer to the
Gentoo X Server Configuration HOWTO (`www.gentoo.org/doc/en/xorg-config.xml`). For
documentation on configuring other parts of your Gentoo system, I recommend that you check
out `www.gentoo.org/doc/en/index.xml` for documentation on other Gentoo subjects.

# Getting software with emerge

Following are some examples of some common uses of the `emerge` command that you can use
with Gentoo. To use some of the examples, you need to either have a connection to the Internet
or have downloaded all package updates to your local computer.

When the `emerge` command is run to install software or to get updated software packages, it
looks on a Gentoo mirror site if it can't find the packages it needs locally. The first example lets
you search (`-s`) the `/usr/portage` directory tree for packages that interest you. For example, to
search for the package named bzflag, type the following:

```
# emerge -s bzflag
```

To build and install a package you choose, simply type **emerge** with the package name:

```
# emerge bzflag
```

To update your Portage directory tree so that it contains the latest information to install software packages, type the following:

```
# emerge --sync
```

To get your Gentoo system up-to-date, use the `-uD world` option. The following command checks all the software packages you have installed on your computer, and then goes to a Gentoo mirror site to download and install the latest versions of each of those packages:

```
# emerge -uD world
```

To view the many other options available with `emerge`, type **man emerge** or run `emerge` with the help option:

```
# emerge -h | less
```

You can use `emerge` to install packages contained on your local computer or have the packages downloaded automatically from Gentoo software mirror sites. During the build process, `emerge` handles getting all the dependencies that the software you choose requires.

The `equery` command can be used to get information about installed packages. Type the following command to page through a list of all installed packages (ebuilds):

```
# equery list | less
```

# Summary

In just a few years, Gentoo distinguished itself as a premier distribution for Linux enthusiasts who are interested in complete control of the components and settings of their Linux systems.

The jewel of the Gentoo system is the Portage package management system. Using the Portage `emerge` command, you can install any of thousands of Gentoo software packages. Those packages can be downloaded and built from scratch, using settings you choose, to tune them for how you use your Linux system.

An improved Gentoo installer that is bootable from the Gentoo live CD has made getting started using Gentoo much easier. Using the more detailed minimal installation, also contained in this chapter, you have more opportunities to tune and tweak your operating system exactly as you want it to be.

# Running Slackware Linux

A sk old-time Linux users about the first Linux distribution they used and many will tell you it was Slackware. Slackware is the oldest Linux distribution still actively developed today. Although it does not have a fancy graphical installer or specialized GUI tools, Slackware still has a loyal following and is a good way to get a basic Linux system that is both secure and stable.

This chapter explores the Slackware distribution, discusses its strengths and weaknesses, and introduces those who use it. It also explains how to install Slackware.

## IN THIS CHAPTER

**Getting into Slackware**

**Characterizing the Slackware community**

**Installing Slackware**

**Starting Slackware**

## On the DVD

**A selection of software from the Slackware 13 three-CD install set is included on the DVD that comes with this book. You can buy the complete Slackware 13 from the Slackware Store (`http://store.slackware.com`) or find out where to download the DVD or other CD images from the Slackware site (`www.slackware.com/getslack`). ∎**

## Getting into Slackware

Although full graphical installs and GUI administration tools can make installing and configuring Linux easy, those tools carry with them some overhead. They also hide some of the details of how Linux is being configured.

Ask Slackware devotees the value of Slackware and they might recite their mantra, the "4S Rule": Stable, Solid, Simple, and Sensible. By keeping things basic, Slackware offers the following advantages:

- **Better comprehension**—Because you use commands and configuration files with Slackware, you learn more about how Linux works on the inside. Most graphical installers and GUI tools hide the actual configuration that is going on and often limit the features you can use. If something goes wrong, it can be hard to debug a problem with many graphical interfaces. The Slackware installer is menu-based, very flexible, and quite intuitive.

- **Less bloat**—In general, graphical interfaces consume far more resources than their command-line counterparts. GUIs require more room on the distribution medium, plus more hard disk space and more RAM. GUIs also may not run well, or at all, on certain underpowered or unsupported video cards. Slackware relies primarily on basic Linux commands, text-based configuration files, and some simple menu-driven administration tools.

- **Better for low-end computers**—Slackware is the first distribution I recommend to run on low-end machines. A special ZipSlack distribution (`www.slackware.com/zipslack`) can be installed from a 100MB Zip drive or floppy disks. ZipSlack can install on a 386 PC with as little as 4MB of RAM. Even with the latest Slackware distribution, if you want a GUI, the installation procedure for Slackware lets you choose small, efficient window managers, Web browsers, mail clients, and other graphical tools.

- **Stable and secure**—Whereas other Linux distributions deliver the latest kernel, glibc, and other critical components of Linux as their default, Slackware opts for more stable, well-tested versions. In Slackware 13, the default kernel is 2.6.27.7. As security issues come up, new packages are made available and announcements are posted by the year that they occurred (`www.slackware.com/security`).

- **Packages as projects intended**—Slackware doesn't mold the software it includes into one look-and-feel. The Apache Web server, KDE desktop, or Samba file/printer sharing projects work pretty much as they are delivered from those projects. So, again, the knowledge you gain from using those projects will transfer fairly easily to those same projects on other Linux systems.

Instead of providing a unified look-and-feel, Slackware gives you the maximum amount of control. It allows the desktop environment or window manager you choose to dictate the desktop presentation. You can change your desktop as you like, using the menus or preference windows that come with those environments. A full KDE desktop environment is included with Slackware. Or you can opt for a lighter, more efficient window manager, such as XFCE4, fvwm2, or twm.

## Note

The GNOME desktop environment was dropped from Slackware 10.2 and remains out of the distribution. Patrick Volkerding, Slackware's creator/maintainer, cited demands of keeping up with GNOME development changes and some GNOME features that don't match Slackware objectives (such as including PAM and replacing some system packages, such as X11). Volkerding suggests `http://gware.sf.net` if you want to add GNOME to your own installation of Slackware. ■

For system administration, Slackware offers some tools based on the ncurses text-mode windowing library. Ncurses allows an application to provide a screen-oriented interface on a character terminal, so you can use forms, menus, and sometimes even a mouse to configure some basic Linux features from any shell (no X-based GUI required).

Recently added Slackware package management tools (such as the `slackpkg` command) have made the tasks of adding, removing, and upgrading packages much easier. For information on `slackpkg` see `http://slackpkg.sourceforge.net`. There are also tools for creating your own Slackware packages (such as the `slacktrack` command). In the true Slackware tradition, Slackware packages are quite simple: basically a tarball of files with an install script.

Anything you can do with other Linux distributions, you can do with Slackware. It might just take a bit more manual work to get there.

## Note

Slackware comes with a good set of libraries that will take care of the dependency needs of most Linux applications. However, for video, audio, and some other types of applications, you may find yourself hunting around for libraries. ■

# Characterizing the Slackware Community

Like many other successful Linux distributions, Slackware was started by a strong-minded individual who created the kind of Linux system that suited him. Slackware users are generally people who pretty much agree with him.

## The Slackware creator

Patrick Volkerding started Slackware in 1993 as a Linux distribution to use for himself and his friends. He was kind enough to answer some questions I had about Slackware, and I want to share his answers with you here.

Patrick originally used a Linux distribution called SLS Linux (named after Soft Landing Linux, the company that made it).

**Question:** Why didn't you just contribute to SLS instead of starting your own distribution?

**Patrick:** I tried. By April of 1993 I had collected a huge list of bugs in SLS, along with the fixes for most of them. Plenty of people tried to get these to Peter MacDonald (SLS's author/maintainer) but the bugs in SLS (many of which were quite obvious) never seemed to get fixed.

Of course, I'd started work on my patched version of SLS with no plan to try to launch a lasting distribution. I figured I'd get it online and SLS would fix the issues, and that might just be that. SLS was a great distribution and isn't given enough credit for all the ideas that started there. Unfortunately it was while Peter was busy working on inventing kernel modules that SLS sat online for a few months full of bugs and not getting any updates.

Patrick decided to take the leap to separate Slackware from SLS after MacDonald suggested that Slackware was infringing on his copyrights (despite the only license on the SLS code saying, "Distribute freely; do not restrict.").

**Question:** So, what did you do?

**Patrick:** I promised Peter that I would write a new installer for Slackware instead of using a modified SLS one, and that the new installer would be the next change made to Slackware online.

**Question:** Did the great success of Slackware from the get-go surprise you?

**Patrick:** Absolutely. I knew it worked better than the other distributions that were out at the time, but I didn't expect the kind of mass exodus from SLS that occurred.

**Question:** What kind of person is attracted to Slackware over other Linux distros?

**Patrick:** It seems to attract the kind of users who want to configure software the old-fashioned way (using a text editor), and who don't want a lot of unnecessary things running in the background. I try to compile software with as few of my own changes as possible, which also makes it pretty easy to update things from source if you decide to go that route.

In the early days of Linux I think most of the users were like this, and as time has moved on and various distributions have focused on different markets, the profile of the average Linux user has changed quite a lot. Most of today's commercial Linux distributions seem to target a user who wants to administer his machine with a point-and-click interface much like Windows. Slackware and other lower-level distributions serve a different niche—users who don't mind a learning curve if it means the operating system will stay out of their way.

Today, Patrick is still the Project Lead and maintains complete control over Slackware's features and release schedule. In this arrangement, Patrick can choose the features to include, and he doesn't add features that don't suit him (even popular ones).

**Question:** How would you characterize the Slackware development process?

**Patrick:** Most of what I do is research—trying to figure out where Linux is going so I can make (I hope) sane choices about what to implement. There's not really a core development team (which really streamlines the development process by sidestepping the usual time-wasting squabbles that happen in any official development hierarchy). But I get a ton of help from people who e-mail me with problems or suggestions that lead to an upgrade or fix somewhere in the system.

The best way to keep up with Slackware development issues is to read the change logs (available from the Slackware home page). Slackware aficionados expect releases on an "it's ready when it's ready" schedule, as the Slackware FAQ notes: "As things are built for the upcoming release, they'll be uploaded into the -current tree. If the -current does not exist, it probably means we have just released a new version of Slackware."

## Slackware users

From a purely subjective perspective, my friends who use Slackware tend to be technically oriented, but not the extreme overclockers and tweakers who might be drawn to Gentoo, for example. They like Slackware because it works so simply and so well that they believe it gives them more time to slack.

Slackware users often think of themselves as loners, despite the fact that they all hang out together at LAN parties and Internet cafes. They like the more purist, less commercial approach of Slackware. For their personal desktop, gaming box, or small-office server, they see no need for the graphical installation and administration tools that you get with Red Hat Enterprise Linux or SUSE Linux systems. They are comfortable with commands and man pages.

I've often heard users refer to Slackware as being easier to use than other Linux distributions. To someone coming from a UNIX or BSD background, this is probably true. You don't have to wait for graphical tools to pop up and almost everything is covered on a man page.

## Note

Man pages are the traditional means of documenting commands, file formats, devices, system calls, and most any other component of a UNIX or Linux system. Man pages date back to the very first UNIX systems. You can read man pages using the `man` command, followed by a component name, from any shell. To learn about how the man page system itself works, type `man man`. ∎

## Slackware Internet sites

The Slackware home page (`www.slackware.com`) is a good place to start looking for information about Slackware. Two main mailing lists plus an IRC channel are available through the Web site, as well as links to download sites, some documentation, and the Slackware Store (`store.slackware.com`).

A Slackware Linux Essentials online book (`www.slackbook.org/`) and four FAQs (`www.slackware.com/faq/`) are available from the Slackware site. There's also no "news" to speak of at the Slackware site, so the best way to keep up on what's happening with the project is to read the change logs (www.slackware.com/changelog/).

For information on the Slackware version described in this chapter (13), refer to the release announcement (www.slackware.com/announce/13.0.php). Refer to the package changes list (ftp.slackware.com/pub/slackware/slackware-current/Changelog.txt) for details on working with this release.

Outside of the official Slackware site, a lot of new sites have been popping up recently that provide information about Slackware. A good place to bring questions about Slackware is http://linuxquestions.org (follow the links: Forums ⇨ Linux-Distributions ⇨ Slackware). The Linux Packages site (www.linuxpackages.net) offers some active forums on different aspects of Slackware.

# Challenges of Using Slackware

There is no commercial organization behind Slackware and no official support, so if something goes wrong with your Slackware system, you are on your own to solve the problem. The Slackware project, however, does maintain a list of third-party organizations that provide technical support at www.slackware.com/support/.

Although functionally Slackware can be used in most any computing environment, in places where you feel the need to have a company behind the computer systems you install (such as a large enterprise), you would do better to look toward a Red Hat or SUSE system.

The lack of official package management tools used to pose another challenge to Slackware users. Although Slackware's packaging tools are a great improvement over just installing from tarballs, those tools have not yet reached the level of sophistication you get with those available with RPM-based (Fedora, Red Hat Enterprise Linux, SUSE, Mandriva, and so on) or Deb-based (Debian, Ubuntu, KNOPPIX, and so on) distributions.

When a software package made to add to Slackware requires a library that is not in the standard Slackware distribution, the developers often build the needed library into the package. If the software fails, however, indicating a missing library, you can try a couple of things:

- Look in the software package's README file for descriptions of the libraries it needs.
- Use the ldd command to determine the libraries a command needs (for example, typing ldd /bin/cat shows the libraries needed by the cat command).
- Search the Web for the terms "Slackware" and the name of the missing library.

## Coming from Windows

As someone comfortable with UNIX and Linux, I find the text-based tools that come with Slackware helpful and fairly simple to use. If you are coming from a Windows environment, however, you may find the lack of GUI-based tools and cohesive end-to-end procedures for setting up features a bit disconcerting. ■

Because Slackware is not backed up by a big support organization, it has not made much headway into the corporate enterprise arena. The fact that most commercial applications are created specifically for Red Hat Enterprise Linux or, to a lesser extent, SUSE distributions, and won't just run out of the box on Slackware, makes Slackware an even harder sell for corporate environments.

# Using Slackware as a Development Platform

Slackware has long been a preferred platform for developing open source software. It contains a large set of libraries and includes nearly every tool you could want for developing applications. There are special spin-off projects for Slackware developers as well, such as the Slackware for ARM processor project for developing embedded Linux applications (www.armedslack.org).

Because Slackware is a clean, basic Linux system, applications that run in Slackware can run on most other Linux systems as well. In other words, you won't be encouraged to add a lot of special Slackware hooks that would prevent software from being portable across a wide range of Linux, UNIX, and BSD systems.

Slackware can easily provide an efficient development workstation environment for technical people because the distribution doesn't get in the way of its powerful features. It's easy to configure a simple window manager and not incur the overhead of background processes that try to "help" you when you insert a CD or need software updates. Slackware simply gives you an efficient desktop that lets you do what you need to do, keeps you as close to the silicon as possible, and otherwise stays out of your way.

If you become interested in building and submitting packages for Slackware, some good descriptions of how to do so are at the Linux Packages site (www.linuxpackages.net). Look for links to building and submitting packages on the site's home page in the Information box.

# Installing Slackware

Slackware is freely available from several different sources. It installs and runs well on low-end computers. Some Linux or UNIX expertise would be useful, especially if something goes wrong.

## Getting Slackware

Slackware 13 comes on a single DVD (about 3.7GB) or six CDs: three installation CDs and three source code CDs. In earlier versions, Slackware included enough software on the first install CD to install a lightweight, but efficient, desktop system. Because that is no longer true, the Slackware software on the DVD that comes with this book includes packages consolidated from several of the official Slackware CDs, so you can install a workable desktop system from that DVD.

The full Slackware distribution set is also available from a few dozen mirror sites on the Web (see www.slackware.com/getslack). Because of disk space issues and to maximize bandwidth, the Slackware project recommends you get the DVD or CD images (ISOs) using BitTorrent. For a list of available torrents, see www.slackware.com/getslack/torrents.php.

## Note

**For many years, Slackware was available on one install CD, but adding KDE to the distribution made additional CDs necessary.** ■

To help support the project, you can purchase the boxed set of Slackware from http://store .slackware.com. At the store, you also can get a subscription to Slackware so that the Slackware Store sends you a new version each time one is released (every six to eight months). The store will just ship it when it's available and charge your credit card. People who like Slackware often pay the subscription fee just to show their support.

## New features in Slackware 13

With Slackware 13, the distribution consists of three installation CDs (plus three source code CDs) and/or a DVD version that holds everything. While still offering a stable foundation (the 2.6.29.6 kernel is used by default, with no 2.4 kernel options still being offered), Slackware includes stable desktop releases (KDE 4.2.4 or XFCE 4.6.1) and applications (the latest Firefox browser and Thunderbird e-mail client).

Here are some applications in Slackware that include new versions for the latest release:

- **KDE 4.2.4**—The plasma desktop, Dolphin file manager and many other features are included with this version of KDE.
- **SeaMonkey 1.1.1**—Contains a combination Web browser, e-mail client, IRC chat client, newsgroup client, and HTML client. In Slackware, SeaMonkey replaces the Mozilla suite as the all-in-one Internet suite.

To work with software packages in Slackware 13, the distribution includes the Slackware Package Browser. This Web application enables you to search a Slackware packages database, making it much easier than it was in the past to find the Slackware software you want.

## Hardware requirements

Although some older versions of Slackware will run on a 386, the Slackware site recommends 486 as a minimum processor. However, Slackware uses i686 optimization to get the maximum performance on Pentium III, Pentium 4, Duron/Athlon, and other i686-class PCs.

Without a graphical interface (X Window System), the minimum amount of RAM required is 16MB. With the GUI, at least 128MB of RAM is recommended. If you intend to use the KDE desktop environments, you can't have too much RAM (KDE in Slackware runs effectively with 256MB RAM or more, depending on your applications).

The ZipSlack distribution is a small Slackware distribution that you can install from a Zip drive or floppy disks. ZipSlack can install on a hard disk with as little as 100MB space. You can find ZipSlack on any Slackware mirror site.

If you are installing Slackware 13, 500MB is the minimum amount of disk space you should have available on your Linux partition. The recommended amount of hard disk space is at least 3.5GB for a full desktop install.

Slackware supports all IDE and SCSI controllers supported by the Linux kernel itself.

## Starting installation

Although the Slackware installer has evolved over the years, its basic look-and-feel hasn't changed much. You still need to do some things manually, such as setting up RAID or doing partitioning.

The following steps describe how to install Slackware from the first installation CD. For the purposes of this book, this procedure demonstrates a minimal installation from the first two Slackware CDs (which are included on the DVD that comes with this book). If you want to install Linux on low-end hardware (slow CPU and minimal RAM), this procedure is a great way to end up with a workable, minimal desktop system.

If you want to do a more complete installation of Slackware, you should obtain the Slackware 13 DVD or the other install CD in the three-CD installation set. For more detailed information (or if something goes wrong during the installation that isn't covered here), refer to the Slackware-HOWTO, which is on the first Slackware CD.

1.  **Obtain a Slackware installation disc.** (As mentioned earlier, you can boot the Slackware selection from the DVD that comes with this book as described in Appendix A, or download official ISO images from a Slackware mirror site and burn them to CDs.)

2.  **Insert the DVD that comes with this book** into the drive and reboot your computer.

3.  **From the boot prompt,** select slackware as shown on the boot screen to start the default boot process. If you are using a Slackware CD instead of this book's DVD, simply press Enter.

    If the Slackware installation boots properly, you are prompted to enter a keyboard map.

## Note
If your Slackware medium won't boot, refer to the BOOTING.TXT file on the Slackware CD for information on things you can try to get around the problem. (If you can't access the CD at all, you can get this file from any Slackware mirror site.) ∎

4. **If you are using a U.S. keyboard map, press Enter.** To use a keyboard map for a different language/country, type 1, press Enter, and then select the one you want. The Slackware login prompt appears.

5. **Type root and press Enter.** A shell prompt appears.

6. **Partition your hard disk.** Chapter 8 explains how to partition your hard disk. Slackware doesn't have a graphical partitioning tool, such as Disk Setup, so you have to use the fdisk or cfdisk command to partition your hard disk (again, refer to Chapter 8 or see the Slackware-HOWTO for details).

   To install Slackware, you should have at least one swap partition (up to twice the size of your RAM, with a maximum of about 2GB) and one Linux partition (such as ext3). You should have at least 500MB of hard disk space available, with a recommended 3GB of disk space available for a full install of Slackware 13.

   Here's an example of an fdisk session which begins with a brand new (or one that can be totally erased) 60GB SATA drive (/dev/sda). The result is a 1GB swap partition and a 3GB Linux partition (that can be used as the root of the filesystem: /).

```
# fdisk /dev/sda

The number of cylinders for this disk is set to 7296.
There is nothing wrong with that, but this is larger than 1024,
and could in certain setups cause problems with:
1) software that runs at boot time (e.g., old versions of LILO)
2) booting and partitioning software from other OSs
   (e.g., DOS FDISK, OS/2 FDISK)

Command (m for help): p

Disk /dev/sda: 60.0 GB, 60011642880 bytes
255 heads, 63 sectors/track, 7296 cylinders
Units = cylinders of 16065 * 512 = 8225280 bytes
Disk identifier: 0xcccdcccd

   Device Boot      Start         End      Blocks   Id  System
Command (m for help): n
Command action
   e   extended
   p   primary partition (1-4)
p
Partition number (1-4): 1
First cylinder (1-7296, default 1): 1
Last cylinder or +size or +sizeM or +sizeK (1-7296, default 7296): +1G

Command (m for help): n
Command action
   e   extended
   p   primary partition (1-4)
```

```
p
Partition number (1-4): 2
First cylinder (124-7296, default 124):
Using default value 124
Last cylinder or +size or +sizeM or +sizeK (124-7296, default 7296): +3G

Command (m for help): t
Partition number (1-4): 1
Hex code (type L to list codes): 82
Changed system type of partition 1 to 82 (Linux swap / Solaris)

Command (m for help): p

Disk /dev/sda: 60.0 GB, 60011642880 bytes
255 heads, 63 sectors/track, 7296 cylinders
Units = cylinders of 16065 * 512 = 8225280 bytes
Disk identifier: 0xcccdcccd

   Device Boot    Start    End    Blocks    Id  System
/dev/sda1            1    123    987966    82  Linux swap / Solaris
/dev/sda2          124    489   2939895    83  Linux

Command (m for help): w
Command (m for help): q
```

**7. Enter setup mode.** Type the following command to enter setup mode:

```
# setup
```

The Slackware Linux Setup screen appears, with the following options:

```
HELP       Read the Slackware Setup Help file
KEYMAP     Remap your keyboard if you're not using a US one
ADDSWAP    Set up your swap partition(s)
TARGET     Set up your target partitions
SOURCE     Select source media
SELECT     Select categories of software to install
INSTALL    Install selected software
CONFIGURE  Reconfigure your Linux system
EXIT       Exit Slackware Linux Setup
```

Type the first letter in the option name (or use the arrow keys) to highlight the option you want, and then press Enter. The following steps describe options you need to configure Slackware.

**8. Select ADDSWAP.** The Swap Space Detected menu appears, listing the swap partitions you have available. Select the one you want (there will usually be just one) and select

Yes to install it as your swap partition. (If you don't have a swap partition, exit the setup screen and run `fdisk` to create one.)

The swap partition will be checked for bad blocks (if you choose), formatted, and activated. Select OK to continue. The Select Linux Installation Partition menu appears.

9. **Select root partition.** From the Linux partition that is displayed, highlight the one that you want to use as your root (/) partition and choose Select. The / partition is where Linux and all your data will go by default. (Other partitions can be added later.)

   Choose to do a quick format (Format) or a slow format that includes bad block checking (Check). Or you can select No to not format the partition.

## Note

Typically you would overwrite your / partition, although you might keep data from another partition. I often maintain a separate data partition that I will attach to the file system in a location such as /home or /mnt/data. With that technique, I can keep my data and still install an entirely new operating system. ∎

Choose the file system type for the root file system. These days, most people select ext3, ext4 or reiserfs file systems as their Linux root partition. All of those file system types do journaling, so they can recover quickly if the system is shut down improperly (such as when someone kicks out the power cord). The ext3 file system is most popular.

Choose the Inode Density. Select 4096 (the default, which is fine in most cases), 2048, or 1024 bytes. (A smaller number allows more inodes on the file system, which is useful only if you have many small files, as you might on a news server.)

10. **Select other partitions.** If you created other Linux partitions, you can assign file system types and format them as well. Identify where in the file system the other partitions are connected. (Again, check Chapter 8 for information on where you might want to attach a partition to your Linux file system.)

    If you have a Windows system partition (FAT32 or NTFS), the setup program detects that and offers to have you mount it automatically when you start Slackware. With a dual-boot PC (Windows and Linux), this is a good way to access your Windows files from Linux. After that, click OK to add partition information to the /etc/fstab file.

11. **Choose your source media.** Select 1, in most circumstances, so that Slackware is installed from the CD. You can also install Slackware from a partition on your hard drive, from an NFS shared file system, FTP/HTTP server, Samba share, or from a pre-mounted directory.

    You can have Setup scan for your Slackware CD or tell it a particular device to use (if you have multiple drives and you want to tell it which to use).

12. **Select the different package series that you want to install and click OK.** General package series include

    - Base Linux system (the core of the operating system and basic utilities)
    - Various applications that do not need X (non-graphical commands)
    - Program Development (C, C++, Lisp, Perl, and so on)
    - GNU Emacs (a text editor)
    - FAQ lists, HOWTO documentation
    - Linux kernel source
    - Qt and the K Desktop Environment for X
    - International support for KDE
    - System libraries (needed by X, KDE, and others)
    - Networking (TCP/IP, UUCP, mail, news, and so on)
    - TeX typesetting
    - Tcl/Tk scripting languages
    - X Window System
    - X Applications
    - Games

    If you are installing from the *Linux Bible* DVD, deselect KDE and KDEI because they are not on this DVD. Later in the installation process, you have an opportunity to select a simple window manager such as XFCE, Blackbox, Fluxbox, or fvwm2.

## Note

Although it's safest just to install everything with the three install CDs so that you're sure to have everything you want and won't miss a dependent package, with the single Slackware CD I had no dependency problems simply deselecting the KDE package group. ∎

13. **Choose how you are prompted to select packages.** After you have selected the package series you want to install, you can choose to further refine the installation of those packages or simply go with the defaults by selecting one of the following:

    - **Full**—Installs everything without prompting or interaction. You can use this option if you have only the first CD or the DVD.
    - **Menu**—Enables you to choose groups of packages interactively. Select this option if you are installing from the DVD that comes with this book.
    - **Expert**—Enables you to choose individual packages interactively.
    - **Newbie**—Shows you a lot about what is being installed on your Slackware system and lets you choose whether to install optional packages. You just have to sit there for a long time and keep pressing Enter.

When prompted, either choose to continue (if you have another Slackware CD you want to install) or Quit (to just install from the first CD). With the single CD install, select Quit. You are asked whether you want to create a USB flash boot device.

14. **Make a USB boot device.** If you have a USB flash drive available (sometimes called memory sticks, pen drives, or thumb drives), you can use it to make a boot disk. It enables you to reboot your computer if your hard disk ever becomes unbootable. If you don't have a USB flash drive, you can use the Slackware install CD as a boot disk in an emergency.

15. **Install the LILO boot loader.** Choose Simple to have the setup process try to automatically install the LILO boot loader, or choose Expert if you want to configure the boot loader to do something special. If you want to add kernel parameters and set framebuffer console features, you can use either mode, but certain tasks require Expert mode, such as

    ● Adding other bootable Linux partitions

    ● Adding a bootable Windows partition

    ● Installing an existing lilo.conf file, instead of creating a new one

    You can have graphics appear on the boot screen by enabling the frame buffer console. Choose the resolution and number of colors (such as 1024 × 768 × 256) to use with the frame buffer console.

    When prompted, add any parameters you want fed to the kernel when you boot. In particular, you might add kernel parameters if you want to turn off autoprobing on certain devices (for example, nousb) or turn off power management features (noacpi). Chapter 21 describes some kernel parameters that might be useful to you.

    LILO is usually placed in the root of the Linux partition or in the master boot record for the entire hard disk. It's safest to put LILO in the superblock (Root) of the Linux partition. For the former, you need to indicate that the Linux partition is bootable (using the fdisk command when you return to a shell prompt). It can be unsafe to put LILO in the master boot record. However, for a system on which only one operating system is installed (in this case, Slackware), the master boot record is a common place to put LILO.

16. **Configure the mouse.** Select the type of mouse connected to your system. (A USB mouse is quite common these days.) You are also given the opportunity to configure gpm, which lets you use your mouse to select, cut, and paste text in virtual consoles (text windows).

17. **Configure the network.** Select Yes to configure your network (that is, your LAN connection from your Ethernet card). You can add a host name and domain name for your computer, then refer to Chapter 8 for information on configuring your network connection. In particular, you need to indicate whether you want IP addresses and related information to be picked up automatically from a DHCP server or you want to add static address information yourself.

18. **Select startup services.** For server software that you installed, you need to tell Slackware whether to start that service at boot time. In general, you should turn on only services you want to have on (you can always turn any others on later). Among the services that will be on by default (assuming you installed the packages) are the sshd service, to enable remote login using ssh; and system logging (rc.syslog), to log system activity. Enable Sendmail to receive e-mail. To share your printer, you may want to enable CUPS; to be a Web server, you should turn on Apache (rc.httpd).

19. **Configure console fonts.** You can try some custom screen fonts. If you find one you particularly like, you can choose to use it instead of the default.

20. **Set hardware clock.** The clock on your computer can be set to local time or to UTC time (Greenwich Mean Time). Most often you will set it to local time, especially if you dual-boot between operating systems (see `http://tldp.org/HOWTO/Clock-2.html` for information on how Linux keeps track of time).

21. **Choose a time zone.** Select your current time zone from the list.

22. **Select a default window manager.** Choices include the KDE and XFCE desktop environments or any of a number of smaller simple window managers, such as Blackbox, Fluxbox, fvwm2 (selections look like Windows systems), and TWM (too lightweight for most people). Refer to Chapter 3 for more information on configuring Slackware to add a lightweight desktop interface.

23. **Set root password.** Select a root password when you are prompted to do so.

    At this point you can click OK to return to the Slackware Linux Setup menu.

24. **Select EXIT to leave the setup screen.**

25. **Press Ctrl+Alt+Delete to reboot your computer.**

# Starting with Slackware

The LILO Boot menu appears when you first boot Slackware. It should contain at least a listing for your Linux partition and possibly for a Windows partition (if one exists on your computer).

Press Enter at the boot prompt to start Slackware. Log in as the root user when you see the login prompt. You are going to be at a Linux command line prompt; if you don't know what that is, refer to Chapter 9.

Here are a few things you might want to do to get started with Slackware:

- **Get mail**—Type **mail** at the command-line prompt. You should have a couple of mail messages there for the root user, including one from Patrick Volkerding. Type the number of that message and page through it (using the Enter key) to read some additional setup steps that may interest you. (Type **q** to exit the message and **x** to exit mail.)

- **Add another user**—Because you shouldn't use the root user account for your daily use of Linux, you should add a regular user account and give it a password. Here's what you run to add a user named robby:

```
# useradd -m robby
# passwd robby
Changing password for robby
New password: ********
Re-enter new password: ********
```

Be sure to use the -m option to useradd (to automatically create the new user's directory) or you will have to create a home directory for that user manually.

- **Start the desktop**—If you installed X and either a window manager or whole desktop environment (KDE or XFCE), you can start it by typing

```
# startx
```

If X and your chosen desktop don't start properly (the screen may be unreadable or X may simply crash), press Ctrl+Alt+Backspace to exit X and return to the shell. Instructions for solving X problems, choosing different window managers, and configuring X are included in the section "Configuring Your Own Desktop" in Chapter 3.

- **Configure sound**—When you first boot Slackware, the ALSA sound system should be set up to work, but the volume is muted. To configure ALSA and check that your sound card is ready to go, as root user run the alsaconf command. It searches for installed sound cards, and when it finds one, it adds any modules needed to use the card, raises the volume, and tests the card.

After your sound card is configured, use the alsamixer command to adjust volume levels for your sound card.

- **Add modules**—If any of your computer hardware was not properly detected and configured, you can add the modules you need after Slackware is running.

## Note

If some of your computer hardware is not being detected properly, and you don't know what module is required for it to work, try booting KNOPPIX (from the DVD included with this book). If the hardware works in KNOPPIX, run the lsmod command to see what modules are loaded. From that list, you should be able to add the necessary modules as just described. ■

- **Configure a printer**—Because Slackware now includes the CUPS facility for printing (replacing LPRng), you can configure your printers using any Web browser. The best way to begin adding and configuring a printer is to type the following into a location box on any Web browser on your Slackware system:

```
http://localhost:631/admin
```

Enter the root username and your root password when prompted. Then select the Add printer button to begin adding your printer to your CUPS printing server on your Slackware system.

- **Configure networking**—If you didn't configure your Ethernet cards at installation time, you can do it now. Type the following command:

  `# netconfig`

  The menu system enables you to configure your network interface using the same screens as at installation.

- **Install additional software packages**—The `slackpkg` command is the preferred tool for downloading and installing software for Slackware. You can download the package from `http://slackpkg.sourceforge.net`. After you have the slackpkg package, install it by typing **installpkg slackpkg***. With slackpkg installed, edit the `/etc/slackpkg/mirrors` file and uncomment a single repository that you will use to get software packages.

  You are now ready to start using slackpkg. First, type **slackpkg update** to get available updates for your Slackware system. Then you can install the packages you want by typing **slackpkg install packagename**, where packagename is the name of the package you want to install.

## Note

**You can find Slackware packages at `LinuxPackages.net`. Likewise, from any open source project (such as `sourceforge.net`), you can install software packages that are either identified as being created for Slackware or simply tar.gz packages that you can build from scratch.** ■

If you are used to other Linux systems, you should familiarize yourself with a few things you might find different in Slackware. For example, system startup scripts are contained in `/etc/rc.d`, rather than a whole series of links to various `/etc/rc?.d` directories.

# Summary

Slackware is the oldest active Linux distribution. It is run by Patrick Volkerding, as it has been for more than a decade, and keeps as its goals stability and security. Slackware has a loyal following, but the project is not geared for wide deployment in enterprise computing situations. Slackware is a great distribution to learn Linux on because it keeps its configuration simple and near to the command line and configuration files.

Look for Slackware to continue to be among the most efficient Linux distributions. There are currently no plans to add a graphical installer, although the project recently began encouraging the use of `slackpkg` for installing packages. You can expect Slackware to remain trim and true to its roots, making it one of the best Linux distributions to run on older computer hardware.

# CHAPTER 25

# Running PCLinuxOS

With many commercial Linux distributions focusing on large enterprise server systems, other distributions have stepped up to go the last mile for desktop users. PCLinuxOS (www.pclinuxos.com) is one such desktop-oriented Linux system.

PCLinuxOS is a Linux distribution that makes it easy for desktop users to be able to run the kind of applications they need and play the type of content they want without jumping through hoops. It's distributed on a live CD, so you can try it first and then, if you like it, follow a simple install procedure that starts from an icon on the desktop.

By offering many popular applications that are lacking in other Linux desktop distributions and adding some great remastering and customization tools, PCLinuxOS has gained a large and enthusiastic following of desktop Linux users. PCLinuxOS makes leaving behind your Windows desktop system for Linux without leaving behind your music, videos, or documents easy.

Besides being able to play MP3 and Flash content from the get-go, PCLinuxOS makes getting software for playing commercial DVD movies, Windows media content, and other content types where it is legal to do so easy. It is set up so that with just a few quick downloads you can play the content you care about most.

Adding to the stability of the PCLinuxOS desktop experience is the fact that PCLinuxOS doesn't always just chase the latest bits of open source software available. By offering stable versions of KDE, Firefox, and other critical desktop components, your desktop might provide more reliable performance than you'll get with the latest Ubuntu or Fedora desktops.

## IN THIS CHAPTER

**Starting with PCLinuxOS**

**Installing PCLinuxOS**

**Remastering PCLinuxOS**

This chapter tells you how to use PCLinuxOS as a desktop system. It also describes some of the many PCLinuxOS remasters you can use for special applications or particular desktop environments. Then it shows how you can create your own remastered PCLinuxOS.

# Starting with PCLinuxOS

PCLinuxOS is often recommended for first-time users because of what you get without having to learn the intricacies of Linux. Many things that don't work out-of-the box with other Linux distributions just work with PCLinuxOS.

Boot up PCLinuxOS from a live CD, open a browser, and go to YouTube.com to immediately begin playing Flash content. Java content is ready to run as well. Open a media player, such as Kaffeine, and start listening to your MP3 music right now. In the case of Kaffeine, it will even warn you about content you can't currently play (DVD movies and Windows media) and what you can do to remedy that (if it's legal to do so where you are).

## On the DVD
A PCLinuxOS live CD is included on the DVD that comes with this book. See Appendix A for information on how to use that live CD. ■

To start using PCLinuxOS, simply insert the CD or DVD you have containing PCLinuxOS. From the DVD supplied with this book, just select PCLinuxOS from the boot screen.

User accounts for a regular user (guest) and administrative user (root) are preconfigured for PCLinuxOS. Select which you want to log in as (guest is recommended) and enter the password (shown on the screen) for the associated user. After a few moments, a desktop should appear that is similar to the one shown in Figure 25-1.

## Checking what you can do

A lot of applications are available on the PCLinuxOS live CD and you can install many more later. But what sets PCLinuxOS apart is how many applications have so many features enabled by default. With PCLinuxOS running, try a few things:

- **Get on the Internet.** Open the Firefox icon on the desktop and type a URL into the location box. If your computer has an available Internet connection, you should be able to browse the Web. If not, select System ⇨Configuration ⇨Network Center and configure your networking as required.

- **Try out Web content.** Plug-ins added to Firefox in PCLinuxOS should allow you to play Flash, Java, MP3, PDF, and other content without any additional software. Some content, such as Microsoft Word files, appear when the browser automatically launches an external application.

**FIGURE 25-1**

Boot PCLinuxOS to the default KDE desktop.

- **Configure your system.** You can perform lots of other configuration on your system from the Control Center. Select System ⇨Configuration ⇨Control Center.

- **Try other applications.** Select the PC icon in the lower-left corner of the screen. From the menu that appears you can select to play games, connect to other systems (e-mail, IM, file sharing, news, and bittorrent), do word processing, or configure your system.

## Adding more applications

If the content you want to play or display cannot be interpreted by your browser or other application (such as those on the PCLinuxOS menus), use Synaptic to install additional software over the Internet. From the bottom panel, select the Package Manager icon. After you type the root password, the Synaptic package manager appears as shown in Figure 25-2.

**FIGURE 25-2**

Add more software with Synaptic package manager.

If this is the first time using Synaptic for this installation, you should reload package information. Select Edit ⮑Reload Package Information. With an active Internet connection, your system will download updated package information to your system.

Every repository that contains software you want may not be immediately enabled. Select Settings Repositories and check for repositories that you may want to enable. For example, a separate repository is available for OpenOffice.org office productivity applications.

With that information updated, you can begin adding the software that you want to your PCLinuxOS installation. Here are some examples:

- **Commercial DVD software.** Because of contention about the legality of open source software for decrypting commercial DVD movies, it is not delivered by default in PCLinuxOS (see the discussion in Chapter 6).

- **Win32 codec binaries.** In the non-free repository are also packages containing codec binaries to play a variety of multimedia content. The win32-codecs-all package includes many such binaries.

- **Office productivity software.** The OpenOffice.org office productivity suite is available for PCLinuxOS (as it is for other Linux distributions). It is not included on the live CD, but you can download it from Synaptic with the OpenOffice.org repository enabled. For US English, select the task-openoffice3-en-US package. (You need about 440MB of disk space for all the packages associated with that metapackage.)

If you miss some other Windows applications, you can try running them using WINE (WINE Is Not an Emulator) software. Install the wine package to give it a try. WINE has been well-tested for running many popular Microsoft Windows applications, including Microsoft Office, Internet Explorer, and Outlook.

# Installing PCLinuxOS

You can install PCLinuxOS to your computer either directly from the medium (DVD or CD) containing PCLinuxOS or by first booting the PCLinuxOS live CD and installing from an icon on the desktop. The following procedure describes how to install from a running live CD.

## Caution

If there is any data on your computer that you want to keep, be sure to back it up before starting this procedure. Although you can choose to not erase selected partitions, you should back up any important data just to be safe. ■

## Starting the install

1. **Boot PCLinuxOS.** Insert the DVD that comes with this book (or otherwise get a copy of the PCLinuxOS live CD) and reboot your computer.

2. **Select to boot PCLinuxOS.** From the Linux Bible DVD, select the entry for booting PCLinuxOS. If PCLinuxOS is unable to boot, refer to the boot options described earlier in this chapter. If it boots properly, a desktop similar to the one shown earlier in Figure 25-1.

3. **Select to install PCLinuxOS.** With PCLinuxOS running on your computer, two icons on the desktop help you begin installing it permanently to hard disk:

   - **Installation Help.** Select this icon to view a description of the installation process if you need more information.

   - **Install PCLinuxOS.** Select this icon to begin the install process.

   Figure 25-3 shows an example of the Installation Help and Install PCLinuxOS icons:

**FIGURE 25-3**

Double-click the Install PCLinuxOS icon to begin hard disk installation.

4. **Enter root password.** When prompted, type **root** as the root password. (This step will happen several times in this procedure.) A dialog appears asking whether you want to remove video drivers.

5. **Remove video drivers?** Click the Remove Driver Now! button. This option removes unused ATI and NVidia video drivers to avoid possible conflicts with future software updates. The PCLinuxOS Installer wizard appears.

6. **Continue installation.** Click Next. A dialog asks you to select your partitioning scheme.

7. **Partitioning.** Select one of these choices for partitioning your computer's hard disk:

## Caution

As soon as you make your selection, PCLinuxOS is installed, erasing any data that exists on the selected disk partitions. ■

- **Use existing partitions.** Choose this option to keep your disk partitions as they are and then pick how you want directories on your system assigned (or not assigned) to those partitions. Don't assign a directory to any partition that you don't want to be erased and reused!

- **Use free space.** Assign space from disk space that is not currently assigned to any partition.

- **Erase and use entire disk.** All data on all partitions will be erased and reused for the new installation.

- **Custom disk partitioning.** Set up disk partitioning yourself.

After you make your partitioning selections, the installer begins writing PCLinuxOS to your computer's hard disk.

8. **Boot loader.** Choose whether you want to use the GRUB boot loader (graphical or text based), the device you want to boot from, and how long to delay before booting the default boot entry if no selection is made (10 seconds by default). If PCLinuxOS is the only operating system installed, you will probably want the boot loader installed to the master boot record (MBR) of the first hard disk (usually /dev/sda). Alternatively, you can install to the root partition where PCLinuxOS is installed and manually add the boot information to the boot loader for another operating system installed on your system.

   If you chose to install the boot loader on a partition, the installer will ask you which drive you are booting from. If that is the case, you are prompted to add, modify, or remove any boot entries you choose. PCLinuxOS will be added to your existing boot loader by default and set as the default entry to boot. Click Next to continue.

At this point, installation is done. As instructed, remove the live CD and restart the computer to run your new PCLinuxOS installation.

## Configuring after installation

The first time you start PCLinuxOS after installation to hard disk, it prompts you to do some basic configuration for your system. Here is what you are asked to do:

- Add a password for the root (administrative) user.
- Add a full name, user name, and password for a user account for everyday use.

After that configuration, you can log in to your PCLinuxOS system, using the information you just entered, and begin using your installed system.

# Remastering PCLinuxOS

Offering tools for remastering PCLinuxOS has encouraged users to create their own custom versions of PCLinuxOS. In many cases, those users have made their remasters available to others. That gives you the opportunity to try out versions of PCLinuxOS that include different desktop environments or special sets of applications.

The DVD that comes with this book includes the official PCLinuxOS live CD, which offers a KDE desktop by default. That and other official remasters are available from official PCLinuxOS download sites such as the following:

```
http://ibiblio.org/pub/linux/distributions/texstar/pclinuxos
```

Official remasters include

- **pclinuxos.** Includes a KDE desktop (about 690MB)

- **pclinuxos-gnome.** Includes the GNOME desktop (about 674MB)

- **pclinuxos-lxde.** Includes the Lightweight X11 Desktop Environment (about 313MB)

- **pclinuxos-minime-kde3.** Includes a stripped-down KDE desktop (about 298MB)

- **pclinuxos-minime-gnome.** Includes a stripped-down GNOME desktop (about 361MB)

Other community-sponsored remasters include PCLinuxOS Xfce (`www.cozmodesigns.co.uk/xfce/download.htm`) and Business Edition Linux PCLinuxOS (`http://belproject.org`).

Creating your own custom remaster of PCLinuxOS is actually quite simple. The result is that you can gather up your running PCLinuxOS system (including all applications, settings, and data) and store that data to a single ISO image that you can burn to CD or DVD and run later.

Most of the procedure centers on the `mklivecd` command. Beyond that, all you need to do is set up your PCLinuxOS system as you like it. Here are the steps for creating your own remastered PCLinuxOS:

1. **Boot up.** Boot PCLinuxOS. You probably want to do this procedure from an installed system, rather than from the live CD (unless you have lots of RAM available to offer all the space needed for the remaster procedure).

2. **Set up.** Install the software, data files, and settings you want to keep on your live CD. A standard DVD can hold about 4GB of data, whereas a CD holds about 700MB of data. For the DVD, that means you can have up to about 12GB of uncompressed data. If you have the ability to burn dual-layer DVDs, you can store a little less than twice that.

3. **Clean up.** Clear out all the junk from your system before you burn your live CD. Here are some suggestions:

   - Don't empty `/tmp` directories (those are ignored anyway).

   - Do clear out things like cached data from your web browser, thumbnails from image applications, and your desktop trash can.

   - Check to see how much space has been used by hidden directories within your home directory. For example, type **du –sh /home/guest/.*** to see space being used by WINE (`.wine`), Thunderbird, and Firefox (`.mozilla`).

   - Unmount any temporarily mounted file systems, such as those from a CD, USB key, or remote system (such as an NFS mount).

   - Check again that everything on your local system is alright to have on your live CD. For example, if you plan to share this live CD with others you probably want to make sure that any private files or privacy data (such as stored passwords or cached URLs you have visited) are cleared away.

4. **Check available disk space.** Make sure that you have enough space on hard disk to not only hold the resulting ISO image, but also the temporary files needed to create that image. The space should **not** be on a Windows FAT partition.

   For example, to create a 4GB DVD image you should have at least 8GB of disk space available. Half of that space must be available from your /tmp partition, because the remastering tool uses that space to store temporary files, and half must be available in the directory where you will store your ISO.

5. **Start the remaster.** To begin the remastering process, select the menu button on the lower-left corner of the screen and choose System ⇨MakeLiveCD and type the root password (or run make LiveCD from the Utilities folder). After a warning about disk space you are asked whether you want to provide advanced options.

6. **Add advanced options.** Click Yes to look at advanced options. If you like you can do such things as force a 1024 × 768 screen resolution or embed md5sums of each stored file on the CD. Type in those options, when prompted, and click OK to continue. You are prompted to provide the name and location for the resulting image.

7. **Name the ISO image.** Select the name of the ISO and the folder in which it will be stored. This folder can be anywhere that can hold the full size of the resulting ISO image. Click OK when you are ready.

At this point, the remastering process begins. You can watch as an initial RAM disk (initrd) is created, filesystem parameters are set, and the compressed image is created. When the process is done, a new ISO image should be stored in the location you named.

With the ISO image complete, you can test it, if you like, before burning it to CD. Use Synaptic to install the qemu package. Then run a qemu command similar to the following, replacing the name and location of the new ISO image with the name you used.

```
# qemu -cdrom /root/remaster.iso
```

You should see a QEMU window displaying your PCLinuxOS boot screen that is similar to the one shown in Figure 25-4.

Click your mouse in the QEMU window and select which entry to boot. Because you are running the image entirely in available memory, it will probably run much slower than the resulting ISO will eventually run from CD or DVD. When you have tested your ISO image, press Ctrl+Alt to release your mouse so you can start using the desktop again.

When you are satisfied that the ISO image works, you can burn that image to CD or DVD using a tool such as k3b or cdrecord. With the image burned to the medium, insert that CD or DVD to a computer's drive and reboot. If all went well, you should be running the same operating system (including its data and settings) that you had when you ran the remaster process.

**FIGURE 25-4**

Test your remastered PCLinuxOS system ISO with qemu before you burn it to CD.

# Summary

The great popularity of PCLinuxOS stems from the interest of many people to replace their current desktop operating systems with an easy-to-use Linux system. PCLinuxOS is often recommended to first-time Linux users because so many features are enabled by default.

To start with PCLinuxOS, you just run one of several available live CD versions. An icon on the PCLinuxOS desktop lets you install your running system to hard disk. After that, adding more applications to do everything you might expect from a full-featured desktop system is easy.

Another feature of PCLinuxOS is the set of tools it offers to remaster your current PCLinuxOS system to an ISO image. You can then use that ISO image to replicate your system to run live, without your having to reinstall the software.

People in the PCLinuxOS community have created custom remasters of PCLinuxOS. These remasters do such things as offer different desktop environments (GNOME, LXDE, and others) or special application sets (such as a set of business tools).

# Running Mandriva

**B**efore becoming Mandriva Linux, Mandrakelinux was created as a fork of Red Hat Linux (in 1998). It initially had such tight ties to Red Hat Linux that the Mandrakelinux installer even stated that you were installing Red Hat.

After those early days, Mandrakelinux became a solid distribution in its own right, with the main focus on an easy-to-use desktop distribution. It was often mentioned along with Linspire, while Linspire was a viable distribution, when people talked about the easiest distributions for someone new to Linux to install and use.

From the beginning of 2005 to the present, Mandrakelinux has gone from the brink of bankruptcy to its current incarnation as *Mandriva,* after MandrakeSoft (the parent company of Mandrakelinux) merged with Conectiva Linux in February 2005. Conectiva Linux was a Brazilian-based Linux company with goals similar to those of Mandrakelinux.

**On the DVD**

The Mandriva live CD, called Mandriva One, is included on the DVD that comes with this book. This desktop-oriented live CD can also be used to install the contents of that live CD to your hard drive. ■

## Mandriva Features

Unlike Linux distributions that are community-driven, Mandriva is a company that sells Linux products. Community-like activities are available through the Mandriva community site (www.mandriva.com/en/community), which provides more of a customer support–type function than a Linux development center.

In addition to the merger with Conectiva, Mandriva also acquired the desktop-oriented Lycoris Linux distribution in June 2005. Since then, Mandriva's product offerings have evolved into a range of desktop, mobile, small-business server, and enterprise products.

Commercial offerings include Mandriva Enterprise Server 5, Mandriva Linux Powerpack, and Mandriva Directory Server. To support those products, Mandriva offers a variety of consulting, support, and training options.

At the time of this writing, the most current version of Mandriva Linux is Mandriva One 2009.1. Version numbers for business-oriented products follow a different scheme, with the latest business server product called Mandriva Enterprise Server 5.0.

Here is a brief overview of the versions of Mandriva that you can download for free:

- **Mandriva One**—A live CD version of Mandriva Linux that contains a well-stocked set of desktop applications. Besides offering the full OpenOffice productivity suite, Mandriva One includes tools for graphics (GIMP and F-Spot), Internet (Firefox, Evolution, and GAIM), and multimedia (Totem movie player, Sound Juicer, and TVtime television viewer). The Mandriva One GNOME desktop live CD is included on the DVD that comes with this book. A KDE version of Mandriva One and more than a dozen different language versions are also available.

- **Mandriva Linux Free**—This three-CD set of free software is aimed at power users. Both i586 and x86-64 versions of Mandriva Linux Free are freely available for download.

You can also purchase Mandriva for individual use:

- **Mandriva Linux Powerpack**—Designed with the entry-level desktop user in mind. The package includes basic productivity software such as OpenOffice, Kdeprintfax, and planning/finance software. Also included are the requisite networking tools for e-mail, FTP, and Web browsing. Several non-free multimedia components are also installed, enabling audio and video playback, image editing, and scanning documents as well as CD recording.

## Coming from Windows

The Mandriva Linux 2009 Powerpack is the product that Mandriva recommends for beginners who are looking to switch to Linux from Windows. By adding commercial software for watching DVD movies (LinDVD), Windows gaming (Transgaming's Cedega), Google Picasa, and 3D desktop effects (drak3D), Mandriva makes transitioning from Windows to Linux a fairly easy proposition. ■

The following is a list of Mandriva product offerings for business:

- **Mandriva Directory Server**—Includes LDAP directory management tools for administering access to Linux and Windows services, such as DNS, DHCP, Squid proxy services, and Samba servers.

- **Mandriva Pulse 2**—A solution for monitoring and managing Linux and Windows networks. It is an open source product that simplifies remote management.
- **Mandriva Enterprise Server**—Along with popular server software (Apache, MySQL, Samba, and so on), business-oriented Mandriva products come with more extensive product support. Both the Enterprise and Premium Enterprise Server products come with 24/7 Web support, with a Web response time of two business days. Both offer unlimited phone support as well, with the premium package offering quicker response time and other extended options. One, three, and five-year maintenance contracts are available.

If you just want to try out Mandriva, you can boot Mandriva One directly from the DVD that comes with this book. When Mandriva One is booted, open the Live Install icon on the desktop to install the contents of the Mandriva One CD to your hard drive if you like. You can also download that same CD ISO image directly from Mandriva (see `www.mandriva.com/en/download`).

# Exploring Mandriva

The Linux distribution that has now evolved into Mandriva has long hung its hat on the concept of "ease of use," the idea being that its distributions should be readily accessible to a large pool of users. Mandrakelinux was heralded early on for its exceptional use of a graphical installer and configuration tools. Its support for hardware, video acceleration, and audio playback also tends to be top-notch.

When coupled with the fact that the Mandrakelinux installer frequently detected and configured hardware that left other distributions' installation routines mystified, you can see why Mandrakelinux has been, and will probably continue, under the name Mandriva, to be a popular distribution.

Mandriva Linux One 2009.1 comes with a number of attractive features, including the following:

- Multiple desktop environments are available. Besides KDE and GNOME, lightweight LXDE and Xfce desktops are included. The user interface is consistent across those desktop environments. You can also get the Sugar desktop, which was designed originally for the One Laptop per Child project.
- Songbird multimedia player provides a full-featured music player, with smart playlists, album artwork support, and connections to upcoming shows by musical artists.
- The largely automated installation process has new features such as the capability to resize NTFS partitions.
- Hardware detection and configuration have been improved over previous Mandrakelinux releases. In particular, the security, printing, and user configuration tools have been completely overhauled to provide additional functionality and ease of use.

- Updated versions of the RPM Package Manager and the Internet update software have improved the ease of installing new software as well as system patches.
- Security maintenance is comprehensive. Mandriva Linux 2009.1 includes easy-to-use configuration tools for setting general system security and setting up a firewall. It also supports a range of security protocols such as SSH, SSL, LDAP, and NIS.

In addition, a few "Drak" tools make a particularly big impact on the usability and consistency of Mandriva. These utilities are DrakX installer, RPMDrake software management window, and Mandriva Linux Control Center.

## Mandriva installer (DrakX)

DrakX is a highly acclaimed and user-friendly installer that has been one of Mandriva's key differentiators against other Linux builds. Included since version Mandrakelinux 7.0, this installer was one of the first attempts at automated installers that most novice Linux users could successfully use.

Although the installer is almost "newbie"-proof, invoking advanced installation options enabling detailed control of the install at any point during the installation process is still possible. As with most versions of Linux, you can install from a boot CD, a hard drive, or a network. The following are the key features of the DrakX installer included in the current version of Mandriva:

- Convenient installation configuration options using predefined packages, rather than requiring you to choose individual packages from the wide selection that is available. You can select individual packages if you do not want to use one of the predefined package options. Workstation and Server Package groups are available for various roles and needs, for example.
- The ability to format hard disks, configure RAID, and resize partitions of many types, including NTFS, FAT32, EXT3, ReiserFS, and XFS.
- Support for a wide range of network file systems.
- Improved upgrade support.
- Automated installation tools.
- Rescue mode for failed/problematic installation.

In addition to the straightforward boot CD, the DrakX installer supports a number of other installation methods, including:

- **Network installs**—If needed, you can start the DrakX installation process and connect to a variety of network servers to access the installation files. This includes NFS, HTTP, SBM, SSH, Web Proxy, and FTP servers.

- **Kickstart installs**—In environments such as customer support call centers, school computer labs, and large offices, you might find yourself needing to install and configure large numbers of computers in a short period of time. Kickstart installations use an answer file to automate most of the installation process. Mandriva's installation routine enables you to create floppies to use when performing kickstart installations. Mandriva enables you to make semi-interactive or completely automated setup floppies.

- **Upgrades**—The DrakX installer supports an upgrade path to bring older installs up to snuff with the newest release.

You can try out the DrakX installer in the walk-through included in this chapter.

# RPM package management with RPMDrake

Adding software to and removing software from your Linux installation should not be a time-consuming chore. RPMDrake provides an intuitive graphical interface for managing installed software. You can easily see what is installed and add or remove packages as needed. To open RPMDrake, select Install & Remove Software from the main menu (bottom-left corner of the screen). Figure 26-1 shows an example of the RPMDrake window.

**FIGURE 26-1**

Add, remove, and update Mandriva software from the RPMDrake Software Management window.

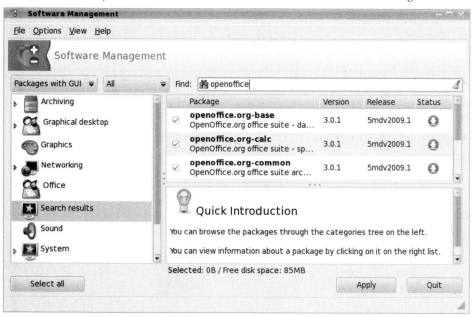

After you open RPMDrake, there are a few things you should know:

- You can configure your list of sources by selecting Options ➪ Media Manager. This enables you to specify the location of installable packages, which could be the local file system, CD-ROM media, RSYNC server, or HTTP/FTP archives of installation packages. One option lets you refresh your list of Mandriva mirror sites, to make sure you're ready to get access to the latest security and system updates.

- From the Packages box, select All Updates to see any updates that are available for your system. You can then select Apply to download and install all available software updates.

- You need the root password when installing packages. RPMDrake prompts you for it as needed.

- RPMDrake offers improved upgrade support. You can use it to scan for software updates, download them, and offer them in the list of installable programs for the user to select.

RPMDrake supports a search feature that enables you to use a variety of criteria to search for desired software within configured sources. You can search by package name, or you can search based on a description. Either way, when you find the package you want, simply select the target package and use the Install/Remove button to get going.

But what if you just want to remove software? This process is very straightforward as well. Locate the package you want to remove under the Installed Applications tab. Select it, and click the Install/Remove button. The package, along with any that depend on it, is removed from the system. (You may also choose not to remove the dependent packages.)

## Mandriva Linux Control Center

The Mandriva Linux Control Center (MLCC), also called DrakConf, provides an intuitive and accessible means of configuring various system resources. You can use this tool to add new hardware, configure installed applications, add or remove applications (by invoking RPMDrake), and change the configuration of your existing hardware.

To open the MLCC, from the main menu, select Tools ➪ System Tools ➪ Configure Your Computer. Figure 26-2 shows an example of the Mandriva Linux Control Center.

You can also use the control center to adjust your default system security levels, change your display options, schedule events, manage user accounts, and even change the system time/date setting. The MLCC uses a number of installation and configuration wizards to help you get rolling. For example, a wizard for Apache Web server setup enables you to get your HTTP server online in just a few minutes. Some of the key improvements and features of MLCC in Mandriva Linux are

- Secure, remote system configuration from any network.
- Automatic detection of hot swappable devices without restarting the system.
- Large icons that are easy to see and appropriately related to the functions they invoke.

**FIGURE 26-2**

The Mandriva Linux Control Center is a simplified tool for system administration.

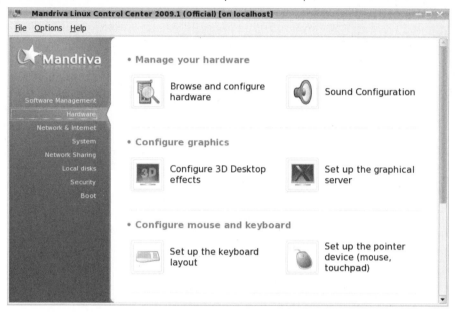

# The Mandriva Community

Like many distributions of Linux, Mandriva Linux has developed a split personality of sorts. Mandriva distributes value-added versions of Mandriva complete with numerous utilities, applications, and support. The core Mandriva development effort produces an unsupported, but just as useful, version of the core Mandriva build.

With this "free" copy, called Mandriva Linux Free, you get the OS and the basic utilities and applications. However, if you purchase the Mandriva Powerpack edition, you have access to extra utilities, such as codecs for playing audio, video, and DVD movies, Google Earth, Adobe Acrobat, Adobe Flash, Opera Web browser, and Skype VOIP telephony. It also comes with three months of Web support.

Whether you purchase Mandriva software or use the free distribution, you have access to the Mandriva community (www.mandriva.com/en/community/start). The Mandriva community offers a Wiki, forums, IRC channels, mailing lists, and security updates.

If you have any interest in tracking product development and maybe getting a little help if you need it, you'll want to keep on top of Mandriva news, forums, and Linux User Groups (LUGs).

User forums are a priceless tool for finding solutions to problems, getting involved in software-related projects, or just connecting with other Mandriva users. The Mandriva forums (`http://forum.mandriva.com/`) include Announcements, Documentation, Community Chat, Requests & Mandriva Services, and many others. The Mandriva Software forum is a great one, with especially in-depth information on installation and configuration.

# Installing Mandriva Limited Edition

To check out Mandriva for the first time, you have several options. As mentioned, Mandriva One is a live CD that you can also use as a basic installer. The other free option is to download the three-CD set of Mandriva Linux Free. If you like the distribution, I encourage you to purchase one of the Mandriva Linux products.

To review your free download options, refer to the Mandriva Linux Download page at `www.mandriva.com/en/download/free`.

To try out the live CD and install the contents of the CD to your hard disk, you can follow the instructions in this section. The contents of the Mandriva One live CD are included on the DVD that comes with this book and can be booted directly from the DVD.

## Note
The DVD that comes with this book includes the English language GNOME version of Mandriva One. If you prefer the KDE version or any of several different free and language versions, refer to the Mandriva Download page (`www.mandriva.com/en/download/`). You can download either Mandriva Linux One or Mandriva Linux Free images from that page. Appendix A explains how to burn the installation CDs from the CD images, if you decide to download Mandriva CDs yourself. ■

## The right hardware for Mandriva

As with software packages, look before you leap. It is important to make sure your hardware is up to the task before you install Mandriva. Fear not, users of less-than-stellar hardware; the hardware requirements are far from onerous. To use Mandriva you need (or you can use)

- **x586 class processor or above**—The Intel Pentium I–IV, AMD K6/II/III, Duron, or Athlon/XP/MP.

- **RAM**—At least 256MB of memory is recommended (although 512MB will work much better). If you need to run Mandriva on a machine with less RAM, consider starting the installation from Mandriva Free instead of Mandriva One, because live CDs generally require more RAM to run effectively.

- **Hard disk**—At least 1GB is recommended for installing Mandriva One.

- **RAID controllers**—There is wide support for SCSI RAID controllers. In addition, 3Ware IDE and Serial ATA controllers are also supported.

- **DVD or CD drive**—To run the installation from a CD/DVD source disk, you need the appropriate drive. This drive needs to support bootable CD/DVD media.

- **Input/Output**—Of course, if you want to interact with your Mandriva install, you at least need a keyboard and a monitor. A mouse is not needed for the installation, but it is handy and recommended.

## Note

**For those who live life on the bleeding edge, a version of Mandriva exists that supports the AMD Athlon64 processor. See the Mandriva Powerpack product (**`www.mandriva.com/en/product/mandriva-linux-powerpack`**).** ■

As you can see from the system specifications, you can use a wide range of hardware to run your Mandriva installation. Do you have an old PIII with 128MB of RAM, a CD-ROM, and a blank 1G hard disk? No problem. How about a "gaming war machine" sporting a 3.2 GHz P4, 1GB of RAM, DVD-R, and an ocean of hard disk space? Bring it on!

The vast assortment of hardware supported includes popular video cards such as NVIDIA FX series and ATI Radeon video adapters. Large numbers of Ethernet and Wi-Fi network adapters, USB 2.0, and other hardware make your chances of installation and configuration success very high.

This installation requires no special hard disk configuration. As mentioned, this install assumes a preexisting Microsoft Windows operating system using the NTFS file system. You will "make room" on the existing partition and install Mandriva there. In addition to using a boot disk (as you will here), you can take advantage of the installation options such as FTP and NFS as outlined briefly in this chapter and in more detail in Chapter 8.

## Caution

**Do not make your first installation attempt on a mission-critical system. Resizing an NTFS partition can have unintended effects. Back up any information you cannot live without, especially if you resize existing partitions as the following instructions show.** ■

## Installing Mandriva with the DrakX installer

The first part of starting a Mandriva install from the Mandriva One live CD is to boot up that live CD. After the live CD is up and running, you start the installation process by opening the Live Install icon from the live CD's desktop.

1. Back up any important data from your computer's hard disk before starting this procedure.

2. Insert the DVD that comes with this book and reboot the computer. The boot screen appears.

3. Type **mandriva** and press Enter. The Mandriva One live CD starts and you are prompted to select your language.

4. Select your language and click Next.

5. You are asked to read and accept the license agreement. After doing so, you are asked to select your time zone.

6. Choose the time zone you are in, based on your country, state, and city. You are asked to choose your keyboard layout.

7. Select your keyboard layout and click Next. Select to accept it and click Next. You are asked to set your time.

8. Choose whether to set your computer's hardware clock to local time or UTC time. As an alternative, you can choose to have your time set by an NTP server (you can choose the server as well). Click Next to continue.

    At this point, Mandriva One continues to boot up to a desktop, such as the one shown in Figure 26-3. In particular, notice the Live Install icon on the left side of the screen. (Notice also the Upgrade to Powerpack icon, which allows you to upgrade an existing Mandriva Linux system.)

**FIGURE 26-3**

Start a Mandriva One installation from an icon on the Mandriva One desktop.

9. Double-click the Live Install icon on the desktop. The Mandriva Live Wizard starts. Click Next to continue. You are asked how you want to partition your disk.

10. The next screen begins the disk partitioning portion of the Mandriva installation. (General guidance regarding the size and types of partitions you'll need is included in Chapter 8.) Select one of the following approaches to configuring your hard disk:

   - **Use Existing Partitions**—Use any available Linux partitions to install Mandriva.

   - **Use free space on the Microsoft Windows partition**—If free space is available on your Microsoft Windows partition (NTFS or VFAT file systems), select here to use that space.

   - **Erase and Use Entire Disk**—Wipes the existing hard disk in preparation for your install. This option is great for critical server systems where you want to start with a completely clean system or if no data exists on the disk you need.

   - **Custom**—Here's where the real magic happens: You can create custom volumes, resize existing volumes, and in general torture your hard drives as much as you like.

Selecting the Custom option opens a new window that shows all the existing hard drives and configured partitions. If your system has only an existing Windows installation on an NTFS partition, all that will be visible are the blue markers indicating a Windows partition.

When you click on the partition that you want to use for your Mandriva installation, a new option appears in the left portion of the disk configuration window. By clicking the Resize button, you can change the size (within limitations) of the existing NTFS partition.

Give it a shot if you have the opportunity. Click the Resize button, and a new window appears. It has a slider that's all the way to the right by default. As you slide the indicator to the left, the corresponding value displayed gets smaller. This number reflects the size (in MB) that the NTFS partition will be after you've completed the resizing operation. For example, if you have a 30GB NTFS partition and you want to free up 10GB of space for the creation of a set of native Linux partitions, simply slide the indicator from the maximum value of 30000MB to 20000MB, and you will have freed the required 10000MB.

The amount of space you can create depends on the size of the disk, how much data is stored, and whether the partition has been defragmented. To find out the degree to which you can resize the partition, move the slider all the way to the left. That displays the smallest size you can make the existing Windows partition.

When you've selected the size you want, click the Next button. You are shown a warning to make sure you have backed up any information you depend on before performing the partition resizing. If you're ready to commit, click OK.

Tinkering with partitions and volumes if you have important information on them and no backup is foolish. Resizing is a pretty predictable process, but the process is not perfect, and you can end up with a working Mandriva install and a sizeable, useless Windows partition.

If all went well, you now have an unformatted partition available. Click the empty partition and create the native Linux partitions you need or want. After you've sorted all your partitions in the manner you want, click Done. A warning message asks whether you're sure you want to do this. Click Next, and the deed is done.

11. In a normal Mandriva installation, you would be given the opportunity to select packages to install at this point. Because this procedure installs from the live CD, however, the operating system on the live CD is simply copied to your hard drive. When that's done, you are asked to choose a boot loader.

12. Choose either the GRUB or LILO boot loader. Then choose the boot device (typically the device representing the first hard disk that is booted on your computer, such as /dev/hda). See Chapter 8 for descriptions of GRUB and LILO. Click the Advanced button to choose other boot options. Click Next to continue. Your current boot entries appear, configured for the selected boot loader.

13. The entries that Mandriva has set up to put on your boot menu appear. You can edit those entries or create some of your own. If you have multiple operating systems on your computer, you can add your own entries so that those systems can be selected from the boot loader. Click Next to continue.

14. You are instructed to restart the computer and remove the live CD. Click Finish and select System ⇨ Shut Down, and then choose Restart.

After the live CD shuts down, the DVD is ejected. Remove the DVD and press Enter to boot your newly installed Mandriva system.

The first time your installed system boots, you have the opportunity to configure settings for that installation. You can configure the following:

- **Network & Internet Configuration**—Configure your Ethernet, wireless, or other Internet connection.

- **Root password**—Enter a password for the root user (twice).

- **Add user**— Enter the real name, login name, and password (twice) for a regular user account.

- **Mandriva account**—You can create a Mandriva online account. With this account, you can take advantage of a variety of services available from Mandriva, such as keeping up with security updates and upgrades.

# Summary

Although Mandriva may not be as widely known as other Linux distributions, it is arguably one of the most accessible versions for novice desktop users. It is especially useful to those who want their Linux installations to exist alongside Windows installations that may not have free partitions for a dedicated Linux installation.

This chapter explores some of the defining features of Mandriva, including the installer, which incorporates the capability to resize existing Windows partitions nondestructively; an RPM package management (RPMDrake); and system configuration tools.

In addition to enabling you to wedge a Linux installation onto a 100 percent Windows partition, the Mandriva installer reliably detects your hardware and provides you with the option of simplified or very granular package selection. The RPM package management enables you to install, uninstall, and update software from a consistent and user-friendly graphical interface.

If you need to add or troubleshoot hardware, Mandriva provides graphical configuration tools (Mandriva Linux Control Center) to make the task easier after the initial installation, and DrakX for detection during the installation. If you join the Mandriva Club, a wealth of support and application downloads are available.

# Running a Linux Firewall Router

The Internet is a potentially hostile place, so you need to be able to protect your computer from attacks coming in from the Internet. One essential element of security for Internet-facing computers is a firewall. A firewall can protect your computer or private network from outside intruders. Placing a firewall on the route between your local network and the Internet gives you tremendous power and flexibility to manage your network traffic. You can react to every packet coming in or going out of your network based on where it's from, where it's going, and what it is requesting to do.

Linux is often used as a firewall. In fact, several Linux distributions are configured to act exclusively as a firewall (running on media as small as a floppy disk). Because firewall tools can also be used to protect personal desktop systems, several Linux distributions include graphical tools for managing firewalls in an appropriate way for desktops. So, in effect, almost any Linux distribution can be used as a dedicated firewall or can simply be configured to use firewall features to protect itself from unwanted outside access.

In this chapter, you explore the features used in nearly every Linux system today for creating firewalls (using iptables features) and discover how to use graphical firewall tools in Fedora and Mandriva Linux. To comprehend how a lot of firewall features can fit in a very small space, you look at how to use the Coyote Linux Floppy Firewall distribution (which comes with this book).

## IN THIS CHAPTER

**Understanding firewalls**

**Protecting desktops with firewalls**

**Managing firewalls with iptables**

**Making a Coyote Linux bootable firewall floppy**

**Getting other bootable firewalls**

## On the CD

The CD that accompanies this book contains what you need to create a bootable floppy-disk firewall with Coyote Linux. The iptables firewall feature is included with every Linux distribution that comes with this book. ■

# Understanding Firewalls

A *firewall* refers to hardware or software tools that limit access to a computer or network based on a defined security policy. As used in this chapter, firewall refers to a piece of software that examines every network packet coming from the Internet, or going out to the Internet, to decide whether it should be allowed in, rejected completely, ignored, or modified.

Every recent Linux system has firewall features available because they are built into the Linux kernel in a facility called *iptables*. But firewalls in Linux can be used differently, depending on what you are doing with your Linux system:

- **Desktop system**—A Linux system used only to run applications and browse the Web may simply use its firewall to block all (or nearly all) incoming requests for services. By doing so, the only data that can come into the desktop system is in response to requests initiated by that computer itself. When that desktop itself is behind a corporate firewall, firewall rules can often be relaxed to allow various kinds of file and printer sharing to take place behind that firewall.

- **Server system**—On a Linux server, a firewall can be used to block requests to all incoming ports except those used to provide the specific services offered by that server. It can also be used to block any requests from addresses known to be particularly abusive or to allow more services to computers known to be friendly.

- **Firewall/router system**—Linux is often used as a dedicated firewall, providing a buffer between a private network and a public network (such as the Internet). Using Linux in this scenario, you can make best use of the full range of firewall features in iptables. Any packet trying to pass through the firewall can be filtered and then allowed to pass, be dropped, or be redirected in some way. The firewall can even hide (masquerade) the identity of private computers coming through the firewall to use the Internet.

Firewalls don't require fancy graphical interfaces (in fact, dedicated firewalls usually don't have X running at all, although they often serve up Web content to others). In fact, a Linux firewall in a home or small-office environment might run on a discarded 486 computer. Its footprint can be so small that it doesn't even need a hard disk—just a bootable floppy or CD that includes (or can access) the needed configuration information.

Firewalls are a prime example of an opportunity to use a special-purpose Linux distribution. (Later in this chapter you see how to build and run your own Coyote Linux firewall distribution, which fits on a floppy disk.) Linux firewall distributions typically

- Are tuned to include primarily those components needed to be a firewall.

- Contain scripts for easily configuring firewall settings.

- Don't include X, which requires that you use the command line or a Web browser from another machine on the network, allowing the distribution to fit in a much smaller space.

- Include a few other tools for diagnosing network problems or serving the local network in some way.

For the average desktop user, however, graphical tools are available with Linux to set up a basic, secure firewall without the user's having to understand the syntax of iptables. Let's examine some of those tools.

# Protecting Desktops with Firewalls

If you are using a desktop Linux system, a simplified GUI firewall tool is a good way to begin protecting your computer. At the very least, you can use your firewall to explicitly allow others to use selected services from your computer, while blocking requests for other services.

Tools that come with Mandriva, openSUSE, Fedora, and Red Hat Enterprise Linux (RHEL) illustrate a few ways to configure a firewall using GUI tools. During installation of Fedora or RHEL, the anaconda installer offers a screen for selecting a simple, secure firewall. Mandriva offers a firewall tool with its Control Center.

## Starting your firewall in Fedora

During the first boot process, after installing Fedora or RHEL systems, the Firewall Configuration screen enables you to put a basic firewall in place. After Fedora is installed, you can use the Firewall Configuration window (select System ⇨ Administration ⇨ Firewall), as shown in Figure 27-1.

---

**FIGURE 27-1**

Change settings for your Fedora firewall in the Firewall Configuration window.

The Fedora Firewall Configuration screen handles almost everything the average desktop user needs in a firewall. Here is what you can do with the settings on that page:

- **Disabled firewall**—Although this option is not generally recommended, some people choose Disabled firewall if they are already protected by a direct connection to a router firewall or feel no threat from their network connection. This allows connection requests through to all ports. Requests to configured services are allowed, whereas requests for other services are ignored. The firewall just passes these requests through without question. (Click the Disable button to disable your firewall.)

- **Enabled firewall**—If your firewall is currently disabled, click the Enable button to enable your firewall to protect from all incoming service requests, except those specifically checked in the pane below the button. After your firewall is enabled, you can choose to allow or disallow selected services to your Linux system using those listed in the pane.

- **Wizard**—Select the Wizard button to create a new, clean firewall configuration. A pop-up window lets you select basic or expert configurations that are appropriate for a desktop or server system as the basis for your firewall.

- **Trusted Services**—If you are offering access to services from your system, select the check box next to the service you want to allow. You can enable access to about 15 different service types from your system by selecting the appropriate check boxes. Services include FTP service (FTP), mail service (SMTP), NFS service (NFS4), remote copy and login service (SSH), Samba service (Samba), Secure Web service (WWW/HTTPS), telnet login service (Telnet), Web service (WWW/HTTP), and others.

- **Other Ports**—To allow access to other ports (which represent particular services), click the Other Ports heading. Click Add, and then type either the port name (such as imap) or number (such as 143) and select the protocol (TCP or UDP). The secure shell service (ssh on port 22) is the only port enabled on this tab by default.

- **Trusted Interfaces**—Select the Trusted Interfaces heading to list all the network interfaces (wired and wireless Ethernet, isdn, VPN tunnels, and so on) available on your system. If you mark the check box for an interface, the firewall won't block any requests for services from computers on that interface. You should not mark an interface as trusted if it is a public interface (such as an interface directly connected to the Internet).

- **Masquerading**—By enabling Masquerading on a selected interface, that interface can be used to allow computers on your LAN to communicate to the Internet through your computer, without exposing their private IP addresses to the outside world. Selecting Masquerading also enables IP forwarding on the interface (so packets entering the computer on one interface can be forwarded out through another interface).

- **Port Forwarding**—Service requests from other computers (such as those on the Internet) to your network interfaces can be forwarded to other IP addresses by selecting Port Forwarding and adding information on this tab (click the Add button). For example, you could select the Source as the eth0 interface facing the Internet, tcp protocol, and port 80. Then choose an IP address on your LAN as the Destination, and all standard Web content requests from the Internet are passed to the Web server at the

IP address. You can also select to have requests forwarded to a different port number (either on the local system or on another IP address).

- **ICMP Filter**—Select this option to enable your firewall to respond to certain ICMP requests. For example, ICMP requests tell your computer to respond to ping requests.

- **Custom Rules**—Select Custom Rules and choose the Add button if you want to add a file of custom rules to your firewall. Choose the address type (ipv4 or ipv6), firewall table (mangle, nat, or filter), and the name of the file containing the custom rules.

After you have made your changes, select Apply (to apply those changes to your firewall rules) and select Reload (to have those settings take effect immediately).

## Note

**Open your IMAP and POP3 ports only if your computer is a mail server. If you're just downloading and reading mail from your computer, you can get your mail just fine from an IMAP or POP3 server without opening those ports.** ■

After you have saved your firewall rules, you can examine the /etc/sysconfig/iptables file to see the firewall rules you created from your selections on the Firewall Configuration window. Those rules are loaded into the kernel from the /etc/init.d/iptables script (which is automatically set to run when you start Fedora). See the later section "Using Firewalls with iptables" for details on how to work with your firewall manually.

## Note

**I like to check a few services just to see the rules that the Firewall Configuration screen creates. Later, if I want to add access to other services on my computer, I can simply copy one of the lines that allow a service and then change the service number or name to the one I want to allow. Standard service numbers and names are included in the /etc/services file. A common service that a desktop system might want to use and offer is Windows file and printer sharing (using Samba in Linux). To share files with Samba, you might need to open TCP ports 137, 138, 139, and 445 in your firewall. (Open Samba ports to local, trusted networks and never to the Internet.)** ■

## Configuring a firewall in Mandriva

Mandriva offers a way to configure your firewall after Mandriva is running:

1. From the Mandriva menu (lower left corner), select Tools ➪ System Tools ➪ Configure Your Computer. (If you are prompted, enter the root password.) Mandriva Linux Control Center appears.

2. Select Security ➪ Set up your Personal Firewall. The Firewall service appears in the window.

3. Select particular services you would like to have available from your desktop system and click OK.

The default settings shown might be appropriate for many desktop systems because they don't allow any incoming service requests. With SSH, FTP, and Echo request on, someone could log in to your system over the network (with appropriate login and password), get files you offer through your own FTP service, and ping your computer to see whether it is up and running on the network. Of course, opening your firewall to allow SSH and FTP service assumes you have those two services turned on and configured as you like.

Other services you can enable from check boxes on this window include Web server, Domain Name System server, and CUPS server (for printing). If your system is configured as a mail server, you can select Mail Server and, optionally, POP and IMAP server (to allow mail users to get their e-mail messages).

If you want to add other ports, click the Advanced button. The Mandriva tool uses a different syntax for adding ports than does Fedora. You need to separate port numbers and protocols with a slash (for example, 123/udp 123/tcp to open network time protocol for those two protocols). Open a range of ports for a protocol by separating them with a colon (for example, 137:139/tcp 137:139/udp to allow Windows file and printer sharing from your computer). Separate multiple entries with spaces instead of commas.

4. Click OK to accept your settings and continue. You are asked if you want to use an Interactive Firewall.

5. With Use Interactive Firewall selected, you will be warned when someone tries to access any of the services you have selected on this page. For example, you can be warned when someone uses a port scanner, presumably in an attempt to find vulnerable ports on your system. You can also be alerted when someone tries to access services you are sharing, such as SSH, FTP, CUPS, or Echo services. Click OK to continue.

6. Select the Ethernet interfaces on which the firewall will be enabled and click OK to continue.

Mandriva uses a facility called Shorewall to set up and manage its iptables rules. So, instead of looking in /etc/sysconfig/iptables for the changes you just made, look in the /etc/shorewall directory for files such as rules, policy, and interfaces. You can have those rules take effect immediately by restarting the Shorewall service (as root user, from a Terminal window):

```
# service shorewall restart
```

When Shorewall restarts, look for any messages displayed. The output can give you information about any problems with the rules you have set up. Periodically check the /var/log/messages file to see whether anyone has tried to intrude on any of your ports.

To find out more about how Shorewall works to configure your iptables firewalls, refer to the Shorewall Web site (www.shorewall.net). You can still use iptables commands to view the current firewall (iptables -L -v) or temporarily flush your firewall (iptables -F). However, other changes you might make with iptables will be temporary because the next time you reboot, Shorewall will take over again.

# Using Firewalls with iptables

Understanding how iptables works will help you with any firewall you have configured in a Linux system. Previous firewall features—ipchains and ipfwadm—are no longer included in the Linux kernel. Unless you are using a Linux with an older kernel (which only a few floppy firewall distributions still have), iptables is your primary underlying facility for firewalls in Linux.

The commands used to configure iptables are not very intuitive. Using the iptables command, you add rules (one by one) to your running Linux kernel. When you have a set of rules you like, save those rules to a file using iptables-save. Then, when you are ready to use them again, you read them back in using iptables-restore.

Although most Linux systems offer some sort of interface to manage and load your iptables firewall automatically, very few offer the full range of features you might want. So you will need to understand iptables to do some configuration by hand if you do more than simply open or close access to ports. Just understanding iptables can help you go from one Linux system to another, regardless of the interface an individual distribution will put on top of it.

## Starting with iptables

If you have a running Linux system in front of you, you can immediately get a feel for how your firewall is working in a number of ways. To go beyond just listing the current firewall rules, however, I recommend that you try the procedure I describe in the next section on a Linux system that is set up for you to play with. Booting KNOPPIX is a great way to try that procedure without doing any harm (because everything disappears at your next reboot). Otherwise, just read along.

### Setting some rules

Studying the following steps can help you understand the syntax of firewall rules and the types of information you can set with them. This procedure is made to run from beginning to end on a computer that you have complete control over.

In the process of setting up your firewall rules, you might temporarily cut off all communications to and from the machine, so do not try this on a machine that must stay connected to the network.

This example procedure illustrates a case where you have two Ethernet interfaces on a computer (as is typical with a dedicated firewall). The interface defined as eth0 is connected to the Internet, and the interface defined as eth1 is connected to a private network of computers that the firewall is protecting. Presumably, the private computers are a bunch of desktop computers that need to go through the firewall to browse the Internet.

The iptables facility enables you to set up tables containing rules for how to handle Internet Protocol (IP) packets that enter the computer. The filtering table is the table you use by default (-t filter) if none is specified on the iptables command line. Other firewall tables you can configure include NAT (-t nat) and mangle (-t mangle). Special uses of NAT and mangle tables are explained later. It's the filter table that's used in this example.

Rules for what to do with packets that enter and leave the firewall are defined within the context of what are called *chains*. Available chains for filter tables are INPUT (packets received by the firewall), FORWARD (packets to be routed through the firewall), and OUTPUT (packets created on the local firewall itself). Filtering is done on those chains based on the set of rules you set up.

When a packet comes to the firewall, it steps through the rules in the chain until it finds a rule that matches. A match might depend on where a packet came from or where it is going, for example. When a match is made, the chain jumps to the action (also called a *target*) for that rule, which might define that the packet should be accepted or dropped, or have some other action done on it.

## Caution

**Setting up a firewall can be serious business. A misconfigured firewall can reject legitimate requests, forward packets to the wrong places, or even make your computer completely inaccessible from the network. Be very cautious if you are trying the following procedure on a computer that you rely on to be safe and accessible from a network. ■**

1. From a Terminal window, become root user:

```
$ su -
Password: ********
#
```

2. Type the following to see what filtering firewall rules are set on your system:

```
# iptables -L
Chain INPUT (policy ACCEPT)
target     prot opt source                destination

Chain FORWARD (policy ACCEPT)
target     prot opt source                destination

Chain OUTPUT (policy ACCEPT)
target     prot opt source                destination
```

The example output shows that no filtering rules are currently set for this Linux system, meaning that all packets are accepted (policy ACCEPT) by default. If you see a complex set of firewall rules, you might consider using a different machine to try this.

**3.** These three commands change the default behavior for how packets are filtered for your computer:

```
# iptables -P INPUT DROP
# iptables -P OUTPUT DROP
# iptables -P FORWARD DROP
```

In this example, the default behavior is changed such that all packets that come into your network interfaces (INPUT), go out of your network interfaces (OUTPUT), or request to travel through them (FORWARD) are dropped. At this point, no packets should be able to come in or go out of any network interfaces. You can run iptables -L again to see that all policies have changed from ACCEPT to DROP. (If this concerns you, don't worry. You can run the commands again, changing DROP to ACCEPT, to make your firewall wide open once more. Likewise, a reboot gets you back to your original state.)

**4.** This step configures how your firewall will accept or reject ICMP packets. ICMP (Internet Control Message Protocol) messages are for reporting error conditions and controlling connections to your server. Your server receives ICMP packets from computers that want to find out the state of your machine, such as whether the machine is currently accessible.

Packets from the Internet that are accepted for ICMP protocol requests in the following example are those for ICMP types 8 and 11. Type 8 service allows your computer to accept echo reply messages, making it possible for people to ping your computer to see whether it is available. Type 11 service relates to packets with a time to live (TTL) that was exceeded in transit, and for which you are accepting a Time Exceeded message that is being returned to you. (You need to accept Type 11 messages to use the traceroute command to find broken routes to hosts you want to reach.)

```
# iptables -A INPUT -p ICMP -i eth0 -s 0/0 --icmp-type 8 -j ACCEPT
# iptables -A INPUT -p ICMP -i eth0 -s 0/0 --icmp-type 11 -j ACCEPT
```

These two lines define rules for ICMP packets that come into the computer on the first Ethernet interface (eth0) from any source (-s 0/0). The first line says to ACCEPT type 8 service and the second says to ACCEPT type 11 service.

**5.** The following are examples of commands that define the packets that will be allowed to come into and go out of the computer from the local computer or the private LAN that the firewall is protecting:

```
# iptables -A INPUT -p ALL -i lo -s 127.0.0.1 -j ACCEPT
# iptables -A INPUT -p ALL -i lo -s 10.0.0.1 -j ACCEPT
# iptables -A INPUT -p ALL -i lo -s 323.45.67.89 -j ACCEPT
# iptables -A INPUT -p ALL -i eth1 -s 10.0.0.0/24 -j ACCEPT
# iptables -A INPUT -p ALL -i eth1 -d 10.0.0.255 -j ACCEPT
```

The result of these commands is that any packets sent from the local host (1o) are accepted, whether the source of those packets is the local host itself (-s 127.0.0.1), an interface to the local LAN (-s 10.0.0.1), or the Internet (-s 323.45.67.89). The IP addresses 10.0.0.1 and 323.45.67.89 are examples of local interfaces to those networks (your addresses will probably be different). The last two lines indicate that the firewall should accept input of packets that are from the private LAN (-s 10.0.0/24) or destined for any address on that LAN (-d 10.0.0.255) network, respectively.

## Note

The 323.45.67.89 address is not a real IP address. You will replace it with the IP address assigned from your ISP for your external Internet interface. No valid IP address can include a part higher than 255. ■

The following commands define acceptable outgoing packets from the firewall computer:

```
# iptables -A OUTPUT -p ALL -s 127.0.0.1 -j ACCEPT
# iptables -A OUTPUT -p ALL -s 10.0.0.1 -j ACCEPT
# iptables -A OUTPUT -p ALL -s 323.45.67.89 -j ACCEPT
# iptables -A OUTPUT -p ALL -s 10.0.0.0/24 -j ACCEPT
# iptables -A OUTPUT -p ALL -d 10.0.0.255 -j ACCEPT
```

As with the input commands, the firewall accepts outgoing packets that come from any of the local firewall interfaces (127.0.0.1, 10.0.0.1 and 323.45.67.89). It also accepts outgoing packets associated with destinations on the private LAN (10.0.0.0/24 and 10.0.0.255).

6. This last set of commands defines which packets originating from the Internet are allowed into the firewall. For packets attempting to enter your computer from the Internet, you want to be more restrictive, allowing in packets only for services you want to provide. Here are some examples of specific rules you might set to allow requests for services from a server:

```
# iptables -A INPUT -p TCP -i eth0 -s 0/0 --destination-port 21 -j ACCEPT
# iptables -A INPUT -p TCP -i eth0 -s 0/0 --destination-port 22 -j ACCEPT
# iptables -A INPUT -p TCP -i eth0 -s 0/0 --destination-port 80 -j ACCEPT
# iptables -A INPUT -p TCP -i eth0 -s 0/0 --destination-port 113 -j ACCEPT
# iptables -A INPUT -p UDP -i eth0 -s 0/0 --destination-port 53 -j ACCEPT
# iptables -A INPUT -p UDP -i eth0 -s 0/0 --destination-port 2074 -j ACCEPT
# iptables -A INPUT -p UDP -i eth0 -s 0/0 --destination-port 4000 -j ACCEPT
```

The first four lines open up the ports for the TCP services you want to provide to anyone from the Internet: for FTP service (--destination-port 21), secure shell service (22), Web service (80), and IDENTD authentication (113), the last of which might be necessary for protocols such as IRC.

## Caution

**You want to ensure that the services on the ports to which you are allowing access are properly configured before you allow packets to be accepted. In other words, don't open port 80 until you have a Web server configured or port 53 before you have a DNS server configured.**

The last three lines define the ports where connection packets are accepted from the Internet for UDP services. This example assumes that DNS service (`--destination-port 53`) is configured on the computer. It also illustrates lines that accept requests for two other optional ports: Port 2074 is needed by some multimedia applications the users on your LAN might want to use, and port 4000 is used by the ICQ protocol (for online chats).

At this point you can run `iptables -L` again to see your new set of rules. If you have a connection to the computer from your LAN, as I illustrated with some options previously, you can try to ping the computer from the LAN. You can also try configuring different services and accessing them from your network interfaces.

With this part of the procedure completed, your new firewall rules are built into the Linux kernel but do not exist anywhere in a configuration file. Unless you save those rules, they will be gone the next time you reboot your computer. The following section discusses saving your firewall settings so you can use them permanently.

### Saving firewall settings

If you think you have a good set of rules in your current kernel, you can save those rules using the `iptables-save` command so they can be reloaded later using the `iptables-restore` command. Here's an example of how to use the `iptables-save` command:

```
# iptables-save > /root/iptables
```

In this example, the current firewall rules are stored in the `/root/iptables` file (you can put them anywhere you like for the time being). These rules can be copied to a location where they can be loaded automatically on some Linux systems. For example, in Fedora systems, copy this file to `/etc/sysconfig/iptables`, and the rules are installed when the computer reboots. If they don't load automatically, you can restore them yourself as follows:

```
# iptables-restore < /root/iptables
```

The previously saved rules are now restored to the currently running kernel.

## Note

**Remember that if you are using a bootable Linux, you need to be sure to save the iptables rules file to a location (such as a directory on a USB pen drive or hard disk partition) that will not disappear when you reboot. Or use some other persistent desktop feature to save the iptables rules file. ∎**

### Checking your firewall

Now that your firewall is configured, you should check it to make sure that it appears to the outside world—in our example, to the Internet on eth0 and your local LAN on eth1—as you would like it to. A popular tool for checking what services are available on a network interface is nmap.

## Caution

**Although nmap is an excellent tool for checking network interfaces on your own computer or private LAN, it should not be used to check for available services on computers that are not yours. Using nmap on someone else's computer is like checking all the doors and windows on a person's house to see whether you can get in. It is considered an intrusive act. Use nmap only to make sure your own "doors and windows" are secure.**

Following is an example of using nmap to scan a large number of ports on the firewall system you just configured to see what services appear to be available from the two network interfaces on the firewall (eth0 and eth1). To do this effectively, you need to run the nmap command from a computer outside your local firewall. That's because you don't want to see what is going on inside your firewall; you want to see the outside world's view of your firewall.

From the firewall computer, you would first get the IP address of the external Internet interface on eth0 by running ifconfig eth0. For this example, that IP address is 323.45.67.89. (Remember that that is not a real IP address; it is used so you don't use nmap to scan a real computer on the Internet.)

Then, from another Linux machine on the Internet, type the following:

```
# nmap 323.45.67.89
Starting nmap 4.76 ( http://namp.org ) at 2009-02-22 14:56 CDT
Interesting ports on 323.45.67.89:
Not shown: 989 closed ports
PORT       STATE  SERVICE
21/tcp     open   ftp
22/tcp     open   ssh
53/tcp     open   domain
80/tcp     open   http
113/tcp    open   auth
4000/tcp   open   remoteanything

MAC Address: 00:0D:61:22:D3:11 (Giga-Byte Technology Co.)

Nmap done:-- 1 IP address (1 host up) scanned in 72.951 seconds
```

The output shows that 989 ports scanned on this address were closed (blocked from access) and 6 were open. Services not filtered include TCP ports 21, 22, 53, 80, 113, and 4000 (which you made available when you set up the firewall earlier). The seven services shown as open in the example all have servers running currently and listening on the open ports.

It's possible that you won't have access to a Linux machine on the Internet to test outside access to your computer. If you have another computer on your LAN, try running nmap from that computer. If you have only Windows machines, you can always run a bootable Linux and try nmap from that.

# Using iptables to do SNAT or IP Masquerading

You can use Source Network Address Translation (SNAT) or IP Masquerading (MASQUERADE) to allow computers on your LAN with private IP addresses to access the Internet through your iptables firewall. Choose SNAT if you have a static IP address for your Internet connection, and use MASQUERADE if the IP address is assigned dynamically.

When you create the MASQUERADE or SNAT rule, it is added to the NAT table and the POSTROUTING chain. For MASQUERADE, you must provide the name of the interface (such as eth0, ppp0, or slip0) to identify the route to the Internet or other outside network. For SNAT you must also identify the actual IP address of the interface.

The following examples assume that the connection to the Internet is provided through the first Ethernet card (eth0). Here's an example of a MASQUERADE rule:

```
# iptables -t nat -A POSTROUTING -o eth0 -j MASQUERADE
```

And here's an example of a SNAT rule:

```
# iptables -t nat -A POSTROUTING -o eth0 -j SNAT --to-source 12.12.12.12
```

You can add several source addresses if you have multiple addresses that provide a route to the Internet (for example, --to-source 12.12.12.1-12.12.12.254). Although MASQUERADE uses some additional overhead, you probably need to use it instead of SNAT if you have a dial-up connection to the Internet for which the IP address changes on each connection.

Make sure that IP forwarding is turned on in the kernel because it is off by default on most Linux systems. To turn it on temporarily, use one of the following commands:

```
# echo 1 > /proc/sys/net/ipv4/ip_forward
```

or

```
# sysctl net.ipv4.ip_forward=1
```

To turn on IP forwarding permanently, add the following line to the /etc/sysctl.conf file:

```
net.ipv4.ip_forward = 1
```

If you require it, here's how to turn on dynamic IP addressing:

```
# echo 1 > /proc/sys/net/ipv4/ip_dynaddr
```

or

```
# sysctl net.ipv4.ip_dynaddr=1
```

To turn on dynamic IP addressing permanently, add the following line to the /etc/sysctl. conf file:

```
net.ipv4.ip_dynaddr = 1
```

## Adding modules with iptables

Some firewall features require that modules be added to the kernel. For example, if a client behind your firewall needs to access an FTP server using passive FTP, special modules are required. With passive FTP, the FTP client sends its IP address and the port number on which it will listen for data to the server. If that client is on a computer that is behind your firewall, for which you are doing NAT, that information must be translated as well or the FTP server will not be able to communicate with the client.

The iptables facility uses modules to track connections, looking inside the FTP data themselves (that is, not in the IP packet header) to get the information it needs to do NAT (remember that computers from the Internet can't talk directly to your private IP addresses). For FTP connection tracking, you need to have the following modules loaded:

```
nf_conntrack_
nf_conntrack_ftp
nf_nat_ftp
```

For client computers to use some chat servers from behind the firewall, you need to add connection tracking and NAT as well. In those cases, addresses and port numbers are stored within the IRC protocol packets, so those packets must be translated, too. To allow clients on your LAN to use IRC services, you need to load the following modules:

```
nf_conntrack_irc
nf_nat_irc
```

The default port for IRC connections is 6667. If you don't want to use the default, you can add different port numbers when you load the connection-tracking modules:

```
# modprobe ip_conntrack_irc.o ports=6668,6669
```

## Using iptables as a transparent proxy

You can use REDIRECT to cause traffic for a specific port on the firewall computer to be directed to a different port. This feature enables you to direct host computers on your local LAN to a proxy service on your firewall computer without those hosts knowing it.

Here's an example of a command line that causes a request for Web service (port 80) to be directed to a proxy service (port 3128):

```
# iptables -t nat -A PREROUTING -p tcp --dport 80 \
      -j REDIRECT --to-ports 3128
```

(This example should actually appear on one line. The backslash indicates continuation on the next line.)

In this example, any packet destined for port 80 (`--dport 80`) is redirected to port 3128 (`--to-ports 3128`). Note that the packet is changed before it is routed (`-A PREROUTING`).

You can use `REDIRECT` targets only in `PREROUTING` and `OUTPUT` chains within a `nat` table. You can also give a range of port numbers to spread the redirection across multiple port numbers.

# Using iptables for port forwarding

What if you have only one public IP address but you want to use a computer other than your firewall computer to provide Web, FTP, DNS, or some other service? You can use the Dynamic Network Address Translation (DNAT) feature to direct traffic for a particular port on your firewall to another computer.

For example, if you want all requests for Web service (port 80) that are directed to the firewall computer (`-d 15.15.15.15`) to be directed to another computer on your LAN (such as 10.0.0.25), you can use the following `iptables` command:

```
# iptables -t nat -A PREROUTING -p tcp -d 15.15.15.15 --dport 80 \
          -j DNAT --to-destination 10.0.0.25
```

You can also spread the load for the service you are forwarding by providing a range of IP addresses (for example, `--to-destination 10.0.0.1-10.0.0.25`). Likewise, you can direct the request to a range of ports as well.

## Getting iptables scripts

Rather than type in all your firewall rules by hand, many scripts are available on the Internet (licensed under the GPL) that you can modify to suit your needs. Many of these scripts contain sections in the front where you can add IP addresses, port numbers, and other information that is specific to your firewall setup.

A nice set of scripts that illustrate how to use iptables comes from Oskar Andreasson, the author of the iptables tutorial. The set can be found at `http://iptables-tutorial.frozentux.net/scripts/`. In particular, the `rc.firewall.txt` is a good file to step through.

## Finding out more about iptables

So far, you've seen an overview of many of the features in iptables and gotten a basic understanding of what it can do. Creating complex firewalls, especially in situations where a lot of people are trying to break in, requires a much deeper knowledge of iptables. I suggest that, from here, you refer to the following:

- **Iptables Tutorial** (`http://iptables-tutorial.frozentux.net`)—This tutorial by Oskar Andreasson is the standard by which other iptables information is measured.

- **Netfilter project** (`www.netfilter.org`)—Get the latest information about iptables development, patches, security issues, mailing lists, and news.

# Making a Coyote Linux Bootable Floppy Firewall

In as little as a 1.4MB floppy disk, you can have a firewall that does a good job protecting your LAN against unwanted access from the Internet. With a CD-ROM, you can add literally hundreds of tools for managing your firewall and keeping your network running smoothly.

A handful of bootable Linux firewall distributions are available today. The rest of this chapter walks you through the setup of Coyote Linux (www.coyotelinux.com) and then describes a few others that might interest you.

## Note

**Coyote Linux Firewall is described here primarily as a demonstration of how small a useful Linux system can be. If you like, you can even use Coyote Linux from a CD (see** http://rzero.com/coyote/bootcd.html**). However, if the computer you plan to use for your firewall has a CD drive, consider using a more feature-rich and up-to-date firewall distribution such as Devil Linux (**www.devil-linux.com**).**

**Also, updates are in the works for a new version of Coyote Linux, so you might want to refer to** www **.coyotelinux.com for the most recent Linux firewall distribution once it is available. ∎**

## Creating a Coyote Linux firewall

Using a single, simple script, Coyote Linux lets you create a bootable Linux firewall that fits on a floppy disk. After you install and boot Coyote Linux, you can manage it from another computer on your LAN. You can use a Web interface or log into it using ssh and manage Coyote Linux from a Linux shell.

Coyote Linux contains an amazing set of features for such a small space. After booting the Coyote Linux boot floppy you create, you have a firewall with which you can

- Route packets between your LAN and the Internet.
- Provide network interfaces to Ethernet LAN (TCP or PPPoE) or dial-up (PPP) network connections.
- Create firewall rules supported by iptables. (It starts with a few basic rules, but you can add your own rules to include IP Masquerading and NAT, port forwarding, transparent proxies, or many other iptables features.)
- Enable DHCP. Coyote Linux can act as a DHCP server, providing IP addresses and other information to the computers on your LAN.
- Log activities. In addition to creating logs of activities on the firewall, Coyote can be set to pass those log files to another computer on your LAN.
- Monitor network activities. Coyote Linux has a few basic administrative tools for checking out your network a bit. Those tools include traceroute and nslookup.

- Log in remotely (ssh) and get around the shell. The sshd daemon in Coyote Linux enables you to log in from another computer on your LAN. The busybox utility (`www.busybox.net/`) provides a good set of basic shell tools.

- Open a Web interface to Coyote Linux. From any Web browser on your LAN, you can open the Coyote Linux Web Administrator interface by typing your firewall's IP address and port 8180 (for example, `http://192.168.0.1:8180`).

The following section shows you how to create a Coyote Linux boot floppy firewall/router. After you have your Coyote Linux firewall up and running, you can change settings for that firewall from another computer on your LAN using the Web browser or shell (ssh) interface to the computer. If you are familiar with the shell and firewall features (described earlier in the chapter), you can do a lot of things, such as routing, demand dialing, and DHCP service, with this nice little distribution.

## Note

**For more information, refer to the Web site of Vortech Consulting, LLC (`www.vortech.net`), which originally created the Coyote Linux project. As with many companies that support open source software, it offers commercial products that relate to its open source project. If you want more advanced products and support, you can consider purchasing its corporate and small-office firewall products. ■**

## Building the Coyote Linux floppy

To get just what you want in your Coyote Linux firewall floppy, you need to build it yourself. That entails the following:

- **Creating the floppy**—You'll need a computer with a floppy drive to which you can write raw data. That machine should be running Linux (KNOPPIX should work fine if you don't have a Linux already installed).

- **Running the firewall**—For this, you want a computer that can boot from a floppy disk and have two network interfaces. That computer can have as little power as a discarded 486 machine. In the example, the firewall computer will have a dial-up modem to connect to the Internet and an Ethernet card to connect it to your LAN (although a better and simpler way is to have an Ethernet connection to the Internet that can basically turn on automatically in most cases).

And, of course, you need a floppy disk.

The computer with which you create the floppy disk and the computer on which you run it may be the same computer (but doesn't have to be).

## Caution

You need to know the Linux driver name for your Ethernet cards before you run the procedure to create your firewall floppy. If you don't know what it is, I recommend starting KNOPPIX on your machine and then using the `lsmod` and `lspci` commands to determine the driver names for your Ethernet cards (they should have been autodetected). Use `modinfo` if you are not sure if the driver name is the right one (for example, `modinfo 8139too`). ∎

If possible, using a broadband or other Ethernet interface to connect to the Internet is better because dial-up modems can require extra configuration to work, provide slower connections, and make you manage bringing dial-up connections up and down all the time. Because this section is meant to illustrate how to use minimal hardware with an extraordinarily compact Linux, it shows how to use an inexpensive connection type as well.

Figure 27-2 shows an example of the firewall configuration you'll create in the following Coyote Linux procedure.

### FIGURE 27-2

A Coyote Linux firewall runs from a floppy disk, managing traffic between your network and the Internet.

To create a firewall with Coyote Linux, follow these steps:

1. On a computer that has a CD drive and a floppy drive, copy the Coyote Linux directory from the CD that comes with this book to your computer's hard drive. Then open a Terminal window (or other shell) and change to that directory. (See Appendix A for the location of Coyote Linux on the CD.)

2. Unzip and untar the Coyote Linux file by typing the following:

```
# tar xvfz coyote*tar.gz
```

3. Change to the `coyote` directory that was just created and start the `makefloppy.sh` batch script to build the Coyote Linux floppy disk, as follows:

```
# cd coyote
# ./makefloppy.sh

Coyote floppy builder script v2.9

Please choose the desired capacity for the created floppy:
1) 1.44Mb (Safest and most reliable but may lack space needed
   for some options)
2) 1.68Mb (Good reliability with extra space) - recommended
3) 1.72Mb (Most space but may not work on all systems or with
   all diskettes)
```

4. Choose the capacity of your floppy disk. I used 3 (1.72MB) and it worked fine. With an older floppy drive, you may have to use a lower capacity, which will include fewer features.

```
Enter selection: 3
Please select the type of Internet connection that your
system uses.

1) Standard Ethernet Connection
2) PPP over Ethernet Connection
3) PPP Dialup Connection
```

5. This example uses a PPP dial-up connection here, so type **3**:

## Note

If you have a broadband (DSL, cable modem, or other Ethernet) connection to the Internet, you would typically select 1 here. Select 2 if your ISP said you have a PPPoE connection. Configuring an Ethernet connection is actually simpler than configuring dial-up. Instead of defining the dialer, you typically just select to connect to the Internet via DHCP and enter a host name (when prompted). ∎

```
Enter Selection: 3

  .

  .

  .

By default, Coyote uses the following settings
for the local network interface:

IP Address: 192.168.0.1
Netmask:    255.255.255.0
Broadcast:  192.168.0.255
Network:    192.168.0.0
```

**6.** You can simply accept the default IP address (and related Netmask, Broadcast, and Network numbers) by typing **N**. If you are creating a new set of addresses for your LAN, this is a common set of IP addresses for you to use (192.168.0.1, 192.168.0.2, and so on). Consider changing the IP address if it conflicts with your current network numbering or if that set of IP addresses is being used on your interface to the Internet.

```
Would you like to change these settings? [Y/N]: N

OPTIONS CONFIGURATION
Demand Dial:
Initiate the link only on demand, i.e. when data
traffic is present.
```

**7.** Now set up your dial-up features (if you are using dial-up to get to the Internet, as this example does). The first question is whether to allow demand dialing. Type **y** if you want the Internet connection to start up every time someone tries to open a connection to that interface (say, for trying to browse the Web or sending e-mail from the local system or any computer on your LAN using this as a route to the Internet):

```
Do you want to enable the demand dial option [y/n]: y
```

**8.** Type the number of seconds of idle time (time when no data is sent over the network connection) after which the dial-up connection to the Internet is dropped. The default is 180 (three minutes). I changed it to 600 (10 minutes).

```
Enter number of seconds for idle disconnect [180]: 600
```

**9.** To connect to the Internet with a particular IP address (assigned from the ISP), type **y** and then add the IP address as requested. In most cases, however, you just have the ISP assign you an IP address by typing **n** here.

```
Did your ISP assign you a static IP ADDRESS? [y/n]: n
Setting up for dynamic PPP Address

Set the local PPP interface IP address. Should not be the
same as 192.168.0.1, but on the same subnet.
```

**10.** You need an initial IP address to start the PPP interface. As noted, you should use an IP address that is on the same network as your LAN.

```
Press enter for [192.168.0.3]: 192.168.0.3
```

**11.** The next several questions relate to setting up your dial-out connection. The tty device is the serial port where your modem is connected (ttyS0 for COM1, ttyS1 for COM2, and so forth). The port speed refers to how fast your computer can talk to the modem (the default, 115200, is fine). ATZ is the normal script for initializing a modem (check your modem manual if you need something else). Type any name representing your ISP (no spaces). Enter the phone number to dial to get your Internet connection. Finally, enter the username and then the password that was provided to you by the ISP for this Internet account.

```
Enter tty device name for modem (ttyS0, etc)[ttyS0]: ttyS0
Enter ttyS0's port speed (115200, 57600, etc)[115200]: 115200
Enter modem init string (Enter = ATZ): ATZ
Enter name of ISP (no whitespace)[isp]: att
Enter phone number to dial: 5551212
Enter username: jsmith
Enter password: tkN0stf
```

**12.** Type **n** to not send clear-text passwords during login. You may need to change this to **y** if your ISP requires CHAP or PAP authentication.

```
If you enable this, your password will be sent in clear
text over the line. Say yes here only if despite having
verified everything, you still cannot connect to your ISP.
Login during chat? [y/n]: n
```

**13.** Because this example firewall will provide IP addresses to the other computers on the LAN, it needs to be enabled as a DHCP server (**y**). Then list the range of addresses it can assign to those computers. If you plan to have 100 or fewer computers on your LAN, the address range in this example should work fine for you:

```
Do you want to enable the coyote DHCP server? [y/n]: y
Enter DHCP range starting IP [192.168.0.100]: 192.168.0.100
Enter DHCP range ending IP [192.168.0.200]: 192.168.0.200
```

**14.** A DMZ is a way of further shielding your local network from the outside world if you want to have a Web server protected by the same firewall. In this case, you can add another Ethernet card to the firewall, connect that to the Web server, and then allow incoming requests for Web services to go through to the Web server. This enables you to still block all incoming traffic to the desktop systems on your LAN. For this example, I just chose N.

```
If you don't know what a DMZ is, just answer NO
Would you like to configure a De-Militarized Zone? [Y/N]: N
```

**15.** Set the domain name with which this firewall is associated, and enter the IP address(es) of the DNS server(s) it will use to resolve addresses (probably provided by your ISP, unless you are running your own DNS server):

```
Enter Domain Name: example.com
Enter DNS Server 1: 123.45.68.799
```

```
Enter DNS Server 2 (optional): 123.45.68.800

If you have a syslog server on your LAN you want Coyote to
send its syslog data to, you can specify the address here.
If unsure or you do not have a syslog server, leave this
entry blank.
```

16. You can have Coyote log its activities to another server on your network. This can be very handy because it removes logs from the firewall (so someone can't tamper with them) and enables you to centrally administer logs on your network. Before you can use this feature, you need to configure support for remote logging on your logging computer. To do this, I recommend reading the syslog daemon man page (man syslogd) on most Linux systems. Look for the "Support for Remote Logging" section. To disable the feature, as in this example, just press Enter to continue.

```
Syslog server address:
```

17. Coyote Linux supports a nice range of Ethernet cards. You must know the name of the Ethernet driver module for each Ethernet card on your firewall and enter it here. (You should already have this information if you followed the Caution at the beginning of this section.) For ISA cards, which you probably don't have unless it's a much older machine, you need to add IO and IRQ information.

```
Enter the module name for your local network card: 8139too
Enter IO address (Leave blank for PCI cards):
Enter IRQ (Leave blank for PCI cards):

Checking module dependencies...
8139too deps = mii

The default language of the Coyote Web Administrator
is English. Do you like to configure a
different language ? [Y/N]: N
```

18. To configure Coyote Web Administrator for a language other than English, select Y. Then choose from more than a dozen available languages. The Coyote setup script will then build the floppy image:

```
Building package: etc
Building package: local
Building package: modules
Building package: root
Building package: dhcpd
Building package: webadmin
```

**19.** Insert a blank floppy into the floppy drive and press Enter to build your floppy-disk Coyote Linux distribution:

```
Make sure that you have a floppy in the first floppy drive
in this system and press enter to continue...

Formatting /dev/fd0u1440
Double-sided 80 tracks 18 sec/track. Total capacity 1440 kB
Formatting ... done
Verifying ... done
bin/mkdosfs 2.2 (06 Jul 1999)
Installing boot loader...
Copying files...
cp: omitting directory 'floppy/config'
'floppy/dhcpd.tgz' -> 'mnt/dhcpd.tgz'
'floppy/etc.tgz' -> 'mnt/etc.tgz'
'floppy/linux' -> 'mnt/linux'
'floppy/local.tgz' -> 'mnt/local.tgz'
'floppy/modules.tgz' -> 'mnt/modules.tgz'
'floppy/root.tgz' -> 'mnt/root.tgz'
'floppy/syslinux.cfg' -> 'mnt/syslinux.cfg'
'floppy/SYSLINUX.DPY' -> 'mnt/SYSLINUX.DPY'
'floppy/webadmin.tgz' -> 'mnt/webadmin.tgz'
'floppy/config/coyote.cfg' -> 'mnt/config/coyote.cfg'
'floppy/config/fireloc.cfg' -> 'mnt/config/fireloc.cfg'
'floppy/config/firewall.cfg' -> 'mnt/config/firewall.cfg'
'floppy/config/hosts.dns' -> 'mnt/config/hosts.dns'
'floppy/config/portfw.cfg' -> 'mnt/config/portfw.cfg'
'floppy/config/qosfilt.cfg' -> 'mnt/config/qosfilt.cfg'
'floppy/config/reserve.cfg' -> 'mnt/config/reserve.cfg'
```

**20.** After the floppy is created, you are asked whether you want to create another floppy disk. Type **y** if you want another floppy disk and insert another floppy disk to create it. Otherwise, just type **n** and you are done:

```
Would you like to create another copy of this disk [y/n]? n
```

Now you're ready to try out your Coyote Linux floppy disk firewall.

## Running the Coyote Linux floppy firewall

To start up your firewall, simply insert the floppy disk into your firewall computer and reboot. The firewall should come up as you configured it to run. There is no direct shell interface from the firewall's console after it's up and running. In fact, you don't even have to have a monitor on the firewall because you won't see a login prompt anyway. Any administration of the firewall should be done over your LAN.

If you configured it as just described, your firewall is now

- Offering addresses to the computers on your LAN using DHCP.
- Launching a dial-up connection from your firewall to your ISP as soon as anyone from your LAN or the firewall itself tries to access the Internet.
- Allowing traffic from your LAN to the Internet.
- Offering login (sshd) and Web administration service to you from your LAN.

If the firewall is not behaving as you would like it to, go to the next section to further tune it.

## Managing the Coyote Linux floppy firewall

With the firewall up and running, you almost surely will want to manage it further. There are a couple of ways to access your running firewall so that you can change its configuration with a Web interface or a remote login. Before you can use the remote login, however, you must change the system (root user) password, and that can be done only through the Web interface.

### Using a Web interface

The Coyote Linux Web Administrator can be run from any browser on your LAN to view and change your firewall configuration. It is available from that machine on port 8180. To access the site you configured in the preceding example, type the following in the location box on your browser: **http://192.168.0.1:8180**.

The first thing you want to do is click the System Password button in the main menu and add a password for the root user. Figure 27-3 shows the Internet configuration that was set up to dial out to the Internet in the previous section.

### Using a remote login

The firewall floppy was configured to run the sshd daemon, enabling you to log in over your LAN (using the ssh command) to access your Coyote Linux firewall from the shell. In the example, you can type the following:

```
# ssh -l root 192.168.0.1
root@192.168.0.1's password: *******
```

Enter the password (that you added from your Web interface as just described) and you are taken to the following Configuration menu:

```
Coyote Linux Gateway -- Configuration Menu
    1) Edit main configuration file    2) Change system password
    3) Edit rc.local script file       4) Custom firewall rules file
    5) Edit firewall configuration     6) Edit port forward configuration
```

```
c) Show running configuration        f) Reload firewall
r) Reboot system                     w) Write configuration to disk
d) Dial PPP connection               h) Hangup PPP connection

q) Exit Menu                         l) Logout
--------------------------------------------------------------------
Selection:
```

**FIGURE 27-3**

Administer Coyote Linux from your Web browser.

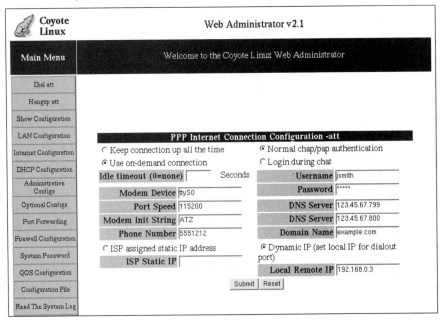

Select the letter of the configuration item you want to change. Type **q** when you are done and you are left at a regular Linux shell prompt. At that point, you can use Coyote Linux as you would any (somewhat limited) Linux system from a shell. (Type **menu** if you want to return to the menu interface.)

As previously noted, the first time you open the browser interface to Coyote Linux, you change the root password. As for basic administrative tasks, you want to read the system log on occasion and back up your configuration changes (which you have made in RAM) so they are copied back to the floppy.

## Note

To use ssh from a Windows machine to get to your firewall, or to get to any other Linux system for that matter, many people use the putty utility. You can get putty from its development home page at `http://chiark.greenend.org.uk/~sgtatham/putty/`. ■

# Using Other Firewall Distributions

Coyote Linux was chosen for this book to illustrate how small, yet still really useful a Linux distribution can be. It also uses the iptables facility, which, after you learn how to use it, is useful in all recent Linux distributions.

However, many other bootable firewalls are available today. I strongly recommend that you check some of these other distributions if you want more or different features than those offered by Coyote Linux.

- **Devil-Linux** (`www.devil-linux.com`) is the live CD firewall distribution that is most often recommended by the people I know. Not only is it recommended because of its excellent features, but also because it is being actively developed. A firewall is your first line of defense against Internet intruders, so choosing a firewall distribution to protect your home or small office computing systems that has an up-to-date firewall with the latest security patches is a very valuable asset.

  In addition to offering common Linux firewall features (such as iptables firewall rules and syslogd logging), Devil-Linux supports a wide range of hardware drivers, including many network cards and SCSI devices. You can configure your own firewall settings to be fed to the live CD from a floppy disk or USB drive. You can also configure many supporting services from the firewall, such as remote login (ssh), DHCP (dhcpd), Web service (httpd), Samba file/print sharing (smbd), and many other services.

- **m0n0wall** (`http://m0n0.ch/wall`) is a BSD-based firewall distribution that was created to run on embedded PCs. It aims to be "free, fast, simple, clean" and include all the facilities a person would need for a full-featured firewall. After answering a few configuration questions, your settings are stored in an XML file.

- **Sentry Firewall CD** (`www.sentryfirewall.com`) is another very nice bootable CD firewall, but one that has not been actively developed for a couple of years. Sentry Firewall CD takes advantage of the additional space on its CD to provide many extra tools for managing and watching your network. You can create a virtual private network connection using FreeS/WAN, manage SNMP services with net-snmp, and set up a variety of servers (using Apache, sendmail, bind, and others).

Sentry Firewall supports many different types of IDE and SCSI hardware (so you are not limited to PCI Ethernet cards and modems). It offers both a shell and Web interface for managing your firewall.

- **IP Cop Firewall** (`http://ipcop.org`) is a stateful firewall distribution based on net-filter. A number of add-ons are available for it and development is constantly underway. As of this writing, the latest version is 1.4.18.

For a list of some additional firewall/router distributions, see the DistroWatch.com site at `http://distrowatch.com/dwres.php?resource=firewalls`.

# Summary

No computer should be connected to the Internet or any public network without either being behind a firewall or being configured as a firewall itself. All the latest Linux systems have iptables built right into the kernel to offer excellent firewall features (earlier Linux systems included ipchains or ipfwadm).

Desktop Linux systems often offer simplified, graphical tools for configuring a firewall. Every Linux system, however, enables you to use the iptables command directly to change the rules in your running Linux system. There are also tools to save and restore your firewall rules.

Coyote Linux illustrates how a Linux distribution with many valuable features can fit on a medium as small as a floppy disk. You stepped through the creation of the firewall floppy, boot-ing it, and configuring the running firewall. For your permanent home or small office firewall, you can use live CD–based firewalls, such as Devil-Linux and Sentry Firewall live CDs.

# Running Bootable Linux Distributions

A *bootable* Linux distribution refers to an entire Linux system that is contained on a removable medium (such as a CD, DVD, or USB flash drive). Because the first full bootable Linux systems were contained on CDs, the common name for this type of Linux system is a *live CD*.

Here are some reasons to use a live CD for your first experience with a new Linux system:

- **Doesn't need to be installed** — As its name implies, the live CD runs live (and immediately) from the removable medium. You don't need to take the time or commandeer the disk space needed to install Linux to your hard disk. Just insert the medium into your computer and reboot to bypass your hard disk and run the CD.

- **Lets you test your computer** — With the live CD, you can check that your hardware is supported before committing to a Linux system. So you will know in advance whether your printer, video card, network card, or other component will just work with your selected Linux system, or whether you might need to do some extra tweaking.

- **Doesn't disrupt your installed computer system** — Because the entire operating system is on the CD or DVD, and uses your computer's RAM to hold temporary data, you can run the live system without touching the contents of your hard disk.

Huge improvements to live CD technology in recent years mean you can do the following tasks with some live CDs:

- **Fix your computer** — If there is a problem with your installed system or a hardware component on your computer, you can often use tool check and possibly fix the problems. Likewise, if you want to prepare to install Linux on your system, some live CDs come with tools for such tasks as backing up data and partitioning your hard disk.

- **Install to hard disk** — If you like the live CD, check the live CD's desktop or menus for a selection that enables you to immediately install the contents of that live CD to hard disk. You will then be able to boot the live CD as you would any operating system from hard disk.

- **Keep your data (persistency)** — A downside of the first live CDs was that, once you rebooted, you would lose any changes you made during the live CD session. Many Linux live CDs now include persistency features that enable you to save desktop settings, data files, or installed software to an alternate medium (such as a USB flash drive or even your hard disk) so the data are available the next time you boot your live CD.

With improvements to live CD technology have also come better tools for building your own live CDs. Those tools range from manual commands for gathering, installing, packaging, and burning live media to single-click GUI tools that can do all that in a single step.

This chapter describes several different Linux live CD distributions (some of which are included on the CD and DVD that come with this book) that you can use to try out different types of Linux systems. It also tells you how to use tools that come with various Linux distributions for customizing or building your own live CDs.

## Note

If you haven't already done so, I recommend you try the KNOPPIX distribution included with this book and described in Chapter 21. It will help you get a good hands-on view of a bootable Linux system by describing how KNOPPIX works, how to use different boot options to start it, and ways of saving changes across reboots. You can also check out Appendix A for a list of other bootable Linux distributions that come on the CD and DVD included with this book. ■

# Overview of Bootable Linux Distributions

By stuffing removable media (CDs, DVDs, floppies, and even USB flash drives) with a select mix of open source software, bootable Linuxes enable you to bypass the hard disk completely (if you like) and have a special Linux distribution running on almost any computer within minutes.

A bootable Linux distribution can offer you some amazing opportunities. On a removable medium, you can take with you:

- Your favorite operating system
- As many of your favorite applications as will fit on your medium
- As much of your music, video, documents, or other data as will fit on your medium
- A fully customized set of features and configuration settings

In other words, if you are willing to build your own custom bootable distribution, the concept of bootable Linux distributions can be extended any way you like. Your bootable business card (mini-CD) or CD can carry all the applications you are used to having, so you can use them anywhere from a handy PC. But it can also hold your presentations, documents, mail-server settings, address books, favorite backgrounds and screensavers, personal photos, and any other kinds of data you want as well.

Most bootable Linux distributions that are created primarily as live CDs are based on established Linux distributions that are typically installed to hard disk. For example, KNOPPIX is based on Debian, as is Damn Small Linux. SLAX is based on Slackware. The SystemRescueCD is based on Gentoo. So if, for example, you want to choose a bootable Linux to customize as a personal desktop or server, you might choose one based on a Linux system you are familiar with.

In recent years, Linux distributions such as Fedora, Ubuntu, openSUSE and Gentoo have begun producing their own live CDs to showcase their distributions. Tools such as the Fedora Project's livecd-creator greatly simplify the task of building live CDs based on packages from the Fedora software repository.

If you don't have a preference regarding which distribution your live CD is based on, however, you will likely want to choose a bootable Linux because it contains a specialized set of tools (such as a security toolkit) or is built to provide a specific function (such as playing multimedia). For example, tools that are included with the BackTrack Network Security Suite live CD are focused on securing, checking, and recovering computers and networks. BackTrack's menus are organized based on the security tools it provides. Components in MoviX$^2$ include those geared toward playing movies, music, and images.

# Trying a Bootable Linux

Whether you choose a bootable Linux to do a special job (security, multimedia playback, gaming, and so on) or as a way of trying Linux before doing a permanent install, several bootable Linux distributions are included with this book that you can try out. For descriptions of those, and other bootable Linux distros, I recommend you visit the following sites:

- **FrozenTech LiveCD List** — More than 300 Linux live CD distributions are listed at this site (www.livecdlist.com). You can sort that list by size, name, primary function, and most votes. This is also a great place to see lists of live CDs based on computer architectures other than x86 (x86-64, PPC, PPC64, Xbox, Alpha, Mips, and so on).

- **Wikipedia List of LiveDistros** — Live CDs based on Linux and other operating systems are listed here: http://en.wikipedia.org/wiki/List_of_LiveDistros.

- **LinuxLinks.com** — This site has a list of mini-distributions, many of which are bootable Linux systems. The page that contains this list is www.linuxlinks.com/Distributions/Mini_Distributions/.

- **DistroWatch.com** — DistroWatch keeps a list of CD-based Linux distributions and live Linux CDs (http://distrowatch.com/dwres.php?resource=cd). Its site also contains information and links to hundreds of distributions.

- **Knoppix Customizations** — The Knoppix Customizations page (www.knoppix.net/wiki/Knoppix_Customizations) lists about 100 distributions based on KNOPPIX. Before live CD creation tools were widely available, simply remastering KNOPPIX was a popular way to create new live CDs.

If you have trouble running any bootable Linux distributions, try adding options to the boot prompt. Because so many of the distributions are based on KNOPPIX, refer to the KNOPPIX boot options (also called *cheat codes*) described in Chapter 21 to help get your Linux distribution to start up the way you would like. View these codes online at www.knoppix.net/wiki/Cheat_Codes.

This book comes with several bootable Linux distributions, which you can find out about in Appendix A. You can get more recent versions of distributions that interest you (some are updated quite often) by following links from the sites just mentioned.

## Caution

**Many bootable Linux distributions are created by individuals and should still be considered experimental in nature. The quality can vary widely and often the controls are not as stringent as they would be for commercial Linux systems, such as Red Hat Enterprise Linux. You can limit your risks by doing such things as mounting all hard disk partitions as read-only (as is usually, but not always, done by default), but remember that this software is distributed with no warranty.** ∎

Although the most popular bootable Linux, KNOPPIX, has already been covered in this book, the following sections describe interesting bootable Linux distributions, based on the type of content they contain.

## Showcasing Linux from a live CD

Most major Linux distributions that were created to install to hard disk also offer live CD versions of their distributions. You can use those live CDs to try that Linux before installing. Then often you can install the contents of the live CD directly to hard disk from the live CD itself.

Here are descriptions of live CDs that are available from major Linux distributions:

- **Ubuntu live CDs** — Official live CDs from Ubuntu (www.ubuntu.com/getubuntu) include desktop and server editions that are available on both x86 and 64-bit AMD (amd64) versions. Both server and desktop (GNOME) editions are available. There are also live CDs for related Kubuntu (KDE desktop) and Edubuntu (education-oriented) projects. By selecting a desktop icon you can install the live CD to hard disk.

- **Fedora live CDs** — GNOME and KDE desktop live CDs are offered by the Fedora project (www.fedoraproject.org/get-fedora). Fedora also offers a collection of what they call live *spins* (`www.fedoraproject.org/wiki/CustomSpins`). Specialty live CDs that are built using live CD creation tools include a games spin, electronic lab spin, developer spin, and Xfce spin. An install icon is available on the desktop.

- **Gentoo live CDs** — Gentoo (`www.gentoo.org/main/en/where.xml`) offers desktop live CDs and DVDs. Builds of those media are available on eight different computer architectures. Each CD and DVD includes an installer.

- **Mepis live CDs** — The Mepis project (`www.mepis.org/mirrors`) offers SimplyMEPIS live CDs that can also be used to install a desktop Mepis system. An offshoot project of Mepis called AntiX also offers a live CD that is tailored to run well on low-end computers.

- **OpenSUSE live CDs** — You can get GNOME and KDE live CDs and DVDs from the openSUSE project (`software.opensuse.org`) for x86, x86-64, and PowerPC architectures. These media also include tools for installing their contents to hard disk.

As you use these live CDs, you can install additional software packages over the Internet to try out other features. Keep in mind, however, that because running the live CD requires more RAM than the same system would need when running from hard disk, many of these Linux distributions will run better after you have installed their contents to hard disk.

## On the DVD
Ubuntu, Fedora, Gentoo, AntiX, PCLinuxOS, and openSUSE live CDs are all available from the DVD that comes with this book. Check Appendix A for details on each of those live CDs. ■

# Security and rescue bootables

Rescuing broken systems and diagnosing network problems are among the most popular uses of bootable Linuxes. At a point where your hard disk might be inaccessible, bootable rescue CDs or DVDs can literally save damaged or infected computers. Some rescue CDs are touted as complete security toolkits, offering a wide range of tools for monitoring Linux or Windows systems, scanning for viruses, debugging networks, and doing forensics.

Most bootable Linux systems will boot up on your network if a DHCP server is on the line. (If there isn't one, many include the netcardconfig utility to let you set up a wired Ethernet card manually.) So, with your computer booted and connected to a network with a bootable Linux, you could proceed to check, fix, back up, and otherwise control the local computer as well as other computers on your network.

## Note
Some security live CD projects note that the tools their live CDs include were chosen, in part, from the Insecure.org "Top 100 Network Security Tools" list (`http://sectools.org`). The list was put together from more than 3,200 responses to a survey on the nmap-hackers mailing list. ■

Here are suggestions of some of the ways you can use most Linux security/rescue CDs, based on open source software that many of these distributions contain:

- **Assessing vulnerability** — Tools for assessing vulnerabilities of your computer include those to let you scan shared Windows SMB folders (nbtscan), CGI scripts (nikto and screamingCobra), and the computer's ports (nmap), as well as scan for viruses (clamAV). You can also check whether someone has used a rootkit to replace critical system files (chkrootkit), or you can use a scanner dispatch (warscan) to test any exploit you like across lots of machines.

- **Running forensics on Windows machines** — If you believe a Windows system has been compromised, there are many tools you can use to find problems and correct them. Boot a security CD, such as KNOPPIX-STD, and you can recover Internet Explorer cookies (galleta), convert Outlook Express dbx files to mbox format (read-dbx and readoe), check system integrity (ftimes), and check the Windows recycle bin (rifiuti).

- **Recovering data** — If a Windows or other operating system won't boot or is otherwise impaired, you can get data off that computer. You can copy files over the network (using rsync, scp, or others) or back up to local CD or tape (cpio, tar, or others). You can selectively recover file types from disk images (foremost) or check and recover lost partitions (testdisk).

- **Dealing with intruders** — Tools such as Snort (`www.snort.org`) enable you to analyze network traffic in real time, as well as log and analyze data as attacks are happening. Honeypots enable you to watch intruders' moves as the honeypots lead intruders to believe they've compromised your system. Honeypots in security-related Linux CDs include honeyd (`http://honeyd.org`), thp, and thpot (`www.alpinista.org/thp`). Kill zombies from DDoS attacks with zz (zombie zapper).

- **Using and analyzing encryption techniques** — Many tools enable you to use encryption techniques to protect your data and find when others have tried to compromise it. GNP privacy guard (gpg) is used for verifying the authenticity of computers and people. For setting up virtual private networks, there are stunnel and super-freeSWAN VPNs. You can find images (giffshuffle, stegbreak, and stegdetect) and music (mp3stego) that contain hidden messages from a technique called *stegonography*.

- **Managing a firewall** — Bring a firewall up quickly or assess what's happening on a running firewall. The blockall script can block all inbound TCP traffic, flushall flushes your firewall rules, and fwlogwatch can monitor firewall logs. The firestarter and floppyfw utilities offer quick ways to start up a firewall. Tools for managing iptables firewalls include gtk-iptables and shorewall.

Popular Linux rescue CDs that illustrate very well how many tools you can get on a single CD include System Rescue CD, BackTrack, Knoppix-STD, and the Inside Security Rescue Toolkit (INSERT) rescue CDs.

## Caution

When you use a rescue CD to change a master boot record, fix partition tables, or clean viruses from a system, you risk doing irreparable damage to your computer system. Remember that GPL software comes with no warranty, so you use that software at your own risk. ■

### BackTrack Network Security Suite

A wide-range of powerful, well-organized security tools are on the Backtrack Network Security Suite (http://remote-exploit.org/backtrack.html) live CD. BackTrack is based on two live Linux distributions used to test whether your computer system has been compromised: Whax and Auditor.

BackTrack offers a good combination of GUI and command-line security tools. The BackTrack menus (shown in Figure 28-1) organize all of those tools together, enabling you to look in one place for all similar tools. When you select a command from a menu, the command runs with the help (-h) option so you can see how it works. It's up to you to then type the command and add the options you want.

## On the DVD

The BackTrack CD is included on the DVD that comes with this book. Refer to Appendix A for information on running BackTrack. ■

---

**FIGURE 28-1**

BackTrack organizes graphical and command-line security tools.

### SystemRescueCd

The SystemRescueCd (www.sysresccd.org) is aimed squarely at recovering crashed systems. Tools included on this distribution include those specifically designed for repairing and saving your data, such as

- **Disk partitioning tools** — You can check, add, remove, move, and resize disk partitions with tools such as parted and qtparted.

- **Logical Volume Management tools** — For file systems with LVM, there are lvm and evms tools. (Logical volume management allows you to add space to areas of a file system without changing the physical partitions.)

- **Security tools** — Check whether the data on your system has been compromised with tools such as chkrootkit (to check for software installed by hackers to let them access your system), as well as clamav and clamd (to scan for existing and incoming viruses). Use nmap (scan network computers for open ports) and nc (the Netcat utility for checking connections to remote hosts) for checking network security.

- **Backup tools** — As you might expect, this distribution contains standard Linux tools for archiving data (tar, cpio, dump, rar, and so on) and compressing data (such as bzip2, gzip, and compress). Likewise, it contains standard tools for copying your data over the network (scp, sftp, ftp, and so on).

Because SystemRescueCd doesn't include a graphical interface, it can get a lot of commands into about 190MB of disk space. Some of the tools however, such as the midnight commander (mc command) file manager, provide a GUI-like interface from a regular Linux shell via the ncurses libraries.

## On the CD

**The SystemRescueCd image is included on the CD that comes with this book. Refer to Appendix A for information on running the SystemRescueCD. ■**

### KNOPPIX Security Tools Distribution

The Knoppix-STD goes lightweight on the window manager to go heavyweight on the diagnostic tools. The distribution contains hundreds of tools that can be used for repairing and assessing computer and network security (see http://s-t-d.org/).

Instead of a full GNOME desktop, Knoppix-STD uses the Fluxbox window manager. It will run on lesser machines, but you'll get a usable GUI on almost any Pentium-class machine with at least 64MB of RAM. With at least 640MB of RAM, you can run the entire distribution from RAM (type **knoppix toram** to boot it to run entirely from RAM). With Knoppix-STD running in RAM, the system operates faster and your CD or DVD drive is available for other purposes.

Go to the project's Tools page (http://s-t-d.org/tools.html) to find out about more features in the project. Or go to the download page (http://s-t-d.org/download.html) to download and try it yourself.

### The Inside Security Rescue Toolkit

INSERT (Inside Security Rescue Toolkit) is another KNOPPIX derivative that includes features from Damn Small Linux as well. INSERT bills itself as a disaster recovery and network analysis system. It contains a more compact set of tools to fit on a bootable business card (about 50MB). Check it out at www.inside-security.de/insert_en.html. Chapter 12 shows you how to use INSERT to check for rootkits.

## On the CD

**INSERT is included on the CD that comes with this book. Refer to Appendix A for information on using INSERT. ■**

The Fluxbox window manager offers some docked system monitors for monitoring CPU, network traffic, memory and swap use, and battery (if you are on a laptop). Another applet displays the Matrix screensaver (double-click it to launch a Terminal window). The mount applet enables you to step through the CD, floppy, and hard disk partitions on your computer. Click the key button on that applet (so it turns green), and you can double-click it to mount and open that device or partition.

Right-click the desktop to see a menu that allows you to select from a handful of graphical tools for troubleshooting your computer and network, most of which will run from the shell. Figure 28-2 shows the INSERT desktop.

**FIGURE 28-2**

Use INSERT to troubleshoot computers and networks.

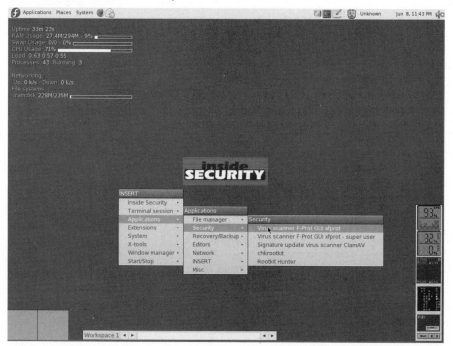

You can find what's in INSERT from the List of Applications page on the Inside Security site (`www.inside-security.de/applicationlist.html`).

## Demonstration bootables

Individuals and organizations that want to promote their businesses or software projects can create custom live CDs to incorporate their own content or display their wares. And software developers can rest assured that the project they want to show off will work because it can be adapted to an entire operating system. An organization that wants to demonstrate what it's about can boot up to play any content (images, presentations, movies, music, and so on) on any existing open source player.

Here are some examples of bootable CDs that are used for demonstration purposes:

- **Software Projects** — There are open source projects that produce a live CD to let people try out their projects. The GNOME Live Media project (`http://live.gnome.org/GnomeLiveMedia`) offers a live CD that can be used to try the features of GNOME.

- **Creative Commons Content** — The Creative Commons projects gathers free audio, video, image, text, and educational resources, covered under the Creative Commons license, and makes that available on a live DVD. The LiveContent DVD (`http://wiki.creativecommons.org/Livecontent`) is a modified Fedora desktop live CD.

- **Any Content You Choose** — Live CDs are becoming a popular medium to hold and play specific content. GeeXBoX Generator and eMoviX$^2$ are spin-offs of GeeXBoX and MoviX$^2$ projects for creating live CDs to play any video you include (see the following section). I've created custom versions of Damn Small Linux that boot directly to a slide show of images from my family vacation.

  Because Linux can act as both a client and server, it is a great medium to demo custom Web applications. The book *Ajax Construction Kit* by Michael Morrison (Prentice Hall, 2008) includes a live CD that contains all the Ajax Web applications described in the book. Because a complete LAMP server package is also on the live CD, that disc is all you need to run the sample projects, display them in a Web browser, and modify them in an HTML editor.

Because open source software can be manipulated as you choose and redistributed, live CDs are becoming an increasingly popular method of demonstrating software projects and content.

## Multimedia bootables

Some bootable Linuxes are tailored specifically to let you play movies, music, and images. Most let you play whatever content you have on your hard disk or can point to from the Internet. Many run in a small enough amount of memory to let you remove the bootable DVD or CD containing Linux and insert your own content (such as a music CD or movie DVD) to play.

### MoviX

With MoviX (http://sourceforge.net/projects/movix/), you run a multimedia player that disregards the operating systems (Windows, Linux, or otherwise) installed on your system. Because MoviX is small enough to run in your system memory, after it has booted you can remove it and insert the CD or DVD containing the content you want to run. With MoviX, you can play

- **Videos** — You can play video from many different formats, including DivX/XVID, MPEG 1 and 2, and MPEG 4. So that MoviX can be freely distributed, it does not include the capability to play most DVD movies.

## Caution

The U.S. Digital Millennium Copyright Act (DCMA) prohibits the creation or distribution of software that is made to circumvent encryption that protects copyrighted material. The libdvdcss library, needed to decrypt DVD movies (even if only for playback), has been the subject of much discussion. Although this library is available on the Internet, most Linux systems in the U.S. have chosen not to distribute this library because using it may be illegal under the DCMA. You should research this issue yourself if you plan to add libdvdcss to MoviX or any other Linux distribution that includes MPlayer or xine media players. ■

- **Music** — You can play audio files in AVI, MP3, Ogg Vorbis, and other formats.
- **Images** — You can run a slide show using the Linux Frame Buffer Image (fbi) viewer that displays images in JPEG, PNG, and a variety of other image formats.

The MoviX player itself doesn't include any video, music, or images for you to play. Instead, it enables you to choose the location of your content. Here are the possibilities, depending on what is available from your computer:

- **DVDs** — If you have a DVD drive on your computer, you can play supported content from there. (As previously stated, that doesn't include most commercial movies, by default.)
- **VCDs and SVCDs** — These are video formats that can be put on standard CDs.
- **Audio CDs** — You can play standard music CDs (including AVI, MP3, and other formats).
- **Hard disk files** — Any supported content on the local hard disk can also be played from MoviX. As with KNOPPIX, MoviX detects hard disk partitions and then mounts them as you request files from those partitions. The mounts are done read-only, by default, so you can play your content without any risk of deleting or otherwise damaging it.
- **Network** — MoviX boots onto the network if a DHCP server is detected. Although the friendly user interface doesn't appear to support it yet, software in MoviX should enable you to get content from your LAN or the Internet to play back using an NFS (UNIX file sharing) or FTP (standard Internet file sharing facility) file server.

MoviX boots right up to MPlayer, so you can eject the MoviX disk, insert a CD, DVD, or VCD into your drive and play any supported content. Right-click the desktop to see your choices for selecting content.

If you are comfortable moving around in Linux, you can go to different virtual terminals while you are using MoviX. Press Ctrl+Alt+F2 to view a sound mixer or Ctrl+Alt+F3 to go to a Linux shell. Then press Ctrl+Alt+F4 to get back to the main screen (with MPlayer). Select Switch to MoviX from the menu, and you can choose to run your audio player, slide show, or TV viewer (the latter if you have a television card installed).

If you think MoviX is cool, you'll really like the idea of the eMoviX project. With eMoviX, you put a mini-MoviX[2] distribution on a CD or DVD with your video, so that your video content comes with its own bootable player! (See `http://movix.sourceforge.net/Docs/eMoviX` for details.)

## Note
**Both eMovix and MoviX are described in the book *Linux Toys II* by Christopher Negus (Wiley, 2006), in a project devoted mainly to creating your own bootable movies. ∎**

### GeeXboX

GeeXboX (`www.geexbox.org`) is another bootable multimedia player distribution. From the screen that appears after GeeXboX boots, you can use your cursor to select the location of the content you want to choose. As with MoviX, you can play a variety of audio and video content. It also boots up on your network, so you can get audio and video content from it.

Because GeeXboX is so small (just a few megabytes), you can fit it easily on a mini-CD, bootable business card, or even a pen drive (provided your computer can be booted from those media). There is no graphical interface; you just use the keyboard to select content and simple controls from menus.

Use arrow keys to move among the few GeeXboX selections (Open, Controls, Options, Help, and Quit). Press Enter to make a selection. You can open a file from hard disk, a music playlist, directory of images, or removable media (DVD, VCD/XCD, or audio CD) containing video content. Press M to show or hide menus and use P to pause.

### KnoppMyth

I've included KnoppMyth (`http://mysettopbox.tv/knoppmyth.html`) because it represents a new and interesting class of bootable Linux distributions. MythTV is a fairly complex set of software used to configure an entertainment center that can include a personal video recorder (complete with downloaded local TV listing and tools for managing recording and playback), music player, weather center, and tools for getting news and other information.

KnoppMyth is a CD distribution based on KNOPPIX that is intended to help simplify getting a MythTV installation up and running. Boot up KnoppMyth, answer a few questions, and MythTV is installed on your hard disk.

KnoppMyth also includes another nice feature: a MythTV front end. With MythTV configured on a computer on your LAN, you can use the KnoppMyth disk to boot up a MythTV front end. That way you can use your MythTV entertainment center from any TV on your local area network.

### Dyne:bolic

The Dyne:bolic GNU/Linux live bootable CD (www.dynebolic.org) provides a full range of multimedia production tools on a single bootable operating system. The distribution is intended for artisans who want to create and work with a variety of digital media: audio, video, digital images, HTML, and so on.

Tools included with Dyne:bolic include MuSE, TerminatorX, GDam, SoundTracker, and PD (for mixing and streaming audio). Video editors include Kino, Cinelerra, and LiVES. For 3D modeling, there is Blender. For image manipulation, Dyne:bolic includes GIMP. Bluefish is included for creating Web pages.

## Tiny desktops

A small CD, shaped in the form of a business card, can fit in your wallet. A USB pen drive can hang from your keychain. There are whole bootable Linux distributions that let you boot up a desktop with which you can connect to the Internet, browse the Web, play music, send and receive e-mail, do instant messaging, write documents, and work with spreadsheets. And they can do all that in about 50MB of space on a removable medium.

### Note
CD business cards are really just regular CDs that have been cut into the shape of a business card. Depending on the one you choose, it can hold from 40MB to 52MB of data. A mini-CD can hold about 180MB of data. You can purchase these CDs in bulk from many locations that sell regular CDs, and you can play them in any CD drive. (However, it's best to use these CDs in trays that have a mini-CD inset because they have been known to fly loose and break CD drives.) ∎

Although the small media size is fun, perhaps the best attribute of these tiny desktop systems is how efficient they are. With their small footprint and scaled-down applications, small desktop live CDs will usually perform fast — even on older, less powerful machines.

Many bootable Linuxes these days are either based on KNOPPIX or the Bootable Business Card project www.lnx-bbc.com/. I know of several Linux Users Groups that have tailored their own bootable business card projects from the lnx-bbc.org BBC project to hand out to represent their groups. Many bootable Linux distributions for media having capacity that is larger than that of a business-card-size CD tend to be based on KNOPPIX.

Two examples of tiny desktop Linux distributions are Damn Small Linux and Puppy Linux.

### Damn Small Linux

If you want your desktop Linux distribution to fit in your wallet, Damn Small Linux is one of your best choices. Damn Small is one of the first distributions based on KNOPPIX to fit on a bootable business card (about 48MB currently).

## On the CD

**Damn Small Linux is included on the CD that accompanies this book. You can use it as described in Appendix A.** ■

With KNOPPIX inside, you have many of the features you get with KNOPPIX: excellent hardware detection and bootup to a desktop with network connectivity (provided you have an Ethernet connection with DHCP). Many features specific to Damn Small, however, are there to let you get a workable desktop system in a small medium (mini-CD) and low RAM. Figure 28-3 shows an example of the DSL desktop.

**FIGURE 28-3**

Damn Small Linux fits a lot of features in under 50MB.

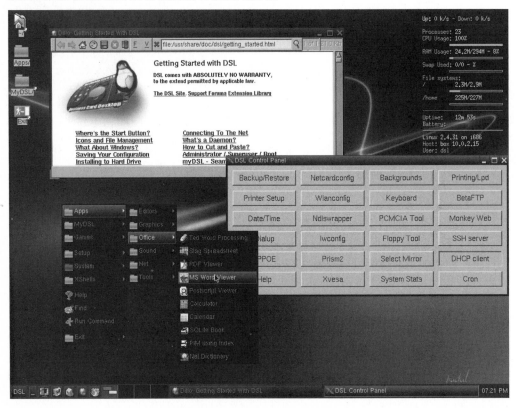

Damn Small's default desktop is pretty simple. The window manager is the powerful, yet efficient, FluxBox window manager (based on BlackBox). Right-click the desktop to see a menu of features you can select. Here are a few things you want to do when you first boot up Damn Small:

- **Change desktop theme** — Right-click to see the Damn Small menu, and then select System ➪ Control Panel. Select Backgrounds, choose a different background from the list, and select the TryIt button to display the new background.

- **Get a network connection** — If you don't automatically get on the Internet at boot time, select Setup ➪ Net Setup from the Damn Small menu. Then you can choose to configure your Ethernet card, DSL connection, dial-up modem, or wireless card.

- **Browse the Web** — Damn Small comes with the Firefox and Dillo Web browsers. Select Apps ➪ Net ➪ Browsers, then choose either Firefox or Dillo to start browsing. The Dillo browser is small and fast, and can run on any X window manager because it doesn't require GNOME libraries.

- **Configure and read e-mail** — The Sylpheed e-mail client is also very compact and runs fast. Select Apps ➪ Net ➪ Sylpheed to open it. Configure it and you can be up and reading your e-mail within a few minutes.

- **Try out other applications** — Right-click and look through the menu for applications that interest you. To see descriptions of those applications, visit `http://damnsmall-linux.org/applications.html`.

- **Get other applications** — Select the MyDSL icon on the desktop to see a selection of application categories you can choose from. If you are connected to the Internet, you can see lists of applications in each category to choose for downloading and installing. ■

## Note

You can get other DSL files that will let you download other applications from your desktop as well. Visit `www.damnsmalllinux.org` and select the link to packages to see the myDSL repository. ■

Damn Small Linux has recently added some excellent customization features. For example, packages you download, desktop settings, and configuration information can be saved across reboots. By creating a list of files and packages you want to save, those files and packages can be saved to a backup file that is stored on your hard disk or any removable medium. The next time you reboot, you can tell Damn Small Linux where to find that backup file and all settings and applications will be inserted into your current Damn Small Linux session.

More information about using Damn Small Linux is available at the project FAQ page, `www.damnsmalllinux.org/faq.html`.

### Puppy Linux

The other heavyweight contender for lightweight Linux bootables is Puppy Linux (`www.puppy-linux.com/`). The Puppy Linux ISO image is about 71MB. So, for example, you can install and boot Puppy Linux on a 128MB flash drive and still have another 50+ megabytes of space left for data.

## On the DVD

**Puppy Linux is included on the DVD that accompanies this book. You can use it as described in Appendix A.** ■

Puppy Linux is built for speed, small size, and ease of use. To emphasize the ease-of-use aspects, Puppy Linux tends to lean more toward open and easy than closed and secure. Here are some examples:

- **Backs up data** — Puppy Linux lets you save files and configuration settings to memory the first time you use it. When you are done with your session, you are asked whether you want to save that information permanently to a USB flash drive, Zip drive, floppy drive, or hard disk partition. If you choose to save your information, it will be backed to a single archive file (named `pup_save.3fs` in ext3 format) on the permanent storage location you selected. You can choose the size of that archive as well. The next time you boot Puppy Linux on that computer, it will find your archive and restore its contents to your Puppy Linux session.

- **Loads to RAM** — When you load Puppy Linux it will, by default, run in RAM. So you should get excellent performance, provided your machine has at least 128MB of RAM available. With Puppy Linux in RAM, that also frees up your CD/DVD drive. So you can pop in a CD or DVD and play it without disturbing the running Puppy Linux system.

- **Sets no firewall rules** — Because Puppy Linux uses a Linux 2.6 kernel, the iptables firewall is built in. However, no firewall rules are set by default. So, if you are thinking of expanding Puppy Linux to offer some services (Web server, mail server, and so on), keep in mind that it is intended for a desktop system and not built to securely offer services.

Every major category of desktop applications is represented in Puppy Linux. For word processing, you have abiword. You can play music with GPlayer and video with Gxine. Much of the SeaMonkey Internet Application Suite (derived from code previously part of the Mozilla Application Suite) is included for Web browsing, mail, news, and HTML editing. For other Internet client applications, you have GAIM (instant messaging), Gftp (FTP client), and several remote login and remote execution tools (secure shell and telnet).

Other personal productivity tools that come with Puppy Linux include calendar (Ical Calendar), spreadsheet (Gnumeric), contacts (Gabby and SeaMonkey Addressbook), finance manager (Xfinans), and personal information (DidiWiki) applications. Most of these applications are lightweight but serviceable utilities.

Puppy Linux is still a relative newcomer to bootable Linuxes, but it seems to have a good following and fairly active forums and development effort. Tools for configuring your network and detecting devices seem to work better in KNOPPIX derivatives, such as Damn Small Linux, at the moment. But look for these areas to improve as Puppy Linux develops.

# Special-Purpose Bootables

As people begin learning about and playing with customizing bootable Linux distributions, I believe more special-purpose distributions will begin to emerge. The eMoviX[2] distribution (part of the MoviX project) is an example of a distribution geared specifically toward a particular function (in that case, playing video content that you package yourself with the distribution).

A firewall is a very good application for a bootable Linux distribution. Using most any PC and a CD (or even a floppy disk) Linux distribution, you can protect your LAN from intruders and provide a route for multiple computers to the Internet. Popular firewall distributions include Devil-Linux (`www.devil-linux.org`) and Sentry Firewall CD (`www.sentryfirewall.com`). Firewall/router distributions are described in Chapter 27.

There are also bootable Linux distributions that are suited for education and for the visually impaired. There are bootable Linux distributions that are suited to be run as a server or to centralize management of clusters. The cool thing is that if there isn't the exact kind of bootable Linux available for you to use, you can start with an existing bootable Linux and customize it yourself.

# Customizing a Bootable Linux

A Linux live CD is like a Linux system running from a hard disk, with a few significant differences. It has to be tailored to run from a read-only medium, it usually doesn't (by default) save information across reboots, and it needs to be able to detect and configure hardware each time it starts. Many live CD distributions have created ways of working around these limitations, including allowing you to customize the CD and to save your customizations across reboots.

If you are setting out to create your own customized live CD, or simply save your own custom settings to go with an existing live CD, you have a few ways to go about it:

- **Customizing data** — Live CD distributions, including KNOPPIX and Damn Small Linux, enable you to save your settings, data files, and even installed applications in a couple of different ways. One approach is to save all your changes to a single archive file to any available writable medium (hard disk, pen drive, and so on), and then restore that archive the next time you boot the CD. Another approach is to create a "persistent desktop" that assigns your home directory and possibly other directories to a writable, mounted file system on your hard disk or other medium. The latter saves your data as you go along.

  Live CDs such as SLAX and Damn Small Linux have their own packaging format that consists of tarballs you can store to be added to the live CD. At boot time, you just point the live CD to the Damn Small MyDSL files or SLAX Modules and the archive containing the application is distributed to its proper location in the file system. (See

Installing_MyDSL_Extension from the `damnsmalllinux.org/wiki` or `www.slax.org/modules.php`.)

- **Remastering** — You can make many more changes to a live CD by remastering it. Remastering is typically done by copying the contents of a live CD to a directory on your hard disk (uncompressing the compressed file system), opening that directory in a chroot environment, adding and deleting software as you please, and then packaging it back up into an ISO image. This approach lets you start with a CD that is basically working, while allowing you to fix problems, update software, and add any data you like so it is included on the CD.

- **Remastersys** — To remaster an Ubuntu live CD, you can use Remastersys scripts (`http://remastersys.klikit-linux.com/repository/remastersys`). Using these scripts, you will be able to set up a remastering environment from an Ubuntu live CD, make the modifications you want, and create a new ISO image in one process.

- **Live CD Projects** — Several projects also focus on building live CDs from the ground up. The Linux From Scratch project has its own tools and procedures for building live CDs (`www.linuxfromscratch.org/livecd`). Linux Live CD/USB scripts (`www.linux-live.org`) enable you to make a live CD from an existing installed Linux system. (The SLAX distribution is made using Linux Live CD scripts.)

Here are links to information about how to customize several popular live Linux distributions:

- **KNOPPIX** — A very extensive KNOPPIX remastering HOWTO is available for those who want to create their own custom KNOPPIX distributions. You can find that document here:

  `www.knoppix.net/wiki/Knoppix_Remastering_Howto`

  To remaster a KNOPPIX CD, you should have at least 3GB of disk space on a Linux (ext2, ext3, xfs, or other) file system along with at least 1GB of available memory (combining RAM and swap space). It's also a good idea to have an active Internet connection during any remastering because there is almost surely some software you will want to download in the process.

- **Damn Small Linux (DSL)** — This is the Linux distribution I have used the most when I want one that runs efficiently on older computer hardware. DSL does good hardware detection and has a good selection of working desktop applications. I can start with the 48MB ISO image, and then add lots of software and customized features to fill up a CD. In fact, the CD that comes with the book *Linux Toys II* (Wiley, 2006) is a remastered version of DSL that includes software for building *Linux Toys* projects as well.

  If you simply want to install DSL to a pen drive or other media, DSL offers an automated feature for doing that. After DSL is on a rewritable pen drive, you can easily add applications (using the MyDSL feature) and customize desktop features in a way that persists across reboots.

- **Puppy Linux** — The project uses its own package management system (called PupGet) that now offers more than 400 packages you can add to Puppy Linux. By adding and deleting these packages, you can create a customized version of Puppy Linux. To see available packages, check out a pet_packages directory from a Puppy Linux mirror site, such as the following:

  ```
  ftp.ibiblio.org/pub/linux/distributions/puppylinux
  ```

- **Gentoo** — Tools for building a potentially more finely tuned live CD are available with the Gentoo distribution. Although creating a Gentoo live CD is supported through the livecd-ng tool, there is currently no complete document describing a simple way to use this, or other tools, to create a custom Gentoo live CD. Here is a link, however, that can get you started:

  ```
  en.gentoo-wiki.com/wiki/Build_Your_Own_LiveCD_or_LiveDVD
  ```

- **Linux Live Scripts** — The Linux Live Scripts (`www.linux-live.org`) can be used to turn an installed Linux system into a Linux live CD. These scripts are used to create the SLAX live CDs. However, the same scripts can be used for other Linux systems as well.

- **LiveCD Project** — The LiveCD project (`http://livecd.berlios.de`) is an initiative aimed specifically at creating a live CD from a Linux distribution. Because the tools currently work only on Mandriva and PCLinuxOS, this project is probably a good place to start if you want to produce a live CD that is compatible with either of those distributions. Currently more than a dozen live CD distributions have been created from the LiveCD project.

Of the projects I've just mentioned, I'd recommend starting with a KNOPPIX or Damn Small Linux distribution for your first attempt at remastering. Because a lot of people are using those, or other distributions based on Debian/KNOPPIX technology, mature procedures and forums are available to help you get over any bumps in the road.

## Building a live CD with Fedora

For the first few years after KNOPPIX was released in 2003, many Linux live CDs were created by simply remastering KNOPPIX. Remastering usually entailed copying the contents of KNOPPIX to hard disk on a running Linux system, setting up a chroot environment to modify the content, then repackaging it all into a new ISO image. Today there are more tools available for creating live CDs and more ways to go about it.

If you want to build Linux live CDs from scratch, the Fedora Project offers some powerful tools for creating a live CD in much the same way you install a Linux system. You can create a live CD or DVD image with the livecd-creator command, a kickstart file, and access to a Fedora software repository. The kickstart file tells livecd-creator which software packages to install and how to set such things as language, keyboard, time zone, authentication, services, and other information needed to run the live CD.

Here is a quick procedure for using livecd-creator to create your own Fedora live CD or DVD. Start with a computer that has a Fedora system running with disk space available that is at least three times the amount of disk space of the CD or DVD created. For a live CD, I would start with at least 5GB of disk space, so there is room for a few live CDs and local downloads of the packages you want.

1. Install the livecd-tools package (other dependent packages will install automatically).

2. Create a kickstart file that contains the packages and settings you want. Look in the /usr/share/livecd-tools directory to choose a sample kickstart file to begin with.

3. Here is an example of a livecd-creator command line you can run as root user from a Terminal window:

```
# livecd-creator -c mylivecd-fedora-12.ks \
    -f F12liveCD \
    -t ~/cache
```

The command just shown uses a kickstart file in the current directory named mylivecd-fedora-12.ks. It stores temporary files in a directory named cache in the user's home directory. The resulting live CD is in the form of an ISO image file named F12liveCD.iso. Within the image, it is assigned a volume name of F12liveCD.

After you have created the live CD, you can test it using a processor emulator program, such as qemu or VMware. Then you can burn the image to a CD or DVD using the cdrecord, k3b, or other CD-burning tool.

# Summary

Dozens of bootable Linux distributions have appeared in the past few years. Those distributions can contain anywhere from 1.4MB of data on a firewall bootable Linux to many gigabytes of data on a bootable DVD. Without needing to touch the computer's hard disk, these distributions can offer full-featured systems that are tailored to be desktop systems, multimedia players, rescue systems, or many other types of systems.

Many bootable Linuxes are based on KNOPPIX (described in Chapter 21), so they feature very fine hardware detection and strong network connectivity. If you want to try out a mini-bootable Linux distribution, try Damn Small Linux or Puppy Linux. For a Linux distribution that fits on a floppy disk, try Coyote Linux (described in Chapter 27).

Nearly all bootable Linux distributions offer ways to access data from the hard disks of the computers on which they are running. Although many bootable Linuxes are still experimental in nature, you can have lots of fun playing with them. Also, with the extraordinary improvements in custom features, you can create your own customized bootable Linux distribution to take with you on a floppy, CD, DVD, or USB flash drive (also referred to as pen drives, thumb drives, or other names).

# Part VI

# Programming in Linux

# Programming Environments and Interfaces

You can slice and dice the topic of Linux programming environments and interfaces in a variety of ways. For example, a list of the programming languages known to have compilers that target or run on Linux easily runs to three single-spaced, typewritten pages. You could also examine the literally hundreds of programming libraries that exist for Linux. Alternatively, you can organize the discussion by dividing everything into three categories: graphically oriented interfaces, command-line interfaces, and other environments.

To some readers, a "programming environment" means a graphical, point-and-click integrated development environment (IDE) such as that provided by ActiveState Komodo or IBM's Eclipse. Yet another way to approach the subject is to look at Linux's development support for certain academic and computing subjects, such as graphics, databases, mathematics, engineering, chemistry, text processing, physics, biology, astronomy, networking, and parallel computing.

Unfortunately, there's no single definitive taxonomy on which everyone agrees, so this chapter takes the easy way out and divides things into environments and interfaces. For the purposes of this chapter, a *programming environment* refers to the setting in which programming takes place, while the *interfaces* (provided by graphical or text-based tools) can be thought of as accoutrement with which someone performs programming tasks.

## IN THIS CHAPTER

**Developing applications for Linux**

**Using graphical programming environments**

**Using command-line programming environments**

**Programming for GUI interfaces**

**Programming for command-line interfaces**

**Using application programming interfaces**

# Understanding Programming Environments

Conventionally understood, a programming environment is either graphically or command line–oriented. However, the Linux programming environment also consists of the services and capabilities provided by the system itself; that is, by the kernel and the core system components. Whether you use a mouse-driven IDE or a text editor and `make`, Linux imposes certain requirements and provides a number of capabilities that determine what the code you write in an IDE or text editor must do and can do.

In this chapter, the term *programming interface* refers to the rules or methods followed to accomplish a particular task. As with programming environments, programming interfaces are usually thought of as graphical or command line:

- **Graphical interface** — Uses the X Window System, or X, to receive and process user input and display information.

- **Command-line interface** — A strictly text-based affair that does not require a windowing system to run.

For example, Firefox, a Web browser, has a graphical interface; it won't work if X isn't running. Pine, a popular e-mail client, has a command-line interface; it works whether X is running or not.

There is a third type of interface, however: an *application programming interface*, or API. An API provides a structured method to write a program that performs a certain task. For example, to write a program that plays sounds, you use the sound API; to write a program that communicates over a TCP/IP network, you use the socket API. Neither playing a sound nor communicating over a TCP/IP network necessarily requires a graphical or command-line interface; both graphical and command-line programs can play sounds or use TCP/IP, provided they use the proper API.

# Using Linux Programming Environments

Linux boasts arguably the richest programming environment of any operating system currently available. As mentioned earlier, this chapter uses the term *programming environment* to describe the tools used to write computer programs on a Linux system and to refer to underlying services that make programming on a Linux system possible (or, perhaps, worthwhile).

This section looks first at the fundamental services and capabilities that inform and constrain programming on a Linux system. Next, you examine a few of the most popular graphical IDEs for creating programs on a Linux system. The section closes with a look at some of the command-line tools used for writing programs.

## Note

**A number of tools are available that simplify cross-platform programming. One such tool is SlickEdit. This interface runs on 7 platforms, supports 40 languages, and emulates 13 editors. More information on it can be found at** www.slickedit.com. ■

As you will discover, some of the graphical IDEs provide comfortable editors for writing code, drawing dialog boxes, and navigating the file system, but use the command-line tools to do the work of compiling the code, hiding the command-line tools beneath an attractive interface.

# The Linux development environment

The Linux development environment consists of the services and capabilities provided by the kernel and core system components, including libraries of prebuilt functions that ship with each Linux distribution. These services and capabilities both define and limit how to write programs that run on a Linux system.

Consider files and the file system. Linux, like the UNIX systems on which it is modeled, is built on the key idiom that "everything is a file." This is a powerful metaphor and model that dramatically simplifies writing application programs to communicate with all sorts of devices. How? You can use the same function, the `write()` system call, to write data to a text file; to send data to a printer; to send keystrokes to an application; and, if you had one, to tell your network-connected coffee pot to brew another pot of coffee.

The file metaphor works this way because Linux treats all devices, such as modems, monitors, CD-ROM drives, disc drives, keyboards, mice, and printers as if they were files. Device drivers, which are part of the kernel, sit between a device and the user and application trying to access it. A device driver translates an application's `write()` call into a form that the device can understand.

So, if an application uses the `write()` system call to write data to a text file on an ext3 file system, the ext3 driver writes the necessary bytes to a file on the disk, but if the application later uses the `write()` system call to write that same data to a printer, the printer driver transmits that data out the parallel port (or across the network) to the printer in a manner that the printer can understand and interpret. This is one way in which the Linux development environment informs, or defines, writing programs on a Linux system.

The catch? If the device you want to use doesn't have a driver (also called a kernel module), you can't use the `write()` call to do anything with that device. You simply do not have a way to communicate with the device. This is how the Linux development environment constrains programming on a Linux system.

What, then, in addition to the file idiom already discussed, are the key features of Linux that characterize its development environment? In no particular order:

- The process model
- CPU and memory protection
- The security model
- Preemptive multitasking
- Its multiuser design
- Interprocess communication
- The building blocks approach

Let's take a closer look at each of these features.

### The process model

The process model is the way that Linux creates and manages running processes. Provided that a process has the necessary privileges, it can create (or spawn) other processes, referred to as child processes. The parent process can also exchange data with child processes. Of course, the capability to create child processes is not unique to Linux, but the particular way in which Linux does so is characteristic of all UNIX-like systems.

When a process calls the fork() system call, it creates an exact copy of itself. After being created by the fork() call, the child process typically calls one of a family of functions collectively known as exec(), providing a program to execute and any options or arguments to that program. Listing 29-1 illustrates the fork()/exec() process in a short program in the C language.

## Note

Actually, the child process created when a process fork()s isn't an *exact* duplicate of the parent. The process ID (PID) of the child process is different, as is the parent PID (PPID); any file locks held by the parent are reset, and any signals pending for the parent are cleared in the child. ∎

### LISTING 29-1

#### Simple fork() and exec() Sequence

```
/*
 * forkexec.c - illustrate simple fork/exec usage
 */
#include <stdio.h>
#include <unistd.h>
#include <sys/types.h>
#include <sys/wait.h>

int main(int argc, char *argv[])
{
        pid_t child;
        int status;

        child = fork();
        if (child == 0) {
                printf("in child\n");
                execl("/bin/ls", "/bin/ls", NULL);
        } else {
                printf("in parent\n");
                waitpid(child, &status, 0);
        }

        return 0;
}
```

Don't worry about what all the code means. The key points to understand are

- The `child = fork()` statement creates a new (child) process.
- The code between `if (child == 0)` and the `else` statements is executed in the child process. In particular, the child uses the `execl()` function call to execute the `/bin/ls` program, which creates a directory listing of the current directory.
- The `waitpid()` statement is executed in the parent process, which means that the parent process will wait for the child process to terminate before continuing execution.

You can compile this program with the following command (if you have the GCC compiler installed):

```
$ gcc forkexec.c -o forkexec
```

and then execute it like this:

```
$ ./forkexec
in parent
in child
28.doc   a.out   forkexec   forkexec.c
```

Your output might be slightly different. The point to take away from this example is that Linux makes it very easy to create new processes programmatically. Because it is so easy, it is a common and powerful programming technique and a characteristic of the Linux programming model. Linux is hardly alone in providing a mechanism by which one program can start another, but the `fork()/exec()` technique is unique to Linux (and the UNIX systems on which Linux is based).

## CPU and memory protection

Another fundamental component of programming on Linux systems is that the operating system itself, which consists of the Linux kernel, is almost entirely insulated from all application programs. The kernel runs in a protected CPU mode known variously as ring 0, kernel mode, or, more prosaically, kernel space. User programs, such as Web browsers, e-mail clients, graphics programs, and games run outside of kernel mode in what is colloquially referred to as *user space*.

The distinction between kernel space and user space is important. The kernel has raw, uncontrolled access to system resources such as the CPU, RAM, and attached peripherals. The kernel mediates all access from user space programs to system resources, funneling it through the *system call*, or syscall, interface. The syscall interface carefully checks the data passed in from user programs before passing that data on to other parts of the kernel. As a result of this careful gatekeeping, it is extremely rare for even the most poorly written user space program to crash the kernel.

The strict division between kernel and user space code is what contributes to Linux's reliability and stability and why you hardly ever see the familiar Windows "Blue Screen of Death" on a Linux system (except in a screensaver).

In addition to the distinction between kernel and user mode code, the kernel and user programs also have their own distinct memory regions. Each process, each instance of a running program, has a virtual memory space, known more formally as the process address space, of 4GB (under most 32-bit processor architectures, as 4GB is $2^{32}$, or two raised to the thirty-second power). Under most circumstances, the kernel gets 1GB of this space, while user space gets the other 3GB. (There are other options for the layout of memory in Linux — this is just the most common.)

User space programs are not permitted to access kernel memory directly. As with CPU and peripheral protection, the motivation for strict memory partitioning is to prevent ill-behaved (or even deliberately malicious) programs from modifying kernel data structures, which can create system instability or even crash the system.

The distinction between kernel and user space is another fundamental feature of the Linux development environment that gives developers considerable flexibility to write almost any code they want with reasonable assurance that if their program crashes, it won't also crash the system. At the same time, the syscall interface that serves as the gateway between user mode and kernel mode code enables user mode programs to access kernel features and services in a safe, controlled manner.

Moreover, the kernel can perform tasks that ordinarily might be executed by user space programs without needing a different programming model. For example, if you implement some sort of user space functionality, such as providing a basic HTTP server, in the kernel, the same syscall interface makes it possible to interact with the HTTP server; there is no need to use a new or different programming interface.

On the downside, the sharp delineation between kernel and user space creates some disadvantages for normal users. For example, unlike Microsoft Windows, user space programs do not have direct access to hardware devices. For user space programs to access a sound card, for example, the system administrator must take steps to permit this sort of access. However, this inconvenience is small compared to the increased stability for which Linux systems are known.

## The security model

As you learned earlier in this book, all users are not created equal. Some users, such as the root user, are effectively omnipotent and can do anything on a system. Most users have more limited access. The user (and group) IDs of these less privileged users control what programs they can execute and the files they can access. The same restrictions apply to the development environment. For example, if you write a program, you might not be able to access a certain feature, such as locking memory with the mmap() system call, unless your program runs with root permissions.

If your program creates files, the default file permissions are controlled by the umask of the user executing the program and/or a umask that you might specifically set at runtime using the umask() system call. Naturally, your program cannot create, delete, or modify files or directories if it doesn't have the necessary privileges. The Linux development environment also makes it possible for a program to drop or add privileges at runtime by calling functions that change its UID or GID.

The impact of the Linux security model on programming is two-fold. First, the same rules and restrictions that affect running programs and other elements of normal system usage also affect the process of creating programs and what those programs can do. This effect is no more than the logical consequence of the Linux security model itself. Programmatically, however, you have more ways, or perhaps more finely grained ways, to interact with the security subsystem than you do as a normal user of the system.

The second effect of the Linux security model for programmers is that writing a program imposes significant burdens on programmers to program securely. An e-mail program, for example, that stores usernames and passwords in a text file that is unencrypted and/or readable by any user (oftentimes called world-readable) is just as insecure as a program that fails to check user input for buffer overflow.

To use a subtler example, when faced with a problem that seems to require root privileges, such as access to a sound card, the initial impulse is usually to run the program as root. However, there are often user space solutions that can accomplish the same goal and that do not require root access. In the case of writing programs that access a sound card, for example, the ALSA (Advanced Linux Sound Architecture) libraries give application programmers access to a rich interface for emitting squeaks and squawks without needing to rely on running a program as the root user.

## Preemptive multitasking

Perhaps the easiest way to express the preemptive multitasking characteristic of programming in a Linux environment is simply to write, "You don't own the CPU; it only seems like you do."

In imprecise terms, the CPU (actually, the CPU scheduler, which is part of the kernel) allocates a quantum of time (on the order of 50 milliseconds) to execute your program, then preempts it (interrupts or suspends it) to spend another 50 millisecond quantum executing another program. It then preempts the second program to execute the third, and so on until the scheduler returns to your program, when (under normal circumstances) the round robin starts again.

The context switch between programs happens so rapidly that you have the illusion that your program is running all the time.

Task preemption happens automatically and unavoidably; very few processes escape preemption. What you might not realize, however, is that a process can voluntarily yield its quantum of CPU time. That is, while a process cannot request additional CPU time, it can voluntarily give it up. The implication of this for a developer is that you can delay executing certain blocks of code if they are either non-critical or rely on input from other processes that are still running. The function that makes this possible is named `sched_yield()`.

Multitasking, while a boon for computer users, poses (at least) three potential problems for programmers: deadlocks, livelocks, and races:

- **Deadlocks** — A deadlock occurs when two or more processes are unable to proceed because each is waiting for one of the others to do something. Deadlocks can happen in several ways. For example, suppose an e-mail client is communicating with a mail server, waiting on the server to send a message. A deadlock occurs if the mail server is waiting for input from the e-mail client before sending the message. This type of deadlock is sometimes referred to as a *deadly embrace*.

A *starvation* deadlock occurs when one or more low-priority processes never get time on the CPU because they are crowded out by higher-priority processes. A third common type of deadlock occurs when two processes are trying to send data to each other but can't because each process's input buffers are full because they are so busy trying to send data that they never read any data sent by the other process. This type of deadlock is colorfully referred to as *constipation*.

- **Livelocks** — A livelock occurs when a task or process, usually a server process, is unable to finish because its clients continue to create more work for it to do before the server can clear its queue. The difference between a livelock and a deadlock is that a deadlocked process doesn't have any work queued; it is blocked or waiting for something to happen. A livelocked process, on the other hand, has too much work to do and never empties its work queue.

- **Races** — A race occurs when the result of a computation depends on the order in which two events occur. Say, for example, that two processes are accessing a file. The first process writes data to the file and the second process reads data from the file to calculate and display a summary value. If the reader process reads the file after the writer completes, the reader calculates and returns the correct value. If the reader process reads the file before the writer completes, the reader will calculate and return an incorrect summary value.

The likelihood of deadlocks, livelocks, or races occurring increases dramatically on multitasking (and multiuser) systems because the number of processes that are potentially competing for access to a finite number of resources is greater. Good design, careful analysis, and the judicious use of locks, semaphores, and other mutual exclusion (or mutex) mechanisms, which mediate access to shared resources, can prevent or reduce their occurrence.

## Multiuser by design

Linux is multiuser by design, an element of the Linux development model that has far-reaching consequences for developers. A program cannot assume, for example, that it has sole access to any resource such as a file, memory, peripheral devices, or CPU time; multiple programs might be attempting to print simultaneously or trying to allocate memory.

Similarly, a program cannot be written with the assumption that only one copy of the program is running at a time. So, if you are writing a program that creates temporary working files in /tmp, you need to ensure that the temporary files created by Bubba's copy of the program are distinct from the temporary files created by Mary Beth's instance of the program. If you don't, hilarity will ensue (if not hilarity, at least confusion and consternation).

Another common need is for programs to honor per-user configurations. At start-up time, a program might apply reasonable global defaults and then read a user's configuration file to apply, say, a custom color scheme.

There are also a number of per-user settings, such as environment variables, that programs need to know how to accommodate. For example, the $MAIL environment variable identifies where the user's mail spool file is kept and the $VISUAL environment variable defines the user's preferred full screen editor (which all true Linux users know is vi). The $PRINTER environment variable stores the name of the user's default printer and, of course, $HOME identifies the user's home directory.

In a pervasively multiuser system such as Linux, programs and programmers must always take into account that most resources a program might want to use are usually shared. Likewise, they must also take into account that most real-world usage scenarios (more formally known as *use cases*) assume that multiple instances of the program are running at the same time.

## Interprocess communication

Interprocess communication (IPC) enables programs to share data and resources with a minimum amount of overhead and is used extensively on all Linux systems. It is especially common with daemons and server processes that spawn child processes to handle client connections. IPC comes in three varieties: shared memory, semaphores, and message queues.

- **Shared memory** — Shared memory is just what the name suggests: a region or segment of memory specifically set aside for use by multiple processes. Because shared memory is never paged out to disk, it is an extremely fast way for two processes to exchange data.

- **Semaphores** — Semaphores, briefly mentioned in the "Preemptive Multitasking" section, serve as flags that indicate a condition controlling the behavior of processes. For example, one process can set a semaphore to indicate a specific file is in use. Before other processes attempt to access that file, they check the semaphore's status and don't (or shouldn't) attempt to access the file if the flag is set.

- **Message queues** — Message queues are first-in-first-out (FIFO) data structures that make it possible for processes to exchange short messages in a structured, orderly manner.

## Note

**Message queues are not necessarily accessed in FIFO data structures. System V UNIX-style message queues are, but POSIX message queues enable readers to pull messages out of a queue in an arbitrary order.** ■

Shared memory, semaphores, and message queues are idiomatic in the Linux development environment. They solve three distinct domains of problems that arise when multiple processes need to exchange data or share resources without having to resort to slow disk files or network connections. All of which is to say that you don't always need IPC, but it sure is nice to have when you do need it.

## The building blocks philosophy

The building blocks philosophy that characterizes the Linux development is best expressed as a short series of rules or principles:

- Do one thing very well.
- Whenever possible, accept input data from standard input and send output data to standard output.
- Keep individual programs as self-contained as possible.
- Remember that someone will use your program in ways you didn't intend and for purposes that you never imagined.

The first rule simply means that programs should not try to be all things to all people: A text editor doesn't need to be able to send e-mail messages and a drawing program doesn't also need to be able to function as a Web browser. Although it is less true today than it used to be, the best Linux programs don't have every imaginable feature (also known as *featuritis*). Rather, developers spend time perfecting the program's intended purpose and making it possible for programs to interoperate.

The second rule allows you to create chains of commands, each of which uses the output of the previous command as its input. A typical use of this behavior is a command pipeline, such as the following rather contrived example:

```
$ cat /etc/passwd | cut -f 5 -d: | tr [:lower:] [:upper:] | sort | head -5
```

The first part of the command pipeline, cat /etc/passwd, writes the contents of the /etc/passwd file to standard output. The second part, cut -f 5 -d:, cuts out the fifth field of its standard input (the contents of /etc/passwd), using the colon character (:) as the field delimiter (the fifth field of /etc/passwd is the comment field, which by convention contains the user's full name).

The third part, tr [:lower:] [:upper:], translates all lowercase characters in the standard input to uppercase characters. The next element, sort, performs an alphabetic sort on the first letter of its input before sending the sorted list to standard output. The final component, head -5, displays only the first five lines of its standard input to standard out. The output of this pipeline might resemble the following:

```
ADM
BIN
DAEMON
GAMES
LP
```

The following command pipeline should prove more useful: it e-mails the current uptime and load average to the root user:

```
$ uptime | mailx -s "System Usage" root
```

The third rule, keeping programs self-contained, is related to the second. The concept behind it is that programs intended for use in command pipelines should make no assumptions about what their input might look like or do any massaging of the output.

Consider the cut command shown in the first command pipeline. It takes arbitrarily formatted input and allows the user to specify on what piece of data to operate (the fifth field in the example, where fields are colon-delimited) and then just displays the requested data on standard output. cut doesn't do any post-processing of the output, allowing the user to do with it as she pleases, probably using another tool.

The fourth rule is really more a philosophical observation that you can't really predict all the ways in which your program might be put to use. Indeed, as S.C. Johnson once noted, "A successful [software] tool is one that was used to do something undreamed of by its author."

The point is that the Linux toolkit, for both developers and end users, is full of small tools and utilities that are building block programs routinely used to create larger programs and tools that, together, perform complex tasks that no single program can do, or can do efficiently. Another element of the building blocks approach is that it enables tasks to be performed in batch mode, without active user intervention or participation. This building block philosophy is another characteristic feature of the Linux development environment, one that can make your life a lot simpler once you grasp the idea. It also helps you to stand on the shoulders of those who have come before because you can build on existing building blocks instead of having to create everything anew.

# Graphical programming environments

If you are sitting in front of a Linux system, chances are pretty good that

- It is running some version of the X Window System.

- Several terminal (or shell) windows (terminal emulators) are running on top of X's graphical interface.

- One or more natively graphical programs are also running, such as a Web browser.

Linux programming environments can be divided into two broad categories, graphical IDEs and discrete collections of command line–based tools. Developers and users coming from a predominantly Windows background will be familiar with IDEs; the 800-pound gorilla in the Windows world is Microsoft's Visual Studio product.

This section looks at some of the full-featured graphical IDEs that collect and merge all the constituent components necessary for the development task, such as an editor, compiler, linker, debugger, class browser, and project manager, in a single, unified interface. The examples discussed include the open source Eclipse environment, KDE environment, Anjuta environment, and Code Crusader environment.

## Eclipse: The universal tool platform

Eclipse is a large, Java-based development platform. In principle and in practice, Eclipse is a universal IDE that is used to create applications as diverse as Web sites, C, C++, and Java programs, and even plug-ins that extend Eclipse itself. Eclipse is amply capable of handling every aspect of Linux development in an astonishing variety of languages. Figure 29-1 shows Eclipse with the "Hello, World" example program, written in Java, on the screen. (Note that the figure actually shows "Hello Word" in a few places.)

**FIGURE 29-1**

The Eclipse IDE

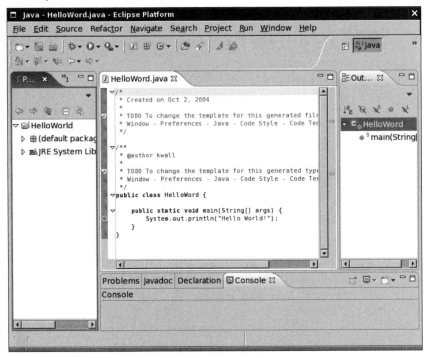

Figure 29-1 illustrates a number of characteristics typical of IDEs. The project view on the left side of the screen provides a project file browser that enables you to see at a glance the contents of the programming project. You can see the primary project folder, HelloWorld, and some of the associated files necessary to support Java projects, such as the default package for Java projects and a folder containing the necessary JRE (Java Runtime Environment) files.

The code editor view in the center of the screen shows the code for the HelloWorld.java program. Although it isn't visible in the black-and-white figure produced for this book, the code editor performs on-the-fly syntax highlighting using color and font-style changes. Java keywords are purple; plain comments appear in green; javadoc-style comments appear in a pale blue; strings are colored blue; and normal code is black. This is all quite customizable to your liking as well.

The right side of Eclipse displays another feature common among IDEs, a class browser. Class browsers enable developers to see the structure of their programs from the point of view of the code modules that make up the program rather than as mere files in a directory. This feature is not terribly useful for a small program such as HelloWorld.java, but larger programs that consist of dozens of classes or code modules are much easier to navigate using a code or class browser.

The bottom of the screen shows various information and status windows. For example, the Problems view shows problems that might have occurred while compiling the program. Eclipse, as with many other IDEs, allows you to double-click on an error in the Problems view to jump right to the error in the associated code file (see Figure 29-2).

**FIGURE 29-2**

Eclipse's Problems view

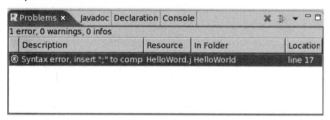

The Javadoc view, which is unique to the Eclipse Java development plug-in, enables you to view the output of Javadoc, a tool that creates documentation from specially formatted Java source code comments. The Declaration view works in combination with the class browser to show you the complete declaration of methods and data types. The Console view shows the actual output of the Java program.

Although much of Eclipse was designed to support developing applications in the Java language, plug-ins provide support for C, C++, Perl, Python, and other languages.

# Note

**For more information about Eclipse, including download information, visit the Eclipse home page at** www.eclipse.org. ∎

### KDevelop: KDE's IDE

KDevelop, another open source IDE licensed under the GPL, was originally created to provide an IDE that interoperated seamlessly with KDE and the Qt framework (a large C++ application framework) on which KDE is based. Over the years, however, KDevelop has evolved into an attractive, feature-rich development environment supporting a number of languages other than C++. Today, KDevelop is a general-purpose IDE, although it works best when used to create Qt-based applications written in C++. Figure 29-3 shows a representative screenshot of KDevelop.

**FIGURE 29-3**

The KDevelop IDE

If you compare KDevelop's appearance to Eclipse's appearance, you will see that both have the same type of components. In Figure 29-3, the class browser is located on the left side of the screen, the project window is located in the upper-right portion of the screen, and KDevelop's version of the Declaration view is displayed in the lower-right portion of the screen.

The log view that occupies the bottom of the KDevelop interface in Figure 29-3 shows the compilation process. As with Eclipse, KDevelop's toolbars and menus are stuffed with buttons and menu items that cater to the needs of developers, just as a word processor is customized with buttons and menu items specific to the task of writing and formatting documents.

## Note

For more information about KDevelop, including download information, visit the KDevelop home page at `http://kdevelop.kde.org/`. The language status support page (`www.kdevelop.org/HEAD/doc/ api/html/LangSupportStatus.html`) shows the current status of programming languages supported. KDevelop is available with most Linux distributions that include the K Desktop Environment. (For example, type **yum install kdevelop** to install KDevelop from Fedora.) ■

### Anjuta: An IDE for GTK/GNOME

To develop C and C++ applications for GTK/GNOME desktop environments, you can use the Anjuta Integrated Development Environment (`http://projects.gnome.org/anjuta`). With Anjuta, you can use editors such as GtkSourceview or Scintilla to view and modify code. You can edit files in the main Documents window, then select to see a tree view in the Project window or open the Symbols window to see a tree of the project's available symbols generated from a ctags parser.

The Anjuta Project Manager plug-in can help you manage most projects based on automake and autoconf. You can create a new project, change its structure, configure build flags and other settings, compile and link source code and execute your programs. By not adding any Anjuta-specific files to a project, Anjuta allows you to work with your project in environments outside of Anjuta.

Anjuta comes with most major Linux distributions. In Fedora, type **yum install anjuta\*** as root user to install Anjuta. To open the Anjuta window, select Applications ➪ Programming ➪ Anjuta IDE. Figure 29-4 shows an example of the Anjuta window.

**FIGURE 29-4**

The Anjuta IDE for GTK/GNOME

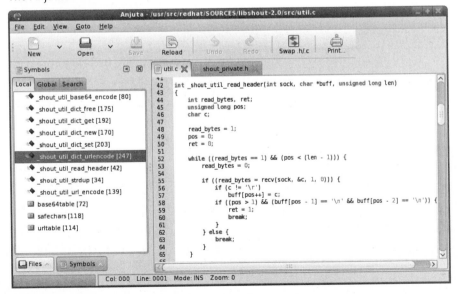

## Code Crusader

Code Crusader is a commercially available and supported IDE written in C++ and specifically targeted at the Linux developer; it is not available for Windows. You can use Code Crusader to write Java, FORTRAN, C++, and, of course, C programs. Unlike the IDEs discussed so far, Code Crusader does not include a built-in debugger. Rather, New Planet Software, developer of Code Crusader, makes its debugger application, Code Medic, available separately (although you can buy the two together as an IDE bundle). Figure 29-5 shows Code Crusader with the `forkexec.c` program from Listing 29-1 open in an editor window.

**FIGURE 29-5**

The Code Crusader IDE

As you can see in Figure 29-5, Code Crusader has a much simpler, cleaner interface than the other IDEs mentioned so far. Another significant difference between Code Crusader and the larger IDEs such as Eclipse and KDevelop is that each IDE component, such as the project browser, the class browser, editor windows, and the log viewer, open in their own, independent windows rather than being part of a single-document interface (SDI).

Having multiple windows is more consistent with traditional Linux and UNIX windowing conventions, but developers coming from a Windows background might find Code Crusader's multiple-document interface (MDI) a little jarring at first. On the other hand, programmers who prefer a leaner, cleaner interface might prefer Code Crusader to the rather overstuffed-looking interfaces that Eclipse and KDevelop offer.

## Note

For more information about Code Crusader, including download information, visit the Code Crusader home page at www.newplanetsoftware.com/jcc/. ∎

There are many more IDEs than the three discussed in this section. Some are less mature or still in beta stage. Others are special-purpose IDEs, such as the Quanta HTML editor, or the GLADE interface designer for GNOME. If Eclipse, KDevelop, and Code Crusader don't appeal to you, a quick search at Freshmeat (use http://freshmeat.net/tags/integrated-development-environments-ide to get right to the IDE category) or SourceForge (http://sourceforge.net/softwaremap/trove_list.php?form_cat=65 takes you straight to the IDE category) should turn up many options from which to choose. There's something available for everyone. This is Linux, after all, so you are free to choose the IDE that appeals to you the most. As you'll learn in the next subsection however, not everyone wants (or needs) a GUI IDE.

# The command-line programming environment

The Linux command-line programming environment or CLI (command-line interface) stands in sharp contrast to the GUI IDEs described in the previous section. It often shocks developers who have only a Windows development background and who aren't accustomed to using a CLI.

To be fair, it must be intimidating to find yourself in front of a command prompt without anything to double-click to start and not the faintest clue how to proceed. That said, while a CLI might seem Spartan to the newcomer, programming at the command line is surprisingly powerful and allows you to mix and match best-of-breed tools in a way that most IDEs cannot begin to approach. The CLI programming environment can match the environment provided by GUIs feature for feature, with the single exception of the graphical interface itself.

The inconvenience, if inconvenience it is, arises from the fact that the CLI programming environment relies on separate tools. For example, assuming you are working in the X Window System, you might be running one or more text editors, such as vi, pico, nano, joe, or emacs, each in its own terminal window. You might use another terminal window for compiling your program, either by invoking the compiler gcc (the GNU compiler collection) directly, or by using the make utility. In still another window you might be running a debugger such as gdb (the GNU debugger). If you are unfamiliar with the library you are using, you might have a Web browser open to view some sort of online documentation, or you might be using a program such as xman that displays Linux manual (man) pages in a graphical format.

It is not a given, however, that graphical IDEs are better than using discrete tools. Rather, it is a matter of which model developers feel most comfortable using, which method makes developers the most productive, and which approach best fits each developer's personal working style. Many long-time UNIX and Linux developers feel more comfortable with and work more productively using command-line tools: vi or emacs for writing and editing code, gcc and make for compilation, and gdb and kgdb for debugging.

In any event, the lines are not so sharply drawn. Emacs, for example, has the facility to invoke both compilation and debugging facilities, has an extremely rich code-editing interface (syntax highlighting and automatic indentation, for example), and also supports other code development features. Emacs also includes features such as source code control, symbol and class browsing, and built-in support for at least three different online help facilities.

If you prefer vi, it also can be configured to support symbol and class browsing using the ctags program, it has basic syntax highlighting (depending on the implementation), and it can also work with the error messages produced by failed compilation.

Perhaps the GUI versus CLI debate boils down to this distinction: CLI-oriented programming environments give developers direct access to the tools and utilities they need, don't consume system resources to draw an attractive GUI, and don't provide so-called point-and-click programming. GUI-oriented programming environments hide the tools and utilities underneath a consistent, unified interface; provide a convenient dashboard or instrument panel for access to the necessary programming tools; and let developers take advantage of some of the conveniences associated with graphical environments.

# Linux Programming Interfaces

As defined at the beginning of this chapter, a programming interface refers to the rules or methods followed to accomplish a particular task. As with programming environments, programming interfaces are usually thought of as either graphical or command line.

Graphical interfaces use the X Window System to receive and process user input and display information. Command-line interfaces, sometimes referred to as text-mode user interfaces (TUIs), are strictly text-based and do not require a windowing system to run. Thanks to the X Window System, however, you can also execute CLI-based programs in terminal emulators running on top of X.

As also mentioned at the beginning of the chapter, there also is a third type of interface: an *application programming interface*, or API. This section of the chapter looks at the ncurses library used to create text-mode user interfaces, examines some of the popular graphical interfaces in use today, and describes a small set of the most popular APIs used by Linux programmers.

## Creating command-line interfaces

There are three primary means of creating programs that interact with users at the command line. Two use libraries of screen manipulation routines, S-Lang and ncurses, to create TUIs and the third just uses standard input and standard output, conventionally known as stdin and stdout, respectively. Using stdin and stdout is trivially simple. Input and output occur one line at a time; users type input using the keyboard or pipe input in from a file, and output is displayed to the screen or redirected to a file. Listing 29-2 shows such a program, readkey.c.

LISTING 29-2

**Reading and Writing to stdin and stdout**

```
/*
 * readkey.c - reads characters from stdin
 */
#include <stdio.h>

int main(int argc, char *argv[])
{
        int c, i = 0;

        /* read characters until newline read */
        printf("INPUT: ");
        while ((c = getchar()) != '\n') {
                ++i;
                putchar(c);
        }
        printf("\ncharacters read: %d\n", i + 1);

        return 0;

}
```

In this program, the ++i syntax is used to increment the variable i by one each time through the while loop.

To compile this program, use the following command:

```
$ gcc readkey.c -o readkey
```

In the preceding code listing, readkey.c reads input from stdin until it encounters a newline (which is generated when you press the Enter key). Then it displays the text entered and the number of characters read (the count includes the newline) and exits.

Here's how it works:

```
$ ./readkey
INPUT: There are three primary means of creating programs that interact with
users at the command line
There are three primary means of creating programs that interact with users at
the command line
characters read: 96
```

The text wraps oddly because of this book's formatting constraints. You can also feed readkey.c input from stdin using the cat command:

```
$ cat /etc/passwd | ./readkey
INPUT: root:x:0:0::/root:/bin/bash
characters read: 28
```

In this case, you see only the first line of /etc/passwd because each line of the file ends with a newline. It should be clear that programmatically interacting with the command line is simple, but not terribly user-friendly or attractive.

## Creating text-mode user interfaces with ncurses

Screen manipulation libraries such as S-Lang and ncurses create more attractive programs, but, as you might expect, the tradeoff for a nicer-looking interface is more complicated code. Ncurses, which stands for *new curses*, is free reimplementation of the classic curses UNIX screen-handling library. The term *curses* derives from the phrase *cursor optimization*, which succinctly describes what the curses library does: compute the fastest way to redraw a text-mode screen and place the cursor in the proper location.

Ncurses provides a simple, high-level interface for screen control and manipulation. It also contains powerful routines for handling keyboard and mouse input, creating and managing multiple windows, and using menus, forms, and panels. Ncurses works by generalizing the interface between an application program and the screen or terminal on which it is running.

Given the literally hundreds of varieties of terminals, screens, and terminal emulation programs available, and the different features they possess (not to mention the different commands to use these features and capabilities), UNIX programmers quickly developed a way to abstract screen manipulation. Rather than write a lot of extra code to take into account the different terminal types, ncurses provides a uniform and generalized interface for the programmer. The ncurses API insulates the programmer from the underlying hardware and differences between terminals.

Ncurses gives to character-based applications many of the same features found in graphical X Window applications — multiple windows, forms, menus, and panels. Ncurses windows can be managed independently, may contain the same or different text, scroll or not scroll, be visible or hidden. Forms enable the programmer to create easy-to-use data entry and display windows, simplifying what is usually a difficult and application-specific coding task. Panels extend ncurses' capability to deal with overlapping and stacked windows. Menus provide, well, menus, again with a simpler, generalized programming interface. The ncurses library even provides support for mouse input.

To give you an idea of how ncurses works and what is involved in writing code to use it, Listing 29-3 shows the readkey.c program (now named nreadkey.c) introduced in Listing 29-2, adapted here to work with ncurses.

**LISTING 29-3**

**Reading Input and Writing Output with ncurses**

```
/*
 * nreadkey.c - reads characters from stdin
 */
#include <stdio.h>
#include <curses.h>

int main(int argc, char *argv[])
{
        int c, i = 0;
        int maxx, maxy;
        int y, x;

        /* start ncurses */
        initscr();

        /* draw a purty border */
        box(stdscr, ACS_VLINE, ACS_HLINE);
        mvwaddstr(stdscr, 1, 1, "INPUT: ");
        refresh();

        /* read characters until newline read */
        noecho();
        while ((c = getch()) != '\n') {
                ++i;
                getyx(stdscr, y, x);
                /* at the right margin */
                if (x == 79) {
                        mvaddch(y + 1, 1, c);
                } else {
                        waddch(stdscr, c);
                }

                refresh();
        }
        echo();
        refresh();

        /* print the character count */
        getmaxyx(stdscr, maxy, maxx);
        mvwprintw(stdscr, maxy - 2, 1, "characters read: %d\n", i);
        curs_set(0);
        refresh();

        /* time to look at the screen */
```

```
    sleep(3);

    /* shutdown ncurses */
    endwin();

    return 0;

}
```

One of the first things you notice is that nreadkey.c is about twice as long as readkey.c. The additional code addresses the need to set up the screen, position the cursor, and so forth. To see whether the additional code is worth it, compile nreadkey.c using the following command:

$ **gcc nreadkey.c -lncurses -o nreadkey**

To run the program, type *./nreadkey*. Figure 29-6 shows the result after typing the same text as typed for readkey.c earlier.

**FIGURE 29-6**

An ncurses-based TUI

Ncurses-based programs can also read input piped from stdin. Figure 29-7 shows the results of the command cat /etc/passwd | ./nreadkey.

As you saw with the command pipeline used with the readkey.c program (shown in Listing 29-2), the input is truncated at the end of the first line because each line in /etc/passwd ends with the newline character, and readkey.c uses the newline character to signal the end of input.

FIGURE 29-7

Displaying input piped to an ncurses-based program.

```
INPUT: root:x:0:0::/root:/bin/bash




characters read: 28
```

## Note

**For more information about ncurses, including download information, visit the ncurses FAQ at**
`http://invisible-island.net/ncurses/ncurses.faq.html.` ∎

### Creating text-mode user interfaces with S-Lang

S-Lang, created by John Davis, is an alternative to ncurses for creating TUIs. In addition to providing screen manipulation and cursor control routines, S-Lang also consists of an embeddable S-Lang interpreter, a large library of built-in (intrinsic) routines that simplify certain parts of programming, and a variety of predefined data types and data structures. Listing 29-4 shows the same program as Listing 29-3, with appropriate updates to reflect use of S-Lang instead of ncurses.

LISTING 29-4

**Reading Input and Writing Output with S-Lang**

```c
/*
 * sreadkey.c - simple S-Lang-based UI
 */
#include <stdio.h>
#include <string.h>
#include <slang/slang.h>

int main(int argc, char *argv[])
{
        int i = 0;
        unsigned int ch;
```

```
/* start s-lang */
SLtt_get_terminfo();
SLang_init_tty(-1, 0, 1);
SLsmg_init_smg();

/* draw a purty border */
SLsmg_draw_box(0, 0, 24, 80);
SLsmg_gotorc(1, 1);
SLsmg_write_nchars("INPUT: ", 7);
SLsmg_refresh();

/* read characters until newline read */
while(1) {
        ++i;
        ch = SLang_getkey();
        if (ch == 13)
                break;
        if (SLsmg_get_column() == 79)
                SLsmg_gotorc(2, 1);
        SLsmg_write_char(ch);
        SLsmg_refresh();
}

/* print the character count */
SLsmg_gotorc(22, 1);
SLsmg_write_nchars("characters read: ", 17);
SLsmg_printf("%d", i);
SLsmg_refresh();

/* time to look at the screen */
sleep(3);

/* shutdown s-lang */
SLsmg_reset_smg();
SLang_reset_tty();

return 0;

}
```

To compile this program use the following command:

```
$ gcc sreadkey.c -lslang -o sreadkey
```

You will need the slang, slang-devel, ncurses, and ncurses-devel packages to compile and run this program.

To run the program, type **./sreadkey**. Figure 29-8 shows the result after typing the same text as typed for `readkey.c` earlier.

**FIGURE 29-8**

An S-Lang–based TUI

As you can see from Figure 29-8, the basic appearance and functionality of `sreadkey.c` is the same as `nreadkey.c`. The differences between the two, which have to do with the TUI framework used to create `sreadkey.c`, are invisible to the user. S-Lang–based programs can also read input piped from stdin.

From a developer's perspective, there are significant differences between ncurses and S-Lang in program structure and the actual library usage, but the output is almost identical.

## Note

**For more information about S-Lang, including download information, visit the S-Lang Web page at**
`www.s-lang.org.` ∎

# Creating graphical interfaces

When it comes to creating GUIs, Linux programmers have more options available than they do for creating TUIs. Probably the most popular and certainly the best known toolkits used to create graphical applications are Qt and GTK+. Qt is the C++ application framework that powers KDE, the K Desktop Environment. GTK+ is the toolkit underneath GNOME, the GNU Network Object Model Environment. GTK+ is written largely in C, but it has language bindings available for many other programming languages, such as Perl, C++, and Python, so you can use GTK+ features in many programming environments. Because of the limited space available, this chapter does not show examples of Qt and GTK+ applications.

## Note

**For more information about GTK+, visit the GTK+ Web site at** www.gtk.org. **You can find information about the Qt framework at** http://qtsoftware.com/. ■

Although Qt and GTK+ are the big hammers of Linux graphical development, you can use many other toolkits, frameworks, and libraries to develop GUI-based applications for Linux. The following list, arranged alphabetically, describes some of the available toolkits. Most of these toolkits and frameworks describe widget sets, which are implemented in one or more programming libraries. *Widget* is the term applied to a user interface abstraction, such as a scrollbar or a button, created using the toolkit.

## Note

**Nearly every programming toolkit described in the following list is available with the major Linux distributions (Fedora, Ubuntu, openSUSE, Debian, and so on) included with this book. Use the appropriate packaging tools that come with your Linux system to find and install the programming tools that interest you.** ■

- **Athena** — The Athena library was one of the earliest (think ancient) widget libraries available for the X Window System. It was a thin layer of abstraction on top of raw Xlib calls that made it slightly less painful to create scrollbars, text entry boxes, and other typical GUI elements. It is part of the standard X11 distribution.

- **3D Athena Toolkit** — The 3D Athena Toolkit was a 3D version of the original Athena toolkit. It gave Athena a 3D look and was a considerable visual improvement over plain vanilla Athena. The 3D Athena toolkit, although no longer widely used, is still available on the Web at http://directory.fsf.org/project/xaw3d.

- **FLTK** — FLTK, which is pronounced "full tick," is an acronym for the Fast Light Toolkit. FLTK is a GUI for X, Mac OS X, and Microsoft Windows. Written in C++, FLTK makes it possible to write GUIs that look almost identical regardless of the platform on which the GUI runs. FLTK also supports OpenGL graphics. You can find more information about FLTK on the Web at www.fltk.org.

- **XForms** — XForms is a GUI toolkit based on Xlib. It isn't highly configurable like the other GUI toolkits discussed in this section, but its simplicity makes XForms easier to use than the other graphical toolkits. It comes with a GUI builder that makes it fast and easy to get working applications up and running. More information about XForms can be found on the Web at http://savannah.nongnu.org/projects/xforms/.

- **OpenGL** — OpenGL is the industry standard 3D graphics toolkit. It provides the most realistic and lifelike graphics currently available for the X Window System. It is generally available as part of XFree86. More information about OpenGL is available on the Web at www.opengl.org.

- **Motif** — Motif was one of the first widget or interface toolkits available for the X Window System that combined both an interface toolkit and a window manager. Originally available only as a commercial product, it is now available in an open source version as OpenMotif from the MotifZone at www.openmotif.org.

- **Xlib** — Xlib is shorthand for the X library, a low-level, C-based interface to the raw X Window System protocol. If you want to write as close to the X graphics core as possible, you write Xlib-based programs. Indeed, most window managers, widget libraries, and GUI toolkits are written using Xlib function. Although using straight Xlib gives you the best performance, it is extremely code intensive. Xlib is an essential ingredient of the standard X distribution. You can learn more about Xlib from the HTML manual page, available on the Web at `http://tronche.com/gui/x/xlib`.

- **Xt** — Xt Intrinsics are a very thin layer of functions and data structures on top of Xlib. Xt Intrinsics create an object-oriented interface that C programs can use to create graphical elements. Without other widget sets, the Intrinsics are not especially useful. Xt, like Xlib, is a part of the standard X distribution and is not available separately.

# Application programming interfaces

Application programming interfaces, or APIs, provide programmers with libraries of code for performing certain tasks. There are many APIs, probably as many as there are types of programming problems that need to be solved. The ncurses library, for example, provides an API that you can use to create text-mode user interfaces. In turn, ncurses works by using either the terminfo or termcap API to perform the actual screen updates in a manner consistent with the underlying type of display device in use.

Developers keep having to perform a specific type of programming task, such as updating a database, communicating over a network, getting sound out of a sound card, or performing complicated mathematical calculations. As a result, there is at least one database API, socket API, sound API, or mathematical API already in existence that they can use to simplify those tasks.

## Note

This section discusses APIs for use in C and C++ programming. You can also make use of these libraries in other programming languages, but you may need to write software to adapt to the C-based API. For example, Perl, Python, and Java all have a means to call on C functions or APIs, but you will need to write the code needed to adapt the actual C library to your programming language. ■

APIs consist of three components:

- **Header file** — Declares the interface (the function calls, macros, and data structures) the developers can use in their own programs.

- **One or more library files** — Implement(s) the interfaces declared in the header files and against which programs must be linked.

- **API documentation** — Describes how to use the API and often provides example code. The documentation might be provided in manual pages, text files, HTML files, GNU TeXinfo files, or some combination of all of these formats.

Table 29-1 describes many popular or widely used APIs, but the list provided here is far from complete.

**TABLE 29-1**

## Common Linux APIs

| API | Category | Description |
| --- | --- | --- |
| aalib | ASCII art | AA-lib is a library that outputs graphics as ASCII art. For an amazing demonstration of AA-lib's capabilities, look into BB Demo or the screenshot gallery links at the aa-project homepage: `http://aa-project.sourceforge.net/index.html`. |
| arts | Sound | The analog real-time synthesizer (aRts) is KDE's core sound system, designed to create and process sound using small specialized modules. These modules might create a waveform, play samples, filter data, add signals, perform effects (such as delay, flanger, or chorus), or output the data to the soundcard. |
| atk | Accessibility | atk is a library of accessibility functions used by GNOME. |
| audiofile | Audio | audiofile, used by the esound daemon (Enlightened Sound Daemon), is a library for processing various audio file formats. You can also use it to develop your own audio file–based applications. |
| db-4 | Database | The Berkeley Database (Berkeley DB) library enables developers to create applications with database support. |
| expat | XML | Expat is a stream-oriented C library for parsing XML. It is used by Python, GNOME, Xft2, and other applications. |
| gdbm | Database | The GNU Database Manager (GDBM) is a set of database routines that work similarly to the standard UNIX dbm routines. |
| gdk_pixbuf | 2-D Graphics | GdkPixbuf is an API for loading, scaling, compositing, and animating images. GdkPixBuf is required by many GTK+ programs. |
| glib | General | GLib is a general purpose API of C language routines. The library includes support for features such as lists, trees, hashes, memory allocation, and many other things. GLib is required by almost every GTK+ application. |
| glut | 3-D Graphics | The GL Utility Toolkit (GLUT) is a 3D graphics library based on the OpenGL API. It provides a higher-level interface for creation of OpenGL-based graphics. |
| gmp | Mathematics | The GNU Multiple Precision (GMP) API implements a library for arbitrary precision arithmetic, such as operations on signed integers, rational numbers, and floating-point numbers. |

| API | Category | Description |
| --- | --- | --- |
| gnet | Network | GNet is an object-oriented library of network routines. Written in C and based on the GLib library, GNet is used by gnomeicu and Pan. |
| imlib | Graphics | ImLib (image library) is an image loading and rendering API designed to simplify and speed up the process of loading images and obtaining X Window System drawables. |
| libao | Audio | libao is a cross-platform audio library used by other libraries and programs that use audio, including ogg123, GAIM, and the Ogg Vorbis libraries. |
| libart_lgpl | 2-D Graphics | Libart is a library for high-performance 2D graphics used by KDE and GNOME. |
| libexif | Graphics | This library provides an API allowing programs to read, parse, edit, and save Exchangeable Image File Format (EXIF) data in image files. EXIF is a format used to store extra information in images, such as the JPEG files produced by digital cameras. |
| libglade | Graphics | The GLADE library, used heavily in GNOME programs, allows programs to load user interfaces from definitions stored in external files. This allows the interface to be changed without recompiling the program. |
| libid3tag | Audio | libid3tag is a library for reading ID3 tags. ID3 tags allow extra information to be embedded in audio files. |
| libieee1284 | Hardware | libieee1284 enables applications that need to communicate with (or at least identify) devices that are attached via IEEE1284–compliant parallel ports, such as scanners. |
| libjpeg | Graphics | The JPEG library provides a rich API for manipulating JPEG-format images, including reading, writing, converting, compressing, and decompressing images. |
| libmad | Audio | libmad provides a high-quality MPEG audio decoder API. libmad provides full 24-bit PCM output, so applications using this API can produce high-quality audio. |
| libmng | Graphics | libmng implements the Multiple-image Network Graphics (MNG) API. MNG provides multi-image animation capabilities similar to animated GIFs, but free of patent encumbrances. |
| libogg | Audio | Libogg is a library for reading and writing ogg format bitstreams. libogg is needed to use the Ogg Vorbis audio format. |
| libpng | Graphics | The Portable Network Graphics (PNG) standard is an extensible file format for the lossless, portable, well-compressed storage of images. PNG provides a patent-free replacement for GIF. (The GIF patent has recently expired.) |

*continued*

| **TABLE 29-1** | *(continued)* | |
|---|---|---|
| **API** | **Category** | **Description** |
| libtermcap | Hardware | libtermcap implements the GNU termcap library API, a library of C functions that enable programs to send control strings to terminals in a way independent of the terminal type. |
| libtiff | 2-D Graphics | The TIFF library provides an API for working with images stored in the Tag Image File Format (TIFF), a widely used format for storing high-quality, high-resolution images. |
| libungif | 2-D Graphics | libungif provides an API unencumbered by patents for loading and saving images in GIF format. |
| libusb | Hardware | libusb allows user space application access to USB devices. |
| libvorbis | Audio | This library supports the Vorbis General Audio Compression Codec, commonly known as Ogg Vorbis. Ogg Vorbis is an open, patent- and royalty-free, general-purpose compressed audio format for audio and music. |
| libwmf | Graphics | libwmf provides an API for interpreting, displaying, and converting metafile images to standard image formats such as PNG, JPEG, PS, EPS, and SVG. |
| libxml2 | XML | libxml2 is the XML parser library used by GNOME and KDE. |
| libxslt | XML | libxslt provides XSLT support for libxml2. XSLT is a language used to transform XML documents into other formats. |
| orbit | CORBA | ORBit is a high-performance Common Object Request Broker Architecture (CORBA) object request broker (ORB). ORBit allows programs to send requests and receive replies from other programs, regardless of the locations of the two programs. GNOME uses ORBit heavily. |
| pango | Text layout | Pango is a library for layout and rendering of text, with an emphasis on internationalization. Pango forms the core of text and font handling in GTK+-2.0. |
| pcre | Regular expressions | The Perl-compatible regular expression (PCRE) library implements an API for regular expression pattern matching that uses the same syntax and semantics as Perl 5. The PCRE library is used by many programs. |
| pilot-link | PalmOS | pilot-link implements a library for communicating with Palm handheld devices and with other devices that adhere to the PalmOS interface standard. gnome-pilot and KPilot use pilot-link. |

| API | Category | Description |
|-----|----------|-------------|
| popt | General | popt is a C library for parsing command-line parameters. popt was heavily influenced by the `getopt()` and `getopt_long()` functions, but improves on them by allowing more powerful argument expansion and allows command-line arguments to be aliased via configuration files. |
| sdl | Multimedia | The Simple DirectMedia Layer (SDL) provides a generic, cross-platform API for low-level access to audio, keyboards, mice, joysticks, 3D hardware via OpenGL, and 2D framebuffers. This is a popular API for many Linux games (see `www.libsdl.org`). |
| t1lib | Graphics | t1lib provides an API for generating character and string glyphs from Adobe Type 1 fonts. |
| taglib | Audio | TagLib is a library for reading and editing the metadata stored in ID3v1 and ID3v2 (MP3 files) and Ogg Vorbis comments and ID3 tags (Ogg Vorbis files). |
| zlib | Data Compression | zlib provides a general-purpose, thread-safe data compression library that implements the data formats defined by RFC1950, RFC1951, and RFC1952 (see `www.ietf.org/rfc.html` to find any of the RFCs just mentioned). |

As you can see, a wide variety of APIs exist for performing an equally wide variety of programming tasks. Chances are pretty good that if you need to perform some sort of programming task, someone has written a library that you can use to do it.

# Summary

The phrase "Linux programming environments and interfaces" is shorthand that masks a rich set of features, which, taken together, only partially characterize the activity of programming on a Linux system.

This chapter looked at both graphical programming IDEs and the less visually attractive but just as powerful command-line or text-mode programming environments. You also learned some of the characteristics of Linux and of Linux systems that define and shape programming and programs on, and for, Linux.

The second part of the chapter looked at the variety of programming interfaces and the methods available for getting particular programming tasks done. You learned that you can create text-mode or command-line interfaces and that you can choose from a variety of graphical interfaces for structuring user interaction with your program. Finally, you took a fast-paced look at some of the many APIs that make it possible to do a variety of things, such as manipulate or create images or interact with a database.

# Programming Tools and Utilities

T he preceding chapter provided a high-level view of Linux programming, focusing on the overall development environment and
introducing the idioms that give programming on a Linux system
its distinctive character. This chapter goes into greater detail and describes
some of the tools and toys found on a typical Linux development system.

The goal of this chapter is not to turn you into a developer in 30 pages or
less, but simply to explore some of the variety of tools developers use so you
will at least know what they are and what they do. You'll also learn how to
use some of the programs and utilities.

## The Well-Stocked Toolkit

Whether you prefer a graphical development environment or the classic
command-line environment, you need a good set of tools if you want to
write, compile, and debug programs for Linux. The good news is that Linux
has plenty of editors, compilers, and debuggers from which to choose. The
bad news is that Linux has plenty of editors, compilers, and debuggers from
which to choose.

The range of programming tool options is good news for developers because
they can pick the best and most appropriate tools for the development task
at hand. The proliferation of choices is bad news for system administrators
who need to install and maintain the tools and for people who evaluate the
tools. Too many choices make choosing the right one a difficult task.

This chapter discusses the most popular programs and utilities of each type. In most cases, alternatives (and sometimes multiple alternatives) exist, but I cover only one to keep the discussion simple. (I try to mention the others just so you're familiar with their names.)

What constitutes a well-stocked Linux development toolkit? The basics include an editor to write the code, one or more compilers to turn source code into binaries, and a debugger to track down the inevitable bugs. Most people have a favorite editor, and you'd have a difficult time trying to persuade them to try a new one. Most editors support some set of programming-related functionality (some more than others, to be sure). There are too many to cover in this space, so suffice it to say: You'll need an editor.

Perhaps the most popular console editors are vi and emacs. vi is a commercial editor, being part of the commercial UNIX offerings, so what you can actually get is usually a clone such as vim, elvis, or (my own personal favorite) nvi (*new* vi). I prefer nvi because it is a port of vi from BSD UNIX to Linux. Other popular editors include pico (the Pine mail client editor made available as a separate program), jed, joe, jove, and nano. If you prefer graphical editors, gedit in GNOME and kedit in KDE also provide basic programming support, as does nedit, a Linux and UNIX-based programmer's editor.

## Cross-Reference

**Chapter 9 has a short tutorial on using the vi editor, as well as short descriptions of several other popular open source text editors. ∎**

When it comes to compilers, GCC is the compiler of choice, or, if you will, the choice of the GNU generation, so this chapter discusses only GCC. Other compilers are available for Linux, such as Intel's C and C++ compiler and a very powerful (and expensive) offering from the Portland Compiler Group. Similarly, GDB, the GNU debugger, is the only debugger described in this chapter.

In Chapter 29, you examined the role that programming interfaces play in simplifying the development task. Interfaces usually include one or more libraries that implement the functionality that interfaces define. Because you need to be able to work with programming libraries, utilities for creating, examining, and manipulating libraries also occupy the well-stocked programming toolkit.

To this list, most developers would add a build automation tool, such as make, because most non-trivial projects need some sort of utility that handles building and rebuilding complicated, multifile projects with a minimum of effort and time.

Another challenge for large projects is tracking source code changes and maintaining a record of what code changed, when it changed, how it changed, and who changed it. This task is the province of source code control systems, and this chapter looks at two: RCS and CVS.

# Using the GCC Compiler

The GNU Compiler Collection (GCC) is by far the most dominant compiler (rather, the most dominant *collection* of compilers) used on Linux systems. It compiles programs written in C, C++, Objective-C, Fortran, Java, and Ada. This chapter focuses on the C compiler.

GCC gives programmers extensive control over the compilation process. That process includes up to four stages: preprocessing, compilation, assembly, and linking. You can stop the process after any of these stages to examine the compiler's output at that stage. GCC can also handle the various C dialects, such as ANSI C or traditional (Kernighan and Ritchie) C. You can control the amount and type of debugging information, if any, to embed in the resulting binary. And as with most compilers, GCC also performs code optimization.

The gcc command invokes the C compiler. To use it, provide it the name of a C source file and use its -o option to specify the name of the output file. gcc will preprocess, compile, assemble, and link the program, generating an executable, often called a binary. Here's the simplest syntax:

```
gcc infile.c [-o outfile]
```

infile.c is a C source code file and -o says to name the output file outfile. The [] characters indicate optional arguments throughout this book. If the name of the output file is not specified, gcc names the output file a.out by default. Not all steps need to be handled by the gcc program itself, as gcc can hand off processing tasks such as linking to ld, the GNU linker.

The following example uses gcc to create the hello program from the source file hello.c. First, the source code:

```
/*
 * hello.c - canonical hello world program
 */
#include <stdio.h>

int main(int argc, char *argv[])
{
        printf("Hello, Linux programming world!\n");
        return 0;
}
```

Now, to compile and run this program, type the following:

```
$ gcc hello.c -o hello
```

If all goes well, gcc does its job silently and returns to the shell prompt. It compiles and links the source file hello.c (gcc hello.c), creating a binary named hello, as specified using the -o hello argument.

If you run the program, here's the output you get:

```
$ ./hello
Hello, Linux programming world!
```

## Caution

**The command that executed the hello program specifically included the current directory, denoted with a period (.) because having the current directory in your path is a security risk. That is, instead of a** $PATH **environment variable that resembles** /bin:/usr/bin:/usr/local/bin:. **, it should be** /bin:/usr/ bin:/usr/local/bin **so that a cracker cannot put a dangerous command in your current directory that happens to match the name of the more benign command you really want to execute.** ∎

With GCC (and any other C compiler), the preprocessing stage handles constructs such as the #include <stdio.h> as well as #define macros. After these are handled, normal processing begins.

GCC relies on file extensions to determine what kind of source code file it is — that is, in which programming language the source code is written. Table 30-1 lists the most common extensions and how GCC interprets them.

**TABLE 30-1**

## GCC's Filenaming Conventions

| Extension | Type |
|-----------|------|
| .a, .so | Compiled library code |
| .c | C language source code |
| .C, .cc | C++ language source code (these may also have .cpp, .cxx, .CPP, .cp, and .c++ as an extension) |
| .i | Preprocessed C source code |
| .ii | Preprocessed C++ source code |
| .m | Objective-C source code |
| .o | Compiled object code |
| .S, .s | Assembly language source code |

# Compiling multiple source code files

Most non-trivial programs consist of multiple source files, and each source file must be compiled to object code before the final link step. To do so, pass gcc the name of each source code file it has to compile. GCC handles the rest. The gcc invocation might resemble the following:

```
$ gcc file1.c file2.c file3.c -o progname
```

gcc would create file1.o, file2.o, and file3.o and then link them all together to create progname. As an alternative, you can use gcc's -c option on each file individually, which creates object files from each file. Then in a second step, you link the object files together to create an executable. Thus, the single command just shown becomes:

```
$ gcc -c file1.c
$ gcc -c file2.c
$ gcc -c file3.c
$ gcc file1.o file2.o file3.o -o progname
```

One reason to do this is to avoid recompiling files that haven't changed. If you change the source code only in file3.c, for example, you don't need to recompile file1.c and file2.c to recreate progname. Another reason to compile source code files individually before linking them to create the executable is to avoid long-running compilation. Compiling multiple files in a single gcc invocation can take a while if one of the source code modules is really lengthy.

Let's take a look at an example that creates a single binary executable from multiple source code files. The example program named newhello comprises a C source code file, main.c (see Listing 30-1); a header file, msg.h (Listing 30-2); and another C source code file, msg.c (Listing 30-3).

## LISTING 30-1

**Main Program for newhello**

```c
/*
 * main.c  driver program
 */
#include <stdio.h>
#include "msg.h"

int main(int argc, char *argv[])
{
        char msg_hi[] = { "Hi there, programmer!" };
        char msg_bye[] = { "Goodbye, programmer!" };

        printf("%s\n", msg_hi);
        prmsg(msg_bye);
        return 0;
}
```

---

**LISTING 30-2**

**Header file for newhello Helper Function**

```
/*
 * msg.h - header for msg.c
 */

#ifndef MSG_H_
#define MSG_H_

void prmsg(char *msg);

#endif /* MSG_H_ */
```

---

**LISTING 30-3**

**Definitions for newhello Helper Function**

```
/*
 * msg.c - function declared in msg.h
 */
#include <stdio.h>
#include "msg.h"

void prmsg(char *msg)
{
        printf("%s\n", msg);
}
```

---

The command to compile these programs to create newhello is

```
$ gcc msg.c main.c -o newhello
```

The gcc command finds the header file msg.h in the current directory and automatically includes that file during the preprocessing stage. The stdio.h file resides in a location known to the gcc command, so this file also gets included. You can add directories to search for such files, called *include* files, with the -I command-line option.

To create the object files individually, you might use the following commands:

```
$ gcc -c msg.c
$ gcc -c main.c
```

Then, to create newhello from the object files, use the following command:

```
$ gcc msg.o main.o -o newhello
```

When you run this program, the output is as follows:

```
$ ./newhello
Hi there, programmer!
Goodbye, programmer!
```

Before it creates the newhello binary, gcc creates object files for each source file. Typing long commands such as this does become tedious, however. The section "Automating Builds with make" later in this chapter shows you how to avoid having to type long, involved command lines.

## GCC command-line options

The list of command-line options GCC accepts runs to several pages, so Table 30-2 describes only the most common ones. (Type **man gcc** to see a more complete list of options available with GCC.)

**TABLE 30-2**

### GCC Command-Line Options

| Option | Description |
|--------|-------------|
| -ansi | Supports the ANSI/ISO C standard, turning off GNU extensions that conflict with the standard. |
| -c | Compiles without linking, resulting in an object file but not an executable binary. |
| -Dfoo=bar | Defines a preprocessor macro foo with a value of bar on the command line. |
| -g | Includes standard debugging information in the binary. |
| -ggdb | Includes lots of debugging information in the binary that only the GNU debugger (GDB) can understand. |
| -Idirname | Prepends dirname to the list of directories searched for include files. |
| -Ldirname | Prepends dirname to the list of directories searched for library files. By default, gcc links against shared libraries. |
| -lfoo | Links against libfoo. |
| -MM | Outputs a make-compatible dependency list. |
| -o file | Creates the output file file (not necessary when compiling object code). If file is not specified, the default is a.out. |

*continued*

| TABLE 30-2 | *(continued)* |
|---|---|
| **Option** | **Description** |
| -0 | Optimizes the compiled code. |
| -On | Specifies an optimization level n, 0<=n<=3. |
| -pedantic | Emits all warnings required by the ANSI/ISO C standard. |
| -pedantic-errors | Emits all errors required by the ANSI/ISO C standard. |
| -static | Links against static libraries. |
| -traditional | Supports the Kernighan and Ritchie C syntax. (If you don't understand what this means, don't worry about it.) |
| -v | Shows the commands used in each step of compilation. |
| -W | Suppresses all warning messages. |
| -Wall | Emits all generally useful warnings that gcc can provide. Specific warnings can also be flagged using -W*warning*, where *warning* is replaced by a string identifying an item for which you want to list warnings. |
| -werror | Converts all warnings into errors, stopping the compilation. |

As mentioned earlier, -o file tells GCC to place output in the file file regardless of the output being produced. If you do not specify -o, for an input file named file.suffix, the defaults are to name the executable a.out, the object file file.o, and the assembly language file file.s. Preprocessor output goes to stdout.

# Automating Builds with make

The make utility is a tool to control the process of building and rebuilding software. make automates what software gets built, how it gets built, and when it gets built, freeing programmers to concentrate on writing code. It also saves a lot of typing because it contains logic that invokes GCC compiler-appropriate options and arguments. Furthermore, it helps you to avoid errors in typing all the complicated commands to build an application; instead, you just type one or two make commands. Use this section to familiarize yourself with the look and layout of makefiles.

For all but the simplest software projects, make is essential. In the first place, projects composed of multiple source files require long, complex compiler invocations. The make utility simplifies this by storing these difficult command lines in the makefile, a text file that contains all of the commands required to build software projects.

The make utility is convenient for both the developer and the user who want to build a program. As developers make changes to a program, whether to add new features or incorporate bug fixes, make makes it possible to rebuild the program with a single, short command. make is convenient for users because they don't have to read reams of documentation explaining in excruciating, mind-numbing detail how to build a program. Rather, they can simply be told to type **make** followed by **make test** followed by **make install**. Most users appreciate the convenience of simple build instructions.

Finally, make speeds up the edit-compile-debug process. It minimizes rebuild times because it is smart enough to determine which files have changed, and recompiles only files that have changed.

So, how does make accomplish its magical feats? By using a makefile, which contains rules that tell make what to build and how to build it. A rule consists of the following:

- **Target** — The "thing" make ultimately tries to create
- **Dependencies** — A list of one or more dependencies (usually files) required to build the target
- **Commands** — A list of commands to execute to create the target from the specified dependencies

Makefiles constitute a database of dependency information for the programs they build and automatically verify that all the files necessary for building a program are available.

When invoked, GNU make looks for a file named GNUmakefile, makefile, or Makefile, in that order. For some reason, most developers use the last form, Makefile. Makefile rules have this general form:

```
target : dependency dependency [...]
        command
        command
        [...]
```

In this syntax, *target* is usually the file, such as a binary or object file, to create. *dependency* is a list of one or more files required as input to create *target*. Each *command* is a step such as a compiler invocation or a shell command that is necessary to create *target*. Unless specified otherwise, make does all of its work in the current working directory.

## Caution

**The first character in a command must be the tab character; eight spaces will not suffice. This often catches people unaware, and can be a problem if your preferred editor "helpfully" translates tabs to eight spaces. If you try to use spaces instead of a tab, make displays the message Missing separator and stops.** ∎

Listing 30-4 shows a sample makefile for building a text editor imaginatively named editor.

---

**LISTING 30-4**

**A Sample Makefile**

```
editor : editor.o screen.o keyboard.o
        gcc -o editor editor.o screen.o keyboard.o

editor.o : editor.c
        gcc -c editor.c

screen.o : screen.c
        gcc -c screen.c

keyboard.o : keyboard.c
        gcc -c keyboard.c

clean :
        rm -f *.o core *~

realclean : clean
        rm -f editor
```

---

To compile editor, you simply type **make** in the directory that contains the makefile. It's that simple.

This example makefile has six rules. The first defines how to create the target named editor. The first target in every makefile is the default target (unless you specifically define one using the .DEFAULT directive, which is not covered in this chapter). The default target is the one that make builds if no target is specified as an argument to make. editor has three dependencies: editor.o, screen.o, and keyboard.o; these three files must exist to build editor. The second line in the first rule is the command that make must execute to create editor: gcc -o editor editor.o screen.o keyboard.o. It builds the executable from the three object files: editor.o, screen.o, and keyboard.o.

The next three rules tell make how to build the individual object files. Each rule consists of one object file target (editor.o, screen.o, keyboard.o); one source code file dependency (editor.c, screen.c, keyboard.c); and a rule that defines how to build that target.

The fifth rule defines a target named clean with no dependencies. When a target has no dependencies, its commands are executed whenever the target is invoked. In this case, clean deletes the constituent object files (*.o), plus any core files (core) as well as any emacs backup files (*~) from previous builds.

The sixth rule defines a target named realclean. It uses the fifth rule as one of its dependencies. This causes make to build the clean target and then to remove the editor binary.

Here is where make's value becomes evident: Ordinarily, if you tried to build editor using the command from the second line, gcc would complain loudly and ceremoniously quit if the dependencies did not exist. make, on the other hand, after determining that editor requires these files, first verifies that they exist and, if they don't, executes the commands to create them.

After creating the dependencies, make returns to the first rule to create the editor executable. Of course, if the dependencies for the components editor.c, screen.c, or keyboard.c don't exist, make gives up because it lacks targets named, in this case, editor.c, screen.c, or keyboard.c (that is, no rules are defined in the makefile for creating editor.c, screen.c, and keyboard.c).

All well and good, you are probably thinking, but how does make know when to build or rebuild a file? The answer is simple: If a specified target does not exist in a place where make can find it, make builds or rebuilds it. If the target does exist, make compares the timestamp on the target to the timestamp on the dependencies. If one or more of the dependencies is newer than the target, make rebuilds that target, assuming that the newer dependency implies some code change that must be incorporated into the target.

## Tip

**You can force** make **to think that a file has changed by using the** touch **command. The** touch **command changes the modified date for a file without altering the file's contents.** ■

# Library Utilities

Programming libraries are collections of code that can be reused across multiple software projects. Libraries are a classic example of software development's ardent goal: code reuse. They collect frequently used programming routines and utility code into a single location.

The standard C libraries, for example, contain hundreds of frequently used routines, such as the output function printf() and the input function getchar() that would be wearisome to rewrite each time you create a new program. Beyond code reuse and programmer convenience, however, libraries provide a great deal of thoroughly debugged and well-tested utility code, such as routines for network programming, graphics handling, data manipulation, and system calls.

You need to know the tools at your disposal for creating, maintaining, and managing programming libraries. The two types of libraries are static and shared, as follows:

- **Static libraries** — Static libraries are specially formatted files that contain object files, called modules or members, of reusable, precompiled code. They are stored in a special format along with a table or map that links symbol names to the members in which the symbols are defined. The map speeds up compilation and linking. Static libraries are typically named with the extension .a, which stands for archive.

- **Shared libraries** — As with static libraries, shared libraries are files that contain other object files or pointers to other object files. They are called shared libraries because the code they contain is not linked into programs when the programs are compiled. Rather, the dynamic linker/loader links shared library code into programs at runtime.

Shared libraries have several advantages over static libraries. First, they require fewer system resources. They use less disk space because shared library code is not compiled into each binary but linked and loaded from a single location dynamically at runtime. They use less system memory because the kernel shares the memory the library occupies among all the programs that use the library.

Second, shared libraries are slightly faster because they need to be loaded into memory only once. Finally, shared libraries simplify code and system maintenance. As bugs are fixed or features added, users need only obtain the updated library and install it. With static libraries, each program that uses the library must be recompiled.

## Note

There can be advantages to static libraries as well, if you want to build an application that does not depend on anything on the host system, or special-purpose commands where you are not sure of the deployment environment. In general, however, shared libraries are recommended. ■

The dynamic linker/loader, `ld.so`, links symbol names to the appropriate shared library in which they are defined at runtime. Shared libraries have a special name, the *soname*, that consists of the library name and the major version number. The full name of the C library on one of my systems, for example, is libc-2.3.4.so. The library name is libc.so; the major version number is 2; the minor version number is 3; and the release or patch level is 4. For historical reasons, the C library's soname is libc.so.6. Minor version numbers and patch level numbers change as bugs are fixed, but the soname remains the same and newer versions are usually compatible with older versions.

I emphasize the soname because applications link against it. How does linking work? The ldconfig utility creates a symbolic link from the actual library, say libc-2.3.2.so, to the soname, libc.so.6, and stores this information in `/etc/ld.so.cache`. At runtime, `ld.so` scans the cache file, finds the required soname and, because of the symbolic link, loads the actual library into memory and links application function calls to the appropriate symbols in the loaded library.

## The nm command

The `nm` command lists all the symbols encoded in an object or binary file. It's used to see what function calls a program makes or to see whether a library or object file provides a needed function. `nm` has the following syntax:

```
nm [options] file
```

The `nm` command lists the symbols stored in *file*, which must be a static library or archive file, as described in the preceding section. *options* controls nm's behavior. Symbols are things such as functions referenced in the code, global variables from other libraries, and so on. You can use the `nm` command as a tool when you have to track down a missing symbol needed by a program.

Table 30-3 describes useful options for `nm`.

**TABLE 30-3**

## nm Command-Line Options

| Option | Description |
|--------|-------------|
| -C | Converts symbol names into user-level names. This is especially useful for making C++ function names readable. |
| -l | Uses debugging information to print the line number where each symbol is defined, or the relocation entry if the symbol is undefined. |
| -s | When used on archive (.a) files, prints the index that maps symbol names to the modules or members in which the symbol is defined. |
| -u | Displays only undefined symbols, symbols defined externally to the file being examined. |

Here's an example that uses nm to show some of the symbols in /usr/lib/libdl.a:

```
$ nm /usr/lib/libdl.a | head

dlopen.o:
00000040 T __dlopen_check
         U _dl_open
         U _dlerror_run
00000040 W dlopen
00000000 t dlopen_doit

dlclose.o:
         U _dl_close
```

# The ar command

The ar command creates, modifies, or extracts archives. It is most commonly used to create static libraries, which are files that contain one or more object files. This command also creates and maintains a table that cross-references symbol names to the members in which they are defined. The ar command has the following syntax:

```
ar {dmpqrtx} [options] [member] archive file [...]
```

The ar command creates the archive named archive from the file(s) listed in file. At least one of d, m, p, q, r, t, and x is required. You will usually use r. Table 30-4 lists the most commonly used ar options.

**TABLE 30-4**

### ar Command-Line Options

| Option | Description |
|--------|-------------|
| -c | Suppresses the warning ar would normally emit if the archive doesn't already exist. |
| -q | Adds files to the end of archive without checking for replacements. |
| -r | Inserts files into archive, replacing any existing members whose name matches that being added. New members are added at the end of the archive. |
| -s | Creates or updates the map linking symbols to the member in which they are defined. |
| -d | Deletes files that are in the archive. |
| -m | Moves files within the archive. |
| -p | Prints files from the archive. |
| -t | Lists the contents of the archive. |
| -x | Extracts files that are in the archive |

## Tip

**Given an archive created with the** ar **command, you can speed up access to the archive by creating an index to the archive.** ranlib **does precisely this, storing the index in the archive file itself.** ranlib's **syntax is**

```
ranlib file
```

**This generates a symbol map in** file. **It is equivalent to** ar -s file. ■

## The ldd command

Although nm lists the symbols defined in an object file, unless you know what library defines which functions, it is not terribly helpful. That is ldd's job. It lists the shared libraries that a program requires to run. Its syntax is

```
ldd [options] file
```

The ldd command prints the names of the shared libraries file requires. Two of ldd's most useful options are -d, which reports any missing functions, and -r, which reports missing functions *and* missing data objects. For example, the following ldd reports that the mail client mutt (which may or may not be installed on your system) requires eight shared libraries.

```
$ ldd /usr/bin/mutt
        libncursesw.so.5 => /lib/libncursesw.so.5 (0x40021000)
        libssl.so.0 => /usr/lib/libssl.so.0 (0x40066000)
```

```
libcrypto.so.0 => /usr/lib/libcrypto.so.0 (0x40097000)
libc.so.6 => /lib/libc.so.6 (0x40195000)
libgpm.so.1 => /lib/libgpm.so.1 (0x402c5000)
libdl.so.2 => /lib/libdl.so.2 (0x402cb000)
/lib/ld-linux.so.2 => /lib/ld-linux.so.2 (0x40000000)
libncurses.so.5 => /lib/libncurses.so.5 (0x402ce000)
```

The output might be different on your system.

## The ldconfig command

The ldconfig command determines the runtime links required by shared libraries that are located in /usr/lib and /lib, specified in libs on the command line, and stored in /etc/ld.so.conf. It works in conjunction with ld.so, the dynamic linker/loader, to create and maintain links to the most current versions of shared libraries available on a system. It has the following syntax:

> ldconfig [options] [libs]

Running ldconfig with no arguments simply updates the cache file, /etc/ld.so.cache. options controls ldconfig's behavior. The -v option tells ldconfig to be verbose as it updates the cache. The -p option says to print without updating the current list of shared libraries about which ld.so knows. To see what ldconfig is doing when updating the cache, the -v option will print out a display of directories and symlinks ldconfig has found.

## Environment variables and configuration files

The dynamic linker/loader ld.so uses a number of environment variables to customize and control its behavior. These variables include

- $LD_LIBRARY_PATH — This variable contains a colon-separated list of directories in which to search for shared libraries at runtime. It is similar to the $PATH environment variable.

- $LD_PRELOAD — This variable is a whitespace-separated list of additional, user-specified shared libraries to load before all other libraries. It is used selectively to override functions in other shared libraries.

The ld.so utility also uses two configuration files whose purposes parallel those environment variables:

- /etc/ld.so.conf — Contains a list of directories that the linker/loader should search for shared libraries in addition to the standard directories, /usr/lib and /lib, as well as /lib64 on 64-bit architecture systems.

- /etc/ld.so.preload — Contains a disk-based version of the $LD_PRELOAD environment variable, including a whitespace-separated list of shared libraries to be loaded prior to executing a program.

You can use $LD_PRELOAD to override installed versions of a library with a specific version; this is often useful when you are testing a new (or different) library version but don't want to install the replacement library on your system. In general, use the environment variables only while you create your programs. Don't depend on these environment variables in production, as they have created security issues in the past, so you may not be able to control the values of the variables.

# Source Code Control

Version control is an automated process for keeping track of and managing changes made to source code files. Why bother? Because:

- One day you *will* make that one fatal edit to a source file, delete its predecessor, and forget exactly which line or lines of code you "fixed."

- Simultaneously keeping track of the current release, the next release, and eight bug fixes manually *will* become mind-numbing and confusing.

- Frantically searching for the backup tape because one of your colleagues overwrote a source file for the fifth time *will* drive you over the edge.

- One day, over your morning chai, you will say to yourself, "Version control, it's the Right Thing to Do."

## Source code control using RCS

The Revision Control System (RCS) is a common solution to the version control problem. RCS, which is maintained by the GNU project, is available on almost all UNIX systems, not just on Linux. Two alternatives to RCS are the Concurrent Version System (CVS), which also is maintained by the GNU project, and the Source Code Control System (SCCS), a proprietary product.

Before you proceed, however, Table 30-5 lists a few terms that will be used throughout the chapter. Because they are used so frequently, I want to make sure you understand their meaning insofar as RCS and version control in general are concerned.

**TABLE 30-5**

### Version Control Terms

| Term | Description |
|------|-------------|
| Lock | A working file retrieved for editing such that no one else can edit it simultaneously. A working file is locked by the first user against edits by other users. |
| RCS file | Any file located in an RCS directory, controlled by RCS, and accessed using RCS commands. An RCS file contains all versions of a particular file. Typically, an RCS file has a ,v extension. |

| Term | Description |
|------|-------------|
| Revision | A specific, numbered version of a source file. Revisions begin with 1.1 and increase incrementally, unless forced to use a specific revision number. |
| Working file | One or more files retrieved from the RCS source code repository (the RCS directory) into the current working directory and available for editing. |

RCS manages multiple versions of files, usually but not necessarily source code files. It automates file version storage and retrieval, change logging, access control, release management, and revision identification and merging. As an added bonus, RCS minimizes disk space requirements because it tracks only file changes.

One attraction of RCS is its simplicity. With only a few commands, you can accomplish a great deal.

## Checking files in and out

You can accomplish a lot with RCS using only two commands (ci and co) and a directory named RCS. ci stands for "check in," which means storing a working file in the RCS directory; co means "check out" and refers to retrieving an RCS file from the RCS repository.

To get started, you need to create an RCS directory. All RCS commands will use this directory, if it is present in your current working directory. The RCS directory is also called the *repository*. When you check a file in, RCS asks for a description of the file, copies it to the RCS directory, and deletes the original. "Deletes the original?" Ack! Don't worry, you can retrieve it with the check out command, co.

Here's how to create an RCS directory:

```
$ mkdir RCS
```

Next, create the following source file (naming it howdy.c) in the same directory in which you created the RCS directory.

```
/*
 * $Id$
 * howdy.c - Sample to demonstrate RCS Usage
 */
#include <stdio.h>

int main(void)
{
    fprintf(stdout, "Howdy, Linux programmer!");
    return EXIT_SUCCESS;
}
```

Now, use the command ci howdy.c to check the file into the repository:

```
$ ci howdy.c
RCS/howdy.c,v  <--  howdy.c
enter description, terminated with single '.' or end of file:
NOTE: This is NOT the log message!
>> Simple program to illustrate RCS usage
>> .
initial revision: 1.1
done
```

With the file safely checked into the repository, you can check it out and modify it. To check a file out for editing, use the co command. Here's an example:

```
$ co -l howdy.c
RCS/howdy.c,v  -->  howdy.c
revision 1.1 (locked)
done
```

The working file you just checked out is editable. If you do not want to edit it, omit the -l option.

## Making changes to repository files

To see version control in action, make a change to the working file. If you haven't already done so, check out and lock the howdy.c file. Change anything you want, but I recommend adding \n to the end of fprintf( )'s string argument because Linux (and UNIX), unlike DOS and Windows, does not automatically add a newline to the end of console output.

Next, check the file back in and RCS will increment the revision number to 1.2, ask for a description of the change you made, incorporate the changes you made into the RCS file, and (annoyingly) delete the original. To prevent deletion of your working files during check-in operations, use the -l or -u option with ci. Here's an example:

```
$ ci -l howdy.c
RCS/howdy.c,v  <--  howdy.c
new revision: 1.2; previous revision: 1.1
enter log message, terminated with single '.' or end of file:
>> Added newline
>> .
done
```

The messages shown in the preceding code may differ depending on whether you modified the file or did not lock the file during check out.

When used with ci, both the -l and -u options cause an implied check-out of the file after the check-in procedure completes. -l locks the file so you can continue to edit it, whereas -u checks out an unlocked or read-only working file.

## Additional command-line options

In addition to -l and -u, ci and co accept two other very useful options: -r (for revision) and -f (force). Use -r to tell RCS which file revision you want to manipulate. RCS assumes you want to work with the most recent revision; -r overrides this default. The -f option forces RCS to over-write the current working file. By default, RCS aborts a check-out operation if a working file of the same name already exists in your working directory. So if you really botch your working file, use the -f option with co to get a fresh start.

RCS's command-line options are cumulative, as you might expect, and RCS does a good job of disallowing incompatible options. To check out and lock a specific revision of howdy.c, you would use a command such as co -l -r2.1 howdy.c. Similarly, ci -u -r3 howdy.c checks in howdy.c, assigns it revision number 3.1, and deposits a read-only revision 3.1 working file back into your current working directory.

The following example creates revision 2.1 of howdy.c. Make sure you have checked out and changed howdy.c somehow before executing this command.

```
$ ci -r2 howdy.c
RCS/howdy.c,v  <--  howdy.c
new revision: 2.1; previous revision: 1.2
enter log message, terminated with single '.' or end of file:
>> Added something
>> .
done
```

This command is equivalent to ci -r2.1 howdy.c.

The next example checks out revision 1.2 of howdy.c, disregarding the presence of higher-numbered revisions in the working directory.

```
$ co -r1.2 howdy.c
RCS/howdy.c,v  -->  howdy.c
revision 1.2
done
```

The handy command shown next discards all the changes you've made to version 1.2 (above) and lets you start over with a known good source file.

```
$ co -l -f howdy.c
RCS/howdy.c,v  -->  howdy.c
revision 2.1 (locked)
done
```

When used with ci, -f forces RCS to check in a file even if it has not changed.

## Source code control with CVS

You may have noticed that RCS has some shortcomings that make it inadequate for use on large projects. First, without some sophisticated wrapper scripts to provide the directory handling machinery, RCS doesn't work very well with a single, centralized repository. And you need such a repository for a programming team with more than a few members.

An RCS repository is always the current directory unless you exert yourself to use a directory located elsewhere. More pertinent for Linux and other open source projects, RCS is utterly unsuitable for distributed development because it doesn't support network protocols. (That is, it doesn't work over the Internet.)

Furthermore, RCS suffers from programmers forgetting commands. If you forget to check out a file with a certain option, you may regret it later. Even if you work alone, you may find CVS a better option.

The Concurrent Versions System (CVS) supports both centralized repositories and network-based access. It is well-suited for use by multiple programmers, and a single CVS repository can support multiple projects. To keep the discussion simple, however, the example in this chapter deals only with a repository accessed locally. The following steps resemble the process described earlier for RCS, but they are slightly more involved and obviously use CVS concepts:

1.  Create a CVS repository:

    ```
    $ mkdir /space/cvs
    $ export CVSROOT=/space/cvs
    $ cvs init
    ```

    The first command creates a directory named /space/cvs in which to establish the repository. The second command defines the environment variable $CVSROOT with this directory. Defining $CVSROOT makes using CVS much simpler. The third command initializes the repository, which creates some administrative directories CVS needs to work properly.

2.  Create a top-level working directory in which to store your various projects and then change into this directory:

    ```
    $ mkdir projects
    $ cd projects
    ```

3.  Check out a copy of the CVS root directory into the directory you just created:

    ```
    $ cvs -d $CVSROOT co -l .
    cvs checkout: Updating .
    ```

    The -d option tells cvs the directory containing the CVS repository ($CVSROOT, or /space/cvs); co means check out (just as with RCS); the -l option, which stands for local, means to work only in the current directory rather than recursing through subdi-rectories; and the . specifies the current directory.

4. Create a directory to hold a project and add it to the repository:

```
$ mkdir newhello
$ cvs add newhello
Directory /space/cvs/newhello added to the repository
```

5. Change into the new directory, copy your project files into it (fill in the your_new_hello_code with the name of the directory where you have the actual source code files for the new project), and then add those files (and any directories that might be present) to the repository:

```
$ cd newhello
$ cp /your_new_hello_code/* .
$ cvs add *c *h
cvs add: scheduling file 'hello.c' for addition
cvs add: scheduling file 'msg.c' for addition
cvs add: scheduling file 'main.c' for addition
cvs add: scheduling file 'showit.c' for addition
cvs add: use 'cvs commit' to add these files permanently
```

6. Do as the instructions recommend: Execute the command cvs commit to make the added files and directories permanent. You'll first see a screen (which is actually a vi edi-tor session) asking you to enter a log message. If you don't want to enter a log message, press Esc, and type **ZZ** to save and exit. After you close the vi session, the output you see should resemble the following:

```
$ cvs commit
cvs commit: Examining .
RCS file: /space/cvs/newhello/hello.c,v
done
Checking in hello.c;
/space/cvs/newhello/hello.c,v  <--  hello.c
initial revision: 1.1
done
RCS file: /space/cvs/newhello/msg.c,v
done
Checking in msg.c;
/space/cvs/newhello/msg.c,v  <--  msg.c
initial revision: 1.1
done
RCS file: /space/cvs/newhello/showit.c,v
done
Checking in main.c;
/space/cvs/newhello/main.c,v  <--  main.c
initial revision: 1.1
done
```

Notice that CVS uses RCS filenaming conventions to work with files in the repository because CVS was built on top of RCS and retains compatibility with the basic RCS feature set.

CVS handles checking files in and out slightly differently than RCS. When checking a file out, it isn't necessary to specifically request a lock to get a writable copy of the file. To work on a file, you do need to use the checkout or co command:

```
$ cd projects
$ cvs -d /space/cvs co newhello
cvs checkout newhello
U newhello/hello.c
U newhello/msg.c
U newhello/main.c
```

The checkout command used in this example specifies the path to the repository using the -d option. This is unnecessary if you set the $CVSROOT environment variable. After you have made changes to files such as main.c, you can check them in using the cvs commit command (commit is comparable to RCS's ci command):

```
$ cd projects/newhello
$ cvs commit .
cvs commit: Examining .
[editor session]
Checking in main.c;
/space/cvs/newhello/main.c,v <-- main.c
new revision: 1.2; previous revision: 1.1
done
```

When you check in a modified file, CVS opens an editor session to enable you to enter a log message that describes the changes you made. The editor used is the editor defined in the $EDITOR environment variable or compiled-in default (usually vi text editor) if $EDITOR is undefined. This example did not use the -d option because the $CVSROOT environment variable is set.

To check out a specific version, or revision, of a file, use the -r option following the checkout or co command, followed by a revision number. For example, to check out revision 1.1 of the main.c file, use the following command:

```
$ cvs checkout -r 1.1 main.c
U main.c
```

To see the differences between two revisions, use the diff command, using the -r m.n, where m.n indicates the revision number you want to check. If you specify -r only once, the indicated version will be compared against the working file (using the diff option). If you specify -r twice, the two versions will be compared against each other. The following example compares revision 1.2 of showit.c to the current working revision (the revision currently in the working directory):

```
$ cvs diff -r 1.2 main.c
Index: main.c
```

```
====================================================================
RCS file: /space/cvs/newhello/main.c,v
retrieving revision 1.2
retrieving revision 1.3
diff -r1.2 -r1.3
9,10c9,10
<       char msg_hi[] = { "Hi there, programmer!" };
<       char msg_bye[] = { "Goodbye, programmer!" };
---
>       char msg_hi[] = { "Hi there, programmer!\n" };
>       char msg_bye[] = { "Goodbye, programmer!\n" };
12c12
<       printf("%s\n", msg_hi);
---
>       printf("%s", msg_hi);
```

The diff output is easier to understand than you might expect. Lines that begin with < appear in the first file (revision 1.2 of main.c) but not in the second (revision 1.3 of main.c). Similarly, lines beginning with > appear in the second file, but not in the first. Each section of diff output begins with an alphanumeric sequence such as 9,10c9,10 or 12c12.

The numeric values of the diff output indicate the lines in the first and second files to which an operation must be applied to get the second file from the first. The operation to perform, such as inserting, deleting, or changing lines, is specified by the alphabetic character. So, for example, the sequence 9,10c9,10 means to create the second file from the first you have to change (c) lines 9 and 10 of the first file to lines 9 and 10 of the second file.

Finally, if you totally botch all of your changes to your working files and want to revert to the most recent versions, use the update command. It updates the specified directory with the most recent versions stored in the repository, as shown in the following example:

```
$ cd ~/projects/newhello
$ cvs update .
cvs update: Updating .
U showit.c
U msg.c
U hello.c
```

There's much more to CVS than the few examples presented here. For additional information, visit the CVS home page on the Web at www.nongnu.org/cvs.

Although CVS improves a lot on the limitations of RCS, CVS has its own limitations. Subversion is a newer source code control system that aims to solve many of the limitations of CVS. See subversion.tigris.org for more on SVN.

# Debugging with GNU Debugger

Software is buggy, and some programs have more bugs than other programs. Although debugging sessions will never be aggravation-free, the advanced features of GNU Debugger (GDB) lighten the load and enable you to be more productive in squashing bugs. A debugger runs a program in a special mode that allows you to view the inner workings of the programs, especially the value of variables at a given point in the code. The theory is that by exposing the inner workings of the program, you can more easily determine what is not correct in the program's source code — that is, where the bug is located.

Time and effort invested in learning GDB is well spent if you can track down and fix a serious bug in just a few minutes. GDB can make this happen. Most of what you will need to accomplish with GDB can be done with a surprisingly small set of commands. The rest of this chapter explores GDB features and shows you enough GDB commands to get you going.

Effective debugging requires that your source code be compiled with the -g option to create a binary with an extended symbol table. For example, the following command

```
$ gcc -g file1 file2 -o prog
```

causes prog to be created with debugging symbols in its symbol table. If you want, you can use GCC's -ggdb option to generate still more (GDB-specific) debugging information. However, to work most effectively, this option requires that you have access to the source code for every library against which you link. Although this can be very useful in certain situations, it can also be expensive in terms of disk space. In most cases, you can get by with the plain -g option.

## Starting GDB

To start a debugging session, simply type **gdb progname**, replacing **progname** with the name of the program you want to debug. Using a core file is optional but will enhance GDB's debugging capabilities. Of course, you'll need a program on which to try out GDB debugging, so Listing 30-5 provides one: debugme.c.

---

**LISTING 30-5**

**A Buggy Program**

```c
/*
 * debugme.c - poorly written program to debug
 */
#include <stdio.h>

#define BIGNUM 5000
#define SZ 100
void index_to_the_moon(int ary[]);
```

```
int main(int argc, char *argv[])
{
        int intary[100];

        index_to_the_moon(intary);

        return 0;
}

void index_to_the_moon(int ary[])
{
        int i;
        for (i = 0; i < BIGNUM; ++i)
                ary[i] = i;
}
```

Compile this program using the command gcc -g debugme.c -o debugme. Then, execute the program using the command ./debugme.

```
$ ./debugme
Segmentation fault (core dumped)
$ file core
core: ELF 32-big LSB core file Intel 80386, version 1 (SYSV
), SVR4-style, SVR4-stylee, from 'debugme'
```

On most systems, when you execute ./debugme, it immediately causes a segmentation fault and dumps core, as shown in the output listing.

## Note

A *core dump* refers to an application failing and copying all data stored in memory for the application into a file named core in the current directory. That file can be used to help debug a problem with the application. The file output may be called core, or have a numeric extension, such as core.12345 (usually the process ID of the program that died). ∎

If you don't see the core dumped message, try executing the shell command ulimit -c unlimited, which allows programs to drop a memory dump in their current working directory.

The program has a bug, so you need to debug it. The first step is to start GDB, using the program name, debugme, and the core file, core, as arguments:

```
$ gdb debugme core
```

After GDB initializes, the screen should resemble Figure 30-1.

FIGURE 30-1

GDB's startup screen

```
xterm
[kwall:~/books/wiley/lb2006/29]$ gdb debugme core
GNU gdb 6.3
Copyright 2004 Free Software Foundation, Inc.
GDB is free software, covered by the GNU General Public License, and you are
welcome to change it and/or distribute copies of it under certain conditions.
Type "show copying" to see the conditions.
There is absolutely no warranty for GDB.  Type "show warranty" for details.
This GDB was configured as "i486-slackware-linux"...Using host libthread_db libr
ary "/lib/libthread_db.so.1".

Core was generated by ` + ,'.
Program terminated with signal 11, Segmentation fault.

warning: current_sos: Can't read pathname for load map: Input/output error

Reading symbols from /lib/libc.so.6...done.
Loaded symbols for /lib/libc.so.6
Reading symbols from /lib/ld-linux.so.2...done.
Loaded symbols for /lib/ld-linux.so.2
#0  0x080483a8 in index_to_the_moon ()
(gdb) []
```

As you can see near the middle of the figure, GDB displays the name of the executable that created the core file: ` + ,'. Obviously, the displayed name is wrong; it should be debugme. The odd characters and the incorrect program name would give an experienced developer an immediate clue that the program has a significant memory bug. The next line in the figure, the text that reads Program terminated with signal 11, Segmentation fault, explains why the program terminated. A segmentation fault occurs anytime a program attempts to access memory that doesn't explicitly belong to it. GDB also helpfully displays the function it was executing, index_to_the_moon.

## Tip

If you don't like the licensing messages (they annoy me), use the -q (or --quiet) option when you start GDB to suppress them. Another useful command-line option is -d dirname, where dirname is the name of a directory, which tells gdb where to find source code (it looks in the current working directory by default). ■

After you load the program and its core dump into the debugger, run the program in the debugger. To do so, type the command run at the GDB command prompt, (gdb), as the following example shows:

```
(gdb) run
Starting program: /home/kwall/code/debugme

Program received signal SIGSEGV, Segmentation fault.
0x0804483db in index_to_the_moon (ary=0xbffff4b0) at debugme.c:24
24                      ary[i] = i;
```

This short output listing shows that the segmentation fault occurred in the function index_to_the_moon at line 24 of debugme.c. Notice the last line of the output; GDB displays the line of code, prefixed with the line number (24), where the segmentation fault occurred. It also shows the memory address (in hexadecimal format) at which the fault occurred: 0xbffff4b0.

You can pass any arguments to the run command that your program would ordinarily accept. GDB also creates a full shell environment in which to run the program. Ordinarily, GDB uses the value of the environment variable $SHELL to create the simulated environment. If you want, however, you can use GDB's set and unset commands to set or unset arguments and environment variables before you use the run command to run the program in the debugger.

To set command-line arguments to pass to the program, type **set args** *arg1 arg2*, where *arg1* and *arg2* (or any number of arguments) are options and arguments the program being debugged expects. Use **set environment** *env1 env2* to set environment variables (again, *env1* and *env2* are placeholders for the environment variables you want to set or unset).

## Inspecting code in the debugger

What is happening in the function index_to_the_moon that's causing the error? You can execute the backtrace (or bt or back) command to generate the function tree that led to the segmentation fault. The backtrace doesn't usually show you *what* the problem is, but it does show you more precisely *where* the problem occurred. Here's how the function trace for the example looks on my system:

```
(gdb) backtrace
#0  0x080483db index_to_the_moon (ary=0x7ffffc90) at debugme.c:24
#1  0x080483a6 in main (argc=104,argv=0x69) at debugme.c:15
```

A backtrace shows the chain of function calls that resulted in the error. The backtrace starts with the most recently called function — index_to_the_moon() in this case — which resides at the hexadecimal memory address shown in the second column of the display (0x0800483db). The function index_to_the_moon() was called by the main() function. As you can see from the output, the most recently called function was index_to_the_moon(), so, somewhere in the function, the segmentation fault occurred. Incidentally, the backtrace also shows that index_to_the_moon() was called from line 15 of the main() function in debugme.c.

## Tip

It's not necessary to type complete command names while using GDB. Any sufficiently unique abbreviation works. For example, back suffices for backtrace. ■

It would be helpful, however, to have some idea of the context in which the offending line(s) of code exist. For this purpose, use the list command, which takes the general form, list [m,n], where m and n are the starting and ending line numbers you want displayed. For example:

```
(gdb) list 10,24
```

would display code lines 10 through 24.

A bare list command displays ten lines of code, including the line where the error was first detected, as illustrated here:

```
(gdb) list
15              index_to_the_moon(intary);
16
17              exit(EXIT_SUCCESS);
18      }
19
20      void index_to_the_moon(int ary[])
21      {
22              int i;
23              for (i = 0; i < BIGNUM; ++I {
24                      ary[i] = i;
```

## Examining data

One of GDB's most useful features is its ability to display both the type and the value of almost any expression, variable, or array in the program being debugged. It can print the value of any legal expression in the language in which your program is written. The command is, predictably enough, print. Here are a couple of print commands and their results:

```
(gdb) print i
$1 = 724
(gdb) print ary[i]
Cannot access memory at address 0xc0000000.
```

This example continues the earlier examples of debugging debugme.c because you are still trying to identify where and why debug me crashed. Although in this example, the program crashed at the point when the counter variable i equaled 724 (the expression $1 refers to an entry in GDB's value history, explained in a moment), where it crashes on your system depends on several variables. Those variables could include the system's memory layout, the process's memory space (especially the kernel's stack space), the amount of available memory on your system, and other factors.

The result of the second command (print ary[i]) makes it pretty clear that the program does not have access to the memory location specified, although it does have legal access to the preceding one.

The expression $1 is an alias that refers to an entry in GDB's value history. GDB creates value history entries for each command you type that produces computed results. The alias numbers increment sequentially each time you execute a command that produces some sort of computed output. As a result, you can access these computed values using aliases rather than retyping the command. For example, the command $1-5 produces the following:

```
(gdb) print $1-5
$2 = 719
```

Notice that the alias incremented to $2. If you later need to use the value 719, you can use the alias $2. The value history is reset each time you start GDB and the values are not accessible outside of GDB.

You are not limited to using discrete values because gdb can display the addresses of data stored in an arbitrary region of memory. For example, to print the first ten memory locations associated with ary, use the following command:

```
(gdb) print ary@10
$3 = {0xbffffc90, 0x40015580, 0x400115800, 0x0, 0x1, 0x2, 0c3, 0x4, 0x5}
```

The notation @10 means to print the ten values that begin at ary. Say, on the other hand, that you want to print the five values stored in ary beginning with the first element. The command for this would be the following:

```
(gdb) print ary[1]@5
$4 = {1, 2, 3, 4, 5}
```

Why go to the trouble of printing variable or array values? Although it isn't necessary in this particular example because you know where the trouble occurs, it is often necessary to see the value of a variable at a particular point in a program's execution so you monitor what is happening to variables. It's pretty clear in this case that the index_to_the_moon() function is suspect, but depending on experience, some people may not see the exact problem within the function.

In the case of arrays, a command that prints the values in an array, such as print ary[1]@5 in the preceding example, enables you to confirm at a glance the values are what you expect them to be. If the values don't match up with your expectations, however, that is a clue that some code is altering the array in a way you didn't intend. As a result, you can focus your bug hunting on a specific section of code.

GDB also can tell you the types of variables using the whatis command. GDB's whatis command is comparable to the man -f command, which searches the whatis database of system commands for short descriptions of those system commands (the manual page whatis database is totally separate from the whatis command used by GDB). Although man's whatis database works on system commands, GDB's whatis command describes the types of variables and other data structures used in a program.

```
(gdb) whatis i
type = int
(gdb) whatis ary
type = int *
(gdb) whatis index_to_the_moon
type = void (int *)
```

This feature may seem rather useless because, of course, you know the types of all the variables in your program (yeah, right!). But, you will change your mind the first time you have to debug someone else's code or have to fix a multifile project for which you haven't seen the source files for a couple of months. The whatis command can also help you track down bugs that result from assigning an inappropriate value to a variable.

# Setting breakpoints

As you debug problematic code, halting execution at some point is often useful. Perhaps you want to stop execution before the code enters a section that is known to have problems. In other cases, you can set breakpoints so you can look at the values of certain variables at a given point in the execution flow. In still other situations, you might find it useful to stop execution so you can step through the code one instruction at a time.

GDB enables you to set breakpoints on several different kinds of code constructs, including line numbers and function names, and also enables you to set conditional breakpoints, where the code stops only if a certain condition is met. To set a breakpoint on a line number, use the following syntax:

```
(gdb) break linenum
```

To stop execution when the code enters a function, use the following:

```
(gdb) break funcname
```

In either case, GDB halts execution before executing the specified line number or entering the specified function. You can then use print to display variable values, for example, or use list to review the code that is about to be executed. If you have a multifile project and want to halt execution on a line of code or in a function that is not in the current source file, use the following forms:

```
(gdb) break filename:linenum
(gdb) break filename:funcname
```

Conditional breakpoints are usually more useful. They enable you to temporarily halt program execution if or when a particular condition is met. The correct syntax for setting conditional breakpoints is as follows:

```
(gdb) break linenum if expr
(gdb) break funcname if expr
```

In the preceding code, expr can be any expression that evaluates to true (non-zero). For example, the following break command stops execution at line 24 of debugme when the variable i equals 15:

```
(gdb) break 24 if i == 15
Breakpoint 1 at 0x80483cb: file debugme.c, line 24.
(gdb) run
Starting program: /home/kwall/code/debugme

Breakpoint 1, index_to_the_moon (ary=0xbffff4b0) at debugme.c:24
24                      ary[i] = i;
```

## Tip

**Verify the line numbers as seen by** gdb. **In this case,** gdb **has line 24 as the assignment of** ary[i] **to the value of** i, **as shown in the preceding code. Use the** gdb list **command to verify the line numbers used by** gdb. ■

Stopping when i equals 15 is an arbitrary choice to demonstrate conditional breaks. As you can see, gdb stopped on line 24. A quick print command confirms that it stopped when the value of i reached the requested value:

```
(gdb) print i
$1 = 15
```

To resume executing after hitting a breakpoint, type **continue**. If you have set many breakpoints and have lost track of what has been set and which ones have been triggered, you can use the info breakpoints command to refresh your memory.

# Working with source code

Locating a specific variable or function in a multifile project is a breeze with GDB, provided you use the -d switch to tell it where to find additional source code files. This option is particularly helpful when not all of your source code is located in your current working directory or in the program's compilation directory (which GCC recorded in its symbol table).

To specify one or more additional directories containing source code, start GDB using one or more -d dirname options, as this example illustrates:

```
$ gdb -d /source/project1 -d /oldsource/project1 \
      -d /home/bubba/src killerapp
```

To locate the next occurrence of a particular string in the current file, use the search string command. Use reverse-search string to find the previous occurrence of string. If you want to find the previous occurrence of the word "return" in debugme.c (refer to Listing 30-5), for example, use the command reverse-search return. GDB obliges and displays the text:

```
(gdb) reverse-search return
17              return ret;
```

The search and reverse-search commands are especially helpful in large source files that have dozens or hundreds of lines. One common use of the reverse-search command is to find the file and/or line in which a variable is first used or in which it is defined. The search command similarly enables you to locate with relative ease each location in which a program symbol (variable, macro, or function) is used, perhaps to find the use that changes a variable unexpectedly or the place where a function is called when it shouldn't be.

# Summary

This chapter took you on a whirlwind tour of a few of the most common programs and utilities used by Linux programmers. You learned how to use GCC to compile programs, how to use make to automate compiling programs, and how to find information about programming libraries using programs such as `ldd`, `nm`, and `ldconfig`. You also learned enough about the source code control systems RCS and CVS to be comfortable with the terminology and how to use their most basic features. Finally, you learned how to use the GNU debugger (GDB) to figure out why, or at least where, a program fails.

# Media

The DVD and CD that accompany *Linux Bible 2010 Edition* contain a variety of Linux systems that you can use. Some of these Linux systems you can boot and run live, whereas you can use others to install a Linux system permanently to hard disk. Some can do both.

Most of the Linux systems included here are slightly remastered versions of official live and installation CDs that come from different Linux projects. Changes made to those CDs were made exclusively to allow each to be booted from a single boot screen on the DVD or CD. After you have selected a Linux to start up, however, it should behave exactly as the original CD from the selected Linux project.

General information on running live or installing the various Linux distributions on the CD and DVD is in Chapter 8. Specific instructions for using and installing each Linux distribution are contained in the other chapters in Part V (see Chapters 17 through 28).

## Caution

The software contained on the CD and DVD is covered under the GNU Public License (GPL) or other licenses included on the medium for each software distribution. Use the software on the DVD and CD (as you would any GPL software) at your own risk. Refer to README, RELEASE-NOTES, and any licensing files delivered with each distribution, and be sure that you agree with the terms they spell out before using the software. ■

# Finding Linux Distributions on the DVD

The following sections describe the Linux distributions on the DVD that accompanies this book. All of these distributions are immediately bootable from the DVD, although some are made to run as live CDs and others are used to install to hard disk.

## Fedora Linux

The DVD that comes with this book includes the Fedora 11 Desktop live/install CD distribution that normally comes on a single CD. Fedora is used as the example for many of the procedures and applications in this book. You can boot Fedora as a live CD directly from the DVD, and then use that live CD to install the same Fedora desktop system permanently to your hard disk.

To begin installing Fedora to your hard disk, insert the DVD into your PC's DVD drive, reboot, and select fedora.

Details on installing and using Fedora are in Chapter 18. If the application is not available as described, use the PackageKit window or the yum command to install the package containing that application from the Internet.

## Note

If you find that you like Fedora, consider getting *Fedora 12 Bible* (Wiley Publishing, 2010) to learn more about that distribution. Although some of the material overlaps with this book's, you will get more complete coverage of installation and different kinds of servers available with Fedora 12. ■

## KNOPPIX Linux

The KNOPPIX 6.0.1 live CD Linux distribution is configured to boot by default from the DVD that comes with this book. KNOPPIX is the most popular bootable Linux and offers some unique features to set it apart from other bootable Linux distributions.

To boot KNOPPIX directly from the DVD, insert the DVD into your PC's DVD drive, reboot, and select knoppix.

Information on using KNOPPIX and configuring it in various ways is in Chapter 21.

## Slackware Linux

The DVD that comes with this book contains software compiled from CD images of the Slackware 13 distribution. Slackware is the oldest surviving Linux system and continues to have a loyal following among Linux enthusiasts. To begin installing Slackware to your hard disk, insert the DVD into your PC's DVD drive, reboot, and select slackware.

Chapter 24 tells you how to install Slackware on your computer from this book's DVD or an official Slackware DVD or CD set. Chapter 3 describes how to configure a simple window manager for you to use with Slackware.

## Ubuntu Linux

The Ubuntu 9.10 (Karmic Koala) installation and live CD is contained on the DVD that comes with this book. You can use that image to run live, and then install, a minimal desktop system. You can do further software installation from the Internet, after the basic install is done.

To boot the Ubuntu live CD image from the DVD that comes with this book, insert the DVD into your PC's DVD drive, reboot, and select `ubuntu`.

Your computer will boot a live CD version of Ubuntu that is intended to be used as a desktop system. An icon on the desktop lets you install the contents of the CD image to your computer's hard disk. The procedure for booting and installing Ubuntu is found in Chapter 17.

## Mandriva Linux

The Mandriva One 2009 Spring live CD is contained on the DVD that comes with this book. This live CD contains a desktop-oriented Mandriva distribution that you can boot live, and then use to install the contents of the Mandriva One live CD to hard disk.

To start Mandriva One from the DVD, insert the DVD into your computer's DVD drive, reboot the computer, and select `mandriva`.

You can run and install Mandriva One as described in Chapter 26. You can also refer to Chapter 26 for information about other versions of Mandriva. In Chapter 27 you can find out how to configure a firewall in Mandriva.

## AntiX Linux

AntiX is a lightweight, desktop-oriented live CD that is suitable for older, less powerful computers. It can run on machines with as little as 64MB of RAM (although 128MB is recommended). AntiX is based on MEPIS. AntiX release 8.2 is included on the DVD.

To start AntiX from the DVD, insert the DVD into your computer's DVD drive, reboot the computer, and select `antix`.

## BackTrack 3 Linux Security Suite

BackTrack 3 is a live CD that contains a set of tools for testing, repairing, and otherwise securing Linux systems, Windows systems, and networks. Use the BackTrack menu on the main menu of this live CD to select from dozens of security-related tools. BackTrack is discussed in Chapter 28.

To boot the BackTrack live CD image from the DVD that comes with this book, insert the DVD into your PC's DVD drive, reboot, and select `backtrack`.

## Gentoo Linux

The DVD that comes with this book includes the Gentoo 2008.0 live/install CD image. With the Gentoo CD, you can install a usable desktop Linux system, to which you can add any of the nearly 7,000 software packages that are available with Gentoo. You can obtain those packages over a network connection or from a local CD, DVD, or hard disk. (Chapter 23 describes a network install of those additional packages.)

To boot the Gentoo live CD image from the DVD that comes with this book, insert the DVD into your PC's DVD drive, reboot, and select `gentoo`.

Refer to Chapter 23 for information on using the Gentoo live/install CD to install Gentoo on your computer. Procedures described in that chapter let you either install a desktop system from binary packages on the CD or build much of the Gentoo operating system from scratch, specifically for your computer hardware, downloading needed packages from the Internet.

## openSUSE Linux

The openSUSE Linux 11.1 live/install CD lets you boot an openSUSE desktop live, and then install it to your hard drive from software downloaded over the network. openSUSE Linux is developed and supported by Novell and a community of software developers. Novell also offers the commercial SUSE Linux Enterprise system, as part of a wider range of Enterprise-ready Linux and NetWare software.

To begin installing openSUSE to your hard disk, insert the CD into your PC's CD drive, reboot, and select `suse`.

To install openSUSE from this DVD, follow the installation instructions in Chapter 20.

## PCLinuxOS

PCLinuxOS is a popular desktop Linux distribution. PCLinuxOS makes it easy to get support for common multimedia content that isn't always so easy to find with other Linux distributions.

To run PCLinuxOS 2009.2 live, insert the DVD into your PC's CD drive, reboot, and select `pclinuxos`.

## Inside Security Rescue Toolkit

Inside Security Rescue Toolkit (INSERT) is a small, bootable Linux distribution that contains a variety of useful tools for checking, repairing, and recovering computers and networks. INSERT is small enough to fit on a bootable business card CD or mini-CD. Although many of its tools are text-based, INSERT includes a simple graphical interface (using X and FluxBox window manager) and a few graphical tools.

To run INSERT live, insert the DVD that comes with this book into your PC's DVD drive, reboot, and select `insert`.

Refer to Chapter 28 for descriptions of what's inside INSERT.

## Puppy Linux

This mini live CD contains a desktop Linux system that you can use for creating documents, playing multimedia content, accessing the Internet, and many other functions. This distribution contains many features for configuring your desktop and saving your features across reboots. Chapter 28 describes Puppy Linux.

To run Puppy Linux live, insert the DVD into your PC's CD drive, reboot, and select `puppy`.

# Finding Linux Distributions on the CD

The CD that comes with this book boots directly to a variety of smaller live and install CDs. The live/install CDs included on this CD include Debian (network install), Damn Small Linux (live/install), INSERT (security CD), and System Rescue CD, and SLAX (live/install CD). Coyote Linux is contained on a tar/gzip that you copy to a hard disk and build into a floppy Linux distribution from instructions in Chapter 27.

## Debian GNU/Linux

The network install ISO image of Debian GNU/Linux distribution (503) is contained on the CD. Debian offers thoroughly tested releases that many Linux consultants and experts use because of Debian's excellent software packaging and stability. Debian is used as the sample distribution for creating a Web server (LAMP) and mail server, as described in Chapters 14 and 15, respectively.

You can start a Debian installation directly from the CD that comes with this book. With a basic install done from the CD, to add the components you need for a desktop or server system, you must have a connection to the Internet.

To begin installing Debian to your hard disk, insert the CD into your PC's CD drive, reboot, and select `debian`.

The procedure for installing Debian is in Chapter 19.

## Damn Small Linux

Damn Small Linux 4.4.10 is set up to boot directly from the CD that accompanies this book. This distribution illustrates how a useful desktop Linux distribution, which includes full network connectivity and some useful productivity applications, can fit in a very small space.

To run Damn Small Linux live, insert the CD into your PC's CD drive, reboot, and select `dsl`.

See Chapter 28 for information on using Damn Small Linux.

## SystemRescueCd

Like INSERT, SystemRescueCd is a bootable Linux that includes a variety of tools for checking and fixing your installed computer systems. It includes tools for managing and fixing file systems, checking for viruses, monitoring the network, and checking whether a machine has been cracked. You can boot the SystemRescueCd version 1.2.3 image directly from the CD that comes with this book.

To run SystemRescueCd live, insert the CD into your PC's CD drive, reboot, and select `rescue`.

Refer to Chapter 28 for further information about SystemRescueCd.

## Coyote Linux

Although not considered a major Linux distribution, Coyote Linux 2.24 is an excellent illustration of a useful Linux distribution that fits on a floppy disk (1.4MB). You can copy the tar file of Coyote Linux on the CD that comes with this book to a Linux system, configure Coyote Linux to suit your needs, and copy the resulting boot image to floppy disk.

See Chapter 27 for information on how to configure and use Coyote Linux as a firewall.

## Tiny Core Linux

Tiny Core Linux 2.1 is a very small Linux distribution in the tradition of Damn Small Linux (in fact it's developed by Robert Shingledecker, lead developer of DSL). Start with a core operating system that is only a few megabytes in size, and you can add only the components you need. Tiny Core is especially good on small devices and older, less-powerful hardware.

To boot Tiny Core Linux from the CD that comes with this book, select `tinycore` from the boot prompt.

## SLAX

The SLAX 6.1.2 CD image is included on the CD that comes with this book. This live CD contains a well-stocked desktop Linux system. Chapter 28 describes SLAX.

To run SLAX live, insert the CD into your PC's CD drive, reboot, and select `slax`.

# Linux Distributions Not on the DVD or CD

Not all the Linux distributions featured in this book are included on the DVD or CD that accompany this book. Some of these did not encourage free redistribution of their products, whereas others were simply too large to include in their entirety and were not available on a single install CD or bootable live CD.

The following Linux distributions described in the book are not on the CD or DVD. The link after each distribution's name indicates the Internet site where you can find out how to purchase or otherwise obtain it.

- **Yellow Dog Linux:** www.fixstars.com
- **Freespire:** http://wiki.freespire.org/index.php/Download_Freespire
- **MEPIS:** www.mepis.org
- **SUSE Linux Enterprise:** www.novell.com/linux
- **Red Hat Enterprise Linux:** www.redhat.com/rhel

Some of these distributions have downloadable versions available on the Internet. I recommend that you try a Linux distribution site such as DistroWatch.com (www.distrowatch.com) to see whether a free or trial version of any of these distributions is available to try out.

If you decide to download or otherwise obtain ISO images of a Linux distribution, the following section describes how to burn those images to a physical CD.

# Creating Linux CDs

You can use several tools to create bootable CDs for either installing or just running Linux from CD images on the DVD or CD. Before you begin, you must have the following:

- **DVD or CD ISO images**—Download the ISO images you want to burn to a physical DVD or CD.
- **Blank DVDs/CDs**—You need blank DVDs or CDs to burn the images to.
- **CD burner**—You need a drive that is capable of burning CDs or DVDs, depending on which you are burning.

Here's how to create bootable Linux CDs from a running Linux system (such as Fedora):

1. Download the ISO images you want to your computer's hard drive. (You'll need between 50MB and 700MB of hard disk space, depending on the size of the CD image you choose. Single-layer DVD images are usually under 4.7GB.)

2.  Open a CD/DVD burning application. For this procedure, I recommend K3b CD/DVD Burning Facility (www.k3b.org). In Fedora, select the Applications menu and choose Sound & Video ➪ K3b (or type **k3b** from a Terminal window). The K3b—CD Kreator window appears.

## Note

K3b may not be installed on your Linux system by default. For Fedora, install K3b by typing **yum install k3b** as root user from a Terminal window. ■

3.  From the K3b window, select Tools ➪ Burn CD ISO Image to burn a CD image or Tools ➪ Burn DVD ISO Image to burn a DVD image. You are asked to choose an image file.

4.  Browse to the image you just downloaded or copied to hard disk and select it. After you select the image you want, the Burn CD Image window appears, as does a checksum on the image. (Often, you can compare the checksum number that appears against the number in an md5 file from the download directory where you got the live CD to be sure that the CD image was not corrupted.) Figure A-1 shows the Burn CD Image window ready to burn an image of Damn Small Linux.

### FIGURE A-1

Use K3b to burn your installation CDs.

5.  Insert a blank CD into the CD burner drive, which may be a combination CD/DVD drive. (If a CD/DVD Creator window pops up, you can just close it.)

6. Check the settings in the Burn CD Image window (often the defaults are fine, but you may want to slow down the speed if you get some bad burns). You can also select the Simulate check box to test the burn before actually writing to the CD. Click Start to continue.

7. When the CD is done burning, eject it (or it may eject automatically) and mark it appropriately (information such as the distribution name, version number, and date).

Now you're ready to begin installing (or booting) the Linux distribution you just burned. Refer to Chapter 8 for general information on installing Linux. Then go to the chapter that covers your particular distribution to find its specific installation procedure.

If you don't have Linux installed or K3b available at the moment, you can burn CDs from any CD-burning application you have available. A nice overview of CD installation tools and how to use them to burn CDs is available at the Gentoo Web site (`www.gentoo.org/doc/en/faq.xml`). It describes disk-burning tools that are available on Windows, Mac OS X, and Linux systems.

If you have no GUI, or don't mind working from the shell, you can use the `cdrecord` command to burn the ISOs. With a blank CD inserted and the ISO image you want to burn in the current directory, here's a simple command line for burning a CD image to CD using `cdrecord`:

```
# cdrecord -v whatever.iso
```

See the `cdrecord` man page (`man cdrecord`) to see other options available with the `cdrecord` command.

## Note
The `growisofs` **command is another useful tool for burning CD and DVD ISO images. See the** `growisofs` **man page for further information.** ■

# Getting Source Code

To offer as many Linux distributions as possible on the limited media available with the book, I have included only binary versions of the software and no source code. However, every distribution included with the book offers the source code used to build it in a form that you can download from the Internet.

The following list contains links to where you can get the source code for all the Linux distributions included with the book. In some cases, you must choose a convenient mirror site from which to download the source code or use bittorrent:

- AntiX: `http://antix.mepis.org/index.php`
- BackTrack: `www.remote-exploit.org/backtrack_download.html`
- Coyote: `http://sourceforge.net/project/showfiles.php?group_id=63552`

- **Damn Small Linux:** `www.damnsmalllinux.org/download.html`
- **Debian:** `www.debian.org/CD/netinst`
- **Fedora:** `http://fedoraproject.org/wiki/Distribution/Download`
- **Gentoo:** `www.gentoo.org/main/en/where.xml`
- **INSERT:** `http://sourceforge.net/projects/insert`
- **KNOPPIX:** `www.knopper.net/knoppix-mirrors/index-en.html`
- **Mandriva:** `www.mandriva.com/en/download/mandrivaone`
- **openSUSE:** `http://download.opensuse.org/distribution`
- **Puppy:** `www.puppylinux.org/user/downloads.php`
- **Slackware:** `www.slackware.org/getslack`
- **SLAX:** `www.slax.org/download.php`
- **SystemRescueCd:** `http://sourceforge.net/project/showfiles.php?group_id=85811`
- **Ubuntu:** `www.ubuntu.com/getubuntu/download`

Because links to Linux download sites change all the time, if the source code is not readily available from the links shown, try contacting the projects directly to find out where downloadable source code currently resides.

# Linux History and Background

ow that you have tried out a few Linux distributions and learned
some things to do with them, are you wondering how Linux came
about? How can a computer operating system and thousands of
applications be free? Well, the truth is that the path to the Linux systems of
today was not a straight line.

This appendix describes the history of UNIX, BSD, and free software development that has led to the Linux systems of today. After that, you can read
some of the most common myths associated with Linux.

## Exploring Linux History

Some histories of Linux begin with this message posted by Linus Torvalds
to the `comp.os.minix` newsgroup on August 25, 1991:

> Hello everybody out there using minix -
>
> I'm doing a (free) operating system (just a hobby, won't be big
> and professional like gnu) for 386(486) AT clones. This has been
> brewing since april, and is starting to get ready. I'd like any feed-
> back on things people like/dislike in minix, as my OS resembles
> it somewhat (same physical layout of the file-system, due to
> practical reasons, among other things) ...Any suggestions are
> welcome, but I won't promise I'll implement them :-)
>
> Linus (torvalds@kruuna.helsinki.fi)

PS. Yes—it's free of any minix code, and it has a multi-threaded fs. It is NOT protable[sic] (uses 386 task switching etc), and it probably never will support anything other than AT-harddisks, as that's all I have :-(.

Reprinted from Linux International Web site

Minix was a UNIX-like operating system that ran on PCs in the early 1990s. Like Minix, Linux was also a clone of the UNIX operating system.

## Note

For a good way to learn more about how Linux was created, pick up the book *Just For Fun: The Story of an Accidental Revolutionary* by Linus Torvalds (2001, Harper Collins Publishing). ∎

To truly appreciate how a free operating system could have been modeled after a proprietary system from AT&T Bell Laboratories, it helps to understand the culture in which UNIX was created and the chain of events that made the essence of UNIX possible to reproduce freely.

## From a free-flowing UNIX culture at Bell Labs

From the very beginning, the UNIX operating system was created and nurtured in a communal environment. Its creation was not driven by market needs, but by a desire to overcome impediments to producing programs. AT&T, which owned the UNIX trademark originally, eventually made UNIX into a commercial product, but by that time, many of the concepts (and even much of the early code) that made UNIX special had fallen into the public domain.

If you are under 30 years old, you may not remember a time when AT&T was "the" phone company. Up until the early 1980s, AT&T didn't have to think much about competition because if you wanted a phone in the United States, you had to go to AT&T. It had the luxury of funding pure research projects. The Mecca for such projects was the Bell Laboratories site in Murray Hill, New Jersey.

After the failure of a project called Multics in around 1969, Bell Labs employees Ken Thompson and Dennis Ritchie set off on their own to create an operating system that would offer an improved environment for developing software. Up to that time, most programs were written on punch cards that had to be fed in batches to mainframe computers. In a 1980 lecture on "The Evolution of the UNIX Time-sharing System," Dennis Ritchie summed up the spirit that started UNIX:

What we wanted to preserve was not just a good environment in which to do programming, but a system around which a fellowship could form. We knew from experience that the essence of communal computing as supplied by remote-access, time-shared machines is not just to type programs into a terminal instead of a keypunch, but to encourage close communication.

The simplicity and power of the UNIX design began breaking down barriers that impeded software developers. The foundation of UNIX was set with several key elements:

- **The UNIX file system**—After creating the structure that allowed levels of subdirectories (which, for today's desktop users, looks like folders inside of folders), UNIX could be used to organize the files and directories in intuitive ways. Furthermore, complex methods of accessing disks, tapes, and other devices were greatly simplified by representing those devices as individual device files that you could also access as items in a directory.

- **Input/output redirection**—Early UNIX systems also included input redirection and pipes. From a command line, UNIX users could direct the output of a command to a file using a right-arrow key (→). Later, the concept of pipes (|) was added where the output of one command could be directed to the input of another command. For example, the command line

```
$ cat file1 file2 | sort | pr | lpr
```

concatenates (`cat`) file1 and file2, sorts (`sort`) the lines in those files alphabetically, paginates the sorted text for printing (`pr`), and directs the output to the computer's default printer (`lpr`). This method of directing input and output enabled developers to create their own specialized utilities that could be joined with existing utilities. This modularity made it possible for lots of code to be developed by lots of different people.

- **Portability**—Much of the early work in simplifying the experience of using UNIX led to its also becoming extraordinarily portable to run on different computers. By having device drivers (represented by files in the file system tree), UNIX could present an interface to applications in such a way that the programs didn't have to know about the details of the underlying hardware. To later port UNIX to another system, developers had only to change the drivers. The applications program didn't have to change for different hardware!

To make portability a reality, however, a high-level programming language was needed to implement the software needed. To that end, Brian Kernighan and Dennis Ritchie created the C programming language. In 1973, UNIX was rewritten in C. Today, C is still the primary language used to create the UNIX (and Linux) operating system kernels.

As Ritchie went on to say in his 1980 lecture:

> Today, the only important UNIX program still written in assembler is the assembler itself; virtually all the utility programs are in C, and so are most of the application's programs, although there are sites with many in Fortran, Pascal, and Algol 68 as well. It seems certain that much of the success of UNIX follows from the readability, modifiability, and portability of its software that in turn follows from its expression in high-level languages.

If you are a Linux enthusiast and are interested in what features from the early days of Linux have survived, an interesting read is Dennis Ritchie's reprint of the first UNIX programmer's manual (dated November 3, 1971). You can find it at Dennis Ritchie's Web site: `http://cm.bell-labs.com/cm/cs/who/dmr/1stEdman.html`. The form of this documentation is UNIX man pages—which is still the primary format for documenting UNIX and Linux operating system commands and programming tools today.

What's clear as you read through the early documentation and accounts of the UNIX system is that the development was a free-flowing process, lacked ego, and was dedicated to making UNIX excellent. This process led to a sharing of code (both inside and outside of Bell Labs) that allowed rapid development of a high-quality UNIX operating system. It also led to an operating system that AT&T would find difficult to reel back in later.

# To a commercialized UNIX

Before AT&T divestiture in 1984, when it was split up into AT&T and seven "Baby Bell" companies, AT&T was forbidden to sell computer systems. Companies that later became Verizon, Qwest, and Lucent Technologies were all part of AT&T. As a result of AT&T's monopoly of the telephone system, the U.S. government was concerned that an unrestricted AT&T might dominate the fledgling computer industry.

Because AT&T was restricted from selling computers directly to customers before its divestiture, UNIX source code was licensed to universities for a nominal fee. There was no UNIX operating system for sale from AT&T that you didn't have to compile yourself.

## BSD arrives

In 1975, UNIX V6 became the first version of UNIX available for widespread use outside of Bell Laboratories. From this early UNIX source code, the first major variant of UNIX was created at University of California at Berkeley. It was named the Berkeley Software Distribution (BSD).

For most of the next decade, the BSD and Bell Labs versions of UNIX headed off in separate directions. BSD continued forward in the free-flowing, share-the-code manner that was the hallmark of the early Bell Labs UNIX, while AT&T started steering UNIX toward commercialization. With the formation of a separate UNIX Laboratory, which moved out of Murray Hill and down the road to Summit, New Jersey, AT&T began its attempts to commercialize UNIX. By 1984, divestiture was behind AT&T and it was ready to really start selling UNIX.

## UNIX Laboratory and commercialization

The UNIX Laboratory was considered a jewel that couldn't quite find a home or a way to make a profit. As it moved between Bell Laboratories and other areas of AT&T, its name changed several times. It is probably best remembered by its last name, which it had as it began its spin-off from AT&T: UNIX System Laboratories (USL).

The UNIX source code that came out of USL, the legacy of which is now owned in part by Santa Cruz Operation (SCO), has been used as the basis for ever-dwindling lawsuits by SCO against major Linux vendors (such as IBM and Red Hat, Inc.). Because of that, I think the efforts from USL that have contributed to the success of Linux are sometimes disrespected.

You have to remember that during the 1980s, many computer companies were afraid that a newly divested AT&T would pose more of a threat to controlling the computer industry than would an upstart company in Redmond, Washington. To calm the fears of IBM, Intel, Digital Equipment

Corporation and other computer companies, the UNIX Lab made the following commitments to ensure a level playing field:

- **Source code only**—Instead of producing its own boxed set of UNIX, AT&T continued to sell only source code and to make it available equally to all licensees. Each company would then port UNIX to its own equipment. It wasn't until about 1992, when the lab was spun off as a joint venture with Novell (called Univel), and then eventually sold to Novell, that a commercial boxed set of UNIX (called UnixWare) was produced directly from that source code.

- **Published interfaces**—To create an environment of fairness and community towards its OEMs (original equipment manufacturers), AT&T began standardizing what different ports of UNIX had to be able to do to still be called UNIX. To that end, Portable Operating System Interface (POSIX) standards and the AT&T UNIX System V Interface Definition (SVID) were specifications UNIX vendors could use to create compliant UNIX systems. Those same documents also served as road maps for the creation of Linux.

## Note

**In an early e-mail newsgroup post, Linus Torvalds made a request for a copy, preferably online, of the POSIX standard. I think that nobody from AT&T expected someone to actually be able to write their own clone of UNIX from those interfaces, without using any of its UNIX source code. ■**

- **Technical approach**—Again, until the very end of USL, most decisions on the direction of UNIX were made based on technical considerations. Management was promoted up through the technical ranks and to my knowledge there was never any talk of writing software to break other companies' software or otherwise restrict the success of USL's partners.

When USL eventually started taking on marketing experts and creating a desktop UNIX product for end users, Microsoft Windows already had a firm grasp on the desktop market. Also, because the direction of UNIX had always been toward source-code licensing destined for large computing systems, USL had pricing difficulties for its products. For example, on software it was including with UNIX, USL found itself having to pay out per-computer licensing fees that were based on $100,000 mainframes instead of $2,000 PCs. Add to that the fact that no application programs were available with UnixWare, and you can see why the endeavor failed.

Successful marketing of UNIX systems at the time, however, was happening with other computer companies. SCO had found a niche market, primarily selling PC versions of UNIX running dumb terminals in small offices. Sun Microsystems was selling lots of UNIX workstations (originally based on BSD but merged with UNIX in SVR4) for programmers and high-end technology applications (such as stock trading).

Other commercial UNIXes were also emerging by the 1980s as well. This new ownership assertion of UNIX was beginning to take its toll on the spirit of open contributions. Lawsuits were being initiated to protect UNIX source code and trademarks. In 1984, this new, restrictive UNIX gave rise to an organization that eventually led a path to Linux: the Free Software Foundation.

## To a GNU free-flowing (not) UNIX

In 1984, Richard M. Stallman started the GNU project (www.gnu.org), recursively named by the phrase GNU is Not UNIX. As a project of the Free Software Foundation (FSF), GNU was intended to become a recoding of the entire UNIX operating system that could be freely distributed. The GNU Project page (www.gnu.org/gnu/thegnuproject.html) tells the story of how the project came about in Stallman's own words.

Although rewriting millions of lines of code might seem daunting for one or two people, spreading the effort across dozens or even hundreds of programmers made the project possible. It turned out that not only could the same results be gained by all new code, but that in some cases that code was better than the original UNIX versions. Because everyone could see the code being produced for the project, poorly written code could be corrected quickly or replaced over time.

If you are familiar with UNIX, try searching the more than 3,400 GNU software packages for your favorite UNIX command from the Free Software Directory (http://directory.fsf.org/GNU). Chances are you will find it there, along with many, many other software projects available as add-ons.

Over time, the term *free software* has been mostly replaced by the term *open source software*. To accommodate both camps, some people use the term *Free and Open Source Software* (FOSS) instead. An underlying principle of FOSS, however, is that, although you are free to use the software as you like, you have some responsibility to make the improvements you make to the code available to others. In that way, everyone in the community can benefit from your work as you have benefited from the work of others.

To clearly define how open source software should be handled, the GNU software project created the GNU Public License, or GPL (you can read the GPL in its entirety at the end of this book). Although many other software licenses cover slightly different approaches to protecting free software, the GPL is the most well known—and it's the one that covers the Linux kernel itself. Basic features of the GNU Public License include

- **Author rights**—The original author retains the rights to his or her software.
- **Free distribution**—People can use the GNU software in their own software, changing and redistributing it as they please. They do, however, have to include the source code with their distribution (or make it easily available).
- **Copyright maintained**—Even if you were to repackage and resell the software, the original GNU agreement must be maintained with the software, which means all future recipients of the software have the opportunity to change the source code, just as you did.

There is no warranty on GNU software. If something goes wrong, the original developer of the software has no obligation to fix the problem. However, many organizations, big and small, offer paid support packages for the software when it is included in their Linux or other open source software distribution. (See the "OSI open source definition" section later in this appendix for a more detailed definition of open source software.)

Despite its success in producing thousands of UNIX utilities, the GNU project itself failed to produce one critical piece of code: the kernel. Its attempts to build an open source kernel with the GNU Hurd project (www.gnu.org/software/hurd) were unsuccessful.

## BSD loses some steam

The one software project that had a chance of beating out Linux to be the premier open source software project was the venerable old BSD project. By the late 1980s, BSD developers at University of California (UC) Berkeley realized that they had already rewritten most of the UNIX source code they had received a decade earlier.

In 1989, UC Berkeley distributed its own UNIX-like code as Net/1 and later (in 1991) as Net/2. Just as UC Berkeley was preparing a complete, UNIX-like operating system that was free from all AT&T code, AT&T hit them with a lawsuit in 1992. The suit claimed that the software was written using trade secrets taken from AT&T's UNIX system.

It's important to note here that BSD developers had completely rewritten the copyright-protected code from AT&T. Copyright was the primary means AT&T used to protect its rights to the UNIX code. Some believe that if AT&T had patented the concepts covered in that code, there might not be a Linux (or any UNIX clone) operating system today.

The lawsuit was dropped when Novell bought UNIX System Laboratories from AT&T in 1994. But, during that critical time period, there was enough fear and doubt about the legality of the BSD code that the momentum BSD had gained to that point in the fledgling open source community was lost. Many people started looking for another open source alternative. The time was ripe for a college student from Finland who was working on his own kernel.

## Note

Today, BSD versions are available from three major projects: FreeBSD, NetBSD, and OpenBSD. People generally characterize FreeBSD as the easiest to use, NetBSD as available on the most computer hardware platforms, and OpenBSD as fanatically secure. Many security-minded individuals still prefer BSD over Linux. ■

## Linus builds the missing piece

Linus Torvalds started work on Linux in 1991, while he was a student at the University of Helsinki, Finland. He wanted to create a UNIX-like kernel so that he could use the same kind of operating system on his home PC that he used at school. At the time, Linus was using Minix, but he wanted to go beyond what the Minix standards permitted.

As noted earlier, Linus announced the first public version of the Linux kernel to the comp. os.minix newsgroup on August 25, 1991, although Linus guesses that the first version didn't actually come out until mid-September of that year.

Although Torvalds stated that Linux was written for the 386 processor and probably wasn't portable, others persisted in encouraging (and contributing to) a more portable approach in the early versions of Linux. By October 5, Linux 0.02 was released with much of the original assembly code rewritten in the C programming language, which made it possible to start porting it to other machines.

The Linux kernel was the last—and the most important—piece of code that was needed to complete a whole UNIX-like operating system under the GPL. So, when people started putting together distributions, the name Linux and not GNU is what stuck. Some distributions such as Debian, however, refer to themselves as GNU/Linux distributions. (Not including GNU in the title or subtitle of a Linux operating system is also a matter of much public grumbling by some members of the GNU project. See www.gnu.org.)

Within the next few years, commercial and non-commercial Linux distributions began to emerge. MCC Interim Linux (www.ibiblio.org/pub/historic-linux/distributions/MCC/) was released in the U.K. in February, 1992. Slackware Linux (described in Chapter 24), which was first released in April 1993, is one of the oldest surviving Linux distributions.

Today, Linux can be described as an open source UNIX-like operating system that reflects a combination of SVID, POSIX, and BSD compliance. Linux continues to aim toward compliance with POSIX as well as with standards set by the owner of the UNIX trademark, The Open Group (www.unix.org).

The non-profit Open Source Development Labs, renamed the Linux Foundation after merging with the Free Standards Group (www.linux-foundation.org), which employs Linus Torvalds, manages the direction today of Linux development efforts. Its sponsors list is like a Who's Who of commercial Linux vendors, including IBM, Red Hat, SUSE (Novell), VA Software, HP, Dell, Computer Associates, Intel, Cisco Systems, and others. The Linux Foundation's primary charter is to protect and accelerate the growth of Linux by providing legal protection and software development standards for Linux developers.

Although much of the thrust of corporate Linux efforts is on corporate, enterprise computing, huge improvements are continuing in the desktop arena as well. The KDE and GNOME desktop environments continuously improve the Linux experience for casual users. Newer lightweight desktop environments such as Xfce and LXDE now offer efficient alternatives that today bring Linux to thousands of netbook owners.

Linus continues to maintain and improve the Linux kernel.

## Note

To get more detailed histories of Linux, I recommend visiting the LWN.net site. LWN.net has kept a detailed Linux timeline from 1998 to the present day. For example, the 2008 timeline is available at http://lwn.net/Articles/Timeline2008. Another good resource is the book *Open Sources: Voices from the Open Source Revolution* (O'Reilly). The entire first edition (published in 1999) is available online (http://oreilly.com/catalog/opensources/book/toc.html). ∎

# OSI open source definition

For software developers, Linux provides a platform that lets them change the operating system as they like and get a wide range of help creating the applications they need. One of the watchdogs of the open source movement is the Open Source Initiative (`www.opensource.org`). This is how the OSI Web site describes open source software:

> The basic idea behind open source is very simple: When programmers can read, redistribute, and modify the source code for a piece of software, the software evolves. People improve it, people adapt it, people fix bugs. And this can happen at a speed that, if one is used to the slow pace of conventional software development, seems astonishing.

> We in the open source community have learned that this rapid evolutionary process produces better software than the traditional closed model, in which only a very few programmers can see the source and everybody else must blindly use an opaque block of bits.

Although the primary goal of open source software is to make source code available, other goals are also defined by OSI in its open source definition. Most of the following rules for acceptable open source licenses are to protect the freedom and integrity of the open source code:

- **Free distribution**—An open source license can't require a fee from anyone who resells the software.

- **Source code**—The source code must be included with the software and there can be no restrictions on redistribution.

- **Derived works**—The license must allow modification and redistribution of the code under the same terms.

- **Integrity of the author's source code**—The license may require that those who use the source code remove the original project's name or version if they change the source code.

- **No discrimination against persons or groups**—The license must allow all people to be equally eligible to use the source code.

- **No discrimination against fields of endeavor**—The license can't restrict a project from using the source code because it is commercial or because it is associated with a field of endeavor that the software provider doesn't like.

- **Distribution of license**—No additional license should be needed to use and redistribute the software.

- **License must not be specific to a product**—The license can't restrict the source code to a particular software distribution.

- **License must not restrict other software**—The license can't prevent someone from including the open source software on the same medium as non–open source software.

- **License must be technology-neutral**—The license can't restrict methods in which the source code can be redistributed.

Open source licenses used by software development projects must meet these criteria to be accepted as open source software by OSI. More than 40 different licenses are accepted by OSI to be used to label software as "OSI Certified Open Source Software." In addition to the GPL, other popular OSI-approved licenses include

- **LGPL**—The GNU Lesser General Public License (LGPL) is a license that is often used for distributing libraries that other application programs depend upon.

- **BSD**—The Berkeley Software Distribution License allows redistribution of source code, with the requirement that the source code keep the BSD copyright notice and not use the names of contributors to endorse or promote derived software without written permission.

- **MIT**—The MIT license is like the BSD license, except that it doesn't include the endorsement and promotion requirement.

- **Mozilla**—The Mozilla license covers the use and redistribution of source code associated with the Firefox Web browser and other software related to the Mozilla project (www.mozilla.org). It is a much longer license than the others just mentioned because it contains more definitions of how contributors and those reusing the source code should behave. This includes submitting a file of changes when submitting modifications and that those making their own additions to the code for redistribution should be aware of patent issues or other restrictions associated with their code.

The end result of open source code is software that has more flexibility to grow and fewer boundaries in how it can be used. Many believe that the fact that many people look over the source code for a project will result in higher quality software for everyone. As open source advocate Eric S. Raymond says in an often-quoted line, "Many eyes make all bugs shallow."

# Linux Myths, Legends, and FUD

The rise in the popularity of Linux has led to rampant (and sometimes strange) speculation about all the terrible things it could lead to or, conversely, to almost manic declarations of how Linux will solve all the problems of the world. I'll try as best I can (with my own admitted bias toward Linux) to address beliefs about Linux and to combat some of the unrealistic fear, uncertainty, and doubt (FUD) being spread by those with a vested interest in seeing Linux not succeed.

## Can you stop worrying about viruses?

Well, you can (and should) always worry about the security of any computer connected to the Internet. At the moment, however, you are probably less likely to get a virus from infected e-mail or untrusted Web sites with standard e-mail clients and Web browsers that come with Linux systems than you would with those that come with the average Microsoft Windows system.

The most commonly cited warnings to back up that statement come in a report from the United States Computer Emergency Readiness Team (CERT) regarding a vulnerability in Microsoft Internet Explorer (`www.kb.cert.org/vuls/id/713878`):

> There are a number of significant vulnerabilities in technologies relating to the IE domain/zone security model, the DHTML object model, MIME type determination, and ActiveX. It is possible to reduce exposure to these vulnerabilities by using a different Web browser, especially when browsing untrusted sites. Such a decision may, however, reduce the functionality of sites that require IE-specific features such as DHTML, VBScript, and ActiveX. Note that using a different Web browser will not remove IE from a Windows system, and other programs may invoke IE, the WebBrowser ActiveX control, or the HTML rendering engine (MSHTML).
>
> *US-CERT Vulnerability Note VU#713878*

Although the note also recommends keeping up with patches from Microsoft to reduce your risks, it seems that the only real solutions are to disable Active scripting and ActiveX, use plain text e-mail, and avoid sites you don't trust when using Internet Explorer. In other words, use a browser that disables insecure features included in Microsoft products.

This announcement apparently caused quite a run on the Mozilla.org site to download a Firefox browser and related e-mail client (described in Chapter 6 of this book). Versions of those software projects run on Windows and Mac OS X, as well as on Linux. Many believe that browsers such as Firefox are inherently more secure because they don't allow non-standard Web features that might do such things as automatically download unrequested software without your knowledge.

Research into hijacked computers being taken over by the thousands to be used as botnets has shown a very high percentage of such incidents to be Microsoft Windows systems. The disturbing thing about the statistics, however, is that many of these systems have been upgraded with Microsoft Service Pack 2 (SP2) or other patches that were supposed to protect from those types of infections. A type of Trojan referred to as SpamThru (resulting in botnets that turn out thousands of spam messages) infected a high percentage of Windows XP systems that have been upgraded to SP2 (see `www.secureworks.com/analysis/spamthru-stats`).

Of course, no matter what browser or e-mail client you are using, you need to follow good security practices (such as not opening attachments or downloading files you don't trust). Also, as open source browsers and e-mail clients, such as those from Mozilla.org, become more popular, the number of possible machines to infect through those applications will make it more tempting to virus writers. (At the moment, most viruses and worms are created specifically to attack Microsoft software.)

# Will you be sued for using Linux?

There have been some well-financed lawsuits against Linux providers. Those with litigation against Linux have gone primarily after big companies, such as IBM, Novell, and Red Hat, Inc. Linus Torvalds himself is the rare individual who has been named in lawsuits. Most threats to individuals have been vague, general declarations from proprietary software companies that claim some infringement of their property, without being specific about what the exact infringement is.

For the past year, most vocal threats to those using Linux systems have come from Microsoft (and companies coincidentally run by ex-Microsoft employees). Before that time, the SCO Group, Inc. spent several years in litigation against major Linux players. Both of those initiatives seem to have more to do with fear mongering than they do with reality.

## Microsoft versus Linux

As of this writing, Microsoft has announced that Linux has infringed on 235 patents that Microsoft holds relating to the desktop. What it has not told us are the exact features that infringe on Microsoft patents and the identity of the patents. Here are some speculations about why Microsoft has not made that information public:

- **Fear is the intent**—The strategy by Microsoft is to get people and companies to pay Microsoft for their use of Linux, without actually telling them specifically what they are paying for. The Linux community has always said that they would replace any code that was shown to impinge on someone else's rights. But if Microsoft doesn't say what their property is, the problem can't ever be corrected and the fear of lawsuits can remain.

- **Too many patents**—There are literally thousands of patents relating to computer operating systems. Many of those patents are held by companies such as IBM, as well as by some open source providers, such as Red Hat, Inc. Opening that can of worms in the court room could mean as much trouble for Microsoft as it does for anyone else.

As lawsuits relate to individuals, few people have been sued because of an association with Linux. However, the level of rhetoric surrounding who *might* be sued has been raised substantially. In the alliance between Microsoft and Novell (see Chapter 20 for details), the two companies agree not to sue each other's customers for intellectual property rights violations. However, Microsoft lawyer Brad Smith had this to say about how open source developers can avoid being sued by Microsoft:

> So Microsoft today is making two, I think, important commitments, or promises to different groups of developers in the open source community. The first is a promise that we won't assert our patents against individual, non-commercial, open source developers. Who are these? These are individuals who are creating code, contributing code, they're not being paid for that code, they're often working in the evenings or at home. They're not creating it as part of their job, but they're acting in an individual non-commercial way. The promise doesn't run to anybody who employs them, because after all, they're not acting in the course of their employment. But, it gives those folks a new commitment from Microsoft.

> The second thing we did in this area was add a promise that goes to developers, even developers who are getting paid to create code to OpenSUSE.org, code that Novell

then takes and incorporates into its distribution, and that is then covered under the patent cooperation agreement between us, because after all Novell is ensuring that our patent rights are respected in an appropriate way, and that gives us the ability to address the needs and interests of those individuals.

`www.microsoft.com/presspass/exec/steve/2006/11-02NovellInterop.mspx`

The actual liability to individual open source software developers, based on statements such as these from Microsoft, is still unclear. That's because there have still been no specific patent claims in connection with Linux from Microsoft. That said, because I am not a lawyer, my opinions on the subject should not be taken as legal advice. However, if you want opinions from lawyers on open source software legality, refer to the Groklaw site (`www.groklaw.net`). Likewise, here is a response from Eben Moglen of the Software Freedom Law Center:

> I and my firm don't take comfort from statement from Microsoft that they won't sue programmers as long as they don't get paid. We represent developers of free and open-source software. If Microsoft or anyone else attempts to sue our clients for doing what they do to create software, because they're being paid for it, then the people doing that will be sorry. We protect our clients.

`http://news.cnet.com/8301-10784_3-6132156-7.html`

## Note

In October 2007, a few days after Microsoft's Steve Ballmer suggested that companies would want Red Hat and others to begin paying for use of their patents, a company called IP Innovation LLC filed a patent claim against Red Hat and Novell. IP Innovation is a subsidiary of Acacia, which recently added Jonathan Taub and Brad Brunell as Vice Presidents. Taub and Brunell were highly regarded executives at Microsoft, with the latter serving as a General Manager of Intellectual Property Licensing. Check out the story here: `http://www.groklaw.net/article.php?story=20071011205044141`. ∎

### The SCO lawsuits

The Linux lawsuits that got the most press a few years ago are the ones involving Santa Cruz Operation (SCO). SCO is the current owner of the UNIX source code that passed from AT&T Bell Labs to UNIX System Laboratories to Univel (a lot of people don't know that one), to Novell, and eventually to the company formed by joining SCO and Caldera Systems. Although the particulars of the claims seem to change daily, and one-by-one the claims have been shot down, SCO's basic assertion in lawsuits against IBM and others is that Linux contains UNIX System V source code that is owned by SCO. So those who sell or use Linux owe licensing fees to SCO.

As of this writing, many of the charges brought by SCO have been dismissed by the judge in the case. SCO, however, is currently stating that it may appeal and believes that there is still a foundation to its charges. A new, recent wrinkle in SCO's case, however, has thrown into doubt how much right SCO even has to the UNIX source code it purchased from Novell.

To a layman (I am not a lawyer!), the assertions seem weak based on the following facts:

- There seems to be no original UNIX code in Linux. And, even if a small amount of code that could be proved to be owned by SCO had made it in there by mistake, that code could be easily dropped and rewritten.

- Concepts that created UNIX all seem to be in the public domain, with public specifications of UNIX interfaces blessed by AT&T itself in the form of published POSIX and System V Interface Definition standards. Although the AT&T UNIX code was covered by copyright, the *concepts* that went into that code were never patented.

- AT&T dropped a similar lawsuit in 1994 against BSD, which had actually started with UNIX source code, but had rewritten it completely over the years.

- Exactly what SCO owns has been brought into question because Novell still claims some rights to the UNIX code it sold to SCO. (In fact, SCO doesn't even own the UNIX trademark, which Novell gave away to the Open Group before it sold the source code to SCO. Attempts were underway in 2004 by SCO to trademark the name UNIX System Laboratories.)

Responses to SCO's lawsuits (which certainly hold more weight than any explanations I could offer) are available from Open Group (www.opengroup.org), The Linux Foundation (formerly OSDL) (www.linux-foundation.org), IBM (ibm.com/linux), and Red Hat (www.redhat .com). The Groklaw site (www.groklaw.net) is another good spot to learn about SCO lawsuits against Linux. If you are interested in the paper trail relating SCO's ownership of UNIX, I recommend the Novell's Unique Legal Rights page (www.novell.com/licensing/indemnity/ legal.html).

## Software patents

Most agree that it is illegal for someone to copy a software company's code and redistribute it without permission. However, the concept of being able to patent an *idea* that a company might incorporate in its code has become a major point of contention in recent years. Can someone patent the idea of clicking an icon to open a window?

Software companies are scrambling to file thousands of patents related to how software is used. Although those companies may never create products based on those patents, the restrictions those patents might place on other software companies or open source software development is a major issue.

In the alliance between Microsoft and Novell, both companies' large patent portfolios have become a major issue of concern among the free and open source community. The fear is that those patents (in other words, the idea represented by code and not the code itself) could be used to claim a tax on every piece of open source software that is freely distributed today.

To deal with the patent issue, the recently released GNU General Public License 3 (GPLv3) includes wording that restricts anyone who delivers software covered under the GPL to exercise their patent rights against those who use or redistribute that software. The hope of the Free

Software Foundation (http://gplv3.fsf.org) is that this will definitively answer the patent issues that might restrict free redistribution of GPL code.

On another front in the patent wars, the Foundation for a Free Information Infrastructure (www.ffii.org) is a group "dedicated to establishing a free market in information technology, by the removal of barriers to competition." The FFII maintains an excellent FAQ page to answer questions surrounding software patents and how they threaten innovation:

> www.ffii.org/Frequently_Asked_Questions_about_software_patents

### Other potentially litigious issues

Particularly contentious legal issues surround audio and video software. In Red Hat Linux 8, Red Hat, Inc. removed support for MP3 and DVD players because of questions about licensing associated with those music and movie formats. Red Hat's advice at the time was to download and install the players yourself for personal use. Red Hat didn't want to distribute those players because companies owning patents related to certain audio and video encoders might ask Red Hat to pay licensing fees for distributing those players (see www.redhat.com/advice/speaks_80mm.html).

To deal with the issue of running proprietary codecs in Linux, Linux distributions such as Fedora, Ubuntu, and others are offering tools to connect their users to sites where they can find legal codecs to use with Linux. See Chapter 4 for information on getting legal software for playing proprietary music, video, and other multimedia content.

# Can Linux really run on everything from handhelds to supercomputers?

Linux is extraordinarily scalable and runs on everything from handhelds to supercomputers. Features in the Linux 2.6 kernel have been particularly aimed at making the kernel easier to port to embedded Linux systems, as well as large multiprocessor, enterprise-quality servers. Yellow Dog Linux even offers a port of its Linux distribution that runs on Sony PlayStation 3 gaming consoles.

# Will Microsoft crush Linux?

As noted earlier, Microsoft has shifted its fear, uncertainty, and doubt (FUD) rhetoric against using Linux to FUD about using any Linux other than Novell's SUSE. Any Linux user or developer who doesn't make an agreement with Microsoft to use Microsoft's as-yet-unnamed intellectual property that is in Linux has, in the words of Microsoft President Steve Ballmer, "an undisclosed balance sheet liability."

In 1998, a series of memos were leaked from Microsoft that became known as the Halloween Documents (www.catb.org/~esr/halloween/). The sudden publicity of these memos forced Microsoft to acknowledge their authenticity. The documents fueled animosity and suspicion about the intentions of Microsoft regarding Linux. At first, some regarded the Novell and Microsoft Patent news as simply Fear, Uncertainty and Doubt (FUD).

However, Microsoft went after GPS car navigation system vendor TomTom for infringing on Microsoft patents related to the File Allocation Table (FAT) file system. TomTom's settlement with Microsoft includes payment for use of Microsoft's intellectual property as TomTom removes features that infringe on that property. Some in the Linux community see this as a way for Microsoft to maintain control over vendors of computing devices that are increasingly moving to Linux rather than pay Microsoft licensing fees.

To many in the Linux community, statements from Microsoft in which Microsoft threatened to sue Linux developers, users, and customers who don't pay a fee to Microsoft (for code that Microsoft had no part in creating) are viewed as extortion. The result has been to divide open source proponents into either the camp for the Novell/Microsoft deal or against it. However you look at it, the battle lines have been clearly drawn.

The U.S. Justice department claimed that Microsoft used the phrase "Embrace, extend, and extinguish" as its policy toward dealing with companies or technologies that it saw as a threat (http://en.wikipedia.org/wiki/Embrace,_extend_and_extinguish). By embracing SUSE Linux, Microsoft has already divided the Linux community. It has announced plans to extend SUSE Linux to better interoperate with Windows. You can only guess what might happen to SUSE when Microsoft's five-year deal with Novell is up and much of the open source community isn't working with Novell anymore.

But it's not all gloom and doom for Linux. Major Linux vendors such as Red Hat, Inc. and the Free Software Foundation have been gearing up for this fight for years. At the time of this writing, it looks like they have a couple of aces up their sleeves as well:

- **GPLv3**—The final text of GPLv3 was released at the end of 2007. Most of the free and open source software community (including the Linux kernel developers) license their software using GPL. However, not all open source software projects covered under GPLv2 have moved to GPLv3 yet, including the Linux kernel itself.

- **Open Invention Network** (www.openinventionnetwork.com)—With sponsors such as Red Hat, IBM, Novell, Philips, Sony, and NEC, the Open Invention Network was formed as an organization for gathering patents to protect open source software. Instead of using those patents as a royalty stream, however, those patents are seen as a defense against someone who might seek to assert patent rights against open source software. It seems to be like an arms race, where it is hoped that no country will attack another since both have ammunition that could inflict damage.

- **Open source community**—So far, there have simply been pleas from the open source community to Novell to abandon the patent portion of its agreement with Microsoft. Projects such as the Samba project have come out publicly against the agreement, but so far no one has taken action. Some believe, however, that many open source projects will not be willing to work with Novell, given that aspects of the alliance with Microsoft seem ready to punish open source developers who do paid work for anyone other than Novell.

It's hard to imagine how any major Linux distribution could survive without assistance from the upstream projects that feed it. So, being set adrift from the open source community is surely not something Novell wants to have happen.

So, the bottom line about whether or not Microsoft will crush Linux is that a fight is brewing, but the jury is still out. It seems, however, that the free and open source community is ready to protect its rights and values.

## Are you on your own if you use Linux?

If you are new to Linux and are concerned about support, several companies are offering well-supported versions of Linux. Those include Red Hat Enterprise Linux (from Red Hat, Inc.) and Ubuntu Linux (from Canonical Global Support Services), as well as a number of other smaller players. In the corporate arena, add IBM to that list.

As noted earlier, many community sites on the Internet also offer forums, mailing lists, and other venues for getting help if you get stuck.

## Is Linux only for geeks?

It doesn't hurt to be a geek if you want to fully explore all the potential of your Linux system. However, with a good desktop Linux distribution, tremendous improvements over the past few years relating to ease-of-use and features have made it possible to do most things you would do on any Macintosh or Windows system without being a Linux expert. The great thing is that, if you ever want to dig deeper, the opportunity is there and the education is free.

Start with a Linux system that uses the KDE or GNOME desktop. Simple menus enable you to select word processors, Web browsers, games, and dozens of other applications you commonly use on other operating systems. In most cases, you'll get along fine just using your mouse to work with windows, menus, and forms.

With Linux distributions that offer graphical tools for basic system administration (such as configuring a printer or network connection), you can be led through most tasks you need to do. Fedora, Red Hat Enterprise Linux, and Mandriva are good examples of Linux distributions that offer simplified administration tools. With a basic understanding of the Linux shell (see Chapter 9) and some help from a Linux forum, you should be able to troubleshoot most anything that goes wrong.

Many inexpensive netbooks are being produced now featuring Linux with lightweight desktop environments such as Xfce and LXDE. With more applications moving into the "clouds" (such as Google's mail, docs, and other Google Apps), the cost, security, and adaptability of Linux have caused netbook manufacturers to move away from Microsoft altogether and toward Linux.

## How do companies make money with Linux?

Open source enthusiasts believe that better software can result from an open source software development model than from proprietary development models. So in theory, any company creating software for its own use can save money by adding its software contributions to those of others to gain a much better end product for themselves.

Companies that want to make money selling software need to be more creative than they were in the old days. Although you can sell the software you create that includes GPL software, you must pass the source code of that software forward. Of course, others can then recompile that product, basically using your product without charge. Here are a few ways that companies are dealing with that issue:

- **Software subscriptions**—Red Hat, Inc. sells its Red Hat Enterprise Linux products on a subscription basis. For a certain amount of money per year, you get binary code to run Linux (so you don't have to compile it yourself), guaranteed support, tools for tracking the hardware and software on your computer, and access to the company's knowledge base.

  Although Red Hat's Fedora project includes much of the same software and is also available in binary form, there are no guarantees associated with the software or future updates of that software. A small office or personal user might take the risk on Fedora (which is itself an excellent operating system) but a big company that's running mission-critical applications will probably put down a few dollars for RHEL.

- **Training and Certification**—With Linux system use growing in government and big business, professionals are needed to support those systems. Red Hat offers training courses and certification exams to help system administrators become proficient using Red Hat Enterprise Linux Systems. In particular, the Red Hat Certified Engineer (RHCE) and Red Hat Certified Technician (RHCT) certifications have become popular (`www.redhat.com/certification`).

  Other certification programs are offered by Linux Professional Institute (`www.lpi.org`), CompTIA (`www.comptia.org` ), and Novell (`www.novell.com`). LPI and CompTIA are professional computer industry associations. Novell centers its training and certification on its SUSE Linux products.

- **Donations**—Many open source projects accept donations from individuals or open source companies that use code from their projects. Amazingly, many open source projects support one or two developers and run exclusively on donations.

- **Bounties**—The concept of software bounties is a fascinating way for open source software companies to make money. Let's say that you are using XYZ software package and you need a new feature right away. By paying a software bounty to the project itself, or to other software developers, you can have your needed improvements moved to the head of the queue. The software you pay for will remain covered by its open source license, but you will have the features you need, at probably a fraction of the cost of building the project from scratch.

- **Boxed sets, mugs, and T-shirts**—Many open source projects have online stores where you can buy boxed sets (some people still like physical CDs and hard copies of documentation) and a variety of mugs, T-shirts, mouse pads, and other items. If you really love a project, for goodness sake, buy a T-shirt!

This is in no way an exhaustive list because more creative ways are being invented every day to support those who create open source software. Remember that many people have become contributors to and maintainers of open source software because they needed or wanted the software themselves. The contributions they make for free are worth the return they get from others who do the same.

## How different are Linux distributions from one another?

Although different Linux systems will add different logos, choose different software components to include, and have different ways of installing and configuring Linux, most people who become used to Linux can move pretty easily from one Linux to another. There are a few reasons for this:

- **Linux Standard Base**—There is an effort called the Linux Standard Base (www.linux-base.org) to which most major Linux systems subscribe. The Linux Standard Base Specification (available from this site) has as one of its primary goals to ensure that applications written for one Linux system will work on other systems. To that end, the LSB will define what libraries need to be available, how software packages can be formatted, what commands and utilities must be available, and, to some extent, how the file system should be arranged. In other words, you can rely on many components of Linux being in the same place on LSB-certified Linux systems.

- **Open source projects**—Many Linux distributions include the same open source projects. So, for example, the most basic command and configuration files for an Apache Web server, Samba file/print server, and sendmail mail server will be the same whether you use Red Hat, Debian, or many other Linux systems. And although they can change backgrounds, colors, and other elements of your desktop, most of the ways of navigating a KDE or GNOME desktop stay the same, regardless of which Linux you use.

- **A shell is a shell**—Although you can put different pretty faces on it, after you open a shell command-line interpreter (such as bash or sh) in Linux, most experienced Linux or UNIX users find it pretty easy to get around on most any Linux system. For that reason, I recommend that if you are serious about using Linux, you take some time to try the shell (as described in Chapter 9). Additionally, Chapters 13 through 16 focus on command line and configuration file interfaces for setting up servers because learning those ways of configuring servers will make your skills most portable across different Linux systems.

Some of the ways that Linux distributions distinguish themselves, however, are with the installers they use, their package management tools, and system administration tools. Also, distributions such as those sponsored by Red Hat will include new features developed by its sponsors to meet its commercial needs. For example, Red Hat has done a lot of work that is useful for enterprise computing environments, such as virtualization, global file systems, and software distribution tools.

## Is the Linux mascot really a penguin?

Figure B-1 shows the penguin logo that Linus Torvalds approved as the official Linux mascot. His name is Tux. Use of this logo is freely available, and you find it everywhere on Linux Web sites, magazines, and other Linux venues. (I used it in my book *Linux Toys II* and on the Linuxtoys.net Web site, for example.)

**FIGURE B-1**

Tux, a gentle and pleasant penguin, is the official Linux mascot.

Tux was created by Larry Ewing. Different versions of Tux are available from his Web site (`www.isc.tamu.edu/~lewing/linux`). Find out more about Tux from the Linux Online Logos and Mascots page (`www.linux.org/info/logos.html`). Refer to the Why Linux Chose a Penguin page (`www.linux.org/info/penguin.html`) if you would like Linus's take on the penguin mascot.

# Summary

The history of the Linux operating system can be tracked from early UNIX systems that were distributed free to colleges and improved by initiatives such as the Berkeley Software Distribution (BSD). The Free Software Foundation helped make many of the components needed to recreate the first UNIX systems as a fully free system; then a Finnish student named Linus Torvalds built the Linux kernel needed to complete the job.

Despite initial attempts to oppose and discredit Linux from major computer companies such as Microsoft and SCO, Linux continues to thrive. From its humble beginnings as a PC-based UNIX-like operating system, Linux is now one of the world's most popular computer operating systems in its own right.

Most Linux software projects are protected by one of a set of licenses that fall under the Open Source Initiative umbrella. The most prominent of these is the GNU Public License (GPL). Standards such as the Linux Standard Base and world-class Linux organizations and companies (such as Red Hat, Inc.) make it possible for Linux to continue to be a stable, productive operating system into the future.

# GNU General Public License

Version 2, June 1991

# Preamble

The licenses for most software are designed to take away your freedom to share and change it. By contrast, the GNU General Public License is intended to guarantee your freedom to share and change free software — to make sure the software is free for all its users. This General Public License applies to most of the Free Software Foundation's software and to any other program whose authors commit to using it. (Some other Free Software Foundation software is covered by the GNU Library General Public License instead.) You can apply it to your programs, too.

When we speak of free software, we are referring to freedom, not price. Our General Public Licenses are designed to make sure that you have the freedom to distribute copies of free software (and charge for this service if you wish), that you receive source code or can get it if you want it, that you can change the software or use pieces of it in new free programs; and that you know you can do these things.

To protect your rights, we need to make restrictions that forbid anyone to deny you these rights or to ask you to surrender the rights. These restrictions translate to certain responsibilities for you if you distribute copies of the software, or if you modify it.

For example, if you distribute copies of such a program, whether gratis or for a fee, you must give the recipients all the rights that you have. You must make sure that they, too, receive or can get the source code. And you must show them these terms so they know their rights.

We protect your rights with two steps: (1) copyright the software, and (2) offer you this license which gives you legal permission to copy, distribute and/or modify the software.

Also, for each author's protection and ours, we want to make certain that everyone understands that there is no warranty for this free software. If the software is modified by someone else and passed on, we want its recipients to know that what they have is not the original, so that any problems introduced by others will not reflect on the original authors' reputations.

Finally, any free program is threatened constantly by software patents. We wish to avoid the danger that redistributors of a free program will individually obtain patent licenses, in effect making the program proprietary. To prevent this, we have made it clear that any patent must be licensed for everyone's free use or not licensed at all.

The precise terms and conditions for copying, distribution and modification follow.

# Terms and Conditions for Copying, Distribution and Modification

**0.** This License applies to any program or other work which contains a notice placed by the copyright holder saying it may be distributed under the terms of this General Public License. The "Program", below, refers to any such program or work, and a "work based on the Program" means either the Program or any derivative work under copyright law: that is to say, a work containing the Program or a portion of it, either verbatim or with modifications and/or translated into another language. (Hereinafter, translation is included without limitation in the term "modification".) Each licensee is addressed as "you".

Activities other than copying, distribution and modification are not covered by this License; they are outside its scope. The act of running the Program is not restricted, and the output from the Program is covered only if its contents constitute a work based on the Program (independent of having been made by running the Program). Whether that is true depends on what the Program does.

**1.** You may copy and distribute verbatim copies of the Program's source code as you receive it, in any medium, provided that you conspicuously and appropriately publish on each copy an appropriate copyright notice and disclaimer of warranty; keep intact all the notices that refer to this License and to the absence of any warranty; and give any other recipients of the Program a copy of this License along with the Program.

You may charge a fee for the physical act of transferring a copy, and you may at your option offer warranty protection in exchange for a fee.

**2.** You may modify your copy or copies of the Program or any portion of it, thus forming a work based on the Program, and copy and distribute such modifications or work under the terms of Section 1 above, provided that you also meet all of these conditions:

**a)** You must cause the modified files to carry prominent notices stating that you changed the files and the date of any change.

**b)** You must cause any work that you distribute or publish, that in whole or in part contains or is derived from the Program or any part thereof, to be licensed as a whole at no charge to all third parties under the terms of this License.

**c)** If the modified program normally reads commands interactively when run, you must cause it, when started running for such interactive use in the most ordinary way, to print or display an announcement including an appropriate copyright notice and a notice that there is no warranty (or else, saying that you provide a warranty) and that users may redistribute the program under these conditions, and telling the user how to view a copy of this License. (Exception: if the Program itself is interactive but does not normally print such an announcement, your work based on the Program is not required to print an announcement.)

These requirements apply to the modified work as a whole. If identifiable sections of that work are not derived from the Program, and can be reasonably considered independent and separate works in themselves, then this License, and its terms, do not apply to those sections when you distribute them as separate works. But when you distribute the same sections as part of a whole which is a work based on the Program, the distribution of the whole must be on the terms of this License, whose permissions for other licensees extend to the entire whole, and thus to each and every part regardless of who wrote it.

Thus, it is not the intent of this section to claim rights or contest your rights to work written entirely by you; rather, the intent is to exercise the right to control the distribution of derivative or collective works based on the Program.

In addition, mere aggregation of another work not based on the Program with the Program (or with a work based on the Program) on a volume of a storage or distribution medium does not bring the other work under the scope of this License.

3. You may copy and distribute the Program (or a work based on it, under Section 2) in object code or executable form under the terms of Sections 1 and 2 above provided that you also do one of the following:

   a) Accompany it with the complete corresponding machine-readable source code, which must be distributed under the terms of Sections 1 and 2 above on a medium customarily used for software interchange; or,

   b) Accompany it with a written offer, valid for at least three years, to give any third party, for a charge no more than your cost of physically performing source distribution, a complete machine-readable copy of the corresponding source code, to be distributed under the terms of Sections 1 and 2 above on a medium customarily used for software interchange; or,

   c) Accompany it with the information you received as to the offer to distribute corresponding source code. (This alternative is allowed only for noncommercial distribution and only if you received the program in object code or executable form with such an offer, in accord with Subsection b above.)

The source code for a work means the preferred form of the work for making modifications to it. For an executable work, complete source code means all the source code for all modules it contains, plus any associated interface definition files, plus the scripts used to control compilation and installation of the executable. However, as a special exception, the source code distributed need not include anything that is normally distributed (in either source or binary form) with the major components (compiler, kernel, and so on) of the operating system on which the executable runs, unless that component itself accompanies the executable.

If distribution of executable or object code is made by offering access to copy from a designated place, then offering equivalent access to copy the source code from the same place counts as distribution of the source code, even though third parties are not compelled to copy the source along with the object code.

4. You may not copy, modify, sublicense, or distribute the Program except as expressly provided under this License. Any attempt otherwise to copy, modify, sublicense or distribute the Program is void, and will automatically terminate your rights under this License. However, parties who have received copies, or rights, from you under this License will not have their licenses terminated so long as such parties remain in full compliance.

5. You are not required to accept this License, since you have not signed it. However, nothing else grants you permission to modify or distribute the Program or its derivative works. These actions are prohibited by law if you do not accept this License. Therefore, by modifying or distributing the Program (or any work based on the Program), you indicate your acceptance of this License to do so, and all its terms and conditions for copying, distributing or modifying the Program or works based on it.

6. Each time you redistribute the Program (or any work based on the Program), the recipient automatically receives a license from the original licensor to copy, distribute or modify the Program subject to these terms and conditions. You may not impose any further restrictions on the recipients' exercise of the rights granted herein. You are not responsible for enforcing compliance by third parties to this License.

7. If, as a consequence of a court judgment or allegation of patent infringement or for any other reason (not limited to patent issues), conditions are imposed on you (whether by court order, agreement or otherwise) that contradict the conditions of this License, they do not excuse you from the conditions of this License. If you cannot distribute so as to satisfy simultaneously your obligations under this License and any other pertinent obligations, then as a consequence you may not distribute the Program at all. For example, if a patent license would not permit royalty-free redistribution of the Program by all those who receive copies directly or indirectly through you, then the only way you could satisfy both it and this License would be to refrain entirely from distribution of the Program.

If any portion of this section is held invalid or unenforceable under any particular circumstance, the balance of the section is intended to apply and the section as a whole is intended to apply in other circumstances.

It is not the purpose of this section to induce you to infringe any patents or other property right claims or to contest validity of any such claims; this section has the sole purpose of protecting the integrity of the free software distribution system, which is implemented by public license practices. Many people have made generous contributions to the wide range of software distributed through that system in reliance on consistent application of that system; it is up to the author/donor to decide if he or she is willing to distribute software through any other system and a licensee cannot impose that choice.

This section is intended to make thoroughly clear what is believed to be a consequence of the rest of this License.

8. If the distribution and/or use of the Program is restricted in certain countries either by patents or by copyrighted interfaces, the original copyright holder who places the Program under this License may add an explicit geographical distribution limitation excluding those countries, so that distribution is permitted only in or among countries not thus excluded. In such case, this License incorporates the limitation as if written in the body of this License.

9. The Free Software Foundation may publish revised and/or new versions of the General Public License from time to time. Such new versions will be similar in spirit to the present version, but may differ in detail to address new problems or concerns.

   Each version is given a distinguishing version number. If the Program specifies a version number of this License which applies to it and "any later version", you have the option of following the terms and conditions either of that version or of any later version published by the Free Software Foundation. If the Program does not specify a version number of this License, you may choose any version ever published by the Free Software Foundation.

10. If you wish to incorporate parts of the Program into other free programs whose distribution conditions are different, write to the author to ask for permission. For software which is copyrighted by the Free Software Foundation, write to the Free Software Foundation; we sometimes make exceptions for this. Our decision will be guided by the two goals of preserving the free status of all derivatives of our free software and of promoting the sharing and reuse of software generally.

# NO WARRANTY

11. BECAUSE THE PROGRAM IS LICENSED FREE OF CHARGE, THERE IS NO WARRANTY FOR THE PROGRAM, TO THE EXTENT PERMITTED BY APPLICABLE LAW. EXCEPT WHEN OTHERWISE STATED IN WRITING THE COPYRIGHT HOLDERS AND/OR OTHER PARTIES PROVIDE THE PROGRAM "AS IS" WITHOUT WARRANTY OF ANY KIND, EITHER EXPRESSED OR IMPLIED, INCLUDING, BUT NOT LIMITED TO, THE IMPLIED WARRANTIES OF MERCHANTABILITY AND FITNESS FOR A PARTICULAR PURPOSE. THE ENTIRE RISK AS TO THE QUALITY AND PERFORMANCE OF THE PROGRAM IS WITH YOU. SHOULD THE PROGRAM PROVE DEFECTIVE, YOU ASSUME THE COST OF ALL NECESSARY SERVICING, REPAIR OR CORRECTION.

12. IN NO EVENT UNLESS REQUIRED BY APPLICABLE LAW OR AGREED TO IN WRITING WILL ANY COPYRIGHT HOLDER, OR ANY OTHER PARTY WHO MAY MODIFY AND/OR REDISTRIBUTE THE PROGRAM AS PERMITTED ABOVE, BE LIABLE TO YOU FOR DAMAGES, INCLUDING ANY GENERAL, SPECIAL, INCIDENTAL OR CONSEQUENTIAL DAMAGES ARISING OUT OF THE USE OR INABILITY TO USE THE PROGRAM (INCLUDING BUT NOT LIMITED TO LOSS

OF DATA OR DATA BEING RENDERED INACCURATE OR LOSSES SUSTAINED BY YOU OR THIRD PARTIES OR A FAILURE OF THE PROGRAM TO OPERATE WITH ANY OTHER PROGRAMS), EVEN IF SUCH HOLDER OR OTHER PARTY HAS BEEN ADVISED OF THE POSSIBILITY OF SUCH DAMAGES.

END OF TERMS AND CONDITIONS

# Index

## SYMBOLS

%, 277
&, 266
[..], 282
|, 255, 265–266
;, 266
* (metacharacter), 282
? (metacharacter), 282
‹ (metacharacter), 283, 284
› (metacharacter), 283, 284
# sign, 247, 398
$ sign, 247, 267
-0 option (GCC), 792
-0n option (GCC), 792

## A

aalib, 780
AbiWord word processor, 126, 127–128
Absolute Beginner Talk forum, 543
.abw, 127
Accelerated Indirect GLX project. See AIGLX
Access (Microsoft), 130
access denied error, 440
AccessConfig, 429
AccessFileName directive, 430
accessibility
    Adriane KNOPPIX and, 616
    atk and, 780
    display managers and, 39
    Firefox and, 175
    GNOME and, 71
    KNOPPIX and, 624
    Ubuntu and, 528, 533
Acer Aspire One, 19
Acronis Disk Director, 222, 223
ActiveX, 177, 837
add-ons, Firefox, 175–176

address books, 161, 165, 170
adfs, 331
administration. See system administration
administrative commands, 305
administrative configuration files, 306–310
administrative log files, 310. See also log files
administrative logins, 310–313. See also root user
Adobe Flash, 8, 177, 181, 528
Adobe Illustrator, 141
Adobe Photoshop, 139. See also GIMP
Adobe Reader, 146–147
Adobe Reader plug-in, 176
Adriane KNOPPIX, 616
Advanced Linux Sound System. See ALSA
Advanced Package Tool. See APT
affs, 332
.aiff, 100
AIGLX (Accelerated Indirect GLX project), 68–71, 555
AisleRiot Solitaire, 192
Ajax Construction Kit (Morrison), 740
Alantik, 193
alias command, 258
aliases, 271–272, 308
ALL wildcard, 395
Allow directive, 431
Almquist, Kenneth, 250
ALSA (Advanced Linux Sound System), 88, 326
    alsa-project.org, 90
    OSS and, 88, 326
    root user and, 759
    Slackware and, 676
    sound drivers, 91
    Wiki, 90

alsaconf command, 676
alsamixer command, 90, 676
alsasound, 649
alternatives system (Debian), 590–591
Amarok, 92–93
ampersand (&), 266
Anaconda, 546, 547–548
analog formats, 87. See also digital media
Anjuta, 767
-ansi, 791
AntiX, 735, 819, 825
Apache Access Log, 385
Apache Error Log, 385
Apache HTTPD, 424, 429, 437, 571. See also LAMP server
    binary, 437
    Coast Grocery business and, 29
    configuration files, 429–431
    httpd -t and, 306
    in LAMP, 424, 426
    SSL-enabled, 410
    SSL/TLS and, 443–444
    virtual hosts added to, 431–433
Apache Software Foundation (ASF), 25, 424
APIs (application programming interfaces), 188, 754, 779–783
Apoteket, 30
AppArmor, 11
Apple BootCamp software, 220
applets, 43, 62–63
application launchers, 41, 42, 58, 63–64, 605
application programming interfaces. See APIs
APT (Advanced Package Tool), 426, 428, 442, 452, 571, 583–587, 590, 592

# C

C++, 16, 766, 767, 768, 777, 779, 786, 788, 797
C compiler. See GCC
-c option, 791, 798
-C option (nm command), 797
C shell. See csh shell
cable modems, 351, 352. See also Ethernet Internet connection
Calc, 124, 126
Call of Duty 2, 206
Camera Device (Link to Device menu), 49
cameras. See digital cameras
Canonical Limited, 526
card games, 194
careers, Linux, 30–31
CAs. See certificate authorities
Cascading Style Sheets (CSS), 50
case, commands and, 259
Casio digital cameras, 119
Ccompris, 28
CD burner (Nautilus), 58
cd command, 280
CD players (audio), 92–93
cdda2wav command, 103, 104
cdlabelgen command, 106–107
.cdr, 100
cdrecord command, 103–104, 750
CD-ROM Device (Link to Device menu), 49
CDs. See also digital media; live CDs
   burning ISO images (Linux distributions), 218–219, 823–825
   K3B CD/DVD Burning Facility, 103, 219, 687, 750, 824, 825
   labels, cdlabelgen and, 106–107
   Linux distributions (on Linux Bible CD), 821–822
   protection schemes, 85, 86
   ripping, 102, 104–106
   tiny. See tiny desktop live CDs
CDWRITER Device (Link to Device menu), 49
Cedaga, 202, 205–207

Celestia, 195
Cell platform, 627
CentOS project, 26, 464, 546, 558, 627, 628, 629, 630, 634, 637
CERT Coordination center, 378
CertCities.com, 24
certificate authorities (CAs), 441, 442, 443, 444, 460, 461
certificate service requests (CSRs), 413–415
certificates
   Crypto and, 53
   e-mail tuning and, 156
   encryption and, 407–417
   Firefox and, 175, 178
   self-signed, 412, 415–417, 441
   SSL, 410–411
   third-party certificate signers, 411–412
   Thunderbird and, 161
   troubleshooting, 417
certification/training (Linux), 30–31
chainloader, 236
ChatZilla, 170
cheat codes, 734
checklist (for security), 374–377
chess programs, 192, 195, 196
chkconfig smb on, 514
chmod command, 280, 286
ci command, 801–802, 803
cifs, 331
CIFS (Common Internet File System), 25, 331, 503
CIN movies, 96
Civilization: Call to Power, 196, 208
ClamAV, 447, 452–454
Click-N-Run service, 94
CLIs. See command-line interfaces
clock (KDE), 43
CLOSED, 403
CLOSE_WAIT, 403
CLOSING, 403
cloud computing, 78, 843. See also LXDE
cluster addresses option, 511
CMS (content management systems), 150
CMYK (cyan-magenta-yellow-black), 139

co command, 801–802, 803
Coast Grocery business, 28–29
Code Crusader, 768–769
codecs, 86–88
color picker, 140
ColorfulTabs, 176
command lines
   completing, 262–263
   editing, 259–262
   keystrokes for, 261–264
   options
      ar, 798
      GCC, 791–792
      nm, 797
   recall, 263–265
command substitution, 266–267
command-line interfaces (CLIs), 754, 770–777
command-line programming environment, 769–770
commands. See also shells; specific commands
   administrative, 305
   arguments and, 256
   background, 266, 276–277
   case and, 259
   directories, 280–287
   environment variables. See environment variables
   expanding, 266–267
   files, 280–287
   foreground, 276–277
   Internet connection and. See Internet connection
   interpreting/managing. See shells
   locating, 256–259
   makefile rule and, 793
   managing/interpreting. See shells
   metacharacters and, 256
   options and, 255
   printing, 479–481
   rerunning, 259
   sequential, 266
   vi text editor, 289–292
comments, # and, 398
commercial Linux games, 201–210